Fodor's
up CLOSE

IRELAND

the complete guide, thoroughly up-to-date

SAVVY TRAVELING: WHERE TO SPEND, HOW TO SAVE

packed with details that will make your trip

CULTURAL TIPS: ESSENTIAL LOCAL DO'S AND TABOOS

must-see sights, on and off the beaten path

INSIDER SECRETS: WHAT'S HIP AND WHAT TO SKIP

the buzz on restaurants, the lowdown on lodgings

FIND YOUR WAY WITH CLEAR AND EASY-TO-USE MAPS

FODOR'S TRAVEL PUBLICATIONS
NEW YORK • TORONTO • LONDON • SYDNEY • AUCKLAND
www.fodors.com

Second Edition

ISBN 0–679–00380–0

ISSN 1098–6766

FODOR'S UPCLOSE IRELAND

EDITOR: Melanie Sponholz

Editorial Contributors: Laurence Belgrave, David Brown, John Daly, Fionn Davenport, Anto Howard, Colin Lacey, M. T. Schwartzman, Cale Siler

Editorial Production: Stacey Kulig

Maps: David Lindroth Inc.; Eureka Cartography, *cartographers*; Robert Blake, *map editor*

Design: Fabrizio La Rocca, *creative director*; Allison Saltzman, *cover and text design*; Jolie Novak, *photo editor*

Production/Manufacturing: Robert B. Shields

Cover Art: ©Pratt-Pries/DIAF

SPECIAL SALES

CONTENTS

3. DUBLIN ENVIRONS 67

4. THE MIDLANDS 83

5. THE SOUTHEAST 106

6. THE SOUTHWEST 126

7. THE WEST 158

8. THE NORTHWEST 188

9. NORTHERN IRELAND 213

PORTRAITS OF IRELAND

TRAVELING
UPCLOSE

G o to a festival. commune with nature. memorize the symphony of the streets. and if you want to experience the heart and soul of ireland, whatever you do, don't spend too much money. the deep and rich experience of ireland that every true traveler yearns for is one of the things in life that money can't buy. in fact, if you have it, don't use it. traveling lavishly is the surest way to turn yourself into a sideline traveler. restaurants with white-glove service are great—sometimes—but they're usually not the best place to find the perfect beef and barley stew. doormen at plush hotels have their place, but not when your look-alike room could be anywhere from dusseldorf to detroit. better to stay in a more intimate place that truly gives you the atmosphere you traveled so far to experience. don't just stand and watch—jump into the spirit of what's around you.

If you want to see Ireland up close and savor the essence of the country and its people in all their charming glory, this book is for you. We'll show you the local culture, the offbeat sights, the bars and cafés where tourists rarely tread, and the B&Bs and other hostelries where you'll meet fellow travelers—places where the locals would send their friends. And because you'll probably want to see the famous places if you haven't already been there, we give you tips on losing the crowds, plus the quirky and obscure facts you want as well as the basics everyone needs.

OUR GANG

Who are we? We're artists and poets, slackers and straight arrows, and travel writers and journalists, who in our less hedonistic moments report on local news and spin out an occasional opinion piece. What we share is a certain footloose spirit and a passion for the land of saints and scholars that we celebrate in this guidebook. Shamelessly, we've revealed all of our favorite places and our deepest, darkest travel secrets, all so that you can learn from our past mistakes and experience the best part of Ireland to the fullest. If you can't take your best friend on the road or if your best friend is hopeless with directions, stick with us.

LAURENCE BELGRAVE • Determined to breathe real air again after a winter spent editing his new short film, director and writer Laurence Belgrave leapt at the chance to roam about Ireland writing for the *Upclose Ireland* guide. English by birth, Laurence attended Trinity College Dublin as a literature major and fell head over heels for his adopted country.

JOHN DALY • In a diverse career that has included stints as a Dublin pub owner, New York horse and cab driver, and Key West fishing guide, John Daly now devotes all his creative energies to travel writing. Based in a seafront cottage overlooking the harbour at Kinsale, County Cork, he contributes regularly to "Hibernia," *The Irish Independent, The Irish Times,* and *The Examiner.* A veteran of most Irish festivals from Kerry's Puck Fair to The Yeats Summer School in Sligo, he can be found anyplace, in short, where the strains of well-played fiddles mingle with accents from foreign lands.

ANTO HOWARD • Northside Dublin native Anto Howard (christened Anthony—Dubliners have a bad habit of abbreviating perfectly good names) studied at Trinity College before acquiring his green card in a lottery and moving to New York, where he works as a travel writer and editor and a playwright.

CALE SILER • Highlights of Cale Siler's assignment to Ireland and Northern Ireland included: two spectacular mountain bike crashes on the Beara Peninsula, writing Belfast manuscript at a Dublin Sinn Féin rally, sea kayaking with three-time national kayaking champion Jim Kennedy, and participating in both Dublin and Galway Gay Pride marches. To top off his tour of Northern Ireland, Cale was unwillingly swept into Derry's Catholic Bogside district by rioting nationalists and some very angry members of the British army. Cale eventually returned to the tranquility of his native California.

A SEND-OFF

Always call ahead. We knock ourselves out to check all the facts, but everything changes all the time, in ways that none of us can ever fully anticipate. Whenever you're making a special trip to a special place, as opposed to merely wandering, always call ahead. Trust us on this.

And then, if something doesn't go quite right—as inevitably happens with even the best-laid plans—stay cool. Missed your train? Stuck in the airport? Use the time to study the people. Strike up a conversation with a stranger. Study the newsstands or flip through the local press. Take a walk. Find the silver lining in the clouds, whatever it is. And do send us a postcard to tell us what went wrong and what went right. You can E-mail us at editors@fodors.com (specify the name of the book on the subject line), or write the Ireland editor at Fodor's upCLOSE, 201 East 50th Street, New York, NY 10022. We'll put your ideas to good use and let other travelers benefit from your experiences. In the mean time, bon voyage!

INTRODUCTION

Throughout the twentieth century ireland has been among the weaker countries of the western world. it is small in area and population and has been slow in achieving success as a producer of non-agricultural wealth.

In five hectic, booming years the opening words to the influential *The Course of Irish History,* last updated in 1994, suddenly sound like they refer to another country. Ireland, recently rated the 19th richest country in the world per capita, has been born again as an economic miracle, a small open economy which does not blush when compared favorably to the perennially prosperous little nations of Denmark and Holland. Unemployment, inflation, emigration are at the lowest since the founding of the state in 1922; immigration, wages, house prices have all soared to new, dizzy heights.

For the visitor this requires a rethinking of all your preconceived ideas about the Aauld Emerald Isle. They may speak English here, but Ireland is every bit as European as Italy or France. The days of isolation, of dependency on Britain, of unquestioning faith in the Catholic church are over: You'll see it in the hordes of foreigners on the streets of Dublin, Cork, and Galway; in the explosion of new ethnic restaurants in these same cities; in the growing willingness of gays to publically display their affections; and in the visible trappings of the new affluence, BMWs, mobile phones, and rocketing prices.

Until Columbus stumbled upon the not-so-New World in 1492, Ireland was on the very edge of the European universe. To the merchants and explorers who chanced upon this storm-battered isle, Ireland was a wild, indomitable place, mysterious and brooding; a land that, viewed from afar, appeared to rise in defiance from the water. To the medieval mind, Ireland was only a short sail away from oblivion.

Though an island has the barrier of the sea to protect it from enemies, the history of Ireland really is the history of its many conquerors, be they the Celts, Vikings, Anglo-Normans, or British. According to myth, Ireland was first conquered by the Fir Bolg, a brawny race of giants who are credited in folklore for building Northern Ireland's Giant's Causeway, a bridge hewn from raw stone, which supposedly once connected Ireland with Scotland. The Fir Bolg "invasion" and the shreds of oral history that document it most likely reflect the coming of the Celts, an Iron-age Continental tribe of warriors who probably arrived in Ireland as early as the BC 6th century. This was an age of glory in Ireland, a time of Druidic learning and bardic poetry, a time when ferocious warriors roamed in search of honor, glory, and of course heads (head-hunting was a common Celtic practice). To judge by the tales that survive, poetry and philosophy were highly developed by the early Celts. So, too, were silver working, wood and stone carving, and weapon making: Those distinctive swirling designs so popular in tatoo parlors originated as ornamentation for Celtic jewelry and stone crosses. The Celts also developed a complex common law code known as the Brehon Law.

The Celts were a tribal people, and the idea of a unified Irish nation never occurred to the numerous chieftains and minor kings who ruled their own little corners of the island. Leinster, Connaught, Ulster, Munster, and Meath were the five provinces, all with their own distinct dialects of the Irish Language (to this day a native speaker from Donegal may have some difficulty understanding a counterpart from Kerry). These provinces were constantly at war, and the great Irish epic cycle, the *Táin Bó Cuailgne*, tells the story of the theft of the great bull of Cuailgne and the heroic war between Ulster and Connaught that followed.

The next conquest of Ireland required no swords. The Christians, under the guidance of St. Patrick himself, appeared around the 4th century AD. Three short centuries later Ireland was famed around the known world as the land of saints and scholars. While continental Europe languished in the so-called Dark Ages, Ireland, basking in its golden age, became a beacon of enlightenment. Irish monks (Columbanus and Colmcille were the most famous among them) braved the terrors of barbarian Europe to reintroduce the faith to a continent ravaged by the heathen Saxons, Anglos, and Franks. Some say Christianity has left a deep scar on the country; others contend it's a sign from God that the Irish are among the chosen. In any case, Christianity and the Catholic Church remain pervasive, if diminishing, forces in Ireland. If you're in doubt, travel to the small village of Knock in County Mayo. Ever since the Virgin Mary was seen on a church wall in 1879, Knock has been inundated with pilgrims. Even today, they can be seen gathered outside the glass-encased shrine 24 hours a day, 365 days a year. But a spate of shocking revelations in the early 1990s concerning sexual abuse by priests, followed by the admission by one of Ireland's premier bishops that he had fathered a child, shook the church's hold on the national psyche. A serious anti-clerical backlash across the country brought the introduction of limited abortion rights and divorce.

The most serious threat to the early Christians were the Vikings, who began their conquest of the coast around 800, establishing settlements in Wexford, Cork, and Dublin. The country's religious orders generally received protection from God-fearing Irish kings, but neither was able to withstand the Vikings' ruthless onslaught. By the 10th century, many Vikings were making Ireland their home, marrying local women, and adopting the language and faith of their new land. It is often forgotten that in the glorious Battle of Clontarf in 1014, when Irish High King Brian Boru (a first among equals of the provincial kings) defeated a troop of Viking raiders near Dublin, a series of local alliances insured Irishmen and Vikings actually fought on both sides. Boru's subsequent murder signaled the end of an era. The Viking threat was subdued if not eliminated, but a new power had arrived in Europe, conquering England in 1066, and little Ireland would not hold out long against the Norman tide. Conquered and subdued, Celtic Ireland would slowly fade into oblivion, its culture and traditions relegated to the imagination, myth, and fairy tale.

It was in this context that, in 1155, English-born Pope Adrian IV boldly granted dominion over Ireland to his fellow Englishman, King Henry II. In retrospect, the move seems presumptuous when you consider that England previously had hardly bothered with Irish affairs; to the Irish, such arrogance simply tells the whole tangled story of Anglo-Irish relations, or the lack thereof. The Norman King's plans for expansion were aided by the constant division and treacheries among the Celtic leaders. Dermot MacMurrough (a name cursed by every Irish schoolchild), the King of Leinster, went to Wales in 1066 to seek Norman allies in his war with the King of Connaught. Richard Fitzgilbert, better known as Strongbow, was only too willing to help, and his troops landed in County Wexford in 1169. The Irish resisted as best they could, but the disciplined Norman troops, with their revolutionary mounted cavalry who fought with lance from the back of a horse, overpowered them. In return for his help, Fitzgilbert demanded MacMurrough's daughter in marriage and thus became the heir to the kingdom of Leinster.

For the next four hundred years or so, the country settled into a period of workable co-habitation between the old Celtic tribes and the Anglo-Normans. While most of Leinster, including Dublin, was firmly in the hands of the Barons of the English King (the area became know as "The Pale"), the rest of the country remained true to its old traditions and rulers; although the major chieftains had to take the title of Earl and promise some type of allegiance to the crown. The Anglo-Norman Barons and Lords, over a few generations, through marriage and the adoption of Irish customs, language, and laws, quickly became more Irish than the Irish themselves. They built up power bases in Ireland which they ran without interference from England. The alarm this caused the English crown can be seen in its passing of the Statutes of Kilkenny in 1336, outlawing intermarriage between English and Irish as well the use of the Irish language. It was too little too late, and by the 15th century English rule in Ireland had more authority on paper than in reality.

Following English King Henry VIII's conversion to Protestantism in 1534, Ireland was divided not only along political lines but also along religious ones. Henry had used all his power and political brilliance to bring to heel his major enemies in England, the barons and the bishops. He had no intention of letting Catholic Ireland, a possible ally of his arch enemies France and Spain, continue on its own merry way. He forced the major Anglo-Irish (as they had become known) families into open rebellion and quickly defeated their forces and divided their lands among the English adventurers who had supported his campaign. As he had done in England, he dissolved the monasteries and absorbed their wealth into his own. Elizabeth I continued her father's policy with vigor, and by the time the last of Ireland's Gaelic kings—the O'Neills and O'Donnells of Ulster— were defeated in battle and had their remaining land confiscated by the British in 1603, Ireland had become a servile colony where English nobles lorded over an adopted homeland. Determined to ensure the loyalty of quarrelsome Ulster for ever, the English Queen pursued the infamous policy of "plantation," whereby new, Protestant settlers from England and Scotland were awarded the land stolen from the defeated chieftains. Ulster was, by royal design, divided along ethnic and religious lines and the seeds of a 400 year-long tragedy were sown.

Cromwell, the name of a hero of democracy to so many Englishmen, is a dirty word in Ireland. In 1641, the Catholic majority of Ireland sided with Catholic King Charles I against the roundheads of the Protestant parliament in the English civil war. Cromwell, a virulent anti-papist and leader of the victorious parliamentary forces, did not forget such treachery. In 1649 he came to Ireland, intent on making it a Protestant country, and unleashed his troops, beginning a campaign of persecution and terror against the already bitter Irish Catholics. Worse was still to come in the wake of Cromwell's Act of Settlement (1652). It called for the forced migration of all Catholics west of the River Shannon. If they removed themselves from the Anglicized and increasingly commercialized east, the Gaels were welcome to relocate, in Cromwell's words, either "to Hell or Connaught."

The 17th and 18th centuries were bitter ones for Ireland. The penal laws, passed in 1695 by the Protestant rulers of Ireland, forbade Catholics from entering the army or legal profession, from bringing up their children as Catholics, from educating them, from playing Irish music, and even from buying land. In 1801, the Act of Union did away with the Irish Parliament (which had been a Protestant-only body based in Dublin) and introduced direct rule from London. Inspired by the republicanism of the French and American revolutions, a group of Irish patriots, led by the Protestant Theobald Wolfe Tone, formed the United Irishmen and organized an armed rebellion against the oppressive crown. The rising of 1798 was bloody and short, with promised help from France never fully materializing. After a few glorious victories, including Father Murphy's triumphs in Wexford, the rebels were defeated and executed en masse; Wolfe Tone committed suicide in his cell before they could make an example of him.

Nineteenth-century Ireland was dominated by the Great Famine of the 1840s and '50s. Throughout the early 19th century, poverty was endemic and disease was a simple fact of life. Irish peasants worked for absentee British landlords and either paid exorbitant rents for land that had probably belonged to their parents or grandparents or they simply starved. The system was harsh and unjust, but somehow the bulk of Ireland survived the lean years prior to 1845. Within a year, however, potato blight ruined crops throughout the country. By 1857, after repeated crop failures, the population of Ireland had decreased from 8 million to 3 million. Starvation was largely to blame for the decline, but this period also marked the first large-scale emigration to America, Australia, and Canada—a draining and disruptive phenomenon that haunted Ireland until very recently. In 1848, nearly a quarter million people were emigrating annually; today, at last, more people are returning than leaving.

The other great victim of the famine was Irish culture. Whole areas of the island were depopulated, and many villages became ghost towns (even today you'll see abandoned famine-era cottages dotting the countryside). As the soul of a centuries-old way of life slipped into oblivion, the English language became the de facto replacement for a people who no longer knew their heritage. The Irish poet Mac Marcus wrote the following in the 17th century, but his words aptly describe the state of post-famine Ireland: "Without laughter at the antics of children; music censored; and Gaelic banned."

Post-famine Ireland was ripe for rebellion. The hatred of absentee English landlords, who sold Irish wheat abroad while thousands starved, was intense. Two separate paths were open for those wishing to end English rule; the ballot box or the bullet. Charles Stewart Parnell, Protestant leader of the Irish party at Westminster (ironically, many of the leaders of Irish nationalism have been Protestant), was a firm supporter of land reform and home rule in Ireland. The brilliant orator and skillful politician quickly became a national hero for the way he stood up to the English; he was dubbed "the uncrowned King of Ireland." He even persuaded the Liberal Prime Minister Gladstone to bring a limited home-rule bill before the House of Commons in 1882. Defections in Gladstone's party saw the bill defeated. But with the help of Michael Davitt and his Land League, Parnell and the Catholic tenants of Ireland achieved a great victory in the "land war," a three-year, sometimes violent struggle that saw the tenants achieve some control over the land they worked. But the daggers were drawn for the golden boy Parnell, and in 1890, when he was named as a party in the divorce case by the husband of Kitty O'Shea, the vultures moved in. The Catholic church, long jealous of his influence, denounced him; his own party split, and Parnell stepped down as leader. Less than a year later he died at the age of 45.

The late 19th century had seen a renewed interest in the culture of Celtic Ireland. W. B. Yeats, along with his friends Lady Gregory, Douglas Hyde, and many others, rediscovered the old tales of Cúchulainn and other mythical heros, and found in them symbols of a new, resurgent Ireland. The Celtic Revival swept the country: the Gaelic League was formed to promote the teaching of the old language, and the GAA (Gaelic Athletic Association) was launched to organize the Gaelic games of football and hurling on a parish level. On the political front, two more Home Rule bills failed to pass the English Parliament, and by the time World War I broke out, there were some Irish nationalists who thought only an armed uprising would rid the country of the British. On Easter Sunday 1916, while the guns of the empire were busy in Europe, a small group of Irish Volunteers seized key buildings in Dublin, including the General Post Office, and declared an independent Irish republic. The British response was swift and bloody, and within days the rebels surrendered. The people of Dublin, having watched their city bombarded by a British gunboat, at first cursed the rebels as irresponsible adventurers; but in a huge miscalculation, the 15 leaders of the rising were executed by firing squad. James Connolly, the last to die, had to be tied to a chair to be shot, because he was so weak from his wounds. The public outcry was immediate, and Irish nationalists seized on the martyrs of 1916 to launch a new attempt at freedom.

The general election of 1918 saw *Sinn Féin* (Ourselves Alone), the new republican party, win a large majority of the seats in Ireland. Refusing to take up their seats in a "foreign parliament," the Sinn Féin deputies set up their own parliament, or *Dáil,* in Dublin. War was inevitable. From 1919 to 1921 the new Irish Republican Army fought a guerilla war with British regular and irregular forces. Under the leadership of the wily fox, Michael Collins, the IRA inflicted great damage on the crown forces, without ever coming close to a decisive military victory. June 1921 saw a truce, and the two sides met in London to negotiate a settlement. The treaty that emerged granted independence to 26 of Ireland's 32 counties. The remaining 6, all in Ulster and with Protestant majorities, would remain part of Britain. Deputies to the Irish parliament would also have to swear allegiance to the British crown.

Sinn Féin split over the treaty, with Collins leading the pro-treaty side, and Eamon De Valera heading up those opposed. A short but vicious civil war broke out, which saw, among its many tragedies, the assassination of "the big fella," Michael Collins, in Cork. In the end, the treaty was accepted, and the two sides who had tried to kill each other in the civil war sat opposite each other in the parliament of the Irish Free State, as it was called. The two parties they eventually formed, Fine Gael (Family of the Gaels) and Fianna Fáil (Soldiers of Ireland) still dominate Irish politics today. The new state was determined to go its own way, remaining stubbornly neutral in World War II, declaring itself a republic in 1948, and withdrawing from the British Commonwealth in 1949. Economically and socially the fledgling nation remained backwards, hidden under the twin shadows of London and Rome. In 1972 Ireland joined the European Economic Community and began a new era of looking outward to the world. Things started to change, slowly at first, but at an accelerating pace as the eighties and nineties came along. Divorce, limited abortion rights, and gay rights, anathemas to 1950s Ireland, were all suddenly on the agenda. The election of Mary Robinson, a liberal, educated, pro-choice woman, as President in 1991 was seen as a watershed. The Celtic Tiger, Ireland's miraculous economic upturn (yearly rates of growth have reached 11%), first began to purr around 1993, and the country has never been the same since. Ireland, despite Marx's warning to the contrary, has awakened from the nightmare of history. But it has cherished the best elements of its difficult years: an identity that is rooted in shared suffering, the subtle twist of a phrase, a strong rural community, and—perhaps most important of all—a love of an unhurried lifestyle, the luxury of the vanquished. In the words of Oliver Goldsmith, another of Ireland's great Anglo-Irish authors: "The natives are peculiarly remarkable for their gaiety . . . and levity; English transplanted here lose their serious melancholy and become gay and thoughtless, more fond of pleasure and less addicted to reason." From an Irish perspective, these are the highest of compliments.

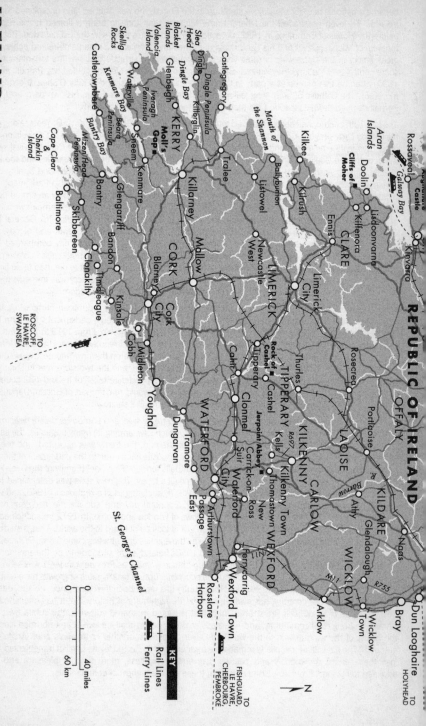

IRELAND

Aran Islands

Rossaveal
Galway Bay

Cliffs of Moher
Doolin
Lisdoonvarna
Kilfenora
Kinvara

Kilkee
Kilrush
Ennis

CLARE

Ballybunion
Listowel
Limerick City

Mouth of the Shannon

Castlegregory
Tralee

Slea Head
Dingle Bay
Dingle
Dingle Peninsula
Killorglin
Blasker Islands
Valencia Island
Glenbeigh
Iveragh Peninsula
KERRY
Moll's Gap

Killarney

Skellig Rocks
Waterville
Sneem
Kenmare

Mallow

Newcastle West

Rosecrea

Portlaoise
LAOISE

OFFALY

REPUBLIC OF IRELAND

Castletownbere
Kenmare Bay
Beara Peninsula

Glengarriff

CORK

Blarney
Cork City

LIMERICK

Cahir
TIPPERARY
Tipperary
Rock of Cashel
Cashel
Thurles

R697

KILKENNY

Kells
Kilkenny Town
Thomastown
Jerpoint Abbey

CARLOW

Athy
KILDARE
Glendalough

Barrow R.

Cape Clear & Sherkin Island
Baltimore
Skibbereen
Clonakilty
Bandon
Timoleague
Kinsale

Mizen Head Peninsula
Bantry Bay
Bantry

TO ROSCOFF, LE HAVRE, SWANSEA

Midleton
Cobh

Youghal

Dungarvan

WATERFORD
Clonmel

Carrick-on-Suir
Waterford City

New Ross

WEXFORD

Naas

Glendalough

Bray
Dún Laoghaire
HOLYHEAD

WICKLOW
Wicklow Town

R755

M11

Arklow

St. George's Channel

Tramore
Passage East

Arthurstown
Ferrycarrig
Wexford Town

Rosslare Harbour

R741

Rosslare

TO FISHGUARD, LE HAVRE, CHERBOURG, PEMBROKE

N

KEY
Rail Lines
Ferry Lines

0   40 miles
0   60 km

IRELAND

BASICS I

I
f you've ever traveled with anyone before, you know that there are two types of people in the world—the planners and the nonplanners. Travel brings out the worst in both groups. Left to their own devices, the planners will have you goose-stepping from attraction to attraction on a cultural blitzkrieg, while the nonplanners will invariably miss the flight, the bus, and maybe even the point. This chapter offers you a middle ground; we hope it provides enough information to help you plan your trip to Ireland without nailing you down. Keep flexible, and remember that the most hair-pulling situations turn into the best travel stories back home.

AIR TRAVEL

AIRPORTS

The major gateways to the Republic of Ireland are Shannon Airport on the west coast, 25½ km (16 mi) west of Limerick City, and Dublin Airport, 10 km (6 mi) north of the city center. Two airports serve Belfast: Belfast International Airport at Aldergove, 24 km (15 mi) from the city, handles all international traffic; Belfast City Airport, 6½ km (4 mi) from the city, handles local and U.K. flights only. In addition, Eglinton, Derry's airport, receives flights from Manchester and Glasgow in the United Kingdom (Loganair).

AIRPORT INFORMATION • Shannon Airport (tel. 011–35361/471444). **Dublin Airport** (tel. 011–3531/8444900). **Belfast International Airport at Aldergove** (tel. 011–441849/422888). **Belfast City Airport** (tel. 011–441232/457745).

BOOKING YOUR FLIGHT

When you book **look for nonstop flights** and **remember that "direct" flights stop at least once.** Try to avoid connecting flights, which require a change of plane.

CARRIERS

When flying internationally, you must usually choose between a domestic carrier, the national flag carrier of the country you are visiting, and a foreign carrier from a third country. National flag carriers have the greatest number of nonstops. Domestic carriers may have better connections to your home town and serve a greater number of gateway cities. Third-party carriers may have a price advantage.

Aer Lingus is the major air carrier to Ireland, with regularly scheduled flights to Shannon and Dublin from JFK, Newark, Boston's Logan, Chicago's O'Hare, and LAX. Delta jointly operates with Aer Lingus's JFK flights and also has a daily departure from Atlanta that flies first to Dublin and on to Shannon. Continental flies daily direct to Dublin and Shannon, departing from Newark Airport in New Jersey.

MAJOR AIRLINES • From the United States and Canada: **Aer Lingus** (tel. 212/557–1110 or 800/223–6537). **Delta** (tel. 800/241–4141). **Continental** (tel. 800/231–0856). From the United Kingdom: **Aer Lingus** (tel. 020/8899–4747). **Ryanair** (tel. 020/7435–7101). **British Airways** (tel. 800/AIRWAYS in the U.S.; 1345/222–1111 in the U.K.) and **British Midland** (tel. 020/7589–5599) have regular schedules to Belfast airport. From Australia: **Qantas** (tel. 800/227–4500 in the U.S.; 02/957–0111 toll-free in Sydney; 0800/808–767 outside Auckland; 09/379–0306 in Auckland).

CHECK-IN & BOARDING

Assuming that not everyone with a ticket will show up, airlines routinely overbook planes. When that happens, airlines ask for volunteers to give up their seats. In return these volunteers usually get a certificate for a free flight and are rebooked on the next flight out. If there are not enough volunteers, the airline must choose who will be denied boarding. The first to get bumped are passengers who checked in late and those flying on discounted tickets, so **get to the gate and check in as early as possible,** especially during peak periods.

Always **bring a government-issued photo ID to the airport.** You may be asked to show it before you are allowed to check in.

CUTTING COSTS

The least-expensive airfares to Ireland must usually be purchased in advance and are nonrefundable. It's smart to **call a number of airlines, and when you are quoted a good price, book it on the spot**—the same fare may not be available the next day. Always **check different routings** and look into using different airports. Travel agents, especially low-fare specialists (*see* Discounts & Deals, *below*), are helpful.

Consolidators are another good source. They buy tickets for scheduled international flights at reduced rates from the airlines, then sell them at prices that beat the best fare available directly from the airlines, usually without restrictions. Sometimes you can even get your money back if you need to return the ticket. Carefully read the fine print detailing penalties for changes and cancellations, and **confirm your consolidator reservation with the airline.**

When you **fly as a courier** you trade your checked-luggage space for a ticket deeply subsidized by a courier service. There are restrictions on when you can book and how long you can stay.

CONSOLIDATORS • Cheap Tickets (tel. 800/377–1000). **Discount Airline Ticket Service** (tel. 800/576–1600). **Unitravel** (tel. 800/325–2222). **Up & Away Travel** (tel. 212/889–2345). **World Travel Network** (tel. 800/409–6753).

COURIERS • Air Courier Association (15000 W. 6th Ave., Suite 203, Golden, CO 80401, tel. 800/282–1202; www.aircourier.org). **Discount Travel International** (169 W. 81st St., New York, NY 10024, tel. 212/362–3636, fax 212/362–3236). **International Association of Air Travel Couriers** (Box 1349, Lake Worth, FL 33460, tel. 561/582–8320; www.courier.org). **Now Voyager** (74 Varick St., New York, NY, tel. 212/431–1616, fax 212/334–5243).

DUTY-FREE SHOPPING

Duty-free shopping is no longer an option within the EU.

ENJOYING THE FLIGHT

For more legroom **request an emergency-aisle seat.** Don't sit in the row in front of the emergency aisle or in front of a bulkhead, where seats may not recline. If you have dietary concerns, **ask for special meals when booking.** These can be vegetarian, low-cholesterol, or kosher, for example. On long flights, try to maintain a normal routine, to help fight jet lag. At night **get some sleep.** By day **eat light meals, drink water** (not alcohol), and **move around the cabin** to stretch your legs.

FLYING TIMES

Flying time to Ireland is 6½ hours from New York, 7½ hours from Chicago, and 10 hours from Los Angeles.

HOW TO COMPLAIN

If your baggage goes astray or your flight goes awry, complain right away. Most carriers require that you **file a claim immediately.**

AIRLINE COMPLAINTS • U.S. Department of Transportation **Aviation Consumer Protection Division** (C-75, Room 4107, Washington, DC 20590, tel. 202/366–2220). **Federal Aviation Administration Consumer Hotline** (tel. 800/322–7873).

RECONFIRMING

Check with your airline before you leave home to find out whether you must reconfirm your return flight a certain number of hours before departure.

BIKE TRAVEL

Ireland is a cyclist's paradise. The scenery is phenomenal, the roads are flat and uncrowded, and the distance from one village to the next is rarely more than 16 km (10 mi). On the downside, foul weather and rough roads are all too common, so rain gear and spare parts are a must. Although most large and midsize towns have some sort of bike shop, if you break down in the country, you're very much on your own. Most ferries will transport your bicycle across the Irish Sea for free, and if there is room bikes can be transported on Irish Rail and Irish Bus for a small fee.

There are plenty of shops offering bike rentals scattered throughout Ireland. Most offer some version of the Raleigh Rent-A-Bike scheme, which consists of a 12- or 18-speed mountain bike with index gears, rear carriers, and heavy-duty pannier bags for about £7 per day or £30 per week. A refundable deposit of £40 is often required. For a £12 fee, you can often rent a bike in one location and drop it off in another.

BIKES IN FLIGHT

Most airlines accommodate bikes as luggage, provided they are dismantled and boxed. For bike boxes, often free at bike shops, you'll pay about $5 (at least $100 for bike bags) from airlines. International travelers can sometimes substitute a bike for a piece of checked luggage at no charge; otherwise, the cost is about $100. Domestic and Canadian airlines charge $25–$50.

BIKE RENTALS • Contact any Bord Fáilte tourist desk or **Raleigh Ireland Ltd.** (tel. 01/6261333).

BOAT & FERRY TRAVEL

There are two principal ferry routes to the Irish Republic: to Dublin from Holyhead on the Isle of Anglesea, and to Rosslare from Fishguard or Pembroke in Wales. Two companies sail the Dublin route: Irish Ferries from Dublin port and Stena Sealink, whose ferries go both to Dublin port and Dun Laoghaire, 4 km (2½) mi south of the city center. SeaCat Ferries have also started service to Dublin from Liverpool. The trip takes about four hours. Prices and departure times vary according to season, so call either company to confirm. In summer, reservations are strongly recommended. Dozens of taxis wait to take you into town from both ports, or you can take DART or a bus to the city center.

Irish Ferries operates the Pembroke–Rosslare route; Stena Sealink operates the Fishguard–Rosslare route. To connect with the Fishguard sailings, take one of the many direct trains from London (Paddington). A connecting train at Rosslare will get you to Waterford by about 8:30 PM, to Cork by about midnight. For the Pembroke sailings, you have to change at Swansea. Sailing time for both routes is 4½ hours.

Swansea Cork Ferries operate a service between Swansea and Cork from mid-March to early January. The crossing takes 12 hours, but easy access by road to both ports makes this longer sea route a good choice for motorists heading for the Southwest. They also sail from Stranraer, Scotland, to Belfast and Larne.

Car ferries run to Northern Ireland from the Scottish port of Stranraer. Trains leave London (Euston) for Stranraer Harbour several times a day. Sealink Ferries crosses the water to the port of Larne, where you pick up a train to Belfast. The whole trip is around 13 hours. Much faster and more convenient is the SeaCat, a huge, car-ferry catamaran that crosses from Stranraer right into Belfast in just 1½ hours. There is also a 9-hour crossing from Liverpool to Belfast, operated by Belfast Ferries. Trains leave London (Euston) for Liverpool throughout the day.

If you're traveling from County Kerry to County Clare and the West of Ireland, you can take the ferry from Tarbert (in County Kerry), leaving every hour on the half hour. Going the other way, ferries leave from Killimer (in County Clare) every hour on the hour. The 30-minute journey across the Shannon Estuary costs £7 per car, £2 for foot passengers.

A 10-minute car ferry crosses the River Suir between Ballyhack in County Wexford and Passage East in County Waterford. It saves you a boring drive through New Ross on the N25 and also introduces you to two pretty fishing villages, Ballyhack and Arthurstown. The ferry operates continuously during daylight hours and costs £3.50 per car, 80p for foot passengers.

You can reach many, but not all, of Ireland's islands by ferry. There are regular services to the Aran Islands from Galway City, Rossaveal in County Galway, and Doolin in County Clare. Ferries also sail to Inishbofin off the Galway coast and Arranmore off the Donegal coast, and to Bere, Sherkin, and Cape Clear islands off the coast of County Cork. The islands are all small enough to explore on foot, so the ferries are for foot passengers and bicycles only. Other islands—the Blaskets and the Skelligs in Kerry, Rathlin, and Tory off the Donegal coast—can be reached by private arrangements with local boatmen. Full details on ferries to the islands are available in a publication from the ITB (see Visitor Information, below).

You can purchase tickets, with a credit card if you like, from the offices listed below. You can also pick them up at Dublin Tourism offices and from any major travel agent in Ireland or the United Kingdom.

FARES & SCHEDULES
BOAT & FERRY INFORMATION • **Irish Ferries** (Merrion Row, tel. 01/6610511). **Stena Sealink** (Ferryport, Dun Laoghaire, tel. 01/2047777 or 01/2047700). **Cork Swansea Ferries** (52 S. Mall St., Cork, tel. 021/271166). **SeaCat** (Donegal Quay, Belfast, tel. 028/9031–2301).

BUS TRAVEL

IN THE REPUBLIC OF IRELAND
Buses are a cheap, flexible way to explore the countryside. Expressway bus services, with the most modern buses, cover the country's major routes. Outside the peak season, services are limited, and some routes (e.g., Killarney–Dingle) disappear altogether. There is often only one service a day on the express routes—and one a week to some of the more remote villages!

Long-distance bus services are operated by Bus Éireann, which also provides local services in Cork, Galway, Limerick, and Waterford. To ensure that your proposed bus journey is feasible, **buy a copy of Bus Éireann's timetable**—80p from any bus terminal.

Many of the destination indicators on bus routes are in Irish, so **make sure you get on the right bus.** Asking someone to translate is often the best way to avoid a mishap. Also, **be aware that bus travel in Ireland is severely curtailed on Sunday** (especially in rural areas).

IN NORTHERN IRELAND
In Northern Ireland, all buses are operated by the state-owned Ulsterbus. Service is generally good, with particularly useful links to those towns not served by train.

FROM THE U.K.
Numerous bus services run between Britain and the Irish Republic, but **be ready for long hours on the road and possible delays.** All buses to the Republic use either the Holyhead–Dublin or Fishguard/Pembroke–Rosslare ferry routes. National Express, a consortium of bus companies, has Supabus (as its buses are known) services from all major British cities to more than 90 Irish destinations. Slattery's, an Irish company, has services from London, Manchester, Liverpool, Oxford, Birmingham, Leeds, and North Wales to more than 100 Irish destinations.

Buses to Belfast run from London and from Birmingham, making the Stranraer–Larne crossing. Contact National Express (see below). The numbers listed are in London, so be sure to add the 44 country code and drop the 0 from the area code when dialing from abroad.

DISCOUNT PASSES • Bus Éireann has a series of passes that allow unlimited intercity bus travel in both the Republic and Northern Ireland. The Irish Rambler Bus Only pass is valid in the Republic of Ireland for either 3 days ($43), 8 days ($105), or 15 days ($152) of travel in any one month. The Irish Rover Bus Only pass is good for travel in all 32 counties of Ireland: 3 days ($56), 8 days ($132), and 15 days ($201). All the above passes are also valid on city services in Cork, Limerick, Galway, Waterford, and Belfast—but not in Dublin. Eurail Pass holders get discounts of up to 20% on the purchase of these passes. Bus Éireann also offers bus and rail passes that are great value for anyone planning extensive travel in more rural parts of the island where trains may not go: the Irish Explorer Rail and Bus covers the Republic only and costs ($140) for 8 days. The Emerald Card allows unlimited use of buses and trains in both the Republic and Northern Ireland and comes in increments of 8 days out of 15 ($163) and 15 days out of 30 ($279).

FARES & SCHEDULES • Pick up a timetable at any bus station or call the numbers below for a schedule. It's best to avoid Friday evening and Sunday morning travel, as this is when throngs of workers from the country return to and depart from Dublin on the weekends.

BUSINESS HOURS

Business hours, generally 9–5, sometimes alter in the larger towns. In smaller towns, stores often close from 1 to 2 for lunch. If a holiday falls on a weekend, most businesses are closed on Monday as well.

BANKS & OFFICES

Banks are open 10–4, Monday–Friday. In small towns they may close from 12:30 to 1:30. They remain open until 5 one afternoon per week; the day of week varies, although it's usually Thursday. Post offices are open weekdays 9–5 and Saturdays 9–1; some of the smaller country offices close for lunch.

In Northern Ireland bank hours are weekdays 9:30–4:30. Post offices are open weekdays 9–5:30, Saturday 9–1. Some close for an hour at lunch.

GAS STATIONS

There are some 24-hour gas stations along the highways; otherwise, hours vary from morning rush hour to late evenings.

SHOPS

Until recently, it was a no-no (thanks to the Church) for stores to remain open on Sunday, but plenty of businesses now do. In small villages, many shops also close for lunch. Pubs are usually open Monday–Saturday 11–11 and Sunday noon–10:30; in summertime they stay open until 11:30.

CAMERAS & PHOTOGRAPHY

PHOTO HELP • **Kodak Information Center** (tel. 800/242–2424). *Kodak Guide to Shooting Great Travel Pictures,* available in bookstores or from Fodor's Travel Publications (tel. 800/533–6478; $16.50 plus $4 shipping).

EQUIPMENT PRECAUTIONS

Always **keep your film and tape out of the sun.** Carry an extra supply of batteries, and **be prepared to turn on your camera or camcorder** to prove to security personnel that the device is real. Always **ask for hand inspection of film,** which becomes clouded after successive exposures to airport X-ray machines, and **keep videotapes away from metal detectors.**

CAR RENTAL

If you are renting a car in the Irish Republic and intend to visit Northern Ireland, make this clear when you get your car. Similarly, if you rent in Northern Ireland and cross the border, make sure the rental insurance applies.

Rates in Dublin begin at $41 a day and $151 a week for an economy car with air-conditioning, a manual transmission, and unlimited mileage. This does not include tax on car rentals, which is 12.5%.

LOCAL COMPANIES • **Argus** (tel. 01/4904444). **Dan Dooley** (tel. 01/6772723). **ECL Chauffeur Drive** (tel. 01/7044062) rents Mercedes Saloons and minicoaches on a journey or daily rate.

MAJOR AGENCIES • **Alamo** (tel. 800/522–9696; 020/8759–6200 in the U.K.). **Avis** (tel. 800/331–1084; 800/879–2847 in Canada; 02/9353–9000 in Australia; 09/525–1982 in New Zealand). **Budget** (tel. 800/527–0700; 0144/227–6266 in the U.K.). **Dollar** (tel. 800/800–6000; 020/8897–0811 in the U.K., where it is known as Eurodollar; 02/9223–1444 in Australia). **Hertz** (tel. 800/654–3001; 800/263–0600 in Canada; 0990/90–60–90 in the U.K.; 02/9669–2444 in Australia; 03/358–6777 in New Zealand). **National InterRent** (tel. 800/227–3876; 0345/222525 in the U.K., where it is known as Europcar InterRent).

CUTTING COSTS

To get the best deal **book through a travel agent, who will shop around.** Also **price local car-rental companies,** although the service and maintenance may not be as good as those of a major player. Remember to ask about required deposits, cancellation penalties, and drop-off charges if you're planning to pick up the car in one city and leave it in another. If you're traveling during a holiday period, also make sure that a confirmed reservation guarantees you a car.

Do **look into wholesalers,** companies that do not own fleets but rent in bulk from those that do and often offer better rates than traditional car-rental operations. Payment must be made before you leave home. **WHOLESALERS • Auto Europe** (tel. 207/842–2000 or 800/223–5555, fax 800/235–6321). **DER Travel Services** (9501 W. Devon Ave., Rosemont, IL 60018, tel. 800/782–2424, fax 800/282–7474 for information; 800/860–9944 for brochures). **Europe by Car** (tel. 212/581–3040 or 800/223–1516, fax 212/246–1458). **Kemwel Holiday Autos** (tel. 914/825–3000 or 800/678–0678, fax 914/381–8847).

INSURANCE

When driving a rented car you are generally responsible for any damage to or loss of the vehicle. Before you rent see what coverage your personal auto-insurance policy and credit cards already provide.

Collision policies that car-rental companies sell for European rentals usually do not include stolen-vehicle coverage. Before you buy it, check your existing policies—you may already be covered.

REQUIREMENTS & RESTRICTIONS

In Ireland your own driver's license is acceptable. An International Driver's Permit is a good idea; it's available from the American or Canadian Automobile Association or, in the United Kingdom, from the Automobile Association or Royal Automobile Club.

SURCHARGES

Before you pick up a car in one city and leave it in another **ask about drop-off charges or one-way service fees,** which can be substantial. Note, too, that some rental agencies charge extra if you return the car before the time specified in your contract. To avoid a hefty refueling fee **fill the tank just before you turn in the car,** but be aware that gas stations near the rental outlet may overcharge.

CAR TRAVEL

A car journey on Ireland's many back roads and byways is the ideal way to explore the country's predominantly rural attractions. Roads are generally good, although four-lane, two-way roads are the exception rather than the rule. Most National Primary Routes (designated by the letter *N*) have two lanes with generous shoulders on which to pass. Brand-new divided highways, or motorways—designated by blue signs and the letter *M*—take the place of some *N* roads. They are the fastest way to get from one point to another, but use caution: They sometimes end as abruptly as they begin. In general, traffic is light, especially off the national routes, although Dublin is always very congested in rush hour and on weekend evenings. It's also wise to **slow down on the smaller, often twisty roads** and **watch out for cattle and sheep**; they may be just around the next bend. Speed limits are 96 kph (60 mph) on the open road, 112 kph (70 mph) on the motorways, and 48 kph (30 mph) in urban areas.

Road signs are generally in both Irish (Gaelic) and English; in the northwest and Connemara, most are in Irish only, so **make sure you have a good road map.** On the new green signposts distances are in kilometers; on the old white signposts they're given in miles. Because of the coexistence of both old and new signs, the route number is not always referred to on the signpost, particularly on National Secondary Roads (*N*-numbered routes) and Regional (*R*-numbered routes). On such roads, knowing the name of the next town on your itinerary is more important than knowing the route number: Neither the small local signposts nor the local people refer to roads by official numbers. At unmarked intersections, a good rule of thumb is to **keep going straight if there's no sign directing you to do otherwise.**

Traffic signs are the same as in the rest of Europe, and roadway markings are standard. Note especially that a continuous white line down the center of the road prohibits passing. Barred markings on the road and flashing yellow beacons indicate a crossing, where pedestrians have right of way. At a junction of two roads of equal importance, the driver to the right has right of way.

The road network in Northern Ireland is excellent and, outside Belfast, uncrowded. Road signs and traffic regulations conform to the British system. Speed limits are 48 kph (30 mph) in towns, 96 kph (60 mph) on country roads, and 112 kph (70 mph) on two-lane roads and motorways.

All ferries on *both* principal routes to the Irish Republic—Holyhead–Dublin and Fishguard/Pembroke–Rosslare—take cars. Fishguard and Pembroke are relatively easy to reach by road. The car trip to Holyhead, on the other hand, is sometimes difficult: Delays on the A55 North Wales coastal road are not unusual.

AUTO CLUBS

IN AUSTRALIA • Australian Automobile Association (tel. 02/6247–7311).

IN CANADA • Canadian Automobile Association (CAA, tel. 613/247–0117).

IN NEW ZEALAND • New Zealand Automobile Association (tel. 09/377–4660).

IN THE U.K. • Automobile Association (AA, tel. 0990/500–600). **Royal Automobile Club** (RAC, tel. 0990/722722 for membership; 0345/121345 for insurance). AAA-affiliated **Irish Automobile Association** (IAA, 23 Suffolk St., Rockhill, Blackrock, Co. Dublin, tel. 01/6779481; 800/667788 for free roadside service) charges a small fee for maps and travel publications.

IN THE U.S. • American Automobile Association (AAA, tel. 800/564–6222).

GASOLINE

You'll find gas stations along most roads. Self-service is the norm in the larger establishments. Major credit cards and traveler's checks are usually accepted.

RULES OF THE ROAD

The Irish, like the British, **drive on the left-hand side of the road.** Safety belts must be worn by the driver and front passenger, and children under 12 must travel in the back. It is compulsory for motorcyclists and their passengers to wear helmets.

Drunk-driving laws are strict. Ireland has a Breathalyzer test, which the police can administer anytime. If you refuse to take it, the odds are you'll be prosecuted anyway. As always, the best advice is **don't drink if you plan to drive.**

Army checkpoints are a thing of the past between the North and the South, though there are some border checkpoints for cattle (in an effort to contain BSE-contaminated livestock).

CHILDREN IN IRELAND

The Irish love children and will go to great lengths to make them welcome. Many hotels offer baby-sitting services, and most will supply a cot if given advance notice. Hotel and pub restaurants often have a children's menu and can supply a high chair if necessary. Unlike laws in Great Britain, Irish licensing laws allow children under 14 into pubs—although they may not consume alcohol on the premises until they are 18, and they are expected to leave by about 5:30 PM (although they may be allowed to stay until 7 PM, depending on how busy the pub gets). This is a boon if you are touring by car because pubs are perfect for lunch or tea stops.

While most attractions and bus and rail journeys offer a rate of half-price or less for children, **look for "family tickets,"** which may be cheaper and usually cover two adults and up to four children. The Irish Tourist Board (ITB) publishes "A Tour of Favorite Kids' Places," which covers a week's worth of sights around the country.

Be sure to plan ahead and **involve your youngsters** as you outline your trip. When packing, include things to keep them busy en route. On sightseeing days try to schedule activities of special interest to your children. Most hotels in Ireland allow children under a certain age to stay in their parents' room at no extra charge, but others charge them as extra adults; be sure to **ask about the cutoff age for children's discounts.**

If you are renting a car don't forget to **arrange for a car seat when you reserve.**

FLYING

If your children are two or older **ask about children's airfares.** As a general rule, infants under two not occupying a seat fly at greatly reduced fares or even for free. When booking **confirm carry-on allowances** if you're traveling with infants. In general, for babies charged 10% of the adult fare, you are allowed one carry-on bag and a collapsible stroller; if the flight is full the stroller may have to be checked or you may be limited to less.

Experts agree that it's a good idea to use safety seats aloft for children weighing less than 40 pounds. Airlines set their own policies: U.S. carriers usually require that the child be ticketed, even if he or she is young enough to ride free, since the seats must be strapped into regular seats. Do **check your airline's policy about using safety seats during takeoff and landing.** And since safety seats are not allowed everywhere in the plane, get your seat assignments early.

When reserving, **request children's meals or a freestanding bassinet** if you need them. But note that bulkhead seats, where you must sit to use the bassinet, may lack an overhead bin or storage space on the floor.

LODGING

Most hotels in Ireland allow children under a certain age to stay in their parents' room at no extra charge, but others charge for them as extra adults; be sure to **find out the cutoff age for children's discounts.**

CONSUMER PROTECTION

Whenever shopping or buying travel services in Ireland, **pay with a major credit card** so you can cancel payment or get reimbursed if there's a problem. If you're doing business with a particular company for the first time, **contact your local Better Business Bureau and the attorney general's offices** in your state and the company's home state, as well. Have any complaints been filed? Finally, if you're buying a package or tour, always **consider travel insurance** that includes default coverage (*see* Insurance, *below*).

LOCAL BBBS • Council of Better Business Bureaus (4200 Wilson Blvd., Suite 800, Arlington, VA 22203, tel. 703/276–0100, fax 703/525–8277).

CUSTOMS & DUTIES

When shopping, **keep receipts** for all purchases. Upon reentering the country, **be ready to show customs officials what you've bought.** If you feel a duty is incorrect or object to the way your clearance was handled, note the inspector's badge number and ask to see a supervisor. If the problem isn't resolved, write to the appropriate authorities, beginning with the port director at your point of entry.

IN AUSTRALIA

Australia residents who are 18 or older may bring home $A400 worth of souvenirs and gifts (including jewelry), 250 cigarettes or 250 grams of tobacco, and 1,125 ml of alcohol (including wine, beer, and spirits). Residents under 18 may bring back $A200 worth of goods. Prohibited items include meat products. Seeds, plants, and fruits need to be declared upon arrival.

INFORMATION • Australian Customs Service (Regional Director, Box 8, Sydney, NSW 2001, tel. 02/9213–2000, fax 02/9213–4000).

IN CANADA

Canadian residents who have been out of Canada for at least 7 days may bring home C$500 worth of goods duty-free. If you've been away less than 7 days but more than 48 hours, the duty-free allowance drops to C$200; if your trip lasts 24–48 hours, the allowance is C$50. You may not pool allowances with family members. Goods claimed under the C$500 exemption may follow you by mail; those claimed under the lesser exemptions must accompany you. Alcohol and tobacco products may be included in the 7-day and 48-hour exemptions but not in the 24-hour exemption. If you meet the age requirements of the province or territory through which you reenter Canada, you may bring in, duty-free, 1.14 liters (40 imperial ounces) of wine or liquor *or* 24 12-ounce cans or bottles of beer or ale. If you are 16 or older you may bring in, duty-free, 200 cigarettes and 50 cigars. Check ahead of time with Revenue Canada or the Department of Agriculture for policies regarding meat products, seeds, plants, and fruits.

You may send an unlimited number of gifts worth up to C$60 each duty-free to Canada. Label the package UNSOLICITED GIFT—VALUE UNDER $60. Alcohol and tobacco are excluded.

INFORMATION • Revenue Canada (2265 St. Laurent Blvd. S, Ottawa, Ontario K1G 4K3, tel. 613/993–0534; 800/461–9999 in Canada).

IN IRELAND

Two categories of duty-free allowance exist for travelers entering Ireland: one for goods obtained outside the European Union (EU), on a ship or aircraft, or in a duty-free store within the EU; and the other for goods bought in the EU, with duty and tax paid.

Of the first category, you may import duty-free: (1) 200 cigarettes or 100 cigarillos or 50 cigars or 250 grams of smoking tobacco; (2) 2 liters of wine and either 1 liter of alcoholic drink over 22% volume or 2 liters of alcoholic drink under 22% volume (sparkling or fortified wine included); (3) 50 grams of perfume and ¼ liter of toilet water; and (4) other goods to a value of £142 per person (£73 per person for travelers under 15 years of age).

Of the second category, you may import duty-free a considerable amount of liquor and tobacco—800 cigarettes, 400 cigarillos, 200 cigars, 1 kilogram of pipe tobacco, 10 liters of spirits, 45 liters of wine, 25 liters of port or sherry, and 55 liters of beer. You'll need a truck!

Goods that cannot be freely imported to the Irish Republic include firearms, ammunition, explosives, illegal drugs, indecent or obscene books and pictures, oral smokeless tobacco products, meat and meat products, poultry and poultry products, plants and plant products (including shrubs, vegetables, fruit, bulbs, and seeds), domestic cats and dogs from outside the United Kingdom, and live animals from outside Northern Ireland. No animals or pets of any kind may be brought into Northern Ireland without a six-month quarantine.

IN NEW ZEALAND

Homeward-bound residents 17 or older may bring back $700 worth of souvenirs and gifts. Your duty-free allowance also includes 4.5 liters of wine or beer; one 1,125-ml bottle of spirits; and either 200 cigarettes, 250 grams of tobacco, 50 cigars, or a combination of the three up to 250 grams. Prohibited items include meat products, seeds, plants, and fruits.

INFORMATION • New Zealand Customs (Custom House, 50 Anzac Ave., Box 29, Auckland, New Zealand, tel. 09/359–6655, fax 09/359–6732).

IN THE U.S.

U.S. residents who have been out of the country for at least 48 hours (and who have not used the $400 allowance or any part of it in the past 30 days) may bring home $400 worth of foreign goods duty-free.

U.S. residents 21 and older may bring back 1 liter of alcohol duty-free. In addition, regardless of your age, you are allowed 200 cigarettes and 100 non-Cuban cigars. Antiques, which the U.S. Customs Service defines as objects more than 100 years old, enter duty-free, as do original works of art done entirely by hand, including paintings, drawings, and sculptures.

You may also send packages home duty-free: up to $200 worth of goods for personal use, with a limit of one parcel per addressee per day (and no alcohol or tobacco products or perfume worth more than $5); label the package PERSONAL USE and attach a list of its contents and their retail value. Do not label the package UNSOLICITED GIFT or your duty-free exemption will drop to $100. Mailed items do not affect your duty-free allowance on your return.

INFORMATION • U.S. Customs Service (inquiries, 1300 Pennsylvania Ave. NW, Washington, DC 20229, tel. 202/927–6724; complaints, Office of Regulations and Rulings, 1300 Pennsylvania Ave. NW, Washington, DC 20229; registration of equipment, Registration Information, 1300 Pennsylvania Ave. NW, Washington, DC 20229, tel. 202/927–0540).

DINING

Rumor has it there has been somewhat of a culinary revolution in Ireland over the last 10 years. In higher-priced restaurants, the soggy vegetables and overcooked meat that once characterized Irish cuisine have become increasingly obsolete. A new generation of imaginative chefs has begun to capitalize on what are some of the best raw materials in the world for gourmet cooking. Ireland is famous the world over for its dairy products (just look at the color and texture of the butter on your table), its meat (especially beef and lamb), its seafood, and its river salmon and trout.

At the truly budget end of the scale, things have also changed for the better. In Dublin and the other major cities a slew of reasonably priced, ethnic restaurants have sprung up with Indian and Chinese establishments a particular strength. Vegetarian eateries, so difficult to find a decade ago, are commonplace, and most restaurants will have at least one vegetarian dish. The ubiquitous chip shop (known as the "chipper") is still a deep-fried standard of the post-pub crowd.

The restaurant price categories used in this book are loosely based on the assumption that you're going to chow down a main course and a drink, and they include an appropriate service charge. Legions of antacids, copious extra pints of stout, and humongous desserts are extra.

MEALS & SPECIALTIES

A typical Irish breakfast includes fried eggs, bacon, black-and-white pudding, sausage, and a pot of tea. A typical lunch might feature a hearty sandwich or smoked salmon on brown bread; dinner meals usually include meat and two vegetables. Some of the best food is found at family bed-and-breakfasts and in inexpensive cafés.

MEALTIMES

Breakfast is served from 7 to 10, lunch runs from 1 to 2:30, and dinners are usually mid-evening occasions.

Pubs are open Monday–Saturday 10:30 AM–11:30 PM May–September, closing at 11 the rest of the year. The famous Holy Hour, which required city pubs to close from 2:30 to 3:30, was abolished in 1988, and afternoon opening is now at the discretion of the owner or manager; few bother to close. On Sunday, pubs are open 12:30–2 and 4–11. All pubs close on Christmas Day and Good Friday, but hotel bars are open for guests.

Pubs in Northern Ireland are open 11:30 AM–11 PM Monday–Saturday and 12:30 PM–2:30 PM and 7 PM–10 PM on Sunday. Sunday opening is at the owner's or manager's discretion.

PAYING

Traveler's checks and credit cards are widely accepted, although it's cash-only at smaller pubs and take-out restaurants.

RESERVATIONS & DRESS

Reservations are always a good idea: we mention them only when they're essential or are not accepted. Book as far ahead as you can, and reconfirm as soon as you arrive. We mention dress only when men are required to wear a jacket or a jacket and tie.

WINE, BEER, & SPIRITS

Ireland's social life is—for good and bad (mostly for good)—synonymous with the pub and the pint of plain, as they like to call their beloved stout. Going to Ireland without venturing into a pub for a Guinness or a Murphys is equivalent to taking a trip to Italy without eating out or a trip to Egypt without checking out the pyramids. The public house is the quintessential Irish experience, where people gather to chat, listen, learn, argue, and gossip about literally any topic under the sun, from horse racing to philosophy. Here, in large, inclusive circles about big round tables, the infamous caustic wit of the Irish is honed and perfected. You don't have to drink to enjoy the atmosphere of "the local," but it certainly helps.

The beer of choice among the Irish is definitely stout, a thick, pitch-black brew with a creamy white head that is flatter than that of regular beer. Ireland produces three brands of it: Murphys and Beamish in Cork and the king of them all, Guinness, in Dublin. Lagers, most familiar to American drinkers, are light-color carbonated drinks that are very popular among younger tipplers, and Guinness-made Harp is the favorite domestic brand. American, Mexican, and European imports have made a big impact on the Irish market over the last decade, to the head-shaking disdain of old-time purists. The British staple, cider, made from apples, can be found in most establishments and is the perfect thirst quencher on warm summer evenings; Bulmers and Strong Bow are names to watch for. Finally, the truly delicious and aesthetically pleasing "black and tan" is a blend of stout and ale sardonically named after the distinctive uniforms worn by hated British irregulars in Ireland in the early part of the 20th century. If poured properly, the dark stout sits majestically atop the amber ale, and the two don't mix until after your first sip.

DISABILITIES & ACCESSIBILITY

Ireland has only recently begun to provide facilities such as ramps and accessible toilets for people with disabilities. Public transportation also lags behind. However, visitors with disabilities will often find that the helpfulness of the Irish often makes up for the lack of amenities.

LOCAL RESOURCES • National Rehabilitation Board (44 N. Great George's St., Dublin, tel. 01/8747503). **Disability Action** (2 Annadale Ave., Belfast, tel. 028/9049–1011).

LODGING

Though not often reviewed in this book, large three- and four-star hotels are much more likely to have elevators and wheelchair-accessible bathrooms; call the U.S. toll-free numbers of such major upscale hotel chains, in most major Irish cities. Always **call hotels ahead to find out about facilities.**

When discussing accessibility with an operator or reservations agent **ask hard questions.** Are there any stairs, inside *or* out? Are there grab bars next to the toilet *and* in the shower/tub? How wide is the doorway to the room? To the bathroom? For the most extensive facilities meeting the latest legal specifications **opt for newer accommodations.**

TRANSPORTATION

In Ireland, not all train stations are accessible. Irish Rail suggests you **call the station a day or two ahead** to guarantee assistance getting on and off trains. Bus Éireann, Ireland's national bus company, will assist travelers with disabilities getting on and off the coach, but none of its buses are equipped with wheelchair lifts. **Give notice when booking if you will need extra help.**

COMPLAINTS • Disability Rights Section (U.S. Department of Justice, Civil Rights Division, Box 66738, Washington, DC 20035-6738, tel. 202/514–0301; 800/514–0301 or 202/514–0301 TTY; 800/514–0301 TTY; fax 202/307–1198) for general complaints. **Aviation Consumer Protection Division** (*see* Air Travel, *above*) for airline-related problems. **Civil Rights Office** (U.S. Department of Transportation, Departmental Office of Civil Rights, S-30, 400 7th St. SW, Room 10215, Washington, DC 20590, tel. 202/366–4648, fax 202/366–9371) for problems with surface transportation.

TRAVEL AGENCIES

In the United States, although the Americans with Disabilities Act requires that travel firms serve the needs of all travelers, some agencies specialize in working with people with disabilities.

The shandy, a mix of lager and lemonade, is a good option if you want to enjoy a few drinks without losing the run of yourself, as the natives might say, and nobody will know the difference because it looks just like a real pint.

TRAVELERS WITH MOBILITY PROBLEMS • Access Adventures (206 Chestnut Ridge Rd., Rochester, NY 14624, tel. 716/889–9096), run by a former physical-rehabilitation counselor. **Accessible Journeys** (35 W. Sellers Ave., Ridley Park, PA 19078, tel. 610/521–0339 or 800/846–4537, fax 610/521–6959). **Accessible Vans of Hawaii, Activity and Travel Agency** (186 Mehani Circle, Kihei, HI 96753, tel. 808/879–5521 or 800/303–3750, fax 808/879–0649). **Accessible Vans of the Rockies, Activity and Travel Agency** (2040 W. Hamilton Pl., Sheridan, CO 80110, tel. 303/806–5047 or 888/837–0065, fax 303/781–2329). **CareVacations** (5-5110 50th Ave., Leduc, Alberta T9E 6V4, tel. 780/986–6404 or 877/478–7827, fax 780/986–8332) has group tours. **Flying Wheels Travel** (143 W. Bridge St., Box 382, Owatonna, MN 55060, tel. 507/451–5005 or 800/535–6790, fax 507/451–1685). **Hinsdale Travel Service** (201 E. Ogden Ave., Suite 100, Hinsdale, IL 60521, tel. 630/325–1335, fax 630/325–1342).

DISCOUNTS & DEALS

Be a smart shopper and **compare all your options** before making decisions. A plane ticket bought with a promotional coupon from travel clubs, coupon books, and direct-mail offers may not be cheaper than the least expensive fare from a discount ticket agency. And always keep in mind that what you get is just as important as what you save.

DISCOUNT RESERVATIONS

To save money **look into discount-reservations services** with toll-free numbers, which use their buying power to get a better price on hotels, airline tickets, even car rentals. When booking a room, always **call the hotel's local toll-free number** (if one is available) rather than the central reservations number—you'll often get a better price. Always ask about special packages or corporate rates.

You can **find discount airfare and hotel deals on the Web.** At most sites you type in how much you want to spend, and the search engine comes up with available offerings in your price range. Some sites act like an auction, where you enter into a bidding war with other people who are logged on at that moment. Be sure to read the fine print before you agree to book anything, since the majority of the air tickets are nonrefundable, and most are not eligible for frequent flyer miles. Also check to see if the site offers secure payment with a credit card.

When shopping for the best deal on hotels and car rentals **look for guaranteed exchange rates,** which protect you against a falling dollar. With your rate locked in, you won't pay more, even if the price goes up in the local currency.

AIRLINE TICKETS • Tel. **800/FLY–4–LESS.** Tel. **800/FLY– ASAP.**

WEB SITES OFFERING DISCOUNT AIRLINE TICKETS AND CHEAP HOTEL PRICES •
www.priceline.com, www.hotfares.com, www.thefarebusters.com; in the UK, www.cheapflights.co.uk.
HOTEL ROOMS • **Steigenberger Reservation Service** (tel. 800/223–5652). **Travel Interlink** (tel. 800/888–5898).

PACKAGE DEALS

Don't confuse packages and guided tours. When you buy a package, you travel on your own, just as though you had planned the trip yourself. Fly-drive packages, which combine airfare and car rental, are often a good deal. If you **buy a rail-drive pass** you may save on train tickets and car rentals. All Eurail- and Europass holders get a discount on Eurostar fares through the Channel Tunnel.

ELECTRICITY

To use your U.S.-purchased electric-powered equipment **bring a converter and adapter.** The electrical current in Ireland is 220 volts, 50 cycles alternating current (AC); wall outlets take Continental-type plugs, with two round prongs.

If your appliances are dual voltage you'll need only an adapter. Don't use 110-volt outlets, marked FOR SHAVERS ONLY, for high-wattage appliances such as hair dryers. Most laptop computers operate equally well on 110 and 220 volts and so require only an adapter.

EMBASSIES

AUSTRALIA • Fitzwilton House, Wilton Terr., Dublin, tel. 01/6761517.

CANADA • 65 St. Stephen's Green, Dublin, tel. 01/4781988.

UNITED KINGDOM • 31 Merrion Rd., Dublin, tel. 01/2695211.

UNITED STATES • 42 Elgin Rd., Ballsbridge, Dublin, tel. 01/6688777.

EMERGENCIES

For **emergencies** dial 999.

GAY & LESBIAN TRAVEL

Although homosexuality is considered "deviant" in many parts of Ireland (and is often met with hostil- ity), there is a huge gay and lesbian subculture. As with most countries, people in more rural areas may have more difficulty accepting gays and lesbians. Many towns have gay/lesbian pubs, bars, or clubs and advertise this fact openly. Gay bashing is a very rare crime in Ireland, but it's always wise to **watch your- self and be careful of public displays of affection.** Dublin, Cork, Galway, and Belfast are the best places to find bars, social events, and publications catering to gays and lesbians. Accommodation-wise, Ireland is not particularly welcoming toward gay travelers—especially if you suggest to a B&B or small hotel owner that you and your significant other would like to share a room.

GAY- AND LESBIAN-FRIENDLY TRAVEL AGENCIES • **Different Roads Travel** (8383 Wilshire Blvd., Suite 902, Beverly Hills, CA 90211, tel. 323/651–5557 or 800/429–8747, fax 323/651–3678). **Kennedy Travel** (314 Jericho Turnpike, Floral Park, NY 11001, tel. 516/352–4888 or 800/237–7433, fax 516/354–8849). **Now Voyager** (4406 18th St., San Francisco, CA 94114, tel. 415/626–1169 or 800/255–6951, fax 415/626–8626). **Skylink Travel and Tour** (1006 Mendocino Ave., Santa Rosa, CA 95401, tel. 707/546–9888 or 800/225–5759, fax 707/546–9891), serving lesbian travelers.

HEALTH

Ireland is a very safe country for travel, with virtually no risk of health problems from food, drink, or insects. The weather, however, is another story; be sure to dress for the cold and rain or you may find yourself plagued by a constant cough and sniffles.

HOLIDAYS

Banks, shops, and most everything you depend on in the Republic close on the following national holidays: New Year's Day; St. Patrick's Day (March 17); Good Friday (the Friday before Easter); Easter Sunday; Easter Monday (Monday after Easter); May Day (the first Monday in May); Summer Bank Holidays (the first Monday in June and August); Autumn Bank Holiday (the last Monday in October); Christmas; and St. Stephen's Day (December 26). Sunday can also pose problems for travelers, especially in smaller towns: Not only do many shops and restaurants close but also bus and train service becomes less frequent or nonexistent.

Holidays in the North are the same as in the Republic except Summer Bank Holidays (last Monday of May and August) and July 12, which celebrates the Protestant victory at the Battle of the Boyne.

INSURANCE

The most useful travel insurance plan is a comprehensive policy that includes coverage for trip cancellation and interruption, default, trip delay, and medical expenses (with a waiver for preexisting conditions).

Without insurance you will lose all or most of your money if you cancel your trip, regardless of the reason. Default insurance covers you if your tour operator, airline, or cruise line goes out of business. Trip-delay covers expenses that arise because of bad weather or mechanical delays. Study the fine print when comparing policies.

If you're traveling internationally, a key component of travel insurance is coverage for medical bills incurred if you get sick on the road. Such expenses are not generally covered by Medicare or private policies. U.K. residents can buy a travel-insurance policy valid for most vacations taken during the year in which it's purchased (but check preexisting-condition coverage). Australian citizens need extra medical coverage when traveling abroad.

Always **buy travel policies directly from the insurance company**; if you buy it from a cruise line, airline, or tour operator that goes out of business you probably will not be covered for the agency or operator's default, a major risk. Before you make any purchase **review your existing health and home-owner's policies** to find what they cover away from home.

TRAVEL INSURERS • In the United States **Access America** (6600 W. Broad St., Richmond, VA 23230, tel. 804/285–3300 or 800/284–8300), **Travel Guard International** (1145 Clark St., Stevens Point, WI 54481, tel. 715/345–0505 or 800/826–1300). In Canada **Voyager Insurance** (44 Peel Center Dr., Brampton, Ontario L6T 4M8, tel. 905/791–8700; 800/668–4342 in Canada).

INSURANCE INFORMATION • In the United Kingdom the **Association of British Insurers** (51–55 Gresham St., London EC2V 7HQ, tel. 020/7600–3333, fax 020/7696–8999). In Australia the **Insurance Council of Australia** (tel. 03/9614–1077, fax 03/9614–7924).

LODGING

Major Irish hotels charge £30–£60 per person. Other, cheaper options include hostels or, for about an extra £9, cozy B&Bs and guest houses. There are also campgrounds scattered throughout the country, many within walking or cycling distance of urban centers; rates are about £3–£5 per tent site and 20p–£1 for each additional person. Most campgrounds are only open from April through September or October. If you plan to do a lot of camping, pick up the handy "Caravan and Camping in Ireland" guide (£1.50) from a tourist office; it is chock-full of maps and information on all registered campgrounds. **During the summer tourist season, reserve as far in advance as possible for all types of accommodation.**

APARTMENT & VILLA RENTALS

If you want a home base that's roomy enough for a family and comes with cooking facilities **consider a furnished rental.** These can save you money, especially if you're traveling with a group. Home-exchange directories sometimes list rentals as well as exchanges.

INTERNATIONAL AGENTS • **At Home Abroad** (405 E. 56th St., Suite 6H, New York, NY 10022, tel. 212/421–9165, fax 212/752–1591). **Drawbridge to Europe** (5456 Adams Rd., Talent, OR 97540, tel. 541/512–8927 or 888/268–1148, fax 541/512–0978). **Europa-Let/Tropical Inn- Let** (92 N. Main St.,

Ashland, OR 97520, tel. 541/482–5806 or 800/462–4486, fax 541/482–0660). **Hideaways International** (767 Islington St., Portsmouth, NH 03801, tel. 603/430–4433 or 800/843–4433, fax 603/430–4444; membership $99). **Rental Directories International** (2044 Rittenhouse Sq., Philadelphia, PA 19103, tel. 215/985–4001, fax 215/985–0323). **Rent-a-Home International** (7200 34th Ave. NW, Seattle, WA 98117, tel. 206/789–9377 or 800/964–1891, fax 206/789–9379). **Vacation Home Rentals Worldwide** (235 Kensington Ave., Norwood, NJ 07648, tel. 201/767–9393 or 800/633–3284, fax 201/767–5510). **Villas and Apartments Abroad** (1270 Ave. of the Americas, 15th floor, New York, NY 10020, tel. 212/759–1025 or 800/433–3020, fax 212/897–5039). **Villas International** (950 Northgate Dr., Suite 206, San Rafael, CA 94903, tel. 415/499–9490 or 800/221–2260, fax 415/499–9491).

B&BS & GUEST HOUSES

B&Bs and guest houses are everywhere, from Dublin's city center to County Donegal's most remote reaches. The typical B&B is a family home with a few rooms given over to visitors. The standard rate is about £15–£18 per person, and most B&Bs accept reservations; any Irish tourist office will make one for you for a £1–£2 fee. Breakfast (generally consisting of coffee or tea, cereal, toast, fried eggs, sausages, and a healthy layer of grease) is nearly always included in the price, and some B&Bs will provide dinner for a small additional charge. If B&Bs will be your primary lodging, consider picking up one of the nationwide B&B books (£2) at tourist offices. Guest houses are really small, informal hotels with 10–30 rooms; they tend to be less friendly than B&Bs but offer more privacy.

CAMPING

This is the cheapest way of seeing the country, and facilities for campers and caravanners are improving steadily. An abundance of coastal campsites compensates for the shortage of inland ones. All are listed in "Caravan and Camping Ireland," available from any tourist office. Rates start at about £4 per tent, £6 per caravan overnight.

HOME EXCHANGES

If you would like to exchange your home for someone else's **join a home-exchange organization,** which will send you its updated listings of available exchanges for a year and will include your own listing in at least one of them. It's up to you to make specific arrangements.

EXCHANGE CLUBS • HomeLink International (Box 650, Key West, FL 33041, tel. 305/294–7766 or 800/638–3841, fax 305/294–1448; $93 per year). **Intervac U.S.** (Box 590504, San Francisco, CA 94159, tel. 800/756–4663, fax 415/435–7440; $83 for catalogs).

HOSTELS

No matter what your age you can **save on lodging costs by staying at hostels.** It is important to remember that almost all hostels in Ireland are open to travelers of all ages; they are not student-only domains. The crowd tends to be a pleasant and exciting mix of university students, professionals with a taste for down-to-earth travel, and older, hardened budget travelers who sometimes come with the whole family. Hostels offer the cheapest beds in the country—generally £5–£9. In more remote areas the local hostel may be one of your only options for affordable accommodation.

The best bet are hostels overseen by Independent Holiday Hostels (IHH), a friendly organization with nearly 90 hostels throughout Ireland. The good news: no IHH membership fee, no curfews or daytime lockouts, and check-in at any time of day. Accommodations generally include small, 6- to 10-bed coed dorm rooms, self-service kitchens, and showers. Singles and doubles are usually an option. Many also have camping facilities. The bad news: IHH is so popular that its hostels are often booked solid during summer, especially in places like Dublin, Cork, and Galway. Conveniently, it now has a book-ahead system that allows you to reserve a bed at another IHH hostel for 50p, plus a £5.50 deposit on your bed (the remainder, if any, to be paid when you arrive). Some hostels accept phone reservations, so call ahead whenever possible. The main office in Dublin or any member hostel can provide you with an IHH map or information book. A handy, free guide to IHH hostels throughout the country is also available at most tourist offices. There is also a growing number of unaffiliated hostels springing up throughout the country.

Membership in any HI national hostel association, open to travelers of all ages, allows you to stay in HI-affiliated hostels at member rates (one-year membership is about $25 for adults; hostels run about $10–$25 per night). Members also have priority if the hostel is full; they're eligible for discounts around the world, even on rail and bus travel in some countries.

ORGANIZATIONS • An Óige (61 Mountjoy St., Dublin 2, tel. 01/8304555), the HI affiliate. **Australian Youth Hostel Association** (10 Mallett St., Camperdown, NSW 2050, tel. 02/9565–1699, fax 02/9565–1325). **Hostelling International—American Youth Hostels** (733 15th St. NW, Suite 840, Washington, DC 20005, tel. 202/783–6161, fax 202/783–6171). **Hostelling International—Canada** (400–205 Catherine St., Ottawa, Ontario K2P 1C3, tel. 613/237–7884, fax 613/237–7868). **Independent Holiday Hostels** (IHH; 21 Store St., Dublin, tel. 01/8364700). **Youth Hostel Association of England and Wales** (Trevelyan House, 8 St. Stephen's Hill, St. Albans, Hertfordshire AL1 2DY, tel. 01727/855215 or 01727/845047, fax 01727/844126). **Youth Hostels Association of New Zealand** (Box 436, Christchurch, New Zealand, tel. 03/379–9970, fax 03/365–4476). Membership in the United States $25, in Canada C$26.75, in the United Kingdom £9.30, in Australia $44, in New Zealand $24.

MAIL & SHIPPING

The Irish mail service is known as An Post. Post offices and smaller substations (generally housed in the back of shops or newsagents) are located in every town in Ireland.

POSTAL RATES

Airmail rates to the United States and Canada from the Irish Republic are 45p for letters and postcards. Mail to all European countries goes by air automatically, so airmail stickers or envelopes are not required. Rates are 32p for letters and postcards.

Rates from Northern Ireland are 43p for letters and 37p for postcards (not over 10 grams). To the rest of the United Kingdom and the Irish Republic, rates are 26p for first-class letters and 20p for second class.

RECEIVING MAIL

You can receive those precious letters from home via "Poste Restante" at any post office (or, if you have an AmEx card, at one of their offices). Here's what you do: Figure out where you'll be in 10 days, and then tell the folks back home the address, town, and (most importantly) the postal code of the post (or AmEx) office where they'll be sending the package. Tell them to write POSTE RESTANTE and HOLD FOR 30 DAYS in the upper left corner of the envelope. You will need to show ID (and/or your American Express card) to pick up this mail.

MONEY MATTERS

Ireland is no longer the cheap destination it once was. For travelers with American dollars, prices for many items in Ireland are more than 1½ times what they are in the United States. It's more than just a bad exchange rate; a booming economy has pushed up prices dramatically, especially in Dublin and other major cities. Even if you stay in hostels or B&Bs and eat only pub grub and cheap chip shop food, be prepared to drop $40 a day. If you plan to stay in hotels and eat in restaurants, your daily bill could top $100 per person.

To add insult to injury, the Irish government slaps a whopping 12%–21% Value Added Tax (VAT) on almost everything. The VAT is usually included in prices, but not always—be sure to ask. VAT refunds are available to all non-EU residents. Look for stores displaying a CASHBACK sticker, where you will receive a voucher with your purchase. Present this voucher at the Cashback desk in the Dublin or Shannon airport for your refund.

In Northern Ireland things cost about the same as in the South, perhaps a little more, except for alcohol and cigarettes. Many southerners who travel north will return with bags full of smuggled cheap beer and cigarettes tucked under their car seat. **To obtain a VAT refund for purchases made in Northern Ireland, you'll need to ask the shopkeeper for the appropriate form and get customs officials to stamp it at the airport;** finally, after you've arrived home you can send the form and a self-addressed Northern Irish–stamped envelope to the shopkeeper, who will then send you a refund.

Lodging will be your greatest expense in Ireland. Expect to pay about £5–£8 for basic hostel accommodations. Prices for bed-and-breakfasts (B&Bs) vary widely, but you can usually find something for £10–£15 per person. Hotels are expensive throughout Ireland, £40 and up. You can camp for as little as £3, though fully equipped campgrounds may charge as much as £8 per site.

Prices throughout this guide are given for adults. Substantially reduced fees are almost always available for children, students, and senior citizens. For information on taxes, *see* Taxes, *below.*

ATMS

To increase your chances of happy encounters with cash machines in Ireland, before leaving home, **make sure that your card has been programmed for ATM use there—ATMs in Ireland accept PINs of four or fewer digits only**; if your PIN is longer, ask about changing it. If you know your PIN as a word, learn the numerical equivalent since most Irish ATM keypads show numbers only, no letters. You should also have your credit card programmed for ATM use (note that Discover is accepted mostly in the United States); a Visa or MasterCard can also be used to access cash through certain ATMs, although fees may be steep and the charge may begin to accrue interest immediately even if your monthly bills are paid up. Local bank cards may not work overseas; **ask your bank about a MasterCard/Cirrus or Visa debit card,** which works like a bank card but can be used at any ATM displaying a MasterCard/Cirrus or Visa logo.

ATM LOCATIONS • Cirrus (tel. 800/424–7787). A list of **Plus** locations is available at your local bank.

CREDIT CARDS

In this guide the words "cash only" in the service information indicate that a property does not accept credit cards.

REPORTING LOST CARDS • American Express (tel. 336/668–5110 international collect). **Diner's Club** (tel. 702/797–5532 collect). **MasterCard** (tel. 1678/70866 toll-free). **Visa** (tel. 1678/177232).

CURRENCY

The unit of currency in the Irish Republic is the pound or punt (pronounced poont). It is divided into 100 pence (abbreviated 100p). In this guide, the £ sign refers to the Irish pound; the British pound is referred to as the pound sterling and is written U.K.£.

Irish notes come in denominations of £100, £50, £20, £10, and £5. Coins are available as £1, 50p, 20p, 10p, 5p, 2p, and 1p, and they are not exchangeable outside the Republic of Ireland.

Ireland is now a member of the European Monetary Fund (EMU) and since of January 1, 1999, all prices have been quoted in pounds and Euros. Noncash transactions, including credit card payments, can be quoted in Euros. January 2002 will see the introduction of the Euro coins and notes, as well as the gradual withdrawal of the local currency.

CURRENCY EXCHANGE

You'll get a better deal if you buy pounds in Ireland rather than at home. Nonetheless, it's a good idea to **exchange a bit of money into pounds before you arrive in Ireland** in case the exchange booth at the train station or airport at which you arrive is closed or has a long line. At other times, for the most favorable rates change **money at banks.** Although fees charged for ATM transactions may be higher abroad than at home, Cirrus and Plus exchange rates are excellent because they are based on wholesale rates offered only by major banks. You won't do as well at exchange booths in airports, rail and bus stations, hotels, restaurants, or stores, although you may find their hours more convenient.

Since tourism is such an important industry, nearly every backwater town throughout Ireland has a Bank of Ireland, an Allied Irish Bank (AIB), or an Ulster Bank branch, making it easy to exchange money. In larger cities, you'll find dozens of banks in the city center. Banks usually take a 1%–3% commission for currency exchanges. In general, Irish banks are open weekdays 10–12:30 and 1:30–3. For weekend exchanges, you generally have two choices: either a gift shop that extorts a large commission or, in larger towns, a post office.

Also, you can often withdraw money with a Visa, MasterCard, or AmEx card. It's better to do so through an ATM machine than through a bank since banks generally charge a £3 commission. Some (apparently randomly selected) AIB, Bank of Ireland, and Ulster Bank ATMs are now linked to the Cirrus and Plus systems, so you can also retrieve money with your bank card if your card is so linked. There will usually be at least one such ATM in towns with populations greater than 10,000, but you may have to hunt for it. Of course, before you leave home, you must get a PIN number (access code) of no more than four digits to use your credit card or bank card at any ATM in Ireland. *See* ATMs, *above.*

EXCHANGE SERVICES • International Currency Express (tel. 888/842–0880 on East Coast; 888/278–6628 on West Coast). **Thomas Cook Currency Services** (tel. 800/287–7362 for telephone orders and retail locations).

TRAVELER'S CHECKS

Do you need traveler's checks? It depends on where you're headed. If you're going to rural areas and small towns, go with cash; traveler's checks are best used in cities. Lost or stolen checks can usually be replaced within 24 hours. To ensure a speedy refund, buy your own traveler's checks—don't let some-one else pay for them: Irregularities like this can cause delays. The person who bought the checks should make the call to request a refund.

PACKING

In Ireland you can experience all four seasons in one day, so pack accordingly. Even in July and August, the hottest months of the year, a heavy sweater and a good waterproof coat or umbrella are essential. **You should bring at least two pairs of walking shoes**: It can and does rain at any time of the year, and shoes can get soaked in minutes.

In your carry-on luggage **bring an extra pair of eyeglasses or contact lenses** and **enough of any med-ication you take** to last the entire trip. You may also want your doctor to write a spare prescription using the drug's generic name, since brand names may vary from country to country. In luggage to be checked, **never pack prescription drugs or valuables.** To avoid customs delays, carry medications in their original packaging. And don't forget to copy down and carry addresses of offices that handle refunds of lost traveler's checks.

CHECKING LUGGAGE

How many carry-on bags you can bring with you is up to the airline. Most allow two, but not always, so make sure that everything you carry aboard will fit under your seat, and get to the gate early. Note that if you have a seat at the back of the plane, you'll probably board first, while the overhead bins are still empty.

If you are flying internationally, note that baggage allowances may be determined not by piece but by weight—generally 88 pounds (40 kilograms) in first class, 66 pounds (30 kilograms) in business class, and 44 pounds (20 kilograms) in economy.

Airline liability for baggage is limited to $1,250 per person on flights within the United States. On inter-national flights it amounts to $9.07 per pound or $20 per kilogram for checked baggage (roughly $640 per 70-pound bag) and $400 per passenger for unchecked baggage. You can buy additional coverage at check-in for about $10 per $1,000 of coverage, but it excludes a rather extensive list of items, shown on your airline ticket.

Before departure **itemize your bags' contents** and their worth, and label the bags with your name, address, and phone number. (If you use your home address, cover it so that potential thieves can't see it readily.) Inside each bag **pack a copy of your itinerary.** At check-in **make sure that each bag is cor-rectly tagged** with the destination airport's three-letter code. If your bags arrive damaged or fail to arrive at all, file a written report with the airline before leaving the airport.

PASSPORTS & VISAS

When traveling internationally **carry a passport even if you don't need one** (it's always the best form of ID), and **make two photocopies of the data page** (one for someone at home and another for you, car-ried separately from your passport). If you lose your passport, promptly call the nearest embassy or con-sulate and the local police.

ENTERING IRELAND

All U.S., Canadian, Australian, and New Zealand citizens, even infants, need a valid passport to enter Ireland for stays of up to 90 days. Citizens of the United Kingdom, when traveling on flights departing from Great Britain, do not need a passport to enter Ireland. Passport requirements for Northern Ireland are the same as for the Republic.

PASSPORT OFFICES

The best time to apply for a passport or to renew is during the fall and winter. Before any trip, check your passport's expiration date, and, if necessary, renew it as soon as possible.

AUSTRALIAN CITIZENS • **Australian Passport Office** (tel. 131–232).

CANADIAN CITIZENS • **Passport Office** (tel. 819/994–3500 or 800/567–6868).

NEW ZEALAND CITIZENS • **New Zealand Passport Office** (tel. 04/494–0700 for information on how to apply; 04/474–8000 or 0800/225–050 in New Zealand for information on applications already submitted).

U.S. CITIZENS • National Passport Information Center (tel. 900/225–5674; calls are 35¢ per minute for automated service, $1.05 per minute for operator service).

STUDENTS IN IRELAND

To save money, **look into deals available through student-oriented travel agencies** and the various other organizations involved in helping student and budget travelers. Typically you'll find discounted airfares, rail passes, tours, lodgings, or other travel arrangements, and you don't necessarily have to be a student to qualify. The big names in the field are STA Travel, with some 100 offices worldwide and a useful Web site (www.sta-travel.com), and the Council on International Educational Exchange (CIEE or "Council" for short), a private, nonprofit organization that administers work, volunteer, academic, and professional programs worldwide and sells travel arrangements through its own specialist travel agency, Council Travel. Travel CUTS, strictly a travel agency, sells discounted airline tickets to Canadian students from offices on or near college campuses. The Educational Travel Center (ETC) books low-cost flights to destinations within the continental United States and around the world. And Student Flights, Inc., specializes in student and faculty airfares. Most of these organizations also issue student identity cards, which entitle bearers to special fares on local transportation and discounts at museums, theaters, sports events, and other attractions, as well as to a handful of other benefits, which are listed in the handbook that most provide to their cardholders. All student ID cards cost between $10 and $20.

STUDENT IDS AND SERVICES • Council on International Educational Exchange (CIEE; 205 E. 42nd St., 14th floor, New York, NY 10017, tel. 212/822–2600 or 888/268–6245, fax 212/822–2699) for mail orders only, in the United States. **Travel Cuts** (187 College St., Toronto, Ontario M5T 1P7, tel. 416/979–2406 or 800/667–2887) in Canada.

TAXES

VALUE-ADDED TAX (VAT)

When leaving the Irish Republic, U.S. and Canadian visitors **get a refund** of the value-added tax (VAT), which currently accounts for a hefty 21% of the purchase price of many goods and 12.5% of those that fall outside the luxury category. Apart from clothing, most items of interest to visitors, right down to ordinary toilet soap, are rated at 21%. Most crafts outlets and department stores operate a system called Cashback, which enables U.S. and Canadian visitors to collect VAT rebates in the currency of their choice at Dublin or Shannon Airport on departure. Otherwise, refunds can be claimed from individual stores after returning home. Forms for the refunds must be picked up at the time of purchase, and the forms must be stamped by customs before leaving Ireland (including Northern Ireland). Most major stores deduct VAT at the time of sale if goods are to be shipped overseas; however, there is a shipping charge. VAT is not refundable on accommodation, car rental, meals, or any other form of personal services received on holiday.

VAT REFUNDS • Europe Tax-Free Shopping (233 S. Wacker Dr., Suite 9700, Chicago, IL 60606-6502, tel. 312/382–1101).

TELEPHONES

COUNTRY & AREA CODES

The country code for Ireland is 353. When dialing an Irish number from abroad, drop the initial 0 from the local area code. The country code is 1 for the United States and Canada, 61 for Australia, 64 for New Zealand, and 44 for the United Kingdom.

DIRECTORY & OPERATOR INFORMATION

For directory assistance in Ireland and Northern Ireland, dial 1190 (free from public phones). Telecom Éireann cards are not good in the North.

INTERNATIONAL CALLS

AT&T, MCI, and Sprint can place collect and credit-card calls to North America from any phone. Otherwise, dial 114 (in Dublin) or 10 (outside Dublin) and place your international call through an Irish operator—a more expensive (to whomever is paying) and time-consuming task. International direct-dial calls can be made from most pay phones. Bring along a phone card or a barrelful of £1 coins because the average international rate is 60p per minute.

LONG-DISTANCE CALLS

When calling a given Irish city from abroad, drop the 0 from the area code. For example, Dublin's prefix is 01 if you're calling from within Ireland, 1 if calling from the United States or the United Kingdom.

LONG-DISTANCE SERVICES

AT&T, MCI, and Sprint access codes make calling long distance relatively convenient, but you may find the local access number blocked in many hotel rooms. First ask the hotel operator to connect you. If the hotel operator balks ask for an international operator, or dial the international operator yourself. One way to improve your odds of getting connected to your long-distance carrier is to travel with more than one company's calling card (a hotel may block Sprint, for example, but not MCI). If all else fails call from a pay phone.

ACCESS CODES • AT&T (tel. 800/550–000). **MCI** (tel. 800/551–001). **Sprint** (tel. 800/552–001).

PHONE CARDS

To cope with card phones, you'll need to **buy a Telecom Éireann** card, available from post offices, Telecom Eireann (the national phone company), or any store displaying the yellow-and-blue CALLCARD sign. Each unit on the card is equivalent to 20p, and cards come in 10-unit (£2), 20-unit (£3.50), 50-unit (£8), and 100-unit (£16) denominations. If you're having any trouble, **dial 10 (free) to speak to an operator.**

PUBLIC PHONES

Within Ireland, the cost of a three-minute local call is 20p. Older phones accept 5p, 10p, and 50p coins. Newer phones will accept all coins except for 5p, but either way there should be a sign stating which coins a particular phone accepts. You'll hear a series of beeps when you need to insert more money.

TIPPING

In Ireland, tip generously only if the service is excellent, and it often is. Standard practice is to tip 10%–15% in taxis and restaurants (unless service is included). Bartenders are almost never tipped, except around Christmas time, when you can tell them to "have one yourself," which translates as tipping them the price of a pint.

TOURS & PACKAGES

On a prepackaged tour or independent vacation everything is prearranged so you'll spend less time planning—and often get it all at a good price.

BOOKING WITH AN AGENT

Travel agents are excellent resources. But it's a good idea to collect brochures from several agencies because some agents' suggestions may be influenced by relationships with tour and package firms that reward them for volume sales. If you have a special interest **find an agent with expertise in that area;** ASTA (see Travel Agencies, below) has a database of specialists worldwide.

Do some homework on your own, too: Local tourism boards can provide information about lesser-known and small-niche operators, some of which may sell only direct.

BUYER BEWARE

Each year consumers are stranded or lose their money when tour operators—even large ones with excellent reputations—go out of business. So **check out the operator.** Ask several travel agents about its reputation, and try to **book with a company that has a consumer-protection program.** (Look for information in the company's brochure.) In the United States, members of the National Tour Association and United States Tour Operators Association are required to set aside funds to cover your payments and travel arrangements in case the company defaults. It's also a good idea to choose a company that participates in the American Society of Travel Agent's Tour Operator Program (TOP); ASTA will act as mediator in any disputes between you and your tour operator.

Remember that the more your package or tour includes the better you can predict the ultimate cost of your vacation. Make sure you know exactly what is covered, and **beware of hidden costs.** Are taxes, tips, and transfers included? Entertainment and excursions? These can add up.

TOUR-OPERATOR RECOMMENDATIONS • American Society of Travel Agents (*see* Travel Agencies, *below*). **National Tour Association** (NTA; 546 E. Main St., Lexington, KY 40508, tel. 606/226–4444 or 800/682–8886). **United States Tour Operators Association** (USTOA; 342 Madison Ave., Suite 1522, New York, NY 10173, tel. 212/599–6599 or 800/468–7862, fax 212/599–6744).

PACKAGES

AIR-HOTEL-CAR • Aer Lingus (tel. 212/557–1110 or 800/223–6537). **Brian Moore Tours** (1208 VFW Pkwy., Suite 202, Boston, MA 02132, tel. 617/469–3300 or 800/982–2299). **British Airways Holidays** (tel. 800/247–9297). **Celtic International Tours** (1860 Western Ave., Albany, NY 12203, tel. 518/862–0042 or 800/833–4373). **CIE Tours** (Box 501, 100 Hanover Ave., Cedar Knolls, NJ 07927-0501, tel. 201/292–3899 or 800/243–8687). **Delta Dream Vacations** (tel. 800/872–7786). **DER Tours** (9501 W. Devon St., Rosemont, IL 60018, tel. 800/782–2424 for brochures). **Irish American International Tours** (Box 465, Springfield, PA 19064, tel. 610/543–0785 or 800/633–0505, fax 610/543–0786). **United Vacations** (tel. 800/328–6877).

FLY-DRIVE • American Airlines Fly AAway Vacations (tel. 800/321–2121). **Delta Dream Vacations** (*see above*). **United Vacations** (*see above*).

THEME TRIPS

BED-AND-BREAKFASTS • Brendan Tours (15137 Califa St., Van Nuys, CA 91411, tel. 818/785–9696 or 800/421–8446, fax 818/902–9876). **Irish Tourist Board** (*see* Visitor Information, *below*). **Northern Ireland Tourist Board** (*see* Visitor Information, *below*). **Value Holidays** (10224 N. Port Washington Rd., Mequon, WI 53092, tel. 414/241–6373 or 800/558–6850).

BICYCLING • Backroads (801 Cedar St., Berkeley, CA 94710-1800, tel. 510/527–1555 or 800/462–2848, fax 510/527–1444). **Butterfield & Robinson** (70 Bond St., Toronto, Ontario, Canada M5B 1X3, tel. 416/864–1354 or 800/678–1147, fax 416/864–0541). **Classic Adventures** (Box 153, Hamlin, NY 14464-0153, tel. 716/964–8488 or 800/777–8090, fax 716/964–7297). **Euro-Bike Tours** (Box 990, De Kalb, IL 60115, tel. 800/321–6060, fax 815/758–8851). **Himalayan Travel** (110 Prospect St., Stamford, CT 06901, tel. 203/359–3711 or 800/225–2380, fax 203/359–3669).

CULTURE • Lynott Tours (350 5th Ave., No. 2619, New York, NY 10118-2697, tel. 212/760–0101 or 800/221–2474, fax 212/695–8347).

CUSTOMIZED PACKAGES • Destinations Ireland & Great Britain (13 Sterling Pl., Suite 4-A, Brooklyn, NY 11217, tel. 718/622–4717 or 800/832–1848, fax 212/622–4874).

FOOD AND WINE • Annemarie Victory Organization (136 E. 64th St., New York, NY 10021, tel. 212/486–0353, fax 212/751–3149).

GOLF • Aer Lingus (*see* Packages, *above*). **Francine Atkins' Scotland/Ireland** (2 Ross Ct., Trophy Club, TX 76262, tel. 817/491–1105 or 800/742–0355, fax 817/491–2025). **Golf International** (275 Madison Ave., New York, NY 10016, tel. 212/986–9176 or 800/833–1389, fax 212/986–3720). **Golfpac** (Box 162366, Altamonte Springs, FL 32716-2366, tel. 407/260–2288 or 800/327–0878, fax 407/260–8989). **ITC Golf Tours** (4134 Atlantic Ave., No. 205, Long Beach, CA 90807, tel. 310/595–6905 or 800/257–4981). **Value Holidays** (*see* Bed-and-Breakfasts, *above*).

HIKING/WALKING • Backroads (*see* Bicycling, *above*). **Butterfield & Robinson** (*see* Bicycling, *above*). **Hiking Holidays** (Box 711, Bristol, VT 05443-0711, tel. 802/453–4816 or 800/537–3850, fax 802/453–4806). **Himalayan Travel** (*see* Bicycling, *above*). **Mountain Travel-Sobek** (6420 Fairmount Ave., El Cerrito, CA 94530, tel. 510/527–8100 or 800/227–2384, fax 510/525–7710). **Wilderness Travel** (801 Allston Way, Berkeley, CA 94710, tel. 510/548–0420 or 800/368–2794, fax 510/548–0347).

HORSEBACK RIDING • Cross Country International Equestrian Vacations (Box 1170, Millbrook, NY 12545, tel. 914/677–6000 or 800/828–8768, fax 914/677–6077). **Equitour FITS Equestrian** (Box 807, Dubois, WY 82513, tel. 307/455–3363 or 800/545–0019, fax 307/455–2354).

TRAIN TRAVEL

Travel on the state-owned Iarnród Éireann is quick, efficient, and free to all InterRail and EurailPass holders, but expect to pay handsomely if you don't have these passes or aren't eligible for the Travelsave stamp (*see* Transportation around Ireland, *below*). If you are under 26 but not a student, you can purchase a Fair Card (also known as the "Under 26 Card") at most train stations for £8; it gives you discounts of 25%–50% on all rail travel. Trains generally run between 5 AM and midnight. Reservations are not accepted for any route, and your ticket does not guarantee you a seat. **On summer weekends, arrive early** if you plan to travel on the popular Dublin–Cork, Dublin–Wexford, or Dublin–Galway route.

CUTTING COSTS

If you plan to ride the rails, **compare costs for rail passes and individual tickets.** If you plan to cover a lot of ground in a short period, rail passes may be worth your while; they also spare you the time waiting in lines to buy tickets. To price costs for individual tickets of the rail trips you plan, ask a travel agent or call Rail Europe, Railpass Express, or DER Tours. If you're under 26 on your first day of travel, you're eligible for a youth pass, valid for second-class travel only (like Europass Youth, Eurail Youth Flexipass, or Eurail Youthpass). If you're older, you must buy one of the more expensive regular passes, valid for first-class travel, and it might cost you less to buy individual tickets, especially if your tastes and budget call for second-class travel. Be sure to **buy your rail pass before leaving the United States**; those available elsewhere cost more. Also, if you have firm plans to visit Europe next year, consider buying your pass this year. Prices for rail passes generally rise on December 31, and your pass is valid as long as you start traveling within six months of the purchase date. The upshot is that a pass bought on December 30, 2000, can be activated as late as June 30, 2001.

If you decide that you'll save money with a rail pass, ask yourself whether you want a EurailPass, an InterRail pass, or a pass issued by Irish Rail (*see below*), the state-owned rail company. InterRail (*see below*) is a great deal and valid for travel throughout the Ireland, but it's available only to European residents and those who have lived in an EU country for more than six months. EurailPasses are a good deal only if you plan to tackle several European countries.

Last warnings: **Don't assume that your rail pass guarantees you a seat on every train.** Seat reservations are required on some express and overnight trains. Also note that many rail passes entitle you to free or reduced fares on some ferries (though you should still make seat reservations in advance).

The EurailPass is valid for unlimited first-class train travel through 17 countries—Austria, Belgium, Denmark, Finland, France, Germany, Greece, Hungary, Italy, Luxembourg, the Netherlands, Norway, Portugal, Republic of Ireland, Spain, Sweden, and Switzerland. It's available for periods of 15 days, 21 days, one month, two months, and three months. If you're under 26, the Eurail Youthpass is a much better deal.

European citizens and anyone who has lived in the EU for at least six months can purchase an InterRail Pass, valid for one month's travel in Austria, Belgium, Bulgaria, Croatia, the Czech Republic, Denmark, Finland, France, Germany, Great Britain, Greece, Hungary, Italy, Luxembourg, Morocco, the Netherlands, Norway, Poland, Portugal, Republic of Ireland, Romania, Slovakia, Slovenia, Spain, Sweden, Switzerland, and Turkey. The pass works much like Eurail, except that you only get a 50% reduction on train travel in the country where it was purchased. Be prepared to prove EU citizenship or six months of continuous residency. In most cases you'll have to show your passport for proof of age and residency, but sometimes a European university ID will do. To prove residency, old passport entry stamps may do the trick, but be forewarned that each time passes are presented, the ticket controller has the option of looking at passports and confiscating "illegitimate" passes. InterRail passes can only be purchased in Europe at rail stations and some budget travel agencies; try the European branches of STA or Council Travel (*see* Students in Ireland, *above*).

The Brit-Ireland Pass—valid for travel on trains throughout the United Kingdom and Ireland and Sealink ferry service between the two—is available in the following increments: 5 out of 30 days ($299) and 10 out of 30 days ($429). All passes are available from most travel agents and from the BritRail Travel Information Office.

Travel on Iarnród Éireann (Irish Rail), the state-owned rail company, is free to InterRail and Eurail pass holders. In addition, you can purchase two passes in the United States and Ireland. The Irish Explorer rail pass ($93) is valid for any 5 days in a 15-day period on all trains in the Republic of Ireland. The Irish Rover rail pass ($116) is good for 15 days on trains in the Republic and Northern Ireland.

INFORMATION ON RAIL PASSES • BritRail Travel Information Office (1500 Broadway, New York, NY 10036, tel. 800/677–8585). **DER Tours** (tel. 800/782–2424). **Irish Rail** (108 Ridgedale Ave., Morristown, NJ 07962, tel. 800/243–7687). **Rail Europe** (tel. 800/438–7245). **Railpass Express** (tel. 800/722–7151).

FARES & SCHEDULES

Stop by any depot or the **Dublin office** (35 Lower Abbey St., tel. 01/8366222).

TRANSPORTATION

Ireland's rail network, operated by Iarnród Éireann (Irish Rail), is modern and comfortable but only serves major cities. Smaller destinations are served by Bus Éireann, Ireland's comprehensive national bus service, and a number of independent, regional bus companies. Rail travel can be pretty expensive, but bus service is about 10%–60% cheaper (and slower). Luckily there are a few deals that can save you some pounds. If you're under 26 and have a valid ISIC card, definitely purchase the invaluable Travelsave stamp (£7), which entitles you to a 30%–50% discount on all rail fares, 10%–30% on bus fares, and a slightly smaller discount on all ferries. The Travelsave stamp is available from major Bus Éireann depots and many tourist offices. Both Iarnród Éireann and Bus Éireann also offer great deals on day-return tickets for their "Expressway" routes: main lines like Dublin to Sligo, Waterford, Rosslare, etc. A number of other train and bus passes are available, but they generally aren't worthwhile.

TRAVEL AGENCIES

A good travel agent puts your needs first. Look for an agency that has been in business at least five years, emphasizes customer service, and has someone on staff who specializes in your destination. In addition **make sure the agency belongs to a professional trade organization.** The American Society of Travel Agents (ASTA), with 27,000 agents in some 170 countries, is the largest and most influential in the field. Operating under the motto "Integrity in Travel," it maintains and enforces a strict code of ethics and will step in to help mediate any agent-client disputes if necessary. ASTA also maintains a Web site that includes a directory of agents. (If a travel agency is also acting as your tour operator, *see* Buyer Beware *in* Tours & Packages, *above.*)

LOCAL AGENT REFERRALS • American Society of Travel Agents (ASTA, tel. 800/965–2782 24-hr hot line, fax 703/684–8319, www.astanet.com). **Association of British Travel Agents** (68–271 Newman St., London W1P 4AH, tel. 020/7637–2444, fax 020/7637–0713). **Association of Canadian Travel Agents** (1729 Bank St., Suite 201, Ottawa, Ontario K1V 7Z5, tel. 613/521–0474, fax 613/521–0805). **Australian Federation of Travel Agents** (Level 3, 309 Pitt St., Sydney 2000, tel. 02/9264–3299, fax 02/9264–1085). **Travel Agents' Association of New Zealand** (Box 1888, Wellington 10033, tel. 04/499–0104, fax 04/499–0786).

VISITOR INFORMATION

TOURIST INFORMATION • Bord Fáilte (Irish Tourist Board), the umbrella organization for Ireland's seven regional tourist boards, can book you a room, recommend a restaurant, and fill your pockets with maps, brochures, and pamphlets—including a number of helpful lodging guides. Bord Fáilte has offices in major cities and other heavily touristed spots throughout Ireland. Its main office (Suffolk St., Dublin) also makes lodging reservations for the whole country; call 01/6057777 in Ireland. Most towns also have some form of a locally run visitor center where you can pick up brochures and inquire about accommodations.

The Northern Ireland Tourist Board offices supply a full range of information on the six counties of Northern Ireland.

IRISH TOURIST BOARD • U.S. (345 Park Ave., New York, NY 10154, tel. 212/418–0800 or 800/223–6470, fax 212/371–9052). **Canada** (160 Bloor St. E, Suite 1150, Toronto, Ontario M4W 1B9, tel. 416/929–2779, fax 416/929–6783). **U.K.** (Ireland House, 150 New Bond St., London W1Y 0AQ, tel. 020/7493–3201, fax 020/7493–9065). **Australia** (36 Carrington St., 5th floor, Sydney, NSW 2000, tel. 02/299–6177). **New Zealand** (Dingwall Building, 87 Queen St., Auckland 1, tel. 09/379–3708).

NORTHERN IRELAND TOURIST BOARD (NITB) • U.S. (551 5th Ave., Suite 701, New York, NY 10176, tel. 212/922–0101 or 800/326–0036, fax 212/922–0099). **Canada** (111 Avenue Rd., Suite 450, Toronto, Ontario M5R 3J8, tel. 416/925–6368, fax 416/961–2175). **U.K.** (11 Berkeley St., London W1X 5AD, tel. 020/7355–5040 for written or telephone inquiries only; BTA's Ireland Desk, 4–12 Lower Regent St., London BW1Y 4PQ, tel. 020/7839–8416).

U.S. GOVERNMENT ADVISORIES • U.S. Department of State (Overseas Citizens Services Office, Room 4811 N.S., 2201 C St. NW, Washington, DC 20520; tel. 202/647–5225 for interactive hot line; 301/946–4400 for computer bulletin board; fax 202/647–3000 for interactive hot line); enclose a self-addressed, stamped, business-size envelope.

WEB SITES

Do **check out the World Wide Web** when you're planning. You'll find everything from up-to-date weather forecasts to virtual tours of famous cities. Fodor's Web site, www.fodors.com, is a great place to start your online travels. Some of the most popular sites (note that their log-on addresses are subject to change) are **Irish Tourism Board** (www.ireland.travel.ie); **Northern Ireland Tourist Board** (www.ni-tourism.com); **Best of Ireland** (www.iol.ie/-discover/welcome.htm); and **Every Celtic Thing on the Web** (www.mi.net/users/ang/angris.html).

WHEN TO GO

The main tourist season runs from mid-April to mid-October, but the real hordes arrive in June, July, and August. During summer prices predictably go up, and many hostels and cheap hotels stop offering weekly rates. Spring in Ireland can also be pleasant—the daffodils and crocuses are in full bloom, and the crowds of foreign tourists are not yet overwhelming. For a very different view of Ireland, come during autumn or early winter. With the tourists all gone, you're more likely to get an honest—albeit cold and wet—view of Hibernia. The West and Northwest are at their most colorful in September and October. Unfortunately, during the off-season many B&Bs, campgrounds, and some hostels are closed; tourist offices and major attractions operate on limited schedules; and public transportation in many regions goes into semihibernation.

Even in summer, rain is an ever-present threat and layering is de rigueur. Summer also means long, long days—sunrise by 6:30 AM and sunset around 10:30 PM. If you're from the United States, you might be forgiven for thinking the miserly gods have cheated you of daylight for all these years.

CLIMATE

Every 10 years, Ireland is blessed with a summer so wonderful that it tides everyone over through the next 9 years of gray skies. The east and south coasts are the driest areas, while the west is famous for its eternal rain. Though the temperature in Ireland rarely falls below freezing in winter, the air is very damp and the cold seems to go right to your bones. The weather in spring is incredibly schizophrenic; a bright, sunny morning is no guarantee that you won't see rain or even hail by teatime.

FORECASTS • Weather Channel Connection (tel. 900/932–8437), 95¢ per minute from a Touch-Tone phone.

FESTIVALS

The following list of major festivals only scratches the surface of the thousands of events staged in Ireland. For information about smaller, local fairs, see the appropriate chapters.

JANUARY • At least six major horse-race meetings (the sport is an obsession to many Irish) are held at centers such as Thurles (Co. Tipperary), Naas (Co. Kildare), Leopardstown (Co. Dublin), and Gowran Park (Co. Kilkenny).

FEBRUARY • The Dublin Film Festival starts at the end of the month, providing 12 days of the best in world cinema, plus lectures and seminars on all aspects of filmmaking.

MARCH • On St. Patrick's Day (March 17), raise a celebratory pint of Guinness with the thousands of other Irish types in pubs throughout the country. The Belfast Music Festival sponsors speech, drama, and music competitions for younger performers.

APRIL • The two-day Irish Grand National race meeting takes place at Fairyhouse, County Meath, about 19 km (12 mi) from Dublin. About 60 choirs raise their voices in the Cork International Choral Festival.

MAY • The County Wicklow Gardens Festival includes flower festivals, musical evenings, and garden tours. Belfast Civic Festival and Lord Mayor's Show lasts 21 days and includes concerts, competitions, and exhibitions, starting on the second Saturday in May with floats in the streets of Belfast.

JUNE • Listowel Writer's Week provides a mix of user-friendly workshops, readings, lectures, and plays. Bloomsday, June 16, is celebrated with great affection in Dublin with a flurry of readings and dramatizations of Joyce's *Ulysses,* preceded by fancy-dress shenanigans over breakfast and pilgrimages around the city.

JULY • The city of the West really swings during the Galway Arts Festival—the largest in the country—which includes theater, parades, film, and rock music, as well as international art exhibits. The Killarney Horse Racing Festival attracts horse fans from around the country and is the perfect place to study the characters of rural Ireland. Battle of the Boyne festivities throughout Northern Ireland celebrate the 17th-century battle in which the Protestant William of Orange defeated the Catholic James II.

AUGUST • The Yeats International Summer School in Sligo is the oldest and most famous of the 15 or so summer schools taking place around the country during this month. Puck Fair is a robust and jovial happening held mid-month at Killorglin, County Kerry. At the end of the month the same county holds the famous Rose of Tralee Festival, a talent show and beauty pageant for women of Irish decent from around the world. Near the end of the month, the Kilkenny Arts Week is an internationally renowned classical musical festival.

SEPTEMBER • The Matchmaking Festival in Lisdoonvarna, County Clare, is the traditional place for bachelor farmers to seek a wife; you'll spot plenty of Yanks who made the trip in hope of finding a partner for life. The Cork Film Festival, the Sligo Arts Week, and the Waterford International Festival of Light Opera all start at the end of the month and run into October.

OCTOBER • The Dublin Theatre Festival is a fortnight of concentrated drama from around the globe, with a special focus on homegrown talent. Cork swings and bops on the last weekend in October when every young fan and old beatnik in the country seem to arrive for the Guinness International Jazz Festival. The Wexford Opera Festival runs for the last two weeks of the month and on into November; directors and performers from all over the world descend on the little city by the sea.

DECEMBER • New Year's Eve celebrations are ubiquitous, but the best place to be at midnight is one of the thousands of parties that people throw in their homes.

DUBLIN

CALE SILER AND ANTO HOWARD

I n the not so distant past, to read Joyce was to know Dublin. In his celebrated work *Ulysses,* the author, in self-imposed exile, provided a detailed map of the city at the turn of the century. And for the next 80 years, except for a few name changes, much of Joyce's Dublin remained intact. The dirty lanes were still here, the soot-covered flats, the dockside slums, and, most of all, the smoky pubs. His infamous portrayal of the people as wits and layabouts trapped by the paralysis of their Catholic, conservative, and chronically poor city also seemed at least partly accurate right up to the late 1980s. Then, in a short few years, everything changed.

To visit Dublin now is to catch it on the crest of a wave of growth and modernization unequaled in the long history of Ireland. In recent years, the white heat of progress, fanned by money from the European Union Structural Fund, has swept through the capital, and many exiles returning after a few years abroad are taken aback by the big-city feel of their old beloved Dublin. All the talk is of the "Celtic Tiger," as the new, vibrant Irish economy has been labeled. There's construction on every second street and a rash of new clubs, coffeehouses, juice bars, cyber cafés, and sushi restaurants. The traffic jam has become the favorite national conversational topic—second only to the insane increase in house prices—and the dreaded cellular phone (much cheaper to use in Ireland than in the United States) is now ubiquitous among the working young. Classic pubs are being replaced by dance-music–inspired, trendy hangouts, reminiscent of London in the mid-1980s, but with a touch more modesty and class.

The population of the greater Dublin area, roughly 1.5 million, is growing rapidly as people from all over the country flock here to find work, and for the first time in the history of the state, the number of returning immigrants outstrips those "taking the boat" of emigration. Don't be surprised if your waitress in a Dublin café speaks English with a delightful mix of Eastern European accenting and pure Dublin idioms. The last few years have seen a sizable (for ultrahomogenous Ireland, that is) influx of immigrants from all over Europe, but especially from former Soviet-bloc countries like Hungary and Romania. Hordes of Spanish students, North and Central Africans studying to be doctors, and Japanese learning English also add to the new, cosmopolitan Dublin scene. It's also a young town, with over half its people under 25. The chic Temple Bar area is the epicenter of this new Dublin and displays its pluses and minuses in microcosm: The energy level on the streets is electric; the bars are packed almost every night; everybody seems to have money to spend; it costs a king's ransom to get an apartment; many classy old bars have been carelessly "revamped"; and you can't go 15 seconds without hearing a cell phone ring.

"My darlin' Dublin's dead and gone," goes the old ballad, and in many ways it is. The price of prosperity, as so many other European cities have discovered, is often a surge in crime and pollution, and a certain loss of innocence and serenity. But the visitor to Dublin, with a little work, can still uncover Joyce's "Dear Dirty Dumpling, foostherfather of fingalls and dotthergills." Dublin is rightly famed for its cobbled streets, its tightly packed rows of Georgian flats, and its dockside warehouses where faded billboards still remind passersby to "Smoke Walnut Plug. It's a Nut!" But as Irish writers like Joyce, O'Brien, Yeats, and O'Casey discovered long ago, people are what make Dublin a great city: portly grandmums complaining about the price of tea in Bewley's café; churlish cart vendors hawking fish and Doc Martens boots with equal ease on Henry and Moore streets; a gruff pub fly soaking himself in stout, triple-checking the horse sheet between cordial hellos and handshakes.

Dublin City hugs the arc of Dublin Bay—from Howth in the north to the Dalkey headland in the south—and continues to creep ever inward to cover most of the county that bears its name. Also to the south, the Dublin and Wicklow mountains stand as a spectacular backdrop to the city on its rare sunny days. The heart of a city is its river, and Dublin's Liffey runs east to west to split the city neatly in two. This divide is not simply physical; the more affluent and slightly snobbish southside can seem a world apart from the more working class, sometimes blighted, and fiercely proud northside.

The capital of modern Ireland, Dublin was first settled by Celtic traders in the 2nd century AD. They christened it Baile Atha Cliath, or City of the Hurdles, a name that is still used by Gaelic speakers (look for it on buses and billboards throughout the city). At the crossroads of four countrywide trade routes, the settlement eventually became prosperous enough to attract the notice of the Greek geographer Ptolemy, who placed Dublin on the very first map of Ireland.

Dublin also attracted the attention of the Vikings, who sailed en masse in their dreaded longboats up the River Liffey. By 850, Dublin was firmly under Viking control, with a Viking king and a brawny city wall. The Norse gold and jewelry found here indicate the importance of Dublin for the Vikings, who established an outpost on the Liffey's southern bank (notice the excavated longboat overlooking the river near Christ Church; it was unearthed in the 1970s). Viking rule, however, was short-lived, and they were soundly trounced in 1014 by Brian Boru, the king of Ireland. Boru was murdered immediately after the battle, and subsequent power struggles left the island divided and vulnerable. Dublin thus declined politically throughout the 11th and 12th centuries, especially after England's King Henry II, with the approval of the pope, landed troops in Counties Wexford and Dublin in 1171, signaling the beginning of the end of Irish home rule for the next seven centuries.

As political ties were strengthened between Ireland and England, Dublin was thoroughly refashioned. Under the rule of the English—who provided the money, artisans, and urban planners—Dublin grew into a modern capital. After Henry II established a secondary court in Dublin in 1173 (mostly to keep a close watch on Ireland's fickle vassal kings), the city was granted a charter, bringing a deluge of skilled immigrants from the Continent. The English influence also led to the creation of Trinity College (1591), a respectable alternative to Cambridge and Oxford for Anglo-Irish Protestants. Politically speaking, the English influence also fueled the much-celebrated Grattan Parliament of 1782, when the English (and Protestant) Henry Grattan demanded Ireland's independence from London. In 1801, the Act of Union brought England and Ireland together in the newly formed United Kingdom. Political power was moved from Dublin to London, and the Irish Parliament was forced and bribed to vote itself out of existence—the only European parliament ever to do so.

Much of the current architectural glory of Dublin belongs to the 18th century. In 1857 the Commission for Making Wide & Convenient Streets began a movement to gentrify and improve the look of the capital. Focusing on the area immediately south of the Liffey, the well-to-do began an extraordinary period of Georgian house-building around Merrion and Fitzwilliam squares that can be appreciated to this day. The 19th century was a period of serious decline for the city, as tenement slums (so movingly evoked in the plays of O'Casey) became the homes of much of the population. The 1916 rebellion, the civil war that followed, and the Troubles inflicted physical and economic damage on the city.

Dublin is a great walking city, compact and easily navigated. The Liffey divides it in two, and the wide boulevard called O'Connell Street runs north–south through its center. A walk up the quays on either side of the river, past the city's many bridges, will bring you to some of the major sites, including Christ Church, the Guinness Factory, Busáras (the main bus station), and Heuston Train Station. The majority of areas of interest to the visitor can be found just south of the river. Temple Bar and Trinity College are just over O'Connell Bridge. A little farther south the major shopping thoroughfare, Grafton Street, leads down to St. Stephen's Green and the city's main museums and Georgian squares.

Overall, the pace of the capital is a lot faster than it was 10 years ago; the streets are more crowded, crime is higher, and the variety of attractions, restaurants, lodgings, and nightlife has increased exponentially. The underlying gentle magic of Dublin remains in the sanctuary of an out-of-the-way hostelry, in the citizens' unceasing search for a good time, and in their indefatigable sense of humor about themselves and their city. In the city of 1,000 public houses, "How do you get from one side of Dublin to another without passing a pub?" the old joke asks. "You go into every one."

BASICS

AMERICAN EXPRESS

This full-service office across from Trinity College changes money, issues and refunds traveler's checks, and holds mail for AmEx cardholders only. There is also a smaller office inside the Dublin Tourism office (*see* Visitor Information, *below*). *116 Grafton St., tel. 01/6772874 or 800/626000 for after-hrs emergency service. Open weekdays 9–5, Sat. 9–noon; bureau de change also open June–Sept., Sun. 11–4.*

BUREAUX DE CHANGE

Banks have the best rates and charge the lowest commissions for changing money. The two main banks, Allied Irish Bank (AIB) and Bank of Ireland, have branches near Trinity College. The AIB is on College Green, to the right of Trinity; and the Bank of Ireland is on Dame Street, just across from the front gates of the college. These two branches also have reliable Cirrus ATMs that will give you pounds from you dollar accounts. If you really need to change money in a hurry, and the banks are closed, various bureaux de changes can be found throughout the city, particularly on Grafton and Westmoreland streets. Interestingly, the bureau with the best rate and no commission can be found inside the Marks & Spencer department store on Grafton Street.

Two classic Dublin jokes: What's the first thing a southsider says when he arrives at work in the morning? Hi Dad. What do you call a northsider in a suit? The accused.

DISCOUNT TRAVEL AGENCIES

CIE Tours. This commission-driven company isn't overly fond of haggard folks looking for cheap deals, but it'll do its best to find you a mid-range plane or ferry ticket. *35 Lower Abbey St., tel. 01/6771871. Open weekdays 9–5, Sat. 9–1.*

USIT. This neon-color office of the Union of Students of Ireland Travel sells ISIC, HI, and EYC cards and Travelsave stamps, and it can book you on any rail, plane, boat, or rickshaw tour imaginable—usually at half the going rate. The office also has heaps of information on budget travel in Ireland, as well as a bulletin board listing job opportunities, apartments for rent, and people looking for travel companions. USIT is usually packed to the gills, so arrive early to avoid hour-long lines. *19–21 Aston Quay, west of O'Connell Bridge, tel. 01/6778117. Open weekdays 9–6 (Thurs. until 8), Sat. 10–5:30.*

INTERNET

There are a number of Internet cafés in the city center, which allow you to access the Internet and E-mail facilities. All charge £4–£6 an hour. **Betacafe** (Arthouse, Curved St., Temple Bar, tel. 01/6715717) is a new Internet café that serves coffee and sandwiches. **Cyberia** (The Granary, Temple La. S, Temple Bar, tel. 01/6797607) is very popular with students, who tend to hog the place for hours playing computer games. **Planet Cyber Café** (23 S. Great George's St., tel. 01/6790583), in the basement of a video store, is the city's best, with top-of-the-range computers and a good coffee bar.

LAUNDRY

No, you can't wear that shirt one more time without washing it! With more and more people choosing to live in inner-city apartments, Dublin's dearth of laundrettes is a thing of the past. On the northside, the **Laundry Shop** (191 Parnell St., tel. 01/8723541) does the job for you. You can listen to music as you spin at the southside's more jovial **All American Laundrette** (40 S. Great George St., tel. 01/4782655). Both are open 9–7.

LOST AND FOUND

Dublin Bus: Contact its headquarters (59 Upper O'Connell St., tel. 01/8734222).

Railways and DART: Contact Iarnród Éireann/Irish Rail (Travel Centre, 35 Lower Abbey St., tel. 01/8366222).

DUBLIN

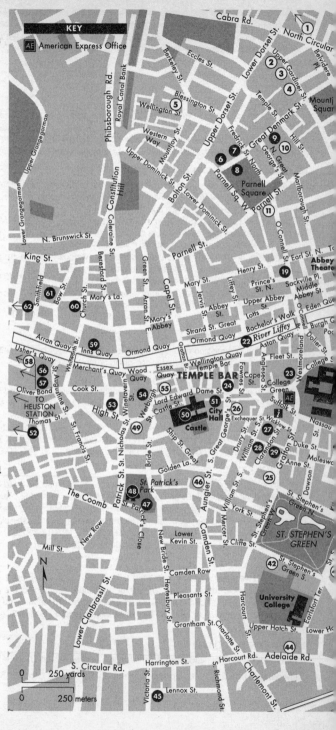

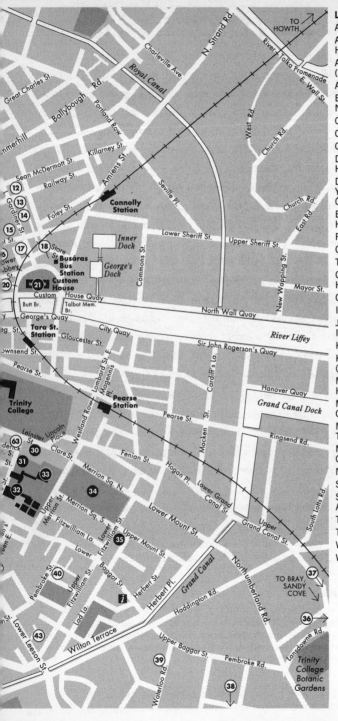

Lodging ○

Abraham House, **14**

Ariel Guest House, **37**

Avalon House (IHH), **46**

Avondale, **15**

Bewley's at Newlands Cross, **58**

Cassidy's Hotel, **11**

Central Hotel, **26**

Charleville Lodge, **1**

Drury Court Hotel, **25**

Dublin International Youth Hostel (An Óige), **5**

Earl of Kildare Hotel, **63**

Fatima House, **3**

Georgian Court, **13**

The Glen, **14**

Globetrotters Tourist Hostel (IHH), **17**

Grey Door, **40**

Isaac's, **18**

Jurys Christchurch Inn, **49**

Kilronan House, **44**

Kinlay/USIT House (IHH), **55**

Marian Guest House, **4**

Montessori Education Centre (MEC), **10**

Morehampton House Tourist Hotel, **38**

Mount Herbert Guest House, **36**

Number 31, **43**

Stella Maris, **2**

Stephen's Hall All-Suite, **41**

The Talbot, **16**

The Townhouse, **12**

Waterloo Lodge, **39**

Wynn's Hotel, **20**

REJOYCE!

If Joyce fans make one pilgrimage in their lives, let it be to Dublin on June 16 for Bloomsday. June 16, of course, is the day Leopold Bloom toured Dublin in "Ulysses," and commemorative events take place all day long and well into the night. Grown men and women stroll the streets attired in black suits and carrying fresh bars of lemon soap in their pockets, imitating the unassuming hero of what is arguably the 20th century's greatest novel. Dedicated Joyceans can start the day at 6 AM with a Bloomsday breakfast (£10) at the South Bank Restaurant in Sandycove. Here, like Bloom himself, they can enjoy "grilled mutton kidneys which gave to his palate a fine tang of faintly scented urine." While in Sandycove, stop in at the Martello Tower (see Just Outside the City, below) for readings and performances by the Dublin Cultural Theatre Group, and general merriment. In Dublin, a number of organized walks retrace Leopold's meanderings. Morning walks leave at 8 AM from the Snug (Dorset St.) and at 9 AM from the Tara Street DART station. You can stop at Davy Byrne's on Duke Street for a midday meal of Gorgonzola cheese sandwiches and red wine. Throughout the day the Balloonatics Theatre Company presents Joycean sketches with a twist—and musical accompaniment—at various locations, including the Dublin Writers Museum (at noon) and the Ormond Hotel on Ormond Quay (at 4 PM).

Don't despair if you miss Bloomsday, because Dublin swarms with all sorts of other Joycean possibilities. The excellent James Joyce Centre (35 N. Great George's St., tel. 01/8788547), set in an 18th-century town house (former home of Denis Maginni, "professor of dancing, etc."), houses a Joycean archive and library and hosts readings and lectures. Admission, including a guided tour of the house, is £2.50. Guides—if you're lucky you'll get Ken Monaghan, Joyce's nephew—conduct walking tours from the center for £5.50, including admission to the house; call for times. Tourist offices also sell the "Ulysses Map of Dublin" (80p), which marks the principal locations of the novel.

LUGGAGE STORAGE

Most hostels, B&Bs, and hotels allow you to leave luggage behind for a few hours after checkout. After that you can store your bags in a locker. **Busáras** (pronounced bus-*r*-us; *see* By Bus *in* Coming and Going, *below*) has lockers (£1.50 daily) and a left-luggage desk, open Monday–Saturday 8–7:45 and Sunday 10–5:45. Or shove your stuff in the lockers (£1.50–£4 for 24 hours) at **Heuston Station** or **Connolly Station** (*see* By Train *in* Coming and Going, *below*).

MAIL

Towering over O'Connell Street is the majestic **General Post Office** (GPO), where Patrick Pearse first intoned the Proclamation of the Irish Republic. You can buy stamps, money orders, and phone cards in the main lobby. To send a postcard to the United States costs 38p, to the United Kingdom 28p. For currency exchange, turn left and follow the signs. This is also the place to pick up poste restante mail. *1 Prince's St., at O'Connell St., tel. 01/7057000. Open Mon.–Sat. 8–8, Sun. 10:30–6.*

MEDICAL AID

Both **General Medical Service** (tel. 01/8343644) and **Dental Service** (tel. 01/6790700) can help foreigners in an emergency. Most hospitals will not charge if your case only requires instant treatment in their accident or emergency unit. This means they'll set a bone or stitch you up for nothing, but any prolonged treatment must be paid for. The only pharmacy chain in Dublin that stays open past 6 PM is **O'Connell's** (55 Lower O'Connell St., tel. 01/8730427). You'll find other branches of O'Connell's throughout Dublin, all open daily until 10 PM. Two of the most centrally located are 21 Grafton Street (tel. 01/6790467) and 6 Henry Street (tel. 01/8731077).

OPENING AND CLOSING HOURS

Dublin is gradually becoming a 24-hour city, even though the bus and DART train services leave you stranded at 11:30. (A few train lines run until dawn on the weekends, and weekend late buses go until 3 AM.) Many taxis run all night, but the demand, especially on weekends, can make for long lines at taxi stands. Many clubs on the Leeson Street strip and elsewhere stay open until 4 AM or later. Sunday, once a day of rest in Dublin, is now often bustling, with some stores open.

The Vikings called their colony here Dubh Linn (Black Pool, pronounced dove-linn), and this Norse name has since made its way into both Gaelic and English.

Banks are open weekdays 10–4, and remain open on Thursday until 5. All stay open at lunchtime. Most branches have ATMs that accept bank cards and MasterCard and Visa credit cards. **Museums** are normally open Tuesday–Saturday and Sunday afternoon; they are usually closed on Monday. **Post offices** are open weekdays 9–1 and 2–5:30, and Saturday 9–12:30. Main post offices are open Saturday afternoons, too (look for green signs that say AN POST). The **General Post Office** (GPO) on O'Connell Street, which has foreign exchange and general delivery facilities, is open Monday–Saturday 8–8, Sunday 10:30–6.

Pubs open Monday–Saturday at 10:30 AM and Sunday at 12:30 PM. They must stop serving at 11 PM in winter and 11:30 PM in summer, but most pubs take another hour to empty out, as patrons drag out their last drink as long as they can. For a memorable glimpse into a ritual repeated all over Ireland every night, hold out in a pub as long as you can and watch the patrons ignore the bartenders pleading with them to leave. A number of bars in the center of the city have permission to serve until 1 AM on weekend nights. **Stores** are open Monday–Saturday 9–5:30 or 9–6, Thursday until 8. Smaller city-center specialty stores open on Sunday as well, usually 10–6. Most department stores are closed on Sunday.

PUBLICATIONS

For current goings-on in Dublin, pick up the biweekly music gospel of Ireland, *Hot Press* (£2), or the weekly *Big Issue* (£1), for which half of the cover price goes to the street vendors who sell it. Both have great coverage of the contemporary Irish music scene. Dublin's theater and cinema listings can be found in the *Irish Times* (85p), Ireland's premier national newspaper and major domestic source for the printed daily news. There are also numerous free newspapers, like the *Event Guide,* that have information on current events, festivals, attractions, and entertainment listings.

RESOURCES FOR PEOPLE WITH DISABILITIES

The **National Rehabilitation Board** (44 N. Great George's St., tel. 01/8747503) provides general information for people with disabilities and an access guide to Dublin, which is also available at Dublin Tourism offices. The **Irish Wheelchair Association** (Blackheath Dr., Clontarf, tel. 01/8338241) is a private group with extensive information on issues of accessibility.

RESOURCES FOR GAYS AND LESBIANS

Gays and lesbians have steadily increased their visibility in Dublin. The city has a small but vibrant gay scene, which culminates each year in Pride Week (usually in June) with a parade and plenty of cultural events. Both the **National Gay and Lesbian Federation** (Hirschfeld Centre, 10 Upper Fownes St., tel. 01/6719076) and the **Gay Switchboard Dublin** (tel. 01/8721055) can give you the scoop on queer happenings. The free monthly *Gay Community News* covers gay and lesbian issues in Ireland and has lists of organizations, restaurants, nightclubs, and pubs that cater to a gay clientele. Most newsagents don't carry this paper; check in the Well Fed Café (*see* Food, *below*) and the Temple Bar Information Centre (*see* Visitor Information, *below*). Lesbians can call **Lesbian Line Dublin** (tel. 01/8729911) from 7 PM to 9 PM on Thursday. The *Big Issue* also has a section on gay and lesbian events.

RESOURCES FOR WOMEN

Well Woman Centre (73 Lower Leeson St., tel. 01/6610083 or 01/6610086) provides general information on women's issues, referrals for legal and medical counseling, and options for pregnant women. The Irish government lifted its ban on all abortion-related information in 1995.

VISITOR INFORMATION

An Óige, the Irish Youth Hostel Association, provides maps and listings of its hostels as well as tons of information on sights, tours, transportation, and the like. You can also pick a copy of the invaluable *An Óige Handbook* (£1.50) which lists all affiliated hostels in Ireland. *61 Mountjoy St., tel. 01/8301766 or 01/8304555, fax 01/8301600. Open weekdays 10–5.*

Dublin Tourism has three offices, but the best is the Suffolk Street location, housed in a former church. You can do almost everything at this tourism nerve center: Gray Line tours, Bus Éireann, AmEx, and Irish Ferries all have offices inside. At any office you can book a room (£1, plus 10% deposit), pick up train and bus schedules, choose from among hundreds of pamphlets on every part of the city and country, and buy walking-tour guides. *2 Suffolk St., tel. 01/6057799 for reservations or 01/550112233 (from Ireland only) for automated 24-hr information (58p per min). Open July–Sept., Mon.–Sat. 8:30–6, Sun. 11–5:30; Oct.–June, daily 9–6. Other locations: Baggot St. Bridge, facing Grand Canal (open daily 9:15–5:15). Dublin Airport, main terminal (open daily 8 AM–10 PM). Dún Laoghaire Harbour, Ferry Terminal (open daily 10–9).*

Temple Bar Information Centre has the scoop on the ultrahip Temple Bar area, along the south bank of the Liffey, with a special concentration on the arts scene. It also publishes the free bimonthly *Temple Bar Guide. 18 Eustace St., tel. 01/6715717. Open June–Sept., weekdays 9–7, Sat. 11–7, Sun. noon–6; Oct.–May, weekdays 9:30–6, Sat. noon–6.*

COMING AND GOING

BY BUS

Busáras, Bus Éireann's sole Dublin depot, is just north of the River Liffey and around the corner from the Connolly rail station. You can reach nearly every town in Ireland from here, but Expressway service is offered only to hub cities. Sample destinations from Dublin are as follows: Belfast (7 per day, 3 on Sun., 3 hrs; £10), Galway (8 per day, 4 on Sun., 4 hrs; £8), and Cork (4 per day, 3 on Sun., 4½ hrs; £12). Inside is an **info desk** and a large bulletin board listing the day's departures. *Store St., tel. 01/8366111. Info desk open daily 8:30–7.*

BY FERRY

Irish Ferries (16 Westmoreland St., tel. 01/6797977) and **Stena Sealink** (15 Westmoreland St., tel. 01/2047700) offer regular ferry service between Dublin and Holyhead, Wales. Irish Ferries (2 per day; £20–£25 single) sails directly into Dublin Harbour. Stena (4 per day; £26–£35 single) docks in Dún Laoghaire, 9½ km (6 mi) south of the city center. Prices and departure times vary according to season, so call the companies to confirm. Irish Ferries offers 25%–50% fare reductions to those with an ISIC card or Travelsave stamp, while Stena offers a 10% discount to ISIC cardholders. During the summer, reservations are strongly recommended. From Dún Laoghaire, a DART train is the most convenient way to reach the city center; from Dublin Harbour, take a bus (£1.10) or taxi (*see* By Taxi, *below*).

BY PLANE

Dublin Airport (tel. 01/8444900) is 10 km (6 mi) north of town. Daily flights to and from Britain and the Continent are offered by the Irish carriers **Aer Lingus** (41 Upper O'Connell St., tel. 01/7056705 for flight info or 01/8444777 for reservations) and **Ryanair** (3 Dawson St., tel. 01/6774422). Inside the airport, you'll find car-rental desks, a **bureau de change,** and a **Dublin Tourism** (tel. 01/2844768) desk, which is open daily 9–8. If you arrive after 11 PM or before 6 AM, most things will be closed and you'll need to take a taxi to reach the city center.

AIRPORT TRANSPORTATION • Airport Express buses (£2.50) make the trip between the airport and the Busáras bus depot every 20 minutes 6 AM–11 PM. You can save some money by taking any bus marked CITY CENTRE or Bus 41 (every 20 mins, £1.10), which stop at Eden Quay in the heart of town. If you're traveling to the airport from downtown, catch Bus 41 at Eden Quay (immediately east of O'Connell Bridge, facing the River Liffey) or at the Busáras terminal. There's also a taxi stop outside the airport's main entrance, usually staffed 24 hours a day; expect to pay about £12–£15 to the city center.

BY TRAIN

Dublin has two train stations that receive intercity trains: **Heuston** and **Connolly** are across town from each other but are connected by Bus 90, which runs frequently and costs 90p. Heuston serves routes to Cork (4 per day, 3 on Sun., 3¼ hrs; £16), Galway (4 per day, 2 on Sun., 2½ hrs; £12), Limerick (9 per day, 6 on Sun., 2¾ hrs; £12.50), Tralee (3 per day, 2 on Sun., 4 hrs; £16.75), and Waterford (4 per day, 3 on Sun., 3 hrs; £11.50), while Connolly serves routes to Rosslare (3 per day, 2 on Sun., 2¾ hrs; £10), Sligo (4 per day, 3 on Sun., 3 hrs; £12), and Belfast (8 per day, 3 on Sun., 2½ hrs; £15). You can buy tickets at either station or at the **Iarnród Éireann** (Irish Rail) office (35 Lower Abbey St., tel. 01/8366222), which has info on domestic passenger routes and sells a comprehensive timetable (50p).

HEUSTON STATION • Heuston Station, on the River Liffey 3 km (2 mi) west of the city center, is a run-down Victorian relic, lined with rows of arched steel spines that support a massive roof. There are dozens of **lockers** (£1.50–£4 per 24 hrs), a small **information desk,** and a **bureau de change.** From downtown, it's not a long walk, but buses leave for the station every 20 minutes from outside USIT on Aston Quay (see Discount Travel Agencies in Basics, above); from the station, take any bus labeled AN LÁR (city center). St. John's Rd., by Stevens La. Call 01/836–6111 weekdays 7:30 AM–10:30 PM, weekends 8 AM–10:30 PM for train info.

Take a clue from the portly Irish matrons keeping close watch on their kids in the Busáras station, and do the same with your luggage.

CONNOLLY STATION • Although Connolly Station has an intricate Georgian facade, its interior is a cement-and-steel monstrosity containing a small **information counter** and **lockers** (£1.50–£4 per 24 hrs). A number of hostels are within an easy walk of the station, or you can take any bus marked AN LÁR (city center) to Trinity College or O'Connell Street. If you're walking from the city center, cross the Liffey at O'Connell Bridge, continue four blocks up O'Connell Street, turn right on Earl Street (which becomes North Talbot Street), and follow the road as it curves left. The walk takes about 15 minutes. 16 N. Amiens St., tel. 01/8363333. Information counter open Mon.–Sat. 7:30 AM–9 PM, Sun. 4:30 PM–9:30 PM.

GETTING AROUND

Historically, the heart of Dublin was on the north side of the Liffey, somewhere between **O'Connell Street** and **Mountjoy Square.** This part of town once sheltered the likes of James Joyce and Brendan Behan, and it's also where you'll find the oldest Georgian town houses, grassy city squares, and Dublin's two most important theaters, the Abbey and the Gate. Today, while areas south of the Liffey get a glitzy, often tacky makeover, Dublin's **northside** is still the place to soak up the pure, unadulterated city. O'Connell Street, which abuts the River Liffey at one end and Parnell Street at the other, is the region's main artery, filled to overflowing with cheap tourist shops and neon-color fast-food outlets. **Henry Street** runs off O'Connell Street and leads into one of the city's main shopping districts, including the glorious **Moore Street** markets, where you're sure to hear the peal of a Dublin accent in all its rough splendor. The statue of Parnell (the 19th-century political hero christened by his contemporaries the "uncrowned king of Ireland") marks the beginning of **Parnell Square,** the oldest square in Dublin, now the site of many good-value bed-and-breakfasts. This part of town has a well-deserved reputation for being dangerous, so consider taking a taxi at night or at least walking in a reasonably large group.

Southside Dublin, on the other hand, is where you'll probably want to spend most of your time. Even though it's littered with sweater shops and overpriced restaurants, the southside still has charm, especially around **Merrion Square,** an impressive Georgian masterpiece, and in the **Temple Bar district,** which is filled with old pubs, narrow streets, and lots of cafés. **Trinity College** and the adjacent Bank of Ireland, a block south of the River Liffey from O'Connell Bridge, are Temple Bar's most famous landmarks. **Grafton Street,** just south of Trinity College, is Dublin's most famous pedestrian street and is always awash with good-looking people checking out the upmarket shops and bars. Walking is the best way to get around and experience Dublin; nearly everything of interest is an easy ramble from Trinity's front gate. Street names change often, sometimes every block or so, but they are usually posted on the sides of the corner buildings.

BY BUS

Between 6 AM and 11:30 PM, Dublin's streets rattle with the hum of its green double-deckers—fondly known as vomit-comets once the pubs close. New, characterless single deckers are fast replacing the old behemoths on many routes. Together they offer comprehensive service between 6 AM and 11:30 PM, but you may need a schedule (£1.40), available at the **Bus Atha Cliath** (Dublin Bus) main office, to choose among the 150 or so routes. If you're headed into town, nearly every bus passes Trinity College or the northside quays; just make sure the sign reads AN LÁR or CITY CENTRE. Fares range between 55p and £1.10. Drivers no longer give change; instead you'll get a receipt for the amount you overpaid, which you can claim at the Dublin Bus central office on O'Connell Street. There are also late-night buses (£3, worth paying just to see young suburban Dubliners letting loose their weekend spirit) that leave from Trinity College and Westmoreland Street on Thursday, Friday, and Saturday at midnight, 1, 2, and 3 AM, but there is no late-night inbound service. Bus stops in Dublin consist of a green pole marked DUBLIN BUS, and many post timetables and route maps. Dublin Bus provides free maps and timetables for all Dublin city bus routes. Call if you're confused about which bus to take. *59 Upper O'Connell St., tel. 01/8734222. Open weekdays 9–5, Sat. 9–1.*

A number of bus passes are available, but don't bother unless you plan to rely heavily on public transport to get around. The **One Day Travel Wide** (£3.30) allows unlimited travel for one day on buses only. The **One Day Bus/Rail Travel Wide** (£4.50) is valid on the buses, DART, and rail service in the greater Dublin area. The **Four Day Explorer** (£10) is also good on buses, DART, and trains. Insert your pass into the scanner on your right as you get on a bus. The **10 Journey Ticket Books** allow 10 trips of the same price (55p, 80p, £1, £1.10, or £1.25) and can save you up to £2.50. All passes are available from Dublin Bus's main office.

BY CAR

The number of cars in Ireland has grown exponentially in the last few years, and nowhere has their impact been felt more than in Dublin, where the city's complicated one-way streets are congested during the morning and evening rush hours and often during much of the rest of the day. If you can, avoid driving except to get you into and out of the city, and be sure to ask your hotel or guest house for clear directions to get you out of the city.

BY DART

The electric DART (Dublin Area Rapid Transport) is a clean, efficient, aboveground train that connects central Dublin with some of the suburbs. Since Dublin is easily navigated by foot, the only times DART comes in handy is for excursions to Sandycove, Dún Laoghaire, Howth, and Bray (*see* Chapter 3). The only downtown stations are at **Pearse Street** (behind Trinity College), **Tara Street** (off Townsend St., near the Liffey), and **Connolly Station.** DART trains run about every 15 minutes between 6:55 AM and 11:30 PM daily. One-way fares range between 75p and £1.30, and tickets are sold at the station. DART is administered by Irish Rail; all inquiries should be directed to them (*see* Coming and Going, *above*). Non-DART train services run from Heuston Station to Kildare Town west of Dublin via Celbridge, Sallins, and Newbridge, and from Connolly Station to more distant locations like Malahide, Maynooth, Skerries, and Drogheda to the north of Dublin, and Wicklow and Arklow to the south.

BY TAXI

There's a slew of taxis in Dublin, but at £1.80 just to get in and £1.60 per 2 km (1 mi) thereafter, you'll do better to explore the city center on foot. Once the pubs close, taxis may look pretty good, but on busy weekend nights you might have to wait in line for up to half an hour. Taxi stands are located beside the central bus station, at train stations, O'Connell Bridge, St. Stephen's Green, College Green, and near major hotels. Otherwise, to grab a cab, stand in the street and hail anything with an illuminated sign on its roof, or call **Castle Cabs** (tel. 01/8319000 or 01/8319947) or **City Cabs** (tel. 01/8727272). City Cabs accept most credit cards (though not American Express) and can provide wheelchair-accessible cabs. Tipping is becoming common.

WHERE TO SLEEP

"An absolute avalanche of new hotels" is how the *Irish Times* characterized Dublin's hotel boom. If you see a major construction site near the city center, and chances are you will, it's probably either luxury apartments or a new hotel. Though much of the new development has been in the high end of the market, many of the lodgings we review below are also in the throes of expanding. Many of those that aren't wish they could—as the demand for rooms continues to be unabated. Why all the new lodgings now? The boom in construction is a response both to Dublin's thriving business climate and its draw for visitors whose only business is fun. Europeans have finally discovered the city as a convenient, happening weekend getaway. What this means is that for all the supply of new rooms, rates are still high by the standards of any major European or American city (and factoring in the exchange rate means a hotel room can take a substantial bite out of any traveler's budget). Service charges range from 15% in more expensive hotels to zero in moderate and inexpensive ones. Be sure to inquire at the time of booking.

Many hotels offer a weekend, or "B&B," rate that is often 30%–40% cheaper than the ordinary rate; some hotels also offer a midweek special that provides discounts of up to 35%. These rates are available throughout the year but are harder to get during high season. Ask about them when booking a room (they are available only on a prebooked basis), especially if you plan a brief or weekend stay. If you've rented a car and you're not staying at a hotel with secure parking facilities, it's worth considering a location out of the city center, such as Dalkey or Killiney, where you won't have to worry about stashing your car on city streets, as parking can be difficult to find.

Lodgings on the north side of the river tend to be more affordable than those on the south. Many bed-and-breakfast establishments, long the mainstay of the economy end of the market, have upgraded their facilities to the "guest house" level, and now provide rooms with private bathrooms or showers, as well as multichannel color televisions and direct-dial telephones, for around £25 a night per person. B&Bs tend to be in suburban areas—generally a 10-minute bus ride from the center of the city. This is not in itself a great drawback, and the savings can be significant.

During July and August it's difficult to find even a mediocre bed in a sleazy hole-in-the-wall, especially if you haven't booked in advance. Ditto goes for big rugby- or football-game weekends. Dublin Tourism can tell you when these are, as well as book you a room for a £1 fee. You can also pick up their "Dublin Accommodation Guide" (£3), which lists every approved hotel, B&B, and hostel in Dublin County. Dublin Tourism has also installed **automated reservation kiosks** at the airport and at the Suffolk Street tourist office. With a credit card, you can choose and book a room at these machines, which will then spit out your confirmation, a map of Dublin, and directions to the lodging.

HOTELS

Central Hotel. Established in 1887, this grand, old-style redbrick hotel is in the heart of the center city, steps from Grafton Street, Temple Bar, and Dublin Castle. Guest rooms are notoriously small but have high ceilings and practical but tasteful furniture; although all have showers, not all have baths, so if you have a penchant for soaking, inquire when booking. A double will cost at least £100. Adjacent to the hotel is Molly Malone's Tavern, a lively hotel bar with plenty of regulars who come to sample the live, trad music played on Friday and Saturday nights. The restaurant and recently opened Library Bar with working fireplace—glorious spot for a twilight, post-shopping pint—are on the first floor. *1–5 Exchequer St., Dublin 2, tel. 01/6797302, fax 01/6797303. 70 rooms.*

Drury Court Hotel. A two-minute walk from Grafton Street and just around the corner from some of the city's best eateries, this small, quality hotel opened in March 1996. You'll pay between £100 and £120 for a double room decorated with some care in subtle shades of green, gold, and burgundy; the fully tiled bathrooms are a joy. The parquet-floored Rathskeller dining room serves breakfast and dinner; lunch is served in the casual Digges Lane Bar, frequented by younger, hipper Dubliners (or so they like to think). *28–30 Lower St. Stephens St., Dublin 2, tel. 01/4751988, fax 01/4785730. 32 rooms.*

Stephen's Hall All-Suite. Dublin's only all-suite hotel is in a tastefully modernized Georgian town house just off St. Stephen's Green. The suites, considerably larger than the average hotel room, include one or two bedrooms, a separate sitting room, a fully equipped kitchen, and bath. It might seem like £200 is a lot for the two-bedroom suite, but for a family or a group traveling together, it can be a good value. Top-floor suites have spectacular city views, and ground-floor suites have private entrances. Morel's Restaurant serves breakfast, lunch, and dinner. *14–17 Lower Leeson St., Dublin 2, tel. 01/6610585, fax 01/6610606. 37 suites.*

SMALL HOTELS AND GUEST HOUSES

Ariel Guest House. This redbrick, 1850 Victorian guest house is a real gem at the heart of the city, just a few steps from a DART stop and a 15-minute walk from St. Stephen's Green. Rooms (£70-plus for a double) in the main house are lovingly decorated with Victorian and Georgian antiques, Victoriana, and period wallpaper and drapes. Thirteen rooms added to the back of the house in 1991 are more mundane, but all are immaculately kept. A Waterford-crystal chandelier hangs over the comfortable leather and mahogany furniture in the gracious, fireplace-warmed drawing room; you'll swear you're in an old gentleman's club. Owner Michael O'Brien is an extraordinarily helpful and gracious host. *52 Lansdowne Rd., Dublin 4, tel. 01/6685512, fax 01/6685845. 40 rooms.*

Bewleys at Newlands Cross. On the southwest outskirts of the city, this drab and predictable four-story hotel is designed for families or small groups of travelers, especially those planning to head out of the city early to avoid the morning traffic crush. The hotel is emulating the dubious formula recently made popular by Jurys Inns, in which functional rooms—here each have a double bed, a single bed, and a sofa bed—are a flat rate (around £50) for up to three adults or two adults and two children. Breakfast is served in the small café, and there's also a small residents' lounge where you can get a decent pint. *Newlands Cross, Naas Rd., Dublin 2, tel. 01/4640140, fax 01/4640900. 126 rooms.*

Cassidy's Hotel. The southside doesn't have a monopoly on Georgian splendor, and this new, family-owned hotel at the top of O'Connell Street is located in a fine example of the wonders of 18th-century architecture. Inside it's a little less spectacular, but the rooms are carefully furnished in deep tones and dark woods. Free parking is available and it's only a five-minute walk to Trinity College. It's a little pricey at £105 for a double (£75 for a single), but it's worth the splurge. The downstairs bar is very popular. *7 O'Connell St., Dublin 1, tel. 01/8780555, fax 01/8780687. 88 rooms.*

Charleville Lodge. It's worth the short commute to the city center (the number 10 bus takes five minutes, and it's a great walk if the weather's good) to enjoy the luxury of the great-value Charleville Lodge. Located in the historic Phibsborough area on Dublin's northside, the lodge is in a beautifully restored Victorian terrace of houses (group of adjoined houses). The dramatically lit residents' lounge with working fireplace is the perfect spot to chat with other travelers who have dared to stray off the beaten path. For £40 a single and £60 a double they even throw in a whopping Irish breakfast. There's also a car park. *268/272 North Circular Rd., Dublin 7, tel. 01/8386633, fax 01/8385854. 30 rooms.*

Earl of Kildare Hotel. Named for the Irish patriot who resisted Henry VIII, the new Earl of Kildare Hotel overlooks Trinity College and is a stone's throw from the National Gallery and Grafton Street. The interior is modern and clean, if a little uninspired, but the Georgian exterior takes care not to disturb the elegant simplicity of Kildare Street as a whole. Rooms (£55 single, £70 double) have TVs and coffeemakers, and a public car park is nearby. The carvery lunch in the bar is a great value. *Kildare St., Dublin 2, tel. 01/6794388, fax 01/6794914. 33 rooms.*

Georgian Court. Gardiner Street is full of budget guest houses and B&Bs of varying quality, and the Court is one of the best. The recently refurbished 1805 terrace house is only a couple of minutes from O'Connell Street and has large, en-suite bedrooms with all the modern conveniences. A double will set you back £70 in season. There is even a private garage. *77–79 Lower Gardiner St., Dublin 1, tel. 01/8557872, fax 01/8555715. 43 rooms.*

The Grey Door. Like Kilronan House and Number 31 (*see below*), the Grey Door offers the cost-conscious visitor the chance to experience the genteel luxury of Georgian Dublin without breaking the bank. Right in the heart of the 18th-century old city, only a couple of minutes from St. Stephen's Green, this place has oversize, en-suite double rooms for only £95. The light-flooded sitting room is the perfect place to chill out and chat with other guests delighted at getting so much for so little. The guest house has two renowned restaurants and a private dining room for guests. *22/33 Upper Pembroke St., Dublin 2, tel. 01/6763289, fax 01/6763287. 7 rooms.*

Jurys Christchurch Inn. Expect few frills at this conveyor-belt budget hotel, part of a new Jurys minichain that offers a low, fixed room rate (£55) for up to three adults or two adults and two children. (The Jurys Custom House Inn, Custom House Quay, Dublin 1, tel. 01/6075000, at the International Financial Services Centre, operates according to the same plan.) The biggest plus: the classy location, facing Christ Church Cathedral and within walking distance of most city-center attractions. The rather spartan rooms are decorated in too-cutesy pastel colors with ultra-utilitarian furniture. A bar offers a pub lunch, and the restaurant serves a mundane breakfast and dinner. *Christchurch Pl., Dublin 8, tel. 01/4540000, fax 01/4540012. 184 rooms.*

Kilronan House. A five-minute walk from St. Stephen's Green, Deirdre and Noel Comer's guest house is a long-standing favorite with in-the-know travelers—thanks in large measure to the hearty welcome they receive. The large, late-19th-century terraced house, with a white facade, was carefully converted, and the decor and furnishings are updated each year. Richly patterned wallpaper and carpets grace the bedrooms (£45 for a single, £75 double), while orthopedic beds (rare in Dublin hotels, let alone guest houses) help to guarantee a restful night's sleep. Homemade breads are served as part of the full Irish breakfast. If you have a dog back home whom you're pining after, you'll appreciate Homer, the gregarious yellow Labrador. *70 Adelaide Rd., Dublin 2, tel. 01/4755266, fax 01/4782841. 15 rooms.*

Mount Herbert Guest House. Budget-minded visitors from all over the world flock to this sprawling guest house, made up of a number of large Victorian-era houses knocked into one. The hotel overlooks some of Ballsbridge's fine rear gardens and is right near the capital's main rugby stadium; you can hear the roar of the crowd on match day. The nearby DART will have you in the city center in seven minutes. The simple rooms (£49 for a single, £79 double) are painted in light shades with little furniture besides the beds, but all of them have bathrooms and 10-channel TVs—true luxury. There is no bar on the premises, but there are plenty of classy hostelries nearby. *7 Herbert Rd., Dublin 4, tel. 01/6684321, fax 01/6607077. 195 rooms.*

Number 31. Two Georgian mews strikingly renovated in the early 1960s as the private home of Sam Stephenson, Ireland's leading modern architect, are now connected via a small garden to the grand town house they once served. Together they now form a top-class guest house, just a short walk from St. Stephen's Green. New owners Deirdre and Noel Comer, who also own Kilronan House (*see above*), serve made-to-order breakfasts at refectory tables in the balcony dining room. The white-tile sunken living room, with its black leather sectional sofa and modern artwork that includes a David Hockney print, might make you think you're in California; but don't fret, it's still Dublin and double rooms are £84. *31 Leeson Close, Dublin 2, tel. 01/6765011, fax 01/6762929. 18 rooms.*

The Townhouse. Lower Gardiner Street, at the top of O'Connell Street, is awash with small guest houses. The Townhouse is probably the best of the bunch. Dion Boucicault, celebrated Irish master of the 19th-century melodrama, once lived in the elegant redbrick building, and the rooms all have literary names. The decor is sumptuous, yet never overbearing, and you wonder how they manage to charge such low prices (single £50, double £80). Rates include breakfast, and they have their own car park. *47 Lower Gardiner St., Dublin 1, tel. 01/8788808, fax 01/8788787. 66 rooms.*

Waterloo Lodge. Tree-lined Waterloo Road is certainly is one of Dublin's most elegant and desirable locations; it's also home to some excellent Georgian guest houses, of which the Waterloo Lodge is the best value. The modern renovation takes care not to spoil the splendor of the old four-story treasure. For £75 you get an ample double room, private parking, and a frighteningly filling Irish breakfast. If the ghost of Howard Hughes ever came to Dublin, the impossibly crisp and clean Breakfast Room might have tempted him to stay here. *23 Waterloo Rd., Dublin 2, tel. 01/6685380, fax 01/6685786. 10 rooms.*

Wynn's Hotel. Fancy a little Yeats after dinner? Right next to the Abbey Theatre, this long-established Dublin hotel is comfortable without bothering with too many frills. Every room has a bathroom and a TV. Singles are reasonable £65, and doubles go for £90 or so. They even have weekend specials. *35 Lower Abbey St., Dublin 2, tel. 01/8745131, fax 01/8741566. 70 rooms.*

BED-AND-BREAKFASTS

If you're in the mood for low-cost privacy, take yourself and your money to one of the hundreds of first-rate B&Bs peppered throughout the city center; most cost about £15–£25 per person, including breakfast. The majority lie just north of the River Liffey, near the bus station and Parnell Square—Talbot and Gardiner are good streets to try—and south of the River Liffey, near Trinity College.

Avondale. Though the plain rooms and pleasantly worn carpets aren't really worth the £20 per person you'd pay on summer weekends, rates are only £17 on weekdays and £13 off-season. Although bathrooms are shared, there's a shower in every room. *40–41 Lower Gardiner St., tel. 01/8745200. 20 rooms. Reception closes at 11:30 PM.*

Fatima House. For £27 per person (£25 off-season), you'll get a simple, comfortable room in a typically plain northside house. Each room has a sink, and rates include a thickly fried breakfast that can't be beat. *17 Upper Gardiner St., tel. 01/8745292. 12 rooms, 10 with bath.*

The Glen. If the Marriott hotel chain started renovating Georgian town houses, it would produce this B&B: very nice but bland. Every room has a shower, telephone, and TV, but you'll pay £27.50 per person for them in summer (£18 in winter). *84 Lower Gardiner St., tel. 01/8551374. 12 rooms.*

Marian Guest House. This clean home is run by a friendly woman who'll ply you with tea and talk your ear off. The rooms (£15 per person) are small, but you'll spend more time chatting in the parlor anyway. *21 Upper Gardiner St., tel. 01/8744129. 6 rooms.*

Stella Maris. High ceilings and an oak staircase grace this beautiful old house. The bedrooms (£50 for a double) are airy and bright, and the snug common room is littered with antiques, books, and old family photographs. The owner will accept traveler's checks of any currency. *13 Upper Gardiner St., tel. 01/8740835. 12 rooms, 9 with bath. Cash only.*

The Talbot. With its brick exterior and lace curtains, this guest house has all the makings of a country retreat (except for the fact that it's in the middle of downtown Dublin). The bright, large, and immaculate rooms cost £35–£40 single, £65–£75 double. *98 Talbot St., tel. 01/8749202 or 01/8749205. 48 rooms, 15 with bath.*

HOSTELS

Hostels in Dublin are not frat houses full of the baseball-cap and university T-shirt crowd. Almost all hostels in the city are open to travelers of all ages. The crowd tends to be a pleasant and exciting mix of university students, professionals with a taste for down-to-earth travel, and older, hardened budget travelers who sometimes come with the whole family.

Abraham House. A five-minute walk from the bus station, Abraham House is a good place to crash after a long bus ride. The happy staff of this large but well-kept hostel can sell you bus and Slow Coach tickets and will wash a big bag of laundry for £4. Beds in 12-bed dorms cost £8.50 (£7.50 off-season), and doubles are £40 (£30 off-season); rates include a decent Continental breakfast, towels, and sheets. Reservations are advised for weekends and July and August. *82 Lower Gardiner St., tel. 01/8550600. 145 beds. Kitchen.*

Avalon House (IHH). Housed in a beautiful Georgian relic two minutes from St. Stephen's Green, the rooms here are bright and cheery, and big plump comforters aid a sound sleep. The Avalon has dorm beds (£11, £8 off-season), doubles (£34, £30), and four luxurious singles (£20, £17); all rates include breakfast. Added conveniences here include a restaurant and bureau de change. *55 Aungier St., tel. 01/4750001. From city center, take Bus 16, 16A, 19, or 22 to the front door. 142 beds. Kitchen.*

Dublin International Youth Hostel (An Óige). Housed in the remains of a 19th-century convent, this enormous northside hostel shares the street with working-class flats and is about a 10-minute walk from the city center. The dorm beds (£10, £8 off-season) are narrow and cramped, but the dorm rooms are large, and luckily there's no curfew or lockout. Doubles are also available for £24 (£22 off-season). A stained-glass-lined dining room and clean, fully equipped kitchen take the edge off communal living. A Continental breakfast is included in the price. There's a bureau de change and laundry facilities (£4). *61 Mountjoy St., tel. 01/8301766 or 01/8301396. From O'Connell St., turn left on Parnell St., right on Parnell Sq. W, and continue 4 blocks to Mountjoy St. 420 beds. Cash only.*

Globetrotters Tourist Hostel (IHH). Globetrotters is a giant step up from many Dublin hostels, with amenities like a pleasant outdoor courtyard; clean, locking dorm rooms with en-suite showers; a turf fire; comfortable bunk beds (with individual lamps for late-night reading); and a delicious, all-you-can-eat breakfast. Plus, you're within walking distance of the city center, one block from the bus station, and two blocks from the train station. Beds cost £15 July–September (£12 off-season). They also have a special deal in the off-season: Stay three weeknights for £30. Sharing the building is the **Town House** (tel. 01/8788808), a cute B&B owned by the same people, with 38 meticulous rooms overlooking the bustling street below. Rooms cost £40 per person (£35 off-season). *46 Lower Gardiner St., near Lower Abbey St., tel. 01/8735893. 90 beds.*

Isaac's (IHH). This noisy northside hostel, underneath the DART tracks, has a pleasantly sleazy nightclub feel to it. Dorm beds in large, institutional rooms cost £6.95–£9.25, doubles £32–£34. Besides tea, sandwiches, and vegetarian entrées, Isaac's small café offers live music on an irregular basis, an outdoor patio, and card games and conversation nightly. They have a lockout from 11 AM to 5 PM. *2–5 Frenchman's La., around corner from Busáras depot, tel. 01/8749321. 400 beds. Kitchen. Cash only.*

Kinlay/USIT House (IHH). This building, in the heart of southside Dublin, looks like something out of a Dickens novel, with red masonry, wrought-iron fixtures, and tall windows. The six-bed dorm rooms are a bit musty, but you'll survive. You're only five minutes from Trinity College and within a stone's throw of Christ Church, St. Patrick's Cathedral, the Guinness Brewery, and the infamous Leo Burdock's (arguably the world's best fish-and-chip shop). Dorm beds are £10.50 (£9 low season), doubles £34 (£30), singles £20 (£18.50). Rates include breakfast, and you get a 10% discount with an ISIC card. There's a bureau de change and laundry facilities. *2–12 Lord Edward St., tel. 01/6796644. From Trinity College, walk west on Dame St. (which becomes Lord Edward St.). 150 beds. Kitchen.*

Montessori Education Centre (MEC). This enormous, three-story, northside hostel feels like a mansion haunted by friendly ghosts: Rickety steps lead nowhere, apparently purposeless closets appear in strange places, and children's voices emanate faintly from nearby classrooms. The rooms are spacious and clean, however, and the bathrooms are in tip-top shape. Dorm beds are £8.50 (£7 off-season), doubles are £21 (£19), and singles start at £13.50 (£10.50). Sheet rental is another £1. *42 N. Great George's St., tel. 01/8726301. From north end of O'Connell St., turn right on Parnell St., left on N. Great George's St. 100 beds. Kitchen. Cash only.*

Morehampton House Tourist Hostel. This hostel's best feature is its location among redbrick Georgian town houses in Donnybrook, an upper-middle-class suburb of Dublin. It's a quick 15-minute bus ride from the city center (80p) or a 25-minute walk. The facilities and dorm rooms (beds £8, £6 off-season) are standard hostel fare, except for private rooms (£50, £40 off-season), which are abnormally large and well lit via huge windows. Reception here is open 24 hours. The two drawbacks to this hostel are the moderate noise from the busy street and the management's policy of jacking up prices on all holidays and concert weekends. *78 Morehampton Rd., tel. 01/6688866. From O'Connell St. or Trinity College take Bus 10, 46A, or 46B. 100 beds. Kitchen.*

STUDENT HOUSING

Trinity College, Dublin City University (DCU), and University College Dublin (UCD) rent dormitory space during the summer holiday (mid-June–mid-September). You won't save any money going this route, but you do get a private or semiprivate room, clean sheets, and modern conveniences. **Trinity Hall** (Dartry Rd., Rathmines, tel. 01/4971772), 3 km (2 mi) from the city center, has neatly decorated rooms with sinks and shared kitchenettes and baths on each floor. Singles cost £16–£25, doubles £30–£50, including breakfast. **Dublin City University** (DCU, Glasnevin, tel. 01/7045736) is a couple of miles outside the city center and offers singles in two-room suites for £17. The rooms at **UCD Village** (UCD, Belfield, tel. 01/2697111) cost £22 per person; they also have more than 100 three-bedroom apartments for £66.

CAMPING

North Beach Caravan and Camping Park. What could be a more peaceful way to spend time in Dublin than camping beside the tranquil beach near the little coastal town of Rush? The 64 (44 with electricity) sites are available on a first-come, first-served basis. They even have indoor beds in case it rains (and it will). *Rush, tel. 01/8437131 or 01/8437602. From city center, take Bus 33 or suburban train to Rush. Electricity (£1), drinking water.*

Shankhill Caravan and Camping Park. Sixteen kilometers (10 mi) south of the city center and 3 km (2 mi) north of Bray, this is not exactly a downtown location. Motor homes and caravans share this 7-acre spread with tents, so don't come here with any hopes of Irish countryside. Tent sites are available on a first-come, first-served basis and cost £4.50 (£5 in summer), plus £1 per person. There's a DART stop 1 km (½ mi) away in Shankhill Town. *Shankhill, tel. 01/2820011. From city center, take Bus 45 or 84 (last bus at 11 PM) to the front gate. Electricity (£1), drinking water, showers (50p).*

FOOD

Though Dublin's cuisine was long dominated by dull sandwiches, bags of greasy chips, eggs and bacon, and Cadbury chocolate, the cosmopolitan spirit sweeping through the city has succeeded in launching a new wave of quality budget eateries. A large influx of immigrants has spawned a number of new, ethnic restaurants including Indian and Japanese. Young Dubliners, who nowadays tend to travel all over the world, are demanding more exciting fare at home. The Temple Bar/Georges Street district in particular has valiantly shaken off the chains of culinary mediocrity and is the place to go for vegetarian, Cajun, Italian, and even Portuguese grub. With a few exceptions the food isn't supercheap, though, so it may be best to adopt the local attitude that Guinness essentially encompasses all four food groups. Many restaurants have recognized that they are priced out of the reach of some diners and offer early bird and/or pre- and post-theater menus with significantly lower set prices at specific times, often from 6:30 to 8 PM.

Besides local chains like **Abrakebabra** (whose pita pockets are very popular with the après-pub crowd) and **Beshoff's** (a fast-food fish place with a popular branch opposite Trinity College), there are innumerable sandwich and tea shops scattered throughout the city center. Another ubiquitous feature of Dublin—and of all Ireland, for that matter—are chippers. These grungy holes-in-the-wall offer deep-fried food at reasonable prices; a burger and chips generally costs around £3, a piece of chicken £2.50, a plate of sausage and eggs around £2.50. If you would rather cook for yourself, stop by the **Moore Street Market** Monday through Saturday 9–6 for great prices on fruit, vegetables, meat, and fish. You can also find a good selection of reasonably priced food at grocery stores like **Dunnes** (50 Henry St., tel. 01/7268333) and **Quinnsworth** (15 Lower Baggot St., tel. 01/6761253).

RESTAURANTS

UNDER £5 • Alpha Restaurant. Even if "Irish cuisine" is sometimes nothing more than a convenient way to group potatoes and stout under the same heading, the shoe-box-size Alpha is a good place for an authentic Irish meal. The food, drawn mainly from the sinewy-beef and soggy-vegetable food groups, is greasy, heavy, strangely satisfying, and popular with working-class Dubliners who appreciate quantity and fair prices above quality. The staff, a couple of older ladies and their young niece, are about as friendly as it gets. Though it's tricky to find (two floors above a shop with a small neon sign in the window), the Alpha may become your home away from home. *37 Wicklow St., off Grafton St., tel. 01/ 7670213. Cash only. Closed Sun.*

Cornucopia. A pioneer among Dublin vegetarian eateries, Cornucopia still serves a menu of fine soups (try the spicy spinach) and sandwiches for £3–£4. The Vegetarian Fry Breakfast includes excellent meatless sausages. The place is a known hangout for some of Dublin's more hippie elements. *19 Wicklow St., tel. 01/6777583. Cash only. Closed Sun.*

Leo Burdock's. Winner of the "Best in Ireland" award, and touted locally as "the *real* reason the Vikings survived," Leo Burdock's has become a favorite of regulars such as U2, Liam Neeson, Mick Jagger, and Rod Stewart. In fact, so popular has Burdock's become that Leo can occasionally afford to close up shop on a whim and take the day off. For £2.50, try the fresh cod, haddock, whiting, or plaice with a side of tomato and tartar sauce. Dash on the salt and vinegar, wrap it in paper, and you've got yourself a meal. There is no seating—it's strictly takeout. *2 Wherburgh St., off Lord Edward St., tel. 01/4973177. Cash only. Closed Sun.*

Marks Brothers. Tasty sandwiches (huge by Dublin standards) and quality salads at a people's price (£2–£3.50), plus a few quiet little nooks hidden away on one of the three floors, act like magnets in drawing the starving Dublin artist and desperate Trinity student to this city-center eatery. The pastries are good, too. *7 S. Great George's St., tel. 01/6671085. Cash only. Closed Sun.*

Munchies. Thick slabs of freshly baked brown bread come filled with your choice of meat (tandoori chicken, tuna, roast turkey) and various side salads (curried rice, couscous, vegetables). A standard sandwich, filled with as many salads as your taste buds can handle, runs £3–£4. Watch out for hungry lunchtime office crowds. *Two locations: 146A Lower Baggot St., and 2 South William St., no phone. Cash only.*

Stag's Head. Sometimes, once in a million, pub grub steps out of the ordinary and becomes something special. The Stag's Head, a public house popular with Trinity students in the evening, is favored for lunch or early dinner by office workers and general layabouts in the know. There's not much variety on the menu, just three or four dishes, but somehow the chips and sausages have a bit more flavor, the peas are a little fresher, and the pies a little spicier. *Egon Ronay*, the well-known European restaurant guide, even gives the place a mention. *Dame St., Dublin 2, tel. 01/6793701.*

Well Fed Café. This Temple Bar co-op, one of Dublin's most famous vegetarian strongholds, serves a rotating selection of decent, wholesome, meat-free and vegan entrées. The school-cafeteria feel (plastic trays and a metallic service counter) is offset by the heartwarming prices—lasagnas and casseroles from £3, soups and salads from 80p—and the fact that you can bring your own wine. *6 Crow St., near corner of Dame and S. Great Georges Sts., tel. 01/6772234. Cash only. Closed Sun.*

UNDER £10 • Bad Ass Café. Sinéad O'Connor (or Sister Mary Bernadette according to her latest handle) used to wait tables at this lively spot in a converted warehouse between the Central Bank and Ha'penny Bridge (a "Rock 'n Stroll" tour plaque notes her presence here). Old-fashioned cash shuttles whiz around the ceiling of the barnlike space, which has bare floors and is painted in primary colors inside and out. A wall of glass makes for great people-watching. Although the food—mostly pizzas and burgers—is unexceptional, the Bad Ass experience can be a giggle. *9–11 Crown Alley, tel. 01/6712596.*

Clery's Restaurant. The famous Clery's department store on O'Connell Street is a well-kept secret on the Dublin budget food scene. It is home to a third-floor restaurant that serves decent meat-and-two-veg standards; an elegant tearoom with a full lunch menu; and a coffee shop with pastries and sandwiches. It's very popular with the older locals. *O'Connell St., tel. 01/8786000. Cash only. Closed Sun.*

Elephant & Castle. This is one of Dublin's most accessible upscale restaurants, in the heart of the cobblestone Temple Bar district. E&C is filled daily with wealthy businesspeople and ragged Trinity students alike, both hungry for the huge hamburgers (£7) or Chinese chicken salads (£9.50). A full meal with appetizers and dessert will easily set you back £12, but it's a wonderful place to purge your system of grease and potatoes. *18 Temple Bar, tel. 01/6793121.*

La Mezza Luna. Good, reasonably priced Italian food is served by a cheerful waitstaff in this hip, eclectic setting. Gobble yummy salads (£4–£5) or dazzle your taste buds with a daily special (£9) like chicken stuffed with cottage cheese or pesto on wild-mushroom pasta. The shamelessly rich Death by Chocolate cake (£3) should not be attempted alone. *Temple La., corner of Dame and S. Great George's Sts., tel. 01/6712840.*

Pasta Fresca. This stylish little Italian restaurant and delicatessen somehow squeezes a lot of people into a small area. Antipasto *misto* (assorted sliced Italian meats) makes a good start—or go for a single meat like prosciutto or *carpaccio della casa* (wafer-thin slices of beef fillet, with fresh Parmesan, olive oil, lemon juice, and black pepper). The main courses consist primarily of Pasta Fresca's own very good versions of well-known dishes such as *spaghetti alla Bolognese*, cannelloni, and *lasagna al forno*. The pasta is freshly made each day. *3–4 Chatham St., tel. 01/6792402.*

Yamamori. Ramen noodle bars offer a staple diet for budget travelers to Japan, but this is the first in Ireland. The meals-in-a-bowl offer a splendid slurping experience, and although you will be supplied with a small Chinese-style soup spoon, the best approach is to use the traditional *ohashi* (chopsticks), which allow you to hoist the noodles and leave you to drink the soup (and spill it all down your front). They also have a more expensive menu of other Japanese dishes. *71 S. Great George's St., tel. 01/4755001.*

UNDER £15 • Chameleon. Run by a young couple, Carol Walsh and Vincent Vis, this informal, two-story Indonesian restaurant is on a Temple Bar side street, off the south quays of the Liffey. Coconut and peanut are the dominant flavors in six *rijstafel* ("rice table") menus, with 20 or more items arranged around a large plate of spiced rice. Typical Indonesian dishes include shrimp croquette; chicken satay; Chinese noodles with pork, bean sprouts, ginger, and garlic; and green beans with butter beans in coconut milk. *1 Fownes St. Upper, tel. 01/6710362. Closed Mon.–Tues. and 1 wk in Nov.*

> To blend in with locals, eat only when faint, scorn all fruits and vegetables, and drink plenty of stout.

Chapter One. The place gets its name from its location, downstairs from the Dublin Writers Museum. The natural stone and wood setting, subdivided into a number of small rooms, gives it a cozy cave feel. The menu is not too adventurous, but fresh fish (river trout and sea cod) and lamb dishes are excellent, and the fillet steak is huge. Try the selection of Irish cheeses after your entrée. *18 Parnell Sq., Dublin 1, tel. 01/8732266.*

Chez Jules. A welcome newcomer on the scene and right across from Trinity College, Chez Jules is something of a budget-priced bistro. The setting is very informal, with long tables and benches. It prides itself on the simplicity and freshness of its French country fare and, as you might expect, the game dishes are especially tasty. The wine list is admirable and has a few good value options. *16 D'Olier St., Dublin 2, tel. 01/6770499.*

Da Pino. Truth is, young Dublin men come here in droves to gawk at the beautiful waitresses who are much more attractive than the bland salmon-and-gray decor of this popular Italian trattoria. Whatever the decorative failings, they are more than made up for by the simple, affordable cuisine. The delicious *zuppa di pesce e crostacei* (fish and shellfish soup) makes a good starter for the pizzas, among the best in the city center. In keeping with the seafaring theme, try the *pizza al salmone*, a thin-crust pie covered in fresh Irish smoked salmon and capers. *38–40 Parliament St., tel. 01/6719308.*

Dish. Open less than a year, Dish has opted for a simple, classy look and a little-bit-of-everything menu. It works. The huge window onto Crow Street throws tons of light onto the wooden floors and navy tablecloths. Lamb, duck, steak, pasta, they do it all—the Asian stir-fry is a favorite. *2 Crow St., tel. 01/6711248.*

Gallagher's Boxty House. The Gallagher brothers, Padraig and Ronan, were so fond of the "boxty" their mother used to make that they opened a restaurant so the rest of the world wouldn't be denied the pleasure of the perfect potato pancake. The key to good boxty, apparently, is to mix boiled and raw potatoes together before frying. The menu features other traditional Irish favs like bread pudding and bacon and cabbage. The fixed-price menu is a bargain, if you're up for a big feed. *20 Temple Bar, tel. 01/6772762.*

Gotham Café. This stylish little place just off Grafton Street is very much in tune with the slightly jaded vogue in Dublin for buzzing restaurants with strong Italian–New York leanings. Zipped-up pasta is typically served with a hot chili sauce and Creole sausage; a dozen gourmet pizzas are inventively done with toppings named after hot neighborhoods in other cities: the "Tribeca" has prawns, roasted peppers, zucchini, cilantro, mozzarella, coriander, and hot sauce. *8 S. Anne St., tel. 01/6795266.*

Il Primo. A few hundred yards from St. Stephen's Green, this lively, two-story Italian restaurant has a bare-bones decor, with bare boards and tables and old-fashioned wooden-armed office chairs. Generous middle-of-the-road Irish-Italian cuisine changes seasonally. Typical offerings include a warm salad of spinach wilted in a balsamic vinegar dressing with shallots and served with Parma ham and new potatoes. Among the main courses, a standout is delicious creamy risotto with chunky chicken breasts, a scattering of chicken livers, and some wild mushrooms. *Montague St., off Harcourt St., tel. 01/4783373. Closed Sun.*

Juice. A slick vegetarian restaurant? In *Dublin?* It's true: Juice serves upscale vegetarian fare (some of it vegan, or dairy-free, and most of it organic) in a large, deep, airy dining room with brushed stainless steel and dark wine-color lacquer walls. Chef Deb Davis's menu offers a platter of homemade dips and pestos to start—including butter-bean and black olive pâté and spinach-pistachio pesto—served with bread and crudités. Main courses include a tasty cannelloni, its fresh pasta filled with spinach, mushroom, hazelnuts, and ricotta cheese, then baked in a creamy tomato and herb sauce. The breads, baked with organic flour, are another treat. *73–83 S. Great George's St., tel. 01/4757856.*

Kilkenny Kitchen. Housed in the Kilkenny Shop, which specializes in superlative (yet sometimes bordering on cheesy) Irish craftsmanship and overlooks Trinity College, this self-service restaurant showcases wholesome (if sometimes a little bland) home cooking in the traditional Irish style. The menu includes a traditional Irish stew, casseroles, an imaginative selection of salads, and a house quiche combining Irish bacon, herbs, and fresh vegetables. Homemade scones, bread, and cakes, as well as Irish farmhouse cheeses, are all good bets. Lunchtime is busy; expect to share a table. *6 Nassau St., tel. 01/6777066. Closed Sun.*

La Mére Zou. Eric Tydgadt is Belgian and his wife Isabelle is from Paris, so—surprise—their small basement restaurant is Continental in emphasis. The lunch menu includes six king-size plates; one of them, La Belge, has a 6-ounce charcoal-grilled rump steak with french fries and a salad with salami, country ham, chicory, and mayonnaise. In the evening, dishes are more elaborate, such as ragout of venison or medallions of monkfish. *22 St. Stephen's Green, tel. 01/6616669. Closed first two wks in Jan.*

Marrakesh. This small spot in Ballsbridge serves authentic food from Morocco—one of the world's most underrated cuisines. Akim Beskri cooks in clay *tagines* (stew pots), the traditional method of desert tribesmen. The tagines' ingredients are a delicate balance of vegetables; meat or poultry; olives, garlic, and preserved lemons; and spices, usually including cumin, ginger, pepper, saffron, and turmeric. There is also a full-blown couscous royale (with beef, lamb, chicken, and spicy sausage), *harira* (a traditional soup with chickpeas), and *mechoui* (a slow-cooked roast side of lamb). *11 Ballsbridge Terr., Ballsbridge, tel. 01/6605539.*

Milano. The open, gleaming stainless-steel kitchen off this well-designed room turns out a tempting array of flashy pizzas. You can expect to find thinner pizza crusts than in the United States, with old standby toppings, like mozzarella and tomato, or more daring combos, such as ham and eggs, Cajun prawns and Tabasco, spinach and egg, or ham with anchovies. Last orders are taken at midnight, so keep this joint in mind if you're looking for a late-night bite. *38 Dawson St., tel. 01/6707744.*

Mitchells Cellars. This perennially popular-with-the-natives lunch spot just off St. Stephen's Green is in the vaulted basement of a posh wine merchant. The quarry-tile floor, whitewashed walls, red-and-white lamp shades above pine tables, and waitresses neatly dressed in navy and white are all virtually unchanged since the early 1970s, as is the menu. Still, a bustling crowd continues to pack the place, drawn to its country French home cooking—fare that includes soups and pâtés, quiche lorraine and salads, beef braised in Guinness, and chocolate-and-brandy meringue. Get here early, or expect a line. *21 Kildare St., tel. 01/6624724. Closed Sun., Sat. June–Aug.*

Odessa. Owned by the same likely lads that started the ridiculously successful Globe bar, Odessa is one of those rarities on the dining scene, a justifiably trendy spot. Dining is on two levels, the upstairs being a little more formal, with great light streaming in the big windows, while downstairs is furnished with couches and big armchairs for an after-dinner chill-out. While the menu is good if not very surprising (the salads are a great deal and the burgers are massive), the staff, who come from all four corners of the world, are always a good laugh. Their coffees are some of Dublin's best, and the full bar keeps folks here long after the last crumb. *13 Dame La., Dublin 2, tel. 01/6707634.*

101 Talbot. Of the few options north of the Liffey, 101 is one of the best. Even though it overlooks uninviting Talbot Street, the place has a cozy upstairs setting where they specialize in vegetarian and pasta dishes. Sandwiches are generous and always fresh. *100–102 Talbot St., Dublin 4, tel. 01/4542028. Closed Sun.*

Shalimar. The food is almost the same in the upstairs and downstairs dining rooms here (larger dishes at higher prices upstairs), but the basement Balti House is more cozy. The house cuisine is from the Punjab, with usual favorites including kormas (chicken, lamb, and beef), koftas, tandooris, and biryanis. *17 S. Great Georges St., Dublin 2, tel. 01/6710738.*

Side Door. Style without the pecuniary guilt! The five-star Shelbourne Hotel ably offers a variation on the usual *très cher* hotel dining room and the uninspired coffee shop. This well-designed budget restaurant has oak floors, cream walls, and art deco wood tables and chairs. You can start off with a bowl of Thai soup, a grilled chicken risotto, or Mediterranean vegetable pizza. Main dishes include supreme of chicken marinated in honey and charcoal-grilled rib eye of beef. Designer beers and a good wine list nicely complement the food. *27 St. Stephen's Green, tel. 01/6766471.*

Trastevere. Walls of glass and a bright Italianate interior with terra-cotta tiles make this restaurant a stylish place for lunch, dinner, snack time, or simply an espresso. Food ranges from crostini to warm prawn salads, various pastas, and charcoal-grilled chicken. From outside you can watch the chef at work through a large glass window. On a warm summer day you can see and hear the buskers playing away in Temple Bar Square. *Temple Bar Sq., tel. 01/6708343.*

UNDER £20 • The Russell Room. Traditional wisdom has it that hotel dining rooms are overpriced eateries of questionable quality. Well, splurge for the £20 fixed-price dinner at the Russell Room, part of the Westbury Hotel, and discover the exception to the rule. The place is really spacious and relaxed. The menu is daring, combining favorites like duck, fresh fish, and lamb with some exotic touches (the salmon in lemon balm for example). *Westbury Hotel, Clarendon St., tel. 01/6791122.*

COFFEEHOUSES

Dubliners may spend their evenings in a pub, but a good part of their day is spent at a **Bewley's Café,** the city's oldest coffeehouse chain. Since its founding in 1847, Bewley's has become synonymous with tea sipping and gossip. Bland pastries, sandwiches, and cafeteria-style lunches are served all day at all locations, but most people rightly venture into these 19th-century Georgian masterpieces simply to drink coffee and ponder the newspaper. *Three locations: 78 Grafton St., tel. 01/6776761; 13 S. Great George's St., tel. 01/6792078; 12 Westmoreland St., tel. 01/6776761.*

Café Kylemore (1–2 O'Connell St., at North Earl St., tel. 01/8722138), smack in the center of town, commands a good view of the teeming streets outside. The coffee is decent at 85p, and you can loiter as long as you like. If you're looking for a hipper, younger crowd, head to the **Globe** (11 S. Great George's St., tel. 01/6711220), which is a café during the day and a damn good pub at night. Dublin's premier northside coffeehouse is **Winding Stair Café and Bookshop** (40 Lower Ormond Quay, tel. 01/8733292), which provides a fabulous view of the River Liffey at the base of Ha'penny Bridge. Housed in an ancient, three-story warehouse, the Winding Stair serves tea, pastries, light meals, and outstanding coffee daily.

WORTH SEEING

Dublin Tourism offices offer several snazzy walking guides (£2.50) that highlight particular aspects of the city: "The Dublin Touring Guide" describes five different walking tours, "The Heritage Trails" highlights historical aspects of the city, and "The Rock 'n Stroll" guide lists pubs, restaurants, and other places frequented by such Irish musicians as Sinéad O'Connor and U2.

Historical Walking Tours (tel. 018780227), run by Trinity College history graduate students, are excellent two-hour tour introductions to Dublin. The Bord Fáilte–approved tour assembles at the front gate of Trinity College mid-May–mid-October, daily at 11, noon, and 3, with an extra tour on Sunday at 2; and mid-October–mid-May, weekends at noon. The cost is £5. The **Jameson Dublin Literary Pub Crawl** (tel. 01/4540228), a guided performance tour of pubs with literary associations, is for writers who like to drink and drinkers who like to write. A couple of Dublin bit players act and sing various texts (Beckett's *Waiting for Godot* gets the most laughs) for two hours while everyone gets loopy on Guinness. Tours (£6) set out from the Duke pub on Duke Street, nightly at 7:30 PM, from Easter to October 21 (Nov.–Mar., Thurs.–Sat. only), and year-round at noon on Sunday. The **Musical Pub Crawl** is led by two professional musicians who tell the story of traditional music over the course of a beer-soaked evening. The crawl visits pubs in the Temple Bar area, and the musicians play a few tunes in each; every crawler gets a songbook and is expected to join in. Tickets (£6) can be purchased in advance at the tourist office on Suffolk Street or on the night of the crawl at Olive Saint John Gogarty's pub on Fleet Street in Temple Bar, where the tour begins. **Gray Line Tours** (tel. 01/6057705) runs popular, 90-minute bus tours (£7) that allow you to get off the bus and check out Dublin's main sights. Buses leave from the Suffolk Street tourist office every 30 minutes from 10 AM to 5 PM. The **Zozimus Experience** (tel. 01/6618646) is an enjoyable walking tour of Dublin's medieval past, with a particular focus on the seedy, including great escapes, murders, and mythical happenings. Led by a guide in slightly hokey costume, the tours are by arrangement only and leave from the main gate of Dublin Castle at 6:45 PM; they only cost £5 a person. Prepare yourself for a surprise! **Colm Quilligan** (tel. 01/4540228) offers highly enjoyable evening walks of the literary pubs of Dublin, where "brain cells are replaced as quickly as they are drowned."

You can choose to save yourself a few bob, as Dubliners like to say (a "bob" was what is now a shilling), and take a self-guided walking tour. The **Old City Trail** begins in front of Trinity and heads up through Temple Bar into the working-class neighborhood called the Liberties. At the other end of the social scale is the **Georgian Heritage Trail,** a southside tour that links many of Dublin's finest homes and streets from the period. The **Cultural Trail** will take you to many of the sights connected with three of Dublin's literary Nobel Prize winners (Shaw, Yeats, and Beckett), as well as Joyce's home, the Dublin Writers Museum, and the Hugh Lane Municipal Gallery of Modern Art. The **"Rock 'n Stroll" Trail** covers 16 sites with associations to performers such as Bob Geldof, Christy Moore, Sinéad O'Connor, and U2. Most of the sites are in the city center and Temple Bar. Information on these trails and others is available from Dublin Tourism.

MAJOR ATTRACTIONS

BANK OF IRELAND

This building was the home of the Irish Parliament in the 18th century, before that body ignominiously (many of the deputies were bribed by the crown) voted to dissolve itself and complete the union with Great Britain. The building was begun in 1729 by Sir Edward Lovett Pearce, who designed the central section; three other architects would ultimately be involved in its construction. A pedimented portico fronted by six massive Corinthian columns dominates its grand facade, which follows the curve of Westmoreland Street as it meets College Green, once a Viking meeting place and burial ground. Two years after the Parliament committed suicide the building was bought for £40,000 by the Bank of Ireland. Inside, stucco rosettes adorn the coffered ceiling in the pastel-hued, colonnaded, clerestoried **main banking hall,** at one time the Court of Requests, where citizens' petitions were heard. Just down the hall is the original **House of Lords,** with tapestries depicting the Battle of the Boyne and the Siege of Derry, an oak-paneled nave, and a 1,233-piece Waterford glass chandelier; ask a guard nicely and he'll show you in. Accessed via Foster Place South, the small alley on the bank's east flank, the **Bank of Ireland Arts Center** frequently exhibits contemporary Irish art and has a permanent exhibition devoted to "The Story of Banking" (no joke!). Visitors are welcome during normal banking hours, and a short but interesting (and free) guided tour is given every Tuesday at 10:30, 11:30, and 1:45. *2 College Green, tel. 01/ 6776801. Admission free. Open weekdays 10–4 (Thurs. until 5).*

BEWLEY'S ORIENTAL CAFÉ

The granddaddy of the capital's cafés, Bewley's Grafton Street location has been serving coffee and sticky buns to Dubliners since 1842. Bewley's trademark stained-glass windows were designed by Harry Clarke (1889–1931), Ireland's most distinguished early 20th-century artist in this medium. It's a fine spot to sit and observe Dubliners of all ages and occupations. The aroma of coffee is irresistible, and the café's dark interiors—with marble-top tables, bentwood chairs, and mahogany trim—evoke a more leisurely Dublin. Until recently, even the waitresses looked appropriately Victorian, garbed in black dress with white collar, hat, and apron, but sadly they've modernized the uniform to black trousers and boring Bewley's tee shirts. The food is infamously overpriced and not particularly good, and yet the place is always full. *78 Grafton St., tel. 01/6776761. Open Sun.–Thurs. 7:30 AM–1 AM, Fri.–Sat. 7:30 AM–4 AM.*

CITY HALL

Prominently situated, facing the Liffey from Cork Hill at the top of Parliament Street, this grand Georgian municipal building (1769–79), once the Royal Exchange, was designed by Thomas Cooley and marks the southwestern corner of Temple Bar. Today it is the seat of the Dublin Corporation (or "the Corpo" as locals call it), the elected body that governs the city. Twelve columns encircle the domed central rotunda, which has a fine mosaic floor and 12 frescoes depicting Dublin legends and ancient Irish historical scenes. Just off the rotunda is a gently curving staircase, a typical feature of most large Dublin town houses. *Cork Hill, tel. 01/6796111, ext. 2807. Admission free. Open weekdays 9–1 and 2:15–5.*

CUSTOM HOUSE

Seen at its best, reflected in the waters of the Liffey during the short interval when the high tide is on the turn, the Custom House is the city's most spectacular Georgian building. Extending 375 ft on the north side of the river, this is the work of James Gandon, a celebrated English architect who arrived in Ireland in 1781, when construction commenced here (it continued for 10 years). Crafted from gleaming Portland stone, the central portico is linked by arcades to the pavilions at either end. Too bad, as many art historians state, the dome is on the puny size and out of proportion. A statue of Commerce tops the graceful copper dome; statues on the main facade are based on allegorical themes. Note the exquisitely carved lions and unicorns supporting the arms of Ireland at the far ends of the facade. Republicans set the building on fire in 1921, but it was completely restored and now houses government offices. The building opened to the public in mid-1997 after having been closed for many years, and with the opening came a new exhibition that traces the building's history and significance. *Custom House Quay, tel. 01/6793377. Admission £1.50. Open weekdays 9:30–5, weekends 2–5.*

DUBLIN CASTLE

If this old castle looks familiar it might be because it played itself—seat and symbol of British rule in Ireland for 7½ centuries—in Neil Jordan's film *Michael Collins.* Understandably, Dubliners tend to have mixed feelings about the place. Just off Dame Street behind City Hall, the castle is one of those sights that are better to look at than to actually visit. Of the original 13th-century Norman castle of King John, only the badly mauled **Record Tower,** an old, weathered stone outcrop, remains. The rest of the site, now used as government offices, is dominated by various 18th- and 19th-century

It's been said that the pub is the poor man's university. If this is true, Dublin has more than 1,000 opportunities for higher education.

additions, done up nice and fancy to impress dignitaries and a ceaseless flow of EU ministers. Even the sprawling **Great Courtyard,** reputed site of the Black Pool from which Dublin got its name, is lined with stretch limos and security guards. Very few rooms are open to the lowly public, and those that are can be seen only on the guided tours. The Beatty Library is in the process of moving into the old barracks. Viking diehards may enjoy the "Undercroft" exhibit, which displays the remains of a 10th-century Viking fortress excavated on the site. *Dame St., tel. 01/6777129. Admission free (£3 for guided tour). Open weekdays 10–5, weekends 2–5.*

FOUR COURTS

Today the seat of the High Court of Justice of Ireland, the Four Courts is James Gandon's second Dublin masterpiece, built between 1786 and 1802, close on the heels of his Custom House (*above*), downstream on the same side of the River Liffey. The Four Courts replaced a 13th-century Dominican abbey that stood here earlier. In 1922, during the Irish Civil War, the Four Courts was almost totally destroyed by shelling. The adjoining Public Records Office was gutted, with many of its priceless legal documents destroyed, including innumerable family records; efforts to restore the building to its original state spanned 10 years. Today the stately Corinthian portico and the circular central hall of the Courts are well worth viewing. Its distinctive copper-covered dome atop a colonnaded rotunda makes this one of Dublin's most instantly recognizable buildings; the view from the rotunda is terrific. Although there is no tour of the building, visitors are welcome to sit in while the courts are in session. *Inns Quay, tel. 01/8725555. Open daily 10–1 and 2:15–4.*

GENERAL POST OFFICE

The GPO is one of the great civic buildings of Dublin's Georgian era, built in 1818 by Francis Johnston. The acronym is burned into the heart of Irish schoolboys by patriotic teachers and parents. Its fame springs from the central role it played during the Easter Rising. It was here, on Easter Monday, 1916, that Republican forces 2,000 strong, under the guidance of Patrick Pearse and James Connolly, stormed the building and issued the Proclamation of the Irish Republic. After a week of relentless shelling, both the GPO and the Citizen's Army lay in ruins, and 13 rebels were executed, including Pearse and Connolly. Most of the original building was destroyed in the uprising—the only part that remains is the front facade, in which you can still see bullet holes. This functioning, full-service post office is always packed with customers, but the magnificent central gallery is worth a quick look. *O'Connell St., tel. 01/8728888. Admission free. Open Mon.–Sat. 8–8, Sun. 10:30–6:30.*

"A PINT OF PLAIN IS YOUR ONLY MAN"

It's said that of the 10 million pints of Guinness produced daily, some 6 million are consumed in Ireland alone—not bad for a country whose population is under 4 million. You'd start to believe infants must be drinking it in their bottles. When the thick, murky brew was first concocted by Arthur Guinness in 1759, it wasn't known as a "stout" but rather as a "porter," a name derived from a heavy, cheaply made drink popular with working-class porters in London. Over the years, the name "stout" has stuck, and it aptly describes the formidable heartiness of this thick black brew (and its effects on the human physique). But if you ask for a "stout," you'll get the more bitter bottled brew, so request "Guinness" if you want the smoother draught. Every Dublin drinker has heard the myths about exactly what goes on at night in the Guinness brewery, and God only knows what they cast into the huge turning vats to make the stuff taste so damned good!

GUINNESS BREWERY

Founded by Arthur Guinness in 1759, Ireland's all-dominating brewer—in fact, at one stage the largest stout-producing brewery in the world—is situated on a 60-acre spread to the west of Christ Church Cathedral. The Guinness Brewery is the most popular tourist destination in town; can you guess why? The brewery itself is off-limits, but the part-museum, part-gift-shop **Hop Store** is open all year. Unfortunately, it's impossible to avoid the "World of Guinness" exhibition, a 10-minute audiovisual show designed to put the brewery into historical context. For all its moving wax figures and silly sound effects, the show merely whets the appetite for what comes next: two free glasses of what's generally considered the best Guinness in the world, poured straight from the adjoining factory. In winter, you can sip your brew leisurely and maybe get a few more out of the servers, but come summer you'll be ushered out of the bar and into the gift shop as quickly as possible. (A good trick is to try to scrounge beer tickets from other, nonimbibing visitors.) Upstairs from the gift shop is a small but worthwhile art gallery that hosts a rotating collection of local and international art. After the tour, spend some time walking the perimeter of the brewery, one of the most Orwellian and genuinely bleak factories in the country. Known as the Liberties, the area is filled with eerie empty streets, ragged brick walls, strange doors, deserted warehouses, and redbrick tenements, which originally housed the Guinness employees and their families. Little has changed since 1759, when Arthur first opened the brewery, and the imposing setting conveys a sense of how austere life must have been for generations of brewers. *Crane St., tel. 01/4536700. From Trinity College, walk west on Dame St. (which becomes Lord Edward St., High St., and Thomas St.), turn left on Crane St; or take Bus 68A from Fleet St., Bus 123 from O'Connell St., or Bus 8A from Aston Quay. Admission £5. Open Apr.–Sept., Mon.–Sat. 9:30–5, Sun. 10:30–4:30; Oct.–Mar., Mon.–Sat. 9:30–4, Sun. noon–4.*

HA'PENNY BRIDGE

This heavily trafficked footbridge crosses the Liffey at a prime spot: Temple Bar is on the southside, and the bridge provides the fastest route to the thriving Mary and Henry streets shopping areas to the north. Until early in this century, a half-penny toll was charged to cross it. Yeats was one among many Dubliners who found this too high a price to pay—more a matter of principle than of finance—and so made the detour via O'Connell Bridge. It's the perfect spot to stand at night and look down the length of the silent Liffey.

KILMAINHAM GAOL

This squat stone building incarcerated some of the country's foremost revolutionary leaders after the 1789, 1803, 1867, and 1916 uprisings. Both Robert Emmet and Charles Parnell did time here, while Patrick Pearse and James Connolly were executed in Kilmainham's front courtyard (as every Irish schoolchild can tell you, the wounded Connolly had to be tied to a chair so he could be shot). Eamon De Valera, future leader of the country, was the last prisoner to be released from the huge gray stone building. Modern visitors are gently escorted through the grounds by informative guides and given the chance to watch an excellent audiovisual presentation. A small museum displays relics from the jail's heyday, and there's also an interesting display of pro-Republican placards that explains the history of Ireland's long struggle for home rule. *Corner of Old Kilmainham and S. Circular Rds., tel. 01/4535984. From city center, take Bus 51, 51B, or 78A. Admission £2. Open Apr.–Sept., daily 9:30–6; Oct.–Mar., weekdays 9:30–5, Sun. 1–6.*

POWERSCOURT TOWN CENTER

Lucky man, this Viscount Powerscourt. In the mid-18th century, not only did he build Ireland's most spectacular country house, in Enniskerry, Country Wicklow, which bears the family name (*see* Chapter 3), but he also decided to rival that structure's grandeur with one of Dublin's largest stone mansions. Staffed with 22 servants, built from granite from the viscount's own quarry in the Wicklow Hills, Powerscourt House was a major statement in the Palladian style. Designed by Robert Mack in 1774, the massive edifice towers over the little street it sits on (note the top story, framed by massive volutes, that was once intended as an observatory). Inside, the decoration runs from rococo salons by James McCullagh to Adamesque plasterwork by Michael Stapleton to—surprise—an imaginative shopping atrium, installed in and around the covered courtyard. The stores here include high-quality Irish crafts shops and numerous food stalls. The mall exit leads to the Carmelite **Church of St. Teresa's** and Johnson's Court. Beside the church, a pedestrian lane leads onto Grafton Street. *59 S. William St. Admission free. Open Mon.–Sat.*

TRINITY COLLEGE

Trinity College is the oldest university in Ireland, established in 1592 by a grant from England's Queen Elizabeth I. The college was intended to instill Oxbridge fundamentals into Dublin's growing population of well-to-do Anglo-Irish settlers (primarily the sons of the country's Protestant and pro-Brit aristocracy). Even though it occupies some 40 acres in the heart of the city, for more than 300 years Trinity seemed to exist independently of Dublin. Its walls were built thick and tall to keep the riffraff out, while its students spoke with lazy West-Brit accents and drank to the queen's health. For centuries Trinity remained the preserve of the Protestant Church. A free education was offered to Catholics—provided that they accepted the Protestant faith. Fat chance. As recently as 1966, Irish Catholics faced the threat of excommunication for attending lectures here, even though Trinity itself had opened its doors to all creeds at the turn of the century (today, nearly 70% of its students are Catholic).

Officially titled Dublin University but still known by all as simply Trinity, the college has sent some great men out into the world over the years, including Dracula creator Bram Stoker, writer and deadly satirist Jonathan Swift, and Nobel Prize winner Samuel Beckett. Although no longer the posh boys' club it once was, Trinity retains some signs of its aristocratic past. The extensive **West Front,** with a classical pedimented portico in the Corinthian style, faces College Green and is directly across from the Bank of Ireland; recently restored, it was built between 1755 and 1759, possibly the work of Theodore Jacobsen, architect of London's Foundling Hospital. The design is repeated on the interior, so the view is the same both from outside the gates and from the quadrangle inside. On the lawn in front of the inner facade are **statues** of orator Edmund Burke (1729–97) and dramatist Oliver Goldsmith (1728–74), two other alumni. Like the West Front, **Parliament Square** (commonly known as Front Square), the cobblestoned quadrangle that lies just beyond this first patch of lawn, also dates from the 18th century. On the right of the square, you'll find Sir William Chambers' theater, or Examination Hall, dating from the mid-1780s, which contains the college's most splendiferous Adamesque interior (designed by Michael Stapleton). The hall houses an impressive organ retrieved from an 18th-century Spanish ship and a gilded, oak chandelier from the old House of Commons; concerts are sometimes held here. The chapel, which stands on the left of the quadrangle, has stucco ceilings and fine woodwork. Both the theater and the chapel were designed by Scotsman William Chambers in the late 18th century. The looming campanile, or bell tower, is the symbolic heart of the college; erected in 1853, it dominates the center of the square. To the left of the campanile is the Graduates Memorial Building, or GMB. Built in 1892, the slightly Gothic building is now home to both the Philosophical and Historical societies, Trinity's ancient, fiercely competitive, and

GRAND CANAL RAMBLE

At its completion in 1795, the 547-km (342-mi) Grand Canal was celebrated as the longest in Britain and Ireland. It connected Dublin to the River Shannon, and horse-drawn barges carried cargo (mainly turf) and passengers to the capital from all over the country. By the mid-19th century, the train had arrived and the great waterway slowly fell into decline until the last commercial traffic ceased in 1960. But the 6-km (4-mi) loop around the capital, with grassy, sheltered banks, is ideal for a leisurely stroll. Walk down the Pearse Street side of Trinity College until you arrive at the Ringsend Road Bridge. Raised on stilts above the canal is the Waterways Visitors Center, which captures the history of Irish rivers and canals in photos, videos, and models. Head west along the bank to the charming Mount Street Bridge. On the southwest corner of the bridge stands a simple monument to the Irish Volunteers who died at this spot in the 1916 rising. Moving along, on the south side you'll pass Percy Place, a row of elegant, three-story terraced houses. On the north side, a small lane leads up to the infamous Scruffy Murphy's pub, where many a political backroom deal has been struck. Detour at the next right, and you'll pass a road that leads up to St. Stephen's, the "pepper canister" church, nicknamed for its unusual shape. Another right takes you into Powerscourt, a classic, inner-city estate of two-up, two-down terraced houses.

Return to the canal and continue your walk along Herbert Place. You can get really close to the dark green water here as it spills white and frothy over one of the canal's many wood and iron locks. James Joyce lost his virginity to a prostitute on the next stretch of the canal, around Lower Baggot Street Bridge. Patrick Kavanagh, Ireland's great lyric poet, spent the later years of his life sitting on a bench here writing about the canal that flowed from his birthplace in the midlands to the city where he would die. A life-size bronze of the poet sits here, contemplative, arms folded, legs crossed, on a wooden bench.

Less than 2 km (1 mi) past Kavanagh's statue the canal approaches Richmond Bridge. Just beyond the bridge is the Irish Jewish Museum (see below). To finish your ramble in style, take a right onto Richmond Street, until you arrive at Bambricks, a public house in the best tradition of Dublin: long, dark-wood bar, half-empty, with a staff whose sharp, grinning humor borders on rudeness. They even sell snuff.

proudly pompous debating societies. At the back of the square stands old redbrick Rubrics, looking rather ordinary and out of place among the gray granite and cobblestones. Rubrics, now used as rooms for students and faculty, dates from 1690, making it the oldest building still standing.

THE LIBRARY AND *THE BOOK OF KELLS* • The *Book of Kells* is generally considered the most striking manuscript ever produced in the Anglo-Saxon world. This 682-page gospel was obsessively illustrated by monks with a penchant for iconographic doodling and frantic spirals. Equally impressive is the smaller and older *Book of Durrow,* essentially a 7th-century coloring book punctuated now and again with religious verse. It has whole pages (known as carpet pages) given over to embellished designs and scribbles, whether a representation of St. Paul with only three fingers or the slithery tendrils of the letter "Q" stretched tightly across an entire page. Both are on permanent display below the library's aptly named **Long Room,** a 210-ft-long exhibition hall that smells heartily of must and old books. Also on display is a wonderful collection of yellowed diaries and old photographs of Dublin, an original copy of the Proclamation of the Irish Republic, and assorted manuscripts of Beckett, Joyce, and Wilde. *Admission £3.50. Open Mon.–Sat. 9:30–5, Sun. noon–5 (shorter hrs Sept.–May).*

Trinity College's stark, modern Arts and Social Sciences Building, with an entrance on Nassau Street, houses the **Douglas Hyde Gallery of Modern Art,** which concentrates on contemporary art exhibitions and has its own bookstore. Also in the building, down some steps from the gallery, there's a snack bar with coffee, tea, sandwiches, and students willing to talk about life in the old college. *Tel. 01/6081116. Admission free. Open Mon.–Wed. and Fri. 11–6, Thurs. 11–7, Sat. 11–4:45.*

MUSEUMS

ARTHOUSE

Apparently this is one of the first purpose-built multimedia centers for the arts in the world. Its modern design—all glass, metal, and painted concrete—is the work of award-winning architect Shay Cleary Doyle, who intended the building to reflect the object glorified within: the computer. Inside is a training center, a performance venue, a creative studio, and an exhibition space that plays host to a variety of art exhibitions throughout the year. Pride of place, however, goes to the Art Information Bureau and the Artifact artist's database, featuring the work of more than 1,000 modern Irish artists working in Ireland and abroad. This useful catalog is open to anyone wishing to buy or admire the work of the listed artists, and it is set up in such a way that you can search for work according to specific criteria. For example, if you want a piece of jewelry in gold from the west of Ireland, just press a few buttons and a list of artists and images of their work fitting your description will appear. Like most monuments to high tech, as of yet this place is more style than substance. *Curved St., tel. 01/6056800. Admission free. Open weekdays 9:30–6.*

CHESTER BEATTY LIBRARY

The library, bequeathed to the nation in 1956 by Sir Alfred Chester Beatty, was closed at press time while it moved to its new premises in the barracks of Dublin Castle. It plans to reopen sometime in late 2000. The library needs more space to cope with its 22,000 manuscripts, rare books, and objects from mainly Middle and Far Eastern cultures. There are no fewer than 270 versions of the Koran, including some illuminated by master calligraphers from the ancient Arab world. The Japanese and Chinese collections include prints and paintings, a large collection of snuff boxes, and cups made from rhino horn. It is also an important center for medieval European woodcuts, including a number by the German master Dürer. *Dame St., tel. 01/2692386. Admission free. Call to confirm opening date and hrs.*

DUBLIN CIVIC MUSEUM

Built between 1765 and 1771 as an exhibition hall for the Society of Artists, this building was later used as the City Assembly House, precursor of City Hall. The museum's small, esoteric collection includes Stone Age flints, Viking coins, old maps and prints of the city, and the sculpted head of British admiral Horatio Nelson that used to top Nelson's Pillar, beside the General Post Office on O'Connell Street; to the delight of many Dubliners the column was toppled by an IRA explosion in 1966 on the 50th anniversary of the Easter Uprising. The museum often holds exhibitions relating to the city. *58 S. William St., tel. 01/ 6794260. Admission free. Open Tues.–Sat. 10–6, Sun. 11–2.*

DUBLINIA

In the old Synod Hall (formerly a meeting place for bishops of the Church of Ireland), attached via a covered stonework Victorian bridge to Christ Church Cathedral, Dublin's Medieval Trust has set up a mildly entertaining and slightly hokey informative reconstruction of everyday life in medieval Dublin. There's a touch of Disney-meets-the-after-school-special about the place. The main exhibit uses audiovisual and computer techniques; there is also a scale model of what Dublin was like around 1500, a medieval maze, a life-size reconstruction based on the 13th-century dockside at Wood Quay, and, best of all, a fine view from the tower. For a more modern take on the city, have a look at the noted James Malton series of prints of 18th-century Dublin hanging on the walls of the coffee shop. *St. Michael's Hill, tel. 01/6794611. Admission £3.95. Open Apr.–Sept., daily 10–5; Oct.–Mar., Mon.–Sat. 11–4, Sun. 10–4:30.*

DUBLIN WRITERS MUSEUM

"If you would know Ireland—body and soul—you must read its poems and stories," wrote Yeats in 1891. Once the home of John Jameson (of the Irish whiskey family), this splendid Georgian mansion is centered on an enormous drawing room decorated with paintings, Adamesque plasterwork, and a deep Edwardian lincrusta frieze (decorated cloth wall covering). The museum is home to rare manuscripts, personal diaries, and a rich collection of portraits, publicity posters, and yellowed photographs commemorating the life and works of Ireland's most famous scribblers. Ireland's four Nobel Prize winners (Shaw, Yeats, Beckett, and Heaney) are especially well represented, along with the likes of Wilde, O'Casey, Behan, Swift, Joyce, and Synge. On display are an 1804 edition of Swift's *Gulliver's Travels,* an 1899 first edition of Bram Stoker's *Dracula,* and an 1899 edition of Wilde's *Ballad of Reading Gaol.* There's even a special "Teller of Tales" exhibit showcasing Behan, O'Flaherty, and O'Faolan. The museum also houses the **Irish Writers Center,** which features periodic readings from local poets and writers, cultural events, and art displays. In the rear is **Books Upstairs** (tel. 01/8722239), a small bookshop that specializes in Irish-interest titles and rare, out-of-print volumes. All in all, it's a fine place to spend the day. *18 Parnell Sq. N, tel. 01/8722077. From O'Connell Bridge, walk north on O'Connell St.; or take Bus 10, 11, 12, 13, or 22. Admission £2.90. Open Sept.–May, Mon.–Sat. 10–5, Sun. 11:30–6; June–Aug., weekdays 10–7, Sat. 10–5, Sun. 11:30–6.*

GENEALOGICAL OFFICE

Are you a Fitzgibbon from Limerick, a Cullen from Waterford, or a McSweeney from Cork? This reference library is a good place to begin your ancestor-tracing efforts. If you're a total novice at genealogical research, you can meet with an advisor (£25 for an hour consultation) who can help get you started. The office also houses the **Heraldic Museum,** where displays of flags, coins, stamps, silver, and family crests highlight the uses and development of heraldry in Ireland. *2 Kildare St., tel. 01/6030200. Genealogical Office open weekdays 10–5, Sat. 10–12:30. Admission free. Heraldic Museum open weekdays 10–8:30, Sat. 10–12:30. Admission free.*

HUGH LANE MUNICIPAL GALLERY OF MODERN ART

Built originally as a town house for the Earl of Charlemont in 1762, this residence was so grand its Parnell Square street was nicknamed "Palace Row" in its honor. Designed by Sir William Chambers in the best Palladian manner, its delicate and rigidly correct facade, extended by two demi-lune (crescent-moon shaped) arcades, was fashioned from the "new" white Ardmulcan stone (now seasoned to grimy gray). Charlemont was one of the cultural locomotives of 18th-century Dublin—his walls were hung with Titians and Hogarths and he frequently dined with Oliver Goldsmith and Sir Joshua Reynolds—so he would undoubtedly be tickled that his home is now the Hugh Lane Gallery. The gallery is named after a nephew of Lady Gregory, Yeats's aristocratic patron who drowned on the *Lusitania* when it was sunk by the Germans off the coast of County Cork in 1915. Lane collected both Impressionist paintings and 19th-century Irish and Anglo-Irish works and bequeathed most of them to Ireland. Yeats and other notables campaigned vigorously to force the government to find a gallery to house the collection. In addition to paintings, the gallery has a good collection of sculptures, contemporary works, and canvases by Jack B. Yeats (W. B. Yeats's brother) and Paul Henry. There's also a small collection of minor European impressionists. *Parnell Sq., tel. 01/8741903. From O'Connell Bridge, walk north on O'Connell St. Admission free. Open Tues.–Thurs. 9:30–6 (Apr.–Aug., Thurs. 9:30–8), Fri.–Sat. 9:30–5, Sun. 11–5*

IRISH JEWISH MUSEUM

In the land of Liam O'Flahertys and Molly Malones, it's surprising to find a museum dedicated to the Paddy Rosenbergs of Irish history, to the handful of Jews who, fleeing persecution on the Continent, came to Dublin in the early 1800s. Ireland has never boasted a large Jewish population (today it hovers around 5,000), but there is an active synagogue on Adelaide Road (mentioned by the Jewish Leopold Bloom in *Ulysses*) as well as this excellent museum, opened in 1985 by Israeli president Herzog (himself Dublin educated). Inside is a restored synagogue and a display of photographs, letters, and personal memorabilia culled from Dublin's most prominent Jewish families. *3 Walworth Rd., off Victoria St.*

near S. Circular Rd., tel. 01/6760737. From city center, take Bus 16, 19, 22. Admission £2. Open May–Aug., Tues., Thurs., and Sun. 11–3:30; Sept.–Apr., Sun. 10:30–2:30.

JAMES JOYCE CULTURAL CENTRE

Not everyone in Ireland has read James Joyce (many will pretend they have), but everyone has heard of him—especially since a copy of his censored and suppressed **Ulysses** was one of the top status symbols of the early 20th century. Today, of course, Joyce is acknowledged to be one of the greatest modern authors, and his *Dubliners, Finnegan's Wake,* and *A Portrait of the Artist as a Young Man* can even be read as poetic "travel guides" to Dublin. Now open to the general public, this restored, 18th-century Georgian town house, once the dancing academy of Professor Denis J. Maginni, is a center for Joycean studies and events related to the author. It has an extensive library and archives, exhibition rooms, a bookstore, and a café. Along with the Joyce Museum in Sandycove, the center is a main organizer of "Bloomstime," which marks the week leading up to June 16's Bloomsday celebrations. *35 N. Great George's St., 01/878–8547. Admission £2.75. Open weekdays 9:30–5, weekends 12:30–5.*

MARSH'S LIBRARY

A short hop west from St. Stephen's Green and accessed through a tiny but charming cottage garden lies a gem of old Dublin: the city's—and Ireland's—first public library. It was founded and endowed in 1701 by Narcissus Marsh, the Archbishop of Dublin, when it was declared open to "All Graduates and Gentlemen." The two-story, brick Georgian building has been practically unchanged inside since it was built. It houses a priceless collection of 250 manuscripts and 25,000 16th- to 18th-century books. Many of these rare volumes are locked inside cages, as are the readers who wish to peruse them. The cages were to discourage students who, often impecunious, may have been tempted to make the books their own. The library has recently been restored with

> St. Stephen's Green, at the south end of Kildare Street, is another magnificent southside park lined by Georgian houses and filled with lakeside paths, gardens, and statues.

great attention to its original architectural details, especially in the book stacks. *St. Patrick's Close off Patrick St., 01/454–3511. Admission £1. Open Mon. and.–Fri. 10–12:45 and 2–5, Sat. 10:30–12:45.*

NATIONAL GALLERY OF IRELAND

Every team needs a star. The National Gallery of Ireland was long known as a decent, if slightly dry, little museum of Irish and European art. Then, while dining at a Jesuit College, an art historian was impressed by the painting he saw on the wall. It turned out to be Caravaggio's *The Taking of Christ* (1602), which was quickly verified and donated to the National Gallery. If for no other reason, visit the gallery just to stand in awe before this monumental work. While you're there, you might as well take in the building itself—all museums should be this airy and well laid out. The simply perfect south wing has been complemented by a new atrium and a beautifully renovated north wing. Built in 1854, the gallery has grown from an original collection of 150 works to more than 3,000 paintings, watercolors, sculptures, and etchings. It boasts numerous examples of 17th-century Italian, French, Spanish, and Irish schools, in addition to a small collection of Dutch Masters. Two of its more notable acquisitions are Reynolds' *First Earl of Bellamont* (1773) and Vermeer's *Lady Writing a Letter with Her Maid* (circa 1670). Another highlight of the museum is the major collection of paintings by Irish artists from the 17th to 20th centuries, including works by Roderic O'Conor (1860–1940), Sir William Orpen (1878–1931), William Leech (1881–1968), and Jack B. Yeats (1871–1957), the brother of W. B. Yeats and by far the best-known Irish painter of this century. Yeats painted portraits and landscapes in an abstract expressionist style not dissimilar from that of the later Bay Area Figurative painters of the 1950s and 1960s. His *Liffey Swim* (1923) is particularly worth seeing for its Dublin subject matter (the annual swim is still held, usually on the first weekend in September). If a particular piece baffles you, head down to the Multimedia Gallery, where you can use the computers to learn about any of the museum's works. *Merrion Sq. W, tel. 01/6615133. From Trinity College, walk 1 km (½ mi) east on Nassau St., turn right at Merrion Sq. Admission free. Open Mon.–Sat. 10–5:30 (Thurs. until 8:30), Sun. 2–5.*

NATIONAL LIBRARY

In most countries saying you're a writer is like admitting you're homeless. In Ireland if you own up to literary aspirations, people will not laugh, nor will they shake their heads—they might even be impressed. Few countries as geographically diminutive as Ireland have garnered as many recipients of the Nobel Prize for Literature. Along with these authors—W. B. Yeats (1923), George Bernard Shaw (1925),

Samuel Beckett (1969), and Seamus Heaney (1995)—the National Library contains first editions of every major Irish writer, including books by Jonathan Swift, Oliver Goldsmith, and James Joyce (who used the library as the scene of the great literary debate in *Ulysses*). In addition, of course, virtually every book ever published in Ireland is kept here, as well as an unequaled selection of old maps and an extensive collection of Irish newspapers and magazines—more than 5 million items in all. The **main reading room** opened in 1890 to house the collections of the Royal Dublin Society. Beneath its dramatic domed ceiling, countless authors have researched and written their books over the years. *Kildare St., tel. 01/6618811. Admission free. Open Mon. 10–9, Tues.–Wed. 2–9, Thurs.–Fri. 10–5, Sat. 10–1.*

NATIONAL MUSEUM OF IRELAND

Situated on the other side of Leinster House from the National Library, Ireland's National Museum houses a fabled collection of Irish artifacts, dating from 6000 BC to the present. The museum is organized around a grand rotunda and elaborately decorated, with mosaic floors, marble columns, balustrades, and fancy ironwork. It has the largest collection of Celtic antiquities in the world, including an array of gold jewelry, carved stones, bronze tools, and weapons. The Treasury collection, including some of the museum's most renowned pieces, is open on a permanent basis. Among the priceless relics on display are the 8th-century **Ardagh Chalice,** a two-handle silver cup with gold filigree ornamentation; the bronze-coated, iron **St. Patrick's Bell,** the oldest surviving example (5th–8th centuries) of Irish metalwork; the 8th-century **Tara Brooch,** an intricately decorated piece made of white bronze, amber, and glass; and the 12th-century bejeweled oak **Cross of Cong,** covered with silver and bronze panels. Another room is devoted to the 1916 Easter Uprising and the War of Independence (1919–21); displays here include uniforms, weapons, banners, and a piece of the flag that flew over the General Post Office during Easter Week, 1916. A recent addition to the museum's collection is a permanent Viking exhibition upstairs, which features a Viking skeleton, swords, leather works recovered in Dublin and surrounding areas, and a replica of a small Viking boat. In contrast to the ebullient late-Victorian architecture of the main museum building, the design of the **National Museum Annexe** is purely functional; it houses temporary shows of Irish antiquities. The 18th-century **Collins Barracks,** the most recent addition to the museum, houses the museum's collection of glass, silver, costumes, furniture, and other decorative arts. The barracks is on Wolf Tone Quay; take Bus 79 from Aston Quay or Bus 66 or 67 from Abbey Street and ask to be dropped off at the museum. *Kildare St.; Annexe: 7–9 Merrion Row, tel. 01/6777444. Admission free. Tues.–Sat. 10–5, Sun. 2–5.*

OLD JAMESON DISTILLERY

Here you'll find yet another temple to booze. Founded in 1791, this distillery produced one of Ireland's most famous whiskeys for nearly 200 years until 1966, when local distilleries merged to form Irish Distillers and moved to a purpose-built, ultramodern distillery in Middleton, County Cork. Part of the complex was converted into the group's head office, while the distillery itself has been recently turned into a museum. Visitors can watch a short audiovisual history of the industry (a little less boring than the Guinness movie), which actually had its origins 1,500 years ago in Middle Eastern perfume making, and tour the old distillery, where you can learn about the distilling of whiskey from grain to bottle. You can also view a reconstruction of a former warehouse, where the colorful nicknames of former barrel makers are recorded. Then, at last, the complimentary tasting (remember: Irish whiskey is best drunk without a mixer—try it straight or with water); attendees are invited to taste different brands of Irish whiskey and compare them against bourbon and Scotch; the staff are confident that you will prefer the Irish to anything else, but who cares—it's all free. *Bow St., tel. 01/8072355. Tour £3.95. Open daily 9:30–5:30; tours every ½ hr.*

ROYAL HOSPITAL KILMAINHAM

Commissioned as a hospice for disabled and veteran soldiers by James Butler, the Duke of Ormonde and Viceroy to King Charles II, the Royal Hospital was completed in 1684, making it the first classical building in the city and, as historians tell us, a precursor of Dublin's golden age. Based loosely on Les Invalides in Paris, with a large stone arcade built around a garden and courtyard, it survived into the 1920s as a hospital, but after the founding of the Irish Free State in 1922, the building fell into disrepair. Over the last 15 years, a huge restoration program has returned the entire edifice to what it once was. The structure consists of four galleries around a courtyard and includes a grand dining hall, 100 ft long by 50 ft wide. The architectural highlight is the hospital's Baroque **chapel,** distinguished by its extraordinary plasterwork ceiling and fine wood carvings. Today the Royal Hospital houses the **Irish Museum of Modern Art,** opened in 1991 in an attempt to improve the country's impoverished visual arts tradition. The museum also displays works by non-Irish, 20th-century greats like Picasso and Miró but concentrates on the work of Irish artists. Richard Deacon, Richard Gorman, Dorothy Cross, Sean Scully, Matt Mullican, Louis Le Brocquy, and James Colman are among the contemporary Irish artists represented. The self-serve Café Musée has soups, sandwiches, and other light, overpriced fare. *Kilmainham La., tel. 01/6129900. Walk west along Liffey, turn left on Steven's La. (about 4 km/2½ mi); or take Bus 68, 68A, 69, 78A, 79, 90, or 123. Admission: Royal Hospital free, but individual shows may have separate charges; Museum of Modern Art permanent collection free, small charge for special exhibitions. Open: Royal Hospital Tues.–Sat. 10–5:30, Sun. noon–5:30, tour every ½ hr; Museum of Modern Art Tues.–Sat. 10–5:30, Sun. noon–5:30; museum tours Wed. and Fri. 2:30, Sat. 11:30.*

HOUSES

NEWMAN HOUSE

One of the greatest glories of Georgian Dublin, Newman House is actually two imposing town houses joined together. The earliest (1738), No. 85 St. Stephen's Green, was designed by Richard Castle, favored architect of Dublin's rich and famous, and has a winged Palladian window on the Wicklow granite facade. Originally known as Clanwilliam House, it features two landmarks of Irish Georgian style: the Apollo Room, decorated with stucco work depicting the sun god and his muses, and the magnificent Saloon, "the supreme example of Dublin Baroque," according to scholars Jacqueline O'Brien and Desmond Guinness, and crowned with an exuberant ceiling aswirl with cupids and gods, created by the Brothers Lafranchini, the finest *stuccadores* (plaster workers) of 18th-century Dublin. Next door at No. 86, built in 1765, the staircase is one of the city's most beautiful rococo examples, with floral swags and musical instruments picked out in cake-frosting white on pastel-color walls.

> *"There is nothing in Ireland from the 17th century that can come near this masterpiece," raves cultural historian John FitzMaurice Mills about the Royal Hospital.*

Catholic University (described by James Joyce in *A Portrait of the Artist as a Young Man*) was established in this building in 1850, with Cardinal John Henry Newman as its first rector. At the back of Newman House lie **Iveagh Gardens,** a delightful hideaway with statues and sunken gardens, that remains one of Dublin's best-kept secrets (you can enter via Earlsfort Terrace and Harcourt Street). *85–86 St. Stephen's Green, tel. 01/4757255. Admission £2. Open June–Aug., weekdays 9–5.*

NUMBER 29

Everything in this exquisite Georgian town house has been meticulously refurbished according to the designs and tastes of the general period from 1790 to 1820. Hand-painted trunks and porcelain dolls lay strewn about the attic; hairbrushes and jewelry sit expectantly on lace-covered mahogany dressers. With every carpet, painting, and bellpull refashioned in exacting detail, Number 29 has a strangely normal feel—as if it were the more eclectic styles of 20th-century Dublin that were unfamiliar and out of place. Arrive early in the morning and you may get one of the museum's superknowledgeable (and supersweet) guides all to yourself. *29 Lower Fitzwilliam St., tel. 01/7026627 or 01/7026165. Opposite Merrion Sq., between Baggot and Upper Mount Sts. Admission £2.50. Open Tues.–Sat. 10–5, Sun. 2–5.*

PARKS & GARDENS

GARDEN OF REMEMBRANCE

Opened in 1966, 50 years after the Easter Uprising, the garden, located within Parnell Square, commemorates all those who died fighting for Irish freedom. A large plaza is at the garden's entrance; steps lead down to the fountain area, graced with a sculpture by contemporary Irish artist Oisín Kelly based on the mythological Children of Lír, who were turned into swans. The garden is a great chill-out spot in the middle of the busy city. *Parnell Sq. Open daily 9–5.*

PHOENIX PARK

Phoenix Park is Europe's largest public park at 1,751 acres, extending about 5 km (3 mi) along the Liffey's north bank. Laid out in the 1740s by Lord Chesterfield, former Lord Lieutenant of Ireland, the park is filled with gardens, woods, and lakes. Several monuments punctuate the grounds, including **Wellington Monument,** an obelisk in honor of the Irish Duke's defeat of Napoléon, and a great cross to commemorate Pope John Paul's visit in 1979, when one in three Irish people turned out to see him. **Áras an Uachtaráin,** formerly the home of the Lord Lieutenant, now houses the president of Ireland. The park is

STROLLIN' DARLIN' DUBLIN

A stroll through the Liberties is a walk through working-class Dublin, past and present, good and bad. The name derives from Dublin of the Middle Ages, when the area south and west of Christ Church Cathedral was outside the city walls and free from the jurisdiction of the city rulers. Begin your walk on Patrick Street, in the shadow of St. Patrick's Cathedral (see above). Look down the street toward the Liffey and a glorious view of Christ Church (see above), the other great Protestant cathedral of Dublin. Take a right onto Dean Street, where you'll find John Fallons, a classy public house with one of the finest "snugs"—small, self-contained rooms with one or two tables, where groups like to gather for a full day's drinking and chatting.

Take a right off Dean Street onto Francis Street, and walk uphill. A host of quality antiques shops line both sides of the thoroughfare. Halfway up Francis Street, on the right-hand side, behind hefty wrought-iron gates, lies Saint Nicholas of Myra's Church, which was completed in 1834 in grand neoclassic style. Inside, the highly ornate chapel includes ceiling panels painted with each of the 12 apostles and a pietà raised 20 ft above the marble altar, which is guarded on each side by angels sculpted by John Hogan while he was in Florence. The tiny nuptial chapel to the right has a Harry Clarke stained-glass window.

Continue on up Francis Street and take the next right up Thomas Davis Street. The street is full of classic, two-story redbrick houses, one window up and down. The area, once the heart of "Darlin' Dublin" and the holy source of its distinctive accent, is rapidly becoming yuppified, as these houses are sold for ridiculous prices to young professionals who want to live near the city center. Back on Francis Street, in an old factory building with its chimney stack intact, the exciting Iveagh Market is well worth a visit. At the top of Francis Street turn left onto Thomas Street. Across the road, on your right-hand side, stands the detailed exterior of St. Augustine and St. John, with its grandiose spire dominating the area around.

Farther up Thomas Street is the National College of Art and Design, whose architecture—a delicate welding of high-tech glass and iron onto the redbrick Victorian—provides a backdrop for students' work in glass, clay, metal, and stone. Finish your day next door in the Clock (tel. 01/6775563), a simple, down-to-earth bar that attracts both students and Liberties locals who, surprisingly, get along famously.

also home to the **Dublin Zoo** (admission £5.50), the third oldest in the world and one of the few places where lions will breed in captivity. It's a bit ratty but still maintains a certain Victorian charm. It costs £2 to visit the **visitor center** (tel. 01/6770095) in the 17th-century Ashtown Castle, which has information about the park's history, flora, and fauna. *Off Parkgate St. From Heuston Station, walk north on Steven's La., turn left on Parkgate St. Open weekdays 9:30–6:30.*

HOUSES OF WORSHIP

CHRIST CHURCH CATHEDRAL

Christ Church, the Church of Ireland's flagship, is also Dublin's oldest standing monument, founded in 1038 by the mead-swilling Sitric, King of the Dublin Norsemen. Construction on the present church—one of two Protestant cathedrals in Dublin (the other is St. Patrick's just to the south; *see below*)—was begun in 1172 by Strongbow, a Norman baron and conqueror of Dublin for the English crown, and went on for 50 years. By 1875 the cathedral had deteriorated badly, so a major renovation gave it much of the look it has today, including the addition of one of Dublin's most charming structures: a Bridge of Sighs–like affair that connects the cathedral to the old Synod Hall, which now holds the Viking extravaganza, **Dublinia.** Despite the fact that Christ Church today is surrounded by new, boxlike flats and concrete office buildings, its squat, gray facade is still captivating, especially the lavishly detailed fenestration, weathered archway chapel, gallery-level carvings, and the famous "leaning wall of Dublin." The interior of Christ Church, filled with a very standard collection of faded murals, tapestries, and men in black robes, is something of a letdown.

The original MGM lion that roared at the start of movies was bred at Dublin Zoo. In truth the big cat was only yawning.

The **crypt,** which is nearly as large as the church itself, contains some fine religious relics and a set of 17th-century punishment stocks. *Christ Church Pl., tel. 01/6778099. Off Lord Edward St., 1½ km (1 mi) west of Trinity College; take Bus 21A, 78, 78A, or 50. Admission £1. Open daily 10–5.*

ST. MICHAN'S CHURCH

This Anglican church, built in 1685 on the site of an older, 11th-century Danish church (Michan is a Danish saint), is architecturally undistinguished except for its 120-ft-high bell tower. However, it has an 18th-century organ, supposedly played by Handel for his first-ever performance of *Messiah*; and its Stool of Repentance, the only one still in existence in the city, was once used by parishioners who were judged to be "open and notoriously naughty livers" and had to do public penance. St. Michan's main claim to notoriety is down in the vaults, where the totally dry atmosphere has preserved a number of corpses in a remarkable state of mummification. Most of the preserved bodies are thought to have been Dublin tradespeople. *Lower Church St., tel. 01/8724154. Admission £2.50. Open Apr.–Oct., weekdays 10–12:45 and 2–4:45, Sat. 10–12:45; Nov.–Mar., weekdays 12:30–3:30, Sat. 10–4:45.*

ST. PATRICK'S CATHEDRAL

Although the present cathedral seems old by most standards (it was built in 1191), the first church built on this site, a tiny wooden shack, was consecrated in 450, reputedly in celebration of Patrick's coming to Ireland. Today, St. Patrick's Cathedral is the oldest and most prominent Christian landmark in Ireland—a bristling Gothic structure meant to awaken the fear of God in its visitors. It's the largest cathedral in the city and the national cathedral of the Church of Ireland. Overall, the place is packed with so many monuments that it can feel like a junk shop at times. The choir and transepts are plastered with the ragged banners of myriad Irish regiments and long-forgotten orders of knights, while the nave is airy and peaceful, bathed in a dusty amber light. Jonathan Swift (1667–1745)—poet, author, wit, and dean of St. Patrick's between 1713 and 1745—is generously remembered with monuments and plaques. Swift's tomb, pulpit, writing table, and death mask are all on display here, along with a memorial to his longtime mistress, Esther Johnson, the poetic "Stella" with whom he had a burning (but supposedly platonic) love affair. Other memorials include the 17th-century **Boyle Monument,** with its numerous painted figures of family members, and the **monument to Turlough O'Carolan,** the last of the Irish bards and one of the country's finest harp players. To the immediate north of the cathedral is a small park, with statues of many of Dublin's literary figures and **St. Patrick's Well.** *Patrick's Close, tel. 01/4754817 or 01/4539472. From Trinity College, walk west 1 km (½ mi) on Dame St. (which becomes Lord Edward and High Sts.), turn left on St. Nicholas St. (which becomes Patrick St.). Admission £2. Open May and*

Sept.–Oct., weekdays 9–6, Sat. 9–5, Sun. 10—11 and 12:30–3; June–Aug., weekdays 9–6, Sat. 9–4, Sun. 9:30–3 and 4:15–5:15; Nov.–Apr., weekdays 9–6, Sat. 9–4, Sun. 10—11 and 12:30–3.

NEIGHBORHOODS

TEMPLE BAR

If change in Dublin has been explosive over the last decade, Temple Bar, the area of cobblestone streets and small lanes bounded by Wellington Quay and Dame Street, is ground zero. In 1991, the area of old factories and warehouses was zoned for a new, dog-ugly bus depot, when some bright sparks decided it was the perfect spot for the most complex and ambitious urban regeneration project since the foundation of the State. It is now the number one tourist draw in the city, with major cultural projects like the **Irish Film Centre, Temple Bar Galleries,** and **ArthouseB** acting as major attractions. Also dotting the area's narrow cobblestone streets and pedestrian alleyways are award-winning new apartment buildings (in fact, inside they tend to be small and uninspired, with sky-high rents), vintage clothing stores, postage-stamp-size boutiques selling £200 sunglasses and other expensive gewgaws, art galleries galore, a hotel resuscitated by U2, hip restaurants, pubs, clubs, and European-style cafés. It all adds up to what the *Irish Times,* in a 1996 headline, called the "Temple of Boom." Its nightlife stays open late, and on weekends its streets are packed with young people from all over Europe. In the last four years, rents in the area have rocketed to Notting Hill levels and cries of gentrification have begun to be heard. The tackiness of some of the newer bars and eateries (Planet Hollywood has muscled its way in) has also caused a little disenchantment, but Temple Bar is still *the* spot to spend an evening.

GRAFTON STREET

It's no more than 200 yards long and about 20 ft wide, but brick-lined Grafton Street, open only to pedestrians, can make a claim to be the most buzzing street in the city, if not in all of Ireland. If you want to find someone in Dublin, just stand on Grafton Street for a few hours and he or she is bound to pass. It is one of Dublin's vital spines: the most direct route between the front door of Trinity College and St. Stephen's Green, and the city's premier shopping street, home to Dublin's two most distinguished department stores, Brown Thomas and Marks & Spencer. Both on Grafton Street itself and on the smaller alleyways that radiate off it, there are also dozens of independent stores, a dozen or so colorful flower sellers, and some of Dublin's most popular watering holes. In summertime, buskers from all over the country and the world line both sides of the street, pouring out the sounds of drum, whistle, pipe, and string.

MERRION SQUARE

This tranquil Georgian square is one of the few places left in southside Dublin where you can feel what the city must have been like 150 years ago. The square has a pristine public garden buffered by a lovely green. Towering over the square on all four sides are some of Dublin's best-preserved Georgian town houses: brick facades overrun with ivy, sporting sooty clay chimneys and black iron gates, punctuated every few steps by the quintessential Georgian masterpiece, the rounded doorway painted thick green, red, or yellow. Leinster House—Dublin's Versailles—along with the Natural History Museum and the National Gallery line the west side of the square, but it is on the other sides that the Georgian terrace streetscape comes into its own, with the finest houses located on the north border. Famous former occupants of Merrion Square include Daniel O'Connell, W. B. Yeats, and the Wilde family, all duly commemorated by a series of brass plaques on the east and south sides of the square. *East end of Nassau St. Open daily sunrise–sunset.*

O'CONNELL STREET

Dublin's most famous thoroughfare and its north–south spine, 150 ft wide, O'Connell Street was previously known as Sackville Street but was renamed in 1924, two years after the founding of the Irish Free State. After the devastation of the 1916 Easter Uprising, the street had to be almost entirely reconstructed, a task that took until the end of the 1920s. The main attraction of the street, **Nelson's Pillar,** a Doric column towering over the city center and a marvelous vantage point, was blown up in 1966, the 50th anniversary of the Easter Uprising. The once-grand street fell into disrepair over the next two decades and is still home to too many fast-food joints and amusement parlors. But a government-inspired spirit of renewal is starting to change the area. After an open design competition, plans are afoot to build a spectacular "Millennium Needle" on the sight of the old column. The new sculpture will be Dublin's tallest man-made structure. The large **monument** at the south end of the street is dedicated to Daniel O'Connell (1775–1847), "The Liberator," and was erected in 1854 as a tribute to the orator's achievement in securing Catholic emancipation in 1829. Seated, winged figures represent the four Victories—courage, eloquence, fidelity, and patriotism—all exemplified by O'Connell. Ireland's four ancient provinces—Munster, Leinster, Ulster, and Connacht—are identified by their respective coats of arms. Look closely and you'll notice O'Connell is wearing a glove on one hand, as he did for much of his adult life, a self-imposed penance for shooting a man in a duel. Also along O'Connell is another noted statue, a modern rendition of Joyce's **Anna Livia,** seen as a lady set within a waterfall, and nicknamed the "floozie in the Jacuzzi" by the natives. **O'Connell Bridge,** the main bridge spanning the Liffey (wider than it is long), marks the street's southern end. **Mary** and **Henry streets,** two of Dublin's main shopping areas, are just off O'Connell Street near the GPO, and Lower Abbey Street, off the other side of O'Connell Street, is home to the famous **Abbey Theatre.**

DUBLIN WEST

This once industrial section of the city stretches west from **Christ Church** to that other holy of holies, the modern plant of **Guinness Brewery.** The area is home to a number of other major attractions listed above, including imposing but benign **Dublin Castle,** more booze at the **Old Jameson Distillery,** the **Royal Hospital Kilmainham,** and the copper-topped **Four Courts.** But the real pleasure here is to walk right to the top of Dame Street and look back down the wide, busy thoroughfare to the glory of Trinity in the distance. Also take a stroll down **Fishamble Street,** the oldest street in the city and home to **St. Michan's Church.**

As St. Patrick's and Christ Church cathedrals testify, the Church of Ireland stole and kept all the best churches.

SHOPPING

In days gone by, travelers would arrive in Ireland, land of leprechauns, shillelaghs, and shamrocks, and quickly realize that the only known specimens of leprechauns or shillelaghs were those in souvenir-shop windows, while shamrocks only bloomed around the borders of Irish linen handkerchiefs and tablecloths. All of this is still true, but today's shopper will find so much more. The variety and sophistication of stores in Dublin now are quite remarkable. But the trade-off, of course, is that prices are competitive with those in most other European cities. Dublin's central shopping area, from O'Connell to Grafton Street, is the top spot in Ireland for concentrated general and specialty shopping. Bargains can be found, and quality, especially when you're buying crafts or clothing, tends to be very high.

Shopping in central Dublin can mean pushing through determined crowds, especially in the afternoons and on weekends. Most large shops and department stores are open Monday–Saturday 9–6. Although nearly all department stores are closed on Sunday, most smaller specialty shops stay open Sunday 10–6. Shops with later closing hours are noted below. Weekday afternoons are the most relaxing times to shop—everyone is just in a better mood. Don't get confused by the two prices quoted on many goods. As of January 1, 1999, all items for sale had to list their price in euros as well as Irish pounds.

SHOPPING DISTRICTS

O'Connell Street. The main thoroughfare of the city has been infested with fast-food outlets, but it also has some worthwhile stores. One of Dublin's largest and most famous department stores, Clery's, faces the GPO. On the same side of the street as the post office is Eason's, a large book, magazine, and stationery store.

Henry Street. Running westward from O'Connell Street, this busy street features Arnotts department store and a host of smaller, supertacky, superfun specialty stores selling records, footwear, and cheap fashion. Henry Street's continuation, Mary Street, has a branch of Marks & Spencer, a splendid store for stocking up on good food for a trip.

Grafton Street. Dublin's main shopping street is now closed to vehicles for most of the day. Two substantial, rather posh department stores face each other here, while the rest of the street is taken up by smaller shops, many of them branches of international chains, such as the Body Shop, Bally Shoes, Next, and Principles. Smaller streets off Grafton Street, especially Duke Street, South Anne Street, and Chatham Street, have expensive crafts and fashion shops that are good for a browse. Grafton Street also has half a dozen outdoor flower sellers with good selections and great attitude. Overall, the street can be a little pricey.

Dawson Street. Just east of Grafton Street, between Nassau Street to the north and St. Stephen's Green to the south, this is the city's primary bookstore avenue, with competitors Waterstone's and Hodges Figgis facing each other like gunfighters from opposite sides of the street.

Francis Street. The Liberties, the oldest part of the city, is the hub of Dublin's antiques trade. This street and surrounding areas, such as the Coombe, have plenty of shops where you can browse. If you're looking for something in particular, dealers will gladly recommend the appropriate store to you. Don't be afraid to haggle—they tend to overprice.

SPECIALTY SHOPPING CENTERS

Blackrock (Blackrock, Co. Dublin) is technically outside of Dublin's city center, but it deserves special mention as one of Dublin's first attempts at a mall. It's built on two levels, looking onto an inner courtyard, with the giant Superquinn Center, cafés, restaurants, and the internationally ubiquitous groups of teenage boys and girls hanging out. Blackrock can be reached conveniently on the DART train line.

Ilac Center (Henry St.) was Dublin's first large, modern shopping center, with two department stores, specialty shops, and several restaurants. A small public library and ample parking are also available. Good deals are certainly to be found, and there is plenty of variety.

Powerscourt Townhouse (S. William St.), a fashionable town house built in 1771, housed a wholesale textile company for many years until it was updated nearly 15 years ago. The interior courtyard has been thoroughly refurbished and roofed over; on the dais at ground-floor level, live piano music is often heard. Two floors of galleries have a maze of small, overpriced crafts shops interspersed with coffee shops and restaurants—a good spot for lunch, but it might be wise to do your purchasing elsewhere. It's also a center for original Irish fashions by designers like Gráinne Walsh.

St. Stephen's Green Centre (northwest corner of St. Stephen's Green), Dublin's largest and most ambitious shopping center, resembles a giant greenhouse, with ironwork in a sort of Victorian style. On three floors overlooked by a vast clock, the 100 mostly small shops sell a variety of crafts, fashions, and household goods. The Dunnes Stores here sells the cheapest groceries in the center of town.

Tower Design Centre (Pearse St.), east of the heart of the city center (near the Waterways Visitor Centre), has more than 35 separate crafts firms in a converted 1862 sugar-refinery tower. As you might expect, they're not giving the stuff away, but a good hunt might unearth a bargain, and the variety available is unmatched anywhere in the country. On the ground floor, you can stop at workshops devoted to heraldry and Irish pewter; the other six floors feature hand-painted silks, ceramics, hand-knit items, jewelry, and fine-art cards and prints.

DEPARTMENT STORES

Arnotts (Henry St. and Grafton St., tel. 01/8721111) has a wide variety of relatively mundane clothing, housewares, and sporting goods filling three complete floors; the smaller Grafton Street branch stocks only new fashion and footwear.

Brown Thomas (Grafton St., tel. 01/6797200), Dublin's most exclusive department store, is worth a people-watching visit even if you're not buying. It stocks the leading designer names in clothing and cosmetics and a wide variety of stylish accessories. It also carries clothing by Irish designers.

Clery's (O'Connell St., tel. 01/8786000) is historically the city's most famous department store and was once the most glitzy spot in town, although its glory has faded somewhat. It has four floors of all types of merchandise, from fashion to home appliances, and it caters to a distinctly modest, traditional sense of style. Shopping for the civilized characterizes Clery's.

Dunnes Stores (major city-center stores at St. Stephen's Green Center, tel. 01/4780188; Henry St., tel. 01/8726833; and Ilac Shopping Center, Mary St., tel. 01/8730211) is Ireland's largest chain of department stores. All stores stock fashion, household, and grocery items and have a reputation for value and variety.

Eason's (major stores at O'Connell St., tel. 01/8733811 and Ilac Shopping Center, Mary St., tel. 01/8728833) distinctive green-and-blue-striped bags have been a favorite with Dubliners for decades. The store is known primarily for its wide variety of books, magazines, and stationery. Recently its biggest outlet on O'Connell Street began to stock music, videos, and other audiovisual goodies.

Marks & Spencer (Grafton St. and Henry St., tel. 01/6797855), the slightly less high-brow rival to Brown Thomas (*see above*), stocks everything from fashion (including lingerie) to tasty, unusual groceries. The Grafton Street branch even has its own bureau de change, which doesn't charge commission.

SPECIALTY SHOPS

An increasing number of Irish-made crafts and souvenir lines reflect an increasing demand by visitors for specifically Irish goods. Some newer specialty shops sell nothing else. Prices can be high, but a little patience usually pays off, and you might just find a bargain.

BOOKS • Books make ideal presents from Ireland, land of saints and scholars and all that. With nearly 1,000 titles now published each year in Ireland, the breadth and choice of material are quite impressive. Best of all, thanks to an enlightened national social policy, there's no tax on books, so if you only buy books, you don't have to worry about getting VAT slips. The range of texts is particularly wide in Irish history, fiction, and travel, and the production quality of such titles compares very favorably with that of books published outside Ireland. **Fred Hanna's** (27 Nassau St., tel. 01/6772544) sells old and new books, with a good choice of titles on travel and Ireland. **Greene's** (Clare St., tel. 01/6762544) carries an extensive range of secondhand volumes. **Hodges Figgis** (54 Dawson St., tel 01/6774754) stocks 1½ million books on three floors. **Waterstone's** (7 Dawson St., tel. 01/6791415), a large branch of a British chain, has two floors featuring a fine selection of Irish and international books. The **Winding Stair** (40 Lower Ormond Quay, tel. 01/8733292) sells secondhand books and has a great chill-out café that overlooks the River Liffey. **Cathach Books** (10 Duke St., tel. 01/6718676) sells first editions of Irish favorites and many other books of Irish interest, plus old maps of Dublin and Ireland.

CDS, RECORDS, AND TAPES • An increasing amount of Irish-recorded material, covering traditional folk music, country and western, rock, and even a smattering of classical music, is now available on records, compact discs, and tapes. **Tower Records** (16 Wicklow St., tel. 01/6713250) now has a branch in Dublin. **HMV** (65 Grafton St., tel. 01/6795334; 18 Henry St., 01/8722095) is one of the larger record shops in town. **Claddagh Records** (2 Cecilia St., tel. 01/6793664) and **Gael Linn** (26 Merrion Sq., tel. 01/6767283) specialize in traditional Irish music and Irish-language recordings and are a great relief from the megastores that dominate the market.

GIFTS • Okay, so gifts from the Emerald Isle are always in mortal danger of being superhokey. But there are some genuine treasures to be unearthed. Ireland is synonymous with Waterford crystal, which is available in a wide range of products, including relatively inexpensive items. But other, slightly less expensive lines are now gaining recognition, such as Cavan, Galway, and Tipperary crystal. **Brown Thomas** (*see above*) is the best department store for gift shopping; the best specialty outlets are listed below.

Blarney Woollen Mills (21–23 Nassau St., tel. 01/6710068) has its fair share of dyed-green rubbish, but it's one of the best places for Belleek china, Waterford and Galway crystal, and Irish linen.

Designyard (East Essex St., tel. 01/6778453) offers beautifully designed but evily priced Irish and international tableware, lighting, small furniture, and jewelry.

Kilkenny Shop (5–6 Nassau St., tel. 01/6777066) specializes in contemporary Irish-made ceramics, pottery, and silver jewelry and also holds regular exhibits of exciting new work by Irish craftspeople.

McDowell (3 Upper O'Connell St., tel. 01/8744961), a straight-up jewelry shop popular with Dubliners about to be wed, has been in business for more than 100 years.

Tierneys (St. Stephen's Green Centre, tel. 01/4782873) carries a good selection of crystal and china. Claddagh rings, pendants, and brooches are popular, affordable buys.

MUSEUM STORES • The little stores attached to major museums are a much-underutilized place to find that special something particular to the country you're visiting. Sure they charge a little over the odds, but you're usually getting the real thing.

National Gallery of Ireland Shop (Merrion Sq. W, tel. 01/6785450) has a terrific selection of books on Irish art, plus posters, postcards, note cards, and a wide array of lovely bibelots.

National Museum Shop (Kildare St., tel. 01/6777444, ext. 327) carries jewelry based on ancient Celtic artifacts in the museum collection, contemporary Irish pottery, a large selection of books, and other gift items.

Trinity College Library Shop (Old Library, Trinity College, tel. 01/6082308) sells Irish-theme books, *Book of Kells* souvenirs of all kinds, plus clothing, jewelry, and other Irish-made items.

VINTAGE • **Flip** (4 Upper Fownes St., tel. 01/6714299) was in Temple Bar before it was cool, selling torn Levis, battered leather jackets, and wild 1940s dresses. It's still a great spot for a snoop.

OUTDOOR MARKETS

Dublin has a number of open-air markets, selling mostly men's and women's fashions. **Moore Street** is open Monday–Saturday 9–6; stalls lining both sides of the street sell fruits and vegetables. The traditional Dublin repartee here is renowned in the city. Other markets are only open on weekends. A variety of bric-a-brac is sold at the **Liberty Market** on Meath Street, open Friday–Saturday 10–6 and Sunday noon–5:30. The indoor **Christchurch Market,** opposite St. Audoen's Church, is open weekends 10–5; come here for antiques and bric-a-brac.

AFTER DARK

Dubliners have always enjoyed a night out, but in the last decade or so, with the influx of new money, they have turned the pleasure into a work of art. First and foremost, of course, comes drinking. If you don't, act like you do and go to the bars anyway—the gaiety is infectious and as inebriating as the strongest whiskey. Whether you're in for a staggering pub crawl or a quiet chat over a pint of plain, head to any one of Dublin's 1,000 public houses. A lot of clichés have been uttered about Dublin pubs, but when you've spent a little time in them, wrapped up in the warm energy that radiates through the best of them, where life is on display in all its guises, you'll understand the hyperbole. If your head is still throbbing from last night's throaty sing-along, go to the movies, the theater, or any one of a dozen music pubs in the city center. Be aware that most of the bars still chuck you out around midnight, though later licensing hours are becoming more and more common on the weekends. If you're stuck for inspiration, pick up the weekly magazine *The Big Issue* (£1), which lists nearly every restaurant, pub, music venue, cinema, theater, art gallery, and late-night hot spot in town.

PUBS

As a general rule, the area between Grafton and Great George's streets is a gold mine for classy pubs. Another good bet is the Temple Bar district (though some of the newer bars are all plastic and mirrors), sandwiched between Dame Street and the River Liffey. In recent years both these areas have been over-run with tourists, so try up around Parnell Square for a few real spit-on-the-floor hideaways.

CITY CENTER The Brazen Head. Dublin's oldest pub (built in 1198) served as the headquarters for the rebellious United Irishmen during the late 18th century. Loaded with character and friendly drunks, the Brazen Head has live, traditional music nightly. It's still a hotbed of Republican sentiment, so be careful with your politics. *20 Lower Bridge St., tel. 01/6779549.*

Brussels. A disorderly sort of metal dive, filled with black leather and greasy longhairs, Brussels features a concert-volume jukebox spewing the likes of Metallica and Soundgarden. *7 Harry St., off Grafton St., tel. 01/6775362.*

Café-en-Seine. With an irony-free, slightly over-the-top approach, this place is a recent conversion to a Parisian-style "locale," with a wrought-iron balcony, art-deco furniture, a vaulted ceiling, and a clientele to match: Most are young, cell phone–carrying professionals. *40 Dawson St., tel. 01/6774369.*

Cassidy's. This is just a quiet neighborhood pub with a pint of stout so good that Bubba Clinton himself dropped in for one during his visit to Dublin. *42 Lower Camden St., tel. 01/4751429.*

The Crane. A smart place about the size of a shoe box, the Crane has recently been renovated in the "old pub" style (dark oak and buckling hardwood floors). It looked better as it was, but it's a popular stop on the Trinity College weekend pub crawl. A variety of music can be heard in the downstairs lounge. *20 Crane La., off Dame St., tel. 01/6715824.*

Davy Byrne's. This is a pilgrimage stop for Joyceans. In *Ulysses*, Leopold Bloom stops in here for a glass of burgundy and a Gorgonzola cheese sandwich. He then leaves the pub and walks to Dawson Street, where he helps a blind man cross the road. Unfortunately, the much-altered pub is unrecognizable from Joyce's day, but it still serves some fine pub grub. *21 Duke St., tel. 01/6711298.*

Dockers. Once a hard man's bar, this quayside spot east of the city center has gone trendy. It's just around the corner from Windmill Lane Studios, where U2 and other noted bands record; at night the area is still a little dicey. *5 Sir John Rogerson's Quay, tel. 01/6771692.*

Doheny & Nesbitt. This traditional spot with snugs, dark wood decor, and smoke-darkened ceilings has hardly changed over the decades it has been open. It gets good and packed on weekends. *5 Lower Baggot St., tel. 01/6762945.*

Doyle's. This small, cozy pub is a favorite with journalists (notorious boozers in Dublin), who hop over from the *Irish Times* just across the street. *9 College St., tel. 01/6710616.*

The Globe. This is still *the* pub for the young and progressive, with massive oak tables, old posters, and ambient sounds. Downstairs is the dance club Rí-Rá, whose atmosphere changes nightly; there's live jazz on Sunday. *11 S. Great George's St., tel. 01/6711220.*

Horseshoe Bar. A classic hotel bar and a popular meeting place for Dublin's businesspeople and politicians, the Horseshoe Bar has comparatively little space for drinkers around the semicircular bar. There's tons of atmosphere, though. *Shelbourne Hotel, 27 St. Stephen's Green, tel. 01/6766471.*

Kehoe's. If you want to hang out with a bunch of Irish students, this is one of the species' favorite watering holes. The main bar is a wonder in wood and brass, and the tiny back room is supercozy. *9 S. Anne St., tel. 01/6778312.*

Lincoln Inn. The Lincoln is a fine pub in all respects: dark, quiet, sufficiently ancient, and frequented by Trinity students and leathery locals. Standard pub grub is available for less than £5. *19 Lincoln Pl., by Trinity College, tel. 01/6762978.*

McDaid's. Most nights you'll hear jazz, blues, or Irish folk music in the upstairs lounge of this popular pub. *3 Harry St., off Grafton St., tel. 01/6794395.*

Mulligan's of Poolbeg Street. Until a few years ago, no women were allowed in Mulligan's. Today, journalists, locals, and students of both genders flock here for what is argued to be the best pint of Guinness on earth. Allegedly, Mulligan's still uses wooden pipes to bring "Arthur's Nectar" (Guinness) up from the cellar of this ancient pub. Sounds like a fib. *8 Poolbeg St., off Pearse St., next to Evening Press building, tel. 01/6775582.*

Mother Redcap's Tavern. The place claims to be an authentic re-creation of a 17th-century Dublin tavern, with stone walls from an old flour mill, beams, and plenty of old prints of the city, as well as trendy Victorian posters. It's a bit twee but can be fun. *Back La., tel. 01/4538306.*

Neary's. The exotic Victorian-style interior is a clue that this was once the haunt of music-hall artists, as well as of a certain literary set including the Goliath of drinkers, Brendan Behan. Join the actors from the adjacent Gaiety Theatre for a good pub lunch. *1 Chatham St., tel. 01/6777371.*

O'Donoghue's. The place is often full of tourists, but on a good night it can be wild: Impromptu musical performances often spill out onto the street, and the barmen have to stand on the counter to serve pints to the throngs. *15 Merrion Row, tel. 01/6762807.*

The only bad thing about Irish pubs is that they close—at 11 PM during winter and 11:30 PM in summer. When the barman shouts "last call" around 10:55, he means it.

Ryan's Pub. Another one of Dublin's last genuine, late-Victorian-era pubs, this one has changed little since its most recent (1896) remodeling. Its dark mahogany counters, old-fashioned lamps, and snugs create a marvelously restful setting. *28 Parkgate St., tel. 01/6776097.*

Stag's Head. No visit to Dublin is complete without lunch at the Stag's Head, one of the city's oldest and best-preserved pubs. The Stag's high oak ceilings and beveled windows give it an open, unstuffy feel. *1 Dame Ct., 1 block south of Dame St., tel. 01/6793701.*

Toner's. This is the epitome of a good pub. Built in the early 1800s, Toner's thankfully retains most of its original furnishings and flavor (old men nursing their pints, antique books and bottles on the walls). It also has the distinction of being the only pub ever visited by W. B. Yeats. Cheap pub grub is available daily. *139 Lower Baggot St., tel. 01/6763090.*

TEMPLE BAR • Oliver St. John Gogarty. This lively bar attracts all ages and nationalities and overflows during the summer. On most nights there is traditional Irish music upstairs. *57 Fleet St., Temple Bar., tel. 01/6711822.*

Palace Bar. Living up to its name, this truly is a temple to the drinking man. Scarcely changed over the past 60 years, its intricate tiled floors and beautiful stained-glass ceiling are the perfect setting for an early evening tipple. *21 Fleet St., tel. 01/6779290.*

GAY BARS • The George. Across the street from the Globe (*see above*), this huge gay-lesbian pub is dimly lit, smoky, and laid-back. The crowd—a good mix of locals and out-of-towners of all ages—wraps itself around the long bar. Wednesday–Monday, the upstairs transmogrifies into the dance club "The Block" from 9:30 PM to 2:30 AM; the cover is free Monday and Sunday, otherwise £2–£5. *89 S. Great George's St., tel. 01/4782983.*

Out on the Liffey. Less frantic than the George (*see above*), Dublin's second gay bar, on the north side of the river, opened three years ago and draws both lesbians and gays plus their straight friends. *27 Ormond Quay, tel. 01/8722480.*

MUSIC BARS

Dublin's music scene is excellent. With more than 120 different clubs and music pubs to choose from, you'll need a copy of *The Big Issue* to get you started. Otherwise, take a walk down Grafton Street and keep your ears open.

Baggot Inn. On the fringe of the city center, the Baggot Inn looks like a dull pub from the street, but head inside to the back rooms and you'll find it dark, sweaty, and loud. There's even a full bar. *143 Baggot St., tel. 01/6761430. Cover: free–£5.*

International Bar. Like a number of other city-center pubs, this one doubles as an independent music venue. Happily, there is rarely a cover. *23 Wicklow St., tel. 01/6779250.*

Slattery's. Music in this full-service pub varies (mostly rock with the infrequent traditional Irish session). The upstairs (£2–£5 cover) hosts more well-known bands, but the live music on the ground floor is always free. *129 Capel St., tel. 01/8737971.*

Whelan's. It's a real in spot for up-and-coming bands from Ireland and the United Kingdom. Big crowds descend on the place for most gigs, so get there early. *25 Wexford St., tel. 01/4780766. Cover £2–£5.*

NIGHTCLUBS

As in most of Europe, the dominant sound in Dublin's nightclubs is electronic dance music (hard techno or break-beat), and the crowd that flocks to the clubs virtually seven nights a week is of the trendy, under-25 generation. However, there are a couple of spots where you're more likely to hear tango than techno, such as the weekend nightclub at the Gaiety Theater, Thursday nights at the Pod, and Sunday nights at Lillie's Bordello. **Velure** (tel. 01/6703750) is one of Dublin's most successful nightclub promoters, offering live music, DJs, and themed parties throughout the year; call to find out what's going on.

The DA Club. The DA Club used to be a place where old farts came for après-theater cheap booze. Now, in the refurbished space, it has become one of the most popular music and dance spots in town. Despite its small capacity, it has a wide variety of nightly entertainment—from comedy acts to live bands to dance parties—often running concurrently, as it has two floors. *3–5 Clarendon Market, tel. 01/6705116.*

The Kitchen. Posh subterranean caves stuffed with velvety crimson lounge furniture surround a tiny dance floor in U2's own club (they own the upstairs hotel, too). Although it's open nightly (11:30ish), only the superglam set gets in on weekends. *East Essex St., tel. 01/6776635. Cover: £4–£8.*

Leeson Street. With the new, more liberal approach to granting late licenses, Dublin's infamous, slightly sleazy "strip" has shrunk to only a few clubs. Dress at these places is informal, but jeans and sneakers are not welcome. Most of these clubs are licensed only to sell wine, and the prices are highway robbery (up to £20 for a mediocre bottle); best to have a few before you arrive. The upside is that most don't charge a cover.

Lillie's Bordello. It's one of those places with airs about themselves that like nothing better than to section off certain areas for V.I.P.s. A popular spot for the trendy, professional crowd, it does draw its share of rock and film stars. On Sunday nights, the strict dress code is relaxed for a night of live music and DJs, and the real people come out of hiding. *Grafton St, tel. 01/6799204. Cover: £5–£10.*

The Pod. The Place of Dance is deservedly Dublin's most renowned dance club, especially among the younger set. Entry is judged as much on clothing as on age; it helps to look either stylish or rich, except on Thursday nights, when the club hosts a no-frills, no-nonsense night of dance-floor jazz and funk. *Harcourt St., tel. 01/4780166. Cover: £5–£9.*

Red Box. Adjacent to the Pod and the Chocolate Bar, Red Box can pack in more than 1,000 people and surround them with state-of-the-art sound and light. It regularly hosts Irish and international rock acts as well as celebrity DJs from Europe and the United States. *Old Harcourt Street Station, Harcourt St., tel. 01/4780166. Cover: £5–£10.*

Rí Ra. Rí Rá. This place is really part of the hugely popular Globe bar. The name means "uproar" in Irish, and on most nights the place does go a little wild. It's perhaps the best spot for no-frills, fun dancing in Dublin. Upstairs you can chill out. *11 S. Great Georges St., tel. 01/6711220. Cover: £5–£7.*

THEATER

Dublin's theater scene is impressive: Scattered around the city center are no fewer than 15 established and experimental stages that host a variety of opera, comedy, and tearjerker dramas. Especially popular (with tourists) are the Irish classics staged every summer, whether it's Brian Friel's hit *Dancing at Lughnasa*, Synge's *Playboy of the Western World* (which sparked massive riots when it opened at the Abbey in 1907), or O'Casey's *Plough and the Stars*. Most theaters offer sizable discounts to students with ID, nearly all productions finish by 11 PM, and, like everything else in Dublin, most theaters are dark on Sunday. Check *The Big Issue* for dead-on reviews and comprehensive listings.

If you're in the mood for low-key entertainment with some good-natured song and dance thrown in, **Olympia Theatre's** (73 Dame St., tel. 01/6777744) "Midnight at the Olympia" program on Friday and

Saturday nights is an excellent choice. Shows cost £7–£10. **City Arts Centre** (2325 Moss St., tel. 01/6770643) also presents experimental works for as little as £2 and hosts a variety of cultural events.

The following theaters offer varied dramatic fare: **Abbey Theatre and Peacock Theatre** (Lower Abbey St., tel. 01/8787222), **Andrew's Lane Theatre** (9 Andrew's La., tel. 01/6795720), **Focus Theatre** (6 Pembroke Pl., tel. 01/6763071), **Gaiety Theatre** (S. King St., tel. 01/6771717), **Gate Theatre** (1 Cavendish Row, tel. 01/8744045), **Project Arts Centre** (39 Essex St., tel. 01/6712321), and the **Riverbank** (10 Merchant's Quay, tel. 01/6773370).

FILM

Most Dublin cinemas offer a standard bag of big-budget Hollywood flicks that were released in the United States ages ago. The boxlike multiplex has replaced the old, cavernous auditorium, except for cinema number one at the **Savoy** on O'Connell Street, still the best place to see a big movie. Dublin's one offbeat art house, **Irish Film Centre** (6 Eustace St., tel. 01/6793477), does its best to keep your brain from turning to mush. O'Connell and Abbey streets have the highest concentration of movie houses. Admission prices are in the £4–£6 range, and reduced rates (£2.50) are available for students and for most showings before 6 PM. Late shows (10–midnight) are common on weekends only.

JUST OUTSIDE THE CITY

SOUTHSIDE

Dubliners are blessed. Few populaces enjoy such glorious and easily accessible options for day trips. Just outside the city, some of the region's most unique sights—the Joyce Tower, the Marino Casino, Malahide Castle, to name a few—beckon, and you need to head either north or south of the city center to see them. Once you cross over the Grand Canal, which defines the southern border of the city center, you enter exclusive Ballsbridge and other southern areas of the city and its suburbs. These areas can have a touch of the Hamptons about them, posh and a little stiff, but the sights make the visit worthwhile. If you do set out for points south and you don't have time to see everything, plan to begin in Ballsbridge. If you have a car, then head to Rathfarnham, directly south of the city. Alternatively, head east and follow the coast road south to Dun Laoghaire (and points even farther south, covered in Chapter 3). Beyond Ballsbridge, these areas are too spread out to cover on foot, and either a car or public transportation (the bus or DART) is the only way to get around. Traveling to and from each of the suburbs will take up most of a day, so you will have to pick and choose the trips you prefer.

RATHFARNHAM

Two parks made for picnic afternoons lie in the suburb of Rathfarnham, due south of the city at the edge of the Dublin Mountains. (You can take Bus 47A from Hawkins Street in the city center to both of them, or drive, leaving the city center via Nicholas Street, just west of Christ Church Cathedral, and following it south through Terenure.) The 18th-century house in **St. Enda's National Historic Park** has been turned into the **Pearse Museum,** commemorating Patrick Pearse, leader of Dublin's 1916 Easter Uprising and great advocate of the blood sacrifice. In the early years of this century, the house was a progressive boys' school, which Pearse and his brother Willie founded to promote the Irish in the Anglicanized city. The museum preserves Pearse family memorabilia, documents, and photographs. A lake and nature trails are also on the park's 50-acre grounds, and guides are available to lead tours of the park or simply to answer questions. *Grange Rd., Rathfarnham, tel. 01/4934208. Admission free. Open: Park year-round, daily 8:30–dusk; museum May–Aug., daily 10–1 and 2–5:30; Sept.–Apr., daily 10–1 and 2–4.*

Marlay Park, leave St. Enda's Park via Grange Road, and walk up the hill for about 1 km (½ mi), turning left at the T junction and continuing another ½ km (¼ mi). The park marks the start of the **Wicklow Way,** a popular but tough walking route that crosses the Wicklow Mountains for 127 km (85 mi), through some of the most rugged landscapes in Western Europe. In addition to its woodlands and nature walks, the 214-acre park has a cobbled courtyard, home to brightly plumed peacocks. It's also a good spot to watch Dubliners at play, especially football (soccer to you), a religion among the young kids of the city. Surrounding the courtyard are crafts workshops, where, even if you don't want to buy, you are welcome to observe the process of bookbinding and the making of jewelry and furniture. *Grange Rd., Rathfarnham, tel. 01/4934059. Admission free. Open Nov.–Jan., daily 10–5; Feb.–Mar., daily 10–6; Apr. and Oct., daily 10–7; May and Sept, daily 10–8; June–Aug., daily 10–9.*

BALLSBRIDGE

Many of Dublin's more upmarket hotels and restaurants are in the northern reaches of Ballsbridge, a leafy, slightly snobby suburb that is directly across the Grand Canal from the city center. Its major cultural sites, however, are considerably farther south—a bit too far to reach on foot for all but the most ambitious walkers. To visit these sites, take the DART train to Sidney Parade, or Bus 7 or Bus 8 from Burgh Quay (on the south bank of the Liffey, just east of O'Connell Bridge).

To reach **Sandymount Strand,** double back to the Sydney Parade DART station and keep heading west the few blocks to the beach. Stretching for 5 km (3 mi) from Ringsend to Booterstown, Sandymount was cherished by James Joyce and his beloved from Galway, Nora Barnacle, and it figures as one of the settings in *Ulysses.* (The beach is "at the lacefringe of the tide," as Joyce put it.) When the tide recedes, the beach extends for 1½ km (1 mi) from the foreshore, but the tide sweeps in again very quickly. A sliver of a park lies between the main Strand Road and the beach.

BOOTERSTOWN

Booterstown lies along Dublin Bay, south of Sandymount along the R118. (You can reach it via the DART local train or by car, picking up the R118 from the corner of Lower Merrion Street and Merrion Square.) The **Booterstown Marsh Bird Sanctuary** is the largest wildlife preserve in the Dublin area. Curlews, herons, kingfishers, and other fairly rare migratory species come to nest here; information boards along the road describe the birds for visitors. Also on this main road you'll pass **Glena,** the house where Athlone-born John McCormack, one of the best and most popular tenors in the first quarter of this century, died on September 16, 1945. *Between the DART line and Rock Rd., tel. 01/4541786.*

BLACKROCK

Fine sea views, swimming, and a major shopping center draw Dubliners down to otherwise boring Blackrock (3 km/2 mi south of Booterstown), a bedroom community where James Joyce's parents lived with their large brood for most of 1892. Above the Blackrock DART station, **Idrone Terrace,** lined with restored, old-fashioned lamps, provides a lovely view across the bay to Howth Peninsula.

MONKSTOWN

One of Dublin's most exclusive suburbs, **Monkstown** (3 km/2 mi south of Blackrock on the R119) boasts two architectural curiosities. John Semple, the architect of Monkstown's Anglican parish **church,** was inspired by two entirely different styles, the Gothic and the Moorish, which he joined into an unlikely hybrid of towers and turrets. Built in 1833 in the town's main square, the church is only open during Sunday services. The well-preserved ruins of **Monkstown Castle** lie about 1 km (½ mi) south of the suburb; it's a 15th-century edifice with a keep, a gatehouse, and a long wall section, all surrounded by greenery.

DUN LAOGHAIRE AND SANDYCOVE

After the British monarch King George IV disembarked for a brief visit in 1821, Dun Laoghaire (pronounced dun-*lear*-ee; it's 2½ km/1½ mi beyond Monkstown along the R119, the Monkstown Crescent) was renamed Kingstown. As you might expect, the natives never liked the imposed title and returned the town to its original Irish name 99 years later, as soon as independence had been achieved. Its Irish name refers to Laoghaire, the High King of Tara, who in the 5th century permitted St. Patrick to begin converting Ireland to Christianity. The town was once a Protestant stronghold of the old ruling elite; in some of the neo-Georgian squares and terraces behind **George's Street,** the main thoroughfare, a little of the community's former elegance can still be felt.

Dun Laoghaire has long been known for its great harbor, enclosed by two piers, each 2½ km (1½ mi) long. The harbor was constructed between 1817 and 1859, using granite quarried from nearby Dalkey Hill. The west pier has a rougher surface and is not as good for walking as the east pier, which has a cute bandstand where musicians play during summer. The workday business here includes passenger-ship and freight-service sailings to Holyhead in north Wales, 3½ hours away. Dun Laoghaire is also a yachting center, with the members-only Royal Irish, National, and Royal St. George yacht clubs, all founded in the 19th century, lining the harbor area. West of the harbor and across from the Royal Marine Hotel and the People's Park, the **National Maritime Museum** is in the former Mariners' church. Its central hall makes a strangely ideal setting for exhibits like the French longboat captured during an aborted French invasion at Bantry, County Cork, in 1796. A particularly memorable exhibit is the old optic from the Baily Lighthouse on Howth Head, across Dublin Bay; the herringbone patterns of glass reflected light across the bay until several decades ago. *Haigh Terr., tel. 01/2800969. Admission £1.50. Open May–Sept., Tues.–Sun. 1–5.*

From the harbor area, Marine Parade leads alongside Scotsmans Bay for 1¼ km (¾ mi), as far as the Forty Foot Bathing Pool, a traditional bathing area that attracts mostly nude older men (not to be witnessed on an empty stomach). Women were once banned from here, but now hardy swimmers of both genders are free to brave its cold waters. On Christmas morning it is the scene for a traditional icy dip before mass.

A few steps away from the bathing pool stands Sandycove's other claim to fame, the **James Joyce Martello Tower.** Originally built in 1804 when Napoléon's invasion seemed imminent, it was demilitarized in the 1860s along with most of the rest of the 34 Martello towers that ring Ireland's coast. Martello towers were originally Italian and were constructed to protect the Italian coastline against the possibility of a Napoleonic naval invasion. In Ireland, they were built by the British to protect Irish shores from the same threat and were remarkable for their squat, solid construction, rotating cannon at the top, and— most importantly—their proximity to one another, so that each one is within visible range of the one next to it. In 1904, this tower was rented to Oliver St. John Gogarty, a medical student and man about town who was known for his poetry and ready wit, for £8 a year. He wanted to create a nurturing environment for writers and would-be literati and liked nothing better than a good party. Joyce spent a week here in September 1904 and wryly described it in the first chapter of *Ulysses,* using his friend as a model for the character of "stately, plump" Buck Mulligan, the first person mentioned in the book. The tower now houses a **Joyce Museum,** founded in 1962 thanks to Sylvia Beach, the Paris-based first publisher of *Ulysses.* The exhibition hall contains first editions of most of Joyce's works. Joycean memorabilia includes his waistcoat, embroidered by his grandmother, and a tie that he gave to Samuel Beckett (who was Joyce's onetime secretary). The gunpowder magazine now holds the Joyce Tower Library, including a death mask of Joyce taken on January 13, 1941. *Sandycove, tel. 01/2809265. Admission £2. Open Apr.–Oct., Mon.–Sat. 10–1 and 2–5, Sun. 2–6; Nov.–Mar. by appointment.*

DALKEY

From the James Joyce Tower at Sandycove, it's an easy walk or very quick drive 1 km (½ mi) south to Dalkey. Along Castle Street, the town's main thoroughfare, you'll observe substantial stone remains, resembling small, turreted castles, of two 15th- and 16th-century fortified houses. During the summer small boats make the 15-minute crossing from Coliemore Harbour to **Dalkey Island,** covered in long grass, uninhabited except for a herd of goats, and graced with its own Martello tower. From Vico Road, beyond Coliemore Harbour, you'll have astounding bay views (similar to those near Italy's Bay of Naples) as far as Bray in County Wicklow (*see* Chapter 3). On Dalkey Hill is **Torca Cottage,** home of the Nobel Prize–winning writer George Bernard Shaw from 1866 to 1874. You can return to Dalkey Village by Sorrento Road.

NORTHSIDE

Dublin's northern suburbs remain predominantly working class and largely residential, but they do offer a few places worth an extra trip. The southside has most of the glamour, but the northside feels somehow more authentic, like it wasn't constructed to attract people like you, tourists. As with most suburban areas, walking may not be the best way to get around. A car is recommended, but not essential. Buses and trains service most of these areas, the only drawback being that to get from one suburb to another by public transport means returning back through the city center. Even if you're traveling by car, visiting all these sights will take a full day, so plan your trip carefully before setting off.

GLASNEVIN

To reach the suburb of Glasnevin, drive from the north city center by Lower Dorset Street, as far as the bridge over the Royal Canal. Turn left, and go up Whitworth Road, by the side of the canal, for 1 km (½ mi); at its end, turn right onto Prospect Road and then left onto the Finglas road, the N2. You may also take Bus 40 or Bus 40A from Parnell Street, next to Parnell Square, in the north city center. **Glasnevin Cemetery,** on the right-hand side of the Finglas road, is the best-known burial ground in Dublin, home to the dead men (they were mostly men, of course) who forged a nation, including Eamon De Valera, a founding father of modern Ireland and a former Irish taoiseach and president, and Michael Collins, the celebrated hero of the Irish War of Independence and victim of an assassin's bullet. Other notables interred here include late-19th-century poet Gerard Manley Hopkins and Sir Roger Casement, an Irish rebel hanged for treason by the British in 1916. The large column just to the right of the main entrance is the tomb of "The Liberator" Daniel O'Connell, perhaps Ireland's greatest historical figure, renowned for his nonviolent struggle for Catholic rights and emancipation, which he achieved in 1829. The cemetery is freely accessible all day.

On the northeastern flank of Glasnevin Cemetery, the **National Botanic Gardens** date from 1795 and have more than 20,000 different varieties of plants, a rose garden, and a vegetable garden. The main attraction is the **Curvilinear Range,** 400-ft-long greenhouses designed and built by a Dublin ironmaster, Richard Turner, between 1843 and 1869, and fully restored in 1995. A complete replanting of the greenhouses was finished in late 1997. The Palm House, with its striking double dome, was built in 1884 and houses orchids, palms, and tropical ferns. Visitors here can stroll along the River Tolka. *Glasnevin Rd., tel 01/837–4388. Admission free. Open Apr.–Sept., Mon.–Sat. 10–6, Sun. 11–6; Oct.–Mar., Mon.–Sat. 10–4:30, Sun. 11–4:30.*

MARINO CASINO

One of Dublin's most exquisite, yet also most underrated, architectural landmarks, the **Marino Casino** (the name has nothing to do with gambling—it means "little house by the sea") is a small-scale, Palladian-style Greek temple, built between 1762 and 1771 from a plan by Sir William Chambers. Often compared to the Petit Trianon at Versailles, it was commissioned as a summerhouse overlooking Dublin harbor by that great Irish grandee, Lord Charlemont (*see* Hugh Lane Municipal Gallery of Modern Art, *above*). While his estate's grand mansion was tragically demolished in 1921, this sublime casino was saved and has now been lovingly restored (thankfully, Sir William's original plans survived). Inside the highlights are the china-closet boudoir, the huge golden sun set in the ceiling of the main drawing room, and the signs of the zodiac in the ceiling of the bijou-size library. When you realize that the structure has, in fact, 16 rooms—there are bedrooms upstairs—Sir William's sleight-of-hand is readily apparent: From its exterior, the structure seems to contain only one room. The tricks don't stop there: The freestanding columns on the facade are hollow so they can drain rainwater, while the elegant marble urns on the roof are chimneys. Last but not least, note the four stone lions on the outside terrace—they were carved by Joseph Wilson, who created the famous British royal coronation coach back in London. To get here, take the Malahide road from Dublin's north city center for 4 km (2½ mi). All in all, this remains, to quote Desmond Guinness, "one of the most exquisite buildings in Europe." You can also take Bus 20A or Bus 24 to the Casino from Cathal Brugha Street in the north city center. It makes a good stop on the way to Malahide, Howth, or North Bull Island. *Malahide Rd., Marino, tel. 01/8331618. Admission £2. Open June–Sept., daily 9:30–6.*

HOWTH

A fishing village set at the foot of a long peninsula, Howth (derived from the Norse *hoved,* meaning head; it rhymes with "both") was an island inhabited as long ago as 3250 BC. Between 1813 and 1833, Howth was the Irish terminus for the sea crossing to Holyhead in north Wales, but it was then superseded by the newly built harbor at Kingstown (now Dun Laoghaire). Today, a marina graces its harbor, which supports a large fishing fleet. Both arms of the harbor pier form extensive walks. To get here from Dublin, either take the DART train, which takes about 30 minutes; Bus 31B from Lower Abbey Street in the city center; or, by car, the Howth Road from the north city center for 16 km (10 mi). Separated from Howth Harbour by a channel nearly 1½ km (1 mi) wide, **Ireland's Eye** has an old stone church on the site of a 6th-century monastery and an early 19th-century Martello tower. In calm weather, local boatmen make the crossing to the island.

At the King Sitric Restaurant on the East Pier, a 2½-km (1½-mi) cliff walk begins, leading to the white **Baily Lighthouse,** built in 1814. In some places, the cliff path narrows and drops sheerly to the sea, but the views out over the Irish Sea are terrific. Some of the best views in the whole Dublin area await from the parking lot above the lighthouse, looking out over the entire bay as far south as Dun Laoghaire, Bray, and the north Wicklow coast. You can also see much of Dublin.

Until 1959, a tram service ran from the railway station in Howth, over Howth Summit and back down to the station. One of the open-topped Hill of Howth trams that plied this route is now the star at the **National Transport Museum,** a short, 800-yard walk from Howth's DART station. Volunteers have spent several years restoring the tram, which stands alongside other unusual vehicles, including old horse-drawn bakery vans. *Howth Village, tel. 01/8480831 or 01/8475623. Admission £1.50. Open Easter–Sept., daily 10–5:30; Oct.–Easter, weekends 2–5:30.*

Next door to the Transport Museum and accessible from the Deer Park Hotel, the **Howth Castle Gardens** were laid out in the early 18th century. The many rare varieties of its fine rhododendron garden are in full flower April–June; there are also high beech hedges. The rambling castle, originally built in 1654 and considerably altered in the intervening centuries, is not open to the public, but you can access the ruins of a tall, square, 16th-century castle and a neolithic dolmen. *Deer Park Hotel, Howth, Co. Dublin, tel. 01/8322624. Admission free. Open daily 9–6.*

DUBLIN ENVIRONS

ANTO HOWARD

alt Disney himself couldn't have planned it better. The small counties immediately north, south, and west of Dublin—historically known as the Pale—seem expressly designed for the sightseer. The entire region is like an open-air museum layered with legendary Celtic sites, grand gardens, and elegant Palladian country estates. Because of its location facing Europe on the Irish sea, and its natural defenses of mountain and coast, the area has always been the first in which successive conquerors have established themselves and over which they exercised the most influence. The traces of each new wave remain: The Celts chose Tara as their hill of kings and the center of their kingdom, the Danes traveled down the Rivers Boyne and Liffey to establish many of today's towns, and the great Protestant houses remind us that the Pale was the starting point and administrative center for the long, violent English colonization of the whole Island.

Dublin Environs consists of three very distinct geographical areas: rugged, mountainous County Wicklow; the lush Boyne Valley of County Meath; and the plains of County Kildare. Like a great outdoor, unspoiled playground, Wicklow lies directly south of Dublin and contains some of the most *et in Arcadia ego* scenery in the Emerald Isle. The rolling granite mountains and hills are the source of the Liffey and attract hikers and climbers from all over Ireland and farther afield. The hermit monks of early Christian Ireland were drawn to the Eden-like quality of some of the valleys in the area, and the evocative monastic settlement of St. Kevin at Glendalough remains to this day a sight to calm a troubled soul. Northern Wicklow, lying so near the capital, became popular with the Anglo-Irish ascendancy, those 18th-century "princes of Elegance and Prodigality" who built some spectacular country retreats, such as those at Russborough and Powerscourt, both with perfectly kept English gardens. Profoundly influenced by the villas of the great Italian architect Andrea Palladio, they spared no expense when it came to ornamentation. Nowadays, somewhat uglier bungalows built by well-to-do Dubliners occasionally blight the small roads and lanes. Farther south the white sandy beaches such as Brittas Bay act as another draw for jaded urbanites.

To discover the history of County Meath, walk in the footsteps of a millennium of explorers and settlers; follow its great river, the Boyne. Directly north of Dublin, the fertile Boyne Valley—stretching all the way north to County Louth—is the cradle of native Irish civilization. Some of the country's most evocative neoliths—including the famous passage graves at Newgrange—are found nestled here in the landscape. It was west of Drogheda—a fascinating town settled by the Vikings in the early 10th century and razed by Cromwell 500 years later—that the *Tuatha De Danann*, onetime residents of Ireland, went underground when defeated by the invading Melesians and became, it is said "the good people" or fairies of Irish legend. When the Celts arrived, they saw the great hill at Tara overlooking the fecund valley and made it the home of Ireland's high kings and center of their druidic religion. Patrick and his successors knew a good thing when they saw it, and Mellifont Abbey and Monasterboice, both major early Christian sites, attest to their determination to conquer this heartland for the new God.

Anyone with even a passing interest in horse racing will recognize the international renown of Irish bloodstock. Well, you can safely bet that the vast majority of those famous Thoroughbreds came from County Kildare. Kildare is as flat as Wicklow is mountainous, the flattest part of the whole country in fact—the perfect spot for racing and training horses. The Curragh racetrack, home to the Irish Derby, is here, as are the less famous Punchestown and Naas. The major towns in the county, Kildare Town, Newbridge, and so on, all have links to the horse trade, with nearly 300 studs, including the world-famous National Stud. To the south it's mostly rich green farmland, with both of Dublin's canals (the Royal and the Grand) crossing the county.

NORTH OF DUBLIN IN THE BOYNE VALLEY

For every dreamy schoolboy in Ireland the River Boyne is a name that resonates with history and adventure. It was on the banks of that river in 1014 that the Celtic chieftain Brian Boru defeated the Danish in a decisive battle that returned the east of Ireland to native rule. It was also by this river that Protestant William of Orange defeated the Catholic armies of exiled James II of England in 1690. In fact this whole area, only 48 km (30 mi) north of cosmopolitan Dublin, is soaked in stories and legends that predate the pyramids. You can't throw a stick in the valley without hitting some trace of Irish history. Great prehistoric, pagan, and Celtic monuments are spread across the wide arc of the fertile, limestone plane with occasional low hills. You don't have to be an archaeologist to be awed by Knowth, and Dowth, and the Hill of Tara. But the jewel in the crown is without doubt the ancient burial site of huge, mysterious Newgrange.

Bus services link Dublin with all the main and small towns in the Boyne Valley. All bus services for the region depart from Busáras, Dublin's central bus station, at Store Street. For bus inquiries, contact **Bus Éireann** (tel. 01/8366111). **Iarnród Éireann** (tel. 01/8366222) trains run the length of the east coast from Dundalk to the north in County Louth. Trains make many stops along the way in larger towns, including Drogheda. If you're driving, follow the N3, along the east side of Phoenix Park, out of the city, and make Trim and Tara your first stops. Alternatively, leave Dublin via the N1/M1 to Belfast. Try to avoid the road during weekday rush hours (8 AM–10 AM and 4:30 PM–7 PM); stay on it as far as Drogheda and start touring from there.

TRIM

BASICS
Located in a fancy Georgian building in the middle of Mill Street, the **tourist office** (tel. 046/37111) is open daily 9–5. On the corner of Emmet and Market streets there's a **post office** and an **AIB** bank.

WHERE TO SLEEP AND EAT
Everybody recommends traditional, cozy **Brogan's Guesthouse** (High St., tel. 046/31237), where a double will cost you less than £30. The food there is also a good value. Right next to the tourist office is the summer-only **Bridge House Hostel** (Mill St., tel. 046/31848), with private rooms for £13. There's plenty of chippers, a Chinese restaurant, and other take-away joints scattered through the town. Pub grub in one of the many bars is another affordable option. For something a little healthier, try the **Salad Bowl Deli** (Market St., no phone).

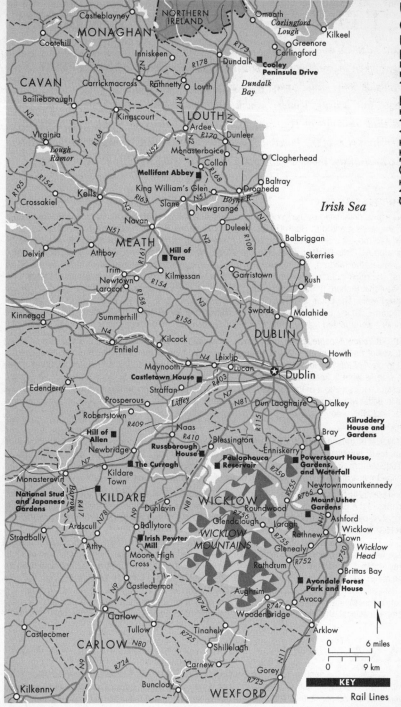

Irish Sea

KEY
——— Rail Lines

N
0   6 miles
0   9 km

THE END OF TARA

Tara's demise was predicted on eventful Easter Eve in the 5th century. It was a night when, according to the Druid religion, no fires could be lit. Suddenly, on a hillside some miles away, flames were spotted. "If that fire is not quenched now," said a druid leader, "it will burn forever and will consume Tara." The fire that the court of Tara saw was lit by St. Patrick at Slane, celebrating the Christian rites of the Paschal. Tara's influence, indeed, waned with the arrival of Christianity; the last king to live here was Malachy II, who died in 1022.

WORTH SEEING

Trim is a town dominated by the glories of its medieval past. It was the main town and administrative capital of the lands granted to Hugh De Lacy by Henry II at the Norman Conquest. In 1173 De Lacy, not known as a modest man, set about building a castle worthy of his new domain and useful in keeping the locals subdued. **Trim Castle** is one of the finest Anglo-Norman fortresses in Ireland, as well as the largest. It dominates the modern, sleepy town from its 2½-acre site, which slopes down to the river's placid waters. The ruins include an enormous keep with 70-ft-high turrets flanked by rectangular towers. Legend has it that Richard II imprisoned young Bolingbroke, Duke of Lancaster (the future Henry IV), in one of these towers. The outer castle wall is almost 500 yards long, and five D-shape towers survive. In the north corner, facing the river, you'll find the ruin of the **Royal Mint.** It was here that coins (called "Patricks") were minted right into the 1600s, a reflection of Trim's importance in the Middle Ages.

The 130-ft **Yellow Steeple,** situated on a ridge opposite the castle, dates from 1368 and was once the bell tower of the 13th-century Augustinian Abbey of St. Mary's. Much of the tower was destroyed in 1649 to prevent it falling into Cromwell's hands. Another part of the abbey, overlooking the river on the north side, is what is know as **Talbot's Castle.** A 15th-century viceroy, Sir John Talbot, converted the monastic buildings into a manor house. His coat of arms can be seen on the north wall. Talbot went on to die in battle with the armies of the Maid of Orleans. In the 18th-century the house became a Protestant school where one pupil was Arthur Wellesley, better know as Napoléan's nemesis, the Duke of Wellington.

The Church of Ireland **St. Patrick's Cathedral** (Loman St.) dates from the early 19th century, but its square tower belongs to an earlier structure built in 1449. Richard, Duke of York, spent time in Trim in the 15th century, and among the relics of his stay are a font and what has been described as the only surviving replica of the grille on the shrine of Thomas à Becket in Canterbury.

Several places just east and south of Trim are also of interest. At **Newtown** (1½ km/¾ mi east of Trim, on the banks of the Boyne) lie the ruins of what was the largest cathedral in Ireland, built in 1210 in early Gothic style by Simon de Rochfort, first Norman bishop of Meath. **Laracor** (3 km/2 mi south of Trim on the R158) is where Jonathan Swift, the great satirist and author of *Gulliver's Travels,* was rector from 1699 to 1714. Only one wall of his rectory remains standing, and not far away are the ruins of a small cottage where Ester Johnson, or Swift's muse "Stella," lived. One of the most pleasant villages of south County Meath, **Summerhill** (8 km/5 mi southeast of Laracor along the R158) has a large square and a village green with a 15th-century cross. Just south of Summerhill is **Cnoc an Linsigh,** an attractive area of forest walks with picnic sites, ideal for a half day's meandering. Many of the lanes that crisscross this part of County Meath provide top-class strolling or driving between high hedgerows, and you're certain to catch occasional, thrilling views of the lush, pastoral countryside spread out before you.

TARA

In the legends and the popular imagination of the Irish this ancient site has taken on mythic proportions. As with much of the glorification of the Celtic past, it was the 19th-century revival led by Yeats and Lady Gregory that was responsible for the near-religious veneration of this Celtic site. The 19th-century ballad by Thomas Moore, "The Harp That Once Through Tara's Halls," was also a major factor in the over-romanticized view of Tara up to recent times. It is not known when people first settled on this rolling hill that commands a view over the plains of Meath. There is evidence of Stone Age settlement, and it was certainly a place of some political importance by the Bronze Age. The golden age came with the Celts when, standing at the juncture of five roads, Tara became a center of ritual, where a great *feis* (national assembly) would be held every three years. From the beginning, the area had held special significance for the druids, and by the 3rd century it had become the seat of the most powerful rulers in Ireland. The Ard Rí (High King, very much a first among equals of the tribal leaders) and his court had a residence here.

At first glance, Tara may disappoint you—a few acres of rolling, green land dotted with the occasional mound marked by an archaeological plaque; not exactly Luxor. But systematic excavation by 20th-century archaeologists has led to the conclusion that the main remains are those of an Iron Age fort that had multiple ring forts. From atop the 300-ft hill, looking out across the flat midlands to the mountains of east Galway rising nearly 160 km (100 mi) away, you have to call upon your imagination to evoke the millennia-old spirit of the place and picture it in its prime, when the tribes were gathered for some great pagan ceremony. In an old Church of Ireland parish on the hillside, the **interpretative center** (tel. 046/25903) will help you re-create the story of Tara and its legends, with aerial views that make sense of the complicated layout. The center is open May–mid-June and mid-September–October, daily 10–5; mid-June–mid-September, daily 9:30–6:30. The greatest crowd ever to gather at Tara came some 800 years after the last king left here. The great Nationalist hero Daniel O'Connell staged one of his "monster meetings" here in August 1843, with more than a million people turning up to hear "The Liberator" cry out for home rule.

A trip to Ireland without going to Newgrange is like going to New York and overlooking the Empire State Building.

KELLS

BASICS

The brand-new Kells **tourist office** (tel. 046/40064) is on Hedfort Place. John Street has a **Bank of Ireland,** and the **post office** is nearby on Farrell Street.

WHERE TO SLEEP

For a little comfort, you might try the **Lennoxbrook Farm House** (4 km/2½mi north of Kells on N3, tel. 046/45902). The Mullans have lived here for 200 years and have opened up five bedrooms to the public. They do a mean breakfast of meats from the farm, and dinner (£10 extra) might include local lamb and produce. A double costs about £60. There's an IHH **hostel** (tel. 046/40100) right next to Monaghan's pub on Garrick Street. It has doubles for £20 a night and dorm beds for £7.50.

FOOD

As usual, you can rely on the **pubs** for substantial if predictable grub. **Penny's Place** (Market St., no phone) is a great-value café, with homemade breads. The **Round Tower** (Farrell St., tel. 046/40144) has good hearty fare built around the meat-and-two-veg tradition.

WORTH SEEING

In contrast to nearby pagan Tara, Kells is one of the centers of early Christianity in Ireland. It is most famous for something that is not here, the **Book of Kells** itself, which is in Trinity College in Dublin (*see* Chapter 2). A monastery was founded here by St. Columba in the 6th century. In the 9th century, a group of monks from Iona in Scotland took refuge at Kells (*Ceanannus Mór*) after being expelled by the Danes and made it the leading Columban monastery in Ireland. Some historians still argue that *The Book of Kells* was created by indigenous monks, but the accepted view is that the exquisitely illustrated Latin version of the four Gospels was brought over by the fleeing Scots. Reputed to have been fished out of a watery bog here in Kells, the legendary manuscript was removed to Trinity for safekeeping during the Cromwellian wars. But a remarkable facsimile of the book is on display in the Church of Ireland **St. Columba's,** in Kells. The churchyard contains a 110-ft-high, roofless **round tower** from the 10th century. In 1076, Murchadh Mac Flainn, a contender for the position of High King, was murdered in one of its rooms. Unusually, the top story has five windows, each pointing to an ancient entrance to the medieval town. The churchyard is also home to some magnificent scriptural **Celtic crosses** telling the stories from the Old and New testaments.

St. Columba's House, a small, two-story, 7th-century church measuring only 24 square ft but nearly 40 ft high, with a steeply pitched stone roof, is similar in appearance to St. Kevin's church at Glendalough (*see below*). Because of the continuous threat of Viking raiders, the church would have been entered by a removable ladder to a small door about 10 ft off the ground. Today there is an entrance at ground level, and if it's locked, you can get the key from the first house on Church View as you come up the hill. An underground tunnel connects the church with the round tower, another option in times of jeopardy.

BRUNA BOINNE

In prehistoric times the Boyne Valley was widely settled, and a variety of burial sites remain today from that mysterious period. They are grouped together under the name Brúna Bóinne ("Palace of the Boyne"). The three major sites are Newgrange, Knowth, and Dowth.

BASICS

The Brúna Bóinne **visitor center** (Newgrange, tel. 041/9824488) is open June–mid-September, daily 9–7; May and mid-September–end of September, daily 9–6:30; March, April, and October, daily 9:30–5:30; November–February, daily 9:30–5. Entrance to all the sites is via the center, and admission is £3 for Newgrange or £5 for Newgrange and Knowth.

NEWGRANGE

Stonehenge and the pyramids at Giza are spring chickens compared to Newgrange. Above ground, Newgrange is a massive, flattened, grass mound. This mundane mound covers a feat of architecture and construction that continues to puzzle and defy belief. How did a people who had only a stone and wood technology sometime in the 4th millennium BC (that's a full 1,000 years before Stonehenge) manage to build such a wonder as this huge neolithic passage grave? Newgrange is constructed with 250,000 tons of stones brought all the way from the Wicklow Mountains. The mound above the tomb measures more than 330 ft across and is 36 ft high at the front. White quartz stones were used for the retaining wall; egg-shape gray stones are studded at intervals. The passage grave may have been the world's first observatory. Its construction is so precise that for five days on and around the winter solstice the rays of the rising sun hit a roof box above the lintel at the entrance to the grave. Then, putting Indiana Jones to shame, rays shine for about 20 minutes down the passageway that leads to the interior and illuminate the **burial chamber.** A visit to the passage grave during the solstice is considered by many to be the most memorable experience of all, due in part to the luck needed to witness the illumination. It has been interpreted as a great metaphor for hope in rebirth. Even if you manage to arrange a visit during the solstice, in Ireland in winter there is certainly no guarantee that the sun won't be obscured by clouds. Don't worry: On your visit, they will reproduce the effect with artificial light.

Much about Newgrange continues to baffle and delight the experts. The geometric designs on some stones at the center of the burial chamber have not been fully interpreted. The inner ring of **kerb stones,** 97 of them, was placed around the mound to prevent it from collapsing. Eleven of them are engraved with designs similar to those on the main entrance stone. It has been argued in recent years that the outer ring of **standing stones** was in fact added by a later civilization, perhaps contemporaneous with the people who put up the famous upright stones at Stonehenge.

KNOWTH AND DOWTH

Knowth is only partially excavated, but the way things are going it might well outstrip Newgrange in size and importance before the diggers are finished. Unlike its more famous neighbor, Knowth was populated continuously right up until the 14th century. The invaluable layers left by civilization allow scientists a unique chance to discover very different phases of settlement. Far larger and more diversified than Newgrange, Knowth has a huge central mound, with 17 smaller ones and nearly 300 carved slabs surrounding it. The earliest tombs date from the Stone Age (ca. 3000 BC). Around 1800 BC, the Bronze Age "beaker people," who buried their dead with drinking cups, moved in. The Celts followed much later, and after them the Christian chiefs turned it into a ring fort. To date only one-third of the site has been excavated and can be visited via the visitor center. You can also watch archaeologists at work on the rest of the site. **Dowth's** central mound is as big as Newgrange, but the site has suffered badly over the years from pillagers, 9th-century road makers, and, even worse, amateur archaeologists. There are two central burial chambers inside, and 50 of the original 100 or so kerb stones remain. At press time, Dowth was closed to the public for conservation work, but you can still walk around it from the outside.

SLANE

BASICS
The **tourist office** (tel. 041/9824010) on Main Street is run by locals who know the place inside out. It's open daily 9–5.

WHERE TO SLEEP
Right across from the tourist office, the reasonably priced **Cunningham Arms** (Main St., tel. 041/9824155) is a quality small hotel with double rooms for £75. It serves a tasty lunch buffet from noon to 3. Nearby, **Ye Olde Post House** (Main St., tel. 041/9824510) has predictable but comfortable doubles for around £20.

FOOD
Newgrange Farm Coffee Shop (N51, tel. 041/9824119) is a family-run eatery that uses the produce and livestock of the adjoining farm. Entrées go for about £5, and the homemade soups and breads are a good bet. **Ye Olde Coffee Shop** is part of Ye Olde Post House and serves Irish lunches and dinners, all for under £5.

Some of the ring forts at Tara were destroyed by 19th-century English zealots who believed they would find the Ark of the Covenant here.

WORTH SEEING
On a hill on the north bank of the Boyne, the small village of Slane was originally a manorial village planned by the Conynghams, successors to the previous Norman rulers of Slane. Four identical Georgian houses face each other from the corners of the main crossroads. Local legend claims the houses were built for four spinster sisters who could not bear to live together but had to keep an eye on what the others were up to. The 16th-century building know as the **Hermitage** was constructed on the site where St. Erc, a local man who was converted to Christianity by St. Patrick, led a hermit's existence.

The 500-ft **Hill of Slane,** where St. Patrick proclaimed the arrival of Christianity in 433 by lighting the Paschal Fire, is just north of town. From the top you can look out over the whole Boyne Valley. Little other than the foundations remains of the 1512 church that once stood here. However, an adjoining **tower** is still in good shape, and the view from the top is impressive.

Dominating the town it inspired, and beautifully situated overlooking a natural amphitheater, **Slane Castle** was almost burned to the ground in a 1991 fire and is still completely closed to the public for the foreseeable future. Since 1981 Slanes's owner, the Anglo-Irish Lord Henry Mountcharles, has staged huge rock concerts in its amphitheater. U2, Bob Dylan, Bruce Springsteen, and the Rolling Stones have all played here to crowds of 70,000 and more. The venue was closed indefinitely following a 1995 show, due, in part, to protests by locals who complained of an army of drunken rock fans bent on destruction.

DROGHEDA

On the County Louth side of the River Boyne, packed tightly between two hills, the historic town of Drogheda (pronounced Dro-*heh*-da) was colonized by the Danes in 911. In the 12th century, Hugh de Lacy, the Anglo-Norman lord of Trim (*see above*), took over the town and fortified it as he did so many other towns on the river. In the Middle Ages Drogheda was one of the country's major walled towns, and many medieval parliaments were held here. Most of the gray, stone, slightly gloomy buildings you see in today's town date from the 18th century.

BASICS
The **tourist office** (Donore Rd., tel. 041/9837070) is open from June to mid-September, daily 9–5. West Street contains the main **post office** and two **banks.**

WHERE TO SLEEP
Harbour Villa (Morington Rd., tel. 041/9837441) has four rooms in a two-story house right on the river. Doubles are £50, and guests have use of a private tennis court. The **Harper House Tourist Hostel** (William St., tel. 041/9832736) is family run and has dorms for £8 and doubles (slightly shabby) for £20.

BLOODY CROMWELL!

In much of the English-speaking world Oliver Cromwell is regarded as something of a hero, a deeply religious self-made man, master general, and leader of the victorious parliamentary side in the English Civil Wars. In Ireland the Lord Protector's name is usually followed by a spit and a curse. In 1649 Old Ironsides arrived in Ireland to subdue a royalist and Catholic rebellion once and for all. His methods were simple: Burn every building, and kill every person that stood in his way. "To Hell or to Connaught" was the dire choice he offered the native population as he drove them ever westward and off the more fertile lands of the east and south. When he approached the walled town of Drogheda, the gates were closed to him. Led by the Anglo-Irish Sir Arthur Aston, the native Catholic population bravely defended their town against Cromwell's relentless siege, twice driving back the advancing army. On the third attempt the town fell, and the order went out that no mercy was to be shown. It is estimated that up to 3,500 men, women, and children were slaughtered. One group hid in the steeple of St. Peter's church, so Cromwell burned it down with them all inside. Sir Arthur was beaten to death with his own wooden leg!

FOOD

For a cheap, hot, traditional meal (that's meat and two veg), head to **Burke's** (St. Peter's St., no phone). It'll set you back less than £4. If you want to splurge, **Buttergates** (Millmount St., 041/9834759) specializes in high-end Irish cuisine, and the view over the town and the river makes the place special.

WORTH SEEING

St. Laurence's Gate is one of the two to survive from Drogheda's original 11 gates. It has two four-story drum towers and is one of the most perfect examples of a medieval town gate in the British Isles. **Butler Gate,** the other survivor to the south, is somewhat less impressive, despite its high, arched passageway. Nearby a piece of the original town wall survives. The Gothic Revival, Roman Catholic **St. Peter's Church** (West St.) is worth a visit to see the preserved head of St. Oliver Plunkett. Primate of all Ireland, he was martyred at Tyburn in London in 1681; his head was pulled from the execution flames by a devotee. It now rests in a glittering gold plate-and-brass case in the north transept, a site of continuing veneration for many Catholics. Nearby is the Anglican St. Peter's, built in a severe, 18th-century style within an enclosed courtyard. It's rarely open except for Sunday services.

Perhaps the main attraction in Drogheda lies across the river from the town center. **Millmount Museum** (tel. 041/9833097) shares space in a renovated British Army barracks with crafts workshops, including a pottery and picture gallery and studio. It was on the hill at Millmount that the townsfolk made their last stand against the bloodthirsty Roundheads of Cromwell. Perhaps in defiance of Cromwell's attempt to obliterate the town from the map, the museum contains relics of eight centuries of Drogheda's commercial and industrial past, including painted banners of the old trade guilds, a circular willow and leather coracle (the traditional fishing boat on the Boyne), and many instruments and utensils from domestic and factory use. The museum is open April–October, Monday–Saturday 10–6 and Sunday 2:30–5:30; November–March, Wednesday and weekends 10–5:30. Admission is £1.50.

MELLIFONT ABBEY

Just west of Drogheda on R168 is Mellifont Abbey, the first Cistercian monastery in Ireland. Founded on the eastern bank of the River Mattock (which creates a natural border between Meath and Louth) in 1142 by St. Malachy, Archbishop of Armagh, it was inspired by St. Bernard of Clairvaux's monastery, which Malachy had visited. It took 15 years to complete and in its prime was the grandest religious structure in the country. Unfortunately today's ruins are a little disappointing, and the visitor has to fill in all the gaps himself. Among the more substantial ruins are those of the two-story chapter house. Built in the 12th-century English-Norman style, and once a daily meeting place for the monks, it now houses a collection of medieval glazed tiles. Four walls of the octagonal lavabo, or washing place (underground pipes brought water from the river), still stand, as do some arches from the Romanesque cloister. At its peak Mellifont presided over almost 40 other Cistercian monasteries throughout Ireland, but the wrath of Henry VIII after his 1539 break with Rome soon led to their suppression. Edward Moore built a Tudor mansion on the site, using material pillaged from the demolition of the monastery buildings. It was to this house, then owned by Sir Garret Moore, that Hugh O'Neill fled after the defeat at the Battle of Kinsale in 1603. The house was later used as King William's headquarters in the Battle of the Boyne. Adjacent to the car park is a small **architectural museum** (tel. O41/9826495) depicting the history of the abbey and the craftsmanship that went into its construction. It's open mid-June–mid-September, daily 9:30–6:30; mid-September–October, daily 10–5. Admission is £1.60.

There is a nine-year waiting list for one of the 20 places available for the viewing of the tombs during the winter solstice at Newgrange.

MONASTERBOICE

Carved-stone high crosses are scattered throughout Ireland, but perhaps the finest collection of them is gathered in the small, secluded monastic enclosure of Monasterboice, a few miles north of Drogheda. Two of these crosses are of particular interest. **Muiredach's Cross** (named after an abbot here) is the smaller of the two and dates from the early 10th century. It stands 20 ft high and is considered the best-preserved high cross in Ireland. Its elaborate panels depict biblical scenes, including Cain slaying Abel; David and Goliath; and a centerpiece of the Last Judgment. The inscription at the foot of the cross reads in Gaelic "A prayer for Muiredach by whom the cross was made." The **West Cross** stands a couple of feet taller than Muiredach's, making it one of the tallest in Ireland. Its engravings are less impressive—many of them have been worn away by centuries of Irish wind and rain. Scenes include Abraham and Isaac and the Resurrection. The enclosure also contains an adjacent **round tower**. It's more than 110 ft high and in the past you could climb to the top to appreciate how extensive the original settlement at Monasterboice must have been. Sadly, safety concerns no longer permit you to enter the tower.

COUNTY WICKLOW'S COAST AND MOUNTAINS

Fall asleep on a Dublin bus going south and you might well wake up in wonderful County Wicklow. From any tall building in the capital that faces south you'll see in the distance—though amazingly, not *that* far off in the distance—the green, smooth hills of the Wicklow Mountains. In other words, Wicklow, the Garden of Ireland, is a very convenient visit, as it lies right on the doorstep of Dublin City. Wicklow is Ireland's little Alps, with bracing fresh air guaranteed among the blue skies and mountain heather and gorse. It is a hiker's paradise, with the famous Wicklow Way the most popular trail winding through most of the county north to south.

Not that the secret isn't out: Rugged Wicklow is a popular day trip with Dubliners, and many of the more wealthy city folk have built somewhat unsightly holiday bungalows along the quite lanes and byways.

Wicklow also contains some of Ireland's earliest Christian settlements, as holy men such as St. Kevin sought solitude in sheltered valleys such as Glendalough. The 18th-century Anglo-Irish were also drawn to the natural beauty of the place and constructed some of the British Isles' finest mansions and gardens in places like Powerscourt.

The DART runs as far as Bray in northern Wicklow, and from there you can jump on a bus or train down the coast. For bus inquiries, contact **Bus Éireann** (tel. 01/8366111), which runs services to most towns in Wicklow. **St. Kevin's** (tel. 01/2818119), a private bus service, runs daily from Dublin (outside the Royal College of Surgeons on St. Stephen's Green) to Glendalough, stopping off at Bray, Roundwood, and Laragh en route. Buses leave Dublin daily at 11:30 AM and 6 PM (7 PM on Sun.); buses leave Glendalough Monday–Friday at 7:15 AM and 4:15 PM (9:40 AM and 4:15 PM on Saturday; 9:40 AM and 5:30 PM on Sunday). The one-way fare is £6; round-trip, £10. The drive down through Wicklow is nothing short of spectacular. Just head south from Christ Church Cathedral, staying on the main road until you reach Rathfarnham village. From there follow the R115, which leads you to Glencree—a beautiful stone village set in a valley—and then on to the Sally Gap. You could opt for one of the bigger roads (N11/M11), but the extra time it might take on the small road is well worth it, as you pass through one of Ireland's most scenic routes of mountaintop passes and steep valley descents.

BRAY

One of Ireland's oldest seaside resorts, Bray is a trim village known for its dilapidated summer cottages, sand-and-shingle mile-long beach, and hokey amusements and dodgem cars. Its heyday was in the late 19th century, after the railway was extended south in the 1850s. With Dublin's rapid growth and spiraling house prices, people are starting to buy property here and commute the 22 km (14 mi) to the city to work (Bray has a DART station), threatening to change the character of the place forever.

BASICS
The **tourist office** (Main St., tel. 0404/69117 daily 9–5) is in the old courthouse and is open daily 9–5. It includes a small heritage center that outlines the history of the town. **Banks, bars,** and the **post office** are all on Main Street.

WHERE TO SLEEP
There's a slew of slightly dingy small hotels and B&Bs on the seafront of Strand Road. Their unpolished, jaded look has a certain charm, and most of the proprietors are superfriendly. **Ulysses** (tel. 01/2863860), near Bray Head, is one of the more recently renovated ones, and a double is only £40.

FOOD
In nearby Greystones, **Poppies Country Cooking** (1 Trafalgar Sq., Greystones, tel. 01/2874228) is a bright and airy place with potato cakes, shepherd's pie, and vegetarian quiche among the traditional favorites. Right on the Seafront, the tiny **Escape** (1 Albert Walk, tel. 01/2866755) is a great vegetarian option with dinners like cheese- and vegetable-filled crepes for under £7.

WORTH SEEING
Bray Head, a rocky outcrop that juts out over the Irish Sea, dominates the town. The steep 9-km (5½-mi) cliff walk up its side offers great views of the town, the sea, and Sugar Loaf Mountain to the south. The start of the trail is at the end of the promenade. The smuggler's cave, Bray Hole, lies at the foot of the Head.

One Martello Terrace (tel. 01/2868407), at the harbor, is Bray's most famous address. James Joyce (1882–1941) lived here between 1887 and 1891 and used the house as the setting for the Christmas dinner in *A Portrait of the Artist as a Young Man*. Today the house is privately owned by an Irish Teachta Dála (member of Parliament, known informally as a "TD"). The phone number we list rings into her constituency office, and someone there should be able to help scholars and devotees arrange a visit (be polite, beg only if you have to); they recommend calling on Thursday, 10 AM–1 PM. Although the residence has been renovated, the dining room portrayed in Joyce's novel maintains the spirit of his time.

Killruddery House and Gardens (tel. 01/2862777) are immediately off the Bray–Greystones road just south of Bray. The rare, 17th-century, precisely laid-out gardens have fine beech hedges, Victorian statuary, and a parterre of lavender and roses. Still owned by the Earl of Meath, the estate also features a Crystal Palace conservatory. The gardens and conservatory are open in summer, daily 9–6, and by appointment the rest of the year; admission is £2.

POWERSCOURT ESTATE

They really had the life, those old aristocrats. At more than 14,000 acres, including stunning formal gardens and a 400-ft waterfall, Powerscourt must have been some place to call home. The grounds, 22 km (16 mi) south of Dublin and directly west of Bray, were originally granted to Sir Richard Wingfield, the first viscount of Powerscourt, by James I of England in 1609. Richard Castle, the German architect, was hired to design the **great house**. His was not an age known for its modesty, and he choose the grand Palladian style. The house took nine years to complete and was ready to move into in 1740, truly one of the great houses of Ireland and, indeed, all of Britain. Unfortunately, you won't be able to see much of it. A terrible fire almost completely destroyed the house in 1974, cruelly on the eve of a huge party to celebrate the completion after a long period of restoration by the Slazenger family. A second program of renovation and rebuilding is currently under way. The original ballroom on the first floor—once "the grandest room in any Irish house," according to historian Desmond Guinness—is the only room in the house that, despite the extensive smoke damage, gives a sense of the place's former glory. It was based on Palladio's version of the "Egyptian Hall" designed by Vitrubius, architect to Augustus, Emperor of Rome.

The **gardens** were impervious to fire and remain for your enjoyment. Laid out first in 1745, they were radically redesigned in the Victorian style between 1843 and 1875, becoming one of the finest examples of the style in Europe. The redesign was the work of the eccentric and often drunk Daniel Robertson, who was inspired by the Villa Butera in Sicily. Whatever Mr. Robertson's mental state, his creation is a marvel of order cut from chaos. The gardens comprise sweep-

Slane Castle looks familiar? Maybe you saw it on the cover of U2's "Joshua Tree" album, which was recorded there.

ing terraces, antique sculptures, and a circular pond and fountain flanked by winged horses. Nature, as if in approval, supplies the stunning backdrop of the Sugarloaf mountain. The grounds include many species of trees, an avenue of monkey puzzles, a parterre of brightly colored summer flowers, and a Japanese garden. The kitchen gardens, with their modest rows of flowers, are a striking antidote to the classical formality of the main sections. The gardens also offer a self-serve restaurant, crafts center, garden center, and a children's play area. They're open March–October, daily 9:30–5:30; entrance is £3.50. You can call 01/2867676 for information.

Trivia question: What are the highest falls in the British Isles? At 400 ft, **Powerscourt Waterfall** is a sudden and spectacular plunge over a rocky cliff. It's best seen after a heavy downpour of rain, as when it so inspired Irish and British painters and writers of the Romantic period. The falls are 5 mi (3 km) from the great house; turn right at the main gate and follow the signs. You can visit February–October, daily 9:30–7; November–January, daily 10:30–dusk. Admission is £1.50.

GLENDALOUGH

WHERE TO SLEEP

Glendalough is only 48 km (30 mi) from Dublin, and you could visit it comfortably in a day trip. If you choose to stay overnight, Laragh is a village just east of Glendalough where numerous **B&Bs** have sprung up to cater to the tourist crowd. A double can cost up to £40. There's not much to distinguish the various B&Bs, but **Valeview** (tel. 0404/45292) overlooks the valley and has a reputation for cleanliness. The **Glendalough Youth Hostel** (tel. 0404/45342) cannot be beat for location, right on the road to the Upper Lake. Doubles go for £20.

FOOD

After a full day's pilgrimage, you might enjoy the convenience of the dining room at the **Glendalough Hotel** (tel. 0404/45135), which is only a short distance from the ruins. The menu is predictable, with potato and meat dishes dominating, but everything is fresh, and the dining room overlooks the River Glendassan. Entrées run £6–£9. In Laragh, the **Laragh Inn** (tel. 0404/45345) has a big fireplace and cheap pub grub.

WORTH SEEING

Gleann dá Loch ("Glen of Two Lakes") is a place of simple natural beauty, nestled in a deep valley in the rugged Wicklow Mountains. The setting involves two lakes, evergreen and deciduous trees, and acres of windswept heather. Stand here in the early morning (before the crowds and the hordes of school-trippers arrive in all their screaming glory), and you can appreciate what drew the solitude-seeking St. Kevin to this spot blessed by nature with a certain calm. A member of the royal house of Leinster who had renounced the profane world, St. Kevin came here on his own and set up a hermitage on the south side of the Upper Lake. Soon this wise and pious man attracted followers, and a monastery sprung up that was visited at its height by thousands of students and teachers. Throughout the Dark Ages Glendalough, along with the other great monasteries of Ireland, kept alive the old learning and then reintroduced it to Europe. In the 9th century, the Vikings came numerous times and sacked the place, but it was painstakingly restored each time. In the end, it was not the fierce pagan Danes but the new religion of the English that led to the dissolution of the monastery in the 16th century.

The **visitor center** (tel. 0404/45352) is a good place to begin your discovery of Glendalough. It is located smack-dab in the middle of the best ruins and tends to get a little crowded during the afternoon. It's open June–August, daily 9–6:30; September–mid-October, daily 9:30–6:30; and mid-October–mid-March, daily 9:30–5. For more solitude and better views, you have to follow in the footsteps of Kevin and head to the Upper Lake.

Probably the oldest building on the site, presumed to date from Kevin's time, is the **Teampaill na Skellig** (Church of the Oratory), on the south shore of the **Upper Lake.** A little to the east is **St. Kevin's Bed,** a tiny cave in the rock face, about 30 ft above the level of the lake, where St. Kevin lived his hermit's existence. It is not easily accessible; you approach the cave by boat, but climbing the cliff to the cave can be dangerous and is not recommended. At the southeast corner of the Upper Lake is **Reefert Church,** dating from the 11th century, whose ruins consist of a nave and a chancel. The saint also lived in the adjoining, ruined beehive hut with five crosses, which marked the original boundary of the monastery. There's a superb view of the valley from here.

The ruins by the edge of the **Lower Lake** are the most important of those at Glendalough. The gateway, beside the Glendalough Hotel, is the only surviving entrance to an ancient monastic site anywhere in Ireland. An extensive graveyard lies within, with hundreds of elaborately decorated crosses, as well as a perfectly preserved, six-story round tower. Built in the 11th or 12th century, it stands 100 ft high, with an entrance 25 ft above ground level.

The largest building at Glendalough is the substantially intact, 7th- to 9th-century **cathedral,** where you'll find the nave (small for a large church, only 30 ft wide by 50 ft long), chancel, and ornamental oolite limestone window, which may have been imported from England. South of the cathedral is the 11-ft-high Celtic **St. Kevin's Cross.** Made of granite, it is the best-preserved such cross on the site. St. Kevin's Church is an early, barrel-vaulted oratory with a high-pitched stone roof. Glendalough is open year-round and admission is a bargain at £2.

MOUNT USHER GARDENS

WHERE TO SLEEP AND EAT

This is the time to spoil yourself. One of Ireland's oldest coaching inns, first opened in the early 1700s, **Hunter's Hotel** (Rathnew, tel. 0404/40106) sits in a lovely rural setting on the banks of the River Vartry, only 1 km (½ mi) east of Rathnew Village. Doubles cost around £100, but the unique experience is worth the price. Period prints, beamed ceilings, and antiques lend an old-world feel enjoyed by both locals (who come here for the excellent restaurant) and guests, and the lovely garden runs right down to the river.

WORTH SEEING

Laid out by Dublin textile baron Edward Walpole in 1868, the 20-acre **Mount Usher Gardens** (tel. 0404/40205) nestle on the banks of the tiny River Varty, 12 km (7½ mi) east of Glendalough. The wonder of the gardens lies in the incredible variety of tree and plant types squeezed into this relatively small area. There are more than 5,000 species from all over the world, including Tibetan lilies, eucalypti, cypress trees, and Burmese juniper trees. Another attraction is the ingenious design that ensures water is visible from nearly every place in the gardens, while numerous small bridges span the river. The twin villages of Ashford and Rathnew are both nearby to the south and east, and tongue-twisting Newtownmountkennedy is to the north. The gardens are open March–October, daily 10:30–6; admission is £3.50.

WICKLOW TOWN

BASICS

On Fitzwilliam Square at the center of town, you'll find the **tourist office** (tel. 0404/69117), which is open year-round, daily 9–5.

WHERE TO SLEEP

Wicklow Town is big enough to have a full range of accommodations. At the top of the price scale is the delightful **Old Rectory Country House** (Dublin Rd., tel. 0404/67048). A 19th-century rectory, the Greek Revival country house stands on a hillside on the northern approach to town. The Saunders family own and run the place with a gentle, warm touch. Double rooms (£104) are big and are full of Victorian antiques. Linda Saunders' excellent "Green Cuisine" makes use of fresh, local produce, and she is fond of sprinkling her famous salads with edible flowers and herbs. In the medium price range, **Thomond House** (St. Patrick's St., tel. 0404/67940) is a standout among numerous B&Bs. It has views of both the mountains and the sea. A double goes for £40 or so. There's only one hostel in town, **Marine House** (The Murrough, tel. 0404/69213); the building feels a little institutional, but it overlooks the sea, and doubles are less than £20.

FOOD

Pizza del Forno (Main St., tel. 0404/67075), with its red-and-white-check tablecloths, low lighting, and pizza oven blazing away, is a great vantage point for people-watching on Main Street. Inexpensive pizzas, pasta, steaks, and vegetarian dishes all hit the spot.

The May Gardens Festival is a great time to visit Wicklow; the county is awash with flowers, and many private gardens open to the public.

WORTH SEEING

The town itself, with its tree-lined Main Street, is pleasant enough without being the most exciting spot in Wicklow. Its main attractions are the **harbor** and **beach.** Take Harbour Road down to the pier; a bridge across the River Vartry leads to a second, smaller pier, at the northern end of the harbor. From this end, follow the shingle beach, which stretches for 5 km (3 mi); behind the beach is the broad lough, a lagoon noted for its wildfowl. The few surviving ruins of **Black Castle** lie south of the harbor. It was built by the all-powerful Fitzgeralds in 1176, in the early years of their 500-year domination of much of Leinster. A walk up **Wicklow Head** makes for a good half-day trip. You can walk right around the top of it, enjoying spectacular views of sea and mountain as you go. Between one bank of the River Vartry and the road to Dublin stands the Protestant **St. Lavinius Church,** a bit of an architectural hodgepodge that incorporates a variety of elements and unusual details: a Romanesque door, 12th-century stonework, fine pews, and an atmospheric graveyard. The church is topped off by a copper, onion-shape cupola, added as an afterthought in 1771. Admission is free and it's open every day.

AVONDALE FOREST PARK AND HOUSE

In 1846 a man was born in Avondale House who was to profoundly affect the course of Irish history. Charles Stewart Parnell (1846–91) rose to prominence as the most vocal and disruptive member of the Irish delegation to Westminster. He quickly came to head the Irish parliamentary party and was on the verge of achieving Home Rule when he was ruined by a divorce scandal in which he was named as the lover of the married Kitty O'Shea. James Joyce, whose father never forgave those who turned their backs on Parnell, dramatizes the conflict in a fiery debate during the Daedalus family dinner in *A Portrait of the Artist as a Young Man*. Avondale House itself was built in 1779. It has been flawlessly restored, with the reception and dining rooms on the ground floor filled with Parnell memorabilia, including some of his love letters to Kitty. It is set on the west bank of the River Avondale, amid the 523-acre **Avondale Forest Park** (tel. 0404/46111), the first national park in Ireland. The park contains an arboretum and a few nature walks. It's open May–September, daily 10–6; October–April, daily 11–5. Admission is £3.

VALE OF AVOCA

"There is not in this wide world a valley so sweet/
As that vale in whose bosom the bright waters meet."

The (overly) Romantic Irish poet Thomas Moore composed his 1807 "Meeting of the Waters" after a day spent beneath a riverside tree in this valley at the confluence of the Rivers Avonberg and Avonmore. It is a forested area, scarred in places by years of mining. The small hamlet of **Avoca** stands right where the rivers meet. The oldest handweaving mill in Ireland, **Avoca Handweavers** (tel. 0402/35105), has been producing quality textiles since 1723. It is famous for its tweeds and knits. Free tours of the mill are available, and the gift store sells clothing made from its fabrics.

COUNTY KILDARE AND WEST WICKLOW

Out of the mountains and down to the plains, Kildare is as flat as most of Wicklow is mountainous. The county can be divided into three regions: the basin of the River Liffey in the northeast, the basin of the River Barrow in the south, and the Bog of Allen to the northwest. Kildare is the horse capital of Ireland, and the sport of kings is truly a passion among the natives. For first-time visitors, the National Stud just outside Naas offers a fascinating glimpse into the world of horse breeding. The Japanese Gardens, adjacent to the National Stud, are among Europe's finest, while Castletown House, in Celbridge to the north, is one of Ireland's foremost Georgian treasures. Buses run from Dublin to all parts of Kildare and West Wicklow. From Heuston Station, the **Arrow,** a commuter train service, runs westward to Celbridge, Naas, Newbridge, and Kildare Town. Contact **Iarnród Éireann** (tel. 01/8366222) for schedule and fare information. To drive, simply follow the quays along the south side of the Liffey (they are one-way westbound) to St. John's Road West (the N7); in a matter of minutes, you're heading for open countryside. Avoid traveling this route during the evening peak rush hours, especially on Friday, when Dubliners are themselves making their weekend getaways.

CASTLETOWN HOUSE

Like the builders of Powerscourt House (*see above*), the designer of Castletown House got caught up in the revival of the architectural style of Andrea Palladio (1508–80) that swept through England in the early 18th century. The Anglo-Irish aristocracy, always prone to a certain inferiority complex, were determined not to be outdone by the extravagant efforts of their English counterparts. Thank the lord for vanity. Castletown, 20 km (12 ½ mi) southwest of Dublin, is arguably the largest and finest example of an Irish Palladian-style house. William Conolly, the speaker of the Irish House and the wealthiest man in the country, hired the Italian architect Alessandro Galilei to design the facade of the main block. The young Irish architect Sir Edward Lovett Pearce completed the house in 1724, adding the colonnades and side pavilions. When Conolly died suddenly before the interior of the house was completed, work resumed in 1758, when his great nephew Thomas, and more importantly, his 15-year-old wife Lady Louisa Lennox, took up residence there. Louisa is said to have taken great interest in the interior decoration. The house had fallen into disrepair by the time it was taken over by the state and the Irish Georgian Society in the 1990s, both of which are now headquartered there.

At press time (fall 1999), the house was closed for yet another campaign of major restoration work and is slated to reopen sometime toward late fall 1999; it's a good idea to call ahead and confirm the opening date. As you walk up the long gravel driveway, the first thing to strike you is the enormous scale of the house, with seemingly endless lines of windows stretching out to each side. Little of the original furniture remains today, but there is plenty of evidence of the ingenuity of Louisa and her artisans. The long **Gallery** (80 ft by 23 ft) is laid out in the Pompeian style and hung with three Venetian Murano glass chandeliers. The Lafranchine brothers, Swiss-Italian craftsmen who were very active in Dublin in the mid-18th century, did much of the plaster work in the halls. The ground-floor **Print Room** is the only example in Ireland of this elegant fad. Like oversize postage stamps in a giant album, black-and-white prints were glued to the walls by fashionable young women who unwittingly anticipated the universal impulse among teenagers to cover their bedroom walls with posters.

The grounds of Castletown also reveal the desire to show off that partly defined the early and mid-1700s. As at many other great houses, there is a **folly** nearby, a strange 135-ft obelisk that was undertaken as part of relief-work efforts during the minor famine of 1739. Castletown (tel. 01/6288252) is open April–September, weekdays 10–6, Saturday 11–6, Sunday 2–6; October, Monday–Saturday, 10–5, Sunday 2–5; and November–March, Sunday 2–5. Admission is £2.50.

NAAS

Not one but two racecourses can be found in the vicinity of Naas, the seat of County Kildare and a thriving market town. **Naas** track can be found just outside the town, and the more prestigious **Punchestown** (the big three-day steeplechase meeting is at the end of April) is about 3 km (2 mi) from town. The town itself is full of pubs with high stools, where jockeys discuss the merits of their various stables and the chances of a precious win.

Robertson liked to be tootled around the gardens-in-progress in a wheelbarrow while nipping at his bottle of sherry.

RUSSBOROUGH HOUSE

Another shockingly grand Palladian house in the middle of nowhere, this extravagance was paid for by beer: In 1741, a year after Joseph Lesson inherited a vast fortune from his father, a successful Dublin brewer, he commissioned Richard Castle (who also designed Powerscourt) to build him a palatial home. Castle, spending another man's money, spared no expense; the result is a confident, majestic, slightly over-the-top house with a silver-gray Wicklow granite facade that extends more than 700 ft.

Modesty did not suddenly strike when it came to decorating the interior, where Baroque exuberance was given free rein. The lavishly ornamented plaster ceilings were created by the popular Lafranchini brothers. After a long succession of owners, Russborough was bought in 1952 by Sir Alfred Beit, the nephew of the German cofounder (with Cecil Rhodes) of the De Beers diamond operation, and it now belongs to Lady Beit, his widow. In 1988, after two major robberies, one a daring heist by a female member of the IRA, the finest works in the Beits' art collection, considered one of the best private collections in Europe, were donated to the National Gallery of Ireland. However, works by Gainsborough, Guardi, Reynolds, Rubens, and Murillo remain, as well as bronzes, silver, and porcelain. The views from Russborough's windows take in the foothills of the Wicklow Mountains as well as a small lake in front of the house; the extensive woodlands on the estate are also open to visitors. Admission to the house is £3. It's open June–August, daily 10:30–5:30; April–May and September–October, Monday–Saturday 10:30–5:30; Sunday 10:30–5:30. For information, call 045/865239.

THE CURRAGH

If the rest of Kildare is flat, the Curragh is a huge pancake. At 36 square km (12 square mi) it's the biggest area of common land in Ireland and for generations has attracted trainers of Thoroughbred racers with its fine grazing and level footing. The **Curragh Racecourse** (tel. 045/441205) is the premier track in Ireland and home to all four Irish classics, including the Derby.

Notorious in Irish history as the scene of a British Army mutiny aimed to defeat Home Rule for Ireland, the **Curragh Main Barracks** is now a large training camp for the Irish Army. It also has a little **museum** (tel. 045/445000), open only by request (admission is free). The prize relic is the armored car once used by the "Big Fella," Michael Collins, general of the Irish side in the war of independence and head of the Free State army in the bloody civil war that claimed his life.

KILDARE TOWN

BASICS

Right in the middle of the main square, you'll find the **tourist office** (tel. 045/522696) in a 19th-century factory building. It's open daily 9–5.

WHERE TO SLEEP

Kildare is a medium-size town and might not be a bad place to base yourself for a couple of days in the area, perhaps to attend one of the many horse meetings. The **Lord Edward Guesthouse** (Market Sq., tel. 045/522389) is nothing special but has the great advantage of being right in the center of town, beside Silken Thomas (*see below*), one of the best pubs in the whole country. Slightly dour doubles are about £35. The **Curragh Lodge** (Dublin St., tel. 045/522144) is a small hotel with decent-size rooms for around £60.

FOOD

If you stop for a bite to eat or a drink in Kildare Town, it would be a crime to miss **Silken Thomas** (tel. 045/522232), named for Lord Thomas Fitzgerald, the Anglo-Irish rebel who was executed in the 16th century, and an institution in these parts. Inside it's all open fires, dark wood, and beautiful leaded lights. They have a little restaurant next to the bar with a seafood and meat menu that never disappoints. Entrées cost around £9. It's right on Market Square. Other dining options in town include numerous fast-food and take-away Chinese joints.

WORTH SEEING

Market Square in Kildare Town is as good a spot as any to sit and watch the Irish go about their daily lives—commercial and social—in an environment not geared toward tourists. The square is dominated by the 13th-century Church of Ireland **St. Bridgid's Cathedral,** built on the site where the eponymous saint (one of the country's favorites) founded a religious settlement in the 5th century. The settlement was unusual because it was "coed," including nuns and monks. Reminiscent of the vestal virgins at Rome, a group of chaste women tended an eternal flame in a special temple where men were forbidden to tread. The **fire pit** can still be seen on the church grounds. There's also a 108-ft-tall 12th-century round tower, the second highest in the country. The tough climb to the top is rewarded with top-class views of the lakelands at the center of Ireland.

How much do the visitors to a stud want to see exactly? County Kildare is the bluegrass, horse-crazy part of Ireland, and the **National Stud** (tel. 045/521617) is its epicenter. Located just outside the town itself, the Stud was established in 1900 by Colonel William Hall Walker, a brewing heir (Ireland seems to have a lot of them). Walker was horse-crazy and perhaps just crazy; when a new foal was born he sometimes had its horoscope done for use in deciding the horse's worth. The place was transferred to the state in 1943 and is home to breeding stallions who are groomed, exercised, tested, and bred within the neat white buildings, which are set around immaculately kept green lawns. There are regular tours that dish out the secrets on getting two horses together (and how soothing music can help). The **Stud Horse Museum** (tel. 045/52167) is open mid-February–mid-November, daily 9:30–6; admission is £5. It recounts the notable history of the horse in Ireland. Its most famous exhibit is the skeleton of Arkle, the hero steeplechaser of Ireland that dominated the sport in the 1960s.

The eccentric Walker also created the nearby **Japanese Gardens** in 1906. He hired the famous master gardener Tassa Eida and his son Minoru to lay out the gardens, which are recognized as among the finest in Europe, although they're something of an East-West hybrid rather than authentically Japanese. The Scotch pine trees, for instance, are an appropriate stand-in for traditional Japanese pines, which signify long life and happiness. The gardens symbolically chart the human progression from birth to death (the focus is on a man's journey, not a woman's). A series of landmarks are situated on a meandering path: The Tunnel of Ignorance (No. 3) represents a child's lack of understanding, the Engagement and Marriage bridges (Nos. 8 and 9) span a small stream, and from the Hill of Ambition (No. 13), you can look back over your past joys and sorrows. It ends with the Gateway to Eternity (No. 20), beyond which lies a Buddhist meditation sand garden. It's a worthwhile destination any time of the year, though it's particularly glorious in spring and fall. The gardens are open mid-February–mid-November, daily 9:30–6; admission is included if you visit the Stud Museum, or £3 if paid for separately.

THE MIDLANDS 4

LAURENCE BELGRAVE

UPDATED BY COLIN LACEY

I rish schoolchildren were once taught to imagine Ireland as a saucer with mountains around the rim and a dip in the middle. The not-so-imaginary dip is the Midlands---or the Lakelands, as Bord Fáilte prefers to call it---and this often-overlooked region comprises seven counties: Cavan, Laois (pronounced leash), Westmeath, Longford, Offaly, Roscommon, and Monaghan, in addition to North Tipperary. Ask people from the rest of Ireland what the sole purpose of the Midlands is and they will jest that the region exists simply to hold the other parts of the island together.

Indeed, the Midlands is usually looked upon with disdain by the Irish people, who consider it dull and mundane (the very worst of offenses in Ireland; better dead than boring). The perception is at least partially true, the Midlands being the kind of place you rush through on the way to somewhere else; with no major city in the region (Dublin lies to the east, Galway and Limerick to the west, and Cork to the south), it remains a quiet and geographically unspectacular place. Night owls should probably head elsewhere—the wildest thing in these parts is the wind. But if you've a little patience and a little time to match you may find you've uncovered a real gem in the making, for the Midlands offers you a chance to see the agricultural-based country of Ireland at work: viable farms and small market towns, whose citizens can be observed simply getting on with their daily lives. They are friendly, of course—around here, there are plenty of folks who have nothing to do but be pleasant—but they are not dependent on the tourist dollar, unlike many other parts of the country. While the area is beginning to increase its profile as an attraction in its own right, in a general sense, residents have not altered their environment to please the big-spending visitors. During the 1980s, emigration from the Midlands left a hole in the region's youth population, but as Ireland's economy gradually improved in the 1990s, the outward trend has reversed. Indeed, some towns in the region—notably along the eastern border of Westmeath—have taken on a new life as satellites of Dublin. It's still a long haul from there to the city, but having a house in the Midlands is considered by many a toiler in the city as worth the lengthy commute.

Even if some Midlands towns are not especially interesting, they will appeal strongly to people hungry for a time when the pace of life was slower and every neighbor's face was familiar. When Ireland's famed film director Neil Jordan shot *The Butcher Boy* in the small town of Clones, he did more for this small town's ego (not to mention regional tourism prospects) than any previous commentator when he remarked: "If I ever want to quantify anything, I measure it against Clones. There is nothing you will ever encounter in life you haven't seen in some form in Clones." Here, as elsewhere in the Midlands, a town's main hotel is usually one of the prime social centers and can be a good place from which to study local life. You might witness a wedding reception (generally a boisterous occasion involving all age groups), a First Communion supper, a meeting of the local Lions Club, a gathering of the neighborhood weight-watcher group, or any one of dozens of social occasions that occur randomly. But for a real sense of regional life, it's important to walk through the main shopping areas or, in the case of smaller towns, the main streets and thoroughfares. It's here you'll get the best taste of the area's daily activity and a sense of its special character and identity. It's here too that you'll begin to distinguish the flatter tones of the Midlands accent; if you spend enough time in the region you might even get to recognize the difference between a Cavan twang and a Tipperary brogue.

A fair share of Ireland's 800 bodies of water speckle this lush countryside. Many of the lakes—formed by glacial action some 10,000 years ago—are quite small, especially in Cavan and Monaghan. Anglers who come to the area boast of having a whole lake to themselves, and many return year after year to practice the sport. The River Shannon, one of the longest rivers in Europe, bisects the Lakelands from north to south, piercing a series of loughs (the Irish term for lakes): **Lough Allen, Lough Ree,** and **Lough Derg.** The **Royal Canal** and the **Grand Canal** cross the Lakelands from east to west, ending in the Shannon north and south of Lough Ree. Stretches of both canals are now being developed for recreational purposes.

But don't think this region is missing out on any number of cultural must-sees. In the countryside you can easily stumble across well-maintained historic homes with carefully tended gardens, including **Strokestown Park House, Birr Castle Gardens, Bellamont Forest,** and **Emo Court.** Examples of the "big house" common in Irish life and literature, including in the poetry of Yeats, these mansions were once objects of scorn for the local population as they generally housed the big-brother Protestant overlord. In times of rebellion it was not unheard of for one of these houses to mysteriously catch fire, and the countryside is dotted with the shells of such once-great houses. You'll also find the impressive monastic remains at **Clonmacnoise, Boyle,** and **Fore.** After days exploring these historic sights—where every stone hides a story—you'll be glad for the region's simpler pleasures: excellent fishing spots, uncrowded parkland golf courses, and numerous lovely country walks along the water.

The main roads from Dublin to the south and the west cross the region, but there is also a network of minor roads linking the more scenic areas. If you're in no particular hurry, these are the ones to take. Traffic tends to move more slowly (although, suffering shamrocks, not always so), and you'll often come across quiet villages where you can spend an hour or so in conversation with locals who'll take an interest in you just because you're an outsider. As you cross the region, you'll note that much of the landscape lies under blanket bog, due to the heavy waterfall hereabouts. For more conventionally attractive hill and lake scenery head to the forest parks of Killykeen and Lough Key.

One of the best ways to immerse yourself in the Lakelands is to meander through the region on a bike. Although the area may not offer the spectacular scenery of the more hilly coastal regions, its level, Netherlands-like terrain means a less strenuous ride. The twisting roads are generally in good (well, good enough) condition, and there are picnic spots in the many state-owned forests just off the main roads. Bord Fáilte recommends two long tours: one of the Athlone-Mullingar-Roscommon area, and another of the Cavan-Monaghan-Mullingar region. The more rural regions of Laois are a cyclist's paradise, and you can spend days exploring beautiful glens, waterfalls, nature trails, and wooded regions around the Slieve Bloom mountains. Try to avoid the major trunk roads that bisect the region—after all, this is a region that deserves thorough and leisurely exploration.

NORTH TIPPERARY AND THE WEST LAKELANDS

This area includes the western part of the Lakelands, skirting the River Shannon, Lough Derg, Lough Ree, and Lough Key. Between these bodies of water much of the land is bog, a fragile ecosystem that rewards closer investigation. The towns are small and generally undistinguished, with the exceptions of Birr and Strokestown, both of which were laid out by architects and designed to complement the "big houses" that share their names.

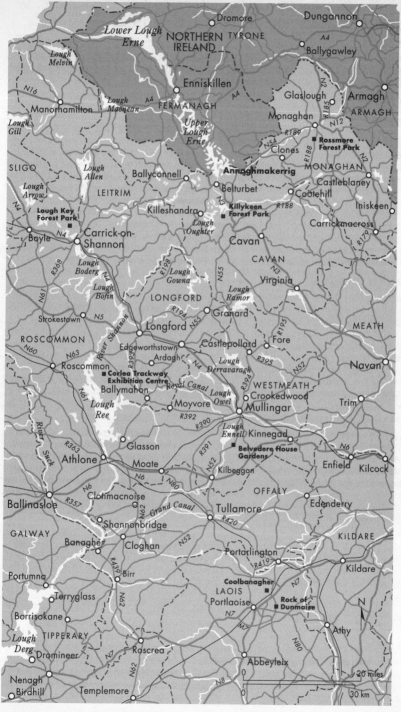

NENAGH & ENVIRONS

BASICS

The **tourist office** (Connolly St., tel. 067/31610) provides all the information you'll need, thanks to its handful of brochures, many of them free. The staff here can also guide you to area accommodations. The office is open Monday–Friday 9:30–1 and 2–5:30.

WHERE TO SLEEP

The volume of traffic that passes through it on the way to and from Limerick gives Nenagh the feel of a busy parking lot at the side of an even busier crossroads, so if early morning traffic is anything other than music to your ears, make sure the B&B you check into isn't on one of the main roads in the town. If you do decide to stay in the town center, there really isn't a whole lot to choose from unless you want to shell out at higher levels. Better to take a walk out along the N53, to the north of the town, where you'll find the spacious and comfortable **Ashley Park House** (Ashley Park, tel. 067/31474), with rooms from £23. West of Nenagh, on the road to Lough Derg, B&Bs are thicker on the ground. One of the best-value spots you'll find is the wonderful and homey **Otway Lodge Guesthouse** (Dromineer, tel. 067/24273), which has rooms from £18 on Dromineer Bay and has fabulous views of Lough Derg and surrounding lakeshore, which includes a ruined castle. The **Country House** (Thurles Rd., Kilkeary, tel. 067/31193) is also good value at £21 per person. It's actually the home of the Kennedy family, situated about 8 km (5 mi) out of town on a few pleasant acres not too far from Lough Derg. Guests are given the run of the place, including the TV room and the peat-burning hearth, and rooms have coffeemakers and hair dryers.

WORTH SEEING

Nenagh, 165 km (103 mi) southwest of Dublin, was originally a Norman settlement; it grew to a market town in the 19th century. Standing 100 ft high and 53 ft across the base, **Nenagh Castle Keep** is all that remains of the town's original settlement. It stands imposingly right in the center of the town and is well worth a quick look, if only to imagine what it might have been like to live in such a weird structure. Pretty much the centerpiece of the town, it was built in 1200 as the Irish home of Theobald Fitzwalter, one of the original Norman conquerors. Just across the road from the castle are the gatehouse and governor's house of Nenagh's old county jail that now compose **Nenagh Heritage Centre** (tel. 067/32633). It's open Easter–October, Monday–Saturday 9:30–5, Sunday 2:30–5; November–Easter, weekdays 9:30–5; and you'll get in for £2. It has permanent displays of rural life in the recent past before mechanization set in, as well as temporary painting and photography exhibits centering on the history and heritage of the region. Unless you've got Nenagh roots, it's not worth spending too much time here.

Lough Derg nudges up against a number of small villages, most of which depend on angling and cruises to attract visitors. Nicest of them all is **Dromineer,** which is also home to **Shannon Sailing** (Dromineer, Nenagh, tel. 067/24295), where you can bring out the seafarer (or at least the lake-farer) in yourself on a cruise of scenic Lough Derg by water bus, cruiser, or sailboat. It can be difficult to get a seat aboard if it's tourist season and the weather is good, so you can save yourself a long wait if you call ahead to book first. If you do take to the waters, wrap up well—even on relatively mild days the breeze on the lake will cut the skin right off you. It's worth it, though, for the amazing views and lulling sound of the lapping of the lake waves.

Southwest of Nenagh, in the picturesque village of **Birdhill,** is the flagship headquarters of Tipperary Crystal (1 Birdhill, tel. 061/379066), one of the country's premier pretenders to the throne occupied by Waterford Crystal. A 200-year-old ex-army barracks with a beautiful stone front has been transformed into a modern visitor center and exhibition space (open weekdays 9—6, weekends 10–6) where, if crystal is your thing, there will be lots of shimmer to engage you.

ROSCREA

BASICS

There's a **Bank of Ireland** on Castle Street that will change money and has an ATM. **Bus Éireann** from Dublin and Limerick stops three times a day on Castle Street. There is no actual tourist office in town, but the **Heritage Centre** in Roscrea Castle (tel. 0505/21850) will have all the information you need, including a free Heritage Walk Map.

WHERE TO SLEEP AND EAT

Cregganbell (Birr Rd., tel. 0505/21421) is a little bed-and-breakfast of four rooms with showers in a modern bungalow. Rooms cost £20 for singles and £17 per person for doubles. **Yellow House B&B** (Main St., tel. 0505/21772) is, surprise, surprise, a yellow house with warm, comfortable rooms (£15 per person) and a friendly atmosphere.

If you're hungry in Roscrea, head for **Kitty's Tavern** on Castle Street, a huge, barnlike bar and restaurant with a giant fireplace (don't sit too close, as it can get smoky). Salads, pastas, and chicken dishes, as well as hearty meat-and-spuds specials for under £5, make it a popular spot with local office workers at lunchtime. At night it's a lively, crowded place, where you can hear live rock and ballads on Tuesday, and Friday through Sunday. Across the street from Roscrea Castle, **Rosewood Inn** (Roscrea Centre, Castle St., tel. 0505/23380) is a handy place to grab a quick snack inside the town's main shopping center, which also has an adjacent deli counter that can make up your choice of sandwich for £2.95. For more substantial fare, head for the **Waterfront Old World Eating House** (The Mall, tel. 0505/22431), tucked away down a side street behind Roscrea Castle. It's bright, airy, and informal and features a good lunch menu for under £5. There's a more expensive à la carte selection in the evenings, when a main course will set you back £9.95 or more.

WORTH SEEING

Thrill seekers beware: The Midlands is sometimes referred to as the biggest farm in the world.

The main road through Roscrea, a town steeped in religious history, cuts through **St. Cronan's Church and Round Tower,** a 7th-century sandstone monastery founded by St. Cronan. It also passes the west facade of a 12th-century Romanesque **church** that now forms an entrance gate to a modern Catholic church. Above the structure's round-headed doorway is a hood molding enclosing the figure of a bishop, probably St. Cronan. Just to the north of the church, you can make out what's left of **St. Cronan's Cross,** a 12th-century stone high cross that originally featured extensive carvings and motif embellishments and, unusually, had originally featured two figures at its base, one a male and one a female. The nearby round tower was reduced to its current height of 25 ft after British authorities lopped off the top floor in 1798 following an incident in which a soldier was shot by a sniper from the roof.

In the very center of town is **Roscrea Castle,** a Norman fortress dating from 1314, given by King Richard II to the Duke of Ormond. Inside are vaulted rooms graced with tapestries and 16th-century furniture. The castle is open daily from June to the end of September, 10 to 6, with an admission price of £2.50. This ticket also gains you entry into the adjacent **Damer House** (tel. 0505/21850), a superb example of an early 18th-century town house on the grand scale. It was used as a barracks during most of the 19th century and only recently rescued from decay by the Irish Georgian Society. It was built in 1725 within the curtain walls of the neighboring Norman castle. In those days, homes were often constructed beside or attached to the strongholds they replaced. Damer House has a plain, symmetrical facade and a magnificent carved pine staircase within. The house contains the collection of the Irish Country Furniture Society, supplemented by pieces from the National Museum—a treat for those interested in antiques. In the adjoining building, exhibits focus on monastic settlements in the Midlands, the old Irish kitchen, and other local and national themes. The house is home to the **Roscrea Heritage Centre** and is open mid-May–September, daily 9:30–6 (rest of year, weekends 10–5).

BIRR

BASICS

The **tourist office** (Rose St., tel. 0509/20110) right across from Birr Castle's front entrance is open May to September from 9 to 5:30. The **AIB** on Emmet Square has an ATM, and you can change money there. **Bus Éireann** from Dublin and Athlone stops in the middle of town.

WHERE TO SLEEP AND EAT

Spinners Town House (Castle St., tel. 0509/21673) is a great option for food and lodging right in the center of town. "Live, sleep, and eat" is the house motto, and you can do it all under one roof here. It's one of the best B&Bs in the entire Midlands, but it doesn't come cheap, with singles costing £25 and doubles £20 per person, including breakfast. If it's raining outside you can amuse yourself with the work of local artists and craftspeople that adorns the walls, and the premises also houses a quality bistro, popular with Birr's trendier set. Main courses of fish, pastas, and tasty burgers are available from £8.95,

THE OFFALY WAY

The Offaly Way has been developed by Offaly's tourism administrators as a long-distance walking route between two other long-distance routes: the Slieve Bloom Way, which cuts through the spectacular bogs and hills of the Slieve Bloom mountain range and crosses an environmental park, and the somewhat less spectacular Grand Canal Way, which follows roughly the route of the Grand Canal, from Ballinasloe in the west to Dublin in the east. If you're a dedicated walker or someone fond of long, lonely hikes through scenic routes, this is the route to head for. If the very thought of a stroll through the mountains leaves you breathless, however, head straight for the Slieve Blooms themselves. Peeking up through the otherwise flat lands of middle Ireland, between the towns of Birr, Portlaoise, and Tullamore, they barely reach 2,000 ft at their highest point, which makes them ideal if your hiking skills are a bit rusty. The tourist offices in any of the surrounding towns will have details on the best routes, and—if you don't mind them thinking you're either crazy or chicken, or both—many of them will advise you on the easiest ones to take.

and there's a full wine list. For a slightly less pricey bed than Spinners, look for a little green door with a glass diamond window: the entrance to **Kelly's B&B** (O'Connell St., tel. 0509/21128), where you'll find nice, clean rooms at £18 for a single, with doubles costing £16 per person.

In the town center, head along O'Connell Street from Emmet Square—many of the bars along the way do decent quality pub grub. If you're driving or can afford a taxi, however, it's worth your while to seek out **The Thatch** (Crinkhill, tel. 0509/20682), a friendly and unpretentious restaurant under a thatched roof that serves quality food at reasonable prices. It's well off the main drag, but you'll be glad you made the extra effort. Back in the town center, **Kong Lam** (O'Connell St.) does a mean Chinese takeout; just witness the crowds after the pubs close.

WORTH SEEING

Birr is a quiet, sleepy place with tree-lined malls and modest Georgian houses, where all roads lead to the gates of **Birr Castle Demesne** (tel. 0509/20056), an imposing neo-Gothic castle dating from the early 17th century that is still the home of the earls of Rosse. The castle isn't open to the common man; however, you can pass a peaceful couple of hours strolling about the surrounding 100 acres of gardens, the oldest of which was planted three centuries ago. The present earl and countess of Rosse continue the adventurous family tradition of undertaking daring botanical expeditions for specimens of rare trees, plants, and shrubs from all over the world. The formal gardens contain the tallest box-hedges in the world (32 ft). Spring is the best time to come: You'll see a wonderful display of flowering cherries, magnolias, crab-apple blossoms, and naturalized narcissi. In autumn, the maples, chestnuts, and weeping beeches blaze red and gold. The grounds are laid out around a lake and along the banks of two adjacent rivers; above one of these stands the castle itself. The grounds also contain the remains of the Rosse Telescope, a giant (72-inch) reflecting telescope built in 1845, which remained the largest in the world for the next 75 years. Allow at least two hours to see all that's here. If you're lucky enough to visit on a sunny day, you can easily find a secluded place for a quiet picnic, in which case you could while away an entire morning or afternoon without noticing it go by. Admission is £3, and the grounds are open year-round from 9 to 6 and on until dusk in the summer.

Everyone ends up at Birr Castle, but the best place to begin exploring Birr itself is the **Birr Heritage Centre** (John's Mall, tel. 0509/20923), which sits in a miniature Greek-style building temple in the town.

Here's where you'll find background on all things Birr, including details on the town's history and the reason why it's been known since the 19th century as "the bellybutton of Ireland." Birr is the perfect departure point for a trip to the Slieve Bloom mountains. The **Slieve Bloom Environmental Display Center** (Railway Rd., tel. 0509/37299) has exhibits on the extensive plant and animal life of the region.

BANAGHER

BASICS

The **tourist information office** is in the **Crank House Hostel** (Main St., tel. 0509/51458).

WHERE TO SLEEP AND EAT

Home to the town tourist office, the excellent **Crank House Hostel** (Main St., tel. 0509/51458) can provide a warm, comfortable room for £8. It's often busy, particularly during the high season, so if you'd like something a little quieter, you could do a lot worse than **Hayes B&B** (Main St., tel. 0509/51360), where rooms cost £22 per person.

WORTH SEEING

Twelve kilometers (10 mi) northwest of Birr, the sleepy but pretty town of Banagher nestles on the banks of the Shannon and is where Anthony Trollope wrote his first two novels. Apart from a squat Martello tower, however, the town has little of interest unless you're a boating devotee, in which case the marina is an excellent point for exploring the Shannon. If you're staying in the area for some time, you can hire a 17-ft, two-person canoe plus all the camping gear you'll need (tent, cooking utensils, etc.) for £215 from **Shannon Adventure Canoeing Holidays** (tel. 0509/51411). A better option for shorter river cruises is **Carrick Craft** (tel. 0509/51187), one of the many operators offering a range of trips on the river. Details on these and other excursions are available at the tourist information office.

Three kilometers (2 mi) outside Banagher, and worth the walk, is the giant **Croghan Castle**, an 800-year-old Norman tower that has been added to over the centuries and has been continuously inhabited since its construction.

CLONMACNOISE

BASICS

The **tourist office** (tel. 0905/74134) outside the ruins (near the parking area) has information on the site and on the whole region. The **visitor center** (tel. 0905/74195) has displays and a surprisingly watchable audiovisual show to educate you about the site.

WHERE TO SLEEP AND EAT

Near the town of Shannonbridge you'll come across **Kajon House** (tel. 0905/74191), where simple but elegant rooms with bath and electric blankets—a lifesaver if you've been out on a wet and windy evening—cost £18 per person. There are also great views out over the silent bog. Breakfast and dinner—good hearty, starchy stuff—are also available.

WORTH SEEING

Clonmacnoise, from the Irish Cluain Mic Nois ("Meadow of the Son of Nos"), was once ancient Ireland's most important ecclesiastical center. In its prime, the site was a complex of houses, workshops, and up to 13 churches and oratories. Thanks in large part to its relatively isolated position—the settlement is flanked on one side by the River Shannon and on the other by a bog that remained virtually impassable for centuries—it almost survived everything thrown at it, including raids by feuding Irish tribes, Vikings, and Normans. The remaining buildings are on an esker, or natural gravel ridge, that overlooks a large marshy area along the river. When the settlement was founded by St. Ciaran in 545, the Shannon was an important artery of communication, so the site was not as remote as it appears now. Survey the surrounding countryside from the higher parts of Clonmacnoise, and you'll get a good idea of the strategic advantages of its commanding riverside location.

Although it's now a tourist mecca, which means that for practically the whole year it's clogged with tour buses and passing traffic, with a little imagination you can picture life here in medieval times, when the

A DAY IN THE BOG

Despite the fact that large clumps of the country are made up of them, in Ireland the word "bog" has defamatory associations—for someone to "come from the bog" in Ireland is roughly the equivalent of being from hicksville in the United States. The tourist board, however, has caught on quickly to the potential inherent in these wild, untamed areas, and the Clonmacnoise and West Offaly Railway is one of the best things they have come up with. A 9-km (5½-mi) tour in a green-and-gold diesel-powered coach train through the Blackwater Bog, one of the most important bogs in the country, this particular trip runs over an area that 12,000 years ago lay beneath a glacier. After 9,000 years, it became a lake and slowly developed into the cutaway bog that lies there today. You can smell the turf in the air as you take in the spectacular, almost surreal scenery and, particularly when it's wet, consider how lucky you are not to have to spend 12 hours there every day, as many locals did to make a living, cutting turf fuel from the land. Tours take place from April to October and cost £4; information is available from the Clonmacnoise and West Offaly Railway (tel. 0905/74114).

nobles of Europe sent their sons to be educated by the local monks, whose reputation as educators and spiritual guides spread throughout the world. Clonmacnoise first found fame as the burial place of the mighty kings of Connaught and of Tara, as well as many other leaders and dignitaries of the ancient Celtic world. The last High King of Ireland, Rory O'Connor, was buried here at the end of the 12th century. (The O'Connor name is still common in the area, and some locals still claim to belong to the original O'Connor line, which would place them among the oldest families in Europe, with roots traceable all the way back to 75 AD.) In 1552, however, the English garrison from Athlone ruthlessly reduced the ancient religious site to ruin, carrying away as booty practically everything of value, including the altars, statues and paintings, books, bells, and even the stained-glass windows, before burning what remained. Any treasures and manuscripts spared can now be found in the National Museum in Dublin (*see* Chapter 2). Surviving buildings include the shell of a small **cathedral, two round towers,** the remains of nine smaller churches, and several **high crosses,** the best preserved of these being the **Cross of the Scriptures,** also known as Flann's Cross. As throughout its long and glorious heyday, Clonmacnoise was a prestigious burial place up until recently; among the ancient stones are many other graves dating from the 17th to the mid-20th century, when a new graveyard was consecrated on adjoining land. The whole place simply reeks of times past, though in mid-summer it can be a little difficult to avoid the throngs of tourists. It costs £2.50 to get into Clonmacnoise and it's open year-round. Guided tours are available on request (tel. 0905/74195).

ATHLONE

Athlone originated as a crossing point of the Shannon, at first as a ford at the southernmost tip of Lough Ree, and it later marked the boundary between the old provinces of Leinster (to the east) and Connaught (to the west). Nowadays it's an incredibly busy town, filled to bursting with traffic, but it is still a place where folks meet, most likely over a cup of tea in a café after a day's hard shopping. Athlone is the commercial hub for the surrounding area, and an important road and rail junction. Despite its place in Irish history—it was the site of many important Cromwellian and Jacobite battles in the 17th century—it contains little of great interest to the visitor. Music fans should note, however, that Count John McCormack (1884–1945), one of Ireland's greatest—and still best-loved—tenors, was born here and is now featured in an audiovisual presentation at Athlone Castle.

BASICS

There is a **tourist office** (tel. 0902/94630) in the castle on the Main Street side of Market Place with information on the town and the surrounding countryside. Ask for the free tourist board handouts; they have as much information as many of the pricier guides. The **Bank of Ireland** and **Allied Irish Bank** on Church Street both have ATMs and, during business hours, will change money. There are also other banks throughout town with ATMs. Bikes can be rented from **M. R. Hardiman** (Irishtown, Co. Westmeath, tel. 0902/78669).

COMING AND GOING

Located almost exactly at the physical center of Ireland, Athlone is in essence a town you pass through, so it is no surprise that there is a plethora of means by which to enter and exit. **Iarnród Éireann** runs trains to Athlone's train and bus depot (tel. 0902/73322) from Dublin (6 per day; fares vary) and Galway (3 per day; fares vary), and **Bus Éireann** has buses to and from Dublin, Galway, Cork, Waterford, and Rosslare. The cost of traveling by bus is low, but times and frequency seem to change without notice, so if you're on a tight schedule, call ahead and then come early, just in case.

WHERE TO SLEEP

The **Athlone Holiday Hostel** (Church St., tel. 0902/73399), right next to the train and bus depot, is one of the most recently established hostels in the country, with still an air of freshness about it. Paintings of Irish myths and legends adorn the common area (TV and pool room). The dorms have 10 beds each (from £8 per person) and are always clean and comfortable. Showers, laundry, and sheets are available, as are decent, hearty meals. The hostel also has Internet access and bike rental facilities. **Lough Ree Caravan and Camping Park** (tel. 0902/78561) is a few miles north of town and is the perfect option if the weather holds out. Tent sites go for £3.50 per person and are available from May through September. Bed-and-breakfast fare in Athlone is plentiful and generally of good quality. Among the better places to lay your head are the **Riverview House** (Summerhill, tel. 0902/94532), which is a short kilometer (½ mi) away from the town center but has clean, sharp rooms for £18, and **Shannonside House** (West Lodge Rd., tel. 0902/94773), which also costs £18 and does a great breakfast. If these happen to be full—and they probably won't—you might try the **Bastion B&B** (Bastion St., tel. 0902/94954), which is more upmarket than the other family-run businesses in town but a good value at £20.

FOOD

Athlone isn't known as one of the best cuisine towns in Ireland, but nevertheless there are a number of charming little places that will entice you right in off the street. Probably the best place in town for reasonably priced good food is the **Left Bank** (Bastion St., tel. 0902/94446), which is popular with Athlone folk because of the ample size of its sandwiches and salads (£5–£8). Dinner at night consists of hearty Mediterranean fare, with entrées beginning at £10. If you're vegetarian, or simply health conscious, then seek out the **Crescent Café,** a casual little eatery connected to the Athlone Holiday Hostel (*see above*). The place specializes in meatless pies and pastas at a people's price. Many of the pubs in town do delicious, if basic, moderately priced lunch specials; check the menus outside for the fare and what it will set you back.

WORTH SEEING

Athlone Castle (Tower Bridge, tel. 0902/94360) was built beside the River Shannon in 1210, on the site of an earlier castle that had served as the headquarters of the King of Connaught. After their ignoble defeat at the Battle of the Boyne in 1691, the Irish retreated to Athlone and made the river their first line of defense. Originally designed for King John of England, the castle structure was extensively renovated in 1991, the 300th anniversary of this rout. It remains an interesting example of a Norman stronghold and houses a small museum of artifacts relating to Athlone's eventful past. Admission (£2.60) includes access to the visitor center (tel. 0902/92912), which features a fairly forgettable multimedia presentation depicting the siege of Athlone in 1691, the flora and fauna of the Shannon, and the life of John McCormack. The castle is open May–September, 10–5. Three excursion boats travel up the Shannon from the castle to nearby Lough Ree in the summer: The M.V. *Goldsmith* is the largest inland waterway boat in Ireland, holding some 200 passengers, offering a Sunday cruise up the river (tel. 0902/85163; ticket price is £6); the M.V. *Ross* is smaller, topping out at 70 passengers (tel. 0902/72892); and the M.V. *Viking* (tel. 0902/73383) is a re-creation of a Viking ship, with room for 70 passengers—no extra charge for Viking attire for photo purposes.

ROSCOMMON

WHERE TO SLEEP AND EAT • If you're staying in town, try the excellent **Gleeson's Guesthouse and Restaurant** (Market Sq., tel. 0903/26954), an award-winning converted 19th-century town house with spacious guest rooms and friendly service. With rooms beginning at £22.50, it's a little pricey, but it's well worth it; the restaurant is good too. Slightly less expensive is **Regans** (Market Sq., tel. 0903/25339), a family-run establishment over a busy bar and restaurant, where rooms cost £20 per person.

WORTH SEEING • Roscommon is the only county in the immediate region without a sea coastline; nevertheless, two-thirds of the county is bounded by water, with the River Shannon and Lough Rea to the east, the unfortunately named River Suck to the west, Lough Ree to the south, and Loughs Key, Gara, and Boderg to the north. And as if that weren't enough dampness, a full third of the county is classified as bog. Tourists, not surprisingly, are generally few and far between. Sheep and cattle farming are the main occupations in the region, although increasingly, manufacturing industries are drawing workers away from traditional employment. The land in the county tends to be flat and featureless, despite the many lakes and the presence, along the eastern border with Longford, of the shores of mighty Lough Ree. Locals will tell you differently, of course, but if you spend more than a day or two in the area, you'll find yourself agreeing with the general Irish consensus that the county of Roscommon can be uncommonly dull.

The county capital is **Roscommon,** which takes its name from the ancient Celtic St. Coman, who founded a monastery in the area in early Christian times. As you enter this pleasant little town on the southern slopes of a hill, you'll pass the remains of the Dominican **Roscommon Abbey.** The principal ruin is a church; at the base of the choir stand eight sculpted figures representing gallowglasses, or medieval Irish professional soldiers, a euphemism for ruthless mercenaries. The abbey has been vacated for centuries, though the religious order actually remained in Roscommon up to the late 1800s. You can roam freely through the ruins. To the north of Roscommon town are the weathered remains of **Roscommon Castle,** a large Norman stronghold dating from the 13th century.

SHANNONBRIDGE

As you pass through the small town of Shannonbridge heading toward **Uisce Dhub,** on either side of the road you'll notice vast stretches of chocolaty-brown bog lands as well as a scattering of industrial plants for processing this natural resource: not exactly the kind of stuff tourists usually flock to see, but it is an ancient industry, long at the heart of the Irish economy. Bog is used in peat-fired power stations; compressed into briquettes for domestic hearths; and made into peat moss and plant containers used in gardening. Ireland's liberal use of a resource that is scarce elsewhere in Europe provoked an indignant reaction from botanists and ecologists in the 1980s, resulting in the setting aside of certain bog areas for conservation. Among these are the **Clara Bog** and **Mongan's Bog** in County Offaly, both relatively untouched, raised pieces of land with unique flora, and the **Scragh Bog** in County Westmeath. Because of the preservative qualities of peat, it is not unusual to come across bog timber 5,000 years old, or to dig up perfectly preserved domestic implements from more recent times—not to mention the occasional cache of treasure. Deer, badgers, and wild dogs inhabit the bog lands, along with a rich variety of birds and plants. These areas are being preserved by Bord na Mona, the same government agency that makes commercial use of other bog lands.

BOYLE

BASICS

The **tourist office** (tel. 079/62145) on Main Street, just inside the main gates of King House, is open every day 9–5 from mid-May to September. Also on Main Street is a **Bank of Ireland** branch with an ATM. There is a **National Irish Bank** on Bridge Street, also with an ATM and a bureau de change. The **train station** (tel. 079/62027) is on the road to Roscommon town and has three services daily to Dublin (£11.50) via Sligo (a single fare to Sligo costs £4.50). **Buses** from Dublin, Athlone, and Sligo stop at the Royal Hotel on Bridge Street in the center of town.

WHERE TO SLEEP

Good-value and good-quality B&Bs are easier to find in Boyle than in any other part of the county. On the outskirts of the town, though still close enough to make the trek to the bars, restaurants, and shops in the main area, is **Avonlea** (Carrick Rd., tel. 079/62538), a spacious, modern family home with comfortable rooms and beds for £18. If you're a nonsmoker, **Carnfree House** (Dublin Rd., tel. 079/62516) is worth checking out. Rooms start at £22, and the owners of this happy, smoke-free house are also Gaelic speakers, so you might be lucky enough to pick up a few words during your stay. You'll get a nice view of the river and the abbey from **Abbey House** (Abbeytown Rd., tel. 079/62385), and the rooms, which cost £18, are decorated attractively enough to make lying in bed seem like a good option. The **Lough Key Caravan and Camping Park** (Carrick Rd., tel. 079/62212), 10 minutes outside Boyle by car, has tent sites for £8 and is open from April to August.

FOOD

The **Una Bhán** (tel. 079/63033) is a restaurant inside the gates of King House (*see below*) offering fried food (chips, fish, etc.) and overcooked vegetables, starting at under £5. There's also a spectacular all-day breakfast, which will set you up for the whole day, as long as you don't mind the damage the fried sausages, bacon, and pudding will do to your waistline. The locals don't seem to mind, and it's one of the most popular eateries for people on the run. If full-blown cholesterol splurges aren't for you, try the more sophisticated **Royal Hotel** (Bridge St., tel. 079/62016), a riverfront establishment with deep roots in Boyle that serves coffee and sandwiches all day and has a meat-carvery lunch as well as full restaurant service at night.

WORTH SEEING

Although it's the county's secondary town (Roscommon is the county capital), **Boyle** has a lot more going for it than anywhere else in the area and therefore gets the lion's share of whatever tourist trade there is. Set at the foot of the Curlieu Mountains, it is a grand, old-fashioned town on the River Boyle midway between Lough Gara and Lough Key.

The ruins of **Boyle Abbey** (tel. 0903/26100) on the N4, dating from the late 12th and early 13th centuries, still convey an impression of the splendor and religious awe this richly endowed Cistercian foundation must have inspired in those who saw it in its prime. The abbey was consecrated in 1220 and for the following 400 years refused to bow to a succession of raids, burnings, and lootings that came about as a result of local tribal wars and later conflicts between the Irish and the English. It is still regarded as one of the finest Cistercian buildings in the country. The nave, choir, and transept of the cruciform church are in particularly good condition and, despite their age, still manage to convey the attention to detail which went into their construction. Strange figures and animals carved into the stone columns near the western end of the abbey seemingly contradict the Cistercian requirements for unadorned houses of prayer and have puzzled historians for some time. Best of all, you can wander about the ruins at your leisure.

Magnificent **King House** (Main St., tel. 079/63242), in the center of Boyle, was built in the 18th century for Sir Henry King, a Member of the British Parliament for the area. The town's main street, which the house still dominates, was originally designed as the approach to this stately home. The King family was one of the biggest and most powerful landowners in the entire country at one time. The family subsequently moved to the Rockingham Estate (*see below*), and the house ended up as a military barracks for the famous Connaught Rangers. It was opened to the public in 1994 after extensive restoration and has multimedia exhibits on the Connaught Rangers, the Kings of Connaught, and the history of the house, which is open to the public Monday–Saturday 10–6. Tours are available, and the last admission is at 5.

Frybrook House, an imposing, three-story Georgian structure at the other end of the town, was built in 1750 for Henry Fry, an English Quaker who settled in the area at the invitation of a local peer. **Lough Key Forest Park** (tel. 079/62214), a popular base for campers and backpackers, is always a big hit with walkers and anglers. Previously the Rockingham Estate, the park is 3 km (2 mi) north of Boyle and consists of 840 acres on the shores of the lake, with a bog garden, a deer enclosure, and a cypress grove; boats can be hired on the lake. A nature trail beginning at Rockingham Harbour will take you through the best of the area, including the cute Fairy Bridge. To get some idea of the vastness of the park, climb to the top of Moylurg Tower, which was built on the site of Rockingham Mansion, destroyed by fire 30 years ago. If you're lucky, or if you manage to get somebody to point you in the right direction, you might stumble upon a castle hidden away in Cloontykilla Wood. The park is so large, you can lose all contact with other visitors without much difficulty, so if it's solitude you're after, this is the place to be—and they don't charge to get in. Lough Key dominates the area northeast of Boyle and, with more than 30 islands dotting the lake, has become internationally renowned among anglers, who come here to try to land one of the pike that are native to the region. There are two other lakes near the town, Lough Arrow to the north and Lough Gara to the west, making the region a favorite destination of fishermen.

Boyle hosts an annual Arts Festival, usually during the last week of July, that is increasingly regarded as one of the leading festivals outside the capital. There is an eclectic lineup of comedy, music, poetry, lectures, and so on, but the best thing about it is that the pubs are generally filled for the week with traditional musicians, who provide a raucous soundtrack to the whole event. For information on the festival, phone 079/63085.

NEAR BOYLE

STROKESTOWN

Like many villages near a "big house," Strokestown was designed to complement the house. The widest main street in all Ireland—laid out to rival the Ringstrasse in Vienna—leads to a Gothic arch, which is the entrance to the grounds of **Strokestown Park House** (tel. 078/33013). As you can see from its facade, this enormous house, seat of the Pakenham Mahon family from 1660 to 1979, has a complicated architectural history. The Palladian wings were added in the 18th century to the original 17th-century block, and the house was again extended in the early 19th century. The interior is full of curiosities, such as Ireland's last surviving galleried kitchen, which allowed the lady of the house to supervise domestic operations from a safe and lofty distance; Monday mornings, menus for the week were dropped by milady from the balcony to the cook below. One wing houses lavish stables with vaulted ceilings and Tuscan pillars. There is also a distillery and a fully equipped nursery. The gardens, which are undergoing an ambitious restoration plan that will include the widest and longest herbaceous borders in Ireland, opened in 1995. Admission to the house is £3 and it's open Tuesday–Sunday 11–5:30 from April to October.

It was somehow fitting that in 1994 Strokestown Park House should also become the site of the **Famine Museum,** Ireland's primary official site commemorating the Great Hunger of 1845–50. During the famine, the house was occupied by the ruthless landowner Denis Mahon, who was responsible for multiple evictions and much consequent hardship and death during the aftermath. In 1847, in an attempt to clear off tenant farmers who could not pay the rent after successive failures of their potato crops, he chartered several ships to transport them to America. They sank off the coast of Ireland, and hundreds perished. Mahon was murdered shortly afterward. The museum, situated in former stables next to the house, details a painful history of the period, which people of sensibility may find rather harrowing to view. Still, to understand anything about Ireland, you have to understand the famine and the echoes that still reverberate a century and a half later, so a visit is almost a duty if you're in the area.

CARRICK-ON-SHANNON

WHERE TO SLEEP • B&Bs are plentiful in Carrick-on-Shannon, particularly out along the Dublin Road, where you'll have a wide choice of comfortable, mostly family-run places to choose from. Try **Ashleigh Guest House** (Dublin Rd., tel. 078/20313), which has bright rooms starting at £18 and—welcome rarities in a small Irish B&B—a sauna and a games room for visitors. Closer to the center of town, **Hollywell B&B** (Liberty Hill, tel. 078/21124) has luxurious rooms and great breakfasts for £25. If you're on a tighter budget, head for the intersection of Main and Bridge streets, where you'll find the **Town Clock Hostel** (tel. 078/20068), which offers clean, well-kept rooms from £8.50. Unfortunately, it's only open from June to September.

FOOD AND DRINK • Finding a place to settle in for a couple of pints and some pub fare is easy in Carrick-on-Shannon; take a walk along Bridge Street and you'll come across half a dozen likely spots within a few doors of each other. Most of them will make you feel welcome as soon as you order a drink, and after a couple, you'll be treated like a regular. One of the best—and noisiest—pubs in town is **Burke's Bar** (Bridge St., tel. 078/20376), which has sessions of traditional music on Thursday and Friday in summer. Also worth your attention is the **Oarsmen** (Bridge St., tel. 078/21733), which caters to a slightly older crowd, while locals flock down the road toward the bridge to **Cryan's** (tel. 078/20409), which features music sessions on Thursday and weekend nights year-round. You'll also find tempting bar food here, starting at £6.95 for a three-course dinner.

WORTH SEEING • Whoever it was that decided to build a town here on the Shannon just south of Lough Key knew what he or she was doing; if any one place in the Lakelands deserves the title of most beautiful setting, this is it. The county capital of Leitrim, Carrick, as it is called locally, is now a major center for boating and pleasure-cruising in Ireland. Anglers, too, flock to the town, hoping to hook pike and a good time in the local bars, of which there are a surprisingly large number. The town is not overburdened with sights, but you should stop at **Costello Chapel** on Main Street, built in 1877 and reputedly the second-smallest chapel in the world. Size apart, the only other aspect of the chapel worth seeing is the pair of lead coffins sunk into the ground on either side of the aisle—they hold the remains of a wealthy local, Edward Costello, who had the place built as a memorial to his young wife, whose remains lie opposite him. Not surprisingly, given the access to waterways, companies offering various forms of river excursions are plentiful, and you should certainly check prices and other arrangements with at least a couple of them before taking to the water. **Moon River Cruises** (tel. 078/21777) provides boisterous, boozy afternoon and evening jaunts on the Shannon in summer, but the best option, if your constitution is strong enough to endure it, is the late-night, post-pub cruise, which leaves at 11 PM on Friday and Saturday throughout the season.

THE NORTHERN LAKELANDS

Leaving the ancient kingdom of Leinster, you come to two counties of Ulster, **Cavan** and **Monaghan**. Beyond Cavan Town you enter the heart of the Northern Lakelands, with lakes both large and small on either side of the road. County Cavan and County Monaghan have at least 180 lakes each. The countryside is distinguished by its drumlins—small, steep hills consisting of boulder clay left behind by the glacial retreat 10,000 years ago. The boulder clay also filled in many of the pre-glacial river valleys, causing the rivers to change course, resulting in the creation of shallow lakes, which provide excellent fishing, with eels, pike, bream, and roach among the most common catches. As well as angling, walking tours are the mainstay of a fairly meager tourist industry, and every tourist office in the area has information on various trails and routes. The River Shannon, the longest natural waterway in Ireland and Britain, rises in County Cavan, in the Cullagh Mountains. **Longford** is rich in literary associations, though after Oliver Goldsmith, the names of the county's writers' pantheon may draw a blank from all but the most dedicated Irish literature enthusiast.

LONGFORD

BASICS

You can't miss the little **tourist office** (tel. 043/46566); it's right on Main Street and has limited but essential information on the town and the county. Trains from Dublin via Mullingar stop at the **Longford Railway Station** (tel. 043/45208) twice a day. Express buses from Dublin also stop at the train station, as does a daily bus from Mullingar.

WHERE TO SLEEP

Despite the fact that tourism is scant in the town, Longford has a fair number of B&Bs to choose from. The **Tivoli** (Dublin Rd., tel. 043/46898) has warm, well-scrubbed rooms for £17 and a breakfast that will leave you satisfied way beyond lunchtime. The nearby **Scancian** (Dublin Rd., tel. 043/46187) is similarly well kept and cozy (rates are £17) and also offers the option of evening meals. In the center of town, the **Annaly Hotel** (Main St., tel. 043/46253) has basic, unadorned rooms from £22 and has a bar and restaurant on the premises.

FOOD

The locally famous **Peter Clarkes** (Dublin Rd., tel. 043/46478) serves top-notch pub grub and is renowned across three counties for its perfect pint of stout.

WORTH SEEING

Although landlocked, County Longford contains bog land, lakeland, and a good deal of wetlands, all of which contribute to the deep greens and dark hills and pastures of the region. Farming remains the county's primary industry, although Longford is best known throughout Ireland as the county where ex-Taoiseach (prime minister) Albert Reynolds made his fortune in pet food manufacturing. The Great Famine hit particularly hard in the county, resulting in a tradition of emigration that has continued right up to the present; the population of the county has actually decreased in the 1990s. In the 19th century, large numbers of Longford natives settled in Argentina, a development that led to the fostering of links between Longford and South America that continue to this day. The county boasts two particularly significant sons, writer Oliver Goldsmith and Joseph Mullooly, the 19th-century priest and archaeologist who discovered the ancient temple of Mithras, one of Rome's most important historic sites.

Longford, the county seat, is a typical small market-town community. The wide streets of the town are unusual for a rural center and give Longford a rather wide-open atmosphere. The town underwent something of a rebirth in the mid- to late-1990s through extensive development and refurbishment. Unfortunately, while the end target is to breathe life into the flagging town center, the extensive construction means that much of the area retains the look of a work site. Longford town itself need delay you no more than an hour or two. The **Longford Museum and Heritage Center** on Lower Main Street has a 4,000-year-old elk's antler, but that's hardly enough to warrant a stop, and you can easily skip it. The **Military Barracks** on Church Street is on the site of a building originally dating from 1619.

The **Corlea Trackway Exhibition Centre** (tel. 043/22386), at the center of a 20-acre site of specially preserved bog land, displays part of an Iron Age timber trackway circa 147 BC, found underneath the bog during turf-cutting activities. The history of the bog is explained through reasonably captivating audiovisual and showcase displays. You'll have to go 22 km (14 mi) southwest of Longford to visit, paying £2.50 for the privilege. It's open from June 1 to October 3, daily 9:30 to 6:30.

For a look at gracious country living in 18th-century surroundings, visit **Carriglass Manor** (tel. 043/45165, £2.50), 5 km (3 mi) northeast of Longford on the R194. The romantic, Tudor-Gothic house was built in 1837 by Thomas Lefroy. His descendants still reside here, and they are proud that as a young man in England, Lefroy was romantically involved with the novelist Jane Austen. Just why they never married is a continuing mystery, but it is believed that she based the character of Mr. Darcy, in *Pride and Prejudice*, on Mr. Lefroy. The house features some good plasterwork and many of the original mid-19th-century furnishings. For security reasons, you must book in advance to visit the house's interior. A magnificent stable yard belonging to an earlier house on the site dates from 1790. Visitors to the stable yard and gardens also have access to a small **costume museum.**

NEAR LONGFORD

GRANARD

The market town and fishing center of Granard, 18 km (11 mi) east of Longford, stands on high ground near the Longford-Cavan border. It's a town that has seen more than its share of strife through the years. In the 13th century, on being refused hospitality by the locals, Edward Bruce burned it to the ground, and during the Rebellion of 1798, a large number of insurgents were captured and executed in the town.

The **Motte of Granard** at the southwest end of town was once the site of a fortified Norman castle. In 1932 a statue of St. Patrick was erected here to mark the 15th centenary of his arrival in Ireland. (At least a dozen statues of the nation's patron saint, all virtually identical, were put up that year; see how many others you can spot on your travels.) Nowadays, however, the town is better known for its **Irish Harp Festival,** which usually takes place during the second weekend in August and attracts harpists from all over the country and the world (for information, contact the Granard Tourist Office, tel. 043/86922). For the weekend of the festival, the town becomes home to hundreds of traditional musicians and turns into what is basically one big traditional-music jam session. Accommodations are difficult to find during the festival; B&Bs tend to be booked up way in advance. You might need to try camping instead; there are two sites set up specially for the event and at night often put on their own impromptu music sessions. **Toberphelim House** (tel. 043/86568) is the best B&B in Granard. It's 2 km (1 mi) outside town, but for £22.50 you'll get a warm and comfortable room in a Georgian farmhouse on a working cattle and sheep farm, a hearty breakfast, and a taste of real Irish hospitality.

ARDAGH

Fourteen kilometers (8 mi) southeast of Longford town, Ardagh is an attractive little village, due largely to its distinctive and exceptional neatness. In 1996, and again in 1998, the village received the National Tidy Town award, a contest held throughout Ireland and designed to reward local communities for their efforts in making their towns and villages more attractive. Ardagh featured strongly in this competition throughout the 1990s, and deservedly so. The town's **Heritage Centre,** located in a century-old school-house, plays heavily on the discovery of significant archaeological remains in the immediate region, as well as the supposition that St. Patrick founded a church here in the 5th century. It's open Monday–Saturday from 9 to 6, and admission is £2; you can pass it by, however, without feeling you've missed something earth-shattering. Still, if you're passing through Ardagh on the way to Dublin, it's worthwhile stopping off just to take in the town's prettiness. If you're enticed into staying, for a good B&B try **Ardken** (tel. 043/75029), a cozy family house with rooms from £22.

CAVAN

BASICS • The **tourist office** (Farnham St., tel. 049/4331942) has all the info you need about the region.

WHERE TO SLEEP AND EAT • There's a healthy choice of B&Bs in the town. Head for **McCaul's Guesthouse** (10 Bridge St., tel. 049/4331327) for charming surroundings, airy rooms, and full meals on request (£20 per person). You'll get a good pint and, unless you arrive on a particularly slow night, some good chat from the locals at **Blessing's Bar** (Main St., tel. 049/4331138).

WORTH SEEING • Cavan is a county of contrasts. In the east, the rich pasturelands along the Westmeath border have for centuries provided the basis for a healthy agricultural base; in the west of the county, the bleak mountain areas provide little in the way of relief. Nevertheless, the county is home to more than 300 lakes, and angling is shaping up as the leading tourist attraction. In the 10th century, the county formed most of the ancient kingdom of Breifne and was ruled over by three clans, the O'Reillys, the O'Rourkes, and the O'Raghallaighs. The county was one of three Ulster counties incorporated into the Irish Free State in 1921, in the aftermath of the War of Independence, and deep ties to communities over the Northern Ireland border remain. Because of its past and its proximity to the border, the county has had a reputation as a sort of "wild frontier," though this is rapidly fading.

Cavan's reputation as something of a "wild frontier" may have originated more than 400 years ago, when, in a fit of jealousy over a man, one of the women of the O'Reilly clan began a fire that burned the town to the ground.

The main urban center of the county is **Cavan,** an undistinguished little town serving the local farming community. The town developed around an abbey, but apart from a somewhat shabby 18th-century tower, little evidence of past glory remains. There are scattered hints of history, including a 19th-century courthouse, but the most striking architectural feature of the town is the unexpectedly large cathedral, built only in the 1940s.

Cavan Crystal (tel. 049/4331800), right in town, is an up-and-coming rival to Waterford in the cut-crystal market. The company offers guided factory tours (free, Mar.–Dec., weekdays 9:30, 10:30, 11:30) and access to its factory shop. If you can't make it to Waterford, this is a good opportunity to watch skilled craftspeople at work.

The **Cavan Folk Museum** (Cornafean, tel. 049/4337248) holds what is called with pride "The Pig House Collection": costumes, kitchen and household goods, farmyard tools, machinery, and other bric-a-brac tracing the rural lifestyle from the 1700s to the present. In some quarters in the area, that way of life has changed so little that the "museum pieces" are still in use around the farms—which may be why the locals dote on this collection. Its owner-curator describes it as "a one-woman show," hence the request that you phone ahead to make sure she is home.

Travel north from Cavan for 13 km (8 mi) to **Killykeen Forest Park** (tel. 049/4332541). Organized within the beautiful mazelike network of lakes called Lough Oughter, this 600-acre park offers a series of planned and signposted walks and nature trails. The park closes in January.

KILLESHANDRA

If you're heading east from Cavan, toward Sligo, you'll pass through **Killeshandra,** a rural village (population 469) surrounded by the forests, lake, and rivers of the upper River Erne and home to a growing water-based tourism wave. After purchasing the Strand, a 1-km (½-mi) stretch on the lakeshore, the

ALL THAT GLITTERS IS NOT GOLDSMITH

Since the early 1990s, the Irish tourist board has attempted to sell the otherwise unremarkable Northern Lakelands to the burgeoning literary tourism market as the region that gave birth to Oliver Goldsmith, the 18th-century writer, poet, and essayist. He is thought to have drawn on memories of his native Longford for his most renowned poem, "The Deserted Village." But despite the number of signs directing you to Goldsmith Country, there is little of the poet to be found anywhere in the region. At Lissoy, in Longford, Goldsmith's childhood home, only the bare walls of the family house remain standing, and they are hardly worth the trip. At Pallas, in County Roscommon, his disputed birthplace, there's a statue in his memory but little else of note. Goldsmith himself left the area as a teenager and returned rarely, if at all. Despite the tourist board's efforts, it seems most visitors take their cue from the man himself and avoid the area altogether.

local community developed a ramp and pier that now serve as the base for the annual **All-Ireland Power Boat Championships,** held at the end of the first week of June. The village is overrun for the weekend by surfers, skiers, and water-sports types of every stripe and hue; it's a great time to be in the area, as long as you don't mind getting wet. For accommodations, check out **Loughbawn O'Reilly's** (Killeshandra, tel. 049/4334423), a smart restaurant, bar, and guest house all in one, which has rooms beginning at £21.

MONAGHAN

BASICS

Walk up Market Street, away from Church Square, to find the **tourist office** (tel. 047/81122). It's open Monday–Saturday 10–5, and Sunday in summer 10–2. **Bus Éireann** buses from Dublin and Belfast stop at the **Monaghan Bus Office** (tel. 047/82377) off Market Square. There are a number of ATMs located throughout the town.

WHERE TO SLEEP

Ashleigh House (37 Dublin St., tel. 047/81227) offers simple, unadorned rooms and a massive, fried breakfast for a very reasonable rate (£20). **Willow Bridge Lodge** (Silver Stream, tel. 047/81054) is a superfriendly B&B situated 3 km (2 mi) outside town in an elegantly decorated house, with lawns and great views of the countryside. For £22.50 you get a spotlessly clean, warm room and a home-cooked breakfast made with the freshest of ingredients. Also well worth considering is **Kilre House** (11 The Corran, Drumbear, tel. 047/84677), a modern family home a short distance outside town where you'll get comfortable, spotless rooms from £17.

FOOD

Supervalu (Church Sq.) shopping center is the best option if you want to pick up groceries. It's open Monday–Saturday 9–6. Many of the bars in town do quality lunches and bar food at reasonable-prices. The **Courthouse Bar** (Church Sq.) is one of the best, with real stomach-fillers for under £7. **Andy's Bar and Restaurant** (Market Sq., tel. 047/82277), a Monaghan landmark, has reasonable quality basic meals at low prices. If you have a more discerning palate, and your wallet can go the distance, head for **Mediterraneo** (58 Dublin St., tel. 047/82355), which has a wonderful atmosphere, an enticingly eclectic menu, and a young-professional clientele. Otherwise, if your belly can stand it, stick to one of the numerous chip shops.

Monaghan has more pubs than a town its size really should have, so there's no shortage of watering holes. The only thing the massive **Patrick Kavanagh's** (Church Sq., tel. 047/81950) has in common with the poet is the name; its clubby atmosphere and hip patrons are more likely to be familiar with the latest dance tracks than with topics literary. When asking for directions, don't mention its actual name, as locals know it as PK's. Tales surrounding **Jimmy's Bar** (Mill St., tel. 047/81694) are legion; a men-only establishment up to 1965, it came up for sale that year and was purchased by its regular customers, making it probably the only bar in Ireland where the drinkers became the owners overnight. It's the place to go if you're looking for quieter, more reflective company. There's also traditional music on Thursday nights, and a boozy jazz session on Sunday mornings.

WORTH SEEING

Monaghan is an attractive county town built around a central diamond. Its old market house, dating from 1792, is now the **County Museum** (Hill St., tel. 047/82928). Entry is free, and its display tracing the history of Monaghan from earliest times to the present is the winner, among other accolades, of a European Community Heritage Award. If you're not rushed, the museum's exhibits offer a pleasant way to spend an hour or two. Make sure to catch the 14th-century Cross of Clogher. Other exhibits include medieval coins and artifacts and relics of the area's past. It's open year-round, Tuesday–Saturday 11–5. Once you've seen what the museum has to offer, check out the nearby **St. Louis Heritage Centre** (Market Rd., tel. 047/83529), which is based in a building that used to be a brewery and is now a convent. The center itself traces the history of an order of locally based nuns from post-revolutionary France to the present day. It's open Monday–Friday 10–4:30 and Saturday–Sunday 2:30–4:30.

On the R189 Newbliss road just outside Monaghan, you'll find **Rossmore Forest Park,** 691 acres of low hills and small lakes with pleasant forest walks and signposted nature trails that are freely accessible. Five kilometers (3 mi) southwest of Newbliss is **Annaghmakerrig,** a small forest park with a lake, and above it Annaghmakerrig House, home of the stage director Sir Tyrone Guthrie until his death in 1971. He left it to the nation as a residential center for writers, artists, and musicians. It is not officially open to the public, but anyone with a special interest in the arts or in its previous owner can ask to be shown around.

NEAR MONAGHAN

INISKEEN

Almost directly on the border separating the southeastern part of Monaghan from Leitrim sits the tiny village of Iniskeen, a featureless spot that would be entirely forgettable were it not the birthplace of Patrick Kavanagh. At the old parish church frequented by the poet (and used as a source for some of his later writings) is the **Patrick Kavanagh Heritage Centre** (tel. 042/78580). If you don't have any interest in Kavanagh, pass right on through on the way south to Dublin, but if you've ever read more than a couple of lines by the poet, the village—which is dedicated almost entirely to his memory—is not to be missed. The center itself features exhibitions on local history with a Kavanagh slant, as well as an excellent audiovisual theater and research library. There are a dozen paintings illustrating some of Kavanagh's poetry and a mishmash of personal effects and memorabilia associated with the poet. Real fans make it a point to view his death mask, proudly displayed. If you're in the area in late November, don't miss the annual Patrick Kavanagh weekend, which attracts academics and fans from around the world and turns the normally sleepy village into something akin to a packed university campus. The Patrick Kavanagh Centre is open weekdays 11–5 and weekends noon–6.

COOTEHILL

The little town of **Cootehill** is in the heart of County Cavan. Fans of the songwriter Percy French (1854–1920) will recall the opening lines of his famous song "Come Back, Paddy Reilly, to Ballyjamesduff," which instruct the traveler in search of that little paradise to "turn to the left at the bridge of Finea, and stop when halfway to Cootehill." In fact, as locals will delight in telling you, if you follow these instructions you will not get to Ballyjamesduff at all—you'll get hopelessly lost. Cootehill is one of the most underestimated small towns in Ireland. It has a lovely setting on a wooded hillside, and its wide streets, with their intriguing old shops, are always busy without being congested. Most of its visitors are anglers from Europe and the rest of Ireland. Only pedestrians are allowed through the gates of **Bellamont Forest,** which lead, after about 2 km (1 mi) of woodlands, to one of the most exquisite hilltop Palladian vil-

THE GREAT HUNGER

In his epic poem "The Great Hunger," generally regarded as one of the masterpieces of Irish literature, poet Patrick Kavanagh summed up his native Monaghan as a place whose peasant populace remained "locked in a stable with pigs and cows forever." The intellectual and sexual paralysis reflected in the work is undoubtedly a thing of the past, but the unremitting barrenness of Kavanagh's vision is still evident in the county's unvarying landscape. Given the acerbic nature of the poem, it's rather ironic that Kavanagh-centered tourism is big business in the region; Kavanagh's bittersweet relationship with Monaghan led to self-imposed exile in Dublin. During his lifetime a lover of controversy, in death Kavanagh remains a source of conflict and debate: In 1998, 31 years after he died, a monument at his grave in memory of his widow, Katherine, was extensively damaged and anonymously replaced by an old wooden cross and stepping stones removed from the garden of his family home at Mucker, a short distance from the village in which he was reared.

las in Ireland, small but perfectly proportioned, and virtually unaltered since it was built in 1728. It is now a private home but is occasionally opened to the public. If you are interested, inquire locally or at the tourist information office in Cavan (tel. 049/31942). Walk up the main street of Cootehill to "the top of the town" (past the White Horse Hotel) and you will see the entrance to the forest.

CLONES

Situated less than 2 km (1 mi) from the border separating the Republic from Northern Ireland, **Clones** was the site of a monastery founded in early Christian times by St. Tighearnach, who died here in AD 458. An Augustinian abbey replaced the monastery in the 12th century; its ruins can still be seen near the 75-ft **round tower.** In the central diamond of the town stands a 10th-century Celtic high cross, with carved panels representing scriptural scenes (images of Adam and Eve, Daniel in the lion's den, and the sacrifice of Isaac by Abraham are among the easiest to decipher). Nowadays, the small agricultural market town is known chiefly for lace making, and a varied selection of lace is on display around the town and can be purchased at the **Clones Lace Centre** (tel. 047/51051), open Monday–Saturday 10–6. For B&B, try the **Lennard Arms Hotel** (The Diamond, tel. 047/51350), a Clones landmark popular with locals as a restaurant and bar and with anyone passing through the town as the best place to find comfortable and clean rooms, which begin at £22.

CASTLE LESLIE

If you're looking for a relaxing excursion in the area, leave Monaghan on the R185 and follow it for 11 km (7 mi) out of town to Castle Leslie (tel. 047/88109), originally a medieval stronghold, which has been the seat of the Leslie family since 1664. The castle sits on the shores of deep, beautiful **Glaslough,** which means "green lake." The present castle was built in 1870 in a mix of Gothic and Italianate styles. The Leslie family, a mildly eccentric one known for its literary and artistic leanings, has many notable relations through marriage, including the Duke of Wellington, who defeated Napoléon at Waterloo, and Sir Winston Churchill. Wellington's death mask is preserved at Castle Leslie, as is a baby dress of Churchill's, along with an impressive collection of Italian artwork. There are 14 acres of gardens with miniature golf and croquet; home-baked goods and teas are served in the tearoom and conservatory. All summer long they have historical tours of the house (£3) from 2 to 6 on the hour.

THE EASTERN LAKELANDS

The Eastern Lakelands fan out from the central point of Mullingar. The region incorporates the larger town of Tullamore as well as the ubiquitous small, solid, quiet villages and hamlets of the Midlands. With richer farmland than in the northern area of the Midlands, the eastern region tends heavily toward beef and dairy farming. Relative proximity to Dublin means that, increasingly, city-based workers are penetrating into the region, bringing a commuter culture and a new sophistication to towns in the region nearest to the capital. Which is not to say that the region has entirely given up its rural ways, but in recent years you're as likely to be delayed on a back road by a badly parked BMW as a slow-moving tractor on its way home from the dairy.

MULLINGAR

BASICS

The **tourist office** (Dublin Rd., tel. 044/48650) is nearly 2 km (1 mi) outside of town. It's open weekdays 9–5:30; June–August, Saturday 10–6. It's more convenient to head for the **Tourist Information Centre** (Market Sq., tel. 044/44044), which has much the same information available anyway. Mullingar is the main town on the Dublin–Sligo train route, and four trains depart and arrive from east and west at the **train station** (tel. 044/48274) every day. A trip to Dublin costs £8.50 one-way. Buses leave for Dublin, Sligo, Galway, and Athlone, where you can get connections to most other towns and cities in the country. You'll find a number of ATMs near the center of town. The AIB on Market Square will change money.

WHERE TO SLEEP

There is no shortage of quality places to bed down in Mullingar. Try the **Ramblers Rest B&B** (Pearse St., tel. 044/48381), a handy town-center base over a popular bar, with clean, well-kept rooms (£20). If you do check in here, though, be prepared to join in the fun downstairs—the hopping bar and club beneath the B&B is one of the most popular local nightclubs with twentysomethings, with live music or a DJ every night until late. The **Wry Mill** (Oliver Plunkett St., tel. 044/49544) is more a hostel than a B&B—there's a relaxed café and fully licensed bar and common area downstairs—but the rooms (which are small and cost a bargain-basement £17) are slightly closer to B&B standards. You can also avail yourself of the Internet access facilities here. **John Daly's B&B** (Main St., tel. 044/42724) is also above a bar (it's quiet enough so you won't really notice), the rooms are bright and cheerful, and there's a great breakfast (£19). If your budget has room, and you want to treat yourself to a little luxury, head for the **Greville Arms Hotel** (Pearse St., tel. 044/48563). In terms of B&B prices, it's expensive (rooms begin at £40) but worth it. Away from the town center, **Avondale** (Old Dublin Rd., tel. 044/48814) is an unassuming, comfortable family premises where you'll be treated well and get a comfortable room for £17. The **Farragh House Holiday Hostel** (Bunbrosna, tel. 044/71446) is 9 km (5½ mi) outside town and has basic, decent rooms from £9.

FOOD

Greville Arms (Pearse St., tel. 044/48052) is a town-center hotel with an unusual second-floor conservatory overlooking a Victorian patio garden. It is famously associated with James Joyce, who set one of his few scenes outside Dublin in the Greville's bar. Though not exactly adventurous, the menu in the dining room is better than average, relying heavily on grilled or roast beef, pork, and lamb, and the prices are excellent. Dishes prepared with local fish are also offered. If you can ignore the ersatz medieval decor and the unusually low ceilings, the **Druid's Chair** on Austin Friar Street has an imaginative and inexpensive menu. Try the excellent steak in garlic sauce (£8.75), or one of the vegetarian dishes for £5.25. There's also a Sunday lunch for less than £7, which will stave off hunger pangs until Monday at least. The **Fat Cat's Brasserie** (41 Pearse St., tel 044/49969) is a far more upmarket affair and one of the hottest restaurants in town for chic young professionals. It's a classy, intimate place with a varied and interesting menu, but make sure you call ahead; even midweek you'll battle for a seat with locals hoping for a cancelled reservation.

ALL HUMAN LIFE IS THERE

Although in terms of its population Clones is a relatively unimportant Midlands town, culturally it has had an impact far beyond its size. Among the more famous citizens of the town are Barry McGuigan, former World Featherweight Boxing Champion and one of the most popular sports figures ever to emerge in Ireland; Thomas Bracken, the man who penned New Zealand's national anthem; and, currently the area's most celebrated citizen, novelist Patrick McCabe, whose novels capture perfectly the vaguely time-locked quality of life in the town. McCabe's novel "The Butcher Boy" put Clones on the map internationally, particularly when Neil Jordan, Ireland's preeminent movie director, filmed the book in and around the town. As he was quoted saying, "If I ever want to quantify anything, I measure it against Clones. There is nothing you will ever encounter in life you haven't seen in some form in Clones."

WORTH SEEING

Mullingar is a busy commercial and cattle-trading center on the Royal Canal midway between two large, attractive lakes, Lough Owel and Lough Ennel. This is an area of rich farmland, and the town is known as Ireland's beef capital; farmers all over Ireland describe a good young cow as "beef to the ankle, like a Mullingar heifer." The buildings in Mullingar date mostly from the 19th century.

The town itself offers a limited range of sights and is probably best used as a base from which to explore the surrounding countryside. As in many other rural Irish towns, the main shopping area turns into a mini–ghost town after the shops close at 6 PM; for the next couple of hours the only people walking the streets are bemused tourists or office workers after burning the midnight oil. Of the sights in the town, be sure not to miss the large Catholic **Cathedral of Christ the King**, which was completed in 1939 in the Renaissance style. Finely carved stonework decorates the front of the cathedral, and the spacious interior has mosaics of St. Patrick and St. Anne by the Russian artist Boris Anrep. The **Mullingar Military and Historical Museum** (Columb Barracks, tel. 044/48391) is home to a display of weapons from the two world wars, boats of oak from the 1st century AD, and uniforms and other articles of the old IRA. You must call ahead to arrange to see the museum. Drop by the sparkling new **Mullingar Arts Center** (Lower Mount St., tel. 044/47777) for its program; you'll catch anything from modern dance to comedy and live music, and there's always an exhibition—usually with free admission—from local or national artists. **Belvedere House Gardens** (tel. 044/40861), 5 km (3 mi) south of Mullingar, is remarkable for a beautiful setting on the northeast shore of Lough Ennel. Terraced gardens descend in three stages to the waters of the lake and provide a panoramic view of its islands. The estate also contains a walled garden with many varieties of trees, shrubs, and flowers, and parkland landscaped in the 18th-century style. Admission is £3. **Mullingar Equestrian Centre** (Athlone Rd., tel. 044/48331) offers riding on the shores of Lough Derravaragh and lessons at all levels.

Mullingar hosts two festivals each year and makes the most of both. The **International Angling Festival,** held over three days early in May, makes use of the town's proximity to great fishing to attract hundreds of anglers, mainly from the United Kingdom. In mid-July, the Mullingar Festival, which lasts a week, takes over the town entirely, showcasing cultural, sporting, entertainment, and craft activities from the area. One of the main attractions of the week is the **Mullingar Guinness International Bachelor Festival,** which is an excuse to keep the bars open longer under the guise of a quest to find the region's "most eligible" bachelor. It's great fun, and the competition itself, which treads the line between ironic and outright ludicrous, is an absolute scream.

NEAR MULLINGAR

KILBEGGAN

Kilbeggan is known mainly for Locke's distillery, which was established in 1757 to produce a traditional Irish malt whiskey and is believed to be one of the oldest distilleries in the world. It closed down in 1954 and was reopened in 1987 by Cooley Distillery. Cooley makes its whiskey in County Louth but brings it to Kilbeggan to be matured in casks. The **Kilbeggan Distillery** (tel. 0506/32134, admission £2) has been restored by the local community as a museum of industrial archaeology illustrating the process of Irish pot-whiskey distillation and the social history of the workers' lives. Restoration of the old distillery is ongoing, and it's open Monday–Saturday, year-round.

TULLAMORE

BASICS • The **tourist office,** open only from May to October (Bury Quay, tel. 0506/52617), has a limited amount of free information on the town and surrounding areas.

WHERE TO SLEEP • For a B&B, try **Oakfield House** (Rahan Rd., tel. 0506/21385), which costs £22.50, or, if you don't mind the short walk from the town center, the purpose-built **Sea Dew Guest House** (Clonminch Rd., tel. 0506/52054), which is new and short on character. The rooms, however, are spotlessly clean and you have breakfast in a cheerful, bright conservatory from where you can look out on the well-kept grounds (£25).

FOOD • Up the road from the Bridge Street Centre mall, the **Bridge** (Bridge St., tel. 0506/21704) is a massive restaurant with a giant horseshoe-shape bar, where locals from the town and surrounding areas grab lunch, a pint, and some respite from the street bustle. There's a carvery in the bar (basic beef, lamb, and pork dishes, primarily, most under £6); head for the top right corner for a nice view of tiny River Tullamore snaking past.

WORTH SEEING • Tullamore, the county seat of Offaly, is a big country town situated on the Grand Canal. County Offaly has the Bog of Allen in the east and to the west is Boora, where turf cutters are in dispute with the Irish government's environmental department over how much turf they can take from the bog without damaging the area's ecology. Set smack in the middle of bog country, Tullamore has been designated a Heritage Town by the Irish tourist board. A couple of hours in the town and surrounding area should be enough to take in most of what is worth seeing. The town makes a handy stopover if you're on the way to Dublin or the west, which is part of the reason that it's an extremely busy place that tends to be choked with traffic during daylight. The other reason, its position on the Grand Canal, has made it traditionally one of the busiest commercial towns in the country. Offaly's agricultural and clothing manufacturing industries have centered on the town for many years (Tullamore is also the home of the whiskey liqueur Irish Mist, but unfortunately, its factory is not open to the public). In the late 18th century, a fire—said to have been caused by the explosion of a hot-air balloon—destroyed the center of the town. As a result, Tullamore is architecturally a relatively young town, with much of the buildings of interest dating from the 19th century. You'll get a good idea of the rhythms of Tullamore life if you hang around a while at the **Bridge Street Centre,** a modern shopping mall with supermarkets, music stores, clothes shops, and delicatessens. It's where the youth of the town congregate on Saturday afternoons to see and be seen.

Charleville Castle (tel. 0506/21279, admission £2.50), 2 km (1 mi) outside Tullamore on the N52, is a castellated Gothic Revival manor house set on about 30 acres of woodland walks and gardens. This magnificent building dates from 1812 and is a fine example of the work of the architect Francis Johnston, who was responsible for many of Dublin's stately Georgian buildings. Guided tours of the interior are available June–September, daily 11–5.

PORTLAOISE

The name of the county capital of Laois derives from the Gaelic for "Fort of Laois" and refers to the town's strife-filled history. Now a prosperous commercial center and administrative center of the county, Portlaoise is known nationally for its prison, which dates back to 1830. The town sits at the junction of a number of important motorways and rail lines between Dublin, Cork, and Limerick. Originally created as an outpost for the defense of settlers in the eastern part of the country against the Irish native hordes, the present town was laid out in the mid-18th century. In terms of its architecture, Portlaoise is rather eclectic—it feels as if bits of other towns were picked up and dropped randomly on the site. Stop in first at the **tourist office** (Lawlor Ave., tel. 0502/21178) and ask for the handy "Guide to Laois County," a free publication that includes all you need to know about the area (the advertisements in it are useful for tracking down B&Bs, restaurants, and bars). **Rosedene** (Limerick Rd., tel. 0502/22345) has good, standard B&B for £22.

PORTARLINGTON

Founded in 1666 by Sir Henry Bennett, Portarlington was settled by British immigrants to the area and later became a colony for Huguenots, who were active in the region until as late as 1861. Thanks in large part to this cosmopolitan background, Portarlington remains a charming old-world town. It straddles the River Barrow, which marks the border between the two neighboring counties of Laois and Offaly. Rivalries sometimes spring up from the opposing sports teams from either side of the river, but everyone agrees the most impressive sight around is **Emo Court and Gardens** (tel. 0502/26573), which lies several miles outside town. The great Palladian-style house was designed by James Gandon, who was also the architect of Dublin's famous Custom House and the Four Courts. Emo Court's domed rotunda, inspired by the Roman Pantheon, is one of the most impressive rooms in Ireland. This vast circular space is lit by a lantern in the coffered dome, which rests on gilded capitals and marble pilasters. The house has been magnificently restored and is a wonderful example of life on the grand scale. Emo's owner donated it as a gift to the Irish nation in 1995. The grounds are open daily year-round and also include formal gardens with classical statuary and rare trees and shrubs. The house is open June–September, Friday–Monday 10:30–5:30; admission by guided tour only is £2 to gardens, £2 to the house. **Coolbanagher** (1 km/½ mi south of Emo Court, no phone) is home to the exquisite Church of St. John the Evangelist, which is open daily from 9 to 6. Gandon's original 1795 plans are on view inside the building, which also has an elaborately carved 15th-century font.

ABBEYLEIX

A town developed as a planned estate in the 18th century, **Abbeyleix** (17 km/9 mi south of Portlaoise on the N8) is one of the most elegant small towns in Ireland. Fine town houses and vernacular buildings dating from the 1850s form the core of the tree-graced town, but the more recent buildings, including the **Market House,** erected in 1906, and the **Hibernian Bank,** from 1900, contribute greatly to the tranquil, refined atmosphere. If you're in the area, don't miss the atmospheric **Morrissey's Public House** (tel. 0502/31233), a combined bar and grocery shop, the exterior of which is virtually unchanged since the early 19th century. The interior is of more recent vintage but still exudes a centuries-old ambience. Built in the same era, **Norefield House** (Old Town, tel. 0502/31059) is a splendid three-story period residence offering great bed and breakfast (including a dangerously good breakfast!) for £20 per person.

EDGEWORTHSTOWN

Those with literary interests may wish to stop in **Edgeworthstown** (also known as Mostrim). This town was the home of the novelist Maria Edgeworth (1769–1849), whose highly original satirical works, the best known of which is *Castle Rackrent,* were admired by such contemporaries as Sir Walter Scott and William Wordsworth, both of whom visited here. The family residence, Edgeworthstown House, at the eastern end of the village, is now a private nursing home and not open to the public. The Edgeworth family vault, where Maria and her father, Richard Lovell Edgeworth, an author and inventor, are interred, is in the churchyard of St. John's Church.

CASTLEPOLLARD

Castlepollard is an unusually pretty village of multicolor houses laid out around a triangular green. Outside the village (1½ km/1 mi), you'll find **Tullynally Castle and Gardens** (tel. 044/61159), seat of the earls of Longford and the Irish home of the literary Pakenham family, whose members include the prison reformer and antipornography campaigner Frank Pakenham (the current earl of Longford); his wife, Elizabeth, and his daughter, Antonia Fraser, both historical biographers; and his brother Thomas, a historian. The original 18th-century building was expanded in the Gothic style in the 19th century, making it the largest castellated house in Ireland, with an elaborate facade of turrets and towers. In addition to a fine collection of portraits and furniture, the house contains many fascinating 19th-century domestic gadgets, as well as an immense kitchen. The grounds also include a landscaped park and formal gardens, which, along with the castle itself, are open May–October, daily 10–5; admission is £3.50.

FORE

Fore is a tiny village 21 km (10 mi) north of Mullingar and is the site of an important monastery founded in the early Christian era by St. Feichin. The ruins of 7th-century **Fore Abbey** are still impressive and constitute the largest Benedictine remains in the country. There are also the remains of a number of early churches, including **St. Feichin's Church,** which has a massive cross-inscribed lintel stone and is reputedly the oldest standing building in Ireland, as well as several crosses and a motte and bailey. But Fore is perhaps best known for its own "seven wonders," which alone make a trip a necessity for aficionados of Irish myth and legend. These "wonders" included water that cannot boil, wood that cannot burn, water without a source, the tree of the Trinity, water that defies gravity by flowing uphill, and a monastery standing on the sodden ground of a bog. Ask the locals about any of them and you'll find yourself on the receiving end of some serious tale-spinning.

THE SOUTHEAST

CALE SILER AND LAURENCE BELGRAVE

Y ou have heard of the Irish weather. It consists of rain. There is a lot of it. Of course, it has been known for the rain to cease, sometimes for as much as two weeks at a time. But when this happens countryfolk complain of drought, pestilence, and imminent bankruptcy. The old saying is true: Nobody ever came twice to Ireland looking for a tan. But if they did, they would head to the country's Southeast region. Here, in "the Sunny Southeast"—as the tourist bodies keenly promote it—you'll find the mildest, sunniest, and also the driest weather in Ireland, as little as 30 inches of rainfall per year, compared with an average of 80 inches on parts of the west coast. This combination of sunshine and sandy beaches makes the Southeast coast a popular vacation area with Irish families. In summer, with children out of school, the eastern stretch of the coast is especially popular with families out from Dublin, a large number of which base themselves in chalets and holiday homes along the coast for the season. This makes the entire area a great spot to watch the Irish amuse themselves and adds a welcome buzz to the often sleepy norm: Outside the summer months, many of these same coastal resorts are depopulated to the extent that you could take a stroll through the length of a town without meeting a soul.

Ask an Irishman, however, if there are any other reasons other than balmy beaches and cloud-free skies for a visitors to spend time here and he will probably shake his head. With few of the country's traditional attractions—no ruggedly romantic coastline or wild bogs or Irish-speaking communities—the region would at first glance appear to have few noteworthy assets. One of the main reasons for coming here, in fact, has always been strictly practical: Rosslare Harbour, 14 km (9 mi) south of Wexford, is one of Ireland's major ferry ports, and it's perhaps the most convenient hub for Eurail and InterRail travelers heading for the Continent or entering Ireland from Britain and France. But the Southeast is steadily growing in popularity as a vacation attraction in its own right, and with good reason.

With evidence of settlements going back some 9,000 years, the region's coastal and inland areas are studded with sites that attest to the area's fascinatingly complex history. County Tipperary is the location of the Rock of Cashel, ancient and ceremonial seat of the kings of Munster, which can be seen from miles around in all directions; in the 7th century this settlement became an important monastic center and bishopric. There were other thriving early Christian monasteries at Kilkenny, Ardmore, and Lismore. But the quiet life of early Christian Ireland was disrupted from the 9th century onward by a series of raucous Viking invasions. The Vikings liked what they found here—a pleasant climate; rich, easily cultivated land; and a series of safe, sheltered harbors—so they stayed and founded the towns of Wexford and Waterford (Waterford's name comes from the Norse Vadrefjord, Wexford's from Waesfjord). Less than two centuries after the arrival of the Vikings, the same cities were conquered by Anglo-Norman barons and turned into walled strongholds. The families of the new invaders and those of the Irish chieftains soon started to intermarry, but the process of integration halted with the Statutes of Kilkenny in 1366, for the English feared that if such intermingling continued they would lose whatever control over Ireland they had.

The next great crisis was Oliver Cromwell's infamous Irish campaign of 1650, which, in attempting to crush Catholic opposition to the English parliament, brought widespread slaughter. The ruined or extensively rebuilt condition of most of the region's early churches is a result of Cromwell's desecrations. His outrages are still a vivid part of local folk memory (partly because of the way history was for years taught in local schools, it's difficult to find someone who doesn't understand the bloodstained significance of Cromwell's edict, "To Hell or to Connaught") but not as vivid as the 1798 Rebellion, an ill-timed and unsuccessful bid for a united Ireland launched by Irish patriots and inspired by the French Revolution. The decisive "battle" took place at Vinegar Hill near Enniscorthy, where some 20,000 rebels, armed only with pikes, were cut down by British cannon fire.

All these waves of conquerors have left Wexford, Waterford, and Kilkenny—the region's main towns—rich in history and romance. Both Waterford and Wexford still pride themselves on their cosmopolitan aura; and though this can sometimes be difficult to discern, a legacy of commercial seafaring and fishing trade has undoubtedly implanted influences beyond those typically found in the towns of Ireland. All three towns have compact town centers best explored on foot—Wexford's town center is pedestrianized from 10 AM to 6 PM every business day—and all also make good touring bases. Wexford's narrow streets are built on one side of a wide estuary, and it has a delightful maritime atmosphere. It also is home to Ireland's most prestigious opera festival. The National Heritage Park, 7 km (4½ mi) outside town at Ferrycarrig, is well worth a visit and will contribute enormously to an understanding of Irish history up to the 12th century. Waterford is less immediately attractive than Wexford, but it offers a richer selection of Viking and Norman remains, some good Georgian buildings, and also the famous Waterford Glass Factory, open to visitors. Kilkenny, an important ecclesiastic and political center up to the 17th century, is now a lively market town whose streets still contain many remains from medieval times, most notably the beautiful St. Canice's Cathedral and a magnificent 12th-century castle. At the top of the list for most visitors, however, are the legendary Rock of Cashel and nearby Cahir Castle—so much so that it's often difficult to navigate through the accumulation of camera-wielding tourists.

The 1798 rebellion was a prime source of quality rebel songs; "The Rising of the Moon," "The Boys of Wexford," and "The Croppy Boy" are three favorites still belted out in local bars.

If you want to escape the tour buses, however, the Southeast can easily oblige you with its tranquil countryside, which often surprises visitors who expect all Irish scenery to be rugged and wild. There are no dramatic, looming mountains, and the nearest the area has to a broad, majestic river is the relatively tame Slaney, which flows south through Enniscorthy before reaching the sea at Wexford. Instead, the region's coastal counties of Wexford and Waterford are low lying and relatively flat, with long sandy beaches and low cliffs; inland, Counties Carlow, Kilkenny, and Tipperary consist of lush, undulating pastureland bisected by relatively peaceful river valleys. In truth, some of the most memorable attractions of the Southeast remain the natural beauty of its landscape and its small, charming fishing villages. So if you're in no particular hurry to get on to Dublin, Cork, or Limerick (all of which are reachable by direct routes from Rosslare), finding a worthwhile spot to visit or a night to remember is far from impossible in the Southeast.

KILKENNY

Dubbed "Ireland's Medieval Capital" by the tourist board, and also called "the Oasis of Ireland" for its many pubs and watering holes, Kilkenny is a 900-year-old Norman citadel 120 km (75 mi) southwest of Dublin. Prior to the 5th century, Kilkenny was a semi-prosperous market town specializing in dyes and woolens, but in the next century St. Canice (a.k.a. "the builder of churches") established a large monastic school here that attracted pupils from as far away as Athens and Istanbul. For this good deed, St. Canice was fondly remembered in the naming of the village, Kil Cainneach (Church of Canice), and his feast day (October 11)

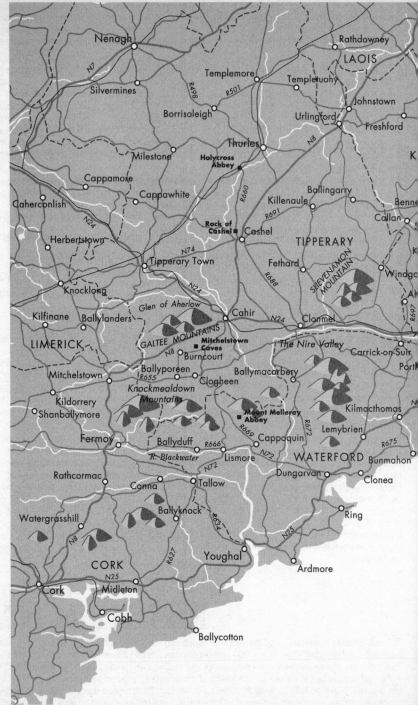

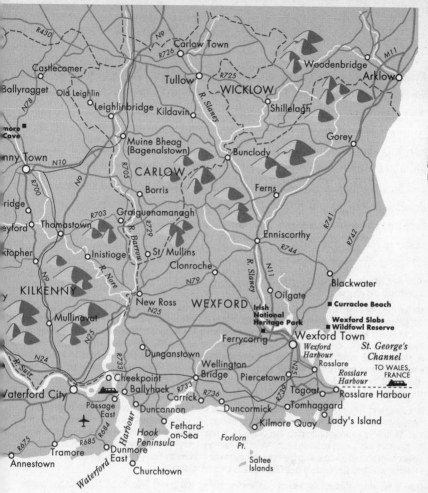

R430
Carlow Town
N9
R726
Castlecomer
Woodenbridge
Ballyragget
Old Leighlin
M11
Arklow
N78
Leighlinbridge
Tullow
WICKLOW
Kildavin
R725
Shillelagh
more
Cave
R. Slaney
Muine Bheag
(Bagenalstown)
Gorey
nny Town
N10
R705
CARLOW
Bunclody
R700
N9
Borris
Ferns
R741
ridge
R703
Graiguenamanagh
R742
eyford
Thomastown
R. Barrow
R729
Enniscorthy
ktopher
Inistioge
St. Mullins
R744
Clonroche
R. Slaney
R. Nore
N79
Blackwater
KILKENNY
N11
Oilgate
Curracloe Beach
Mullinavat
New Ross
WEXFORD
Irish
National
Heritage Park
Wexford Slobs
Wildfowl Reserve
N25
N25
Ferrycarrig
Wexford Town
N24
R. Suir
Dunganstown
Wexford
Harbour
St. George's
Channel
R731
Wellington
Bridge
Piercetown
Rosslare
TO WALES,
FRANCE
Cheekpoint
Rosslare
Harbour
Waterford City
Ballyhack
R733
Carrick
R736
Tagoat
Rosslare Harbour
Passage
East
Duncannon
Duncormick
Tomhaggard
R675
R685
R684
Fethard-
on-Sea
Kilmore Quay
Lady's Island
Tramore
Dunmore
East
Hook
Peninsula
Forlorn
Pt.
Annestown
Churchtown
Waterford Harbour
Saltee
Islands

Celtic Sea

N

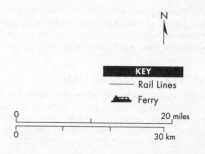

FROM STAKE TO STEAK

Kyteler's Inn (Kieran St., tel. 056/21064) is famous for having been owned by the notorious Dame Alice Kyteler—a beautiful enchantress from the Middle Ages who went through four wealthy husbands quicker than you can say "poison." Her behavior aroused suspicion in the superstitious Kilkenny farm folk, and she was charged with witchcraft and finally convicted of sacrificing animals to an evil demon she referred to as "Art." Equipped with a quick tongue and a chance to flee, Dame Alice left her poor maid Petronilla to be burned at the stake in her place in 1324. Kyteler's is now a popular pub-restaurant serving excellent bar food for under £5, as well as traditional meals and good-quality steaks in the £9–£14 range.

is celebrated with zeal—although offering £200 to new parents who name their baby after the saint, as one local politician did after the unveiling of a new statue in 1999, is probably taking it a little too far.

Credit for the city's medieval appearance goes to the anglicized Normans, who fortified the city with a castle, gates, and a brawny wall, all of which still lend to the city an air of historical significance and elegance. In recent years, the city has become something of a haven for artists and crafts workers seeking an escape from Dublin and currently has a thriving artistic community. The town's lively pub and traditional music scene explodes during one of the best and more progressive festivals in Ireland: **Kilkenny Arts Week,** a showcase for film, theater, and music performances. This weeklong event, generally held the third and fourth weeks of August, attracts large crowds and big-name national and international artists; call the Arts Council (tel. 056/63663) or the tourist office for current schedules.

During June and July, practically the only topic of conversation in the city is sports: Like its neighbor and archenemy, Wexford, Kilkenny has a long history of success in the ancient game of hurling, and as the annual All-Ireland Hurling Championship draws to its final stages, interest in the success (or otherwise) of the county's team runs to fever pitch. Although home games in the championship are relatively rare, on no account should you pass up the opportunity to see the county team and their supporters in action. Call Kilkenny County GAA Board (tel. 056/65122) for match details.

Despite a fair degree of tourist kitsch and roaring traffic, Kilkenny's links to its Middle Ages origins remain, as witnessed by Kilkenny Castle—now gorgeously restored, it remains the town's pride and joy.

BASICS

MONEY

You can change money at one of the many banks along High Street, or in the tourist office on weekends. There is a **Bank of Ireland** on Parliament Street with an ATM that accepts Visa, Plus, and Cirrus. **Allied Irish Bank** on High Street has two more. You can also cash traveler's checks and change currency at the **bureau de change** at Dore's Restaurant (65 High St., tel. 056/63374). A **Western Union** service is also available here.

VISITOR INFORMATION

In the city center, the **tourist office** offers extensive information on the city, including free maps with practical information about Kilkenny (including taxi numbers, bus and train details, parking areas, and business hours for shopping). It's just a few steps from Kilkenny Castle, on the south side of the River Nore. *Shee Alms House, Rose Inn St., tel. 056/51500. Open May–Sept., Mon.–Sat. 9–6, Sun. 11–1 and 2–5; Oct.–Apr., weekdays 10–1 and 2–5, Sat. 10–2.*

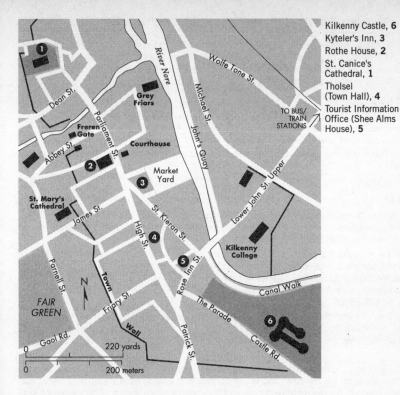

Kilkenny Castle, **6**
Kyteler's Inn, **3**
Rothe House, **2**
St. Canice's
Cathedral, **1**
Tholsel
(Town Hall), **4**
Tourist Information
Office (Shee Alms
House), **5**

COMING AND GOING

McDonagh Station (Dublin Rd., tel. 051/879000 for trains, 051/879000 for buses) serves as both bus and rail terminal and has a staffed information desk open Monday–Saturday 8:30–8, Sunday 10–noon, 3–5, and 6–8. The office is sometimes closed despite these posted times, reopening approximately 20 minutes before a train departs, so make sure you call ahead before turning up in person, just in case. From McDonagh Station, **Bus Éireann** offers four daily departures to four nearby gateway cities: Dublin (£11), Waterford (£5), Cork (£23), and Galway (£18). Kilkenny is also on **Irish Rail**'s frequently serviced Dublin (Heuston Station)–Waterford line (£10). Transfer in Kildare for all western and northwestern stops. For bike rentals, head to **J. J. Walls** (88 Maudlin St., tel. 056/21236), which offers bikes for £8 per day or, if you plan on being in the area for longer than it really takes to see everything, £50 per week.

WHERE TO SLEEP

If you're stuck for accommodations and don't want to have to search too hard, drop in to **Bedfinders** (23 Rose Inn St., just up the road from the tourist office), an accommodations reservation service that will find you a room in your price range—for a fairly modest charge. If you feel like saving a few pounds and doing it yourself head for Waterford Road (south of Patrick St.), where many of Kilkenny's bed-and-breakfasts are located. Of the B&Bs grouped here, **Beaupre House** (Waterford Rd., tel. 056/21417) and **Ashleigh** (Waterford Rd., tel. 056/22809) are among the nicest—family-run establishments with large, airy rooms (£16–£18 per person) and modern bathrooms. If these happen to be full, you'll find within a couple of hundred yards other houses offering much the same kind of rooms and service. But while it can be slightly more expensive, staying in town is a better option if you plan on hitting the bars and clubs—finding a taxi after closing time can be difficult. **J&K Dempsey B&B** (26 James St., just off High St., tel. 056/21954) has small, frilly rooms (£18 per person) and a cozy breakfast nook. Parliament Street is dotted with B&Bs, many of which are above fairly noisy bars and face onto the street, so be careful—if you mind boisterous, late-night crowds and the noise of early morning traffic, you'll probably be better off elsewhere. **Fennelly's** (13 Parliament St., tel. 056/61796) has recently changed hands, but its spacious, tidy rooms are still among the best in the city (£22 per person). The **Bailey** (10 Parliament St., tel. 056/70422) is clean, sharp, vaguely Continental, and a short walk from some of the city's best pubs for nightlife (£20 per person). Pricier, but worth it if you can afford to dish out, **Berkeley House** (5 Lower Patrick St., tel. 056/64848) is a clean and comfortable town house with en-suite bedrooms and friendly, efficient service (£27.50 per person) close to the center of town.

HOSTELS

Easily the best hostel in town, the IHH **Kilkenny Tourist Hostel** (35 Parliament St., tel. 056/63541) is threadbare, though warm and comfortable. The building has plenty of oak, high ceilings, a kitchen that opens into a courtyard, and, in summer, a bustling, cheerful atmosphere. Dormitory-style and private accommodations cost from £7 to £12. Best of all, it's in the city center and surrounded by a bunch of good pubs.

FOOD

Many of Kilkenny's best restaurants are geared toward big spenders and AmEx-carrying tourists. However, if you know where to look (*see* the Under £5 places, *below*), there's plenty of good eating to be had that won't break the bank, especially if you make lunch the main meal of the day.

UNDER £5 • One of the best places for food in the city—expensive or otherwise—is **Caislean Ui Cuain.** The lunch menu is extensive, with upwards of seven main courses most days as well as a range of sandwiches (try the Kitchen Sink Special—it's got everything you could possibly eat, and more). Best of all, the menu rarely rises above the £4.95 mark, even for the soup–main course–dessert specials. *2 High St., tel. 056/65406.*

Kyteler's Inn. This also offers a solid and inexpensive bar menu during the day in atmospheric surroundings and opens its downstairs restaurant at night. But because it appears in every tour guide going, you're likely to have to listen to tourists talking about the place as you eat. *Kieran St., tel. 056/21064.*

Lautrec's. You'll find surprisingly daring fare at this elegant wine bar and café. Other cuisines are on tap but the main highlights are vegetarian and Tex-Mex dishes, with specials often around the £5 mark during the day. Again, it's more expensive at night (but their license allows them to continue serving wine after the bars close) so make sure you check the prices in the window before you sit down. They stay open until 12:30 AM during the summer; for the rest of the year last orders are at 9:30 PM. *9 Kieran St., tel. 056/62720. Cash only. Closed Sun.*

Ristorante Rinuccini. Moody and atmospheric, this Italian spot is directly opposite Kilkenny Castle. There's a fine menu, with quick lunch specials available daily at £4.95. Make sure you get there before the menu changes for dinner, however; it's far more expensive at night. *1, The Parade, tel. 056/61575.*

UNDER £10 • **Italian Connection.** This is a decent low-priced eatery, nothing more, but a tasty meal here won't set you back an entire day's budget. Lunchtime (daily noon–3) offers the best bargains, including pastas (£5), pizzas (£6.50–£9), and grilled entrées in a spiffy, paisley-bedecked dining room. *38 Parliament St., tel. 056/64225. Cash only.*

M. L. Dore. Cluttered and homey, this little café is definitely worth a visit not just for the food but for its ambience, which is considered so quintessentially Kilkenny. After sampling the coffee (95p), warm fruit scones (55p), and tasty sandwiches (various prices), you can also explore dozens of grocers and butchers along nearby High Street, as well as the usual late-night chip shops and kebab stands. *Kieran St., at High St., tel. 056/63374. Cash only.*

Paris, Texas. Who can resist this huge bar specializing in chilies, Tex-Mex, and Cajun? There's a separate restaurant, but eating at the bar is cheaper (under £5 for many dishes)—check out the chili dish of the day. The restaurant opens at 6 PM and features everything from noodles to pasta to chili, which means nothing is high style, but you'll come away filled for under £10. *92 High St., tel. 056/61822.*

WORTH SEEING

The city center is small and, unless you decide to take the tour of Kilkenny Castle (which you should), can be covered in less than three hours if you hurry. Better to take it easy, though—remember, Kilkenny is a medieval site, and if you speed-walk, you're certain to miss something you really shouldn't. After taking in Kilkenny Castle and the **Riverfront Canal Walk,** an overgrown pathway that meanders alongside the castle grounds, mosey down High and Kieran streets. These parallel avenues, considered the historic center of Kilkenny, are connected by a series of horse-cart-wide lanes and are fronted with some of the city's best-preserved pubs and Victorian flats. Be sure to look up over the existing storefronts to catch a glimpse of how the city looked in years past, as many of the buildings still have second-floor facades dating way beyond the commercial premises below. Both streets eventually merge into Parliament Street, which stretches on down to Irishtown. Parliament Street is the commercial main street, and still houses the **Tholsel,** an important 18th-century financial center. You can check out local musical talent here for free, as the arched roof and pillars offer street buskers decent acoustics as well as shelter from the weather. During summer, **Tynan Walking Tours** (tel. 056/52066) organizes excellent guided walks of Kilkenny (£3.50). If you'd rather tour alone, pick up one of the free city guides and maps, available from the tourist office, which point out everything of interest.

KILKENNY CASTLE

A striking marriage of Gothic and Victorian styles, Kilkenny Castle was founded in 1127 and has served since 1391 as the seat of the Butler family, one of the more powerful clans in Irish history. The Butlers presented the castle and its 50-acre gardens to the people of Kilkenny in 1967. During its long history it has undergone countless renovations. The central block of the castle has received the most extensive restoration but retains a convincing air of authenticity. Most impressive is the Long Gallery, a refined, airy hall that contains a collection of family portraits and frayed tapestries. More interesting than the art is the Long Gallery's decorated ceiling, whose oak beams are carved in the manner of Celtic strapwork; the roof was designed to look like the inside of a Viking longboat. You should also see the Butler Gallery, which features exhibitions of contemporary art. You can see the interior of the castle only by taking a guided tour, and in summer it's essential to book ahead. Kilkenny

Built in 1710 on the site of the St. Francis Abbey, Smithwicks Brewery (tel. 056/51500) is a testament to the fabled brewing skills of Dominican monks; it's open for tasting (June–Sept., daily 3 PM).

Castle receives upwards of 130,000 visitors a year, and with tours limited to groups of 20, admission is strictly controlled. Tours set out on the half hour and last about 45 minutes. *The Parade, tel. 056/21450. Admission £3. Open June–Sept., daily 10–7; Oct.–May, daily 10:30–5 (Oct.–Mar., Sun. 11–5).*

ROTHE HOUSE

This typical Tudor-period, middle-class home was built in 1594 by wine merchant John Rothe. Renovations of the structure have recently been completed and the rooms have been restored to their Tudor splendor. Some of the rooms function as a makeshift County Kilkenny museum, with a motley collection of Bronze Age artifacts, smithy tools, ogham stones (ornamented with ogham, an ancient Irish system of writing, using marks cut into stone), and coal-mining gear. *Parliament St., tel. 056/22893. Admission £2. Open Apr.–Oct., Mon.–Sat. 10:30–5, Sun. 3–5; Nov.–Mar., weekends 3–5.*

ST. CANICE'S CATHEDRAL

While Kilkenny Castle pretty much defines the city, the name Kilkenny actually derives from Cill Cheannaigh—Gaelic for "the Church of Canice." Kilkenny's most famous cathedral is also the second longest (212 ft) in all Ireland. St. Canice's was founded in 1285 and later used to store volumes of the Irish Annals and other one-of-a-kind religious manuscripts. Cromwell, however, deemed the cathedral better fit for a stable and quartered his army's 500 steeds within its walls. The resulting smell was so powerful, it is said, that the troops were eventually driven to smash open the stained-glass windows. Since then, the cathedral's interior has been restored, but the complex's biggest attraction remains the 102-ft **round tower,** built in 847 by King O'Carroll of Ossory. The church walls and floor are filled with medieval tombstones, and—not for nothing is Kilkenny known as "the Marble City"—the grounds are dotted with 16th-century marble sculptures, some of which supposedly depict the Butler family. Weather permitting, admission to the tower is £1 and worth it, not only for the tremendous 360-degree view of the city you'll get from the top but also for the thrill of climbing 102 ft on makeshift wooden stairs. *Coach Rd., at northern foot of Parliament St., tel. 056/64971. Open Apr.–Oct., Mon.–Sat. 9–1 and 2–6, Sun. 2–6; Oct.–Apr., Mon.–Sat. 10–1 and 2–4, Sun. 2–4.*

AFTER DARK

If you're craving a pint, there are plenty of pubs to choose from along Parliament and High streets; several of them, including **John Cleare's Pub** (28 Parliament St.), **Widow MacGrath's** (29 Parliament St.), and **Phelans** (30 Parliament St.), also feature traditional music. Among the pubs on nearby John Street, **Langton House** (69 John St., tel. 056/65133), voted "Best Pub of the Year" for five years in a row in the mid-1990s, has four bars and a classy restaurant, and remains one of the better spots in the city. If historical pubs turn you on, try **Kyteler's Inn** (*see box, above*). For rock and traditional music sessions and a game of pool, try the hopping **Pump House** (Parliament St., tel. 056/21969), opposite the hostel. Popular **Caisleán Ui Cuain** (High St., opposite Kilkenny Castle, tel. 056/65406) and **Peig's** (John St., tel. 056/63671) also have traditional music during summer. **Syd's Bar** (25 Rose Inn St.) has won a James Joyce Award as one of the country's most authentic (i.e., not "renovated" so as to look older than it actually is) Irish pubs. The stone and wood floors date back to the 19th century, when poet Thomas Moore proposed to his mistress on the premises. If you're feeling romantically inclined, you can do the same on the flagstone that commemorates the event. The **Watergate Theatre** (Parliament St., tel. 056/61674) hosts opera, plays, concerts, comedy, and other entertainment at reasonable prices.

ROSSLARE HARBOUR

If you're coming to Ireland from England or the Continent, chances are you'll end up on a ferry bound for Rosslare Harbour, 19 km (12 mi) south of Wexford, one of Ireland's busiest ferry ports. Indeed, taking the ferry is the only reason you should find yourself in this otherwise dull little town. If you do need to stay, forget about the half dozen luxury hotels—they're probably out of most budgeteers' price range—and head instead for one of the many, many B&Bs that line the road coming off the ferry and into Wexford. Most are small, welcoming places, where you'll get a nice room in a family house for a reasonable price. Try **Old Orchard Lodge** (Kilrane, Rosslare Harbour, tel. 053/33468) or **Clifford House** (Rosslare Harbour, tel. 053/33226), both of which offer rooms from £17. If you're stuck, try the **An Óige hostel** (Goulding St., tel. 053/33399), which has beds for £6.50. Reception is open until 10:30 PM.

If you do find yourself with a couple of hours to spare in the area, it's worth checking out **Yola Farmstead Folk Park,** a restored farmhouse surrounded by beautifully thatched replica cottages, a working windmill, and a four-pew miniature church. There's also an unusual menagerie and an extensive herb garden, complete with local legends and details of curative powers. *Tagoat, Rosslare, Co. Wexford, tel. 053/ 31177. Open May–Oct., daily 10–6; Mar.–Apr. and Nov., weekdays 10–4.30.*

COMING AND GOING

The **Rosslare Harbour rail depot** (tel. 053/33162), adjacent to the ferry terminal, is serviced by frequent trains to Dublin's Connolly Station (£10) and Cork (change at Limerick Junction, £12). For most other destinations, you have to go back up through Dublin. **Bus Éireann's Rosslare Harbour depot** adjoins the rail station; look for the row of neatly parked Expressway Coaches. Buses go to Dublin (£9), Galway (£16), and Cork (£13), among other places.

BY FERRY

The two ferry companies serving Rosslare Harbour have small information kiosks in the ultramodern terminal, which also has a **tourist office** (tel. 053/33622), lockers, and a sprawling waiting room. There's also a mediocre café, where you can get cheap food and coffee. You can purchase ferry tickets at the terminal, but try to reserve a space in advance through the companies' Cork or Dublin office to avoid the frequent sellouts, particularly in summer and any time the Irish soccer team is playing in a major tournament abroad. Reservations are also a must if you're traveling by car or motorcycle because onboard parking space is at a premium. ISIC cardholders are (begrudgingly) given discounts on most ferries. The journey from France to Ireland is free for EurailPass holders.

Irish Ferries (tel. 053/33158 or 01/6610511) makes the 3¾-hour crossing to Pembroke, Wales, twice daily. Departure times vary from season to season; call ahead for schedule. Fares are £20 one-way. Irish

Ferries also makes the 22-hour journey to Cherbourg and Roscoff, France, once daily and charges £40–£80 one-way, depending on the season; call for current prices and departure times. **Stena Sealink** (tel. 053/33115 or 01/2808844) sails twice daily to Fishguard, Wales; again, call ahead for schedules. The journey takes approximately 3 hours and costs £22–£33 one way.

WEXFORD

Wexford's history goes back to prehistoric times, though you'll find scant traces of it now. Much more obvious are the Viking and Norman associations, evident in winding, narrow streets and alleys as well as in the town walls, some of which are still standing. The legacy of Oliver Cromwell, who sacked Wexford in 1649 and murdered more than 1,000 citizens, has remained as a dark folk memory for centuries and is only now beginning to fade; a new housing development at the old Cromwell's Fort is one of the ritzier developments in the town. The first (and short-lived) Irish Republic was declared in Wexford during the 1798 rebellion. Up to recently, the single most memorable facet of Wexford was the extensive wooden quay, which ran the length of the town's River Slaney waterfront and housed a fleet of tiny fishing boats owned by local fishermen. A massive, and seemingly endless, project to develop a marina on the river has not only robbed the town of the wooden works but created havoc on the quays since the mid-1990s. Once a haven of calm, where locals relaxed along the river, it's now a heaving, 2-km-long (1-mi-long) construction site, a mechanical blemish on the otherwise splendid mouth of the Slaney. Despite this, though, Wexford is a pleasant town, with a reasonably good nightlife for a rural center. If you can find a street without at least one bar on it, you're not still in Wexford.

BASICS

MONEY

Both the AIB on South Main Street and the **Bank Of Ireland** on the Quay have 24-hour ATMs that accept Visa and Cirrus. You can change money at bank branches during opening hours (Mon.–Fri. 10–5).

VISITOR INFORMATION

Wexford's **tourist office** (tel. 053/23111), open Monday–Saturday 9:30–6, is on Crescent Quay, opposite the statue of John Barry, the Wexford-born founder of the American Navy. You'll find basically everything you need here, from free touring guides and maps to recommendations for B&Bs and hotels. You can use their free service to book you into a local B&B and, for a fee, you can also book a room anywhere in Ireland. On the way back out, take a look at the sills on the windows around the corner—they're blunted and worn from the knives of sailors and fishermen who used them to sharpen their blades.

COMING AND GOING

North Station (Redmond Square, tel. 053/22522) is the bus and rail terminal for the town. Theoretically, you can call its information staff from 7 AM until the last train of the night, but, particularly during off-peak times, you may be calling a long time before someone answers. There are three daily train services to and from Dublin (£10.50 single fare) and nine buses (£7, single or day return). Private bus companies also do the Dublin trip, and if you're tight on cash, this is the way to go. Best is Ardcavan Coaches (tel. 053/22561; £5), but make sure you call to check the departure point. If at all possible, avoid Sunday-night travel to Dublin, when buses and trains are filled with students and government workers returning to the city after a weekend in the country and seats are at a premium.

WHERE TO SLEEP

Wexford town has fairly substantial B&B options, though you'll find little difference in prices throughout the town. Try **Darral House** (Spawell Rod., tel. 053/24264), a cozy, family-run establishment next to leafy Redmond Park and within minutes' walk of the town center, or **Saint George** (George St., tel. 053/43474), both of which have quiet, comfortable rooms from £18 per person. At the south end of the town, the **Faythe Guest House** (The Faythe, Swan View, tel. 053/22249), built on the grounds of a former castle, has bright and airy rooms from £17. Ask for a room at the back and you'll get a good view

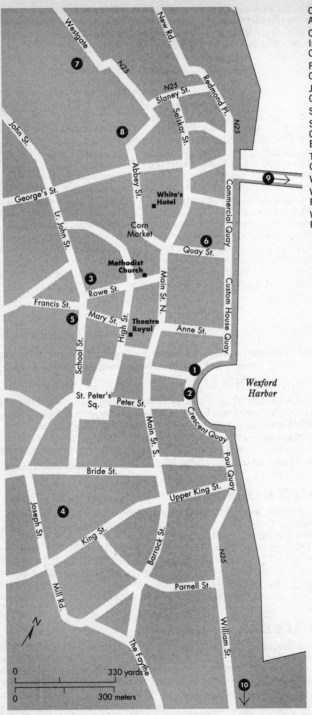

WEXFORD TOWN

Church of the Assumption, **4**

Church of the Immaculate Conception, **3**

Franciscan Church, **5**

Johnstown Castle Gardens, **10**

Selskar Abbey, **8**

Statue of Commodore John Barry, **2**

Tourist Information Office, **1**

Westgate Tower, **7**

Wexford Bull Ring, **6**

Wexford Wildfowl Reserve, **9**

Westgate

New Rd.

N25

Redmond Pl.

Slaney St.

N25

Selskar St.

John St.

George's St.

Lr. John St.

Abbey St.

White's Hotel

Corn Market

Commercial Quay

Quay St.

6

Methodist Church

Rowe St.

Francis St.

Mary St.

Main St. N.

High St.

Theatre Royal

Anne St.

Custom House Quay

1

2

Wexford Harbor

School St.

St. Peter's Sq.

Peter St.

Main St. S.

Crescent Quay

Paul Quay

Bride St.

Upper King St.

Joseph St.

4

King St.

Barrack St.

Mill Rd.

Parnell St.

N25

William St.

The Faythe

0   330 yards

0   300 meters

10

7

8

3

5

9

of Wexford Harbour. If you're on a really tight budget, **Kirwan House** (3 Mary St., tel. 053/21208), a 35-bed hostel in the center of town, has beds from £7.50 to £10.

FOOD

Wexford is filled with interesting places to eat. Main Street and the Quays are the best bets to restaurant-shop, and you'll find many options that are inexpensive as well as tasty. A converted wine bar, **Lig Do Scith** (Crescent Quay, tel. 053/22998) has a solid if unexciting menu with mid-range prices. There's an early bird à la carte menu from 6:30 to 8, which offers a three-course meal for £9.95. Two hundred yards away, **Asple's Irish Pub** (The Crescent, tel. 053/24197) is a better option if you'd like a pint with your meal. The standard bar menu won't win many awards but will fill you up for less than £6 in a bright, piazza-style atmosphere. The entrance to **Westgate Design Cafe** (Main St., tel. 053/23787) is through a store filled with expensive tourist baubles and even more expensive home accessories, but downstairs, the bright and bustling café itself has an extensive menu of soups, sandwiches, and breads at very reasonable prices. The refined **La Riva** (The Crescent, tel. 053/24330) is a classy place with an excellent French- and Mediterranean-based menu from £10 for a main course. One of the best places in town, however, is the relatively new Italian restaurant, **La Dolce Vita** (Westgate, tel. 053/23935). Lunch specials (from £7.95) are probably your best bet if money is a concern; otherwise, the excellent dinner menu, which features possibly the best food in the area, is a worthwhile splurge.

The best place for traditional Irish breakfasts is **Sidetracks** (Paul Quay, tel. 053/21666), the only spot open at 7 AM in the whole town. Truckers and construction workers from the development across the Quay make up the clientele in this no-frills greasy spoon, but you won't get a better breakfast (£3.50) anywhere. For late-night snacking, the **Premier** (South Main St.) is the best chip shop in town, by a mile. It's got unbelievably good chicken breasts and battered fish, as well as sausages and burgers and a local delicacy not found outside Wexford—the rissole, a sort of spicy bread and onion ball battered and deep-fried in oil. Terrible for your health, but a treat for your palate.

AFTER DARK

Wexford is a place of many pubs, though on any weekend night there are only a handful that everyone under the age of 35 seems to gravitate toward. Chief among these is the dark and cavernous **Centenary Stores** (Charlotte St., tel. 053/24424), for years one of the most popular places in town. Noisy and smoky, the Stores, as everyone calls it, is packed to bursting almost every night, so arrive early if you don't want to be refused entry. There's a late-night dance club on weekends, traditional music on Sunday mornings, and a blues session every Monday. Around the corner, **Mooney's** (The Quay, tel. 053/24483) is one of the town's more raucous pubs, particularly on weekends, when young twentysomethings clamor to see and be seen and, for many, compete to get seriously drunk. Live music (rock covers, mainly), flashing lights, and jostling crowds are part of the attraction, so if it's a quiet pint you're after, go elsewhere. Similarly, seekers of solitude had better avoid **O'Faolains** (Monck St., tel. 053/23877), which is, if anything, even more crowded and raucous than Mooney's. If the **Thomas Moore Tavern** (Cornmarket, tel. 053/24348), is busy, you won't get your foot in the door; on other nights, it's quiet enough to hear a pint of Guinness settle. It's worth a visit, though, if only for a chance to check out the arty crowd (the Wexford Arts Centre is just up the hill) and hear the impromptu traditional sessions that occasionally pop up unannounced. At the other end of town, one of Wexford's newest bars, the **Sky & the Ground** (112 South Main St., tel. 053/21273), has music most nights, a young, vibrant clientele, and a ground floor of nooks and crannies to hide in, if you feel like losing yourself.

WORTH SEEING

Wexford is a small town, and you can quite comfortably take in all the historic sights in an afternoon. The thing that will strike you most immediately about the place is the width of Main Street. Barely 30 ft, it obviously evolved in a pre-car era; now the street is pedestrianized and offers a great opportunity for observing locals while strolling its length. As you do, watch out for the even narrower lanes that open off the Main Street and offer access to the Quays. The recently redesigned **Bull Ring** features an imposing 1798 monument (as well as **Macken's Pub,** a local landmark and a place it seems you almost never have to leave—as well as serving spirits, the premises famously includes a grocery store and an undertaking business). The Bull Ring takes its name from the bull baiting that was once held here, though now it's more a hangout for local youth.

SMALL TOWN, BIG OPERA

Held in October, the 18-day annual Wexford Opera Festival is the biggest social and artistic event not just in the town but in the entire southeast of the country. From mid-September until the final curtain comes down, Wexford becomes home to a colorful international cast of singers, designers, and musicians as the town prepares for the annual staging of three obscure grand opera productions at the tiny Theatre Royal (High St., tel. 053/22400). The festival has a huge international cachet, and the actual productions are expensive, full-dress affairs. Current prices are £50 per ticket, but the extensive fringe events are far less pricey, and often far more fun. Best thing about the festival for non–opera buffs, though, is the atmosphere in the air: Art exhibitions, street music, parades, and window dressing competitions are held every year, and local bars compete in a Singing Pubs competition, which means that there's almost as much music and song in the hostelries as on the stage. Most bars have extended hours throughout the festival too. Now the bad news: Nearly every single bed within a large radius of Wexford is booked up during the festival weeks, usually for months before the actual event kicks off. So be warned—book well ahead of arrival.

WESTGATE HERITAGE CENTRE

The well-preserved **Westgate,** now the home of Westgate Heritage Centre, is the only section of the town's original Norman wall still in one piece. An audiovisual presentation at the wall's tower presents an excellent overview of the town's history. *Off Spawell Rd, tel. 053/46506. Admission £1.50. Open weekdays 10–4, weekends 11–4. Audiovisual show presented every ½ hr.*

SELSKAR ABBEY

There's just about enough left of **Selskar Abbey,** conveniently close to the Westgate Heritage Centre, to allow you to imagine what must have been a splendid medieval structure. King Henry II visited here to do penance for the murder in 1170 of Thomas à Becket. You'll get a great view of the town from the top of the tower, and the site also features a spooky old graveyard, which is worth a quick walk-through. *Not formally open, but keys are available for the abbey gates by knocking at the door of 9 Selskar St. during daylight hrs only.*

THE FRIARY

You should also drop in to the Friary church, home to the town's community of Franciscan monks since the 13th century. There's a mural that gives background on the town's Cromwellian history and a weird, centuries-old monument to a boy martyr murdered by his Roman father. The Friary is open from morning services at 8 AM to approximately 8 in the evening. As it is a working church, visits should be limited to nonservice times. *School St.*

Other addresses worth noting as you wander the town's narrow, winding streets are Oliver Cromwell's temporary residence at 29 South Main Street and, on King Street, the birthplace of William Cody, father of the famous American showman "Buffalo" Bill Cody.

NORTH OF WEXFORD TOWN

IRISH NATIONAL HERITAGE PARK

The Irish National Heritage Park at Ferrycarrig is a sort of outdoor museum, with reconstructions of monuments, houses, fortifications, and tombs from different eras throughout Irish history. It's all completely fake, of course, but it does give a wonderful taste of times past, from the Megalithic period up to the late 19th century. If you've always wondered what it might have been like to live in a hut made entirely from mud, sticks, and manure, this is obviously the place for you. Set in stunning surroundings—don't forget to visit the Norman castle across the Ferrycarrig bridge—the park also features woodlands, a heritage trail, and a 90-minute guided tour (not formally organized; call ahead to arrange). *Irish National Heritage Park, Ferrycarrig, tel. 053/20733. Open daily 10 AM–6 PM (last admission 5 PM, Mar. 17–Oct. 30).*

WEXFORD WILDFOWL RESERVE

Colloquially known by the charming title the Slob, this natural preserve was originally developed in the mid-19th century when more than 1,000 acres of mudflats were reclaimed from the sea. The Slob—incidentally, the name probably derives from the old Irish word *slab,* meaning muddy or wet lands (or, indeed, a slimy individual, whence our use of the word comes)—3 km (2 mi) outside of Wexford town on the Castlebridge Road, now forms a world-renowned reserve, with more than 190 species of bird visiting the area regularly, including almost half the world's population of Greenland white-fronted geese. The Slob offers bird-watchers the opportunity to see these, and other large fowl, in the wild. Bring your binoculars and some heavy clothing—it's damp and wet, and there's no way to avoid the weather when it turns nasty. *Wexford Wildfowl Reserve, North Slobs, Wexford, tel. 053/23129. Admission free. Open Apr.–Sept., daily 9–6; Oct.–Apr., daily 9–5.*

CURRACLOE BEACH

A couple of miles north of the Slob is the wild and wonderful Curracloe Beach, one of the most unspoiled and popular bathing beaches in the entire Southeast. Miles and miles of white sand backs up onto deep green grasses and forest: No wonder Stephen Spielberg chose it to stand in for Normandy in *Saving Private Ryan.* Locals worried about the effects of the film on the surrounding areas and objected to their much-loved amenity being taken over by Hollywood, but the beach survived and remains a fabulous place to escape to. Bring a picnic if you're going—the only shop in the immediate area is devoted to video games and candy floss.

ENNISCORTHY

Twenty five kilometers (13 mi) north of Wexford on the main Dublin road, Enniscorthy is the kind of town you forget about as soon as you've traveled a couple of miles beyond it. Despite a commercial overhaul in recent years, it remains relatively run-down and retains all the signs of its status as a county's secondary town. The **Castle Museum** (Castle St., tel. 054/35926) is dreary, dark, and oppressive, and the Gothic **St. Aidan's Cathedral,** designed by Pugin, is—sad to say, as he was designer of London's Houses of Parliament and is one of the greatest Victorian-era architects—tiny and singularly unimpressive. Enniscorthy does have one thing going for it, however—the absolutely astonishing, utterly unmissable **National 1798 Visitor Centre.** This brand-new, state-of-the art multimedia interpretive center tells the story of the 1798 Rebellion from a range of perspectives and is so well done it seems almost out of place in otherwise dreary Enniscorthy. The only reason to skip it is if you're even mildly depressed—the graphic representation of the Battle of Vinegar Hill, the last stand of the 1798 rebels, will leave you either in tears or ready to start another revolution. Walking back to the somber streets of Enniscorthy is quite a comedown after it. *National 1798 Visitor Centre, CBS Monastery, Enniscorthy, Co. Wexford, tel. 054/37198. Admission £4. Open daily 10–5.*

SOUTH OF WEXFORD TOWN

SOUTH COUNTY WEXFORD

This is the area in which the Normans first gained a foothold in Ireland as well as where the Baronies of Forth and Bargy were the last to shake off the remaining vestiges of Norman culture and language. All that survives of the medieval era now is an impressive range of castles and churches. Among the most impressive is **Tintern Abbey,** named after its more famous counterpart in Wales. Built at the beginning of the 13th century, the abbey sits, surrounded by rivers, hills, and woods, on what must be the most tranquil spot in the county. The remains consist of nave, chancel, tower, chapel, and the cloister; now a national monument, it has undergone extensive restoration in recent years and also marks the base for a series of hiking trails through the immediate area. *Tintern Abbey, Saltmills, Co. Wexford, tel. 053/ 562650. Admission £1.50. Open June–Sept., daily 9:30–6:30.*

BALLYHACK CASTLE

This large and mightily impressive five-story tower house is believed to have been built in the mid-15th century by the Knights Hospitallers of St. John, one of the two great military orders founded at the time of the Crusades. The castle is now the centerpiece of a small coastal village. *Tel. 051/389468. Admission £1. Open June–Sept., weekdays 10–1 and 2–6, weekends 10–6.*

KILMORE QUAY

If you're looking for those icons of rural Ireland, thatched cottages, you'd be hard-pressed to find them in a greater concentration than in Kilmore Quay, 26 km (12 mi) southwest of Rosslare Harbour. This part of the county was long known for the quality of its thatching and clustered in the center of this charming little fishing village are a good dozen or so examples of thatching at its best; most of the houses are private, however, so you won't get an up-close look unless you knock on a door and ask, and since a good number of them are holiday homes owned by nonresidents, you'd be lucky to catch them at home. Still, you can soak up the atmosphere just walking by. Also at Kilmore is the unfortunately dilapidated **Maritime Museum** (tel. 053/29655), open June–September, daily noon—6; admission is £2. Previously docked quayside in Wexford, the rusting ex-lightship that houses the museum was dry-docked at Kilmore in the early 1990s. Despite an uninspiring selection of artifacts, the chance to check out the salty old innards is alone worth the price of admission.

WATERFORD

The name Waterford brings to mind the dazzling cut glass that has carried this city's name to the banquet halls of the world. Today, the crystal factory (*see box, below*), along with its handful of historic sights and its traditional pubs, remains the main attraction. Built on the banks of the grimly industrialized River Suir, Waterford claims to be the oldest city in Ireland. It was founded between 856 and 914 by Viking raiders who fortified the town against competing waves of Flemish, Gaelic, and French intruders: On Manor Street, near the intersection of John and Parnell streets, are three towers and a crumbling section of the wall that once surrounded the town. The most striking example of Waterford's Viking legacy is **Reginald's Tower** (The Mall, tel. 051/873501), an impressive circular battlement with 12-ft-thick walls built in 1003 by Reginald the Dane. The oldest civic structure in Ireland, it was here that Strongbow, head of the Anglo-Norman force that took Waterford in 1170, met Aoife, daughter of the King of Leinster. Their marriage forged a family tie between Irish and French rulers, and altered the course of Irish history. You won't find much in the way of romance here now, but the Tower played a key role in the development not just of the southeast region, but of the entire country. Three centuries after Strongbow's strategic marriage, the Irish Parliament established a mint here, and in subsequent centuries it was used variously as a prison, an arms store, and a private residence.

Around the corner from Reginald's Tower, the **Heritage Centre** (Greyfriars St., tel. 051/871227) is a one-room museum displaying Viking and medieval artifacts unearthed during excavation of the city center. The collection includes leather work, brooches, and other doodads, such as pewter pilgrim badges worn by medieval folk as proof of their shrine-hopping. Admission to the tower and center costs £1.50, and both are open weekdays 8:30–8:30, weekends 10–5.

Right behind the tower is the city's other medieval treasure, the **French Church.** Also known as Greyfriars, from the gray habits worn by the Franciscan friars based here, this ecclesiastical center was built in 1240 and features heavily in the history of the city. It was used by French Huguenots as a place of refuge and devotion from the 17th to the 19th century, hence the name.

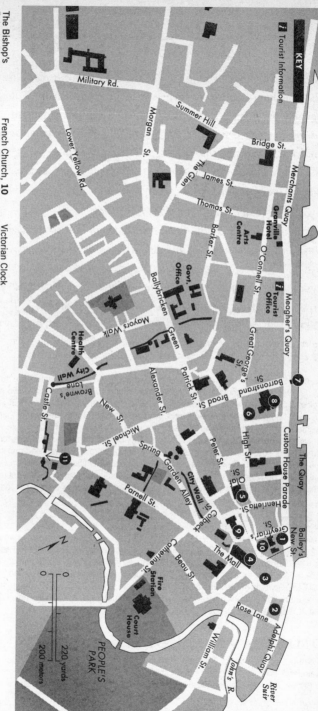

KEY

i Tourist Information

The Bishop's
Palace, **4**
Blackfriars
Abbey, **6**
Christ Church
Cathedral, **9**
City Hall, **3**

French Church, **10**
Holy Trinity
Cathedral, **8**
Reginald's
Tower, **2**
St. Olaf's
Church, **5**

Victorian Clock
Tower, **7**
Waterford Glass
Factory, **11**
Waterford Heritage
Centre, **1**

Military Rd.

Summer Hill

Bridge St.

Morgan St.

The Glen

James St.

Thomas St.

Lower Yellow Rd.

Barker St.

Merchants Quay

Granville Hotel

Arts Centre

O'Connell St.

Meagher's Quay

Tourist Office

Govt. Office

Ballybricken Green

Mayor's Walk

Great George's St.

Health Centre

City Wall

Browne's Lane

Barronstrand

Custom House Parade

The Quay

Castle St.

New St.

Alexander St.

Patrick St.

Broad St.

Michael St.

Spring Garden Alley

City Wall

Peter St.

High St.

St.

Henrietta St.

Greyfriar's St.

Bailey's New St.

Parnell St.

Colbeck St.

Catherine St.

Beau St.

The Mall

Rose Lane

Adelphi Quay

River Suir

Fire Station

Court House

PEOPLE'S PARK

William St.

John's R.

0   0
220 yards
200 meters

ROLLS-ROYCE
OF CRYSTAL

Silica sand + potash + litharge = Waterford crystal: It reads like cold science, but something magical happens when the craftsmen of Waterford produce arguably the finest crystal on the planet. When the Waterford Glass Factory opened in 1783, it provided English royalty with a regular supply of ornate handcrafted flatware, chandeliers, and decorative knickknacks. Over the years, its clientele has diversified along with its product line, and today the United States is the biggest market for its crystal.

If you're in Waterford, a tour of the nearby factory is a must, even if you can't afford the expensive crystal. From April through October, guided tours (£2.50), which include glassblowing and glass-carving demonstrations, are given daily 8:30–4. The rest of the year, tours operate weekdays 9–3:15. The adjacent crystal gallery is open April–October, daily 8:30–6, November–March, weekdays 9–5; bargains are sometimes available in the adjoining gift store. Both are 1½ km (1 mi) west of Waterford on the N25/Cork Road, an easy walk or hitch from the city center. For information call 051/873311.

These days Waterford is a tourist-oriented city, and shopping opportunities are so abundant that the entire downtown area seems to have sprung up around the development of two malls. The principal shopping district stretches from the River Suir and Barronstrand Street to Broad and Michael streets, where you'll find the bustling **Broad Street Shopping Centre.** But the real action happens a block west, at the intersection of Barronstrand and George streets, where droves of fashionable Waterford youth chill out between forays to the very modern and chic **City Centre** shopping mall. Waterford's student population (mostly from the Waterford Institute of Technology) ensures good weekend pub crowds and gives the town a youthful feel. If you want a sense of Waterford's other life, continue down George Street toward O'Connell and Bridge streets. This undeveloped and seemingly forgotten quarter of town is dominated by gray buildings and crumbling Georgian-era warehouses, evocative of Waterford's industrial past.

BASICS

The **tourist office** (41 The Quay, tel. 051/875788) stocks Irish-interest books and tourist information (ask for *Waterford, A Touring Guide,* which costs £2; others are complimentary) and has a competitive bureau de change. Considering Waterford's relatively limited choice of accommodations, you may want to book a B&B here for a service fee of £1. The office is open weekdays 9–6 and Saturday 9–1 and 2–5. **USIT** (37 Georges St., tel. 051/872601), open weekdays 9:30–5:30 and Saturday 11–4, also has lots of travel info and can book ferry and plane tickets. Mountain bikes (£10 per day, £45 per week) can be rented at **Wright's Cycle Depot** (Henrietta St., off The Quay, tel. 051/74411).

COMING AND GOING

The joint bus and rail depot, **Plunkett Station** (Dock Rd., tel. 051/879000 for bus info or 051/873401 for train info), is on the River Suir's north shore, west of the city center. Turn left out of the station, cross Rice Bridge, and head left on the riverfront quay for the tourist office and Barronstrand Street shops.

Inside the station are an info desk, open Monday–Saturday 9–6, and a left-luggage desk (£1) open slightly longer hours. Trains run to Rosslare Harbour (2 per day; £6), Cork (1 per day; £10), and Dublin's Heuston Station (3–4 per day; £12). If you're heading to Cork, take the bus. It's cheaper (£8), more frequent (eight daily), and won't backtrack like the train, which heads first to Kilkenny and then on to Cork. There are also buses or connections to most other towns and cities, including Rosslare (3 per day; £8.80) and Dublin (7 per day; £6).

WHERE TO SLEEP

Waterford is a city where much of the nonhotel accommodation has been converted into student flats and apartments, so quality B&Bs are relatively hard to find. Ask to see your room before booking into one of the many dingy B&Bs in downtown Waterford, to avoid an unpleasant surprise. Some exceptions are **Beechwood** (7 Cathedral Sq., off Greyfriars, tel. 051/876677), which is located on a residential street near Christ Church Cathedral and has lovely rooms for £18 per person, and the elegant 19th-century residence, **Derrynane House** (19 The Mall, tel. 051/875179), which has simple, spacious rooms for £15–£18 per person. There are better B&Bs outside the city, on the Cork Road, so if you're fussy about where you lay your head, the extra 2-km (1-mi) or so trek will be worth it. Try **Saint Albans Guesthouse** (Cork Rd., tel. 051/358171), which has ample, comfortable rooms in a family-run house from £20 per person. Also good value is **Roncalli Guest House** (Ballynaneeshagh, Cork Rd., tel. 051/375632), a no-smoking establishment with clean, airy rooms (£18 per person) and a bright garden for visitors' use. If it's full, try nearby **St. Anthony's** (Ballinaneeshagh, Cork Rd., tel. 051/375887), another solid family-run B&B, with comfortable rooms from £18 per person.

HOSTELS

There are only two hostels in the city worth considering. If these are full, find someplace else to stay— the other hostel in Waterford is best avoided if at all possible.

IHH Viking House Holiday Hostel. This new, friendly hostel is smack in the center of town and has dorm beds in bright, clean rooms from £8, breakfast and sheets included. There's also a beautiful 15th-century stone fireplace in the large and relaxed common room. *Coffee House La., off Greyfriars St., tel. 051/853827, fax 051/871730). From Plunkett Station, cross the river, walk left along the riverfront, turn right on Henrietta St., and make a quick left. Kitchen, laundry.*

Waterford Hostel. Smaller and a pound cheaper, the friendly and unpretentious Waterford Hostel serves a Continental breakfast and has free city maps showing which of Waterford's many pubs are having traditional music sessions scheduled for any given night. At the height of the summer season, *definitely* make a point of reserving a bed because rooms fill up quickly. *70 Manor St., tel. 051/850163. Kitchen, laundry.*

FOOD

Expensive restaurants line Waterford's main shopping avenue, but finding someplace with a reasonably priced menu is not difficult. Fast-food joints litter the main shopping area, so you'll never be stuck if you need a fix of burgers and fries, but there are far more worthwhile ways of spending your lunch money. **Haricots** (11 O'Connell St., at western foot of Georges St., tel. 051/841299) is a small, intimate whole-food restaurant with an extensive menu, including vegetarian, most of which is under £6. It's closed after 8 PM, so get there early. You should also consider the informal ambience of **Chapman's Pantry** (61 The Quay, tel. 051/873833), where delicious homemade soups, breads, and sandwiches for under £3 and full meals for slightly more make it a popular choice for locals, and particularly with office workers at lunchtime. Waterford's most popular Chinese restaurant is the **Happy Garden** (53 High St., tel. 051/55640), noted for its prawns and beef chop suey and prized for its late hours (daily until 12:30 AM, Friday–Saturday until 1 AM—you'll be surprised how busy it gets late at night, particularly after the bars close, so if you want to avoid a long wait, get there before 11:30). Prices go up 50% if you sit down, so you may want to order your food to go. You can also pick up a filling meal for under £7 at the more trendy **Cafe Luna** (53 John St., tel. 051/843539).

You'll find decent pub grub in many of the city's bars. Two of the better such spots are the **City Arms** (Arundel Sq., tel. 051/872220) and **Lords of Waterford** (6 Arundel La., tel. 051/875041). They're both busy around midday most days, so you should also remember **Egan's** (Barron Strand St., tel. 051/

875619) and **Muldoon's** (John St., tel. 051/873693), both of which feature a variety of cheap main courses.

AFTER DARK

The weekly *Waterford News & Star* (£1) and *Waterford Today* (free) both provide exhaustive accounts of the goings-on in the city. Waterford's large student population gravitates to the most city-center pubs, especially the ones on John Street, which are packed to capacity seven nights a week. The undeniable favorite is the **Pulpit** (10 John St., tel. 051/879184), a dark, old-style place endowed with a wooden pulpit and a handful of semiprivate snugs. After 10:30, **Preacher's** nightclub opens upstairs, playing mostly modern indie rock and disco from the 1970s. It's extremely popular with students and Waterford's trendy young things. Next door is a Waterford drinking landmark, **Geoff's** (9 John St., tel. 051/874787), another cavernous pub furnished with large oak tables and antique billboards that attracts a wide mix, from after-work tipplers to the seriously fashion-conscious. **Club LA** (Manor St., tel. 051/857474) is an insufferably trendy student nightclub above the **Junction,** a similarly annoying bar, but there are regular drinks specials and promotions, and the music is a good mix of dance and rock. For tunes, check out **Old Ground** (The Glen, tel. 051/852283), which features traditional music every Friday night with no cover charge, or **Fitzgeralds** (High St., tel. 051/875612) for disco and hip-hop.

If your idea of a good time runs more to poetry readings and lectures, head to **Garter Lane Arts Centre** (22A O'Connell St., tel. 051/77153), which coordinates daytime photography and art exhibits with evening entertainment. If you're in town at the right time, try not to miss any performances by Red Kettle Theatre Company, widely recognized as one of Ireland's best companies outside Dublin. **Theatre Royal** (City Hall, The Mall, tel. 051/74402), Waterford's public theater, stages everything from modern Irish and international drama to musicals and opera during its May–September season. Ticket prices vary and student discounts are often available. On the first weekend of August, Waterford hosts the **Spraoi Festival,** billed as the largest "rhythm festival" (lots of percussion and African music) in the country; call the tourist office for details.

CASHEL

Cashel owes its fame to the surrounding **Rock of Cashel,** a ragged outcrop of limestone that, over the centuries, has been endowed with churches, towers, and stone crosses by a successive stream of religious orders. The "Rock," as it's known, stands like an ominous beacon in the middle of a sloped, treeless valley, as if it had been upthrust by some subterranean violence. Set atop the limestone is an entirely restored Romanesque church, a complete round tower, the 15th-century Hall of Vicars, a handful of carved stone crosses, and a buttressed medieval cathedral—all in all, a stunningly comprehensive collection of Irish religious architecture. It's also one of the tourist board's prized gems and the favorite of Dublin-bound tourist coaches. The Rock (admission £2.50) is open mid-June–mid-September, daily 9–7:30, mid-March–mid-June, daily 9:30–5:30; the rest of the year it closes at 4:30. Crowds are at their worst after noon, so try to arrive as early as possible. Unfortunately, renovation of the cathedral walls is under way indefinitely, and the scaffolding definitely detracts from the scenic beauty of the Rock. An audiovisual presentation is shown every half hour. Guided tours run less frequently but are wheelchair accessible. For more info, stop by the **tourist office** in the Cashel Heritage Center (Town Hall, Main St., tel. 062/61333).

Unless you're arriving by road, the easiest way to get to Cashel is from Dublin or Cork. **Bus Éireann** has four departures per day from Cork (£8) and four services from Dublin (£9) and Clonmel (£4.80). It's also possible to reach Cashel from Waterford or Kilkenny, but the trip involves about three hours and three transfers. Bus tickets and schedules can be purchased at **Rafferty's Travel** (102 Main St., tel. 062/62121). The closest train station is 19 km (12 mi) away, in Cahir, which can be reached on any of three daily buses (£2.50).

WHERE TO SLEEP AND EAT

There really isn't much to warrant an overnight in Cashel—unless, of course you want to catch the Rock before the tourist buses begin to pile up in the morning. If you do want to stay, finding a place to sleep isn't difficult; Cashel has evolved as an entirely tourist-oriented town, and B&Bs line every approach road and town street. There are also a number of good hostels. The excellent **Cashel Holiday Hostel** (John St., 2 blocks from tourist office, tel. 062/62330) has dorm beds from £7.50, doubles from £16, and amenities like a blazing fire nightly in the common room, an impressively equipped kitchen, and 7-ft-long beds for tall hostelers.

Equally good value is **O'Brien's Farmhouse Hostel** (St. Patrick's Rock, Dundrum Rd., tel. 062/61003), which would be worth checking into for the view of the Rock alone. Dorm beds are from £7, but the pine floors and comfortable conditions will make you feel like you've paid a lot more.

One of the best B&Bs in town is **Maryville** (17 Bankplace, tel. 062/61098), a prim guest house with tremendous views of the Rock. It has eight meticulously cleaned and decorated rooms from £18. Even better views can be had around the corner at **Rockville House** (Rock Pl., tel. 062/61760), where rooms start at £16 and include breakfast in a super-posh dining room. **Bailey's of Cashel** (Main St., tel. 062/61937) is an early 18th-century Georgian town house beautifully restored by its current owners. One of the classiest B&Bs in the entire area, it also has an excellent, though expensive, restaurant. Rooms start at £22.50.

It was at Cashel that St. Patrick preached the doctrine of the Trinity, using a handy shamrock as an example.

Some of the better places to get cheap eats in Cashel are at **O'Dowds** (103 Main St., tel. 062/62650), the **Royal Oak** (49 Main St., tel. 062/61441), and the **Bakehouse Coffeeshop** (Main St., tel. 062/61680), all of which serve sandwiches and soup for less than £5.

THE SOUTHWEST

CALE SILER AND ANTO HOWARD

A varied coastline, spectacular scenery (especially around the famous lakes of Killarney), and a mild climate have long attracted visitors to this romantic region; the place has become so popular in the last decade that some locals whisper of being a little overwhelmed by the well-intentioned invasion. But the area's most notable attractions are rural and still very much intact: miles and miles of country lanes meandering through rich but sparsely populated farmland. Even in the two main cities the pace of life remains perceptibly slower than in Dublin. To be in a hurry in this region is to verge on demonstrating bad manners. It was probably a Kerryman who first remarked that when God made time, he made plenty of it.

Cork, Kerry, and Limerick are the three counties that make up the Southwest, and as you look over thick fuchsia hedges at thriving dairy farms, or stop off at a wayside restaurant to sample the region's seafood and locally raised meat, it is hard to imagine that some 150 years ago this area was decimated by famine. Thousands perished in the fields and the workhouses, and thousands more took "coffin ships" from Cobh in Cork Harbour to the New World. Many small villages in the Southwest were wiped clean off the map. The region was battered again in the civil war that was fought with intensity in and around "Rebel Cork" between 1919 and 1921, and it was in his home county of Cork that the "Big Fella," Michael Collins, was assassinated by a rebel bullet. Economic recovery only began in the late 1960s, which led to a boom in hotel construction and renovation—not always, alas, in the style most appropriate to the area's aesthetic. The 1990s "Celtic Tiger" has increased prosperity and unleashed on the area even more Dubliners in search of holiday homes.

Outside of crazy Killarney (oh, and it is crazy, an emerald green Orlando), tourist development remains fairly low-key. The area is trying to absorb more visitors without losing too much of what attracts them in the first place: uncrowded roads, unpolluted beaches and rivers, easy access to golf and fishing, and unspoiled scenery where wildflowers, untamed animals, and rare birds (which have all but disappeared in more industrialized European countries) still thrive. The jury is still out on their success.

The city of Cork and its environs dominates the eastern portion of the Southwest. In the last few years, with high prices and overcrowding in Dublin, Cork has become the new hot spot for urban thrills. Groups of Europeans pop over for a weekend of partying, and the city makes a great base from which to explore the whole of the south.

The southwest coast of the region is formed by three peninsulas: the Beara, the Iveragh, and the Dingle; the road known as the Ring of Kerry makes a complete circuit of the Iveragh Peninsula. Killarney's sparkling blue lakes and magnificent sandstone mountains, inland from the peninsulas, have a unique wild splendor, though in July and August the area is packed with and tamed by visitors. Around the Shannon estuary you move into "castle country," littered with ruined castles and abbeys as a result of Elizabeth I's attempt to subdue the old Irish province of Munster in the 16th century. Limerick City, too, bears the scars of history from a different confrontation with the English, the Siege of Limerick, which took place in 1691.

As in the rest of Ireland, social life centers on the pub, and a visit to your local is the best way to find out what's going on. Local residents have not lost their natural curiosity about "strangers," as visitors are called. You will frequently be asked, "Are you enjoying your holiday?" "Yes" is not a good enough answer: What they're really after is your life story, and if you haven't got a good one you might want to make it up.

Tourism reaches a frenzied crescendo, which borders on the ugly, in Killarney, a largish market town and the best base for exploring the adjacent Ring of Kerry. Cape Clear, an island just south of Mizen Head, is another area famed for its rural wonders—a terrain of sea cliffs, thatched cottages, and rolling farmland. North of Killarney, Tralee makes a good base for extended trips into the picturesque Dingle Peninsula, though recent development has "Killarnized" the town to an extent. Although Dingle Town itself is becoming a popular stop on the tour-bus circuit, the peninsula's thinly populated Slea Head and Blasket Islands are everything Ireland is meant to be—harsh, rugged, and spectacularly scenic.

Between 1846 and 1849 the population of Ireland fell by an estimated 2.5 million and has not recovered to this day.

CORK CITY

Dublin is home to more than half of Ireland's 3.5 million people. So when you hear Cork is Ireland's second-largest city, with a population of only 150,000, you might expect it to be small and provincial. This is certainly how Dubliners view Ireland's "second city." For them, a trip to Cork is a trip to the country, a place to come for hurling, Gaelic football, and locally televised plowing contests.

Cork has few "don't miss" attractions, but that's not the point. Unlike so many other towns in Ireland, Cork is very much alive. After weathering a severe recession and the pullout of a number of major foreign companies in the grim 1980s, the city's economy bounced back with that of the rest of the country. It has a formidable pub scene, some of the country's best traditional music, a respected and progressive university, art galleries, and offbeat cafés. Next to Galway, it also has one of the largest communities of hippies, dropouts, artists, musicians, and poets outside Dublin. Cork can be very "Irish" (music pubs, sheep, and peat smoke). But depending on what part of town you're in, Cork can also be distinctly un-Irish—the sort of place where hippies, gays, and conservative farmers drink at the same pubs, and the sort of place where a Catholic church, a motorcycle bar, and a vegetarian café can share the same street without causing too much of a ruckus. Since 1998 it has begun to enjoy a spillover of European weekend tourists from overcrowded Dublin. You can't mistake these groups: They're usually young, drunk, and singing.

At the heart of it all is Cork's sprawling, partially pedestrian shopping district—though cheaper shopping and meals can be had if you wander down the less-traveled alleys. Cork (or *Corcaigh* in Irish) means "marshy place" and takes its name from the Great Marsh of Munster, atop which the city is built. The original 6th-century settlement was spread over 13 small islands in the River Lee, and as late as 1770 Cork's major streets—Grand Parade, Patrick Street, and the South Mall—were submerged (notice the street-level boathouses in the modern city center). In the 9th century the Danes arrived, bringing violence and terror, but also new crafts and town-building skills. The Normans arrived in 1172 and, as was their wont, immediately fortified the town with thick stone walls that survived everything, including the rage of Cromwell, only to be destroyed by the armies of William of Orange. Around 1800, the river was partially dammed, nearly tripling the amount of arable land in the city center. As a result, Cork's center

ATLANTIC OCEAN

Ennistymon • C

CLARE

N67

Kilkee

Kilrush

Killimer
Tarbert • Gli

N69
N

Mouth of
the Shannon

Ballybunion

Listowel

R523

Abbeyfeale

N69

N21

Tralee
Brandon
Bay
Tralee
Bay

Mt. Brandon

N21 Castleisland

Kilcummin R559 Blennerville
Connor
Pass
DINGLE PENINSULA

Castlemaine

N70

R577 R5

Ballydavid

Ballyferriter
Dunquin
Slea Head
Ventry
Dunbeg

Dingle R561
Town

Annascaul Inch

Killorglin

N22 Killarney

N72

Rossbeigh
Glenbeigh
Kerry

Caragh
Lake

R562

Dingle Bay

Blasket
Islands

Ring of N70

IVERAGH PENINSULA

KERRY

Lake
Leane

Muckross

Upper
Lake

KILLARNEY
NATIONAL
PARK

Cahirciveen

R568

Valentia
Island

Ballinskelligs
Bay

Kerry

Sneem
Tahilla

N70
Kenmare

R569

R584

Waterville

Ring of Kerry

Parknasilla R571

N71

Gougane Ba
Forest Park

Skellig
Islands

Caherdaniel

Kenmare River

BEARA PENINSULA

Glengarriff

Garnish
Island

Ballylickey

R586

Dursey
Island

Castletownbere

R572

Bere Island

Bantry Bay

Durrus

N71

Bantry

Ballydehob

N71

Skibbereen

Schull R592

Goleen

Mizen Head
Signal Station
Crookhaven

Liss Ard
Foundation

R596

R595

Baltimore

Roaring Water Bay

Cape Clear
Island

Sherkin
Island

Cc

rofin

Ennis

Quin

Tuamgraney

Lough Derg

Craggaunowen Project

Killaloe

Nenagh

N52

N62

■ **Knappogue Castle**

Bunratty Castle and Folk Park

Shannon

River Shannon

Foynes

Plassey

Limerick City

Thurles

N75

TIPPERARY

Askeaton

R521

Adare

LIMERICK

N20

N24

R497

N8

Rathkeale

Croom

Holycross

Cashel

N74

N21

Newcastle West

Kilmallock

Tipperary

N8

Cahir

N24

Milford

Kilfinnane

Clogheen

R516

R579

Kanturk

Mitchelstown

WATERFORD

Castletownroche

N8

N72

N72

Mallow

Fermoy

River Blackwater

Lismore

Dungarvan

N20

Rathcormac

N8

CORK

Youghal

N25

Blarney

R579

R617

Cork City

Midleton

Macroom

N22

Fota Island

Fota Demesne

Cloyne

Shanagarry

Cobh

Ballycotton

R600

Cork Harbour

Dunmanway

N71

Bandon

Kinsale

Charles Fort

R600

N

Timoleague

R597

N71

Clonakilty

Courtmacsherry

Rosscarbery

Glandore
Union Hall
etownshend

Celtic Sea

KEY
—— Rail Lines
Ferry

0   20 miles

0   30 km

CORK CITY

Sights ●

Beamish Brewery, 6
Bishop Lucey Park, 7
Cork Arts and Theater Club 12
Cork City Gaol, 1
Crawford Art Gallery, 9
Elizabethan Fort, 3
Fitzgerald Park and Sunday's Well, 2
Murphy's Brewery, 13
St. Fin Barre's Cathedral, 5
Shandon Church and Steeple, 10
Triskel Arts Centre, 8
University College Cork, 4

Lodging ○

Alma Villa, 19
Antoine House, 25
Clare D'Arcy, 24
Clon Ross, 21
Cork City Independent Hostel, 23
Isaac's (IHH), 15
Jury's Cork Inn, 26
Kent House, 18
Kinlay House/USIT, 11
Metropole Hotel, 16
Oakland's, 20
Sheila's Cork Tourist Hostel, 17
Tara House, 22
Victoria Hotel, 14
Victoria Lodge, 27

Fitzgerald Park

Sunday's Well Rd.
Blarney St.
Western Rd.
River Lee
Donovan's Rd.
(S. Channel)
River Lee (N. Channel)
The Mardyke
Connaught Ave.
College Rd.
Gill Abbey St.
Dean St.
Lancaster Quay
Dyke Parade
S. Crawford St.
Bishop St. Proby's Quay
Wandesford Quay
Washington St.
Sheares St.
Peter's St.
Henry St.
Grattan St.
North Mall
Grenville Pl.
Bachelor's Quay
Adelaide St.
Liberty St.
Pope's Quay
Old Market Pl.
Boyce's St.
Blarney St.
Shandon St.
Church St.
Dominick St.
Ferry St.
Upper John St.
Leitrim St.
Richmond Hill
St. Patrick's Hill
Pine St.
St. Patrick's St.
MacCurtain St.
York St.
Summer Hill
Wellington Rd.
Belgrave Pl.
MONTENOTTE
Lower Glanmire Rd.
TO KENT STATION
S. Main St.
N. Main St.
Kyle St.
Cornmarket St.
Castle St.
Paul St.
Emmet's Pl.
Academy St.
Camden Pl.
Lavitt's Quay
St. Patrick's Quay
Brian Boru Bridge
Alfred St.
Hargans Quay
Hanover St.
Grand Parade
Market Parade
Princes St.
Marlboro St.
Cook St.
Winthrop St.
Oliver Plunkett St.
Merchant's Quay
Patrick St.
Morgan St.
Mayor St.
Parnell Pl.
Anderson's Quay
Penrose's Quay
Bus Station
Custom House Quay
Sullivan's Quay
Cove St.
South Main St.
Mary St.
Ft. Mathew Quay
St. George's Quay
Union Quay
River Lee
Lapp's Quay
Albert Quay
Albert St.
Anglesea St.
Victoria Quay
Albert Rd.
Victoria Rd.
South Gate Br.
Clarke's Bridge
Grand Parade

N

0   440 yards
0   400 meters

grew at a furious but even pace: Cork does have slums and a few bleak warehouse districts, but most of the present city was built in the same style at the same time by the same people, giving the city a homogeneous feel. Cork also has many bridges and quays that, although initially confusing, add to the unique character of this ancient port town. All this makes compact Cork a great walking town.

BASICS

LAUNDRY

If your jeans are standing and you're not in them, lug them over to **Cork City Laundry Service.** Washers cost £1, dryers 50p. *14 MacCurtain St., tel. 021/501421.*

MAIL

The **General Post Office** has a bureau de change, phone cards, and a stamp kiosk. *Oliver Plunkett St., at Pembroke St., tel. 021/272000. Open Mon.–Sat. 9–5:30.*

VISITOR INFORMATION

Cork Kerry Tourism has maps, brochures, walking guides, B&B info, and a bureau de change. *Grand Parade, near Washington St., tel. 021/273251. Open July–Aug., Mon–Sat. 9–6, Sun. 10–1; June and Sept., Mon.–Sat. 9–6; Mar.–May and Oct., Mon.–Sat. 9:15–5:30.*

USIT. This student-run travel shop, with two Cork locations, offers the best deals on rail, bus, and air tickets. It's also quite skilled at changing return dates on tickets or finding you a cheap connecting flight from Cork to Calcutta, Santiago, and the like. *10–11 Market Parade, tel. 021/270900. UCC Travel, Boole Library, University College, tel. 021/273901. Both open weekdays 9:30–5:30, Sat. 10–2.*

> *Cork's port served as the departure point for millions of emigrating Irish, was the chief recipient of the survivors and casualties of the "Lusitania" (which was torpedoed off the coast), and was the last port of call for the "Titanic."*

COMING AND GOING

Cork's city center can be thought of as an island, surrounded by the River Lee and dominated by a maze of pedestrian shopping alleys impaled upon the crescent-shape Patrick Street; all the sights are easily reached on foot from here. Local buses arrive and depart from Parnell Place Station, though most serve the suburbs rather than the city center.

BY BUS

All **Bus Éireann** buses depart from the city-center **Parnell Place Station** (tel. 021/508188 or 021/506066), which faces the water on the south side of the River Lee. The bus station has a bureau de change and a left-luggage desk (£1.30 per day) open weekdays 8:30–6:15, Saturday 9:30–6. The station's information counter is staffed daily 9–6. Buses leave for Galway (£13), Cashel (£11), Limerick (£9), Killarney (£12), and Dublin (£13).

BY FERRY

Cork's ferry port is in **Ringaskiddy** (tel. 021/378401 or 021/378111), a desolate industrial complex 16 km (10 mi) south of town. Bus Éireann runs nine daily coaches (45 mins; £3 one-way) from 7 AM to midnight to the ferry port from Parnell Place Station. **Brittany Ferries** (42 Grand Parade, tel. 021/277801) sails Saturday at 3:30 PM to Roscoff, France, arriving the next day at 7 AM. One-way fares are £34–£65. Eurail passes are not valid. **Swansea-Cork Ferries** (52 South Mall, tel. 021/271166) sails every day except Tuesday (daily in summer) to Swansea, Wales. Off-season they saiil every second day. Ferries generally leave Cork at 9 AM and arrive in Swansea at 7 PM. Fares are £22–£32.

BY PLANE

Cork Airport (Ballygarvan, tel. 021/313131) is 9½ km (6 mi) south of town. A taxi to or from the airport runs about £6, or you can take the airport shuttle, which runs every 45 minutes from the bus station (£2.50 one-way). **Aer Lingus** (Union Quay, tel. 021/327155) offers direct service to Dublin, London, Paris, Manchester, Frankfurt, and Amsterdam. Other flights go through Dublin.

REBEL CITY IN A REBEL COUNTY

If County Cork is the "Rebel County"—a label it wears proudly—Cork City can claim to be the heart of that tradition of stout resistance. Since its formation the city has gallantly resisted domination, in turn defying the Vikings, Cromewell, and King Billy's Protestant army. In more recent times Cork was a beehive of IRA activity (Michael Collins, the IRA's greatest tactician and leader, was a Corkman) and a constant thorn in the side of the crown forces. In the 1920s the infamous Black and Tans were unleashed with great ferocity on troublesome Cork City. They quickly murdered Thomas MacCurtain, the mayor. His successor, Terence MacSwiney, was arrested and died on hunger strike with his comrade Joseph Murphy in Brixton prison, London. The two men refused food for 76 days, one of the longest strikes in history, and their names have become myths in the Republican cause, especially in the Southwest. In the bloody civil war that followed victory in the War of Independence, Cork remained staunch IRA country and in general opposed the new State and its army. Michael Collins was killed by a sniper as he drove through Beal-na-Blath not far from the city.

Practically speaking, Cork is a good base for touring the Southwest of Ireland— particularly the villages and sights that flank the city to the south and west. Cork is well serviced by international ferry, so it's also a logical stop for those headed to or from the Continent. In late summer and early autumn, Cork hosts an incredible range of festivals. At the end of October, the huge Cork Jazz Festival draws about 50,000 visitors from around the world. Although you can often buy tickets for music events on the day of the performance, make room reservations at least a month or so in advance or risk spending your nights—all night—in a pub. At the beginning of August, the nearby town of Yougal has its annual Busking Festival, which draws street musicians from all over the world, and in early September look for the Cork Folk Festival. Cork's International Film Festival, held the second week in October, is one of the best in the British Isles. Call Cork Kerry Tourism (see Visitor Information, below) to find out the exact dates.

BY TRAIN

Cork is easily reached from all parts of the country. Inside Cork's **Kent Station** (Lower Glanmire Rd., tel. 021/504777 or 021/506766), open daily 7 AM–8:30 PM and for all departures and arrivals, are an info counter, bureau de change, and lockers (£1 per day). Destinations from Kent Station include Dublin (9 per day; £16), Tralee (5 per day, 3 on Sun.; £9.50), Killarney (5 per day, 3 on Sun.; £7.75), Limerick (6 per day; £7.75), and Rosslare (2 per day, 1 on Sun.; £13.50).

WHERE TO SLEEP

With city-center hostels, a few small hotels, and hundreds of good B&Bs, Cork is hardly ever short of moderately priced beds. Reservations are a good idea if you want a bed near the train station during July and August, and they're absolutely imperative during the October Jazz Festival, when beds are at a premium; try to book at least two months in advance. If you'd rather camp, **Cork Camping Park** (Togher Rd., tel. 021/961866), 1½ (1 mi) southwest of Cork University, has tent sites for £5 (plus £1 per person) available May–October. The park is accessible by Bus 14 and has a nearby food shop.

SMALL HOTELS AND GUEST HOUSES

Jurys Cork Inn. Opened in 1994, this unexciting budget hotel pursues the same function-over-form policy as its Dublin and Galway counterparts. Rooms are £58 a night, and each sleeps three adults or two adults and two children. Beside a busy bridge over the River Lee, the inn is a short walk from the city center and bus and rail stations. *Anderson's Quay, Co. Cork, tel. 021/276444, fax 021/276144. 133 rooms.*

Metropole Hotel. If Cork City were ever in the international news, this is where the journalists would stay. Located near all the action, the grand dame of accommodations in the city, the Metropole has been refurbished to bring out its original Victorian class. All bedrooms are en-suite, with cable TV. There's a brand-new swimming pool and health center. It can get noisy on MacCurtain Street, so ask for a room in the back. In-season doubles aren't cheap at £98 (including breakfast), but they have bargains throughout the rest of the year. *MacCurtain St., Co. Cork, tel. 021/508122, fax 021/506450. 113 rooms.*

Victoria Hotel. Built in 1810, the restored Victorian has seen its share of famous guests, including Charles Stewart Parnell. In *A Portrait of an Artist,* Joyce recounts his stay in the place. It's right smack in the middle of town; a wonderful marble stairway leads to the entrance on pedestrian Cook Street. Inside they have tried to regain the lost charm of the place, with a black-and-white tiled floor and the elegant Vic Bar. The rooms are surprisingly large and wouldn't look out of place in a more expensive hotel. A double costs £70. *Cook and Patrick Sts., Co. Cork, tel. 021/278788, fax 021/278790. 30 rooms.*

Victoria Lodge. This guest house, originally built in the early 20th century as a Capuchin monastery, is a five-minute drive from the town center; it's also accessible by several bus routes. Breakfast is served in the spacious old refectory, with its intact polished benches and paneled walls; the common room is now a television lounge where you can catch up on old episodes of the best (and worst) American shows. Singles go for £36, doubles £52. *Victoria Cross, Co. Cork, tel. 021/542233, fax 021/542572. 42 rooms.*

BED-AND-BREAKFASTS

Cork's B&Bs are mainly clustered around the train station on Lower Glanmire Road (turn right as you leave the train station), near Cork University on Western Road, and on Wellington Road. The cheapest is **Kent House** (47 Lower Glanmire Rd., tel. 021/504260), which has airy rooms for £14–£19 per person. Three other comfortable B&Bs within a two-block radius are run by the Murray family: **Clon Ross** (85 Lower Glanmire Rd., across from the train station, tel. 021/502602), **Oakland's** (51 Lower Glanmire Rd., tel. 021/500578), and **Alma Villa** (50 Lower Glanmire Rd., tel. 021/502602). At all three the rates are £18–£24 per person. **Tara House** (52 Lower Glanmire Rd., tel. 021/500294) charges £15–£22 per person. **Antoine House** (Western Rd., tel. 021/273494) and **Clare D'Arcy** (7 Sidney Pl., Wellington Rd., tel. 021/504658) both offer doubles for about £20 per person.

HOSTELS

Cork City Independent Hostel. Opposite the train station on the north side of Cork, this unaffiliated hostel is an easy 10-minute walk from the pubs and shops. It doesn't look like much, situated among the quay's ramshackle port facilities, but the interior—with brightly painted doors and mismatched furniture—is folksy and fun. Dorm beds are £7, doubles £18. Bikes can be rented for £5 a day. *100 Lower Glanmire Rd., tel. 021/509089. 30 beds. Kitchen, laundry.*

Isaac's (IHH). This is definitely Cork's best-looking hostel (inside and out), and it's close to both the bus and rail stations. In addition to the hostel building, with its dorm-style accommodations, there's a little hotel with double rooms. Too bad the staff are curt, there's an 11–5 lockout (for hotel guests, too), and the main common room is only open for four hours a day; the rest of the time, two chairs, a table, and a TV constitute the common area. Dorm beds are £7–£9.25 and doubles £40. Bike rental is £7 a day.

48 MacCurtain St., tel. 021/500011. From train station, turn left and continue for ½ km (¼ mi). 190 beds. Kitchen.

Kinlay House/USIT. The large and thoroughly modern Kinlay House isn't a true hostel but rather an upscale holiday complex that happens to rent cheapish beds. Kinlay House offers a range of accommodations: singles (£15), doubles (£25), and dorm beds (£8), all of which include a Continental breakfast. *Bob and Joan Walk, Shandon, tel. 021/508966. From bus station, turn left on Merchant's Quay, right on the second bridge (Opera House Bridge), walk north on Upper John St. (past the Northern Infirmary) and look for steps on the left. 140 beds. Kitchen, laundry.*

Sheila's Cork Tourist Hostel. Commanding citywide views from its perch at the top of steep York Street, Sheila's is housed in a big, comfortable, ramshackle building. Dorm beds cost £8.50, singles £18 (£13 off-season), and doubles £22; sheet rental is available (50p). The hilly front yard has tables and chairs where you can sip your morning coffee. There's even the posh touch of a sauna to relax in. *Belgrave Pl., Wellington Rd., tel. 021/505562. From bus station, cross the river on Brian Boru St., turn left on MacCurtain St., right on York St., right on Wellington (which funnels onto Belgrave Pl.). 130 beds. Reception open 8 AM–3:30 AM. Kitchen, laundry.*

FOOD

Cork has a good collection of upscale restaurants and unpretentious, affordable cafés. Most are scattered in the city center between the Grand Parade and the River Lee, notably in the network of narrow pedestrian lanes that slice across St. Patrick and Oliver Plunkett streets. For breakfast and afternoon snacks, snag an outdoor table at **Gingerhouse** (10 Paul St., tel. 021/276411), famous for its authentic cappuccinos and buttery, flaky croissants. Cork's slackers, longhairs, and gays tend to gather at the **Other Side** (South Main St., between Castle and Washington Sts., tel. 021/278470), where they sip coffee leisurely over newspapers and fill up on cheap salads and vegetarian soups (£1.50–£3.50). For pub grub and solid pints, try the **Lobby** (1 Union Quay, tel. 021/319307), **Dan Lowrey's** (13 MacCurtain St., tel. 021/505071), or the **Long Valley** (10 Winthrop St., off Oliver Plunkett St., tel. 021/272144), all famed for their old-style decor and high-quality bar food. Enter the wrought-iron arch opposite Bishop Lucey Park to reach Cork's **City Market,** a pungent indoor bazaar that runs between the Grand Parade and Princes Street. **Natural Foods** (26 Paul St., tel. 021/277244) has organically grown produce and yummy baked goods. For groceries go to the **English Market,** built in 1881, which houses numerous traditional market stalls selling a range of fresh food. There are entrances on Grand Parade, Patrick Street, Princes Street, and Oliver Plunkett Street. It's open from 9 to 5:30. **Quinnsworth** (Paul St., tel. 021/270791) has the biggest selection and best prices of all the supermarkets.

UNDER £5 • Noble Grape. The best little greasy spoon in the city, the Grape has as its special "anything on toast," the jumbo sausages on toast being the number one choice. It has all the other unhealthy but delicious stuff Irish people seem to crave all the time. The big window looks right out onto the Lee. *George's Quay, tel. 021/319025. Cash only.*

Quay Co-op. It's Cork's most happening vegetarian hangout, especially on weekend mornings when the local veg-heads stumble in for coffee and a hand-rolled cigarette. The Co-op's couscous salad, blue-cheese cannelloni, curried eggplant, and broccoli soup make a welcome change from chips and toasted sandwiches. During the afternoon, the second and third floors of this riverside complex open as a self-service café, with dishes starting at £2. Around 6 PM, the second floor is transformed into a semi-posh sit-down restaurant, offering the same foods at slightly inflated prices. *24 Sullivan's Quay, 1 block south and across the river from tourist office, tel. 021/317660. Cash only. Closed Sun.*

Triskel Arts Café. This quiet tearoom in the top floor of the Triskel Arts Centre serves simple but delicious salads (£3–£4) and hearty soups and sandwiches. Bow down and worship the chocolate-and-pear tart (£2). Everything here is made daily from scratch. *South Main St., off Washington St., tel. 021/272022. Cash only. Closed Sun.*

UNDER £10 • Bewleys. A very much smaller, and perhaps cozier version of the Dublin Original, Bewleys Cork has the elegant Victorian brass and tiles look that is distinctive of what now, sadly, must be called the chain. The grub is the same, too—slightly overpriced fried fare and top-class sticky buns. *4 Cook St., tel. 021/270660. Cash only.*

Farmgate Café. On a terrace above the fountain at the Princes Street entrance to Cork's English Market, this simple restaurant-café is one of the best-value lunch spots in town. One side of the terrace is open to the market and operates as self-service; the other is glassed in and served by waiters (reservations advised). A piano player does his stuff at lunchtime most days. Tripe is always on the menu, while daily specials include less challenging but no less traditional Irish dishes such as corned beef with *colcannon* (mashed potatoes with onions and cabbage) and loin of smoked bacon with *champ* (potatoes with scallions or leeks). A large share of the food prepared here comes from the market below. *English Market, Cork, tel. 021/278134. Closed Sun.*

New Maharajah. It looks shabby, but this family-run restaurant serves the best and cheapest Indian food in Cork. The fixed-price lunch menu (appetizer, tandoori entrée, dessert, and tea) is a steal at £5, or choose from the à la carte tandoori menu (£7.50) for slightly larger portions. *19 Cook St., tel. 021/ 276576.*

Pierre's. This superb restaurant in an old country house is refined and stately, decorated with mahogany panels, an open fire pit, and a beautifully carved high ceiling. Surprisingly, it's also reasonably priced. The menu changes daily and features a variety of fish, steak, and pasta dishes. Lunch is around £6–£8, dinner £7–£9.50, but even if you're broke, Pierre's is highly recommended for late-night coffee or wine and divine homemade desserts. *17 Church St., tel. 021/278107.*

UNDER £15 • Michael's. The eponymous Michael Clifford is a talented local chef, and this is his latest venture. He has abandoned the world of haute cuisine to cater, bistro-style, to the diner on a budget, and does so exceptionally well. The large dining room has dark walls and cheerful bright yellow curtains, with well-spaced oilcloth-covered tables. Start with a warm smoked haddock salad dusted with fine herbs followed by traditional bacon and cabbage or Irish lamb casserole. *71–72 Patrick St., tel. 021/277716. Closed Sun.*

UNDER £20 • Manor Room. Part of the high-end Hayfield Manor hotel, this award-winning (no, really!) dining room has one of the finest wine selections in the whole country—French, German, Italian, Spanish, and New World, you'll find it all. The rich Continental menu includes a starter of smoked Barbary duck salad with Crisp Westphalian ham and truffle cream, and a main dish of stuffed breast of guinea fowl with turnip gratin and beetroot jus. If you're going whole hog, finish with the rhubarb parfait and brandy snap wafers. *Perrott Ave., College Rd., tel. 021/315600.*

WORTH SEEING

Cork's historical sights are spread out and easy to overlook, especially if you're unfamiliar with the city's confusing layout. Consider buying the useful "Tourist Trail Walking Guide" or the "Cork City Area Guide" (each £1) from the tourist office. The walking guide outlines a three-hour walk covering the city's history and architecture. The tourist office also sponsors free guided tours of historic Cork that depart at 7:30 PM on Tuesday and Thursday July–August. **Cork Harbour Cruises** (44 Grand Parade, tel. 021/277085) offers pleasant harbor cruises (£5) past the area's many waterside sights and a short day trip to **Cobh** (£10, including admission to the Cobh Heritage Centre).

BEAMISH BREWERY

Beamish has been brewing its mild, fruity stout since the early 19th century. Over the years, it's become the pint of choice and a point of pride for locals. It has a slightly sweeter taste than Guinness and is often quite a few pence cheaper. The brewery is a Cork landmark and is easily found by following the smell of boiling hops from the tourist office (or simply head north on Grand Parade, left on Washington Street, and left on South Main Street). Keep your eyes peeled for the brewery's brooding Tudor frontispiece, cupola, and clock. You can take a free tour with tastings Thursday 10–noon, but only if you write one week in advance to Chris Reynolds. *Beamish Inc., S. Main St., Cork, tel. 021/276841.*

BISHOP LUCEY PARK

This park was opened in 1985 in celebration of the 800th anniversary of the town's Norman charter. During excavation for the park, workers unearthed portions of Cork's original fortified walls, now preserved just inside the arched entranceway. Adjacent to the site is the 18th-century **Christ Church,** built on the foundation of an older (1199) Norman church. The building currently houses the city and county archives and is not open to the public. *Grand Parade, tel. 021/277809. Park open daily sunrise–sunset.*

CRAWFORD ART GALLERY

This is Ireland's most active and respected provincial art gallery. Its permanent collection of second-rate Irish landscapists and portrait painters is completely forgettable, except for a couple of excellent works by Jack B. Yeats and a few examples of the St. Ives school. However, the Crawford regularly mounts superb exhibitions of modern Irish and foreign work. The building itself was originally the city's custom-house, dating from 1724. *Emmet Pl., tel. 021/273377. Admission free. Open Mon.–Sat. 10–5.*

ELIZABETHAN FORT

At the top of Keyser Hill stand the ruins of a fort built in 1601, right after the English defeated the disorganized armies of O'Neill, O'Donnell, and their Spanish allies at Kinsale on the coast. A few ivy-covered remnants of the original structure remain, but the view of the old city from here is worth the visit.

FITZGERALD PARK AND SUNDAY'S WELL

Cork's largest public green is 2 km (1 mi) southeast of the city center, on the south bank of the River Lee. The **Mardyke,** a small footpath along the River Lee, makes for a good afternoon stroll. Near the park's entrance is the free **Cork Museum** (tel. 021/270679), home to a large, hodgepodge collection of Republican memorabilia and local artifacts; particularly good is the glass, silversmith, and coopering section. Across the water is the quiet suburb of **Sunday's Well,** a stately redbrick Victorian district. On the hill across the river (use the footbridge) is the foreboding **Cork City Gaol,** a creepy 19th-century jail that looks like a castle. On view are the prison cells (inhabited now by life-size replicas of some of the jail's most notorious criminals, complete with cheesy sound effects) and two walls of graffiti left by Republican prisoners in the early 20th century. *Park open May–Aug., daily 8 AM–10 PM; Sept.–Apr., daily 8–5. Cork City Gaol and Museum, tel. 021/305022. Open Mar.–Oct., daily 9:30–6; Nov.–Feb., daily 10–5. Admission £3.50.*

MURPHY'S BREWERY

Rival to Guinness and Beamish for the heart of a nation of stout drinkers, Murphy's began brewing here in 1856, but the company's purchase by Heineken in 1983 has led diehards to lament that the ol' familiar "hasn't been the same since." The brewery isn't open to the public, but you can taste for yourself in the Brewery Tap Pub across the road. **Lady's Well,** the brewery's second name, refers to a celebrated well across the street that's supposedly been blessed by the Virgin Mary herself. *Lady's Well, Leitrim St., tel. 021/503371. Walk west on MacCurtain St. and follow the road as it veers right.*

PATRICK STREET

Patrick Street, which cuts a graceful curve, lies to the south of Patrick Bridge. If you look up above some of the standardized plate-glass and plastic shop facades here, you'll see examples of the bowfront Georgian windows that are emblematic of old Cork. The street saw some of the city's worst fighting in the years 1919–21, during the War of Independence. Roches Stores is the largest department store in town; Cash's, next door, is the most upscale. Tall ships that once served the butter trade used to load up on Patrick's Quay, at the end of Patrick Street, before heading downstream to the open sea on Merchant's Quay. The design of the large shopping center on the site today evokes the warehouses of old.

ST. FIN BARRE'S CATHEDRAL

Built on the site of the original settlement of 606, this Protestant church was designed by Victorian architect William Burgess and completed in 1879. From the looks of it, Will had a lot of fun with the design, sprinkling leering gargoyles in every nook and cranny of the cathedral; there's even one under the book rest on the pulpit. The rich and lofty interior also contains mosaics, wood carvings, stained-glass windows, and a 3,000-pipe organ, which is sunk 15 ft into the floor. *Bishop St., off S. Main St., tel. 021/963387. Admission free. Open daily 10–5.*

SHANDON CHURCH AND STEEPLE

One of Cork's most famous landmarks, the church of St. Ann Shandon was built in 1722 on the site of a derelict Viking fort (Shandon, or Sean dun, means "old fort" in Irish). The steeple's motley faces of red sandstone and bleached limestone inspired Cork's official city colors—red and white—while the 11-ft-long, salmon-shape weather vane is a tribute to the River Lee and Cork's founder, St. Fin Barre. For 50p, you can make the treacherous climb to the top of the 170-ft tower and ring Shandon's famous bells. *Church St., off Shandon St., tel. 021/505906. Admission £1 (additional 50p for tower). Open daily 10–5:30.*

UNIVERSITY COLLEGE CORK

Along with Maynooth College, U.C.D. (Dublin), and U.C.G. (Galway), U.C.C. is part of the National University of Ireland. The extensive campus is on the western edge of the city. The original buildings were built in the 1840s in gray granite. There are plenty of open fields good for a long stroll by the river. Students run regular tours of the campus, and their favorite story is that Professor Moriarty, the fictional archenemy of Sherlock Holmes, was based on an old teacher at the college. The main quadrangle is a fine example of 19th-century university architecture in the Tudor-Gothic style, reminiscent of many Oxford and Cambridge colleges. Several ancient ogham stones are on display, as well as occasional exhibitions of archival material from the old library. The **Honan Collegiate Chapel,** to the east of the quad, was built in 1916 and modeled on the 12th-century, Hiberno-Romanesque style. The stained-glass windows are by that Irish master of the medium, Harry Clarke. When the students are around there's always something going on (except study, of course), including films, plays, and concerts.

SHOPPING

For general bygones and curiosities, try **O'Regan's Antiques** (27 Lavitt's Quay, tel. 021/273528), where to look around is a pleasure, and—who knows?—you might find a bargain hidden away. For inexpensive rainwear (a real necessity in these parts), go to **Penney's** (27 Patrick St., tel. 021/271935). **Matthews** (Academy St., tel. 021/277633) has a wide selection of sporting gear. **Great Outdoors** (23 Paul St.) caters to most outdoor-sports needs. **Cash's** (18 Patrick St., tel. 021/276571) is Cork's leading department store and has a good selection of Waterford glass. The **Lavit Gallery** (5 Father Mathew St., tel. 021/277749) displays a representative selec-

In a country where accents come in all shapes and sizes, the Cork twang is deemed the thickest of the thick—a blunt and guttural lilt that, in the words of one Dubliner, "reeks of the farm and field."

tion of oils and watercolors by members of the Cork Arts Society and other Irish artists, all of which are for sale. Fans of Irish music should visit the **Living Tradition** (40 MacCurtain St., tel. 021/502040), a specialist Irish music shop. Book buyers should head to **Mercier Bookshop** (18 Academy St., tel. 021/275040), off Patrick Street, which sells new books and publishes its own list of Irish and local interest titles. The **Merchant's Quay Shopping Centre** (Merchant's Quay, Cork, tel. 021/275466) is the largest indoor mall in downtown Cork. **Coal Quay Market** (Cornmarket St.) is a slightly seedy flea market with hidden bargains in a great 19th-century setting.

AFTER DARK

Like Galway and Dublin, Cork is best appreciated from inside a pub, especially during the chaotic **Jazz Festival** in October. Cork's theaters and art centers also mount a diverse selection of productions year-round, most with substantial student discounts. **Triskell Arts Centre** (Tobin St., just off S. Main St., tel. 021/272022) presents a variety of plays, concerts, performances, films, art exhibits, and even dance lessons throughout the year. Tickets usually cost £3–£8; sometimes, they're free. **Cork Arts and Theatre Club** (7 Knapps Sq., tel. 021/508398) also presents theater, comedy, and musicals; tickets usually go for £5. For entertainment listings, pick up a copy of the free weekly *What's On* or the extremely useful *Guide to Cork* from the tourist office or the *Evening Echo* (50p) from any newsagent.

PUBS

Cork has some of the best pubs in Ireland, especially for those into loud traditional music and rowdy crowds of college students. Right in the center of town, on Marlboro Street, you'll find **Fanny Adams** (tel. 021/272703) friendly and full of students. Connie, who runs it, will give a 15% discount to any traveler who asks; he also has some derring-do stories about windsurfing and lifeboat rescues. At lunchtime you can get large doorstop chapters 7 and 9 have doorstep-sandwiches (that is, big enough to act as a doorstop) for £1.60. One of the most popular stops is Union Quay, on the south side of town opposite the South Mall and River Lee. Here three excellent pubs stand side by side: **An Phoenix** (tel. 021/964275), famed for its old-style decor; the **Lobby** (tel. 021/319307), a folk/traditional music pub packed with yuppies and middle-age slackers; and **Donkey Ears** (tel. 021/964846), home to a drunken horde of bikers and youthful fashion slaves. The Lobby has free traditional-music sessions Tuesday and Friday, country and blues on Monday, and a variety of folk and local rock upstairs the rest of the week (for a small cover). Farther down the river, **Callagan's** (24 George's Quay, tel. 021/274604) is an unpretentious (okay, shabby) pub frequented by professional alcoholics and grandmotherly sorts, but its spur-of-the-moment, untouristy music sessions are not to be missed. Across the river, the popular **An Bodhrán** (42 Oliver Plunkett St., tel. 021/274544) and **An Spailpín Fánac** (28–29 S. Main St., tel. 021/277949) host regular traditional music during the summer. The only gay pub in town is **Loafers** (Douglas St., tel. 021/311612), which is papered with gay and lesbian community info and hot-line numbers. Saturday night at the **Other Side** (*see* Food, *above*) is gay disco night; the first Friday of each month is lesbian dance night. **An Bros** (72 Oliver Plunkett St., no phone) spins mainstream Top 40 music, and **Mojo's** (George's Quay, tel. 021/311786) hosts blues bands for a slightly older crowd. Depending on who's playing, these pubs often charge a £1–£3 cover.

NEAR CORK CITY

JAMESON HERITAGE CENTRE

At the Jameson whiskey distillery—once fourth largest in the world—nearly 10,000 gallons of the dry, malty Irish brew known as *Uisce Beatha,* or Water of Life, were made each day until the 1970s, when production was moved to a new, modern factory in Middleton. The impressive distillery itself, built in 1795 and transformed into a heritage center in 1975, covers 11 acres. Everywhere you turn are stone-faced warehouses, redbrick smokestacks, mills, still houses, and kilns, all interspersed with working waterwheels, whiskey barrels, and a 30,000-gallon, copper-plated pot—still the largest ever built. From March to November, if demand warrants, tours and free tastings are given weekdays 10–4. Even if you miss the tour, it's worth making the trek just to walk the distillery grounds. Inside is an exhibition center, museum, and, of course, gift shop. Bus Éireann runs coaches (17 per day; £4.50 round-trip) here from Cork's Parnell Place Station; take the bus going to Midleton and ask the driver to stop at the gate. *Midleton, tel. 021/631594. Admission £3.50. Open Mar.–Oct., daily 10—6; Nov.—Feb., weekdays guided tours only at noon and 3 PM.*

BLARNEY CASTLE

Blarney Castle, 8 km (5 mi) northwest of Cork City, is one of Ireland's best-known historic sites. In other words, it's plagued by herds of tourists and nearly impossible to enjoy; try to visit in the very early morning or be prepared to wait in long lines. That said, it's hard to deny the allure of the **Blarney Stone,** set in a wall below the castle's battlements. Tradition holds that all who kiss the Blarney Stone will gain the gift of "the blarney," meaning eloquence and a crafty tongue. To receive this blessing, you lean backward from the second-story parapet and stick your head through a small opening, grasping an iron rail for support lest you fall into a murky shaft. Despite the difficulty, there's generally a long line of overweight retirees waiting to scale the skeletal remains of Blarney Castle, a strangely derelict edifice in this otherwise neatly groomed setting. *Admission £3, £5 for combined ticket with Blarney House (see below). Open daily 9–6:30 (slightly shorter hrs in winter and on Sun.).*

The restored **Blarney House** (tel. 021/385252), 200 yards from the castle, is a Scottish baronial mansion graced with a series of asymmetrical spires and stone chimney spouts. Inside are some fine Elizabethan and Victorian antiques showcased alongside period furniture and a handful of dark, ceiling-high portraits. *Admission: £2.50. Open July–Aug., Mon.–Sat. 12:30–5:30.*

BASICS

From Cork's Parnell Place Station, **Bus Éireann** offers 15 daily coaches (30 mins; £2.60 round-trip) to Blarney Square, an easy walk from the castle. You can also walk (2 hrs) or drive from Cork by taking the N8 past the train station and following the signs, or the N20 past Murphy's Brewery on Upper St. John Street. In Blarney itself there's a small **tourist desk** (The Square, tel. 021/381624) with a bureau de change.

KINSALE TO SKIBBEREEN

The "high road" to Skibbereen from Kinsale is definitely the N71, but it's a bit slower and more fun to take the "low road" along the coast of West Cork, with its delightful small towns, like Union Hall, and inspiring Celtic Sea views.

KINSALE

BASICS

Right on the harbor, next to the cinema, the **tourist office** (tel. 021/772234) has information on town goings-on; it's open daily 9–5. There's a **Super Value** supermarket and an **AIB bank** on Pearse Street. **Bus Éireann** (tel. 021/508188) runs buses to and from Cork three times a day. It takes under an hour and costs £6 round trip.

WHERE TO SLEEP

Kilcaw House (Pewter Hole Cross, tel. 021/7741550) is a guest house that offers value for money and the personal attention of Henry and Christina Mitchell, the enthusiastic owners. The building is only four years old and its location, 2 km (1 mi) outside town, guarantees peace and quiet. Doubles go for £44–£50. The town is full of quality B&Bs, but nearly all are closed in the off-season. **Sea Gull House** (Cork St., tel. 021/772240) is one of the best, with doubles for around £40. **Castlepark Marina** (tel. 021/774959) is a bit out of the way—3 km (2 mi) west of town— but it's the best hostel in the area, with doubles for around £22 and dorm beds for as little as £9.

FOOD

Kinsale is arguably the gourmet capital of Ireland. That usually means two things: quality food and high prices. If you want to splurge a little, try the dining room of the **Blue Haven Hotel** (Pearse St., tel. 021/772209). It is famous for its seafood, which includes the Blue Haven Seafood Pie topped with creamed potato gratinée. The hotel also serves the "Wine Geese" selection, plucked from the numerous vineyards around the world started by Irish "Wild Geese" families who emigrated over the centuries. On the same theme, the **Wild Geese** (69 Main St., no phone) restaurant is an 11-table café serving a stupendous Irish breakfast (£3) and homemade soups (£1.50). **Max's** (48 Main St., tel. 021/772443) has a fantastic-value early bird special for £12. It's three courses, and you get a choice of three dishes for each. The wine list is impressive.

WORTH SEEING

On a straight line 29 km (18 mi) south of Cork lies the historic seaside village of Kinsale. Through an organized effort by the local community (note the bright colors used to paint the houses), the once-dilapidated ex–fishing town has become one of the most picturesque villages in Ireland. Kinsale has also garnered quite a reputation as a center for fine dining. Fame has its price, of course, and tourist overcrowding and higher prices are a problem; the throngs are particularly thick during the **Gourmet Festival** in the first week of October.

Situated at the tip of the wide, fjordlike harbor opening out from the River Bandon, the town center is nestled among small streets lined with upscale shops and eateries. The steep, narrow streets climb up to the slopes of Compass Hill. Tall, slate-roof and unusual slate-front houses have an unmistakable Spanish influence. That's not as surprising as it might seem; in 1601 Spanish troops landed to join Irish forces against the English at the Battle of Kinsale. After 1601 the town developed into an important shipping and fishing port.

Frightened by the landing of the Spanish, the British picked a spot on the harbor shore, on the east side of the Bandon's estuary, and built **Charles Fort** in the late 17th century. One of the best-preserved "star forts" in Europe, it encloses 12 acres on a cliff top. Take a stroll along the footpath signposted "Scilly Walk"; it winds along the edge of the harbor under tall, overhanging trees, and then through the village of Summer Cove. The fort is open weekdays year-round and daily in the summer. Admission is £2. When the dreaded Spaniards landed in 1601 they immediately occupied **Desmond Castle** (Cork St.) There is little left to see of the castle except its structure, but the tour is worth taking, as it relates the history of the building as a British prison for French and American soldiers and as a workhouse during the Great Famine. The castle is open April–October; admission is £1.50.

TIMOLEAGUE

WHERE TO SLEEP AND EAT

Lettercollum House. Here's your chance to play lord of the manor without breaking the bank. This country manor house dates from 1861 and looks back across the estuary to Courtmacsherry Bay. It's now an excellent guest house, run by chef-proprietors Con McLoughlin and Karen Austin. Rooms are big and airy, but Lettercollum is a TV-free zone (addicts be warned). The restaurant in the old chapel makes use of the organic herbs, salad greens, and fruits from the walled garden, and your pork chop might be from a pig raised on site. In summer, doubles go from £48 to £60; rates include a great breakfast. *Timoleague, tel. 023/46251. 9 rooms. Closed Nov.–Jan.*

WORTH SEEING

The town of Timoleague sits at the eastern end of the small Seven Heads Peninsula. The highlight here is the 13th-century **Franciscan Abbey** at the water's edge. It was sacked by the English in 1642 but continued to be used as a burial site until recent times. A tower and walls with Gothic-arched windows still stand, and you can trace the ground plan of the old friary—chapel, refectory, cloisters, and wine cellar (at one time the friars were highly profitable wine importers). The entrance is around the back. **Timoleague Castle Gardens** (tel. 023/46116) are right in the village. Although the castle is long gone—it has been replaced by a dull early 20th-century house in gray stone—the original gardens have survived. Palm trees and other frost-tender plants flourish amid the mature shrubbery. The gardens are open June–August; admission is £2. **Coutmacsheerry,** the postcard village of multicolored cottages glimpsed across the water, has sandy beaches that make it a fave spot for holidaymakers.

CLONAKILTY

This small but happening seaside village, about 51 km (32 mi) southwest of Cork, has become something of a buzzword in the Cork-area live-music scene. Strung along **Pearse Street,** the main thoroughfare, are a handful of pubs that host excellent traditional, folk, and blues bands almost every night of the week. The locals mingle peaceably with the growing immigrant musician population and are often, in fact, their loudest supporters. This mix makes for a true West Cork experience: hippies clad in Indian cotton sharing a bar with wizened local men, all tapping their feet to the sounds of a visiting folk duo. Popular, cluttered **De Barra's** (Pearse St., tel. 023/33381) usually has the best music lineups. Check their window for the night's entertainment. Other good bets are **Shanley's** (Connolly St., no phone), which hosts everything from blues and jazz to trad and folk seven nights a week in the summer, and **An Teach Beaj** (in O'Donovan's Hotel, Pearse St., tel. 023/33250), which rocks with traditional music every evening. Clonakilty's other draw is the nearby beaches. **Inchydoney** beach, about 5 km (3 mi) south, was once an island and is now a gorgeous stretch of sand connected to the mainland. From Cork, there are two buses a day to Clonakilty (£5.90 one-way, £7.90 round-trip). Only one bus is direct; the other is via Skibbereen.

ROSSCARBERY, GLANDORE, AND UNION HALL

WHERE TO SLEEP AND EAT

Rosalithir (N71, between Clonakilty and Rosscarbery, tel. 023/48136) is a small, family-run accommodation that allows you to cook your own meals. Doubles go for £18 per person.

WORTH SEEING

The N71 briefly meets the coast at **Rosscarbery**. The 12th-century **St. Fachtna's Cathedral** there is worth a visit for its intricately carved doorway. Just outside of Rosscarbery on the small R597, you'll come across one of the many stone circles in West Cork, and one of the finest. The 17 stones probably date from the Bronze Age and are in a field with a stunning view of the Celtic Sea. Continuing along the R597, you come to **Glandore**. In the 19th century William Thompson established a short-lived socialist commune here that earned a mention in Marx's hefty *Kapital*. The picturesque fishing village is set at the foot of grassy slopes, on the edge of the dark blue sea. There's not much to do in the town, except kick back with some seafood and a pint and glory at the surroundings.

No, **Union Hall** was not a center for labor activism; it gets its name from the 1800 Act of Union, which abolished the parliament in Dublin and brought Ireland (along with Scotland) under the direct rule of Westminster. Jonathan Swift and family favored the place for vacations. Between Union Hall and Castletownsend is the tiny **Ceim Hill Museum** (tel. 028/36280), which is home to a weird gathering of odds and ends collected by owner Teresa O'Mahony, including tools used in her folk medicine practice. The museum is open daily 10–7; admission is £2.

Alexander Selkirk departed from Kinsale on the voyage that left him stranded on a desert Island; his story would later become the model for Daniel Defoe's Robinson Crusoe.

CASTLETOWNSEND

The first thing you'll notice about this town is the unusual number of graciously designed, large stone houses, mostly dating from the mid-18th century when it was an important trading center. Its main street runs steeply down a hill to the sea. The sleepy town awakens in July and August, when its sheltered harbor bustles. Sparkling views await from the cliff-top perch of **St. Barrahane's Church,** which has a medieval oak altarpiece and three stained-glass windows by Harry Clarke. In late July and early August, the church is the venue for an international festival of classical music (tel. 028/36193) that focuses on chamber music. The low-beamed interior of **Mary Ann's** (tel. 028/36146), one of the oldest bars in the country, is frequented by a very friendly mix of visitors and locals and is a good place for a pint and a bite. Writer Edna O'Brien calls it her favorite pub in the whole world.

SKIBBEREEN

WHERE TO SLEEP AND EAT

For a little luxury, try the **West Cork Hotel** (Bridge St., Skibbereen, tel. 028/21277), which has a certain old colonial charm. Rooms, big and decorated with period pieces, go for £18 per person. The restaurant specializes in great steaks. West of town on the Castletownsend Road, the **Russagh Mill Hostel** (tel. 028/22451) is a converted mill (and still looks like one too). The rooms are unusually large for a hostel, and dorms cost £8, doubles £25. The restaurant at **Eldon's Hotel** (Bridge St., tel. 028/21300) is a good spot for the ubiquitous meat-and-two-veg done to perfection.

WORTH SEEING

Skibbereen is the main market town in this neck of southwestern Cork and is a perfect base for the sights nearby. If you really want to see the place at its liveliest, come on a Wednesday when the cattle market is in full swing and the sound of men spitting and shaking hands fills the air. Just outside town, the **Lis Ard Foundation** has developed one of the most daring and unusual gardens in Ireland. More than 40 acres set around a number of small lakes have been planted with complex flora that highlights the natural beauty of the landscape in an ecologically sound way. Each area of the garden is supposed to aid the your emotional well-being in a distinct way. Most exciting of all is the **Sky-Garden,** a huge earth sculpture designed by American artist James Turrell. You can walk right into the huge mound of earth, and from inside it perfectly frames the sky in an oval of pristine green grass. The gardens are open all summer; admission is £5. The **West Cork Arts Center** (North St., Skibbereen, tel. 028/22090) is a cen-

WAY, WAY OFF THE BEATEN PATH

If you want to unwind in one of Ireland's best hostels, come to Maria's Schoolhouse (Union Hall, tel. 028/33002), 11 km (7 mi) east of Skibbereen. Maria has transformed a 19th-century schoolhouse into an eclectic, superbly decorated hostel (beds £8) and B&B (doubles £40). While there you can take her dogs for walks to isolated coves, or grab some old fishing rods, hop on the free bikes, and catch your dinner. Better still, take a kayaking lesson (£5 per hour) from Maria's partner Jim, a champion kayaker. To get to the hostel, take any bus going between Clonakilty and Skibbereen, get off at Leap, and call to have someone pick you up.

ter for art and performance in the region, including films, poetry readings, and art exhibitions. The on-site crafts shop also sells items made by area artists.

BALTIMORE, CAPE CLEAR, AND SHERKIN ISLAND

BASICS

The waterfront **tourist office** (tel. 028/20226), open Monday–Saturday 9:30–5:30 in summer, can provide bus schedules and book accommodations.

COMING AND GOING

To reach Baltimore you will have to change buses in **Skibbereen.** Buses go between Skibbereen and Baltimore four times a day Monday–Saturday (£2.10). Buses run from Cork to Skibbereen (4 per day; £6) and in the summer from Killarney (2 per day; £7.60).

WHERE TO SLEEP

Comfortable bed-and-breakfast rooms from £15 per person are available in Baltimore at **Algiers Inn** (tel. 028/20145), above its adjoining pub and around the corner from the waterfront pubs. If that's full, try the nearby **Sunbury House** (tel. 028/20150), a cozy place that's less atmospheric and lively but also £15 per night. Near the harbor on Cape Clear, **Cluain Mara House** (tel. 028/39153) has a virtual monopoly on the area's B&B business. Fortunately, it doesn't abuse this privilege, and all five of its rooms (£16 per person, £14 without a bath) are immaculate and endowed with sag-free beds. They also offer a two- to three-person studio for £25. When the weather is fine (June–September), you can camp at **Cuas An Uisce** (tel. 028/31149) in South Harbour, 1½ km (1 mi) from Cape Clear's main ferry port. Its 20 pitches (£2 per person) hug the rocky coast: a beautiful setting on a clear day, miserably damp and dreary when it's raining.

Baltimore is blessed with the phenomenal IHH **Rolf's Hostel** (tel. 028/20289), ½ km (¼ mi) east of town on a rural farm road (follow the signs). Besides being amazingly friendly and relaxed, Rolf's has stone-faced cottages with pine interiors (dorm beds £8–£9, doubles £25), a welcome change from the dusty-couch-and-peeling-paint category of hostels. Inside is a luxurious common room and self-service kitchen—though for £3.50–£8 you can try the Malaysian and Italian dishes, served nightly in the common room (prices in the restaurant next door are steeper).

FOOD

Baltimore's food scene is pretty dreary, composed mostly of pricey restaurants catering to the yachting crowd. Your best bet is to try the pub grub at **Bushe's Pub** (near the harbor, tel. 028/20125), grab a burger and chips at a kiosk on the pier, or head to Rolf's Hostel (*see above*). **Cotter's** (tel. 028/20106), across from the pier, sells produce and groceries. On Sherkin Island, **Jolly Roger Tavern** (tel. 028/20379) has decent pub eats and a terrace with incredible views. You can pick up grocery items at **Abbey Store** (tel. 028/20181), which also doubles as the post office. Cape Clear's the **Club** (tel. 028/39184) serves cheap sandwiches during the day.

WORTH SEEING

Despite the look-alike holiday homes that infest the area, the crescent-shape port village of **Baltimore** is beautiful and not touristy. Its well-protected harbor attracts the occasional sailboater during the summer season, along with a handful of Irish and German families on holiday. Baltimore was sacked in 1631 by a band of Algerian sailors, who after razing an abbey on Sherkin Island, kidnapped an Irish fisherman and forced him to pilot their two frigates into the bay. As a result, watchtowers were installed at the harbor mouth to protect the town. Today, you can walk to a modern version of the watchtower—a phallic, whitewashed weather beacon—southwest of the pier; the view is particularly stunning when the fishing trawlers head for port around sunset.

Baltimore's most famous attractions are **Sherkin Island** and **Cape Clear,** both accessible by regular ferry. Sherkin, 2 km (1 mi) off the coast and visible from Baltimore's waterfront pubs, receives the bulk of visitors, mainly because it's only 10 minutes away by boat. The island has recently been featured in the popular works of young playwright Sebastian Barry. **Bushe's Pub** (tel. 028/20125) provides info on the **Sherkin Island Ferry Service,** which runs seven boats per day in the summer (three per day off-season) that will drop you at Sherkin's port and collect you later the same day for £4. On the island, you'll find the ruins of **Dun Na Long Castle** and **Sherkin Abbey,** both built around 1470 by the O'Driscolls, a seafaring clan known as the "scourge of the Irish seas." On the island's northwestern shore, stop by the **Sherkin Island Marine Station,** 1 km (½ mi) from the pier, for nice views.

More impressive by far is **Cape Clear,** a 10-square-km (3-square-mi) island 6 km (4 mi) offshore. The most southerly port in Ireland, Cape Clear has as its unofficial slogan "Next Parish: America." With its sparse population (about 200), the island is rugged and unblemished, perfect for hiking. In the 17th century, before the famine, Cape Clear's population was nearly 10 times its present size. Near the pier in North Harbour, the cape's principal port, are the ruins of **St. Chiaran's Church.** It was here in 351 that Ireland's first saint, Chiaran of Clear, was born and taught the gospel of Christianity some 70 years before St. Patrick reached Ireland. The ferry *Naomh Chiaran* (tel. 028/39135) leaves Baltimore harbor for Cape Clear three times per day July–August, twice per day September–June, and four times every Sunday year-round (45 mins; £8 round-trip), weather permitting.

MIZEN HEAD PENINSULA

COMING AND GOING

Bus Éireann buses depart from Skibbereen and Ballydehob and rumble down the peninsula as far as Goleen (£5.50). Buses leave three times per day in summer (once daily in winter). From Goleen to Barley Cove and the Mizen Head, you'll need to drive or cycle.

MULLING OVER A LITTLE YEATS

A few hundred years ago, the O'Mahonys built a tiny town on an equally minuscule island about 45 minutes off the coast road between Schull and Goleen. These days, you'll probably be the only person enjoying this gorgeously remote bit of Ireland, with lapping waves and wildflower-ensconced views. Unless, of course, Tim Hyde (the occasional inhabitant of the tower) is home, in which case you may (if you ask nicely) receive a personal tour of the tower.

To reach the castle from Schull, bike or hike along the coast road toward Goleen; turn left on the unmarked road across the street from the barn with the red, corrugated-metal door; turn right at the extremely overgrown footpath at the white house (which, incidentally, belongs to Fred Astaire's daughter); then meander across the fields and over several gates (they're meant to stop the cows, not you) until you reach the bridge to the tower.

WHERE TO SLEEP AND EAT

The excellent and outdoorsy **Schull Backpacker's Lodge** (Colla Rd., tel. 028/28681) is a five-minute walk from Schull. Dorm beds are £7, private rooms £10, and tent sites £5. Smack in the center of town is Mrs. McSweeney's **Schull Central B&B** (Main St., tel. 028/28227), with large, plain rooms for £14–£17 a head. The place has a well-worn, homey feel—probably because Mrs. McSweeney has lived here her entire life. The **Barley Cove Holiday Park** (Barley Cove, tel. 028/35302) is a campground that overlooks the beach but swarms with RVs and their owners at the height of summer. Tent sites cost £9.50–£12 depending on the number of people. A far better choice is to camp at the nearby beach for free (and it's even legal).

Also in Schull, **Bunratty Inn** (Main St., tel. 028/28341), on the main square, serves seafood chowder (£2.50), smoked mackerel salad (£4.50), and sandwiches (£2.50). It also puts on frequent, foot-stomping traditional music shows. **Courtyard Bar** (Main St., tel. 028/28209) bakes bread on the premises and serves sandwiches and the like for about £4. In Goleen, **Heron's Cove Restaurant** (Goleen Harbour, tel. 028/35225) serves cheap soup, sandwiches, and fish-and-chips in a secluded courtyard overlooking a cove. You'll find grocery stores in every town.

WORTH SEEING

Poor Mizen Head. Though still incredibly scenic, it doesn't have jaw-dropping views like the Ring of Kerry or Beara Peninsula. But it *does* have a marked dearth of tourists (which certainly can't be said of Kerry) and accessibility via public transport (Beara's Achilles' heel), which make it well worth a couple of days of exploring. The main highlight is the Mizen Head itself, where the peninsula ends in a series of cliffs. The **Mizen Head Signal Station** (tel. 028/35225), admission £2, is perched on one of these cliffs. At the entrance to the station is a narrow bridge that affords dizzying views of the rocks below and access to a lookout point offering an amazing view. The station is open April–October, daily 11–5, and November–March, weekends noon–4.

Small towns dot the peninsula's southern coast. With a great hostel, bike-rental shops, and plenty of pubs, **Schull** makes the best base for exploring the peninsula. It's a cute, little harbor town where you can take scenic walks along the bay. Rent a bike from **McCarthy's Garage** (Main St., £7 per day) and head west along the less-trafficked road along the coast. You'll pass an incredibly remote 16th-century castle (*see box, below*) and a heather-and-cow landscape, which soon begins to include coves and inlets. About 11 km (7 mi) west, you'll reach the tiny town of **Goleen,** where you can grab picnic supplies or lunch. From Goleen, it's another 11 km (6½ mi) to Mizen Head. Other spots worthy of exploration are **Barley Cove** (18 km/11 mi from Mizen Head), a sandy beach with craggy rocks on one side and brilliant blue water on the other, and **Crookhaven,** at the end of a smaller peninsula, which has a few markets and a pub.

BEARA PENINSULA

BASICS

Beara has two **tourist offices:** one in Glengarriff (Main St., tel. 027/63084) that's open May–September 9–9, and one in Kenmare (The Square, tel. 027/412331) that's open daily 9–5, which is more oriented to Kerry. The local Raleigh Rent-A-Bike agent operates out of **Jem Creations Craft Workshop** (Main St., Glengarriff, tel. 027/63113), where bikes cost £7.50 per day, plus a £40 deposit. Pick up the excellent "Walking Around Glengarriff" brochure (5p) from the tourist office or Jem Creations Craft Workshop. Castletown's information trailer doesn't have a phone or address; look for it on the road to Dursey, west of the square.

COMING AND GOING

Bus Éireann offers regular daily service from Glengarriff to Cork (3 per day, 1 on Sun.; £9) and Dublin (1 per day; £16), and summer-only service to Kenmare (2 per day; £3.50) and Killarney (2 per day; £7.30). All buses stop on Main Road in front of the Harrington's office. Bus Éireann does not operate at all on the peninsula itself, but **O'Donoghue's** (tel. 027/70007) and **Harrington's** (tel. 027/74003) offer service from Glengarriff to Castletown (£4–£5) once a day Monday–Saturday. It is extremely important that you call these companies to find out when they are going through Glengarriff: You must literally flag down the O'Donaghue bus, but the Harrington's bus will pick you up if you call.

WHERE TO SLEEP

GLENGARRIFF

At the east end of Glengarriff's two-block-long center is **Cottage Bar and Restaurant** (Main Rd., tel. 027/63331), which triples as a B&B (£15 per person), hostel (beds £7.50), and restaurant. All rooms have en-suite bathrooms, and there's also a small kitchen. There are also two excellent campgrounds outside town on the road to Castletown. **O'Shea's Camping Park** (Castletown Rd., tel. 027/63140) has 30 tent sites peppered throughout a small forest adjacent to Bantry Bay. A stone's throw away is **Dowling's** (Castletown Rd., tel. 027/63154), which is larger (90 sites) and more crowded, thanks to the nearby food shop and the traditional-music pub on the grounds. Both charge £6–£7 per site and are open mid-March–October.

CAHERMORE

Adjacent to the Tibetan Buddhist Retreat outside Cahermore is the **Garranes Hostel** (tel. 027/73147), touted as the best hostel on the peninsula. This cliff-side farmhouse—with stunning views of the Atlantic and the peninsula—has 18 beds (£7), but in a pinch, they sometimes allow tent camping. Inquire about free meditation classes at the retreat next door.

ALLIHIES

Smack in the middle of Allihies is the well-kept and mellow IHH **Village Hostel** (Main St., tel. 027/73107), with 14 beds (£7) tucked into small, bright rooms, as well as three doubles (£18) and laundry facilities (£3). The hostel has a common room–kitchen with a wood-burning stove and is closed October–February.

FOOD

The **Cottage Bar and Restaurant** (*see above*) serves the best non-pub eats in Glengarriff. On Allihies, choices are very limited, but **O'Neils Pub** (no phone) does the usual soup and sandwiches menu.

WORTH SEEING

The Beara Peninsula (pronounced *bar*-a) is one of Ireland's better-kept secrets. Despite its proximity to Killarney and the heavily trod Ring of Kerry, Beara sees only a handful of cyclists and hitchhikers during the summer season, and only locals and sheep during winter. Bus service is very minimal, so you may want to rent a car for the trip. The rewards, however, are substantial. Much of the road hugs either the coast or the ridge of the Slieve Miskish Mountains and gives phenomenal views. Come nightfall, when the air is pungent with peat smoke and farm smells, the greatest reward may be a small, smoky pub filled with the sort of locals who are actually impressed when they meet foreigners. The 141-km (88-mi) Beara Loop is best explored by a lengthy hike or a few days of cycling. The loop is accessible via **Kenmare** from the north or west and **Glengarriff** from the south and east. If experiencing Beara's strikingly desolate beauty is your goal, stop in one of these tourist towns to buy a map and rent a bike, and then hit the road. If you're hiking, the well-marked **Beara Way** is an excellent way to see the peninsula—it stays off the roads and strays near hundreds of prehistoric monuments sprinkled across Beara. Both the trail and monuments are shown on the superb "Discovery Series Map 84" (£4.20), useful for hikers and bikers alike. Pick one up at post or tourist offices.

As you travel counterclockwise from Kenmare, the first town you'll hit is **Lauragh,** an outcrop of pubs and newsagents surrounded by woods and small lakes stocked with trout and salmon. From here, you can head south via the steep but wildly scenic **Healy Pass** or continue west for the postage stamp–size town of **Eyeries,** possibly the most beautifully remote settlement on the entire peninsula. Sweeping views and the wonderfully deserted beach fascinate during the day. Come Thursday night the entire town turns out at local pubs for untouristy traditional-music sessions that often lead to dancing in the street. Farther west is tiny **Allihies,** from where you can begin the return leg toward Glengarriff or make an 8-km (5-mi)—and highly recommended—detour to **Dursey Island.** To reach the island, take a rickety cable car (£3 round-trip) from Garnish Point, a trip that involves swinging violently 50 ft above the ocean on a journey that many fear will be their last. The carriage—which can carry six people, two cows, or 10 sheep—makes crossings year-round, Monday–Saturday 9–11, 2:30–5, and 7–8, with irregular times on Sunday; call 027/73016 or 027/73095 for schedules. Back on the main road are the towns of **Cahermore** and **Adrigole,** from where it's 19 km (12 mi), uphill, to Glengarriff.

Castletown (which also appears as Castletownbere or Castletown Bearhaven on some maps) has the distinction of being the most westwardly town on Beara to be served by buses. Near Castletown are the decent **Beara Hostel** (3 km/2 mi west, tel. 027/70184), with dorm beds for £7 and doubles for £17, and **Dunboy Castle** (admission 50p), 3 km (2 mi) southwest. You can rent bikes at **Supervalue** (Main St., tel. 027/70020) for £8 per day. **Glengarriff** lies at the foot of one of Ireland's most scenic roads, the 27-km (17-mi) stretch of N71 that connects Glengarriff with Kenmare. This mountaintop route twists and turns through desolate valleys and 100-year-old, rough-carved rock tunnels—a steep ascent from either side but a favorite among veteran travelers. Luckily, the bus from Glengarriff to Kenmare keeps to this route, so all is not lost if you don't have a bike. If you do plan to cycle this route, start out early in the day so you can take your time with the killer climbs.

KILLARNEY

BASICS

AMERICAN EXPRESS

East Avenue Rd., tel. 064/35722. Open weekdays 9–8, weekends 10–7.

In case you want to see the world.

At American Express, we're here to make your journey a smooth one. So we have over 1,700 travel service locations in over 130 countries ready to help. What else would you expect from the world's largest travel agency?

do more

Travel

Call 1 800 AXP-3429 or visit
www.americanexpress.com/travel

In case you want to be welcomed there.

We're here to see that you're always welcomed at establishments everywhere. That's why millions of people carry the American Express® Card – for peace of mind, confidence, and security, around the world or just around the corner.

do more

In case you're running low.

We're here to help with more than 190,000 Express Cash locations around the world. In order to enroll, just call American Express at 1 800 CASH-NOW before you start your vacation.

do more **AMERICAN EXPRESS**

Express Cash

And in case you'd rather be safe than sorry.

We're here with American Express® Travelers Cheques. They're the safe way to carry money on your vacation, because if they're ever lost or stolen you can get a refund, practically anywhere or anytime. To find the nearest place to buy Travelers Cheques, call 1 800 495-1153. Another way we help you do more.

do more AMERICAN EXPRESS

Travelers Cheques

BIKE RENTAL

The local Raleigh Rent-A-Bike agent is **O'Callaghan's Cycles** (College St., tel. 064/31175). It rents 18-speeds for £6 per day, £30 per week. A half block toward Main Street, **O'Neill's Cycles** (Plunkett St., tel. 064/31970) also rents 18-speeds for the same price. Your best bet, however, is **O'Sullivans** (High St., tel. 064/31282), which rents 21-speeds with all the extras for £5 per day and a mere £25 per week.

MAIL

Post New St., tel. 064/31288. Open weekdays 9–5:30, Sat. 9–1.

VISITOR INFORMATION

The **tourist office** books B&B rooms (£1 fee) and organizes guided tours of the Ring of Kerry through the coach companies that have offices across the street. It's best to visit the tourist office first if you want an objective rundown of Ring tours. New Town Hall, south end of Main St., tel. 064/31633. Open July–Aug., Mon.–Sat. 9–8, Sun. 10–6; June and Sept., daily 9–6; Oct.–May, Mon.–Sat. 9:15–5:30.

COMING AND GOING

BY BUS

Killarney's **bus station** is adjacent to the rail depot and the Great Southern Hotel, both of which are off East Avenue Road, east of the city center. Inside the bus annex is an information desk and a listing of daily departures. To reach town, turn left from the depot and follow the main road as it curves right. There are buses to Cork (5 per day; £12), Dublin (3 per day; £15.50), and Tralee (8 per day; £6). East Avenue Rd., tel. 064/34777. Information desk open Mon.–Sat. 8:30–5:45, Sun. 8:30–1 and 1:45–4.

Commercialized Killarney feels like a movie set. The day-to-day life of locals has been elbowed out of existence by the needs of tourists, and you'll be lucky to hear an Irish accent on the Babel-like streets.

BY TRAIN

Killarney Station, roughly 30 yards from the bus depot, has a staffed information counter. Killarney is on both the main Tralee–Dublin line and the Tralee–Limerick line, with connections to Cork (sometimes via Mallow). Four trains per day go to both Dublin (£17.50) and Tralee (£5.50). A one-way fare to Cork is £13.50, while a trip to Galway costs £15. East Avenue Rd., tel. 064/31067. Information counter open Mon.–Sat. 7:30–6, Sun. for train departures.

WHERE TO SLEEP

Killarney has nine hostels, 35 hotels, and hundreds of B&Bs. Things fill up fast in the summer, so book ahead. Reservations are particularly essential and must be made far in advance, if you plan on visiting in mid-May or the last weekend in July, when Killarney hosts its biannual horse races.

BED-AND-BREAKFASTS

Muckross Road and New Road have the largest selection of B&Bs, but in Killarney nearly one house in three seems to provide accommodations during the summer season. Try **Innisfallen House** (Muckross Rd., tel. 064/34193) or **Killarney View Guest House** (Muckross Rd., tel. 064/33122), both of which charge £22–£25 per person. The Killarney House is probably the nicest, decorated in a cutesy grand-motherly style of antiques and flowery wallpaper. The **Arch House** (East Avenue Rd., near train station, tel. 064/32184) has rooms with bath starting at £20 per person. If you want to spend a little more for comfort, try the **Arbutus** (College St., tel. 064/31037), which has been run by the Buckely family since it was built in the 1930s. The lobby has an open fire where guests congregate. Try to get a room in the newer second-floor section; they're bigger. A double costs between £60 and £90. Only a five-minute walk from the town center, **Lime Court** (Muckross Rd., tel. 064/34547) has 16 rooms in a modern building with great bay windows at the front. The rooms are plenty big enough and look out over green pasture. A double costs £52.

HOSTELS

Four Winds (IHH). There's a fire-warmed common room and dorm rooms with new beds (£6–£7.50) at this large and generally crowded hostel. It's comfortably modern and situated in the heart of Killarney. Doubles are £19 (£25 high-season). *43 New St., tel. 064/33094. From train station, turn left on East Avenue Rd., left on New St. 56 beds. Reception open until midnight (until 3 AM weekends). Kitchen.*

Neptune's. Neptune's is your standard huge hostel, but it's surprisingly quiet for being in the city center. Comfortable 6- to 10-bed dorm rooms (beds £7.50) and a large kitchen help to make up for its rather sterile and vast common room. Singles are also available for £18, and doubles for £23. Sheet rental is 50p. *Bishop's La., just off New St., tel. 064/35255. 102 beds. Kitchen.*

CAMPING

The best of the three campgrounds near Killarney is **Whitebridge Camping Park** (tel. 064/31590), 2 km (1 mi) east of Killarney on the banks of the River Flesk; take the Cork Road and follow the signs. Its 40 sites (£3.50–£5, plus £2.50 per person) are developed and crowded, although there's good hiking on nearby Lough Leane. Bicycles (£6) can be rented on the premises, and a food shop and pub are nearby. The park is closed November–mid-March. Five kilometers (3 mi) west of Killarney, along St. Margaret's Road (which becomes the N70 just outside of town), is **Beechgrove** (tel. 064/31727), which has 50 sites available from mid-March to mid-October. A little farther is **Fossa Caravan and Camping Park** (Killorglin Rd., tel. 064/31497), which has 120 sites and is open mid-March–October. Neither is particularly scenic, but Fossa has an on-site restaurant and food shop. Beechgrove's rates are £4 per person (£6 July–August). The rates at Fossa are £3.50–£5 per site, plus £2.50 per person.

FOOD

Sheila's (75 High St., tel. 064/31270) has fed the people of Killarney for more than 30 years—it was recently passed on from mother to daughter. The menu has no frills (entrées run anywhere from £8), with corned beef and cabbage the number one choice. They serve wine. The **Súgán Hostel** (Lewis Rd., tel. 064/33104) serves delicious "vegetarianish" three-course meals for around £10 (£7 for hostel guests) in its intimate dining room, which features live traditional music on summer weekends. The restaurant is open October, Tuesday–Sunday 6 PM–9:30 PM. Nearby, **Mayflower Chinese Restaurant** (Church La., off Plunkett St., tel. 064/32212) serves chow mein (£5–£6), tofu dishes (£5), and inventive chicken concoctions like crispy chicken with plum sauce (£5) daily until midnight (a little later on weekends). Both the food and the ultracozy feel of the vegetarian **An Taelann** (Bridewell La., tel. 064/33083), open daily 12:30–4 and 6:30–10, make this place popular with carnivores and veg heads alike. It serves unusual pastas, such as spinach pasta with blue cheese and broccoli (£6). Lunches are a bargain, but the same dishes cost £3 more in the evenings. Do not leave without trying the rhubarb crumble (£2). At the other end of town, **Grunts** (New St., tel. 064/31890) whips up good soups and sandwiches for less than £3. For late-night, post-pub feasts, **Busy B's Bistro** (15 Upper New St., tel. 064/31972) serves all things deep-fried Monday–Saturday until 3 AM. For groceries and such, **Dunnes** (New St., tel. 064/31560) has it all.

AFTER DARK

For information on current Kerry events, pick up the weekly *Killarney Advertiser,* free and available at the tourist office. Most of Killarney's pubs are unabashedly devoted to the tourist trade. The **Laurels** (Main St., tel. 064/31149), a beautiful old-style public house, charges a scandalous £4 cover for the simple privilege of singing "Danny Boy" with a choir of drunken foreigners; however, the front bar isn't too bad and has no cover. **O'Connor's** (High St., tel. 064/31115) is a worn 1960s pub that balances large tourist crowds with solid pints and traditional music on Monday and Thursday nights. A sure bet for traditional acoustic music in the summer is **Fáilte Bar** (College St., tel. 064/31893), which also irregularly hosts rock bands. Stake your claim on a seat by 8 PM or prepare to stand. **Yer Man's Pub/The Strawberry Tree** (Plunkett St., tel. 064/32688) is mobbed by local twentysomethings most nights. At closing time, they move to the adjoining **Rudy's Nightclub**, which stays open until 1:30 AM. The cover charge for Rudy's is free before 10:30 and £3–£45 thereafter. **Gleneagles** (Muckross Rd., tel. 064/31870) is the spot for gloriously cheesy cabaret. The **Killarney Cineplex** (tel. 06437007), a four-screen cinema opposite Killarney Towers Hotel, might be your only means of escape from the tourist glut.

WORTH SEEING

Killarney is the most heavily touristed city in southwestern Ireland, so much so that you feel it's on the verge of ceasing to be a town at all and becoming a Celtic theme park instead. Its proximity to Shannon Airport ensures a constant flow of wealthy foreigners, and most coach companies use Killarney as a base for their bus tours. Another reason this prim tourist village is at the top of everyone's must-see list is its location on the eastern fringe of the **Ring of Kerry** (*see below*) and the fabled **Lakes of Killarney.** Behind the lakes the beautifully named **Macgillycuddy's Reeks** rise up, the highest mountain range in Ireland. If you're planning to explore the Ring by bicycle or tourist coach, you will inevitably find yourself in Killarney for at least one night, and that's probably enough.

Massive, glacial rocks form the side of the **Gap of Dunloe,** one of Killarney's primary sights. The rocks create strange echoes; give it a shout to try it out. The gap is 7 km (4½ mi) west of town and the road through it stretches for 6 km (4 mi). The **Upper Lake** comes into view at the head of the Gap, with the lonely Black Valley stretching into the hills at the right. From **Lord Brandon's Cottage**—a tea shop serving soup and sandwiches in summer—a path leads to the edge of the lake. From there you can take a boat out to the 30 little islands of the **Middle Lake.** The impressive **Killarney National Park** (tel. 064/ 31440), a pristine, 25,000-acre wood whose principal entrance is 1½ km (1 mi) east of the city, is a good reason to visit. Much of the park straddles **Lough Leane** (Lower Lake), a tranquil, windswept lake that's littered with rocky islets and dozens of hard-to-reach (and rarely visited) waterfalls. On an island in the center of the lake the romantic ruins of **Innisfallen Island** date from as early as the 6th century. From the mid-10th to the 14th-century the fabled *Annals of Innisfallen* were compiled by the monks who set up residence here. The book survives in the Bodleian Library in Oxford. You can rent a rowboat at Ross Castle (*see below*) to reach the Island. It would take three or four days and a good map to fully explore the park, but a few good day hikes are signposted at each of the park's entrances. The park's gates are open daily 9–6, but technically the park is accessible 24 hours and admission is free.

At the end of the Gap is **Ross Castle,** a fully restored 14th-century stronghold. It was the last place in the whole province of Munster to fall to the bloody army of Cromwell in 1652. A later building has 16th- and 17th-century furniture. It's open from May to October, and admission is £2.50.

RING OF KERRY

Running along the perimeter of the Iveragh Peninsula, the 176-km (110-mi) Ring of Kerry can be accessed at any number of places, although Killarney (*see above*) is the traditional—and most practical—starting point. On sunny days, the two-lane highway that handles the bulk of traffic is choked with rental cars, tourist coaches, and cyclists, all engaged in the vain struggle to find the real, rural Ireland promised by the tourist board. Many are disappointed to find that the Ring is one of the country's busiest roads, overflowing with cars, buses, fumes, gift shops, restaurants, and other tourists. Most of the loop is not recommended for serious cyclists or hikers who are looking for beautiful rugged countryside; for that, time could be better spent in the Beara (*see above*) or Dingle (*see below*) Peninsula.

Yet as long as you don't mind sharing the road, you will encounter some incredibly stunning coastal and mountain views. To do the Ring justice, you'll need a minimum of two days on bike, more if you're traveling by bus. Most prefer to tackle the Ring in a counterclockwise direction, starting from Killarney, then pausing for a night in Glenbeigh, Caherciveen (also spelled Cahersiveen), Valentia Island, Ballinskelligs, Waterville, or Kenmare. You can also begin the loop in Kenmare, but during the winter, it will be difficult to get around in this direction unless you have a car. The Ring can be explored in as little as a day, either by car or on a guided tour, but most of the Ring's best sites are found on spontaneous detours and winding back roads—the sort of pleasant traps that take time to fall into. Another reason to spend more time here is to do the 36-km (22½-mi) **Skellig Loop,** a short but scenic circuit ignored by most luxury coaches. Touring this smaller loop will add an additional day or two to your itinerary, but it may well be the highlight of your Ring of Kerry tour.

BASICS

Bord Fáilte's only Ring of Kerry tourist desk is in Kenmare's **Courthouse** (The Square, tel. 064/41233), open May–September, daily 9–5:30 (closed Sun. 1–2:15). Most towns on the Ring have numerous pubs, restaurants, food stores, a bureau de change, and street-side triangular billboards crowned with a Bord Fáilte shamrock that contain town maps and a brief list of B&Bs. In Caherciveen, the privately owned **Old Oratory** (Main Rd., tel. 066/72996) stocks regional maps and brochures and changes money. The **post offices** in Kenmare (Bridge St., tel. 064/41490), Killorglin (The Square, tel. 066/61101), and Waterville (Main St., tel. 066/74100) also change money. The post office in Glenbeigh has tourist brochures and free guides to the Ring.

GETTING AROUND

BY BICYCLE

Though the roads teem with luxury coaches, the 176-km (110-mi) Ring of Kerry is easy to navigate and generally quite flat. Youth hostels and restaurants are found every 32 km (20 mi) or so, making it possible to tackle the loop in a piecemeal fashion. A fast-paced bike tour will take at least two days, but most cyclists prefer to do it in three to four days in order to have time to explore a few unmarked backroads and/or to detour through Valentia Island and the Skellig Loop. No matter where you're headed, however, storms are a year-round threat, so rain gear is a must, as are spare parts and a good map. The most convenient place to rent cycles is in Killarney (*see above*), but a few shops are scattered throughout the area. In Killorglin there's **O'Shea's Cycle Centre** (Lower Bridge St., tel. 066/61919), which rents bikes for £6 per day. In Kenmare, **Finnegan Cycles** (37 Henry St., tel. 064/41083), the local Raleigh Rent-A-Bike agent, rents bikes for £6 per day and £35 per week, with a £40 deposit. Be sure to time your departures so that you miss the cavalcade of coaches that could leave you headfirst in a ditch, bike and all, or worse; keep in mind that the coaches leave Killarney between 9 and 10, stop in Waterville and Sneem for lunch at noon, and then head back to Killarney.

BY BUS

Killarney has four competing companies that offer three nearly identical tours at identical prices: a full-day tour of the Ring of Kerry (£10), a half-day tour of the Ring of Kerry (£7.50), and a boat-bus combo trek through the Gap of Dunloe and the Lakes of Killarney (£13); some companies give a £2 discount to students or hostelers. The companies are **Castle Lough Tours** (High St., tel. 064/32496), **Deros Tours** (Main St., tel. 064/31251), **O'Connors** (Ross Rd., tel. 064/31052), and **Cronin's Tours** (College St., tel. 064/31521).

If you're short on time, one of the cheapest ways to see the Ring is on **Bus Éireann's Ring of Kerry route** (tel. 064/34777), which departs Killarney twice daily (less often late Sept.–May), stopping at Killorglin, Glenbeigh, Caherciveen, Waterville, Caherdaniel, Sneem, and Moll's Gap, before returning to Killarney. The entire loop costs £9.70, £12.20 if you want to get off (once) and then continue on in the next bus. At no extra cost, you can extend the loop as far as Tralee. For Valentia Island or Ballinskelligs, take the bus to Caherciveen or Waterville, respectively, and walk from there.

WHERE TO SLEEP

GLENBEIGH

Breens Diner and the **Village House** (Main Hwy., tel. 066/68128) are two functional B&Bs run by the same people. Rooms are £17–£20 per person. **Glenbeigh Hotel** (Main Hwy., tel. 066/68333), a country house thick with rural charm and cutesy antiques, has rooms for £25–£30 per person. It's small enough to avoid large tour groups and quite luxurious in its own way. Slightly cheaper (£20 per person) is **Ocean Wave House** (Main Hwy., tel. 066/68249), closed November–March, a family-run B&B 1 km (½ mi) east of town. Campers should try **Glenross Caravan and Camping Park** (Main Hwy., tel. 064/68456), which is open mid-May–early September and charges £4 per person. It is clean and well kept, with showers (50p) and a small laundry for washing and drying (£4.50).

CAHERCIVEEN

The IHH **Sive Hostel** (15 East End, tel. 066/72717) is three blocks from Caherciveen's small square; you can't miss the smart yellow-and-blue exterior. Inside it's tidy and comfortable. The hostel charges £7.50 for a bed and £4 for a tent site. There are doubles for £18. The hostel also arranges day trips to the Skellig Islands (£20). Paul, who runs the place, is bubbling over with information on local musical events and might even be able to get you invited to play in a session if your talents lie in that direction. The most comfortable B&B in town is in the village center: **Dun An Oir** (New St., tel. 066/72565), a four-room, family-run place that charges £14 per person. If it's full, there's a cluster of dull B&Bs on the road to Valentia Island. From mid-March to mid-October, when the weather is good, try **Mannix Point Campground** (tel. 066/72806), which has 42 pitches (£4 per person) on the waterfront. Nearby is a semi-stocked food shop and a common room with an open fireplace and a 160-year-old piano.

VALENTIA ISLAND

Of the two hostels on the island, only the **Royal Pier Hostel** (Knightstown, tel. 066/76144), housed in a brooding manor house, offers private rooms (£8.50) as well as dorm beds (£7.50) and tent spaces (£4.50 per person). There's also a pool table and a restaurant. **Mrs. Lyne's B&B** (Knightstown, tel. 066/76171) is well tended and cozy. All of its rooms come equipped with thick comforters and an assortment of religious icons for around £15. It's closed October–March.

WATERVILLE

Peter's Place (no phone) is an amazingly mellow town house 300 yards west of town. Some of the rooms have exceptional views out to sea. Beds are £7.50, tent sites £4, but rates are negotiable—Peter is a very laid-back guy and has the lowdown on how best to explore the local area. He can also arrange bike rentals (£6) and trips to the Skelligs (£20). **Waterville Leisure House** (Main St., tel. 066/74400) is generally packed with families and school-age tour groups. Dorm beds cost £7.50, singles £10. **Clifford's** (Main St., tel. 066/74283), closed November–February, is a nice B&B with en-suite rooms for £17 per person. The **Ashling House** (Main St., tel. 066/74247) has rooms starting at £16.

CAHERDANIEL

It's not a big stopping-off point for coaches or one-day Ring of Kerry visitors, so Caherdaniel is one of the more pleasant spots to rest your limbs. The **Old Forge** (tel. 066/75140) is a pleasant B&B in a historic old building. Doubles are around £35. The **Travellers Rest Hostel** (tel. 066/75175) on the main road is comfortable and clean. Dorm beds are £7–£8; doubles are £19. If no one answers the phone, inquiries should be made across the road at the gas station.

SNEEM

Tahilla Cove Country House (Tahilla Cove, tel. 064/45122) is in an idyllic location, with its own jetty in a sheltered private cove. The sitting room has an open log fire and the terrace overlooks 14 acres of subtropical gardens and the cove. Big, comfortable double rooms go for under £60. The **Old Convent House** (tel. 064/45181) is past the bridge and next to the church. Doubles in the grand old building go for around £40. The owners have a **campsite** next door with sites for £4.50. The **Harbour View Hostel** is at the Kenmare end of town and has dorm beds for £7–£8.50 and doubles for £20.

KENMARE

Kenmare's IHH **Fáilte Hostel** (Henry St., tel. 064/42333) is a comfy town house with a spacious sitting room and oak-paneled bedrooms. Its rooms, spread over three floors and accessed via a Georgian staircase, are clean, small (six to eight beds), and airy. Doubles are £20, dorm beds £7.50. If you're looking for B&Bs, there's a large cluster just outside town on the Killarney Road. None are particularly outstanding; the best value is **Ardmore House** (Killarney Rd., tel. 064/41406), closed December–February, where doubles cost £34–£40. On the N70, 4 km (2½ mi) west of Kenmare, is **Ring of Kerry Camping Park** (tel. 064/41648), closed January–March. Its 60 sites (£4.50 per person) have good views of Kenmare Bay and the Caha Mountains, and there's a food shop, kitchen, and common room with fireplace.

FOOD

The **Ring Lyne** (Chapeltown, tel. 066/76103) is a famous seafood joint on Valentia Island; the scallops are out of this world. The fixed price lunch at £8 is a great deal. The **Smugglers Inn** (Cliff Rd., tel. 066/74330) is Waterville's gourmet surprise, with seafood the specialty. It's not cheap, but the fixed-price deals are worth the £15. The **Purple Heather Bistro** (Henry St., tel 064/41016), in Kenmare, has classy bistro fare at very moderate prices. Try the excellent sandwiches.

WORTH SEEING

As you travel west from Killarney, the first major stop on the Ring of Kerry is **Killorglin**, 16 km (10 mi) west, a quiet riverside village on the slope of a gentle hill. The flat and only vaguely scenic road from Kil-

THE SKELLIGS

Sure, £20 is a lot to spend on a boat ride, but the wet, wonderful ride to Skellig Michael is worth it for adventurers with plenty of Dramamine. During the 1½-hour journey you'll pass the Lesser Skellig, a sanctuary where 40,000 birds careen around the island's jagged spires. Farther out is the phenomenal Skellig Michael: home to an amazing 6th-century village of monastic beehive dwellings and vertigo-inducing views. To get here, book at least one day in advance via Joe Roddy (tel. 066/74268) or Sean Feehan (tel. 066/79182), both of whom leave from Ballinskelligs; or Michael O'Sullivan (tel. 066/74268), who departs from Portmagel or Waterville. Be warned: The pinnacles of this ancient Christian (possibly pagan) center of worship will haunt you for days.

larney to Killorglin disappoints many travelers, but once they regain the rural road west of Killorglin, the flat bog turns into hilly, sylvan pastures. Despite its small size, Killorglin has a handful of budget restaurants and is a popular lunch stop with Ring of Kerry cyclists. If at all possible try to be in town for the three days in mid-August when the truly unique and lively **Puck Fair** takes over the place. The bacchanalian event gets its name from the tradition of capturing a wild goat (or puck) and crowning it king. It's really an excuse for boozing and carousing, and special opening hours ensure nobody's fun is tampered with.

Because Killorglin is so close to Killarney, most travelers prefer to cycle or bus straight through to **Glenbeigh,** 11 km (7 mi) west of Killorglin. Set on a boggy plateau by the sea, Glenbeigh is one of those block-long towns where everyone knows what everyone else had for breakfast. A detour leads to a long stretch of pristine beach at the end of the R564. Glenbeigh's only other attraction is the **Kerry Bog Village Museum** (tel. 066/69184), a small place with exhibits on bogs and peat and reconstructed 18th-century houses. At £2.50, it's worth a quick look, especially since a mug of Bewley's coffee at the pub next door is half off with admission. The museum is just west of town on the main highway, signposted from the village center. It's open June–September, Monday–Saturday 10–6, Sunday 2–6; March–May and October, weekends 9:30–5:30. West of Glenbeigh, the highway curves toward the coast, where it ultimately changes into a creeping cliff-side road, battered on one side by the Atlantic and overshadowed by steeply rising mountains on the other. Nearby **Caragh Lake** and its surrounding area offer some of the best hill and mountain views in Kerry.

The next stop is **Caherciveen** (pronounced care-sha-*veen*), 26 km (16 mi) southwest of Glenbeigh. Large by Ring of Kerry standards, Caherciveen is a tiny town with lots of long-standing hardware stores and butcher shops. Following the tradition in this part of the world, the town's modest, terraced houses are painted in different colors—the brighter the better. Refreshingly undeveloped and old-fashioned for this part of the country, its bay-side quay has a few weathered storehouses, but its only official attraction is the **Barracks** (tel. 066/72777), which highlights local history and also houses a tourist desk. For a quiet pint, try the worn **Kelly's Pub** or **Anchor Bar**; both are on Main Street and host live music during summer. The **O'Connell Memorial Church,** also on Main Road, is a large and elaborate neo-Gothic church that dominates the center of town. It was built in 1888 of Newry granite and local black limestone to honor the local hero, Daniel O'Connell.

Caherciveen marks the Ring's western fringe; from here the road turns south and inland, rejoining the coast at **Waterville,** 13 km (8 mi) south. If you'd rather continue along the coast, 5½ km (3½ mi) south of Caherciveen is the turnoff for **Skellig Loop.** The first 11 km (7 mi) of this 35-km (22-mi), semicircular detour are unimpressive, but at Portmagee you'll find the turnoff for **Valentia Island,** accessed via a two-lane bridge or a shuttle ferry that leaves from Renard point. The fastest route from Caherciveen, the ferry runs April–October, daily from 8:15 AM to 9:30 PM, and it costs £1 for foot and bike passengers. The island itself is mostly flat and studded with fields of sheep and cattle. Its two principal villages are Chapeltown and Knightstown. You can easily cycle the 11-km-long (7-mi-long) island in less than two hours. Besides its untouristy roads and ocean views, Valentia's major attraction is the **Skellig Heritage Centre** (tel. 066/76306), open April–

September, daily 10–6. Here you'll find a good collection of Skellig artifacts and photos, along with a 15-minute audiovisual show that charts Skelligs' development as a monastic site. Admission is £3.

South from Portmagee, the Skellig Loop keeps to the coast and passes through the villages of **Ballynahow** and **Killonecaha**. This 26-km (16½-mi) stretch affords unbeatable views of the Atlantic and, on a clear day, the Skellig Islands. If you're in the mood for yet another detour, take any of the rough dirt roads to the short cliffs that guard St. Finan's Bay. Or continue south 4 km (2½ mi) toward **Ballinskelligs**, a small fishing village with an old monastery, a pub, and **An Óige hostel** (tel. 066/79229) that will give you a fairly gruff and unfriendly reception. Unless you're spending the night, the only reason to stop here is to catch a ferry to the Skellig Islands (*see box, above*). From Ballinskellig, it's an easy 9½-km (6-mi) ride east (via the R567) to rejoin the main Ring road at Mastergeehy.

Like so many villages on the Ring, **Waterville** has a few restaurants and pubs, but little else. Many people end up calling it a day here, but be warned, there is no bank machine in town. Three kilometers (2 mi) south of Waterville is **Coomakesta Pass.** Its summit gives stunning views of the Kerry coast, but cyclists should be prepared for a long, grueling, 1,014-ft ascent. A rugged, signposted trail by the parking lot atop the pass leads to **Hog's Head.** On foot, it takes 45 minutes to reach the point, which affords a clear view of the Scariff Island and, to the left, the stunning Derrynane National Park with its immaculate white sandy beach and dunes. Your last chance for accommodation before you reach Kenmare is in **Caherdaniel.** This tiny village has two hostels and is a great base from which to walk Derrynane National Park and visit Derrynane House, home of Daniel O'Connell, great patriot, who fought for Catholic emancipation and home rule. Every major city in the south of Ireland, including Dublin, has an O'Connell Street. The house is open May–September, Monday–Saturday 9–6 and Sunday 11–7. Admission is £2. Caherdaniel is also popular with divers. Once past Caherdaniel, the road becomes relatively flat and dull for the next 53 km (33 mi), never regaining the rugged splendor of the northern circuit. For tour-bus travelers, this means time for a sweater-shop stop in **Sneem.** For cyclists and those with rental cars, on the other hand, it means getting to Kenmare as quickly as possible.

> O'Connell Memorial Church is the only church in Ireland named for a layman.

Situated slightly inland without a clear view of Kenmare Bay, **Kenmare** is a natural stopover for buses and cyclists, mainly because it's the last large town before Killarney, 42 km (26 mi) north. Kenmare is also well served by bus, making it a good first or last stop on the Ring if you're looking to avoid the more touristy Killarney completely. On summer evenings, Kenmare's pub scene is surprisingly lively, boasting frequent music sessions and lots of drunken conversation. The **Kenmare Heritage Centre** (near Fair Green, tel. 064/41233) explains the history of the town and supplies a walking route pointing out places of interest. On Old Killarney Road you'll see **Holy Cross Church.** Built in the 1860s, it has a beautiful roof, all of wood with intricate carvings of angels. Also worth visiting is the nearby **Druid Circle**, a 3,000-year-old monument that dates from the early Bronze Age. It consists of 15 large stones arranged in a circle around a center stone. Its precise use is unknown, but it is believed to have served in the rituals of the ancient Druid priests. The beauty of the site is somewhat marred by industrial garbage littering the surrounding area. There's also a worthwhile walk down to the harbor with a great view of Kenmare Bay and boat trips around the bay (£9–£11). Call **Sea Fari Cruises** (tel. 064/83171) for times and details.

DINGLE PENINSULA

The Dingle Peninsula stretches 48 km (30 mi) between Tralee (pronounced tra-*lee*) in the east and Slea Head in the west. It is home to the villages of Castlegregory, Ventry, Inch, Dingle Town, and, just off the coast, the Blasket Islands. Its small size makes it one of Ireland's most accessible and popular summer retreats, especially for cyclists who don't have time to cover the larger Beara or Ring of Kerry circuit. Despite its size, the Dingle Peninsula is topographically diverse and brazenly scenic. Driving or cycling over its high mountain passes, in fact, may conjure images of the Alps or Rockies, and the lushly forested mountains along the shore look like they belong on a South Pacific island.

Culturally, however, the Dingle Peninsula is uniquely Irish. It's part of County Kerry's Gaeltacht (Irish-speaking region), where Irish is still spoken on a daily basis. You won't come across many locals openly

WHERE'S THE HONEY?

If you travel west along the coast road beyond Dunbeg, you'll see a number of puzzling signs indicating "Prehistoric Beehive Huts"—clocháns in Irish. Built of unmortared stone on the southern slopes of Mount Eagle, these huts were actually cells used by hermit monks in the early Christian period. The ultimate isolation you might think, a man alone in a tiny stone hut—only problem is there are some 414 of these between Slea Head and Dunquin. Seems like every second person was dropping out. Farmers, quick to spot a profit, have started to charge for the privilege of visiting one of these huts on their land. The usual price is about 50p.

From Dingle, an excellent walk or cycle is to Ventry, a small outcrop of pubs and newsagents 3 km (2 mi) west. If you keep to the R559 coast road from Ventry, you'll soon end up on the 32-km (20-mi) Slea Head Loop, an incredible circuit that skirts the foot of Mt. Eagle (1,692 ft) and eventually curves north past Dunmore Head, Dunquin, and An Óige's Dunquin Hostel. This road offers views of the coast and Blasket Islands that are unforgettable— two notches above "don't miss." A few miles west of Ventry lies the prehistoric ruins of Dunbeg, a promontory fort from the Iron Age. A fortified stone wall cuts off the promontory, and the landward side is protected by an elaborate system of earthworks and trenches. Within the enclosure is a ruined circular building, with walls up to 22 ft wide.

engaged in Irish conversation, but during summer, the region is swamped with school-age children who have enrolled in one of the peninsula's Irish-language courses. Folk customs and handicrafts are still integral to the Dingle lifestyle, especially now that tourism has become its principal industry. A day or two in Dingle Town, and another few busing or hitching the perimeter, are sufficient to behold the peninsula's best sights, particularly if good weather allows a trip to the impressive Great Blasket Island.

BASICS

The town of **Tralee** is not actually on the peninsula but is the main local transportation hub. Tralee also has a **tourist office** (Ashe Memorial Hall, tel. 066/21288) that's generous with brochures and information about the Dingle Peninsula and is open year-round, Monday–Saturday 9–6 (also Sun. July–Aug.). **O'Shea's Tours** (2 Oakpark Dr., tel. 066/27111) runs tours of the Ring of Kerry (£10) from here. They depart Tuesday and Saturday (additional Thurs. tours in Aug.). You'll find plenty of banks and bureaux de change around town. The closest to the bus/train station is **AIB** on Denny Street. Tralee's **post office** (Edward St., tel. 066/21013) is open Monday–Saturday 9–5:30.

The peninsula's lone **tourist office** is in Dingle Town (Main St., tel. 066/51241) and is open daily 9–6, mid-April–October only. Grab their handy map of Dingle and the peninsula for £1. Another good source for maps and peninsula-related literature is Dingle's **Café Liteartha** (Dyke Gate La., tel. 066/51388), a small bookshop with an intimate, budget-friendly soup and sandwich bar. Along Main Street in Dingle, you will also find a **post office** (tel. 066/51661), open weekdays 9–1 and 2–5:30 and Saturday 9–1, and plenty of bureaux de change.

Most peninsula hostels rent bikes for local day trips, but for long-term rentals try Dingle's **Paddy's Bike Shop** (Dyke Gate La., next to the Grapevine Hostel, no phone), which rents the best bikes in town for £5 per day or £25 per week, plus a £50 deposit. Or try **Foxy John Moriarty Bikes** (Main St., tel. 066/51316), the local Raleigh Rent-A-Bike agent, with 18-speeds for £5–£7 per day or £25 per week, plus a £30 deposit.

COMING AND GOING

Tralee makes a good springboard for exploring the Dingle Peninsula. **Irish Rail** offers daily service to Tralee from Killarney (3 per day; £5.50), Cork (2–4 per day; £17), and Dublin's Heuston Station (3 per day; £16.75). The joint **bus/rail station** is on J. J. Sheehy Road, at Oakpark Road; call 066/23522 for rail information, or 066/23566 for bus information. From Tralee, **Bus Éireann** offers year-round Expressway service to Dingle five times a day, three per day on Sunday. Fares are £5.90 one-way, £8 round-trip. During summer there's also service to Dunquin (direct to youth hostel, 2 per week; £7.70). Buses to Castlegregory (£3.80) leave Tralee on Friday at 8:55 AM and 2 PM. Bus Éireann offers slightly more frequent service to the peninsula's smaller towns and Dingle and Dunquin in the summer; get a schedule at the Tralee bus station.

WHERE TO SLEEP

Because it is the most popular stop on the peninsula, Dingle has the largest selection of value accommodations. There are also a few hostels scattered throughout the region, convenient for cyclists but too far off the beaten track to be easily reached by bus. One of these is the IHH **Bog View Hostel** (tel. 066/58125), a small place with a modern kitchen, common room with open turf fire, clean doubles (£18), and dorm beds (£7). Open May–October, the Bog View is 8 km (5 mi) southwest of the town of Camp on the N86, on the far side of Caherconree Pass. It is also near Inch Beach, where parts of *Ryan's Daughter* were filmed.

Gallarus Oratory, 1½ km (1 mi) from Smerwick Harbour, is one of the best-preserved early churches in Ireland. Built by monks in the 7th or 8th century, the corbeled structure is still waterproof today.

DINGLE

The landmark **Alpine House** (Mail Rd., tel. 066/51250) is a plain, three-story block but happens to be one of the original guest houses in Dingle, dating from 1963. It is still run by the O'Sheas. The location is right over Dingle Bay. Big, bright doubles cost £50. **Greenmount House** (tel. 066/51414) is a classy B&B overlooking the harbor and uphill from the town center. The modern bungalow has 12 impeccable, comfortable rooms (around £50) with big pine beds. Breakfast is served in the conservatory. The incredibly friendly people at **Avondale House** (Corner of Dyke Gate La. and Avondale, tel. 066/51120) offer cozy rooms for £15–£16.50 per person, which includes a stunning breakfast. Some rooms have just been renovated and are quite nice, while others are just okay—ask to see the room first to ensure you get a good one. **Mrs. Russell** (The Mall, tel. 066/51747) has luxurious, en-suite rooms (£17 per person) in a small but cozy town house. Both the Avondale and Mrs. Russell offer vegetarian breakfasts for those who just can't stomach another drop of grease. **An Dreoilin** (Lower Main St., tel. 066/51824) offers smaller, less comfortable rooms in a standard row house from £13 to £15 per person.

There are several hostels in and around Dingle, but many are seasonal, so be sure to call ahead. The best hostel is **Rainbow Hostel** (The Wood, tel. 066/51044), a 15-minute walk from town toward Ventry; a free shuttle also whisks hostelers to and from the bus stop. Set in a secluded farmhouse on a country lane, it has an awesome kitchen, common room, dorm rooms (beds £7), campsites (£4) and, perhaps best of all, it offers 1½-hour massages (£20) to soothe your weary body. For £6 the owner leads trips to see Fungi the dolphin, a superfriendly aquatic mammal who has made his permanent home just off the coast. On Dingle Bay lies **Marina Hostel** (The Wood, tel. 066/51065), a small, plain house with dorm rooms (£7 beds), private rooms (£9 per person), and camping (£4 per person).

TRALEE

Tralee is blessed with a slew of B&Bs. There's not a lot to distinguish one from another, and most have rates around £20 per person. **Castle House** (Upper Castle St., tel. 066/25167) is right in the center of the bustling town. If you want to splurge a little, the **Abbey Gate Hotel** (Main St., tel. 066/29888) is an elegant option in the center of town. Doubles go for £30–£45 per person. Around the corner from the tourist office is the magnificent **Finnegan's Holiday Hostel** (17 Denny St., tel. 066/27610). Most of the

RYAN'S DAUGHTER

Ask any of the older residents of Dunquin and they'll tell you with some pride that the town was the filming site for David Lean's overambitious Irish epic "Ryan's Daughter" in 1969. The movie gave the area its first taste of tourism, and the stars and crew were famed for their fondness for the "old drop." The film was lambasted by critics—"Gush made respectable by millions of dollars tastefully wasted," lamented Pauline Kael. The failure sent Lean into a dry spell (a lean period?) he didn't come out of until 1984's "A Passage to India."

Dunquin itself is a loose collection of sheep fields and isolated, peat-smoke-spouting cottages. Here you can stop for lunch at Kruger's Pub (tel. 066/56127) and catch the Blasket Island Ferry (Dunquin Pier, tel. 066/56455). During summer (weather permitting), boats leave daily on the hour, starting at 10 AM, for the 20-minute ride (£7) to this desolate island, where you'll find the ruins of 15th- and 16th-century monasteries and dozens of good hiking trails. The beautifully designed Blasket Centre (tel. 066/56371) tastefully highlights the history and surprisingly strong literary tradition of the islands. The center is open Easter–September, daily 10–6; July–August, daily 10–7. Admission is £2.50. The cafeteria offers good views and moderately priced food. North of Dunquin, the Slea Head Loop continues past Clogher Head and its ragged cliffs—another popular spot for picnics—before veering south toward Dingle and Ventry via the publess and shopless village of Ballynana. To extend the circuit, continue north-east from Dingle over Connor Pass (2,020 ft), a steep, rough road that clings to the side of Brandon Mountain as it curves its way toward Castlegregory, 22 km (14 mi) north. Like the Slea Head's southern leg, this high-altitude pass affords incredible views but is dauntingly steep and narrow; it is recommended only for serious cyclists. Over the pass is Castlegregory, a sleepy resort town that sees only a handful of cyclists and foreign families on holiday but attracts a number of windsurfing fanatics.

It used to be that the only good things to come out of Tralee (the capital of County Kerry) were the buses shuttling travelers elsewhere. To a certain extent, that is still the case: There are no ruins or quaint architecture. Accordingly, however, there are no tourists, and the local folk (21,000 strong) have slowly but surely been fashioning worthwhile sights (and accommodations) that deserve a look. Aesthetically, Tralee is bland, with a medium-size-town-with-no-character feel to it. The Kerry Kingdom Museum (Ashe Memorial Hall, next to tourist office, tel. 066/27777) is Tralee's star attraction.

rooms of this 19th-century mansion, including the vast kitchen and wood-beamed common room, have been painstakingly restored. Dorm beds are £8.50, private rooms go for £12 per person, and there's a superb (yet pricey) restaurant downstairs. Farther out is **Collis-Sandes House** (Oakpark, tel. 066/28658), where dorm beds in sunny, spacious rooms cost £7. There are also doubles (£20) and a nice garden. Call for a free shuttle from the bus/train station.

FOOD

Outside Dingle, your meals will either be pub grub or sandwiches at cafés irregularly sprinkled about the peninsula. Most eating establishments close October–February, so be sure to bring your own food during the winter, or prepare to exist solely on fish-and-chips. There are a few chippers and a grocer in Castlegregory, but head for Dingle Town or Tralee for anything substantial. In Dingle, **Sméara Dubha** (The Wood, tel. 066/51465) serves pricey but satisfying vegetarian cuisine 6 PM–10 PM. Bean and hazelnut bake and peppers stuffed with fruited couscous both cost £8. Slightly cheaper are **Cois Farraige Café** (Strand St., no phone) and **Nell's Coffee Shop** (Strand St., no phone). Both conjure up soups, sandwiches, and fried things in the £2–£4 range. Near the church is **Cúl an Tí/Café Ceol** (Green St., tel. 066/52083), a wholesome vegetarian café-restaurant tucked into a pretty courtyard. Crepes (£2–£3) filled with goodies like spinach and cheese, sweet-and-sour vegetables, or apples and cinnamon are the specialty. During summer, it hosts traditional musicians on the weekend. **An Grianán** (Dyke Gate La., next to Grapevine Hostel, tel. 066/51910), open weekdays 9–6 (Sat. 10–6), stocks an array of dairy-free foods and organic fruits and vegetables. Two to three kilometers (1–2 mi) south of Dunquin lies the work of a deranged children's book illustrator—the annoyingly cute **Enchanted Forest Museum and Café** (tel. 066/56234). Inside the pink, teddy bear–laced facade are cheap sandwiches (£1.50), excellent views, and a toy museum based on pagan Celtic holidays. Really. Between Ballyferriter and Dunquin lies the cozy **Tig Aine** (tel. 066/56214), which serves up a dynamite veggie stir-fry and salad (£5) with the ubiquitous stunning views of the sea.

Dick Mack's pub on Green Lane in Dingle Town appears not to have changed since it opened in 1899. The little snug was where women, not allowed into the pub proper, used to wait for their husbands to get sloshed.

In Tralee, **Blasket Inn** (Church St., tel. 066/28095) serves filling, standard fare for £4 and is the only pub that serves food on Sunday. **Brats** (18 Milk Market La., no phone) whips up vegetarian entrées and salads for £4–£5. For groceries, try **Dunnes** (tel. 066/28333) on North Circular Road.

WORTH SEEING

Dingle Town is a small, lively fishing village that makes an excellent base for exploring the surrounding peninsula. Although many expect Dingle to be a quaint and undeveloped Gaeltacht village, it's popular with tourists and has become a haven for pricey seafood restaurants and a handful of luxury hotels. Things get so bad in summer that the label "little Killarney" is starting to stick. In many of its music pubs—**O'Flaherty's** (Bridge St., tel. 066/51983) and the **Small Bridge Bar** (Main St., tel. 066/51564) are the best—you'd be hard-pressed to find more than two or three locals among the summer video-camera crowds. That said, Dingle is blessed with a beautiful harbor and encircled by low-lying hills that offer good views of the peninsula. Since 1985, the harbor has been home to a bottle-nosed dolphin named **Fungi,** notorious for playing with swimmers and boaters. Ask anyone in Ireland who Fungi is and a stupid, childlike smile will come over his or her face. People travel from all over the country just for the chance to say "I met Fungi." Boat trips to visit Fungi are led by a variety of operators and cost about £6; ask at the tourist office or the Rainbow Hostel (*see* Where to Sleep, *above*) for more information. More tactile interaction with marine life can be had at Dingle's **Oceanworld** (Waterside, tel. 066/52111), where you can pet sea rays and ogle sharks from within an underwater tube. It's open daily 9:30–9:30 and charges £4. The local archaeologists at **SCIUIRD** (Holy Ground, tel. 066/51937) lead two- to three-hour walking tours of some of the peninsula's more interesting prehistoric—and more recently created—sites. Dingle's main streets—the Mall, Main and Strand streets, and the Wood—can be covered in less than an hour, so plan to spend most of your time walking or cycling in the countryside.

THE WEST

JOHN DALY

When Oliver Cromwell delivered his infamous ultimatum, "To Hell or to Connaught," back in the 1600s, it's clear he had no idea how attractive the latter option would be 500 years later. Back in those harsh and repressive times, when barren rock and piercing sea spray were the only things on offer, the West of Ireland was the last stop before oblivion for countless dispossessed unfortunates. Today, however, as W. B. Yeats might put it, "all is changed, changed utterly, a terrible beauty is born."

This most distinct region of Ireland has always been a place of contrasts—ancient history, sacred and savage; culture and literature, illuminating and unique; and a landscape where the thundering Atlantic forms the pounding backbeat to the limestone hills and bog-land valleys. There's something special about the West. It's the kind of place that can make even a streetwise Dubliner get misty eyed and thoughtful at the prospect of a visit. With its remote islands that proclaim themselves "the last parish before America," and silent, hidden lakes dripping in history, the West is a place that draws you in, bidding you leave your burden of 21st-century angst at the border.

Unlike most of Ireland where the marks of Viking, Norman, and English invaders blotted out much of the rich heritage of the ancient Irish kingdoms, the West retained, by virtue of its remoteness, those essential Celtic characteristics of rebellion and individuality. These traits survive, despite the purges of conquering genocide by Cromwell and his ilk and the all-pervasive trauma of the Great Famine (1845–49) that wiped out an entire generation. The West remains a place where melancholic antiquity sits comfortably with modern progress and whose spirit has always spoken clearly to the hidden poet within all who travel there.

A stronghold of Celtic culture, the West holds the highest concentration of Irish-speaking communities and traditional musicians in the country. A distinct appreciation for the gifts of ancestry is evident here, heard in the Gaelic dialects still flourishing in parts of the Aran Islands and in the haunting melodies of a well-played fiddle in a country pub at midnight. If Galway City has assumed the identity of the ultrahip destination of a younger, newer, more confident Ireland, the surrounding countryside retains a traditional personality that's more in keeping with old men at country crossroads who can recite their family trees going back to the 12th century.

As in the Southwest, the population of the West was decimated by famine in the mid-19th century and by mass emigration from then until the 1950s. A major factor in the region's recovery from economic depression has been the attraction of visitors to its sparsely populated mountain landscape and long,

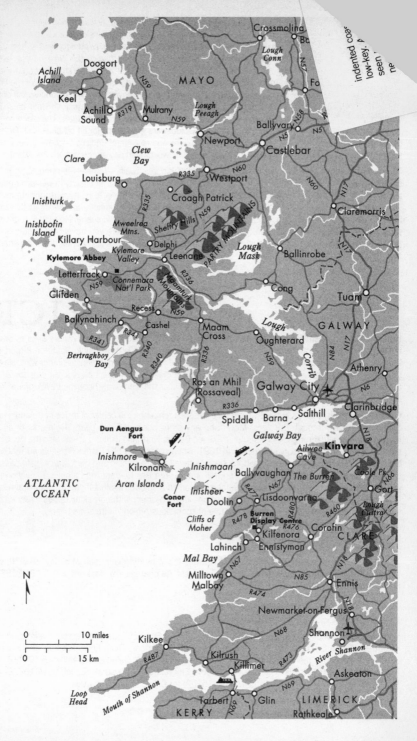

THE WEST

Achill Island
Doogort
Keel
Achill Sound
Mulrany
R319
R319
N59

MAYO

Crossmolina
Lough Conn
Ba
N57
Fo
N58

Lough Peeagh
Newport
Ballyvary
N5
N5
Castlebar

Clew Bay
Clare
Louisburg
R335
R335
Westport
N60
N60
Claremorris
N17

Croagh Patrick
Inishturk
Mweelrea Mtns.
Sheffry Hills
N59
Partry Mountains
Lough Mask
Ballinrobe
N17

Inishbofin Island
Killary Harbour
Delphi
Leenane
Kylemore Valley
Kylemore Abbey
Letterfrack
Connemara Nat'l Park
N59
Maamturk Mountains
R336
N59
R336
Cong
Tuam

GALWAY

Clifden
Recess
Cashel
R340
R341
Ballynahinch
R341
N59
Maam Cross
Lough Corrib
Oughterard
N18
N59
Athenry
N17
N6

Bertraghboy Bay
R340
R336
Ros an Mhil (Rossaveal)
R336
Galway City
Clarinbridge

Dun Aengus Fort
Inishmore
Kilronan
Aran Islands
Conor Fort
Inishmaan
Spiddle
Barna
Salthill
Galway Bay
Ailwee Cave
Kinvara
N18

ATLANTIC OCEAN

Inisheer
Doolin
Ballyvaughan
N67
The Burren
Coole Pk.
N66
Gort

Cliffs of Moher
R477
Lisdoonvarna
Burren Display Centre
R478
Kilfenora
R476
Corofin
R460
Lough Cutra
N18
CLARE

Lahinch
Mal Bay
Kilfenora
Ennistymon
N67
N85
Ennis

Milltown Malbay
R474
Newmarket-on-Fergus
N68
N18

N

Shannon

0   10 miles
0   15 km

Kilkee
R487
Kilrush
Killimer
R473
River Shannon
Askeaton

Loop Head
Mouth of Shannon
Tarbert
N69
Glin
LIMERICK
Rathkeale

KERRY

line with its many lakes and rivers. Tourism's development, however, has been mercifully
part from a seaside promenade and fun palace at Salthill, just outside Galway, the area has
major investment in public amenities. Instead, additional land has been acquired for the Con-
nara National Park. The existence of some of the best angling in Europe on the West's rivers, lakes,
and seas accounts for many regular visitors. Most holiday cottages, so often a concrete blight on the Irish
landscape, are built according to the model of the traditional thatched cabin. The residents of the West
have encouraged the revival of such cottage industries as knitting, weaving, and woodworking; the provi-
sion of bed-and-breakfast in existing homes; and informal sessions of traditional music in small bars. The
lack of razzmatazz makes the West an ideal destination for travelers on a tight budget. The place comes
alive between June and September. April, May, and October are good times for an off-peak visit. Outside
these months many places will be closed; nightlife options and restaurant choices become limited. During the winter, weather can be harsh, with gales and rain sweeping in day after day from the Atlantic.

You may start your explorations of the West in Limerick, since it awaits you near Shannon Airport. The
city is oft-neglected by tourists but possesses a rich history. Galway, the other big city in western Ireland,
gets far more attention as a major hub for travelers, offering connections to many surrounding towns.
The barren Aran Islands—with their Gaeltacht (Irish-speaking) communities—are serviced by ferries
from Galway and nearby Doolin, a tiny village with a huge traditional-music scene. No matter your path,
you'll witness western Ireland's beauty from the bus window everywhere you travel, and a stop at the
famed Cliffs of Moher or a cycle through the desolate limestone Burren will really bring home the strange
beauty of the west.

LIMERICK

Limerick, Ireland's third-largest city, has an infamous reputation with locals and visitors alike as one of
the dullest places for travelers to find themselves. Perhaps, given its proximity to Shannon Airport (24
km/15 mi west of the city), it suffered from being too close for just-arrived visitors to bother with. Having
undergone both an industrial and cultural renaissance in the last few years, however, the city now offers
not only a lively pub scene but also a number of ancient sites that can easily hook the traveler for at least
a day or two.

Originally settled by Vikings in the 10th century, Limerick remained the center of much of Ireland's troubled history down through the ages. More than any other place, the city bears the marks of all the
invaders rampaging through the Republic—Vikings, Danes, Normans, Britons. It was also the site of the
signing of the infamous Treaty of Limerick in 1691, when patriots lead by Patrick Sarsfield surrendered
to Cromwell's forces after a valiant yearlong siege. After allowing Sarsfield and his followers safe passage
to France, the English promptly reneged on their treaty promises to grant the Catholic population religious and property rights and instead instituted draconian measures against them. In a national history
filled with broken promises, awesome betrayal, and dashed dreams, the breaking of this treaty encap-
sulated as much as anything the traditional role of "perfidious Albion" in Ireland's history.

BASICS

There's a **tourist office** (tel. 061/317522) at Arthur's Quay, by the river, open weekdays 9–5:30, with
longer hours in summer months. There is also a bureau de change. The **post office** (tel. 061/315777)
is on Lower Cecil Street.

COMING AND GOING

Railway and bus depots are both in Colbert Station (tel. 061/315555), just southeast of the town on Parnell Street. There is regular rail service to Dublin (£25), Waterford (£17), Ennis (£5.50), and Killarney
(£15). Bus service is more frequent and cheaper—Dublin (£10), Galway (£9), Killarney (£9.50), and
Rosslare Harbour (£12). Bikes can be rented from Emerald Cycles (Patrick St., tel. 061/416938) and
McMahon's Cycleworld (Roches St., tel. 061/415202) for £7 a day or £30 a week.

WHERE TO SLEEP

SMALL HOTELS AND GUEST HOUSES

Cruises House (Denmark St., tel. 061/315320), a new guest house in the center of town, has many hotel-like amenities, including direct-dial phones, TV, and good tubs. B&B rate is £20 per person. Hanratty's Hotel (5 Glentworth St., tel. 061/410999) is a smartly renovated town house with 22 en-suite rooms with all the usual appliances, including TV, hair dryer, tea/coffeemaker, and telephone. The building dates from 1796 and is right by the city center. B&B rate is £22.50 per person. Jurys Inn (Lower Mallow St., tel. 061/207000), part of the large Jurys chain of hotels, offers rooms that are clean and airy if a bit bland. It overlooks an urban stretch of the Shannon, a short step from the main shopping and business district. Rooms are priced at £44–£51 per person.

HOSTELS

The independent Limerick Hostel (Barrington's House on George's Quay, tel. 061/415222) is a spacious affair, close to the city-center action, with rooms for three or four costing £8.50 and £7.50 per person. Single rooms go for £10, and doubles for £20. The latest addition to the city's growing hostel scene (another sign of the city's regeneration as a tourist destination) is Finnegan's (6 Pery Sq., tel. 061/310308). A refurbished Georgian mansion overlooking People's Park, this hostel offers beds in the dorms for £7.50 and private rooms for £10 per person.

FOOD

Freddy's Bistro (Theatre La., tel. 061/418749), closed Monday, serves a variety of decent stews, pastas, and veggie dishes for about £10 a person. The Green Onion Café (Ellen St., tel. 061/400710) does good pasta and pizza, as well as tasty coffee and sticky buns, and is open from 10 to 10. Lunch is the best value. On George's Quay, try Moll Darby's Pizzeria (tel. 061/411511) for full meals running from £10 to £14. There are outside tables in the summer. O'Flaherty's Basement Restaurant (O'Connell St., tel. 061/316311) serves hearty lunch and dinner food. You can take in the historical relics that festoon the walls as you tuck into your spicy spaghetti calabresi.

The pub scene in Limerick is somewhat of a movable feast of late with many of the places changing hands and undergoing face-lifts. A cookie-cutter approach to decor, usually something in pine and brick, seems to be the trend. Luckily there are exceptions. Most places also serve a hearty and inexpensive lunch and dinner menu. Nancy Blake's (Upper Denmark St., tel. 061/416443) always has a trad or jazz session going on in its sawdust-strewn bar, as does South's Pub (tel. 061/318850) on the Crescent. The Locke (George's Quay, tel. 061/413733) is worth checking out as well for its pleasant quayside location. You can also check out PJ's Place (Little Catherine St., no phone), which you'll recognize by its mock-thatched roof.

WORTH SEEING

KING JOHN'S CASTLE

The castle, town center's most notable monument, is located near Thomond Bridge. It was built as a Norman fortress in the 13th century. It has changed hands several times in its tumultuous history and underwent a major restoration after a 17th-century pounding during the Siege of Limerick. The tower is the castle's oldest section and housed a British garrison until the birth of the Irish Free State in 1922. A well-laid-out visitor center offers good audiovisual presentations on the city's history, as well as a display of siege-warfare weapons in its outer yard. Across the river from the castle, the Treaty Stone marks the spot where the infamous Treaty of Limerick was signed. *Castle St., tel. 061/411201. Admission: £3.80. Open Apr.–Sept., daily 9:30–5; Oct.–Mar., weekends 9:30–5.*

ST. MARY'S CATHEDRAL

Although Limerick is a predominantly Catholic city, this Protestant cathedral is the oldest religious building in the city, founded by Donal Mor O'Brien in 1172. A Romanesque doorway survives from that period, as do the 15th-century chancel and chapels. The cathedral contains huge tombs, memorial stones, and some exquisite black oak choir stalls carved with animals and other figures in a depiction of the struggle between good and evil. *Bridge St., tel. 061/416238. Admission free. Open Mid-June–September 15, Mon.–Sat. 9—1 and 2–5.*

THE CITY OF ANGELA AND DOLORES

If you happen to be one of the estimated 10 million people around the world who've already read Frank McCourt's Pulitzer Prize–winning book, "Angela's Ashes," about his youth in Limerick, you will arrive in the city, no doubt, with fixed expectations of a place that the author certainly didn't recall through rose-tinted glasses. His witty but devastating memoir of his poverty-stricken family is not exactly a public-relations piece for growing up Irish-Catholic in the 1940s and '50s. The book isn't a favorite among locals who feel he overstated his case at their expense, and many residents of Limerick see red at McCourt's mention. With director Alan Parker ("The Commitments") having just finished filming the screen version of the book, it seems that McCourt mania is far from over. Some walking tours of the city include "Angela's Ashes" sites on their itineraries. However, Limerick's citizens will be happy to tell you that the slums around Limerick's Windmill Street and Pery Square are long gone, and the filmmakers were forced to use the back lanes of Cork City as a substitute.

If you're a fan of that other global success story, the band the Cranberries, you'll find many local barflies in Limerick who'll tell you they "knew 'em when they were nothing." The band's lead singer, the elfin Dolores O'Riordan, she of the searing soulful vocals and see-through wedding dress, sold her Dingle mansion to move back to this, her native county. Consistently producing million-selling albums, this tight little outfit owns a stud farm, a radio station, a pub, and numerous properties in and around the city. They normally keep a low profile but do often pop up at various cultural events and gatherings.

HUNT MUSEUM

The finest collection of Celtic and medieval treasures outside the National Museum in Dublin is found here in the Custom House, on the banks of the Shannon. The Antrim Cross and a Bronze Age shield are among the objects displayed. A good selection of 20th-century European paintings are also on view. *Rutland St., tel. 061/312833. Admission £3.90. Open Oct.–Apr., Tues.–Sat. 10–5, Sun. 2–5; May–Sept., Mon.–Sat. 10–5, Sun. 2–5.*

THE BURREN

The Burren, a limestone escarpment in the western part of County Clare, ranks as one of Ireland's fiercest landscapes. No matter from which direction you approach the Burren, rolling green hills and smooth valleys quickly give way to jagged shelves of green-gray rock, rough and porous and bordered by a series of stark mountains. Even on a sunny day, the Burren seems stuck in mourning, silent except for the pound of the surf or the cry of a seagull scavenging the shore. Because it's so inhospitable, few actually live in the heart of the Burren, a narrow strip that hugs the coast from Black Head in the north to Doolin and the Cliffs of Moher in the south; the few villages you pass seem barely to grip the rugged terrain, grateful to have even a small clutch of earth in this otherwise unaccommodating region.

A military Humvee may seem at first like the best mode of transport through this bleak and eerie landscape, but careful negotiation of the twisting roads and tight corners is relatively easy by car or bike, once you get used to rubbernecking the awesome stone formations. The road through the heart of the Burren runs between Ballyvaughan and Corofin, via Leamenah Castle, and the trip takes just a few hours of leisurely driving. If there's no sign of rain clouds, get a picnic, a pair of strong boots or shoes, and head off on the Burren Way, a 29-km (18-mi) trail running toward Doolin that can be broken into smaller stages depending on your enthusiasm.

Just outside Ballyvaughn, the Aillwee Caves (tel. 065/77036) are a grand place to pass a rainy afternoon. The main passage penetrates 1,968 ft into the mountain and widens into larger caverns the deeper in you go. One cavern has a waterfall. Our particular guide switched off his flashlight about 650 ft in and bade all of us to pause a moment and listen to the silence, then with typical Irish understatement said: "If you were awake in your coffin, this is what it would be like." Carved out by water almost 2 million years ago, the caverns contain the remains of a brown bear, extinct in Ireland for more than 10,000 years. You can get a guided tour for £4.50.

About 6 km (4 mi) inland from Aillwee is the Poulnabrone Dolmen (Portal Tomb), surely one of the country's most photographed ancient monuments. A large three-legged tomb sitting on a sea of limestone rock, with not a sign of civilization in any direction, this is truly a mystical place.

Like the desert, the Burren nourishes abundant animal and plant life despite the harsh conditions. Every crack and hollow in the weatherworn rock contains some fragile vegetation. In fact, the Burren plays host to 1,000 of the 1,400 forms of plant life found in Ireland. Volumes have been written on the diverse species of plants and birds that manage to thrive here, and the best way to discover these is on foot. Dozens of signposted walks run through both coastal and inland areas, and most hostels stock topographic maps and organize reasonably priced day trips. The villages of Lisdoonvarna and Doolin (the unofficial music capital of Ireland) are also good bases for exploring the Burren. Both have comfortable accommodations and are regularly serviced by Bus Éireann, though you can easily walk or cycle the short distance from one village to the next when the weather is good. The Burren is no secret, however, and summer crowds are a given, especially in Doolin. Unless you want to pitch a tent on a bed of rock, reservations (even if only one day in advance) are strongly encouraged in July and August.

LISDOONVARNA

BASICS

There is a not-so-useful tourist office (tel. 065/74630) outside town in Spa Wells, downhill from the Imperial Hotel. Much better is Kincora House (*see below*), which stocks maps and cycling guides and rents sturdy 18-speed bicycles (£6 per day, £30 per week). They also have a good idea of when buses come and go. Expressway buses stop at Lisdoonvarna's village square, once daily (twice in summer) from Dublin (£12) and at least twice daily on summer weekdays from Galway (£7.30), Ennis (£6), and Doolin (£2). Both the post office (Church St., tel. 065/74110) and the Imperial Hotel (Lisdoonvarna Ave., tel. 065/74042) have a bureau de change.

WHERE TO SLEEP

Finding accommodations is not a problem except during September, when the Matchmaking Festival and the World's Barbecue Championship collide in a saucy mélange of chefs and hopeful bachelors. You'd never guess Kincora House and Burren Holiday Hostel (tel. 065/74300) only charges £6 (£6.50 July–Sept.). This 19th-century mansion looks like an upscale hotel, and has a bureau de change, a good pub, and a popular restaurant (entrées £4.50–£7). The four- to six-bed rooms are comfortable, the common room is huge and bright, and they rent bikes for £6 per day. Coming from the coast, this resort-style hostel is on your right just before town. For comfortable B&B accommodations March–November, try the homey, family-run Ravine House (The Square, tel. 065/74043) or the classy O'Loughlin's (Church St., tel. 665/74038). They and the other 20 or so B&Bs in town have rooms for £16–£20 per person.

Ballinalacken Castle (Lisdoonvarna, tel. 065/74025), a sprawling Victorian lodge on a hill 4 km (2½ mi) outside Lisdoonvarna, offers location, location, location—100 acres of wildflower meadows and

LOOKIN' FOR LOVE

If you happen to hit town anytime during the month of September, don't be surprised at the unusual sights of Lisdoonvarna's Matchmaking Festival (tel. 065/74005). Held annually after harvest time, the festival has an honorable history of being the time farmers paired off their eligible sons and daughters, via a matchmaker, for the appropriate dowries of cattle or horses. Eventually, it became a dating agency for the famously shy bachelor farmers of rural Ireland, who flocked there as their one social outlet of the year in search of a bride. The whole deal has become big business of late, with one tour operator flying in a 747 full of Midwest matrons from Kansas. Unfortunately, the event has acquired some unwelcome modern additions, such as the weekend arrival of drunken townies prone to annoying the earnest revelers. However, this hasn't dampened the optimism of the many red-cheeked hill farmers of 65 or 70, who, dressed in their Sunday suits with a twinkle in their eyes, determinedly search for the "real thing." The recent Viagra explosion is even said to have kick-started a whole other generation of hardy 80-year-olds. Men usually outnumber women two to one, and the whole thing has to be entered into with an open mind (not to mention a strong constitution). One of the main personalities of the festival is Willie Daly, a white-haired rogue with a heart of gold who has devoted his life to matching the needs of his lovelorn clients. You'll spot him rushing from one place to the next, forever clutching a sheaf of marital CVs under his arm. His standard answer to all inquiries is: "If God's fortune smiles upon us, there'll be matches made today." If you're on the lookout, who knows, you might just get lucky!

panoramic views of the Atlantic, the Aran Islands, and the Connemara hills. The 12 rooms all come with baths, and some come with ocean views. Ocean-view rooms are £36 per person; those with less-stunning vistas can be had for £30 per person. Sheedy's Spa View (Lisdoonvarna, tel. 065/74026), a small, friendly hotel housed in a 17th-century farmhouse near town center, offers 11 rooms with bath for £27.50 per person a night. The Orchid Restaurant here is more pricey than the lodgings but serves award-winning French-Irish cuisine.

FOOD

With its memorabilia-covered walls and rustic charm, Roadside Tavern (Coast Rd., no phone) provides some of the best and most affordable pub grub in town. You can get soups (£2), sandwiches (£1.50), and lasagna (£4). Dolmen Restaurant (The Square, tel. 065/74760) offers entrées for less than £6. The Orchid Restaurant (Sheedy's Spa View; *see above*) is known for its French-Irish cuisine, including fresh local lobster and panfried sirloin steak. Entrées run from £10 to £17.

WORTH SEEING

Lisdoonvarna's location, 8 km (5 mi) inland from the sea and set atop a small hill, is well suited to excursions into the surrounding Burren. Particularly fun is the 6½-km (4-mi) walk or cycle to Corkscrew Hill, reputedly the curviest road in Ireland. From the top of this zigzag road there's an incredible view of

County Clare, the Burren, and the Aran Islands. In the village of Kilfenora, 8 km (5 mi) south of Lisdoonvarna, is the Burren Centre (tel. 065/88030), open March–October, daily 10–5, and June–September, daily 9:30–6. For £2.50 you get to see a representative model of the Burren, an extensive display of the region's flora and fauna, and a short audiovisual show that does a good job of explaining the Burren's geology and topography. Adjoining the center is the Kilfenora Cathedral, whose graveyard is worth a look for the ruins of six crosses, including the 12th-century Doorty Cross. These high crosses commemorate Kilfenora's being made a diocesan seat in the 12th century. It's possible to camp in the fields behind the churchyard for £5 for two or more people; ask for Dermot Hogan at the shop across from the fields. Summer evenings in Lisdoonvarna are filled with the sounds of excellent traditional music. Weekend nights there are sessions (and dancing) in Lisdoonvarna's hostel, and top-rate music is played nightly at the nearby Roadside Tavern (Coast Rd., no phone), one of County Clare's best pubs.

DOOLIN AND THE CLIFFS OF MOHER

BASICS

There's a tourist office (tel. 065/81171) at the Cliffs of Moher, open Easter–October, daily 10–6, with longer hours in summer. It has maps of the Burren (around £2) and a bureau de change. There's no tourist information office in Doolin, nor is there a bank, so, if you're living off your credit card or ATM card, stock up on punts before arriving. You can exchange cash or buy maps at the front desk in Doolin Hostel (see below), which also serves as both the local Raleigh Rent-A-Bike outlet and the Bus Éireann depot.

Surveying the region for Oliver Cromwell in 1651, General P. Ludlow wrote that the "Burren is a country where there is not water enough to drown a man, wood enough to hang one, or earth enough to bury him."

COMING AND GOING

Doolin is shaped like a long hourglass, with the Rainbow Hostel, Aille River Hostel, and McGann's and McDermott's pubs at one end and the Doolin Hostel and O'Connor's pub at the other, ½ km (¼ mi) down the main road. In the summer, Expressway buses run twice daily (once on Sunday) to Dublin (£12), Tralee (£9.70), Killarney (£12), Cork (£12), and the Cliffs of Moher (£1.35). Buses to Galway (£8.20) and Lisdoonvarna (£1) run four times per day in the summer (twice on Sunday). Often cheaper is the West Clare Shuttle (tel. 088/517963), which operates a daily service to Galway (£5) and Lisdoonvarna (£1) March–October. West Clare will also pick you up from wherever you're staying and transport bikes for £2. Call to see when the shuttle runs and to tell them where to pick you up.

WHERE TO SLEEP

It has finally happened: Doolin now has more B&Bs than residential houses, so pick one that strikes you. For great views of the cliffs, stay at Atlantic View (The Pier, tel. 065/74569), which has six clean rooms starting at £12. The Westwind B&B (Upper Village, tel. 065/74227) added a feather to its cap when filmmaker Quentin Tarantino stayed there while scouting locations for an Irish gangster film (it hasn't been made yet). Adjacent to McGann's pub, it has a pleasant, laid-back atmosphere and includes a hearty breakfast in its £12-per-person rates. Of Doolin's three hostels, Aille River (tel. 065/74260) is the most comfortable. Its well-equipped kitchen, spacious common room, and free laundry facilities attract a lively crowd. It's open mid-March–early November and has dorm beds (£7), doubles (£15), and campsites (£3.50 per person).

FOOD

Considering its size, Doolin has a staggering number of upscale restaurants. Of these, Ivy Cottage (Fisher St., near O'Connor's pub, tel. 065/74244) is the best. Housed in a cozy, candlelit cottage, it offers a tremendous selection of home-baked breads, fresh seafood, and grilled meats nightly 6–9. A full meal with wine runs £11–£14. For a good mid-range meal, Doolin Café (tel. 065/74795) prepares vegetarian and vegan dishes for £4–£7. Doolin's post office (opposite Doolin Café, tel. 065/74209) doubles as the village's grocery store.

THE FAMINE DAYS

*The West of Ireland suffered more than most regions during the famine.
Everywhere you travel you'll see plaques and monuments dedicated to that
terrible chapter of history. Seeing the tragedy as an opportunity for
indoctrination, some Protestant landlords attempted to lure their starving
tenants away from the Catholic Church by offering converts food, better
housing, and education. One such convert, Edward Synge, became a
passionate preacher who would stand in town squares beseeching the destitute
to follow his path. An attempt made on Synge's life was thwarted when a
leather-bound Bible in his pocket stopped the bullet—an occurrence that made
the preacher all the more determined in his conversion efforts. The Bible,
complete with bullet hole, is displayed at the Clare Heritage Centre in Corofin
(tel. 065/76105).*

WORTH SEEING

Although this small village boasts a larger population of sheep than people, Doolin is the place to come
for traditional music. Its international reputation has attracted many—if not all—big names in Irish music,
who spend a summer or two here learning their trade from old-timers and any players who happen to
drop in for a pint and a tune. Traditional music greats like Michael Russell, Kevin Griffin, and Sharon
Shannon have all played here. Doolin's three pubs—McGann's, McDermott's, and O'Connor's—host top-
rate music sessions nightly throughout the year. Summer, especially, draws crowds of tourists, but the
music is unbeatable. Happily, the three pubs also habitually defy the puritanical 11:30 PM closing time by
bolting the doors and drawing the curtains, obeying the "be a good man and pour us another pint" law
of the country. Given the ever-increasing popularity of Irish traditional music with locals and tourists alike,
it must be said that actually getting into pubs can often be as much of a problem as getting out.

Doolin's other main draw is its proximity to both the Cliffs of Moher and the Aran Islands (*see below*),
visible off the coast. The preferred way to see the Cliffs of Moher is to hike the 4-km (2½-mi) Burren Way
from Doolin. Known also as the "Old Road," this rugged dirt trail (walk past the Doolin Hostel, cross the
riverbed, and continue straight) keeps entirely to the coast, providing great views of the sea and the
occasional village of run-down thatched cottages. Best of all, the trail approaches the cliffs from the less-
touristed north side, where you can fearlessly walk to the very edge and have a picnic without being disturbed by the putter of tour buses. Be warned: At some points, the only thing separating you from the
sea, 700 ft below, is a patch of slippery heather and a jagged overhang that may or may not offer a last-
chance handhold. For other walks and a good rundown of the area's history, pick up Martin Breen's
Doolin Guide & Map (£2), available in shops and at the Doolin Hostel.

As any trip around Ireland will quickly illustrate, there's a tall tale behind most sites. The Cliffs of Moher
episode concerns one Red Mary, a lusty woman who lived hereabouts in the 17th century and attracted
a great many suitors. As proof of their undying love, the lady required her would-be Romeos to ride her
fierce stallion right to the edge of the cliffs—whereupon the horse would make a sudden stop, throwing
the rider into the air and on to his doom on the jagged rocks down below. Needless to say, they weren't
forming a line to take Red Mary to the prom. One man did eventually manage to ride the stallion and
keep his mount but returned to Mary's stronghold only to find the gates barred. Urging the horse to leap
the walls resulted in the deaths of both man and beast. Hence the name of Mary's castle was Lea-
managh, or "horse's leap." Though history doesn't record it, we can surely assume that Red Mary
remained unwed.

The Aran Islands are accessible from both Doolin and Galway (*see below*). Doolin Ferries (Doolin Pier,
tel. 065/74455) makes the 30-minute to two-hour (depending on the weather) trip to the islands of

Inisheer (£15 round-trip) and Inishmore (£20 round-trip) daily between mid-April and late September. If demand warrants, they also head to Inishmaan (£18 round-trip). Departure and arrival times are notoriously unpredictable (due largely to the ornery weather in these parts), so be flexible.

GALWAY

Galway, Ireland's fourth-largest and fastest-growing city, is a progressive student town with a flair for the hip and offbeat. Despite its block houses and factories, Galway's small city center has the atmosphere of a bustling market town, especially in the streets that lead from the River Corrib to Eyre Square, the city's main social hub. Founded by the Normans in 1240 and later fortified and transformed into a prosperous trading outpost by the Lynch clan, Galway has since become western Ireland's most prominent music and arts center. Because of its close relation with the surrounding Gaeltacht, Galway's music scene is happily and predominantly traditional. Lacking a large number of historic sites, Galway seems to cherish its traditional-music pubs with a vengeance, recognizing their importance to the town's cultural (and touristic) appeal. Civic pride also stems from the city's famed academic institution, the University College Galway (UCG). Opened in 1846 to promote the development of local industry and agriculture, UCG today has become a center for Irish-language and Celtic studies, attracting crowds of youthful misfits, buskers, New Age prophets, and wandering hippies. The Galway-based Druid Theatre Company and An Taibhdhearc Theatre also sustain Galway's commitment to Irish culture by staging a variety of raucously celebratory summer festivals. One of these, the Galway Arts Festival (tel. 091/583800), held in late July, showcases Irish and international drama in dozens of city-center venues. During the festival, Galway is packed with musicians (and tourists) from all over Ireland, so book a bed in advance and get to the pub early if you want a seat.

Galway also makes a good base for exploring western Ireland, since it's well served by train and bus from most major cities. During the day you can visit the Aran Islands (*see below*), Kinvarra Bay, or, if you're short on time, take in the Burren on a reasonably priced tour, but stay in town for the unbeatable nighttime pub scene. There are no fewer than nine hostels in Galway, a sure sign that it's neither the "hidden jewel" nor "quiet coastal village" that the tourist brochures would have you believe.

BASICS

LAUNDRY

Take your grubby clothes to Bubbles Inn Laundry, in the center of town, for a cheap (£4) wash and dry. *Mary St., tel. 091/563434. Open Mon.–Sat. 8:45–6:15.*

MAIL

Take care of all your postal needs at Galway's main post office. *21 Eglinton St., tel. 091/562051.*

VISITOR INFORMATION

The tourist office exchanges money, arranges tours of the city and county, and can book ferry tickets to the Aran Islands. It can also book you in a cheap B&B (£1 fee) or call hostels to check for vacancies. *Victoria Pl., tel. 091/563081. From station, turn left on Eyre Sq., left on Merchants Rd. Open June–Aug., daily 9–8; Sept.–Apr., weekdays 9–5:45, Sat. 9–12:45.*

USIT, the student-run travel organization, has two offices in Galway. One is on the UCG campus (New Science Building, tel. 091/524601), open weekdays 9:30–5. The other is directly across from the tourist office on Merchants Road (tel. 091/565177) and is open weekdays 9:30–5:30, Saturday 10–1 (July–Aug. until 3).

COMING AND GOING

Ceannt Station (tel. 091/562000 for bus info, 091/561–444 for train info), on the east corner of Eyre Square, doubles as the rail and bus depot. Inside the station is a bureau de change and an information and left-luggage desk. Galway is served by six daily trains from Dublin (£12); for any other destination you'll have to change in Athlone. Bus Éireann Expressway buses make daily hauls to Dublin (8 per day;

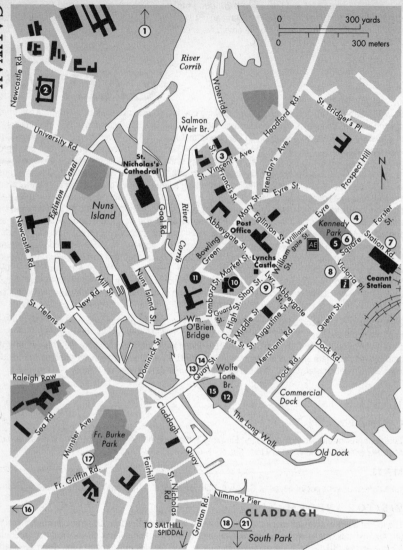

GALWAY

Sights ●
Civic Museum, **15**
Collegiate Church of
St. Nicholas, **10**
Eyre Square, **5**
Nora Barnacle
House, **11**
Spanish Arch, **12**
University, **2**

Lodging ○
Adare Guest
House, **17**
Corrib Haven, **21**
Cregg Castle, **1**
Eyre Square
Hotel, **4**
Great Southern
Hotel, **6**

Great Western
Hostel, **7**
Inishmore Guest
House, **16**
Jurys Galway
Inn, **13**
Kinlay House, **8**
Knockrea B&B, **18**
Lydon House, **9**
Norman Villa, **20**

Ocean Crest
House, **19**
Quay Street
House, **14**
Salmon Weir
Hostel, **3**

£8), Donegal (3 per day; £10), Sligo (4 per day; £10.50), and Cork (3 per day; £12). To reach the hostels, shops, and pubs from the station, walk to the opposite corner of Eyre Square, turn left down Williamsgate Street, and cross the River Corrib.

If you want to cycle around the area, Europa Bicycles (Earl's Island, tel. 091/563355) rents bikes for £5 per day, £25 per week, plus a £30 deposit. They'll transport you and your bike up to Connemara (or other biking musts) for £6. The local Raleigh Rent-A-Bike agent is Celtic Cycles (Queen St., off Victoria Pl., tel. 091/566606), which rents bikes for £7 per day, £30 per week, with a £40 deposit.

WHERE TO SLEEP

SMALL HOTELS AND GUEST HOUSES

Cregg Castle. Set on a 165-acre wildlife preserve about 15 km (9 mi) north of Galway, this 17th-century castle is surprisingly informal. The Brodericks, the owners, all play instruments, and traditional sessions often take place around the huge, log-and-turf fire in the Great Hall. The bedrooms (£40 for a single, £60 for a double) vary in shape and size and are mainly decorated with sturdy Victorian bygones. Breakfast is served until noon around an antique dining table that seats 18 people, so be prepared for chatting. *Corrandulla, Co. Galway, tel. and fax 091/791434. 10 rooms, 5 with bath. Closed Nov.–Feb.*

Eyre Square Hotel. You can't be much more centrally stationed than this hotel overlooking the bustling square, right in the middle of the pub action and theaters. Additional lures include cable, direct-dial phones, decent-size bathtubs, and the adjoining Red Square pub, which is a favorite happy-hour spot for locals—quite a deal for £60 per double room. *Eyre Square, Co. Galway, tel. 091/569633, fax 091/ 569641. 45 rooms.*

Great Southern Hotel. If it happens that Lady Luck shines on you at the Galway races, and you feel like splurging, there's nowhere better than the venerable Great Southern, also on Eyre Square. Built in 1845, it's a marriage of 19th-century elegance and top-of-the-line amenities. A double room will set you back about £116, but the big rooms, great views across the city, terrific swimming pool, and health club are worth every penny. The cocktail bar, O'Flaherty's, is always jammed with punters keen to share their betting tips. Inquire about weekend-rate specials. *Eyre Square, Co. Galway, tel. 091/564041, fax 091/ 566704. 3 suites, 112 rooms with bath.*

Jurys Galway Inn. This four-story hotel offers boring but budget accommodations (£66 per room, £99 July–Sept.). The atmosphere unavoidably tends toward anonymous-international, but each room is big enough for three adults or two adults and two children, and Jurys' fixed-price policy applies to all of them. Try to get one overlooking the river; they're quieter than those in front. *Quay St., Co. Galway, tel. 091/566444, fax 091/568415. 128 rooms.*

Norman Villa. Dee and Mark Keogh's Victorian town house, midway between the city center and the seaside promenade of Salthill, is away from the bustle but within easy walking distance of both places. Brightly painted walls, Victorian brass beds with Irish linen sheets, varnished floorboards, working wooden shutters, and fun, offbeat paintings and artifacts make for lively, pleasant decor. Vegetarians are readily accommodated at breakfast. Double rooms cost £50. *86 Lower Salthill, Galway, Co. Galway, tel. and fax 091/521131. 5 rooms. Cash only. Closed Jan. 10–31.*

BED-AND-BREAKFASTS

Galway has more than 150 B&Bs scattered throughout its suburbs, and there are a few in the city center. One of the most convenient is **Lydon House** (8 Lower Abbeygate St., tel. 091/564914), a city-center home with cozy doubles (£36) available March–October. Many B&Bs are clustered along Father Griffin Place, a five-minute walk from downtown along Quay Street. Try the very modern **Adare Guest House** (9 Father Griffin Pl., tel. 091/582638), which has nine rooms with bath starting at £20 per person, or the charming **Inishmore Guest House** (109 Father Griffin Pl., tel. 091/582639), with singles at £25 and doubles at £40. Prospect Hill, which meets Eyre Square at its north corner, also has a string of look-alike B&Bs near the station. Otherwise, hop on Bus 1, labeled SALTHILL, and head for Lower Salthill Road, where you'll find at least 20 competitively priced B&Bs. **Corrib Haven** (107 Upper Newcastle, tel. 091/ 524171) is a bright, new all en-suite hotel with massaging "power showers," cable, direct-dial phones, etc., with singles from £25 and doubles from £30. The gorgeous, pine-floored rooms at **Knockrea B&B** (55 Lower Salthill, tel. 091/520145) are available for a bargain £18 per person. **Ocean Crest House** (Seapoint Promenade, Salthill, tel. 091/589028, fax 091/529399) is a hefty modern house with some great views across Galway Bay and the Burren mountains. The rooms even have trouser presses should your shorts require a sharp crease. Rates are £20 per person.

HOSTELS

Even during the summer, it's not very difficult to find a bed in one of Galway's many hostels. However, if you're planning to be in town during July or August, you should definitely book a bed at least two weeks in advance.

Great Western Hostel. This block-long hostel beckons weary backpackers from its perch directly opposite Ceannt Station. You can stay in an immaculate dorm room (£9.50), a four-bed room with bath (£12.50), or a double with bath (£32). All rates include a Continental breakfast. There is even a bureau de change, a sauna, and a pool table. *Frenchville La., tel. 091/561150. 230 beds.*

Kinlay House. Relive your college dorm days at this monstrous, muraled hostel two minutes from Ceannt Station. Sure, it's institutional, but it has everything, including a free Continental breakfast. Dorm beds cost £8.50, doubles £28, with bath £32. It's also got a bureau de change, a laundry room, and 24-hour Internet access for £5 per hour. *Merchants Rd., across from tourist office, tel. 091/565244. 150 beds.*

Quay Street House. This is the serious pub goer's paradise: It's just across the street from Quays Bar (one of Galway's most popular pubs) and steps away from a slew of great restaurants and coffee shops. Take your pick of a bed in a plain, overfilled dorm (£7–£8.50); a four-bed room with bath (£9.50–£12); or a double with bath (£24–£29). All prices are £1–£2 higher June–September. The common room rocks until the wee hours, which ensures that the hostel is pretty noisy. You'll find the usual services— bureau de change, laundry, kitchen. *10 Quay St., tel. 091/568644. From station, head west along Eyre Sq., turn left on Williamsgate St. (which becomes Quay St.). 97 beds.*

Salmon Weir Hostel. Salmon Weir does what no other Galway hostel can—combine an intimate, homey town house with small but extremely well kept rooms. The happy staff organizes Monday-night pub crawls and Thursday-night barbecues (£3). In summer rates are £7.50 for four- to six-bed dorms, £20 for doubles; off-season they drop to £7 and £18. *3 St. Vincent's Ave., tel. 091/561133. Head north from station, turn left on Eyre St., right on Eglinton St., right on St. Vincent's Ave. 40 beds. Curfew 3 AM.*

CAMPING

Twenty-eight grassy sites right on the water go for £3 per person at the Salthill Caravan and Camping Park (tel. 091/523872). It's 1 km (½ mi) west of Salthill, open May–September, and has showers, laundry, and a TV room.

FOOD

Galway has an abundance of cheap and offbeat whole-food restaurants and cafés, most of which are south of Eyre Square between Abbeygate Street and the River Corrib. For bulk supplies and fresh vegetables, head to one of the many grocers along Shop and High streets. Evergreen Health Food Store (High St., tel. 091/564215) has a good selection of fresh sandwiches, juices, breads, and organic foods, or visit the fruit and vegetable market, held Saturday mornings on Market Street, near St. Nicholas Church.

UNDER £5 • Couch Potatas. Wonderful smells waft from this immensely popular restaurant serving monstrously huge potatoes filled with almost anything you can imagine for £4. Plain 'ole spuds and butter are £1.75. The menu also includes delicious brown bread, soups, vegetarian dishes, and homemade pies. *40 Upper Abbeygate St., tel. 091/561664. Cash only.*

Food for Thought. Good, unfussy homemade soups, sandwiches, and veggie casseroles for less than £3 are indeed food for thought. While this living-room-size café doesn't look like much, it's one of the cheapest and least pretentious places around. *Lower Abbeygate St., no phone. Cash only. Closed Sun.*

The Home Plate. Galway's local youth and visiting backpackers come here in droves for generous portions of excellent home-cooked food. The most popular dish is the chicken or vegetarian pita fajita (£3.25–£4), which comes with a heaping plate of mixed salad, fresh veggies, rice, refried beans, pita bread, and a non-alcoholic drink. For breakfast there's all things fried with French bread for £3. *Mary St., off Abbeygate St., tel. 091/561475. Cash only.*

McDonagh's. Ask locals where to get a cheap meal and they'll steer you to McDonagh's, Galway's most popular chipper. You can tell it's a classy chippy because there are actually tables to eat at while the aquarium-bound lobsters glare at you. *22 Quay St., tel. 091/565001. Cash only.*

The River God Café. This is a branch office of the original restaurant in Dingle, offering everything from good scones and excellent coffee right through to stews, quiches, and hearty soups. Located right over Tigh Neachtain (*see* Worth Seeing, *below*), it's handy for a bite after a serious night of trad and chat. *2 Quay St., tel. 091/566172.*

The Round Table. A 15-ft-high stone fireplace makes a splendid centerpiece to this 16th-century dining room. The popular, down-to-earth eatery specializes in hearty pork, beef, and chicken dishes and tasty desserts. The mammoth breakfast is also worth a try. *6 High St., tel. 091/564542. Cash only.*

Runner Bean. This comfy little place with brightly painted tables and stools has vegetarian dishes like quiche (£3.75) and vegetarian curry (£4). There are also chicken-and-pineapple sandwiches (£2) and tacos for the carnivorous. *20 Mary St., tel. 091/569292. Cash only.*

UNDER £10 • Brannagans Restaurant. The old pitch-pine tables here are packed on weekends, and there's always a good buzz of conversation. The menu runs the full gamut of pizzas, burgers, steaks, and seafood, and you can have a pint with your meal. *Upper Abbeygate St., tel. 091/565974.*

Bridge Mills. A 400-year-old former grain mill right beside the River Corrib has been renovated into a minimall (oh no, they're everywhere!), and this restaurant dominates the ground floor. You can sit outside beside a bubbling stream and watch local fishermen pulling salmon out of the river. During the day, the fare includes freshly made salads and sandwiches and hot daily specials, with desserts like fresh fruit tarts and homemade crepes. The evening menu is more substantial: roast rack of lamb with mustard and tarragon, 10-ounce sirloin steaks, and vegetarian specials like the spinach-and-ricotta cannelloni. *O'Brien's Bridge, Galway, tel. 091/566231.*

Fat Freddy's. This place makes good pizzas and pastas priced in the £5–£6 range. It's the only cheapish sit-down place that's open on Sunday (daily 10–10). Try the beef-and-Guinness stew for £5.45. *Quay St., tel. 091/566231.*

House of Bards. Come here for refined, upscale dining in a beautiful 16th-century villa. Surprisingly, this family-run place caters less to the AmEx crowd than to locals looking for candlelighted intimacy and superbly conceived menus. Lunch (£4–£5) and dinner (£5–£14) menus change regularly but generally include a steak, lamb, and fresh-fish course, complemented by homemade soups and desserts. If you're looking to splurge, this is the place. Reservations are recommended on weekends. *1 Market St., tel. 091/568414. Cash only.*

McDonagh's Seafood Bar. The McDonaghs are one of Galway's most entrepreneurial families, and this spot is a longtime town landmark. It's now partly a fish-and-chips bar and partly a "real" fish restaurant. If you've yet to try fish-and-chips, this is the place to take the plunge: Cod, whiting, mackerel, haddock, or hake is deep-fried in a light batter and served with a heap of freshly cooked chips. Or try Galway oysters au naturel or a bowl of mussels steamed in wine and garlic. *22 Quay St., Galway, tel. 091/565001.*

Trattoria Pasta Misa. Regardless of one's quest for authentic national cuisine, Galway, like most other large towns in Ireland, now has a serious number of more Continental eateries. Most, including this trattoria, are surprisingly good. Owners Sergio and Mary Magnetti have developed a strong following among those who dig the ambience and genuine Italian cooking. They also do a roaring trade with hungry students eating off the starters menu. *12 Quay St., tel. 091/563910.*

WORTH SEEING

Your first impression of Galway is bound to be Eyre Square, opposite Ceannt Station in the center of town. Formerly a green where livestock and produce were sold, it's not much to look at today, but the park in its center (named Kennedy Park in honor of JFK's 1963 visit to Galway) is a fine place for a picnic or an afternoon snooze. To the north of the square is a statue commemorating Galway-born Padraig O'Conaire (1882–1928), a pioneer of the Irish literary revival as well as noted hell-raiser in his day. He and 1916 Insurrection leader Patrick Pearse are recognized as two of the most important Irish-language short story writers of the early 20th century. The bronze cannons across the square commemorate the heroic deeds of the Connaught Rangers Brigade at the battle of the Alma Valley during the Crimean War in 1854.

From Eyre Square's west corner, Galway's main shopping artery leads to the River Corrib. Confusingly known at different points as Williamsgate Street, William Street, Shop Street, High Street, and Quay Street, this is where you'll find the best pubs, restaurants, tourist shops, and most of Galway's youth hostels. On nearby Market Street is the **Nora Barnacle House** (4 Bowling Green, Market St., tel. 091/

LITTLE EYE OPENERS

While Galway is home to many grandiose monuments of ancient history, it also holds many obscure yet fascinating relics of days gone by—things that are only glimpsed on foot by eagle-eyed visitors whose eyes are, hopefully, not too fogged after the previous night's late session. Footscrapers: In the 18th century, many areas of the city were unpaved and very mucky in wet weather. Gadgets called footscrapers became popular outside the front doors of prosperous houses, enabling guests to divest themselves of the street ooze before entering for dinner. The best examples of these intricately styled cast-iron contraptions can be seen on either side of the main door of the Great Southern Hotel in Eyre Square. Jostle Stones: These small conical stones were usually placed at corners of narrow lanes and gateways to prevent overenthusiastic carriage drivers from cutting corners too finely and breaking their wheels. One still remains outside Eason's bookshop in Church Lane. Mermaids: Galway has more carvings of these sea nymphs than anywhere else in Ireland, and some fine examples can be seen in the windows of St Nicholas's Collegiate Church. A recent book by local historian Jim Higgins, "Irish Mermaids," documents the many myths surrounding these creatures, including one that dubbed the siting of a mermaid as a warning of a crime committed and a portent of severe bad luck. Marriage Stones: Throughout the city, over many doorways, the more observant visitor will spot stone plaques bearing two interlinked coats of arms. The plaques were fashioned to commemorate marriages between the Merchant Tribes families and placed on prominent positions on the mansions and castles for all to see. Water Troughs: These stone creations have all but disappeared now, but one fine example still remains—albeit filled with flowers—at the entrance to the Fairgreen car park in Forster Street.

By the western mouth of the River Corrib is the remains of an Irish-speaking fishing community known as the Claddagh. It still oozes a certain nautical atmosphere in the shade of the original city walls. If you're in love or have hopes of achieving that status some day, one of the best Irish keepsakes you can take home must be the famous Claddagh ring. Ornaments of silver or gold depicting two hands holding a heart surmounted by a crown, they symbolize a promise of eternal love, friendship, and respect. Often passed down from mother to daughter, the heart worn outward signifies that the wearer is available, while worn inward it becomes a statement of being spoken for.

564743), birthplace of James Joyce's wife. Joyce and Nora Barnacle first met in Dublin on June 16, 1904, a date known to most Joyce fans as Bloomsday because Ulysses follows its hero, Leopold Bloom, on that day. Inside the house is a mediocre collection of photographs and letters and a small gift shop. The house is open mid-May–mid-September, Monday–Saturday 10–5, and admission is £1.

Lynch's Castle, on the corner of Shop and Abbeygate streets, now houses an AIB bank. Check out the gargoyles that leer down at you from the stonework on the outside of the building. In the bank foyer (open weekdays 10–4) is a detailed history of the castle, with old prints and drawings displaying its original state and surroundings.

The Lynch Memorial, a marble plaque found over a Gothic doorway near St. Nicholas Church on Market Street, commemorates yet another Celtic legend dripping equal amounts of blood and sentimentality. James Lynch Fitzstephen, a city mayor in the early 1800s, tried and convicted his own son Walter for killing a Spanish sailor who had made advances on his beloved. Judge Lynch felt morally obliged to hand down the same sentence on his son as he would anyone else—death. However, since no one was willing to place the noose around Walter's neck, the judge was forced to carry out the deed himself. He retired into seclusion soon afterward, a broken man. Those who would give further legs to the tale will attest that this is where the term "lynching" came from. Who knows, it could be true.

Kirwan's Lane, just off Quay Street, is one of Galway's last remaining late medieval lanes. It was here that Galway MP Richard Martin built a 100-seat theater for his actress wife in 1783. Among the many who tread the boards there was the Republican patriot Theobald Wolfe Tone.

Close by is the **Collegiate Church of St. Nicholas** (Market St., tel. 091/564648), one of the best-preserved medieval churches in Ireland. Built in 1320, the interior is filled with interesting carvings, and rumor has it that Christopher Columbus stopped in here to pray before sailing off to distant lands.

The building that now houses Tigh Neachtain pub on Cross Street was once the town house of Richard Martin of Ballinahinch, whose notoriety as a duelist in the 18th century earned him the name "Hair-Trigger Dick." Out of keeping with this moniker was his other source of notoriety—his instrumental role, as a member of parliament, in creating the anti-cruelty laws that led to the founding of the Royal Society for the Prevention of Cruelty to Animals. This welcome sea change in character earned him the new nickname "Humanity Dick."

At the southern end of town are the **Spanish Arch** and **Civic Museum** (tel. 091/567641), both visible along the river near Quay Street. The arch, built in 1594 to shelter stores of Spanish wine unloaded to the docks, is easily (and often) mistaken for a pile of weathered stones. The museum (open daily 10–1 and 2:15–5:15; admission £1), built into the arch's base, houses an exhibit of old photographs and miscellaneous antiques, from fishing hooks to rusty food tins.

Galway's other main draw is the **university,** on the opposite side of the River Corrib from town and clearly visible from the Salmon Weir Bridge. Much of the campus is modern and unfriendly looking; only the Tudor-style courtyard and the administrative block (1845) save it from the aesthetic trash heap. The university library (tel. 091/524411), open weekdays 9:30–5, has an impressive collection of dusty manuscripts and volumes of Galway's municipal records, mostly penned between 1485 and 1820.

SALTHILL

Just 3 km (2 mi) west of Galway (just hop on Bus 1, labeled SALTHILL), you'll find Salthill. It may not have the same regularity of sundown celestial action as, say, Mallory Square in Key West, but the Blackrock Tower at the end of the 3-km (2-mi) promenade must rank high for those of us who want to emulate the famous song and "watch the sun go down on Galway Bay." A longtime favorite resort for locals, Salthill has moved way beyond its blue-collar heritage of cloth caps and Queen Victoria–style bloomers into a snappy modern conglomeration of leisure, culture, and music that stays just the right side (barely) of tacky. Originally Salthill was a haven for the city's merchant princes who built summer homes back in the 1800s when it was separated from the city by farmland, yet its more recent fame grew up around the ballroom dancing craze of the 1950s and '60s when national stars like Dickie Rock, Joe Dolan, and the Royal Showband had thousands flocking to cavernous arenas in search of romance and a slow number under the glitterballs. These dance-hall days are now a forgotten aspect of Irish cultural interaction that formed the basis for most marriages of anyone over, say, 45 whom you might meet on your travels. A taste of the old-fashioned romance can still be sampled in the Warwick Hotel (tel. 091/521244) every Sunday night (admission £5) when many of the remaining showbands provide the beat for veterans to strut their stuff. And if you think that your jiving is up to par, just wait 'til you've seen a pair of 65-year-olds cutting up the dance floor—amazing.

PUB ETIQUETTE

Even if you're a veteran barfly who's been booted out of gin mills and clip joints from Bombay to Baton Rouge, there are still some aspects of Irish public house behavior that can perplex even the most seasoned drinker. Most of these complexities come down to language and the way the locals use it. The word "whore," for instance, has many interpretations—in much the same way that the Eskimoes have 84 different words for snow. For starters, it's gender-flexible but is usually applied by males to other males. Go figure. For instance, "He's a cute whore" signifies that the so-described person is a canny man to seal a business deal and is a phrase much heard in towns where cattle are being bought and sold. Likewise, all the other swear words that are little heard in other developed countries find liberal employ here. The Irish have always been experts at giving a sentence even greater poetry with the inclusion of one of these epithets—they have no intention of giving offense, it's simply another tool used to spin a good yarn. Another source of amusement to outsiders is the rush to the counter when the owner flicks the lights to signify last call. Were Marilyn Monroe herself to offer all her charms to a sheep farmer from the Connemara highlands, at 11:30 he'd put her on hold to get up there for that last pint. Maybe our pubs close too early, maybe that final pint sipped amidst the publican's plaintive cry, "Have ye no homes to go to?," is the sweetest of them all. Who knows? Either way, clear a path for the rush when the clock strikes half-past. The round system is also, unfortunately, a mystery to many visitors. If you get into conversation with them, locals will automatically include you in the round—it's good manners as far as they're concerned, and the strongest means they have of saying, "Good to meet you." Having accepted, woe betide you if the compliment is not returned. Even if you live in Ulan Bator 12 months of the year, with only the wind for company, such an absence of required etiquette will not go down well. And finally, a word to the ladies—please remember that most Irishmen under the age of 85 are driven with an all-consuming desire to flirt outrageously with strangers. You'll hear poetry (Yeats continues to be the best aphrodisiac known on the island) and sonnets, and, as we witnessed at midnight on a rain-drenched street in Corofin last year, you might see a man of 70 doing his version of a Fred Astaire tap dance for a group of astonished Scandinavian women. You may just want to play along with it, consider the whole thing another form of theater, and take it as good fun. After all, that's what Irish women have been doing for generations.

AREA TOURS

If you want to explore nearby regions in western Ireland, Western Heritage (34 Carragh Hill, tel. 091/521699) offers tours of both the Burren and Connemara for £8–£11. The five-hour Burren tour departs Galway at 11:30 AM daily and includes stops at the Cliffs of Moher, Kinvarra, and Poulnabrone Dolmen. The Connemara tour leaves Galway daily at 1 PM and stops at the Ross Erilly Medieval Friary, the *Quiet Man* village of Cong, and Hen's Castle. Bus Éireann (Ceannt Station, tel. 091/562000) and Lally's Coach Tours (19 Shop St., tel. 091/562905) offer similar tours at basically the same rates, as well as tours of Galway Town for about £4. Lally's tends to focus more on Yeats and *The Quiet Man* than the others. *The Corrib Princess* (tel. 091/592447) sails from Galway's Woodquay on a tour of Lough Corrib, taking visitors for trips around the lake (£5).

SHOPPING

Cobwebs (7 Quay La.) stocks small antiques and gifts with an accent on nostalgia. Stop at Claddagh Jewellers (Eyre Sq.) for jewelry; the store has a wide selection of traditional Claddagh rings. The Galway Woolen Market (21–22 High St.) offers good value in sweaters. Kenny's Bookshop (High St.) offers five floors of books of Irish interest, mainly secondhand and antiquarian, as well as prints, maps, and a small art gallery. Check out the Cornstore (Middle St.), a stylish shopping mall. The Eyre Square Shopping Centre (Eyre Sq.) offers a wide range of mid-price clothing and household goods. Design Ireland Plus (Unit 14, Eyre St. Shopping Centre, Eyre Sq.) has an excellent range of Irish-made crafts and clothing.

AFTER DARK

Given Galway's great pubs, and live music and theater scenes, there's no lack of options for evening entertainment. Pick up the *free Galway Advertiser,* a weekly newspaper available in stores and at the tourist office, for listings of Galway events.

PUBS AND CLUBS

There are dozens of good pubs scattered throughout Galway's eminently crawlable city center. For traditional music, Taaffes (19 Shop St., tel. 091/564066) and King's Head (15 High St., tel. 091/566630) are musts, though a recent deluge of video-camera-bearing and green-sweater-wearing folks threatens the authenticity of its summer sessions (winter sessions, however, are still tourist-free). Two underpublicized old-style pubs that have good reputations with local traditional-music fans are An Púcán (11 Forster St., tel. 091/561528) and Crane Bar (2 Sea Rd., tel. 091/587419). Tigh Neachtain (Cross St., tel. 091/566172) hosts impromptu trad sessions seven nights a week, with many musicians from Connemara and other outlying areas making the weekend pilgrimage into the center. The Snug (Shop St., tel. 091/564771) is popular with UCG students and classic-rock lovers. Lisheen Bar (Bridge St., tel. 091/563804) and Sally Long's (33 Upper Abbeygate St., tel. 091/565756) are dependable for jazz and folk. Taylor's (Dominick St., tel. 091/589385) is another of those untouched old pubs still resisting a pine and brick makeover: real locals, few tourists. McSwiggan's (Eyre Sq., tel. 091/568917) is a huge place with everything from church pews to ancient carriage lamps contributing to its eclectic character. It's packed with visitors and students, and the buzz is always "mighty." Roisin Dubh (Dominick St., tel. 091/586540) is another place where the junk your granny threw out years ago now adorns the walls. A serious venue for emerging rock and trad bands, it often showcases big talents while they're still struggling. It sometimes has a £5 cover for major bands. For late-night sounds heard from the comfort of your table, try the Sevn'th Heav'n Restaurant (Courthouse La., Quay St., tel. 091/563838), where blues and folk sounds pour forth from 11:30 PM onward.

From an aesthetic point of view, the Quays (Quay St., tel. 091/568347) is Galway's most impressive pub. The never-ending, wood-paneled, cavernous interior—including a sunken back room—is outfitted in brass, including several long bars. The Quays is even the setting for its own TV show, featuring performers like Sharon Shannon, Mary Black, and Dolores Keane. Despite the fact that it's become almost too popular with natives and visitors alike, a noisy pint in its atmosphere-laden environs is a definite must.

Galway's postpub nightclub scene is formidable. In the center of town is Central Park Disco (36 Upper Abbeygate St., tel. 091/565974), popular with the twentysomething crowd. The cover hovers around £3–£5. Otherwise, most everyone heads to Salthill, a small suburban community 3 km (2 mi) west of Galway. The main road, Upper Salthill, is lined with clubs. Try Liquid (tel. 091/722715) for nightly indie and techno music, or Warwick (tel. 091/521244, cover £3–£7.50), which plays 1970s, '80s, and indie music, except for Sunday, when the dance-hall days return (*see* Salthill, *above*).

THEATER

Galway's theater scene is nearly world famous, and if either of its two home companies are in town, do not fail to lay your hands on some tickets. The Druid Theatre Company (Quay St., tel. 091/568660), which produces lunchtime and evening shows in its Chapel Lane Theatre (tel. 091/568617), has built an international reputation with its revivals of Anglo-Irish classics and a slew of Irish-language plays. More touristy, but no less entertaining, An Taibhdhearc Theatre (Middle St., tel. 091/562024) is famous for its bilingual productions of lesser-known Irish plays, generally accompanied by live traditional music and bawdy pantomime. Productions are most frequent during summer; stop by its Middle Street theater for performance schedules or inquire at the tourist office. The Punchbag Co. (6 Quay La., tel. 091/565422) does successful commercial shows (in English) that attract the unpretentious masses. Tickets for performances range from £6 to £10, and student discounts are often available.

FESTIVALS

Local lore has it that festivals have now become so commonplace around Ireland that the sight of crowds clustered around two flies climbing up a wall can't be too far away. Often just another excuse for small-town publicans to unify in hopes of getting pub extension hours from the courts (late-night drinking and festivals go together like, uh, Guinness and oysters), most hamlets and small towns are now performing their own celebrations in everything from the blessing of fishermen's nets at the start of the season in Donegal to pig wrestling in County Cork (don't ask). Thankfully, Galway, as the cultural hub of the West, doesn't have to try too hard in attracting punters to an already-full festival calendar. The absolute biggie of the year takes place the last two weeks of July and the first week in August—this is a combination of the Galway Arts Festival and Galway Race Week. On a definite par with New Orleans Mardi Gras for local enthusiasm and color, the Arts Festival is fast becoming an international event, with a film and theater festival attracting big names from across the world to display their productions to sold-out forums. Factor in street theater, impromptu dance sessions on street corners, established music acts from the United States and Europe, and a city bursting at the seams with all manner of creed, color, and humanity, and you have a melting pot Irish-style to rival any other event around the country. A definite must: The local theater group Macnas always stage a dazzling parade on a given day during the festival, and depending on the particular theme it has chosen for that year, you can thrill to the sight of 30-ft-high papier-mâché creations ambling down Main Street to a background of intoxication and fiddle tunes. This is big, brash, and right in your face—irresistible. Contact the festival office (tel. 091/583800) or the main tourist office for details and times. The Galway Races, going on at the time of the Festival, are one of the major meetings on the Irish sporting calendar. Horse-lovers enjoy not only the fun at the track but the entire festival atmosphere that surrounds the area during this time. Do listen to the conversations that waft by when the racing crowd hooks up with the movie crowd in the wee hours. Last year we overheard an avid gambler in earnest discussion with an enthusiastic movie buff on the strange similarities between Arkle's hindquarters and Ava Gardner's thighs in her heyday.

Another well-established event with slightly more upmarket and adult appeal is the Galway International Oyster Festival (tel. 091/527282), which takes place the last weekend in September. Based around the World Oyster-Opening Championship, which sees worthy types with their tiny knives ripping into stacks of waiting mollusks, this is, again, a good opportunity for late nights, free small concerts, and, everywhere, Guinness and oyster combos waiting to kick-start unaccustomed taste buds to this most delicate combination. Sixteen kilometers (10 mi) south of Galway, just off the main Limerick road in the tiny hamlet of Clarinbridge, another oyster festival takes place a week earlier, centered on the thatched Paddy Burke's Pub (tel. 091/961070) and the quaint Moran's Oyster Cottage (tel. 091/96113). Just a few feet away are the oyster beds, which can be seen at low tide. You can see 'em, gather 'em, and eat 'em all at one go. For information, call the Festival Office (tel. 091/796342).

NEAR GALWAY

KINVARA

COMING AND GOING • Bus Éireann sends buses (£5) to Kinvara from Galway once daily during winter, four times daily in the summer. If you're cycling, avoid the N67 and stick to the coast. Although the coast road adds a good 5 km (3 mi) to the ride, it's less congested and infinitely more scenic.

WHERE TO SLEEP AND EAT • The semi-isolated IHH Johnston's Hostel (tel. 091/37164), on Kinvara's main (and only) road, is open June–September and offers comfortable four- to six-bed dorm rooms (beds £7.50) and tent sites (£4.50 per person). For B&B accommodations, try Kinvarra House (tel. 091/37118) or Cois Cuain (tel. 091/37119). Both charge £16–£18 per person; they're closed November–February. Also, check out the Hollyoak B&B on Kinvara Road (tel. 091/637165), a pleasant family home with manicured gardens run by Maureen Fawle. Singles are £18 per night. The Merriman Inn (Main St., tel. 091/638222) is a new addition to the Kinvara scene. Boasting the largest thatched roof in Ireland, this slightly Alpine-looking hotel on the edge of the Burren fits in well despite its grand size. Singles are £25.50 a night.

Kinvara has a solid handful of great pubs. Try the Ould Shawl (tel. 091/637400), Winkles (tel. 091/637137), or Café on the Quay (tel. 091/37654), overlooking the bay. The café is one of the best restaurants in County Galway. Particularly exceptional are the salmon pasta (£6), Irish stew (£6), and ginger sponge cake (£1.65)—reason enough to visit this sleepy village. The café is open daily 9–9 in summer, irregularly in winter. Also, try Tully's (tel. 091/637146), an old-time grocery-cum-pub with trad sessions always on the go, and Greene's (tel. 091/637110), an old premises, dating from 1873, with ancient adornments and lively young locals.

WORTH SEEING • Kinvara is not as striking as the Burren or as lively as Doolin, but it is a picture-perfect seaside village 18 km (11 mi) southeast of Galway that is easily reached by bus or bicycle. Kinvara's most notable attraction is Dunguaire Castle (1 km/½ mi west of town, tel. 091/37108), a squat tower set atop a rock on the fringe of Galway Bay. It was originally built by merchants between 1450 and 1650; its two previous owners, Oliver St. John Gogarty (surgeon and model for Joyce's Buck Mulligan) and Lady Ampthill, both commissioned modest restorations. The castle is open May–September, daily 9:30–5; admission is £2.35.

"An ancient bridge and a more ancient tower/A farmhouse that is sheltered by its wall/An acre of stony ground/Where the symbolic rose can break in flower" — "Meditations on the Civil War," W. B. Yeats

Kinvara's long association with the sea is everywhere to be found in house names, local lore, and the presence of nets drying on the pier. The weekly voyages made in bygone times by Galway hookers bringing turf from the Aran Islands onto the mainland in exchange for local farming produce are now celebrated at the annual Crinniu na mBad Festival (Aug. 7–10). (Lest there be confusion here, folks, the Galway hooker is an ancient and venerable skin-built boat crafted exclusively in these parts.) The other big annual affair occurs on the May bank holiday weekend (first Monday of the month), when the town rises from the winter slumber with the Cuckoo Fleadh, a trad festival that attracts scores of local and national musicians.

Kinvara is also famous for having been the adopted home of the Waterboys rock band back in the early 1990s when they recorded their Irish-influenced album *Fisherman's Blues* in the area. Many other established international musicians cruise through the town to hook up for impromptu sessions during the year. On our visit there, we spotted Elvis Costello sipping a peaceful and unmolested pint with Irish legend Christy Moore. Ireland, in general, has become a haven for movie stars and music icons over the last few years. With a huge number of them locating all over Ireland, and in particular West Cork, don't be at all surprised if you do a double-take at a famous face buying sausages in the deli of a small town. The number of those who own homes over here grows by the week—a combination of resident tax breaks and unspoiled country seems to form the main attraction for regulars like Jeremy Irons, Mick Jagger, David Puttnam, George Michael, Tori Amos, Oliver Reed, Mike Oldfield, and even Julia Roberts, who's fallen hook, line, and sinker for Dingle. When it comes to letting superstars get on with their lives, Irish people are as cool about fame as New Yorkers.

THOOR BALEE

In 1917, when Yeats found this peaceful location to deliberate upon the aftermath of the 1916 Insurrection, it became the muse from which much of his greatest works were born. "I, the poet William Yeats/With old mill-boards and sea-green slates/And smithy work from the Gort forge/Restored this tower for my wife George/And may these characters remain/When all is ruin once again."

Thoor Balee was originally a fortified residence built by the Norman family the de Burgos during the 14th century. It was purchased for the princely sum of £35 by the poet, and he took up residence here with his new bride, George Hyde-Lees. It figured strongly in much of his work, particularly "the winding stair" leading to his study in the ancient tower. In 1928 a desire for warmer climes and a disillusionment with Irish

A TASTE OF ANCIENT EVENINGS

Now it may be that you're the kind of traveler who wouldn't wish to cover any ground that your parents might have trod before you, but a visit to a medieval banquet in a genuine Irish castle does still exert a powerful tug. A popular tourist attraction throughout the country almost since Irish tourism began, the experience ranks up there with climbing the Empire State or having your photo taken beside a beefeater guardsman in front of Big Ben, a been-there-got-the-T-shirt kind of thing. Despite their distinctly hokey reputation, these showcase events have progressed beyond the leprechaun and blarney stage of yesteryear into something in tandem with today's more demanding and hip tourist. As well as plentiful food—chicken, beef, lamb, and all the trimmings—served by, yes, red-haired colleens in traditional garb, it provides four hours of often unexpected entertainment that includes songs, poems, and extracts from chosen Irish writers like Yeats, Synge, and Gogarty. Don't expect anything too highbrow or authentic and you'll be pleasantly surprised. While most of the elderly visitors automatically head for Bunratty Castle, a few miles in from Shannon Airport, the best setting and atmosphere are found at Dunguaire Castle (tel. 091/37108) close to Kinvara. Cost of the banquet and reception runs £30 per person.

politics led Yeats to abandon the place. He died in France a decade later, in 1939. Situated 32 km (20 mi) south of Galway, just 2 km (1 mi) off the main Limerick road, it is open to the public May–September and offers a decent audiovisual history of the poet, as well as a bookshop, café, and gardens (tel. 091/631436).

COOLE PARK

Conveniently located near Thoor Balee is the home of Yeats's patron, Lady Gregory, at Coole Park. A canny widow of independent means who smiled upon the fortunes of many aspiring writers and poets around the turn of the century, she was a cofounder of the Abbey Theatre and vital to the resurrection of Irish literature in those times. After her death in 1932, the grand house fell into ruin and was eventually demolished during the Second World War. The well-kept grounds are now administered by the Office of Public Works and are ideal for picnicking, strolling, or soaking up the atmosphere of what was once a great hive of artistic endeavor. A huge copper beech tree on the grounds still retains many of the autographs put there by the literary greats who enjoyed the hospitality of the house—George Bernard Shaw, Sean O'Casey, and Douglas Hyde. Coole Park (tel. 091/631804) is about 5 km (3 mi) northeast of Gort and is open April–mid-June, Tuesday–Sunday 10–5:30, and mid-June–September, daily 9:30–6:30. Admission is £2.

ARAN ISLANDS

No one knows for certain when the Aran Islands—Inishmore, Inishmaan, and Inisheer—were first inhabited, but judging from the number of Bronze and Iron Age forts found here (especially on Inishmore), 3000 BC is a safe guess. Why scraggly nomads in deerskin jerkins would be attracted to these barren islets remains a greater mystery, not the least because fresh water and farmable land were (and

Finally, a travel companion that doesn't snore on the plane or eat all your peanuts.

MCI *WORLDCOM*   *WorldPhone*

123 456 7891 2345
J.D. SMITH

When traveling, your MCI WorldCom Card is the best way to keep in touch. Our operators speak your language, so they'll be able to connect you back home—no matter where your travels take you. Plus, your MCI WorldCom Card is easy to use, and even earns you frequent flyer miles every time you use it. When you add in our great rates, you get something even more valuable: peace-of-mind. So go ahead. Travel the world. MCI WorldCom just brought it a whole lot closer.

You can even sign up today at www.mci.com/worldphone or ask your operator to make a collect call to 1-410-314-2938.

EASY TO CALL WORLDWIDE

1 **Just dial the WorldPhone access number of the country you're calling from.**
2 **Dial or give the operator your MCI WorldCom Card number.**
3 **Dial or give the number you're calling.**

France ◆	0-800-99-0019
Germany	0800-888-8000
Ireland	1-800-55-1001
Italy ◆	172-1022
Spain	900-99-0014
Sweden ◆	020-795-922
Switzerland ◆	0800-89-0222
United Kingdom	
To call using BT	0800-89-0222
To call using CWC	0500-89-0222

For your complete WorldPhone calling guide, dial the WorldPhone access number for the country you're in and ask the operator for Customer Service. In the U.S. call 1-800-431-5402.

◆ Public phones may require deposit of coin or phone card for dial tone.

EARN FREQUENT FLYER MILES

AmericanAirlines
AAdvantage

Continental Airlines
OnePass

▲Delta Air Lines
SkyMiles

✈ MILEAGE PLUS.
United Airlines

US AIRWAYS
DIVIDEND MILES

MCI WorldCom, its logo and the names of the products referred to herein are proprietary marks of MCI WorldCom, Inc. All airline names and logos are proprietary marks of the respective airlines. All airline program rules and conditions apply.

MCI *WORLDCOM*

Distinctive guides packed with up-to-date expert advice and smart choices for every type of traveler.

Fodor's. For the world of ways you travel.

still are) scarce commodities. Much of the islands' arable land, in fact, is the by-product of centuries of erosion. After clearing as many loose stones as possible (which now form stone walls all over the islands), early farmers carpeted the ground with seaweed and kelp. Years and countless rain showers later, this decomposed to make soil suitable for shallow-rooted crops and grass. Add sheep, horses, and cows, their attendant tons of manure, and a few generations of backbreaking labor, and you have a proven recipe for transforming rocky wasteland into reasonably productive cropland.

During the 1800s, the islands, wracked by famine and mass emigration, were virtually forgotten by mainland Ireland. At the turn of the 20th century, however, they became the focus of renewed attention. Intrigued by the islanders' rugged lifestyle and centuries-old traditions, the playwright J. M. Synge spent four summers on Inishmaan between 1898 and 1902. Both his book *The Aran Islands* and his play *Riders to the Sea* prompted Gaelic revivalists to study and document this isolated bastion of Irish culture and to work for the islanders' economic development. Liam O'Flaherty (1897–1984), one of the most famous sons of Inishmore, was a novelist and historian who also made his name around the turn of the century, with his classic novel *Famine* becoming one of the more revered tracts of modern Irish literature. O'Flaherty wandered around North and South America for years before finally coming home to write. He also fought on the Republican side during the bloody civil war of 1921. In 1934, American director Robert Flaherty filmed his classic documentary *Man of Aran* (screened daily in Kilronan town hall on Inishmore), bringing the islands into the world spotlight. Much has changed since the film was made, but the islands continue to preserve a way of life that's all but disappeared on the mainland. This alone is reason enough to make the ferry ride from Galway, Doolin, Rossaveal, or Liscannor.

While traditional Irish culture fights a rear-guard battle on the mainland, the islanders continue to preserve as best they can a culture going back generations. Irish is still the native tongue here. It's spoken in these barren parts with a panache and gusto that come from a tradition of vocal entertainment far predating the days when satellite TV brought a stranger into every living room. A handful of people still wear the traditional Aran dress—red skirts and black shawls for the women and baggy trousers and colorful belts, called chrios, for the men. The classic white Aran sweater that has long been a trademark around the world, as well as being the ultimate protection from wind and rain, carries complex patterns of stitching that designate different parts of the region. Individual family patterns also helped in identifying the bodies of drowned fishermen in sea tragedies.

To appreciate the fierce loneliness of the islands you must spend the night on one. Because all the islands, especially Inishmore, crawl with day-trippers between 11 AM and 6 PM, it's difficult to let the rugged beauty of the islands sink into your soul until around 10 PM, when the sky is dark, the wind howling, and the pubs filled with the acrid smell of peat smoke and Guinness. Without a police presence on the islands, local gatherings in the pubs are free-flowing affairs. Hard work and the toils of the day often result in places just starting to get going at 2 AM. For mainland locals confined to the usual pub closing times of 11:30 PM, there is an undoubted thrill, to say nothing of potential intoxication, in visiting pubs without clocks. It's all about the disregard for time when you give yourself over to life on the islands, or, as one local laconically observed when we raged over missing the last boat back one evening: "What'll the world do without ye at all when ye're in the grave?"

COMING AND GOING

BY FERRY • Island Ferries (Merchant Rd., next to tourist office, Galway, tel. 091/568903) serves all three islands year-round, departing from Rossaveal, 37 km (23 mi) from Galway. Island Ferries buses depart from the tourist office to meet the three ferries bound for Inishmore, daily April–October at 9:15 AM, 12:15 PM, and 5:15 PM. The ferry journey takes 45 minutes and costs £19 round-trip, including the bus ride. Island Ferries also depart once a day to Inisheer and to Inishmaan at 11:15 AM; catch the 9:15 bus from the tourist office. Ferries from Inishmaan and Inisheer leave for Inishmore around 4 PM daily. The interisland trips cost £6. In the winter, service to Inishmore is reduced to once per day, with additional trips (for any of the three islands) dependent on demand and weather. Reservations at least one day in advance are strongly advised during July and August.

O'Brien Shipping/Doolin Ferries (Victoria Pl. tourist office, Galway, tel. 091/567283) sends ferries once a day June–September from Galway Harbour to all three islands. The trip takes about 90 minutes and costs £15 round-trip. They travel directly to the smaller islands on Wednesday and Thursday in the summer. They also travel to Inishmore every other day in the winter, weather and demand permitting.

INISHMORE

WHERE TO SLEEP AND EAT

If you want to stay through the witching hour, when dusk turns Inishmore hauntingly barren, be sure to book early into the IHH Mainistir House (tel. 099/61169). Located 1 km (½ mi) west of Kilronan's ferry port (walk uphill and follow the main road) and built on a rock plateau overlooking Galway Bay, the Mainistir House offers comfortable B&B accommodations (dorms £8, singles £11, doubles £24). In the evening Joel's "vaguely vegetarian" buffet costs £7 (£8 for nonguests) and is highly recommended. Mainistir House also offers an off-season deal with Island Ferries: transportation to the island and one night's accommodation for £21.

Otherwise, Dun Aengus House (tel. 099/61318), 6½ km (4 mi) west on the far side of the island, offers dorm beds (£7) April–October. This place is quiet and scenic, but you'll have to depend on its erratic shuttle bus to reach town unless you have a bike and don't mind a long, winding ride through the country. You'll find B&Bs along most of the main roads on the island. One of the nicest is Clai Bán (tel. 099/61111), open mid-March–September; it's a five-minute, signposted walk from Kilronan's small center, with rooms for £15 per person. Down the road, An Crugan (tel. 099/61150), open March–November, is also a safe bet, with rooms for £15 per person.

Inishmor Camp Site (tel. 099/61185) has a blissful location near the beach in Mainistir, a 20-minute walk from the pier. Facilities are basic and clean and cost £3.50 per night. If you hit a patch of good weather, stargazing on a deserted beach at midnight is hard to beat.

The best two bars in town are Joe Watty's (on the main road between Kilronan and Mainistir House, tel. 099/61155) and Joe Mac's (right off the pier, tel. 099/61248). Another good bet for hearty local food is Teach Nan Phaidt (tel. 099/61330), a thatched restaurant close to Dun Aengus. It specializes in home-baked bread with smoked salmon, shellfish, and vegetarian dishes. For lighter fare, try Peig's Coffee Shop (no phone) near the Lucky Star bar and the Ould Pier (no phone) snack bar—both serve good coffees, teas, and sandwiches.

WORTH SEEING

Inishmore (Inis Mór, or Large Island) is the biggest, most popular island of the three. Most people visit only for the day, content to see the island from the window of a minibus before catching the last ferry back to Galway. Once these folks clear out, Inishmore's stunningly fierce and brooding beauty is disturbed only by the "baa" of sheep and the incessant rush of the wind. Even if you only have a few hours to explore Inishmore, spend £5 on a rental bike (available next to the pier) and head straight for Dun Aengus, a 4,000-year-old stone fort perched on the edge of a 300-ft cliff, on the far side of the island, 8 km (5 mi) from the port. Along the way, about 5 km (3 mi) from the fort, you'll pass a cluster of religious ruins—a few small churches, a monastery, and some crosses—called the Seven Churches. At the southern end of the island, Black Fort (Dun Duchathair) is Inishmore's other archaeological treasure, built around 1000 BC into a cleft of razor-sharp rocks. According to military historians, this cliff-top fort was probably the most defensible in Ireland, evident by the fact that it was never overrun in battle. Unfortunately, erosion and landslides have done what military might could not, and sections of the stone battlements have been destroyed. An intriguing history of the islands is provided by the Aran Heritage Centre (Kilronan, tel. 099/61355), which is open April–October, daily 10–7. For £2 you'll discover fossils, ingenious farming techniques, a few cheesy models, and a cliff rescue cart for saving shipwrecked sailors. Buy the £3.50 combo ticket to watch one of the frequent showings of Robert Flaherty's famous *Man of Aran*.

A number of locals also offer minivan tours of Inishmore. Prices range from £3 to £7 per person, depending on your ability to haggle, and most last two or three hours. The islanders know the ferry timetables by heart and congregate on the pier at the appropriate hours. Several bike shops lie on the harbor and charge £5 per day. Toward sunset a handful of locals pedal their squeaky bicycles down the long road to Kilronan, the island's port and largest village. A few pubs share this block-long, harbor-front settlement with a chipper, a grocery store, and a tourist office (tel. 099/61263), open late May–mid-September, Monday–Saturday 10–6ish, depending on the weather and crowd. Day-trippers can leave their luggage here (75p) or with one of the bike shops for free if you rent from them.

INISHMAAN

WHERE TO SLEEP AND EAT

Inishmaan's tourist industry is in its infancy, which means that accommodations here are strictly B&B. In fact, there are only two Bord Fáilte–approved B&Bs on the island and, confusingly enough, both are run by a Mrs. Faherty (not related). Angela Faherty's B&B (Creigmore, tel. 099/73012) and Ard Alainn B&B (West Village, tel. 099/73027) are open April–October and cost £13 per person. Reservations are a must.

For refreshment, pull up a stool at O'Conghaille's Pub (tel. 099/73003), a smoky, friendly drinking room that serves sandwiches and soup and often hosts traditional music on summer weekends.

WORTH SEEING

Inishmaan (Inis Meáin, or Middle Island) is both less touristed and, in many ways, more scenic than Inishmore. Though it doesn't have a wealth of archaeological sites, the ruins of Dún Conchúir (*see below*), a 3rd-century stone fort overlooking a valley, and Cill Cheannannaech (½ km/¼ mi from the pier), a church from the 8th century, make interesting stops. Inishmaan is surprisingly lush—compared with Inishmore's rock-strewn terrain—and is dominated by smooth patches of heather and pasture. Still, there isn't much arable land, and Inishmaan's 350 residents rely mostly upon fishing for their livelihood, so you're more likely to see people sporting cable-knit sweaters, knee-length boots, and woolen caps here than on the other islands. Around 8 PM on summer nights you can sometimes see the currachs, hide- and tar-covered fishing skiffs, unload the day's catch at beachfront landings all along the shore. There's none of the hard tourist sell on Inishmaan that's often found elsewhere; the locals seem content to let the visitors find them. If that doesn't happen, nobody's going to lose sleep over it. The presence of an export knitwear factory that gives decent local employment probably helps in constructing their laid-back attitude.

As you pedal around Inishmore, keep your eyes peeled for faded signs pointing the way to the impressive sets of ruins scattered about the island.

To get a sense of the island's antiquity, head to Dún Conchúir (Connor's Fort), the largest of all Aran stone forts. Measuring 225 by 115 ft, with walls 20 ft high, the fort dominates the landscape from its position atop a cliff in the island's center, brooding over a sunken valley. To the east, a small footpath leads to Cathaoir Synge (Synge's Chair), one of the playwright's favorite sea-viewing points, carved neatly into the rock. A tourist desk (inside the An Cora shop, tel. 099/73092) is open June–September, daily 11–6, and has maps and hiking info.

INISHEER

WHERE TO SLEEP AND EAT

At sunset, you'll find most people ambling slowly toward the pier-side village and its pubs. Inisheer's two most popular pubs are attached to hostels. One hundred yards from the pier, Radharc na Mara (tel. 099/75024) offers standard dorm-style accommodations (£7) for 40 people. It doesn't look like much, but its cozy common room has a blazing peat fire whenever the weather is gray (i.e., always). Next door is the hostel's excellent pub and restaurant, the latter serving soups, sandwiches, and stews for £3–£5. Nearby, Ostan Inis Oír (tel. 099/75020) offers hotel-style accommodations (£15–£17 per person) to herds of tourists between mid-April and August. Its restaurant (open to nonguests) is a better deal: Hearty steak and seafood dishes are £5–£10. Fisherman's Cottage (tel. 099/75073) serves fish dishes for lunch in the £3.30–£7 range. Between May and September, you can camp at Lathair Campala (tel. 099/75008), 1 km (½ mi) north of the ferry port and well signposted from the docks. The 40 sites (£2) all have good views of the coast.

WORTH SEEING

Inisheer (Inis Oírr, or Eastern Island) is the smallest island in the Aran chain, but its proximity to Doolin in County Clare (11 km/7 mi) means it's often packed with day-trippers. On the plus side, Inisheer's relative prosperity means you'll find a hostel, a cheapish hotel, numerous B&Bs, pubs, and restaurants near the ferry dock. On a visit more than a decade ago, there were still a few thatched cottages left.

LIGHTS, CAMERAS, ACTION!

If "The Quiet Man" (filmed around Cong by John Ford in 1951) represented the 1950s Ireland and the practically nonexistent film business back then, "The Field" in 1990 is a marker of just how far things have progressed for the home-based industry. Always seen as a cheap and stunning location by visiting productions, the area has gained even more notice from the film industry since Richard Harris and John Hurt played out the richly textured drama by John B. Keane around the village of Leenane. This was Ireland's first Oscar-nominated film and prompted the government to back the production of more Irish movies made by Irish people. Result? It's gotten to the stage where locals are now shocked if there's not at least one Irish Oscar-nominated film every year. Movies like "My Left Foot," "In the Name of the Father," "Michael Collins," "Dancing at Lughnasa," and "The General" are just some of the high-profile exports doing serious business beyond these shores. An unfortunate by-product of all this cinematic activity, however, is the constant refrain heard in pubs late in the evening: "We've got such a dynamite script, if only we can find the money to make it." Don't be surprised at all to be engaged in conversation, especially if you're from Los Angeles, by earnest would-be writers and directors keen to take you step-by-step through their latest opus. Ireland has long been a country full of writers if only they had the time to sit down and write—now add scriptwriter-director to that list.

Sadly, these are no more, replaced by a more functional modern bungalow style whose whitewashed walls do actually manage to blend quite well upon this ancient landscape. The island is suitable for an overnight stay, especially since you can (and should) walk its entire length, 3 km (2 mi), in the dark without fear of getting too lost (there are only two roads). By day, you'll want to check out the ruins of O'Brien Castle, set inside a stone-ringed fort that's clearly visible from the pier. The castle itself was built in the 15th century by the O'Brien clan, which ruled Inisheer from 1150 to 1585. Another ancient island site, Arkin's Castle, dates from Cromwellian times when it operated as a garrison in the 17th and 18th centuries. To the west of Kilronan is the Church of St. Enda, the saint most associated with the spread of Christianity on Aran.

CONNEMARA

The Connemara region, in the northwest corner of County Galway, is wild and desolate. Its geography—expanses of windswept bog land buffered by mountains, white-sand beaches, and glacial lakes—provides endless fodder for the "rugged and rural" Irish stereotype. Part of Connemara's appeal stems from the extremes of its landscape, noted for such features as the Twelve Pin Mountains, Lough Corrib, and Killary Harbour. Botanists and rangers from the Connemara National Park Visitor Centre (tel. 095/41054), open May–September, daily 9:30–6:30, near Letterfrack, lead walking tours at 10:30 AM Monday, Wednesday, and Friday during July and August. The walks highlight the varied features of the park's bog lands, megalithic tombs, and flora and fauna and cost £2, including admission to the center. Aside from the stunning geography, Connemara is equally popular for its lazy country feel and for the rugged characters who live in the area. Although Connemara is not heavily Irish-speaking, its relative isolation has helped to insulate it from the nastier effects of mass tourism, which in turn has helped to foster a more traditional, some even say a more authentically Irish, style of living. On the downside, Connemara's rugged conditions present certain travel problems, especially for those traveling in winter when Bus Éireann goes into semihibernation. Not a distinct geographical area like the Burren, Connemara shelters in the shadow of the massive mountainous outcrops looking south across a plain dotted with lakes, bog land, and rocks—lots of 'em. Those keen on some serious hillwalking must attempt this terrain. With many well-marked trails and brochures of the various options available in most pubs and hotels, it's the kind of country where the always-threatening rain only adds to the stark beauty of the place.

CONG

BASICS

Cong's tourist office (Abbey St., tel. 092/46542), open March–September, daily 10–6, has brochures and maps on Cong and Connemara and a bureau de change. If you plan to hike the area, pick up the booklet "Cong: Sights, Walks, Stories" (£2.50), which details some excellent, scenic walks. Buses go to and from Galway (£5.50) once per day (except Sun.). The stop is in front of Ryan's Hotel on Main Street. Cong's post office (Main St., tel. 092/46001) is open weekdays 9–1 and 2–5:30.

WHERE TO SLEEP

HOSTELS • Cong theoretically has two hostels, but one is closed most of the year and the other lies a good distance from the village. Both charge £6 per person, have a laundry, are utterly spotless, and show *The Quiet Man* every night at 9 PM. The Quiet Man Hostel (Abbey St., tel. 092/46511), a prim town house in the center of town, is the cozier of the two but is only open June–August. Down the Galway Road (1½ km/1 mi) is An Óige's Cong Hostel (Lake Quay Rd., tel. 092/46089), a thoroughly modern and clean place with a huge kitchen and cozy TV room. It also offers a shuttle to town; has flat, grassy camping sites (£3.75 per person); and rents fishing rods (£1) to snag the many trout and salmon in the adjacent and stunningly beautiful Lough Corriband. Neither has a strict lockout or curfew.

SMALL HOTELS AND INNS • If you're looking for some privacy, the White House (Abbey St., tel. 092/46358) charges £16 per person and is across from the Cong Abbey. There's a TV and a bathroom in every room. Less comfortable is Rising of the Waters Inn (Main St., tel. 092/46316), which charges £14 per person and has a run-down pub downstairs with sandwiches under £2. Both are closed for the winter. **Villa Pio** (Gurtacurra Cross, tel. 092/46403) is situated near *The Quiet Man* film locations, a 5-minute walk from Lough Corrib. Modern rooms with bath en-suite are £18 per person B&B.

WORTH SEEING

Resting on a narrow isthmus between Lough Corrib and Lough Mask on the County Mayo border, Cong is dotted with ivy-covered thatched cottages and dilapidated farmhouses. Just two blocks long, and bisected by the chocolate-brown River Cong, the village is surrounded on all sides by thickly forested hills. Unfortunately, there is something a little too refined about the place; perhaps all those film stars left a lot of airs and graces behind. Also nearby is the immensely posh Ashford Castle (tel. 092/46003). Built by the de Burgos family in 1228, the castle was purchased by the Guinness family and transformed into a luxury hotel in the early 1970s. You'll need upward of £200 per person to spend the night here, but visitors are encouraged to walk the castle's grounds (admission £3). If you can manage it, poke your head inside the lobby, which is decorated in period style and oozes aristocratic elegance. An infinitely more romantic way to see the castle is via rowboat, which you can rent (£6 for 2 hrs) from the Cong Hostel (*see above*).

Cong's other main attractions are the remains of Cong Abbey, built in 1120 by Turlough Mór O'Connor, king of Connaught and now open (free) to the public. There's not much to this roofless, skeletal ruin, but if you continue past the abbey toward the banks of Lough Corrib, about 2 km (1 mi) south, you'll get a clear view of the stupendous natural beauty that surrounds the town. Take a short detour on one of the signposted footpaths that meander through the Cong Hills and you'll end up in dense, old-growth forest. Cong is also surrounded by many caves, stone circles, and burial mounds. The impressive Pigeon Hole cave is 1½ km (1 mi) from town on the road to Clonbur, and Giant's Grave, one of Ireland's megalithic burial chambers, is 1 km (½ mi) farther. Ask at the tourist office for hiking information and maps.

CLIFDEN

BASICS

Clifden's small tourist office (Market St., tel. 095/21163) is open May–September, Monday–Saturday 9—6, also July–August, Sunday noon–4. The office distributes maps and brochures, exchanges money, and organizes day trips to Inishbofin Island (*see below*), starting at £10. The Bus Éireann depot is in front of Cullen's on Market Street. Expressway buses from Galway (£7) stop here five times daily July–September, once daily in other months. Other destinations include Cong (1 per day in summer, £7) and Cleggan (2 per week, £3). Pat Lydon's Mini & Midi Coach Hire (tel. 095/41043) is the local bus company, offering daily trips between Clifden and Westport, stopping in Cleggan along the way, for £7 round-trip. The bus runs twice daily Monday–Saturday in the summer (if there is demand). Michael Nee's Connemara Bus (tel. 095/51082) runs between Cleggan and Galway twice daily in the summer (£7 round-trip, £5 one-way) and once a day otherwise. The local Raleigh Rent-A-Bike agent is Mannion's (Bridge St., tel. 095/21160), just off Main Street on the east side of town, which rents bikes for £7 per day, £30 per week, plus a £10 deposit. Change your money at AIB bank (The Square, tel. 095/21129), open weekdays 10–12:30 and 1:30–4.

WHERE TO SLEEP

HOSTELS • For a town its size, Clifden has more than enough hostels to accommodate the summer rush. The very modern Clifden Town Hostel (Market St., ½ block west of the bus stop, tel. 095/21076) has comfy dorm beds (£7–£8), triples (£20), and doubles (£27). Unfortunately, the staff has more than a little attitude. The IHH Leo's Hostel (The Square, tel. 095/21429) commands the best views of any hostel in town: Most rooms (and even one choice toilet) look out over the bay and surrounding mountains. Standard dorm beds cost £7–£8, doubles £12–£16; an excellent campsite with great views out over the bay and full use of the hostel facilities costs £3 per person. The hostel also rents bikes at £5 a day.

BED-AND-BREAKFASTS • There are a dozen good B&Bs huddled together on Bridge Street, east of the square off Main Street. Try Ben View House (Bridge St., tel. 095/21256), which has 10 refined rooms with bath from £18 per person, or Errismore House (Bridge St., tel. 095/21360), which has 5 rooms starting at £17 per person. Both are in small, family-inhabited flats—the sorts of places where the fried breakfasts are lovingly steeped in grease and served in huge portions.

FOOD

O'Grady's Seafood Restaurant (Market St., tel. 095/21450) offers a solid local reputation and sizable portions for about £12 a meal. Doris's (Market St., tel. 095/21427) does good steak, seafood, and Continental dishes for about £10 a head. Farther out at Claddaghduff, Acton's Restaurant (Cleggan Rd., tel. 095/44339) has another excellent menu with the added bonus of stunning views right out across the Atlantic from its cliff-top location.

WORTH SEEING

During summer, Clifden is painfully overcrowded with snap-happy tourists and luxury coaches from Galway, proof that Clifden is indeed the unrivaled "capital" of Connemara. For the past few years the town has been subject to intense tourist development in the style of Killarney. Although not yet tainted to the same degree as that southern town, some of Clifden's old charm and timelessness have disappeared forever. Despite the crowds, however, its old rural market-town flavor is especially ripe during August's world-famous Connemara Pony Show (tel. 095/21863), usually held during the third week of the month. It's worth booking a bed well in advance for this festival, which features horse traders from a dozen countries parading their yearlings and stallions and bartering over a pint or two. Admission to the principal market runs around £3, but there are always a few ponies on parade in the streets or at the nearby beach, which is also the site of informal races when the weather is good.

The town's main attraction for visitors is its location: perched above Clifden Bay on a forested plateau and flanked in the east by the impressive Twelve Ben Mountains (also known as the Twelve Pin Mountains). At the western edge of Connemara, Clifden is regularly serviced by bus in the summer months, making it a convenient hub for exploring the mountains and nearby coast. To appreciate the scenery, you need to get out of and above Clifden, preferably on one of the small hillocks that form its western border. Here, down Sky Road, you'll find the derelict ruins of Clifden Castle, built in 1815 by the town's founder, John D'Arcy. To the west, just below Clifden's main cluster of tourist shops and pubs, the Owenglin Cascades are also worth a quick tour. Formed by large limestone boulders jammed into the mouth of the River Owenglin, the steep cascades are believed to have the power of healing. Hikers should head for the Connemara Walking Centre (Market St., tel. 095/21379), which has maps, plenty of advice on the best hiking around, and archaeologists who lead half-day (£10) and full-day (£20) hikes. After conquering the Maamturk or Twelve Pin mountains, give your aching muscles the Guinness treatment at Guy's (Main St., tel. 095/21130) or Humpty's (Market St., tel. 095/21511). Both feature the best of, well, the Clifden live-rock scene.

Eight kilometers (5 mi) out of Clifden on the N59 is Dan O'Hara's Homestead, an accurate rendering of a pre-famine farm (circa 1840). Also part of this 8-acre attraction are reproductions of a prehistoric lake dwelling—a crannog—dating to 1500 BC, a neolithic tomb 5,000 years old, a prehistoric dolmen tomb, pony rides, a restaurant and crafts shop, and audiovisual presentations about the history of the region. The unfortunate Dan O'Hara, by the way, was evicted from here due to rent arrears. He emigrated to the United States in the mid 1800s, where he sold matches on street corners before dying of consumption.

OUGHTERARD

BASICS

Tourist information and bike rental can be found in the same premises on Main Street (tel. 091/82808); the office is open Monday–Saturday 9–5:30 and Sunday 10–2. The thoroughfare is also the site of banks, the post office (tel. 091/552201), a launderette, and the inevitable gift shops. Galway buses to and from Clifden make regular stops in Oughterard throughout the day. Internet access can be found at Clearview Solutions (Camp St., tel. 091/552351) for £5 per half hour.

WHERE TO SLEEP AND EAT

B&Bs abound in this area, but some of them have become quite pricey of late due, no doubt, to the many wealthy Europeans arriving to fish in the area. Check out Forest Hill (Gleann Rd., tel. 091/552549), a large bungalow set on acres of its own grounds, where serious comfort can be bought for £22.50 per head. Also, there's Pine Grove (Hill of Doon Rd., tel. 091/552101), where a turf fire burns all day in a friendly home; rooms are £22.50 per person. Restaurant-wise, Oughterard is more pub oriented than most towns, with good solid fare to be had in the Boat Inn and Keogh's Bar, both on the square. On Bridge Street, the more upmarket Water Lily (tel. 091/82737) sits right on the river and serves, appropriately enough, excellent poached salmon. Prices run around £14 a head.

Heading out of Oughterard through Maam Cross on the N59, you'll hit the tiny village of Recess, having passed Lough Shindilla and Lough Oorid on route. Just a row of houses on a single street, it might be a handy stop for a coffee or a pint in Paddy Resty's (tel. 095/34673); it also serves excellent smoked salmon on brown bread. The village serves as a gateway to one of the more spectacular routes in the region, with the Twelve Pins towering up ahead and the Maamturks brooding on the right. Turning north here brings you into the dazzling Lough Inagh Valley, one of the most scenic routes in the region. With Loughs Derryclare and Inagh accompanying the route for most of the way, and the desolate mountain ranges always dwarfing your progress, this is one time you'll insist on stopping every few miles for photographs. For some curious reason, the road is never crowded with other cars, a fact that only enhances the beautiful desolation of it all. Halfway up the valley is the distinctly upmarket Lough Inagh Lodge (tel. 095/34706), a classic country house hotel. Built in 1880, this is a world of oak paneling, open blazing fires, and stunning views from every window. Doubles cost £110 and are worth every penny if you're splurging; if not, settle for tea and scones in the deep comfort of ancient sofas around the fire.

WORTH SEEING

Calling itself "the gateway to Connemara," this basic one-street town seems like the last stop for provisions before heading deep into the panorama of lakes, mountains, and bogs that await you farther west. It's a major center for anglers keen to test their skills on Lough Corrib, particularly during the mayfly period (mid-May to mid-June), when both fish and their pursuers become frenzied in search of that springtime fly. "Dapping" is the best method of catching them—an activity in which the line is given gentle tugs, enabling the bait to hop lightly on the water. Large spring salmon of 15 pounds and upward, as well as excellent brown trout of up to 10 pounds, are on offer for those keen to try. An experienced boatman (vital for the uninitiated) plus his boat and motor can be hired for £45 for the day; your B&B or the tourist office can arrange it.

A longtime hideaway for city folk from Dublin and Galway who keep country cottages down the leafy lanes, Oughterard doesn't have much in the way of ancient sites other than Aughnanure Castle (tel. 091/82214), about 2 km (1 mi) east of the town. Built in the 16th century by the O'Flaherty clan who controlled the region for hundreds of years after fighting off the Normans, the six-story tower house stands on a rocky outcrop overlooking Lough Corrib. True rebels in every sense, the O'Flaherty clan were definitely not to be messed with. One of their favorite pastimes was sending the heads of tax collectors to the opposing chieftains in Galway in a woolen sack. Amazingly, their daily activities around the castle were distinctly civilized, with family members employed as physicians, standard bearers, judges, poets, genealogists, collector of revenues, and beekeepers. Underneath the castle foundations, which are currently being renovated, the lake washes through a series of natural caves and caverns. The castle is open daily in the summer, from 9:30 AM to 6:30 PM; entrance is £3.

Inchagoill Island forms the biggest island of the 360 found in Lough Corrib. At one point seriously far back in the mists of time, an ancient monastic settlement existed there whose signs are still to be found. A lonely place with an eerie atmosphere, the island's most fascinating site is a burial marker that reads "Lia Luguaedon Macc Meneuh," meaning "the stone of Iuaguaedon son of Menueh," standing beside the remains of the Saints Church. Historians claim that the Latin writing on the stone is the oldest Christian inscription in Europe apart from those in catacombs in Rome. Of early Romanesque design, the church dates from the 9th or 10th century. Boats can be hired for the crossing to the island from either Oughterard or Cong, at a cost of about £5 a head.

ROUNDSTONE

WHERE TO STAY AND EAT

The recently built Eldon's Hotel (Main St., tel. 095/35933) has comfortable rooms, some overlooking the town, for £25 per person. Under the same management is the Beola Restaurant (tel. 095/35871), serving mainly seafood in the £12–£15 range. Roundstone House Hotel (tel. 095/35864) is a whitewashed family hotel right on the bay with great views across Connemara. Singles run £32.50 per person. The Gurteen Beach Caravan & Camping Park (tel. 095/35882) is 2 km (1 mi) west of the town, by the beach, and charges £8 a night for two. O'Dowd's Pub (Main St., tel. 095/35809) in the village has fine bar food, as well as a restaurant specializing in seafood. Expect to pay around £10 a head.

WORTH SEEING

Right across the other side of the peninsula, heading south from Lough Inagh, is Roundstone, a picturesque fishing village on the western extension of Bertaghboy Bay. Sitting at the foot of Errisbeg with wonderful views of the Twelve Bens from another angle, this picture-postcard town has the regulation old stone pier, gaily painted fishing boats, lobster pots drying in the sun, and rows of weather-bleached houses arcing down to the sea. At the head of the pier is the home of Tim Robinson, the man behind Folding Landscape Maps—the compact maps of the Burren, Connemara, and the islands that you've probably already bought. His home, where local advice and information can be found, is open to visitors during the summer. South of the village is the IDA (Industrial Development Authority) crafts complex where those goatskin bodhrans beloved of all Irish musicians are made. As you move southward from the town, the superb beaches of Gorteen and Dog's Bay can be found just 3 km (2 mi) away.

If you cut inland instead of heading down along the coast, you'll see upclose one of the last stretches of Irish blanket bog land. At last given due recognition as an important ecosystem and not just a cute source of fuel by the EU, vast stretches of this ancient soil are now preserved. Wear boots and be careful when venturing upon certain sections—especially when the entire ground beneath your feet wobbles like jelly—you're on thin crust: Move very, very carefully.

CLEGGAN, LETTERFRACK, AND INISHBOFIN ISLAND

BASICS

A tourist desk in Cleggan at Oliver Coyne's Pub (tel. 095/44640) stocks brochures, maps, and bus info. Between June 22 and August 27, Bus Éireann offers one Expressway bus each Monday and Thursday to Letterfrack and Kylemore Abbey from Clifden; local service operates once a day year-round. You can exchange money at the Cleggan post office (Main St., tel. 095/44655), open weekdays 9–5:30 and Saturday 9–1.

WORTH SEEING

Northwest Connemara is famous for the rugged barrenness of its land and the harsh beauty of its coast, where desolate bog land and ragged mountains are tempered by the sea. In towns like Clifden, those striking contrasts are often muted or ruthlessly exploited by the tourist board for mass consumption. But you can encounter pure and unblemished Connemara in a village like Cleggan, a tiny fishing settlement 9½ km (6 mi) northwest of Clifden. Cleggan has its fair share of tourist shops, along with a well-developed harbor and fishing industry, but its pace is soothingly rural and its scenery stunning. Enveloped by mountains and perched on the cusp of Cleggan Bay, the village is crisscrossed by hundreds of good hiking trails and by the sort of curvy coastal roads that give cyclists a reason to live. The IHH Master's House Hostel (tel. 095/44746) has become more of a horseback-riding center than a hostel, with riding at £12 an hour. Closed October to May, it offers top-rate dorm accommodations (£7) and private rooms (£8 per person). The hostel is a three-minute walk from the village's minuscule center; just follow the signs.

If Masters House Hostel is full, head for the village of Letterfrack, which has a very laid-back and welcoming hostel set behind the church on your right as you come from Clifden. The Old Monastery Hostel (tel. 095/41132) has beds from £7 to £9. The price includes a hearty breakfast with home-baked bread. They also do evening meals for £5 and offer bike rental for £6 per day and Internet access for £2.50 per hour. Letterfrack itself is really just three pubs, an excellent village shop, and a couple of houses at a crossroads. Veldons (tel. 095/41046) is a pub and shop in one, with an excellent selection of fresh fish. Traditional musicians gather and play most evenings in the pub. Letterfrack is also a good point from which to visit Kylemore Abbey (tel. 095/41146) on the road to Westport. Built in the 19th century, the abbey is set alone beside Kylemore Lake in a perfect, postcard setting. It's still in use as a convent boarding school run by nuns, but it's open to the public; admission is £3. There is a serene walk beside the lake, and you can stroll up the hill to the life-size statue of Jesus, usually surrounded by grazing sheep. The view out over the lake is well worth the effort.

Master's House Hostel can arrange summer boat trips (£10 per hosteler) to nearby Inishbofin Island, an amazingly laid-back outcrop of rocky farmland 9½ km (6 mi) northwest of Cleggan Harbour. You can also book ferries for yourself at Coyne's Shop (tel. 095/44750) and King's Shop (tel. 095/44642). Coyne's will book you on Dun Aengus, the island's mail boat, while King's sells tickets for The Queen, the better and larger boat of the two. Check at the shops for sailing times and prices, both of which vary according to demand and weather. Inishbofin has a deserved reputation for attracting Euro-hippies and unrepentant boozers looking to commune with nature and a pint or two. During the day, the island's protected beaches are littered with longhairs and the strains of Bob Marley; at night, the three pubs overflow with locals and bleary-eyed Guinness-pounders of all nationalities. If you stick around for the strange and wonderful pub scene here, check into the excellent IHH Inishbofin Island Hostel (tel. 095/45855), near the island's harbor. Besides its modern kitchen, dorm rooms (£6.50), and double rooms (£20), the hostel has an airy conservatory that's perfect for rainy-day cups of tea and meaningful conversation.

THE NORTHWEST

JOHN DALY

I n the wild, wet, grass-and-heather hills of the Northwest you'll find some of Ireland's most majestic scenery and some of its least-touristed areas. Cool, clean waters from the roaring Atlantic Ocean slice the landscape into long peninsulas of breeze-swept rocky crests, each one remote from the next. The lower country, at least where it is covered by layers of moist bog, cuts open to reveal dark brown peat underneath; although this area may be thought less pretty than the rest of the region, it has a haunting, lonely appeal.

Comprising the counties of Mayo, Sligo, Leitrim, and Donegal, this most inaccessible and isolated corner of Ireland provides rich rewards for intrepid travelers willing to overcome vast distances and poor transportation. While the rest of the Island finds the tourist season extending to a year-round commerce nowadays, the Northwest can still proclaim itself "the hidden Ireland"—and that's no blarney. From the lonely expanses of bog land in Mayo's Belmullet Peninsula to the varied cultural footprints of W. B. Yeats around Sligo and onward to the ultimate inspiration of walking the Bloody Foreland or Slieve League cliffs in Donegal, this is indeed a place that still resonates with what William Makepeace Thackeray described in 1842 as "one of the most wild and beautiful districts that it is ever the fortune of the traveler to examine."

Tucked into the folds of the Northwest's hills, modest little market towns and unpretentious villages with muddy streets go about their business quietly. In the squelchy peat bogs, cutters working with long shovels pause to watch and wave as you drive past. Remember to drive slowly along the country lanes, for around any corner you may find a whitewashed thatched cottage with children playing outside, a shepherd leading his flock, or a bicycle-riding farmer wobbling along in the middle of the road. Yes, it may sound too cute to be true, but that's just the way it is with Ireland.

Keep in mind, though, that the whole region—and County Donegal in particular—attracts a good share of visitors during July and August; this is a favorite vacation area for people who live in nearby Northern Ireland. To be frank, a few places are quite spoiled by popularity with tourists and careless development; the coast between Sligo Town and Donegal Town, a cheap and cheerful family beach resort full of so-called "Irish gift shops" and "amusement arcades," is another place to pass by rather than visit. On the whole, though, the Northwest is big enough, untamed enough, and grand enough to be able to absorb all of its summer (and weekend) tourists without too much harm.

County Donegal has the country's largest Gaeltacht (Irish-speaking area). Drivers in this part of the country, you'll be amused to notice, often end up frustrated whenever they come to a crossroads: Signposts show only the Irish place-names, often so unlike the English versions as to be completely unrec-

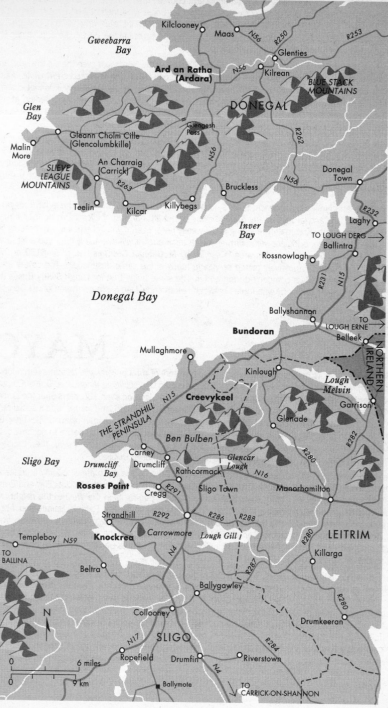

Gweebarra Bay

Kilclooney

Maas

N56

R250

R253

Glenties

Glen Bay

Ard an Ratha (Ardara)

N56

Kilrean

BLUE STACK MOUNTAINS

DONEGAL

Glengesh Pass

Malin More

Gleann Cholm Cille (Glencolumbkille)

R262

SLIEVE LEAGUE MOUNTAINS

An Charraig (Carrick)

N56

R263

Bruckless

N56

Donegal Town

R232

Teelin

Kilcar

Killybegs

Inver Bay

Laghy

TO LOUGH DERG →

Ballintra

Rossnowlagh

R231

N15

Donegal Bay

Ballyshannon

Bundoran

TO LOUGH ERNE →

Belleek

Mullaghmore

Kinlough

Lough Melvin

NORTHERN IRELAND

Creevykeel

N15

THE STRANDHILL PENINSULA

Garrison

Glenade

Ben Bulben

R282

Carney

Drumcliff

Glencar Lough

R280

Sligo Bay

Drumcliff Bay

Rathcormack

N16

Rosses Point

R291

Cregg

Sligo Town

Manorhamilton

Strandhill

R292

R286

R288

Templeboy

N59

Knockrea

Carrowmore

Lough Gill

R280

LEITRIM

TO BALLINA

Beltra

N4

R287

Killarga

Ballygawley

Collooney

R280

N17

SLIGO

Drumkeeran

Ropefield

Drumfin

Riverstown

R284

0   6 miles

0   9 km

Ballymote

N4

TO CARRICK-ON-SHANNON

N

189

ognizable. All is not lost, however—maps generally give both the Irish and the English names, and locals are usually more than happy to help out with directions (in English), sometimes with a yarn thrown in. County Donegal was part of the near-indomitable ancient kingdom of Ulster, which was not conquered by the English until the 17th century. By the time they were driven out in the 1920s, the English had still not eradicated rural Donegal's Celtic inheritance.

If the whole of Ireland is a land of seemingly infinite diversity, in the Northwest even the air, the light, and the colors of the countryside change like a kaleidoscope. Look once, and scattered snow-white clouds are flying above tawny-brown slopes. Look again, and suddenly the sun has brilliantly illuminated some magnificent reds and purples in the undergrowth. The inconstant skies brighten and darken at will, bringing out a whole spectrum of subtle shades within the unkempt gorse and heather, the rocky slopes merging into somber peat and grassy meadows of scintillating green.

Not only close to the bracing ocean shore but also farther inland, water in all its forms dominates the Northwest; countless lakes, running streams, and rivers wind through lovely pastoral valleys. Be prepared for plenty of rainfall as well; don't forget to carry a raincoat or umbrella—although, as a kind local may inform you, the "brolly" acts purely as a talisman: "For it's only when you *don't* have it with you that the rain will really come down" is a piece of local wisdom.

With no train and limited bus service, there's no denying that northwestern Ireland is a hard region to traverse. Steep hills and winding roads frighten away all but the hardiest of cyclists, as do the frequent cold weather and rain. Fortunately, hitching is fairly easy here: Even if you get stuck in what seems like the middle of nowhere, odds are some farmer with a thick accent will eventually offer you a lift to the next pub. Besides Bus Éireann, the area is served by **McGeehan Coaches** (tel. 075/46150 or 075/46101), which offers competitively priced service to many of the same destinations and covers areas ignored by the national bus company during winter. The same holds true for **Lough Swilly Buses** (tel. 074/22400), a private company with routes between Letterkenny, Derry, and northern County Donegal.

MAYO

While it shares with its neighbors Galway and Sligo a history of rural poverty and desolate reminders of the famine, Mayo is still for many natives and visitors alike an undiscovered landscape. One of Europe's most underpopulated regions, this county is still racked by emigration even 150 years after the famine. Yet it holds firmly to its peculiar identity of cultural introspection, hidden landscapes, and a social ethos that more resembles the Ireland of 30 years ago than the rampant cosmopolitan Celtic Tiger that presently roams cities like Dublin and Cork. The people in these parts have no desire to become better acquainted with the outside world: If snappy Dublin folk will speak of "remote Mayo," then the sentiment is neatly rebounded by locals hereabouts talking of "remotest Dublin."

Covering an area of 5,398 square km (2085 square mi), Mayo is the third-largest county in Ireland. It stretches from Lough Corrib and the long fjord of Killary Harbour in the South to Killala Bay and Erris in the North, and from Achill Island, Clew Bay, and the Mullet peninsula in the West to the neighboring counties of Sligo and Roscommon in the East. It is the county of Croagh Patrick, Balintubber Abbey, numerous medieval friaries, and the Marian Shrine of Knock. With the main towns of Castlebar, Westport, and Ballina providing a tight geographical triangle of commerce in the center, the rest of the county reaches out with wild desolate shorelines, stunning vistas from remote peaks, and silent ghostly valleys that stretch along for miles.

Apart from the main tourist routes, this is a distinctly quiet region to travel across; and because of their relatively untouched position, the natives still provide a glimpse of the real Ireland. "When God made time, he made plenty of it" is a constant refrain in Mayo. These folks will pause for 20 minutes to give directions and, in the process, extract your family history, how bad the winter was in your country, and whether you have any intention of making an honest woman of the gorgeous creature sitting beside you. In addition to the flocks of sheep and herds of cattle that block the byroads at every turn, the sight of two cars parked right in the middle of the white line while their drivers engage in serious discussion, oblivious to your revving engine behind them, is definitely something you might want to get used to.

WESTPORT

Traveling up from Connemara, with the Sheffry Hills to the west and the towering Partry Mountains to the east, the N59 leads right on to **Westport,** one of the most gentrified and Anglo-Irish heritage towns in the whole western region. Its Georgian origins are clearly defined by the broad streets skirting the gently flowing river and, particularly, by the lime-fringed central avenue called the **Mall.** Originally built as an O'Malley stronghold, with the castle and adjoining hovels flanking a pivotal entrance from the sea, the entire town received a face-lift when the Brownes, who came from Sussex in the reign of Elizabeth I, constructed Westport House and much of the modern town.

BASICS

The **tourist office** (tel. 098/25711) on the Mall is open year-round, 9 AM–5:30 PM. It's got all the info you need on the town—beds, bars, bike rentals, and so on. The **post office** (tel. 098/25475) is on the North Mall. It's open Monday–Saturday 9–noon and 2–5.

The **Westport Washeteria** on Mill St (tel. 095/25261) offers a cleansing salvation to your dirty socks for £4, self-service. It's open Monday–Saturday 9:30–6 (Wednesday only until 1). **Internet Access** at Dunning's Cyberpub at the Octagon (tel. 095/25161) is £5 for a half hour. **Bicycles** can be hired for £7 a day from Club Atlantic Hostel (tel. 098/26644) or from Breheny Bike Hire on Castlebar Street just north of the Mall.

In northwestern Ireland, it's said that sheep outnumber people by roughly 100 to 1.

COMING AND GOING

Buses (tel. 095/41043) depart regularly from the Octagon monument for Achill (£5.50), Ballina (£6.70), Belfast (£15.80), Castlebar (£2.50), Dublin (£9), Galway (£8.80), and Knock (£6.70). The **railway station** (tel. 098/25253) is on Altamont Street and provides daily connections to Dublin (£15) and points east through Athlone.

WHERE TO SLEEP

The **Club Atlantic Hostel** on Altamont Street (tel. 098/26644) near the railway station charges £6.50 for dorms, £9 for singles, and £17 for doubles. It also provides a camping area close by. B&Bs abound in Westport, and the tourist office can find you rooms even at late notice. Try **Plougastel House** (tel. 098/25198), a well-appointed modern town house on Distillery Road. Rooms are £18 per person. There's also **Woodside** (tel. 098/26436) on Golf Course Road, a family-run affair in a solid two-story house built on a historical site a pleasant 10-minute walk from town center. Rooms are £18 per person. The **Clew Bay Hotel** (town center, tel. 098/28088) has all the amenities you'd expect in a family-run hotel right in the town center, as well as a cozy bar called Tubbers and riverside restaurant overlooking the Carrowbeg, all for £32.50 per person.

FOOD

There's nothing exceptional about the eateries in Westport—good plain food and plenty of it seems to be the order of the day. **McCormack's** (Bridge St., tel. 098/25619) has good lunch specials for under £5, and **Café Circe** (Bridge St., no phone), just down the street, does likewise but with a more vegetarian flavor. Dinner needs are best served by visiting the **O'Malley Restaurant** (Bridge St., tel. 098/27308), whose menu of pizza and steak staples gets you out for about £10. The **Urchin** (Bridge St., tel. 098/27532), across the street from O'Malley's, has a rather spartan appearance but does have a fairly inventive menu, with the emphasis on pasta. Cost per person is around £12. For a quick bowl of sturdy soup and doorstop (huge) sandwiches, try **O'Cee's** (no phone) near the Octagon. **Matt Molloy's** (Bridge St., tel. 098/26655) is owned by the flautist of the Chieftains and attracts trad folk of all persuasions, while **Henehan's Bar** (tel. 098/25561), farther down the street, is a rockin' joint where locals, young and old alike, congregate to discuss the visitors.

WORTH SEEING

Westport House (tel. 098/25430), about 3 km (2 mi) outside town, is the main visitor attraction. Designed by James Wyatt for the Browne family in the 1730s, it is Mayo's only stately home open to the public. Despite its scenic location and gardens rolling down to a glittering lake, the house has gone headlong along the tacky commercialization route—an unfortunate necessity to cope with the enormous running costs, one supposes. Everything from the "genuine dungeon" to cheap souvenirs competes for the visitor's attention. Ignore them all and instead enjoy the Jamaican mahogany doors, the huge collection of Georgian and Victorian silver, Waterford crystal, Chinese wallpapers, and a fine collection of paintings including *The Holy Family* by Rubens. It's open mostly in the afternoons from April to September (call for hours), and the admission is a steep £8.50.

Ten kilometers (6 mi) west of Westport on the Louisburgh road is **Croagh Patrick,** one of Mayo's famous landmarks and "the most holy mountain in Ireland." Soaring to a height of 2,510 ft, it overlooks Clew Bay and the entire western coastline. This is a climb you might want to consider for both the stunning visual rewards and the opportunity to become part of a unique annual Irish pilgrimage. In AD 441, as legend has it, Ireland's patron saint, Patrick, who is celebrated with rainy parades and much revelry on March 17, came here to fast for 40 days and nights as part of his effort to convert the country to Christianity. The aftermath of this included, among other things, his chasing all the snakes from the country (unfortunately, he didn't add crooked politicians and lawyers to the list of undesirables). Throughout the year, people from all corners of the country come to make the steep ascent to the top for all sorts of personal and religious reasons. On the last Sunday in July, called Reek Sunday, the mountain is thronged with 60,000 souls, all intent on making it to the top. You can join the crowd, which starts out before dawn with lighted torches to guide the way. The unique blend of pilgrims is quite a spectacle: Kids of 5 or 6 scampering up along the loose shale path, grandfathers of 80-plus gripping their stout sticks and passing you along the way, and, this one has to be seen to be believed—huge numbers of people piling on the penance by making the climb in their bare feet. A simple stone statue of St. Patrick crowns the summit. At its base, people leave their staffs and little bunches of wildflowers picked on the way up. With the stunning views from every side, the weather that can deliver four seasons in 10 minutes, and the often eerie calm that surrounds the place, this is an atmosphere-laden location even for nonbelievers. The ascent of Croagh Patrick starts at **Murrisk Abbey**—check at any tourist office for details.

CLARE ISLAND

BASICS

There's no tourist office on the island, but any questions will be answered at the **Bay View Hotel** (*see* Where to Sleep, *below*). Bike rental can be found at **O'Leary's** (tel. 098/25640), right beside the harbor, for £5 per day.

COMING AND GOING

Two ferry services operate to the island (return fare £10). **Ocean Star Ferry** (tel. 098/25045) operates regularly from Roonage Pier in Louisburgh, and **Clare Island Ferries** (tel. 098/26307) leave from Westport Harbour (tel. 098/26307).

WHERE TO SLEEP AND EAT

There's no shortage of free camping sites around the island, and the locals are very welcoming in this regard. Just ask before pitching your tent. There are also a few B&Bs. **Mary O'Malley's** (tel. 098/26216), 3 km (2 mi) from the harbor, has clean, comfortable accommodations from £18 per person. It's on an unnamed road, but any local can give you directions. More unique is the **Clare Island Lighthouse** (Clare Island, tel. 098/45120), an actual lighthouse that was built in 1806 and decommissioned in 1965. It offers all the comforts of home, plus some superb views, for £24 per person. The **Bay View Hotel** (Harbour Rd., tel. 098/26307) is the main accommodation center by the harbor, with singles going for £27 per person. Food is available in the hotel; light snacks and dinners run £5–£15. All the B&Bs offer evening meals for nonguests and can produce some terrific seafood for just £10 a head. If you're day-tripping across, take a good picnic and enjoy it while gazing across all those miles of blue.

WORTH SEEING

The island, at the mouth of Clew Bay, is Mayo's only island with a regular ferry service. Unlike the well-trodden Aran Islands, this is a paradise of peace and tranquillity, if you're lucky enough to hit some good weather. Just 150 people live on the island now, but in pre-famine times it supported a thriving community of more than 2,000. There are magnificent views to dazzle the senses at every turn on these solitary roads—southward toward Connemara, eastward toward Clew Bay, and north toward mighty Achill Island. A climb of **Croaghmore** mountain when the sun and gentle wind are at your back is a tonic for self-exploration more potent than a thousand therapist visits (and a whole lot cheaper).

Granuaile, or Grace O'Malley, was Ireland's only female pirate and ruled the waters around Mayo in the 1500s. Definitely the feminine template from which many aspiring Thelma and Louises took note, she was born in 1530 to a clan who owned lands from Achill to Inisbofin. She was married in her teens, and the murder of her husband by the rival Joyce clan spurred Grace to rally her people and establish a base on Clare Island. From her secure island fortress, no cargo vessel in the surrounding waters was safe. Her power grew to such an extent that the merchants of Galway, fearing her expansionist intentions, pleaded with the English governor to do something. In 1593, when the viceroy Sir Richard Bingham set about suppressing Grace, she headed bravely to the English court to plead her case with Queen Elizabeth I. Impressed by Grace's bravery, the English monarch granted her pardon and freedom and even offered her the title of countess. Grace O'Malley politely declined, protesting that she was already Queen of Connaught. She died peacefully in 1603. The ruined tower is all that stands of her stronghold, while the sturdy 13th-century Cistercian abbey nearby is said to contain her remains. The **Granuaile Visitors Centre** (tel. 098/25711) has an audiovisual display that recounts the remarkable story of this woman. Admission is £2.

ACHILL ISLAND

Ireland's largest island, and one of its most spectacular, is joined to the mainland by bridge at Achill Sound on the N59 at Mulrany. Combining a neat package of moorland, mountains, and dramatic beaches that stretch for miles, **Achill** is a place that has all but been overlooked by tourism over the last 20 years. Unfortunately, due to the lack of employment, the community continues to dwindle and most of the homes that come on the market are snapped up by city folk looking for country getaways. With most of the houses closed up for large parts of the year, it only adds further to the remoteness and tranquillity for the first-time visitor.

BASICS

The **tourist office** (tel. 098/45385) is in Cashel, on the main road from Achill Sound to Keel, and is open 10 AM to 5:30 PM, Monday–Saturday. The office can provide schedules for the regular **bus** service that operates throughout the year across the island; it runs from farthest Dooagh on to Keel, Cashel, Achill and onward to Westport, Belfast, and Ballina. **Bikes** can be hired from the **Achill Sound Hotel** (tel. 098/45245) or **O'Malley's** (tel. 098/43125) in Keel for £6 a day or £30 a week.

WHERE TO SLEEP

Camping is available at **Lavelles** (The Valley, Dugort, tel. 098/47232) for £7 and at **Seal Caves Caravan Park** (tel. 098/43262), which is between Dugort beach and Slievemore Mountain, for £5.50 per tent. The **Railway Hostel** (tel. 098/45187), on the east side of the bridge over Achill Sound, charges £6 for dorms and £7 per person for a private room. The **Wild Haven Hostel** (tel. 098/45392), an excellently appointed place just across the bridge and near the church, has a basic rate of £7.50; private rooms are £10 a person. At the extreme west of the island **Mrs. Quinn** (Keel, tel. 098/43385) operates a neat bed-and-breakfast where singles run about £23. The **Achill Sound Hotel** (tel. 098/45245) on the west side of Achill Sound bridge has singles for £26, and the **Slievemore Hotel** (tel. 098/43224) at Dugort charges £20 per person. The **Strand Hotel** (tel. 098/43241), also in Dugort, is on a pretty beach and has great views across the sea; rooms are £22.50 per person.

FOOD

Nearly all the hotels and B&Bs serve light snacks and dinner to nonguests; check the menus as you amble along. The **Atoka Restaurant** (tel. 098/47229) in Dugort serves a conventional menu of seafood and meat dishes at around £12 a head; and **Manamon's** (tel. 098/45272), close by, is also worth a call. At Keel the most popular place is the **Boley Restaurant** (tel. 098/43147), with an extensive menu ranging around £14 for dinner. **Calvey's** (tel. 098/43158), farther down the street, is similarly priced. There's music in most of the pubs and hotels during the summer, especially during the first two weeks of August, when the **Achill School** presents lectures, talks, and musical gatherings to promote Irish music, language, and culture.

WORTH SEEING

Beaches are the name of the game on Achill—massive tracts of white sandy soil that stretch tantalizingly off into the shimmering horizon. They are never crowded, and it's quite possible to snooze or lie around on your own personal stretch of sand without being disturbed by a single soul all day, even in

ST. PATRICK

St. Patrick is not only Ireland's patron saint but one of the most revered saints in Catholic hagiography. Born the son of a minor Roman official in western Britain at the turn of the 5th century, he was captured by Irish raiders at the age of 16 and spent six years in slavery as a shepherd on Slemish Mountain in County Antrim. Eventually escaping to France, he trained as a cleric and, haunted by a vocation to convert his captors to Christianity, returned to Ireland. He spent an energetic 30 years preaching around the country, all the while founding churches wherever he went. His huge importance to the country is evident from the massive number of place-names associated with him, as well, of course, as the continuing popularity of Patrick, Pat, and Paddy as Christian names. There's even a whiskey named after him. The shamrock, a trifoliate cloverlike plant worn expansively on lapels on March 17, is also closely associated with Patrick, having been used by him to illustrate the doctrine of the Trinity. Criticize anything you want during a trip to Ireland, but be mighty careful about casting any aspersions on Ireland's patron saint.

good weather. The beaches at **Keel** and **Keem** are particularly glorious, as are Golden Strand and Ridge Point. All of them have received the prestigious European Blue Flag beach award.

Achill's steep hills rise dramatically from the sea, giving the island some of the most inspiring cliff faces in Ireland. The famous **Atlantic Drive** encompasses all the variations of scenery found on the island: Bog land and poor farm soil mingle with the heather and fuchsia that burst forth from hedges all around. On the southern coast are the atmospheric **Cathedral Rocks,** and at the western end is **Croaghaun,** which rises from the sea to a height of 2,129 ft. **Slievemore Mountain** is a handy walk, even for the inexperienced, and its lower slopes contain the deserted village that was once home to the **Colony,** a Protestant mission established in 1834 to help convert Catholics. It offered education, food, and shelter in exchange for conversion to Protestantism. At the southern entrance to Achill Sound are the remains of **Kildavnet Castle,** another 15th-century stronghold belonging to the pirate queen Granuaile.

The island has long been a refuge to artists and writers attracted by its solitude and the savage elements that buffet the landscape. One of the more famous residents was the 1972 Nobel Prize winner **Heinrich Boll,** who lived in Dugort. He chronicled his life on the island in his novel *An Irish Diary,* and his house has become a refuge for international literary figures who stay there for periods of the year. Irish landscape artist **Paul Henry** was also a resident here for a number of years.

The **Achill Seafood Festival** (tel. 098/43317), now in its sixth year, has quickly established itself as one of Mayo's prime holiday weekends in mid-July. As well as presenting cuisine in all its seafaring glory, the island fairly hops with visiting traditional musicians lured with promises of free Guinness and oysters.

KNOCK

BASICS

The **tourist office** (Main St., tel. 094/88193) is open May–September, daily 10–5. **Buses** operate in and out of Knock to all the major towns around Mayo and points beyond. Fares are as follows: Dublin £10, Westport £9, Sligo £7.50. The bus stop is at Lennon's Shop on Main Street, and schedule information can be found at the tourist office.

WORTH SEEING

The **Knock Shrine.** The Apparition of Our Lady at Knock was unusual in that it was silent. No word was spoken, no message was given. The 15 witnesses, ranging in age from 6 to 75, who saw the apparition on the evening of August 21, 1879, heard nothing during the two hours that the Virgin Mary appeared to them. When they realized that it was the Mother of God before to them, they fell to their knees and said the Rosary in thanksgiving. More than a hundred years later, people still flock to Knock to celebrate the event in a union that crosses all ages, genders, and persuasions. When the apparition took place, it was to a backdrop of a nation suffering from starvation and eviction, as well as enduring diseases like cholera and the myriad demons of poverty. Mary came at a time when the people were broken, and in the spirit of that time, people still come here with pleas for curing sickness, emotional turmoil, fear, and loss of hope. Miracles have happened here, as upheld by a church commission convened in 1936. Today the Knock industry that's built up around the event has taken away much of the sacred gloss with tacky stalls selling everything from plastic Jesus statues to wristbands that glow in the dark. It's kind of a peculiar Celtic version of Lourdes–meets–Las Vegas. The basilica of Our Lady, Queen of Ireland, can hold 12,000 people. Nonetheless, there is a silence and peace about the place that's hard to ignore. The **Knock Folk Museum** (tel. 094/88100), on the grounds of the basilica, has plenty of info on the apparition, the commissions of proof, and, with a nod to Lourdes, many rows of crutches left behind by souls who found their cure. Admission is £4.

BALLINA

Located on the banks of the River Moy, Ballina has become a hub for many Continental fishermen from France and Germany keen to cast a line in search of the elusive salmon. A solid commercial town full of healthy florid-faced farmers selling their livestock and produce on market days, it sits at the mouth of Killala Bay, nestled between the Nephin Beg mountains to the west and Sligo's Slieve Gamph range to the east. With nothing of exceptional note for the visitor, the town does make for a reasonable pit stop en route to the wilds of Sligo and Donegal farther north.

BASICS

The **tourist office** (tel. 096/70848) is on Cathedral Close next to St. Muredach's Cathedral; it's open Monday–Saturday 9:30–5:30. **Internet access** is available in the same building at **Moy Valley Resources.** The **post office** (tel. 096/21498) is on Casement Street and is open Monday–Saturday 9–5:30. The **train** (tel. 096/71818) and **bus** (tel. 096/71800) stations are on, appropriately enough, Station Road. Train service to Athlone and onward to Dublin happens three times per day and costs £15. Buses to Galway (£9.70), Westport (£6.30), Donegal (£10), Dublin (£8), and Sligo (£7.30) also run on a daily basis. Bike rental can be found at **Gerry's Cycle Centre** (Lord Edward St., tel. 096/70455) for £7 a day and £30 a week. Dirty laundry can be dealt with at the **Moy Launderette** (tel. 096/22358) on Cathedral Road. It's open Monday–Saturday 9–6; a wash and dry is £4.50, self-service.

WHERE TO SLEEP

Hogan's American House Hostel (tel. 096/70582) is well located close to the train and bus stations and provides comfortable if unimaginative accommodations in a family-run atmosphere for £15 a single and £25 a double. **Corrigan's Greenhill** (tel. 096/22767) is adjacent to the tourist office on Cathedral Close and costs £36 for a double. Just a few doors down, **Walsh's Suncraft** (tel. 096/21573) offers doubles with bath for £34. The **Belleek Camping and Caravan Park** (tel. 096/71533) is 3 km (2 mi) from Ballina on the Killala road, in a prime location on the edge of the Belleek woods, and charges £4 per person sharing a tent.

FOOD

If you're searching for epicurean delights, Ballina isn't a town overstocked with four-star establishments. **Humbert's Restaurant** (Pearse St., tel. 096/71520) is a popular coffeehouse-restaurant where good home baking and hearty lunchtime specials will fill the empty space. **Brogan's Bar and Restaurant** (Garden St., tel. 096/21961), close by the bridge, has a good pub atmosphere with excellent, if slightly pricey, seafood on the menu. Expect main courses at around £10. The best pub action can be found in **Gaughan's** (O'Rahilly St., tel. 096/21151), a place where TV and music have been banned in favor of the beguiling sounds coming from well-made arguments. This place gets the real farmers. **Murphy Bros** (Clare St., tel. 096/22702) is an oak-paneled place that's frequented by the younger generation—it has

CAPTAIN BOYCOTT

Another global colloquialism is traced to Ireland. The Captain, whose name has entered the English language as a word meaning to ostracize, was a land agent for Lord Erne in the late 19th century. Boycott remained firmly opposed to Charles Stewart Parnell's Land War of 1880, a campaign to reduce the rents payed by a hard-pressed population by 25%. While the other landlords got hip to the notion of trying to keep at least some income coming in from lands often unfit for anything agricultural, Boycott refused to budge an inch. As a result, he became isolated by the local community who refused to work for him or speak to him and who would turn their backs on his approach. Proving that peaceful revolution can sometimes be mightier than the pitchfork, Captain Boycott was eventually forced to leave Ireland and return in disgrace to England.

great pub grub. **An Bolg Bui** (Bridge St., tel. 096/22561), also near the bridge, makes much of its angling angle, selling lures, fishing rods, and waders right next to the best pint of Guinness in town.

WORTH SEEING

Belleek Woods provide the main focal point for visitors who are willing to head into the forest in search of the abundant wildlife. **Belleek Castle** (tel. 096/22400) is a distinctly upmarket establishment right in the middle of the woods. Stop by its **Armada Bar,** built from the actual shell of a 500-year old Spanish galleon. Good sessions take place there on weekends. Tours of the castle cost £2.50.

Right behind the railway station is the **Dolmen of the Four Maols,** or "the Table of the Giants." Dating back to 2000 BC, it is said to be the burial ground of the Maols who murdered Ceallach, a 7th-century bishop. After they were hanged, their deed was commemorated by a huge rock—go figure.

The year 1998 marked the bicentenary of the **1798 Rebellion** in Ireland, an event with very strong connections in County Mayo. In August of that year, a French expeditionary force sailed from La Rochelle to aid the rebellion that was breaking out all across Ireland. The force of more than 1,000, led by **General Humbert,** landed at Kilcummin, near Killala, and was quickly joined by local patriots before marching deep into English territory. The army marched through Killala and on into Ballina, along a route known to this day as the Old French Road. The road into Ballina was lit by burning straw and is still called Botharnasup, or "the Road of Straw." The town was successfully captured, and the English were forced to retreat. Castlebar was the site of the next battle, and once again the Franco-Irish army won the day, with the English beating such a hasty retreat that it became known as "the races of Castlebar." The efforts of Humbert's army would undoubtedly have changed the face of Irish history forever had their success continued. However, a superior English force defeated the army at the Battle of Ballinamuck in County Longford.

The **Tour de Humbert** is a new, signposted trail, initiated during the bicentenary celebrations, that allows you to cycle or walk on that famous route that might have led to glory and freedom. It faithfully follows Humbert's route through Mayo, Sligo, Leitrim, and Longford. Sites of historical interest are clearly indicated by explanatory panels, as well as by the signposts set out at regular intervals. The main towns along the trail are Killala, Ballina, Castlebar, Swinford, Tubbercurry, Drumshambo, Cloona, and Ballinamuck. For further info contact the **Westport tourist office** (tel. 098/25711) or the **Mayo Cycling Club** (tel. 094/25220).

If biking, rather than hiking, is your bag, you can head into the wilderness for a day trip into the lonely **Ox Mountains** east of Ballina. It makes a perfect one-day jaunt. With trails and routes crisscrossing the woods, where every new turn reveals another solitary lake or vista, this is an often exhausting but rewarding activity, especially if the weather's good. Parts of the route form the Western Way that meanders from the Ox Mountains right into Connemara.

SLIGO

Considering its location, straddling the mouth of Lough Gill at the foot of Sligo Harbour, Sligo ought to be a picturesque and thoroughly enjoyable market town. The Great Famine reduced the town's population by nearly half, but even then Sligo's port and shipping industry profited from the mass emigrations, transporting as many as 400 people per week to America during the 1850s and 1860s. Over the past 20 years, however, Sligo has fallen victim to its own prosperity. Companies from Dublin and the Continent continue to refashion the small city center with bleak, modern shopping malls, giving Sligo an artificial and anonymous look. A few historic buildings survive intact—Hargadon's Pub on O'Connell Street is a good example—but even these look strangely out of place in a city where every second shop blazes in neon.

As the city to which William Butler Yeats was fervently attached, Sligo benefits from the Yeats Museum and Yeats Summer School and from its proximity to the poet's grave in Drumcliff. But Sligo remains little more than a functional stopover on the way to somewhere else, preferably County Donegal and its wildly gorgeous coastline. Since Sligo is the last stop on all northbound trains, train travelers headed for County Donegal or Northern Ireland must transfer to a bus, an awkward process that may require you to spend at least one night in town.

BASICS

The **tourist office** (Temple St., tel. 071/61201), open weekdays 9–5 (longer and weekend hours in summer), stocks a full range of maps and brochures, can book you into a bed-and-breakfast for a £1 fee, and houses a competitive bureau de change. From the train and bus depot, walk down Lord Edward Street and turn right on Adelaide Street; then veer left on Temple Street. The **post office** is on Wine Street (tel. 071/42593). It's open Monday–Saturday 9–5:30 (not until 9:30 on Wednesday). Both **Gary's Cycles** (Quay St., tel. 071/45418) and **Conway Bros.** (6 High St., tel. 071/61370) rent 15-speed mountain bikes for £7 per day, £30 per week, plus a £40 deposit. Bike repairs can be had at **PJ Coleman's** (Stephen St., tel. 071/43353). You can do your **laundry** at **Pam's** on Johnson Court (tel. 071/44861). It's open Monday–Saturday 9–7; a wash and dry cost £5. **Internet access** is at **Futurenet** on Pearse Road (tel. 071/50345) for £6 per hour.

COMING AND GOING

Bus Éireann and Irish Rail offer regular daily service to Sligo, though only Bus Éireann makes the journey northward to County Donegal and Derry. Conveniently, their two depots are right next to each other. The rail station, **McDiarmada Station** (Lord Edward St., tel. 071/60066 for bus info and 071/69888 or 071/69889 for rail info), is an easy 10-minute walk to the city center (walk downhill and turn left). Inside there's an info desk (open weekdays 9:15–6 and Saturday 9:30–5) and a left-luggage desk (open weekdays 9–6, Saturday 9:30–6:30), which will store your luggage for £1.50 per day. The only major destination served by rail from Sligo is Dublin (4 per day; £12). Even if you're traveling to nearby Galway or Belfast, you must transfer in Dublin first. In other words, take the bus. Bus Éireann destinations include Belfast via Enniskillen (1–3 per day; £12.40), Cork via Galway (1–2 per day; £16), Derry (2–6 per day; £10), Dublin (3 per day; £9), and Galway (5 per day; £10.50).

WHERE TO SLEEP

Sligo has a slew of mid-range B&Bs, most of which are on Lower and Upper Pearse roads. Finding a bed isn't usually a problem, but things fill up during August, when the Yeats Summer School draws poets and Yeats fans from around the world. If everything is booked, you can always camp in nearby Rosses Point. Of the city-center B&Bs, **Parkmore** (32–34 Wolfe Tone St., opposite bus station, tel. 071/60241) has rooms for £16–£18 and provides good information about touring the area. The **Anchor Guest House** (Quay St., tel. 071/42904) offers standard rooms and lovely fried breakfasts for £17–£19 per person. **Renate Central House** (Upper John St., tel. 071/62014 or 071/69093), only a short walk from the bus station, is a spotlessly clean and homey three-story house, with a comfortable lounge and TV room and guest rooms for £16–£18 per person.

THE VISIONARY PREACHER

Another personality who will crop up continually in any conversations you'll have with the locals in these parts is Monsignor James Horan, the man who created his own modern miracle in this remote spot and was made even more famous in a hilarious Christy Moore tune. The guiding light behind the formation and eventual construction of Knock International Airport, it was he who announced 20 years ago to a disbelieving government that the then tiny airstrip should be upgraded to handle 747s. Proving himself every inch the fund-raiser and an indefatigable preacher on par with Billy Graham, he pushed ahead despite the howls of "White elephant!" coming from the opposition. Mgr. Horan was convinced that a bigger airport would bring more pilgrims and thus pay for itself—a situation that's happened in spades since it opened in 1986.

CAMPING

Greenlands Caravan & Camping Park. Eight kilometers (5 miles) northwest of Sligo at the tip of Rosses Point, the Greenlands has 25 tent sites, all with good views of the bay. Sites cost £5, plus 50p per person. *Rosses Point, off R291 Hwy., tel. 071/77113. From city center, take the Rosses Point bus. Showers. Closed mid-Sept.–mid-May.*

Strandhill Camping Park. More secluded than the Greenlands, the seaside Strandhill is generally filled with no-stress families and goofy dropouts touring the world on £5 a day. It, too, is 8 km (5 mi) outside Sligo Town, and it's the place to come for outstanding ocean views. Sites cost £3.50, plus 50p per person. *Strandhill, off R292 Hwy., tel. 071/68120. From city center, take any bus marked STRANDHILL. 100 suites. Laundry, showers (50p). Closed mid-Sept.–May.*

FOOD

Food in Sligo is like American televangelism: cheesy, shameless, tasteless, and often hard to stomach. One of the few places that defy the Jim Bakker school of cooking is **Bistro Bianconi's** (44 O'Connell St., tel. 071/41744), which serves delicious antipasto platters (£3.75), exotic pizzas (£6–£7), and pastas (£6–£9.50). **Gourmet Parlour** (Bridge St., tel. 071/44617) creates superb take-out meals of mostly organic ingredients and breads baked fresh on the premises. Try the salmon salad (£3.20), whole-wheat sandwiches with a choice of fillings (£1.50), or a loaf of sun-dried-tomato bread (60p). The **Cottage** (4 Castle St., tel. 071/45319), a café on the second floor of a thatched-roof building, has a vegetarian menu that includes pizza, lasagna, quiche, and vegetable curry with rice for around £3.80, Monday–Saturday 9 AM–10 PM. The well-stocked **Quinnsworth** (O'Connell St., tel. 071/62788) is the place to go for groceries.

WORTH SEEING

Sligo's city center is small and walkable. From the intersection of O'Connell and Wine streets, head east down Stephen Street for Sligo's **County Museum, Municipal Art Gallery,** and **Yeats Museum,** all housed in the local library (Stephen St., tel. 071/42212). Admission is free, and the library is open Monday–Saturday 10–12:30 and 2:30–4:30 (shorter hours in winter). The Yeats hall houses a comprehensive collection of Yeats's writings from 1889 to 1936, various editions of his plays and prose, and the Nobel

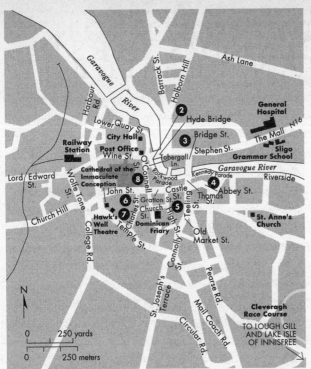

Courthouse, **5**
Hargadon's, **8**
Niland Gallery, **3**
St. John's
Cathedral, **6**
Sligo Abbey, **4**
Tourist Information
Office, **7**
Yeats Memorial
Building, **2**

Prize medal that was awarded to him in 1923. The penmanship is dreadful, but Yeats's letters to James Stephens and Oliver St. John Gogarty offer insight into Yeats's obsessive love for Sligo. Out the door and around the corner, the art gallery contains a respectably large collection of Irish and Anglo-Irish canvases. Of note are the oils and watercolors by Jack B. Yeats, Bill's brother.

On nearby Abbey Street, you'll find the ruins of Sligo's **Dominican Friary,** commonly known as the Abbey. Founded in 1252 by Maurice FitzGerald, ancestor to the Earls of Kildare, the abbey was accidentally burned in 1414 and had to be completely rebuilt. In 1642, during the English Civil War, Sir Frederick Hamilton and a troop of Puritan soldiers sacked Sligo and once again demolished the abbey, an event described by Yeats in *The Curse of the Fires and the Shadow*. Today the abbey consists of a ruined nave, aisle, transept, and tower. It's the sort of isolated hideaway popular with Sunday lovers and wild dogs. The ruins are open daily 9:30–6:30, mid-June–mid-September, and admission is £1.50.

Back in town, the **Yeats Memorial Building** (Hyde Bridge, at O'Connell St., tel. 071/45847) houses a tiny art gallery, open Monday–Saturday 10–5:30, and the headquarters of the **Yeats Society** (tel. 071/42693). During the Yeats Summer School in the first two weeks of August, the society organizes lectures and Yeatsian theatrical performances, some of which are open to the public; call for current listings. You can also sit in on a lecture for £5. Across the street is a photo-worthy sculpture of the poet himself, draped in a flowing coat overlaid with poetic excerpts. It was unveiled in 1989 by Michael Yeats, W. B.'s son, in commemoration of the 50th anniversary of his father's death.

The **Hawk's Well Theatre** on Temple Street (tel. 071/61526) presents a usually decent selection of modern and traditional Irish dramas. The **Blue Raincoat Theatre Company** on Lower Quay Street (tel. 071/70431) is also worth checking out for the more risqué and challenging productions emerging from the pens of Ireland's young theatrical turks. The **Sligo Arts Festival** (tel. 071/69802) in June celebrates theater and film and is fast becoming a major European event.

MARY ROBINSON, IRELAND'S FIRST WOMAN PRESIDENT

If modern Ireland had to choose a spokesperson to communicate to the world just how far the nation has progressed, the nation would undoubtedly select Mary Robinson. Ireland's first female president, Robinson took office in 1990 and served for seven glorious years before going on to a larger world stage as the present UN High Commissioner for Human Rights. Ballina-born Mary Robinson (née Bourke) graduated with first class honors from Trinity College and then accepted a fellowship at Harvard. She then became the youngest person ever to be appointed Professor of Law in Trinity College at just 25. After a career as one of the country's most distinguished lawyers, she was elected to the Irish Senate in 1969 and eventually crossed all party loyalties to win the presidential election. After decades of presidents who were all too remote for the real people, Mary Robinson brought a breath of fresh air to the entire nation by continually getting out there and talking to people. For that alone, she has already achieved an almost mystical status. That rarest of creatures on the Irish political landscape, she had no enemies and is generally credited with helping to kick-start the overpowering sense of confidence and self-worth that now reigns in Ireland. When she decided to seek further challenges, championing the underprivileged on the world stage, it was to the lament of a distraught population. One newspaper poll asking whether she should stay a second term got a staggering 100% affirmative response.

NEAR SLIGO

Beach-going locals love the **Strandhill Peninsula** for its 3 km (2 mi) of sandy dunes that lie in the shadow of mighty Knockrea on the tip of Sligo Bay. Surfers from all over the county come here to catch the breakers, despite the dangerous currents. You can get here from Sligo town via Bus Éireann, which makes the hour-long run at regular intervals during the day (£1.65).

Carrowmore, 5 km (3 mi) southwest of Sligo, is the site of ancient megalithic tombs and stone circles that date back to 4840 BC. Some of the original 120 tombs and dolmens were removed by quarriers, but about 30 of those that remain can be visited. An interpretative center (tel. 071/61534) that offers tours (£1.50) is open May–September, daily 9:30 AM–6.30 PM.

According to Celtic legend, **Knockrea Mountain** (1,078 ft) on the south shore of Sligo Bay is the final resting place of Queen Maeve, who was buried standing up to face her enemies in Ulster. The cairn at the top of the mountain that marks the grave was almost ruined by visitors who took little stones as souvenirs. The Office of Public Works, with a suitable Irish solution to an Irish problem, put out the myth that anyone taking a stone from the cairn would be cursed forevermore. They also declared that any single woman adding a small stone to the cairn from the land below would find herself married within the year. Result? The cairn is now back in its former glory.

Lough Gill, a large mass of water just southeast of Sligo town, has a wonderful drive circling its edges. The 40-km (25-mi) loop is too long to hike but is an ideal car trip. You'll pass **Holywell,** a shrine marking the place where outlawed masses were said during the penal days, the period during the 18th century when the English forbid Catholics (who made up 90% of the population at the time) from practicing their religion. The road carries on to **Dooney Rock**—made famous by the Yeats poem "The Fiddler of Dooney"—on the south shore of Lough Gill near Cottage Island. The center of the lake is dominated by **Inisfree,** the island of the Yeats poem "The Lake of Isle of Inisfree": "I will arise and go now/And go to Inisfree/a small cabin built there of clay and wattles made/Nine beanrows will I have there and a hive for the honey bee/And I will find some peace there for peace comes dropping slow." The local boatman, John O'Connor (tel. 071/64079), will row you across to the island for £3.50; his house is right beside the jetty. Farther along the route you'll come to **Dromahair,** sit of the ruins of **Creevelea Abbey.** Founded in 1508 as the Friary of Killanummery, it became another victim of Oliver Cromwell in 1650. Heading back to Sligo town on the final leg of the tour, stop at **Parke's Castle** (tel. 071/64149). The Anglo Parkes built the stronghold in 1623 as a defense against angry and dispossessed peasants. It's on the site of an earlier fort that belonged to the O'Rourke clan. The manor house and turret walk, which have excellent views across the lake, are open to the public April–May, Tuesday–Sunday 10–5; June–September, daily 9:30–6:30; and October, daily 10–5. Admission is £2.

Drumcliff churchyard, 6 km (4 mi) from the Sligo town, is where W. B. Yeats is buried. It's heavily trafficked but worth a visit. Buses from Sligo to Derry make regular stops here (£2.60 return from Sligo town). "Under bare Ben Bulben's head/ In Drumcliff churchyard Yeats is laid," wrote Yeats in 1938, a year before his death in France. Since he was brought home by his wife, George, to his final resting place in the simple churchyard, his grave has become to Celts what Jim Morrison's grave in the Père Lachaise cemetery in Paris is to rock fans. North of Drumcliff is **Ben Bulben** itself, the massive flat-domed plateau that dominates the bog land below. Dating to 574 when St. Columcille founded a monastery on its top (these guys were seriously into inaccessibility), it became a major religious destination until, again, the drive of Oliver Cromwell extinguished it. The 1,729-ft climb is worth the effort for the superb views across the surrounding country. Be advised, though—it's always windy on top and frequently soggy underfoot.

Also close to Drumcliff is **Lissadell House** (tel. 071/63150), the home of poet Eva Gore Booth and her sister Constance Markiewicz, a major figure in the 1916 Rising and confidante of Yeats's. The mansion is still occupied by Markiewicz's great-nephew; sadly it's showing signs of age and neglect. The interior is a strange mix of badly frayed carpets, peeling wallpaper, dry rot, and a jumble of relics from Eva and Constance's father, Henry Gore Booth, who was an Arctic explorer and big-game hunter. Yet, even in its dilapidated state, Lissadell still carries a sense of "auld" grandeur, a feeling of times past and the ghosts that walked there. The house is open June through September, Monday–Saturday 10:30–12:15 and 2–4:15; admission is £2.50.

AFTER DARK

Sligo's most famous pub is **Hargadon's** (4–5 O'Connell St., tel. 071/70933), a dark, old-style public house filled with sepia photographs, antique whiskey jugs, and a maze of private oak-lined snugs. Top-rate grub is available Monday–Saturday for less than £3. Otherwise, the dilapidated **Cullen's Bar** and **Thomas Connolly,** both on Markievicz Road near the White House Hostel, are good for quiet pints in the company of rough-hewn locals. For a concert-volume dose of Hendrix and Bach, **Shoot the Crows** (Grattan St., no phone) is another solid choice. Traditional music is most common during the summer season; pick up a copy of the weekly *Sligo Champion* (75p), or the *Weekender,* a free weekly available at all newsagents, to see who's playing where and when. There's also a rather run-down looking, four-screen cinema on Wine Street called the Gaiety.

DONEGAL

Donegal thrives despite its isolated location on the Bloody Forelands and a climate that leaves it permanently marked by rain clouds on TV weather maps. Due to its dramatic coastline and ancient bog lands, it is regarded by many as the runner-up to Kerry in the contest for the most scenic county in Ireland. The picture-postcard scenes of whitewashed cottages, the reek of turf, and the by-now-familiar herds of idly wandering animals on main roads preserve a rural atmosphere that's been steamrolled elsewhere in the country by unforgiving progress. Beauty notwithstanding, Donegal, like its neighbor Mayo, continues to lose its residents to more metropolitan areas; scores of young people desert it for jobs in Dublin and Cork. The aging population is supported by the small farms that somehow survive the weather's insults. Much of the county's rugged beauty is the result of the continuing struggle between man and the elements.

DONEGAL TOWN

Despite the fact that it is not served by Irish Rail, Donegal Town is still a popular stop with day-trippers from Sligo. Throughout July and August, the town feels like a tacky amusement park, and most establishments charge outrageous prices to match.

BASICS

The **tourist office** (Quay St., tel. 073/21148) overlooks the water south of the Diamond. It has maps, a list of B&Bs, and info on guided tours of the Donegal coast. It's open weekdays 9–1 and 2–5, Saturday 9–1 (June–August, Monday–Saturday until 8 and Sunday 10–1 and 2–5). The **Bank of Ireland** and **AIB** are both on the Diamond, open weekdays 10–4, and have ATMs that accept Plus, Cirrus, Visa, and MasterCard. To change money on weekends, try one of the large hotels or tourist shops on the Diamond, all of which offer dreary rates made worse by hefty 2%–5% commissions. Both **Doherty's Fishing Tackle** (Main St., tel. 073/21119) and the **Bike Shop** (Waterloo Pl., tel. 073/22515) rent mountain bikes for £6 per day.

COMING AND GOING

Lacking an official bus depot, all **Bus Éireann** coaches arrive and depart from the Diamond, outside the Abbey Hotel, where a small schedule lists common departure times. The Quay Street tourist office also provides information for all departures. Destinations from Donegal Town include Derry (6 per day; £7.70), Sligo (5 per day; £6), Letterkenny (6 per day; £5.90), Galway (4 per day; £10), Dublin (5 per day; £10), and Glencolumbkille (2 per day in summer, 1 per day in winter; £7). **McGeehan Coaches** (tel. 075/46101 or 075/46150) also runs buses to Dublin (£10) and day trips to Glencolumbkille (£3) and other nearby towns twice daily late-June–September.

WHERE TO SLEEP

B&B accommodations are easy to come by. **Riverside House** (tel. 073/21083) has beds for £17. **Castle View** (tel. 073/22100), right across from Donegal Castle, provides spacious private rooms for about £15 per person. Both are a three-minute walk south of the Diamond, on Waterloo Place just off Bridge Street, and overlook the River Eske. Larger and more modern is **Windemere House** (Quay St., tel. 073/21323), near the tourist office. The rooms (from £15 per person) are comfortable and spotless, and Mr. Ryle's breakfasts are unbeatable. **Aranmore House** (tel. 073/21242) on the Killybegs Road has clean, comfortable rooms in a very friendly setting. All rooms have coffee/tea makers and baths. Singles are £18, doubles £30.

The IHH **Donegal Town Independent Hostel** (Killybegs Rd., tel. 073/22805) has 44 beds (£7) spread generously about a large, whitewashed house. Doubles are available for £16. The rooms are well kept, and the cozy kitchen has all the amenities, including a microwave and washing machine. You can also camp (£3.75 per person) on the lawn surrounding the hostel, which is 1 km (½ mi) from the Diamond on the road to Killybegs. Closer to the center of town and in pristine condition is **Cliffview Budget Accommodation** (tel. 073/21684), on the Coast Road as it heads out of town toward Killybegs. The modern, well-designed accommodation costs from £9 for a dorm bed to £15 for a single. The price includes a simple breakfast. A proper "fry up" is £2 extra.

FOOD

Donegal's small size means budget travelers can expect little more than pub grub and greasy bags of chips. There are a few upscale restaurants in town, notably in the Abbey and Hyland hotels, but expect generic atmosphere and the din of tourists comparing their new sweaters. **Atlantic Hotel Café** (Main St., tel. 073/21080) does reasonable lunches and dinners for less than £8—mostly steaks, fish, and pastas—and is surprisingly cozy, considering the number of tourists ushered through. Cheaper and less crowded is **McGinty's No. 11 Café** (Main St., tel. 073/22416), a self-service sandwich shop with good sandwiches (£2) and burgers (£2.70). Otherwise, the best affordable meals are done by the **Blueberry Tea Room** (Castle St., off the Diamond, tel. 073/22933). This second-floor restaurant and café serves excellent (and excellently priced) specials ranging from roast chicken (£4.50) to a bacon-and-broccoli quiche (£3.25). Although **Just Williams** (in the Hyland Central Hotel, the Diamond, tel. 073/21027) seems geared toward the tour-bus crowd, it serves heaping lunch specials, like lamb curry and a seafood pancake, for £5. **Foodland** (The Diamond, tel. 073/21006), open Monday–Saturday 9–7, is a well-stocked market smack in the center of town. For a trustworthy greasy chip shop, try **Beavers** on Main Street, which offers good cod in batter with chips for £2.80. The **Harbour Restaurant** (tel. 073/21702), opposite the tourist office, has an excellent fish menu (£3.50–£8). **Sam's Deli** on Main Street is also worth a call for the endless tea refills and the delicious overstuffed sandwiches (£2.50).

Schooner's Pub (tel. 073/21671) on Upper Main Street is the best place for music and craic (Irish slang for "having a good time"), with trad sessions seven nights a week. With the smoke-stained ceiling, the dark oak walls, and the terrific seafood for around £5, it is a one-stop shop for the weary traveler. If you're just in the mood for a pint, try **Charlie's Star Bar** (Main St., tel. 073/21158) or **McGroarty's** (The Diamond, tel. 073/21049), which, between the two, have live traditional music most summer nights. Two other colorful pubs are **Tirconnail** (The Diamond, tel. 073/22188) and the **Scotsman** (Bridge St., tel. 073/22470). The Scotsman occasionally hosts low-key music sessions on summer weekends.

WORTH SEEING

Donegal Town is a small outpost of pubs and shops overlooking the River Eske. The entire village can be walked in 10 minutes, and nearly everything of interest is centered on the **Diamond,** which was once a marketplace but is now used as a parking lot. The town was founded in 1200 by the O'Donnell clan. Its Gaelic name, Dun na nGall (Fort of the Foreigners), pays tribute to the Norse raiders who first settled in County Donegal during the 9th century. In 1474, Red Hugh O'Donnell commissioned a castle (now destroyed) and the **Donegal Monastery,** on the riverbank south of the Diamond. The ivy-covered ruins are impressive, considering that the complex was burned to the ground in 1593, razed by the English in 1601, and ransacked again in 1607, at which time the monastery was abandoned. Prior to leaving, however, the monks had time to copy down a series of Old Irish legends in what they called *The Annals of the Four Masters*. For their efforts, the monks are remembered by a 20-ft obelisk (1937) in the Diamond's busy parking lot. Donegal's other prime attraction is **Donegal Castle**, half a block southwest of the Diamond. The castle was built in 1474 by Red Hugh the Younger. Restored in a tastefully simple manner in the mid-1990s, the castle harbors the so-called chimney piece, a gargantuan, sandstone fireplace wrought with minute reliefs. The castle is open June–October, daily 9:30–6, and admission is £2.

NEAR DONEGAL TOWN

LOUGH DERG

BASICS • The **visitor center** (Main St., tel. 072/61546) in Pettigo, the small town on the shores of the lake, is the place to purchase your boat ticket (£17), which includes admission to Station Island. The first boat leaves at 11 AM, the last at 3 PM. They're usually on an hourly schedule, with more frequent departures as demand dictates. The center also provides information about Lough Derg's past and St. Patrick's role in its history. It's open daily from April to September, 10 AM to 5 PM.

COMING AND GOING • From Donegal, turn off the main Sligo–Donegal road (N15) in the village of Laghy onto the minor Pettigo road (R232), which hauls itself over the Black Gap and descends sharply into the border village of Pettigo, about 21 km (13 mi) from the N15. From here, take the Lough Derg access road for 8 km (5 mi). During the pilgrim season (June–Aug.), special buses service Pettigo from Donegal, Laghey, and Ballybofey.

WHERE TO SLEEP AND EAT • You can stay in **Pettigo at the Avondale** (tel. 072/61520) on Lough Derg Road or **Hill Top View** (tel. 072/61535) at Billary on the road from Donegal. Both B&Bs are spartan but clean and reasonably comfortable. Prices are about £17 per person. Accommodations in the very basic dormitories of the hostels on the island (where the pilgrims stay) are included in the £17 ticket charge for the boat crossing and island admission. There is no food available on the island, so bring your own supplies.

WORTH SEEING • **Lough Derg,** with tiny Station Island in its middle, is in a desolate moorland and bog east of Donegal. The island is also known as St. Patrick's Purgatory, since he is said to have fasted here for 40 days and nights, and it is one of Ireland's most popular pilgrimage sites. From Whitsunday to the Feast of the Assumption (that is from June to mid-Aug.) devotees converge here seeking inner solitude and peace. An octagonal basilica and a number of hostels have sprung up to cope with the 15,000-plus people who arrive here each summer. Pilgrims stay on the island for three days, beginning with a 24-hour vigil during which all fast, except for taking in black tea and toast, and no one sleeps.

They then walk barefoot around the island, on its flinty stones, performing the stations of the cross. The tired and hungry pilgrims are also usually subject to a downpour at some point. Nonpilgrims may not visit the island June–mid-August. For more information about the island or how to become a pilgrim, contact the Reverend Prior on the island (tel. 072/61518).

THE DONEGAL COAST

The Donegal coastline is a complex and perplexing affair— all the more so if you're trying to travel it on foot or by public transport. If your wallet allows, this is the one region in Ireland where you might consider shelling out for a rental car for a few days. The investment will pay you returns in the form of jaw-dropping vistas. Starting from Donegal Town, traveling along the N56, you'll encounter the sculpted rocks at Crohy Head just north of Maas. As you continue you'll reach the headland dubbed the **Bloody Foreland** for the many shipwrecks that have occurred off its coast. Following roads rutted with potholes and deep cracks (take it slow), you'll come upon the panoramic seascapes around **Horn Head** and **Rosguill.** Continuing farther, if time allows, you can take in the gorgeous scenery around **Fanad Head,** at the entrance to serene Lough Swilly. An essential for this journey is some Enya or Chieftains on the tape deck.

GLENVEAGH NATIONAL PARK

U-turning from the coast and venturing inland, you can head through the 25,000 acres of glaciated valleys and open moorland that make up the ever-changing aspects of **Glenveagh National Park.** Within its borders, a thick carpet of russet-color heath and dense woodland rolls down the Derryveagh slopes into the broad open valley of the River Veagh (or Owenbeagh), which opens out into the Glenveagh's spine: long and narrow, dark and clear **Lough Beagh.** On one side of the lough stands **Glenveagh Castle,** begun in 1870 by a ruthless gentleman farmer, John George Adair. Due to his harsh eviction of all his tenants after the killing of one of his estate managers, Adair was eventually forced to move to America, though his wife did return some years later to create the 27 acres of superb gardens around the castle. The estate was eventually bought by American philanthropist Henry McIlhenny in the 1940s, who bequeathed it to the State. The park is open all year, while the visitor center is open Easter through October from 10 AM to 6:30 PM. The entrance fee is £4. No camping is allowed in the park. Glenveagh Castle is open the same hours as the visitor center and admission is £4.

Gartan Lough and the surrounding mountainous country, though 13 km (8 mi) southeast of Glenveagh on R251, are technically within the national park. On the northwest shore of the lough sits **Glebe House,** a fine Regency building that was built as a rectory in 1828 and was for 30 years the home of landscape and portrait artist **Derek Hill.** Born in England in 1916, Hill worked in Germany before traveling extensively in Russia and the East. He visited Armenia with Freya Stark and became interested in Islamic art and all things Oriental. Hill furnished the house with care and detail in a mix of styles using art from all over the world. Included are Oriental and Middle Eastern tapestries and ceramics, Victoriana and original William Morris papers and textiles, as well as Donegal art from many local painters. In an adjacent gallery are works by Picasso, Bonnard, Kokoschka, Renoir, Jack B. Yeats, and Augustus John. The house is open May–September, Saturday–Thursday, from 11 AM to 6:30 PM. Admission is £4.

KILCAR, DERRYLAHAN, AND SLIEVE LEAGUE

BASICS • Both **Bus Éireann** and **McGeehan Coaches** (tel. 075/46101) stop outside John Joe's Pub in the center of Kilcar. There's no staffed bus depot or tourist office in town, but most shop owners have a sense of which bus leaves when for where. The town doesn't have an official bank, so change your foreign currency in one of Main Street's grocery stores. Most are open Monday–Saturday 9–6, and all offer equally poor rates.

WHERE TO SLEEP • The centrally located **Molloy's/Kilcar Lodge** (Main St., tel. 073/38156) is open March–October and offers comfortable private rooms from £14.50 per person. The IHH **Derrylahan Hostel** (Carrick Rd., tel. 073/38079) is one of the most popular hostels in Ireland. Dorm beds are £6, double rooms £16, and tent sites £3. The 32-bed hostel is a steep 3 km (2 mi) north of Kilcar on the road to Carrick and overlooks Teelin Bay and the mountains. If you call from Kilcar or Carrick, one of the staff will come to get you. The hostel's well-stocked food shop sells enough to make a half dozen different meals, the reception desk is open all day, and all guests are treated to biscuits and tea.

WORTH SEEING • The village of Kilcar would probably be forgotten were it not for its proximity to IHH's Derrylahan Hostel. In fact, pretty much the only time people venture into Kilcar is to catch a bus or have a few pints in one of the village's lively pubs. **Piper's Rest** (Main St., tel. 073/38205), probably the most attractive pub in town, serves up decent food and usually hosts music sessions on Wednesday and weekends, as does **John Joe's Pub** (Main St., tel. 073/31093), a few doors away.

Most visitors, however, spend their day at the isolated hostel, which provides access to some of the best hiking in northwestern Ireland. Within 3 km (2 mi) of the Derrylahan Hostel are trailheads to both **Slieve League** (2,972 ft) and the **Bunglass Cliffs,** the highest sea cliffs in the country. Slieve League (Sliabh Liec, or Mountain of the Pillars) is a ragged, razor-backed rise bordered by the River Glen and, at its foot, the village of Teelin. The mountain looks deceptively climbable from the back (the inaccessible front side borders the Atlantic Ocean), but once the fog rolls in, the footing can be perilous. At some points, the jagged trails wind within a foot of the cliff's edge, and the green heather that somehow thrives in the rocky soil is always slippery.

To access the mountain yourself, drive or hike from the hostel to **Carrick,** a small two-pub town 5 km (3 mi) northwest. Go just under 2 km (1 mi) south on the road for Teelin and turn right at the sign for Bunglass. The hike to Bunglass is fairly easy, and the views are nothing short of incredible. Continue past Bunglass and head for the summit of Slieve League. On the way, you'll traverse trails with names like Fog Ridge and the aptly named One Man's Pass. Be extra careful on windy days here—inexperienced hikers have been blown off the ridge by 50-mph gusts. Once you reach the summit, take a well-anchored peep over the cliff's edge. Almost 2,000 ft below, the pounding waves and white-water spray seem to move in slow motion, soundlessly. After you've humbled yourself before ocean, cliff, and sky, take the alternative route down, heading south for Cappagh and Teelin (follow the occasional weathered sign). Here you can grab lunch at **Rusty Mackerel Pub** (Teelin, tel. 073/39101), a hideaway filled with pipe-smoking fisherfolk. The entire circuit, from Carrick to Slieve League to Teelin, takes roughly five hours of medium-paced hiking, slightly more when heavy fog calls for extra vigilance.

GLENCOLUMBKILLE

BASICS • The **tourist office** (Main St., tel. 073/30116) is open mid-April–mid-October, Monday–Saturday 10–6. It has maps, walking guides, and a bureau de change. The **post office** (near Biddy's pub, tel. 073/30001), open weekdays 9–1 and 2–5, also has a bureau de change. Both **Bus Éireann** and **McGeehan Coaches** (tel. 075/46101) stop three blocks from the tourist office. During summer, they both offer twice-daily service to Kilcar (£1.40), Killybegs (£1.80), and Donegal Town (£3.20).

WHERE TO SLEEP • **Dooey Hostel** (tel. 073/30130) has fantastic views of the Glen Head cliffs and beach. One side of the hostel is, quite literally, carved right out of the hillside, complete with jutting rocks and cascading plants. When it rains (and it *will* rain), water trickles through the rock formation and gurgles quietly by the dorm rooms. Dorm beds are £6, private rooms £6.50, and tent sites in the beautiful camping area cost £3.50. The hostel is a 1½-km (1-mi) walk from the tourist office (head west toward the beach and follow the signs). Otherwise, both **Mary Cunningham's** (Brackendale House, tel. 073/30038) and **Mrs. Byrne's** (Corner House, tel. 073/30021) offer standard B&B accommodations for around £16 per person; the latter is open April–September only. Look for them on the road to Carrick, 1 km (½ mi) outside Glencolumbkille. There are also a bunch of B&Bs near the folk museum and on the road to Malinbeg.

FOOD • **An Chistan** (Main St., adjacent to Ulster Cultural Institute, tel. 073/30213), named "The Kitchen" in Gaelic, serves excellent soups, sandwiches, and stews at lunchtime. Evening fare is more elaborate, with good seafood platters, pasta, and meat dishes. The **Lace House Café** (Cashel St., no phone), located over the tourist office, specializes in fried food—everything from great hand-cut chips to batter burgers (a beef patty coated in egg yolk) to the fish of the day.

WORTH SEEING • Glencolumbkille (pronounced glen-colm-*keel*) lies on the coast 13 km (8 mi) northwest of Kilcar. Although tiny even by Irish standards, Glencolumbkille manages to balance rural solitude with the occasional crafts shop and, best of all, a lively pub scene. It has yet to be "discovered" by mass tourism, but each year there's increased interest in this remote village. Part of the reason is that Glencolumbkille is at the heart of County Donegal's shrinking Gaeltacht. This gives the Glen a strong, rural Irish flavor, as do its affable country pubs and brightly painted row houses.

For a good overview, start at the beachfront **Folk Museum** (tel. 073/30017), where you can explore thatched-roof buildings on your own, or take one of the guided tours (£1.50) that start every half hour daily, 10–6, mid-April–September (Sunday from noon). Then cross the strand and climb up to Glen Head (769 ft). Along the way, you'll pass a series of stunning cliffs studded with ancient hermit cells. Also of note is yet another squat **Martello tower,** built by the British in 1804 to protect against an anticipated French invasion that never happened. Another good walk is the 8-km (5-mi) trek to **Malinbeg,** reached by following the coast road past both Doon Point and the Glencolumbkille Hotel. Look for the ruins of no fewer than five burial cairns, a ring fort, a second Martello tower, and one of the best beaches in Ireland (renowned for its calm waters, dramatic scenery, and lovely golden sand).

LETTERKENNY

If nothing else, Letterkenny is a useful hub for those headed deeper into northern County Donegal. Both Bus Éireann and Lough Swilly Buses offer a variety of routes from here north to the beautiful Inishowen Peninsula and Fanad Head. If you're coming from Northern Ireland, particularly from Derry, Letterkenny is the last large town you'll come across for miles. For this reason, Letterkenny's restaurants, pubs, and two hostels are popular with backpackers and cyclists looking to rest and stock up on supplies (or those ravenously hungry after a week on the remote coast). Letterkenny gets most active during early August's **International Folk Festival,** which brings together musicians from all over Ireland and the world. For details on performances, contact the festival office (52 Main St., tel. 074/21754). If you're suffering from electronic-image withdrawal symptoms, there's an up-to-date, four-screen cinema on the main street where you can get a fix.

BASICS

The **tourist office** (Derry Rd., tel. 074/21160) is 1 km (½ mi) outside of town on Derry Road. It's open June–September, Monday–Friday 9–5; July–August, Monday–Saturday 9–8. Letterkenny is small enough to navigate without a map, so the only reason to walk out here is for Saturday currency exchange and B&B information. Weekday exchanges can be made more conveniently at the **AIB** (61 Upper Main St., tel. 074/22877), open Monday–Friday 10–4, Thursday until 5. **Church St. Cycles** (11 Church St., off Main St., tel. 074/26204) rents bikes for £7 per day, £30 per week, plus a £40 deposit.

COMING AND GOING

The **bus station** (Port Rd., tel. 074/21309) is a five-minute walk from the city center; turn left out of the depot, cross to the far side of the roundabout, and follow the CITY CENTRE signs. From here, **Bus Éireann** serves Derry (3 per day; £4.40), Sligo (3 per day; £9, or £6 for the first bus of the day), Galway (3 per day; £14), and Dublin (4 per day; £10). Most of northern Donegal is served by the **Lough Swilly Bus Co.** (tel. 074/22863), which also operates out of the Port Road Station. It provides an excellent means to explore the Northern Donegal coastline, with services running to Dungloe, via Creeslough, Dunfanaghy, Falcarragh, Gweedore, and Crolly, to name a few of the towns. There are four buses a day (£8 to Dungloe), two of which go via the Bloody Foreland, a trip highly recommended for its scenic beauty. Pick up a free timetable at the bus station. If you show them an ISIC card, they'll take 50% off the regular fare.

WHERE TO SLEEP

There are a number of B&Bs outside town on the roads to Sligo and Derry. **Ard na Greine** (Sentry Hill, tel. 074/21383) has rooms from £18. Closer to the bus station is **Covehill House** (Port Rd., tel. 074/21038), a comfortable five-room guest house with similar rates and excellent fried breakfasts; it's closed late-December–January.

Letterkenny has three hostels. The most spacious and best equipped is IHH's the **Manse Hostel** (High Rd., tel. 074/25238), set atop a hill and surrounded by a pleasant, sloping lawn. The dorm rooms (£6) and doubles (£14) are airy and clean. From the bus station, walk down Port Road toward the town center and make a sharp right on High Road.

FOOD

The most popular restaurant in town is **Pat's Pizza** (9 Market Sq., tel. 074/21761), where a 9-inch pizza with five toppings costs £5. You'll be privy to all the hot gossip around town, as the seating arrangements will have you elbow to elbow with Letterkenny's youth. The sign outside **Bakersville** (10 Church St., tel. 074/21887) promises "damn fine coffee," which it delivers along with piping-hot baked goods. Letterkenny is also well endowed with pubs. **Peadar McGeehin** (46 Main St., tel. 074/29564) has a quiet, mostly local crowd, while the **Orchard** (High Rd., tel. 074/21615) and the **Cottage** (25 Main St., tel. 074/21338) have livelier atmospheres. **Pulse** (Port Rd., tel. 074/24966) is the hottest club in town, occasionally featuring live bands.

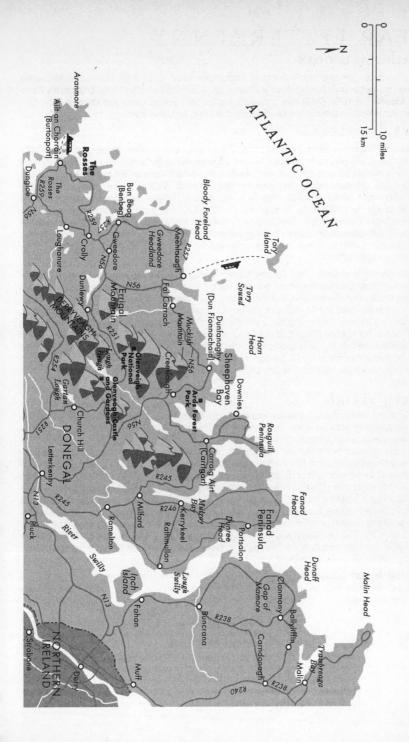

ATLANTIC OCEAN

Aranmore
Allt an Chorráin
(Burtonport)
Dungloe
The Rosses
R259
The Rosses
N56
R259
Crolly
R257
Loughanure
N56
Dunloe
Gweedore
Headland
Bun Beag
(Benbeg)
Gweedore
Errigal Mountain
R251
DERRYVEAGH MOUNTAINS
R254
Gartan Lough
Meehataragh
R257
Fal Carrach
Muckish Mountain
Bloody Foreland Head
Tory Island
Tory Sound
Dunfanaghy
(Dún Fionnachaidh)
Horn Head
Sheephaven Bay
Downies
Creeslough
Ards Forest Park
Rosguill Peninsula
Fanad Head
Carraig Airt
(Carrigan)
Mulroy Bay
Kerrykeel
R246
Milford
Rathmullan
Fanad Peninsula
Portsalon
Dunree Head
Dunaff Head
Malin Head
Lough and Gardens
Glenveagh National Park
Glenveagh Castle and Gardens
Church Hill
DONEGAL
Letterkenny
R245
R251
R245
Ramelton
Pluck
N13
River Swilly
N13
Fahan
Inch Island
Lough Swilly
Buncrana
R238
Carndonagh
Gap of Mamore
Clonmany
Ballyliffin
Malin
Trawbreaga Bay
R238
R240
Muff
Derry
NORTHERN IRELAND
Strabane

0
10 miles
15 km
N

NEAR LETTERKENNY

COMING AND GOING

Some private bus services run to the more inaccessible areas in the high season. Try **McGeehan Coaches** for coaches from Donegal Town northward (tel. 075/46150 or 075/46101). **O'Donnell's Trans-Ulster Express** (tel. 075/48356) runs once-daily service from Belfast, Derry, and Donegal Town. This service passes through Letterkenny, Dunfanaghy, and Crolly, and other towns.

WHERE TO SLEEP

The roads leading to Dunfanaghy are full of B&Bs; the closest to town is the **Willows** (tel. 074/36446). Clean but small, with only six beds (£16 a person), it's open year-round and is on the main street. About 2 km (1 mi) on the road west is a hostel that's an attraction in itself; **Creggan Mill Hostel** (tel. 074/36507 or 074/36409) set alone among lush greenery. You can sleep in either the beautiful, rustic old kiln house, where dorm beds cost £6–£8, or in the newly installed, 120-year-old railway carriage, which has romantic doubles for £10 a person or dorm beds from £8–£10. The hostel also has a camping site with good facilities for £4 per person. The hostel and garden are littered with quirky objects, and there is a very special feel to the place. Laundry facilities are available and cost £2. The hostel also arranges trips to Tory Island and other local sites. Be sure to arrive well stocked, as there are no shops nearby—or anything else, for that matter.

Near the tiny village of **Crolly,** you'll find the isolated **Screag An Iolair (Eagle's Nest) Hostel** (tel. 075/48593). Eammon, who runs the hostel, will have instant respect for you if you've conquered the one-hour uphill walk, past wild bog land, rushing streams, and a beautiful mountain lake to get to his hostel. If you're not in the mood to hike, he'll pick you up or you can take a taxi (£3). The hostel has a spartan, rustic feel, but it's very cozy. It also has a peculiar meditation room, with the naked torso of a young woman carved out of wood and placed in a Buddha-type position in the corner. Eammon's explanation is that this is a shrine to the Celtic goddess Brid (the goddess of fertility and young women). Dorm beds are £6.50 and private rooms are £8 per person. You can do laundry for £3 a load. Be sure to buy food in the village before you head up. The only problem is that the nearest pub is 5 km (3 mi) away, an Irish nightmare.

WORTH SEEING

Head west and north out of Letterkenny, and you'll be entering an area that is perhaps the least developed and populated of all the scenic glories of Ireland. This may make the area difficult to explore without independent transport, but don't be put off; some buses do brave the region (*see above*), and you will be richly rewarded by the wild and rugged landscape that typifies northwest Donegal. Head for **Dunfanaghy,** a small seaside resort that overlooks the impressive Sheephaven Bay. The town itself is heavily frequented in summer by tourists from Derry, but it's a good spot to stock up on provisions. **Horn Head,** with its impressive cliffs and view of the surrounding coastline, is a must-see, and some distance away (bicycling is probably the best way to cover the 16-km/10-mi trip) are **Doe Castle** and **Lackagh Bridge.** At Lackagh Bridge, looking upriver, you can see distinctive Muckish Mountain, and downriver is the beginning of Sheephaven Bay, with Doe Castle perched on its low promontory fringed by a white sandy beach. In 1544, Doe Castle was the focus of internecine wars between the sons of McSweeney Doe, and in the 17th century it was the scene of bloody conflict between the Irish princes and the Crown, changing hands many times.

The **Screag An Iolair** hostel is set right in the middle of the mountains of Glenveigh National Park and makes a perfect base from which to set out on some serious and spectacular walks. **Mt. Errigal** is a three-hour walk away.

THE DONEGAL GAELTACHT

BASICS

Dungloe is the unofficial capital of the Rosses, the market town where provisions are bought before heading off into the wilds. The tourist office (just off Main St., tel. 075/21297) is open June–September, Monday–Saturday 10–1 and 2–6. It has all the info you'll need to bone up on the surrounding area. The **post office** is on Quay Road (tel. 075/21179); it's open Monday–Friday 9–1 and 2–5:30.

COMING AND GOING

While Bus Éireann doesn't operate up this far, **McGeehan Coaches** (tel. 075/46150) have a regular schedule to Dungloe from most main towns in Donegal.

"Where the wave of moonlight glosses/The dim grey sands with light/Far off by furthest Rosses/We foot it all the night/Weaving olden dances/mingling hands and mingling glances/Till the moon has taken flight" — W. B. Yeats, *"The Stolen Child"*

WHERE TO SLEEP

Greene's Independent Holiday Hostel (Carnmore Rd., tel. 075/21943) has several dorm rooms with six to eight beds (£7), as well as singles (£8), doubles (£16), and family rooms (£30). **Park House** (Carnmore Rd., tel. 075/21351) has decent-size beds with duck-down quilts and a communal kitchen where you can cook your own food. Singles are £20, and doubles £32. Good views of the water and nice, freshly decorated rooms await at **Hillcrest B&B** (Barrack Brae, tel. 075/21484). Camping can be had at **Dungloe Camping and Caravan Park** (tel. 075/21943) and costs £6 per tent.

FOOD

Check out the **Riverside Bistro** (Main St., tel. 075/21062) for a pretty universal selection, including pastas, curries, and even Tex-Mex, at about £10 per head. The **Bay View Bar** (Main St., tel. 075/21186) is good for pub grub, especially the steamed mussels and seafood chowder. For music, try **Breedy's** (Main St., tel. 075/21219), which is thronged with itinerant musicians from all over the county on weekends. Across the street, the **Atlantic Bar** (tel. 075/21066) packs them into a large old-style bar where the strains of fiddles fill the air until the wee hours (dawn when we visited).

WORTH SEEING

While every corner of Ireland would have you believe that its particular landscape is unique, out among the **Rosses** (Na Rosa in Iriah, meaning "the headlands") even the seasoned traveler must pause at the windswept lonely beauty of it all. This vast plain of sweeping bog land, dotted with craggy rocks and dark pools, encompasses the area around **Glenties, Dungloe,** and **Burtonport.** You can often travel for miles here without seeing another living soul. It's a land of weather-beaten faces and hard, unforgiving soil that ain't never going to make anyone a millionaire from farming. The Rosses is where the few old customs of bog cutting and draught-net fishing still keep old dreams alive. The Irish language also continues to survive here, despite the flight of the youth into the cities. While everyone has English at the ready for lost visitors, it's a joy to listen to the seductive rhythms of locals conversing in full flight. It may be a dying language, but it's spoken here with true passion.

The **Mary from Dungloe Festival** (for information, tel. 075/21254) held the last week of July has built up a serious following from all over Ireland in the last few years. Basically a beauty contest (without the swimsuits), the 10-day shindig swells the town population up to 50,000. However, the hordes aren't just there to see the new Queen of the Festival crowned; they come to hear the incredible array of great trad

BIG TOM & THE MAINLINERS

Leitrim has produced more than its share of Irish country-and-western singers. You know the type, a hybrid of Nashville and the Emerald Isle, singing songs that run toward loneliness and despair. One of the most potent of these was Big Tom, a local lad of 6 ft 7 inches and righteous girth, who warbled his way around the country singing of love disasters and terminally sick aunts to an adoring audience of 50-year-olds and upward. Semiretired now, he still sings around Leitrim, so if you happen to see a notice do go and catch the gig. The name of his band leads some of the uninitiated to expect a group of heroin junkies. Imagine their surprise at the sight of six middle-aged men in tight-fitting 1950s blue suits with starched shirts and ties. The name, you see, refers to railway tracks. There ain't nothin' psychedelic about country music in these parts.

sessions performed by the wealth of top-notch musicians who visit for the week. Of course there's also that local lad who still loves his Mammie, **Daniel O'Donnell** (a proud self-professed virgin, still waiting for the right one to come along), who performs a few concerts during the week. Women of all shapes, creeds, and ages converge for this event alone.

LEITRIM

Since Leitrim is a relatively small county, with its sites all within easy reach of one another, there's no need to relocate every night. The easiest way to plan your tour is to make the town of Carrick-on-Shannon your base for your travels around the area.

BASICS

Carrick-on-Shannon, on the border with Roscommon, is the main town of the county and marks the upper limit of navigation of the Shannon. Apart from a healthy commerce around the renting and sup-plying of pleasure boats on the waterway, there isn't a whole lot to keep the visitor here. The **tourist office** (tel. 078/20170) is on West Quay beside Carrick Bridge and is open May–September from 9:30 AM to 1 PM. The **post office** is on St George's Terrace (tel. 078/20020); it's open Monday–Saturday 9–5:30. **Internet access** can be found at Gartlan's on Bridge Street (tel. 078/21735) for £4.50 per hour. You can take care of your laundry at **McGuire's Washeteria** on Main Street (tel. 078/20339). It's open Monday–Saturday 10–6; a wash and dry will run you £4.50.

COMING AND GOING

The bus stop in Carrick-on-Shannon is outside **Coffey's Pastry Case** (tel. 071/60066), a restaurant on the corner near the tourist office at the Marina; they can provide schedule information. **Bus Éireann** (tel. 071/60066) express between Dublin (£8), and Sligo (£5), stops here on a daily basis. There are also services to Cork, Waterford, Limerick, and Galway. The **railway station** (tel. 078/20036) is a short walk over the bridge on the Roscommon side of the border, and has daily services to Dublin (£11.50), and Sligo (£7).

GETTING AROUND

Bicycles can be hired from **Geraghty's** (Main St., tel. 078/21316) for £7.50 a day or £25 a week; you can also rent rods and tackle for fishing in the lakes if you're interested.

WHERE TO SLEEP

The IHH **Town Clock Hostel** (tel. 078/20068) is at the junction of Main and Bridge streets. It's a very spartan affair with dorm beds going for £6 and private rooms with bath for £8.50 per person. Like most towns, Carrick (as the locals call it) is well served by B&Bs. **Villa Flora** (Station Rd., tel. 078/20338), a modernized Georgian house within easy walking distance of the town center and railway station, has singles for £22. There's also **Corbally Lodge** (Dublin Rd., tel. 078/20228), a quiet house furnished with tasteful antiques that has a big garden that's ideal for an afternoon siesta. Singles are £22.50.

FOOD

Coffey's Pastry Case (West Quay, tel. 078/20929), near the tourist office, is a busy self-service place where all the locals seem to be found. Next door is **Cryan's** (tel. 078/20409), where you can get hearty lunches for around £4. On Bridge Street, the **Mariner's Reach** (no phone) has lunch specials for under £5 and serves bar food right up to 10 PM.

WORTH SEEING

Rather like the plain sister in the family who often gets taken for granted, the county of Leitrim has a much lower tourist profile than Donegal or Galway and, indeed, most travelers might have difficulty pointing it out on a map. It is a pretty, if unspectacular, county with Lough Allen basically splitting it in two. The northern half, marked by the dramatic Manorhamilton limestone ridges, adjoins Sligo. The southern half is a mixture of lush fields, hidden lakes, and undulating drumlins. Not many people live here and the towns are often grim one-street arrangements with houses wearing the same weary looks. Lacking the craggy mountain majesty of its more famous neighbors toward the west, Leitrim wears a stolid visage of low-lying farmland dotted everywhere with lakes. A rainfall that can even impress a native with its unrelenting regularity feeds the hearty hedgerows and bursting vegetation found along seemingly every route in the county. Irregular outcroppings of whitethorn, ash, green oak, holly, wild cherry, sloe, and sycamore provide a contrast to vast rushy fields, bright yellow gorse groupings, and plains of white-reeded bog land.

Like the neighboring Cavan man, the Leitrim native has a national reputation for thrift. Canny small farmers used to scraping the last crumb from a cattle deal, and shopkeepers who store broken twine for reuse, are some of the characters found hereabouts. As well as that, there's a closeness about the people: They'll stop and ingest your inquiry for minutes before giving their considered reply. In this regard, it's well not to find yourself in too much of a hurry when idling about the county.

Outdoor activities abound in Leitrim. The county is famous for the sport fishing on its lakes. Bream, perch, roach, and pike are the draw at the angling centers in Ballinamore, Carrigallen, Drumshambo, Mohill, and Roosky. Biking and walking are also popular in the county, due to the relatively flat terrain and the abundance of trails. These trails include *Sli Liatroma,* the Miner's Way, the Kingfisher Cycle Trail, the Leitrim Glens Walking Trail, and the Cavan Way walking trail. This is also horse-riding country, with equestrian centers at Ballinamore, Leitrim Village, and Roosky. The **Carrick-on-Shannon tourist office** (*see above*) can provide information on all of these activities.

Turlough O'Carolan (1670–1738) is the famous blind poet associated with Leitrim. He's buried at **Kilronan Church** in the town of Mohill, just north of the village of Leitrim, where there's also a 12th-century doorway. O'Carolan spent most of his life in Mohill where his patron, Mrs. MacDermot Roe, lived. A sculpture on Main Street there commemorates this connection.

The **Lough Rynn Estate** (tel. 078/31427), just outside Mohill on the N4 road to Dublin, was the home of the Clements family, the earls of Leitrim, and many of the various 19th-century buildings constructed by the last earl are open to the public. The terraced, walled garden is more than half an acre in size; its Victorian pleasure-garden design reflects the period of its creation in 1859. The romantic turreted house has excellent views across the lake. It's open May through September, 10 AM to 7 PM, with an admission charge of £1.50 per person.

About 8 km (5 mi) north of Carrick-on-Shannon, on the southern shores of Lough Allen, **Drumshambo** is mainly an angling center. The **Sliabh Iarainn Visitor Centre** (Main St., tel. 078/41522) is about the only thing to see. It has an audiovisual display on the history, life, and culture of the area. There is also a nonfunctioning replica of an ancient Irish sweathouse. These small stone structures with just a small doorway for access were used to cure aches and pains. A turf fire would be lit inside for several hours, then removed when the house was heated enough. The patient would then enter and lie upon a pile of rushes or straw until he felt he'd sweated enough. Finally, in true Finnish fashion, he would emerge to take a dip in the nearby lake. The center is open April–September, 10 AM–6 PM. Admission is free, but there's a £1 charge to see the audiovisual show.

The 224 km (140 mi) of linked rivers and lakes that compose the **Shannon-Erne Waterway** are a major source of revenue for Leitrim. Many visitors and locals opt for a week of cruising, and they keep many little pubs and groceries hopping during peak season. If you have a group of six or eight people, a boat can provide an interesting way to see the counties of the midlands, and lazing on the bow of a boat is a fine way to chill out. With 34 bridges and 16 locks along the waterway's length, there's quite a bit of nautical traffic, especially during July and August. For information on cruiser rental, try **Emerald Star** (tel. 01/6798166).

NORTHERN IRELAND

JOHN DALY

Northern Ireland is small—about half the size of Delaware and less than one-fifth the size of the Republic of Ireland, its neighbor to the south. Because of its size, and because it wasn't a separate country prior to 1921, Northern Ireland is often lumped together with the Irish Republic. Both countries, after all, share more than just a similar climate and heritage. Both are dominated by rolling pastureland, craggy coasts, meandering stone fences, and isolated farm villages. The Irish traditions of hospitality and artful conversation also prevail in Northern Ireland.

The similarities, however, generally stop here. Politically speaking, Northern Ireland is administered and governed by England, much like Scotland and Wales. Northern Ireland, which nowadays includes six of Ulster's nine counties (the other three—Donegal, Monaghan, and Cavan—lie in the Republic), thus derives its social, economic, and political orientation from the British, who have maintained some presence in Ulster since the late 12th century. Over the past 20 years, in fact, Britain has spent millions of pounds in support of the province, mostly to sustain its heavily armed security forces but also to install better roads and a dependable phone system. The English presence also accounts for Northern Ireland's currency (the British pound), its bright red "postboxes" (they're lime green in the Republic), and the preponderance of some very un-Irish names like William Smyth and Victoria Browne.

At its closest point, Northern Ireland is only 27 km (17 mi) from Scotland, so there's always been a strong Scottish influence here. Ulster's Scottish connection meant that when England underwent its 16th-century conversion to Protestantism (thanks to Henry VIII), so did the majority of Ulster. And when James VI of Scotland was crowned James I of England, whole parts of Ulster were opened up for settlement by Protestant immigrants (read: confiscated by the Crown). These were generally farmers and merchants who competed with the native Irish for everything from grazing land to political favor. Being Protestant, of course, gave you certain advantages when dealing with Ulster's English administrators. Simply put, Protestants received free lands and Catholics didn't. English became Ulster's "first" language, replacing Irish, and the Gaelic culture was systematically repressed. As discriminatory practices became enshrined in law, Catholics rightly felt excluded, disenfranchised, and persecuted.

In terms of Catholic-Protestant relations, the pivotal event was the 1649 arrival in Ireland of Oliver Cromwell, a staunch Protestant who unseated (and beheaded) the pro-Catholic Charles I during the English Civil War. Cromwell was a despot who earned the everlasting hate of Catholic Ireland with his 1653 Act of Settlement, which stipulated that all Catholics were to relocate west of Ireland's Shannon

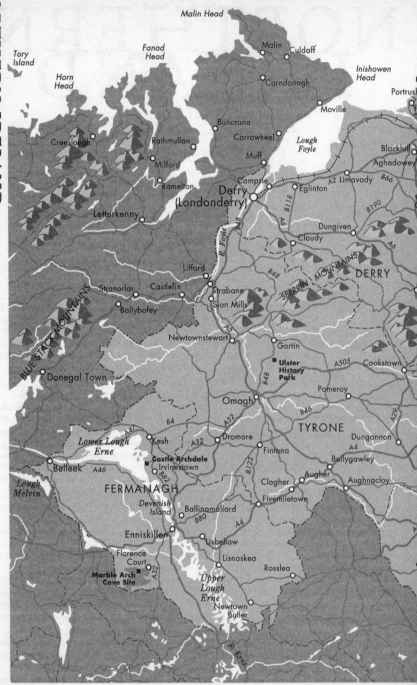

Tory Island

Malin Head

Fanad Head

Horn Head

Malin
Culdaff

Carndonagh

Inishowen Head

Portrush

Creeslough

Rathmullan

Milford

Ramelton

Buncrana

Carrowkeel

Moville

Lough Foyle

Blackhill

Aghadowey

Muff

Campsie

Derry (Londonderry)

Eglinton

A2 Limavady

B66

Letterkenny

B118

A6

Dungiven

B190

Claudy

Lifford

R. Foyle

B48

B48

SPERRIN MOUNTAINS

DERRY

Stranorlar

Castlefin

Strabane

Sion Mills

A5

Ballybofey

Newtownstewart

Gortin

A505

Cookstown

BLUE STACK MOUNTAINS

Donegal Town

Ulster History Park

B48

Pomeroy

A29

Omagh

A32

B46

TYRONE

Dungannon

A4

Lower Lough Erne

A7

Kesh

B4

A32

Dromore

Fintona

Ballygawley

Belleek

A46

Castle Archdale
Irvinestown

B82

B122

Clogher

Augher

Aughnacloy

Lough Melvin

FERMANAGH

Devenish Island

Ballinamallard

B80

Fivemiletown

A4

Florence Court

Enniskillen

A32

Lisbellaw

Lisnaskea

Rosslea

Marble Arch Cave Site

Upper Lough Erne

Newtown Butler

R. Erne

Kintyre
(Scotland)

Rathlin Island

Bull Pt.

Giant's
seway

Ballintoy   Rue Pt.
A2   Carrick
B15   -a-rede
Ballycastle

Bushmills
art

Armoy   Cushendun

Cushendall   Red Bay
A44   Glenariff   A2
Ballymoney

A26   Glens of
Antrim

Carnlough Bay

ANTRIM   Carnlough

North Channel

Larne
A43   Harbour

Larne   Ballygally
A12   Larne

Ballymena
A36

TO STRANRAER,
CAIRNRYAN,
SCOTLAND

A26   A8
Randalstown   Ballyclare

Toome   Whitehead
Antrim
Magherafelt

TO STRANRAER,
ISLE OF MAN

Belfast
International   Newtownabbey
Airport   A52

Eden
Carriekfergus
Belfast Lough

Bangor

Lough
Neagh

Crumlin

Belfast
City   A20   Newtownards
Airport

Ardboe

vartstown

Comber

Greyabbey

Lisburne

Strangford
Lough   Ards
Peninsula

ortadown

rmagh

Lurgan   Hillsborough
Cragavon

A1   A24   Saintfield

Killyleagh

Portaferry
A20

A3

Ballynahinch

Strangford   Car Ferry

Banbridge

DOWN
Downpatrick

rkethill

A25

ARMAGH   Castlewellan   Dundrum
A25   A2   Ardglass

Bessbrook

Dundrum Bay

Camlough   Newry   Newcastle

N

KEY

Slieve Donard
Mountain   Rail Lines

Warrenpoint   Ferry Lines

A2

Carlingford Lough

Kilkeel

0   10 miles

0   15 km

215

AN UNPRECEDENTED RETURN TO VIOLENCE

In 1996, the IRA began a full-scale campaign of terror in Northern Ireland, the Republic of Ireland, and England. The bombs in London's Canary Wharf and Manchester (which killed two, injured hundreds, and caused millions of dollars in damage) and the bizarre murder of Irish policeman Jerry McCabe were but a prelude to the worst violence in decades. The critical incident was the so-called Siege of Drumcree. Essentially, the Orange Order (a Protestant group) decided to reroute its annual march through a Catholic neighborhood—knowing full well it would incite the wrath of the residents as well as Nationalists across the province. To prevent violence, the RUC, the Northern Irish police force, blocked the marchers, and a three-day standoff ensued. Protestants from all over the province poured into the city to support the Orangemen, and the RUC reversed its decision and allowed the Orangemen to march. Watching the peaceful Nationalist protesters get forcibly yanked from the roads and Catholic residents forced from their neighborhood to clear a way for the marchers enraged the Catholic community and unleashed the most violence—in virtually every Northern Irish city—seen since the late 1960s. Belfast and Derry were particularly hard hit: Dozens of cars were hijacked and set afire, stores were ransacked, and for a week the world had the chilling experience of watching Nationalist mobs and police exchange plastic bullets and gasoline bombs in almost nightly battles (one man was killed).

River. Thousands were forcibly removed to Ireland's barren extremes, while the English nobility granted itself vast tracts of land throughout the country; later, they would rent the very same soil back to locals at extortionate rates.

England eventually relented in its policies, but the damage had already been done. Catholics understandably viewed England—and, by extension, most Protestants—as exploitative in the extreme. After Ireland gained its independence in 1921, England was left with a troublesome problem. Roughly 85% of Ulster was Protestant, but the newly created Republic of Ireland was emphatically Catholic. In the 1918 parliamentary elections most southerners voted for Sinn Féin, or "We, Ourselves," the Nationalist pro-Catholic party. Ulster, on the other hand, voted to remain a part of the United Kingdom. Even though people saw themselves as Irish first and foremost, Ulster's Protestants feared they would be mistreated by the new countrywide Catholic majority. The solution: the creation on June 22, 1921, of Northern Ireland, a political entity governed and safeguarded by the British Crown and a country where Protestants far outnumbered Catholics. Needless to say, this solution opened a Pandora's box of problems.

For a small country, Northern Ireland has received more than its fair share of international press coverage in the last few decades—mostly along the lines of ". . . the IRA claimed responsibility today for a bombing that has left three dead and dozens wounded." This new wave of sectarian violence began in the late 1960s, after two decades of relative peace. The northern state had for years denied Catholics basic civil rights, and in the spirit of the 1960s, a radical but peaceful movement for social justice sprang up all across the province. The government tried to suppress this movement and violence soon erupted. The participants were mainly the reborn IRA (Irish Republican Army), the RUC (Royal Ulster Constabulary, the province's police force), and Ulster's numerous Loyalist paramilitary factions (those who support British rule in Northern Ireland are often called Loyalists or Unionists). Particularly hard hit was Derry, Northern Ireland's second-largest city. On August 13, 1969, following a march by Derry Protestants through mostly Catholic ghettos, rioting forced Britain to dispatch an armed regiment. This was the first time in modern history that England had assumed an active military role in Ulster. At first, the presence of troops had a calming effect, as they protected Catholics who were being burned out of their homes by Protestant mobs with the tacit and sometimes active support of the police. But in time the IRA became angered by the sight of British troops on Irish soil and by the continuing biased actions of the government, and, intent on driving the British out, they initiated a ruthless bombing campaign in Belfast. To combat the rise in violence, the Northern Irish prime minister, Brian Faulkner, instituted an emergency power known as "internment without trial." In the climate of resentment that followed, the IRA stepped up its bombing attacks in Belfast and Derry. On the Protestant side, two new paramilitary organizations were born, the Ulster Volunteer Force (UVF) and the Ulster Defense Association (UDA), both outlawed Loyalist groups committed to Ulster's union with Britain.

These developments simply provided fuel for the watershed event in Northern Irish history, the civil rights march in Derry on January 30, 1972—better known as Bloody Sunday. The British have their own story of what happened on that day, but the generally accepted version is that 13 unarmed Catholic civilians were shot dead by British paratroopers during the march. Countrywide protests ensued, as did a surge of sectarian tit-for-tat violence. On July 21, known as Bloody Friday, 20 IRA bombs exploded within hours of one another in Belfast. The UVF responded with the beating and execution of Catholic civilians. Recognizing that the situation in Northern Ireland was about to degenerate into full-scale civil war, Britain took control on March 24, 1973 by establishing direct rule

Like the modern state of Israel, Northern Ireland is a political entity that draws its mandate from religion and history—a country where God and politics are tightly interwoven and where ancient quarrels still affect the tone of everyday life.

over the North and dispatching troops to occupy several "no-go" areas in Belfast. By the end of 1973, more than 800 people had been killed as a direct result of the Troubles, as they became known.

On August 31, 1994, after 25 years of political and sectarian conflict, the IRA declared a cease-fire and committed itself to the creation of a lasting peace and the reunification of Ireland. On October 12, 1994, the Loyalist paramilitary groups also declared a cease-fire. Sinn Féin (acting as the IRA's political wing) and the British government then began to wage a verbal war in the courtrooms over such issues as decommissioning arms, withdrawing British troops, and disbanding the Protestant police force. For a time the citizens of Northern Ireland were able to experience what many of us take for granted: living without the constant fear of bombs, bullets, and terrorist threats. Tourism increased in Northern Ireland, new businesses opened in anticipation of a lasting peace, and a new wave of optimism swept the island as the world community waited and hoped.

After a year and a half of delays by the British government, coupled with a continuing refusal to talk directly with Sinn Féin, a bomb exploded in London's Canary Wharf in February of 1996, heralding the renewal of the IRA's bloody campaign to reunite Northern Ireland with the Republic. Months later the Troubles–related violence reached a crescendo in the aftermath of the so-called Siege of Drumcree (*see box, above*). In summer 1997, the situation seemed to be deteriorating: "All party" talks had stalled, and with Sinn Féin barred from the discussions, many questioned the effectiveness of the talks.

On April 10, 1998, Good Friday, delegates from all the major political parties in the province approved a draft of the 1998 Northern Ireland Peace Agreement. On May 22, 1998, in the first vote taken in the North and South of Ireland since 1918, a vast majority of both the Republic (94%) and the North (71%) voted the agreement into law. The vote struck a telling blow for the silent peace-loving majority on both sides of the border against the traditional conflict of the petrol-bomb and the Armalite. This vote in turn initiated the 108-seat Northern Ireland Assembly, the governing body composed of all sections of the political sphere, including previous sworn enemies who now sat side by side to grapple with the bigotry and hatreds of centuries. With David Trimble of the Ulster Unionist Party (UUP) and Seamus Mallon of the Social Democratic & Labour Party (SDLP) as First Minister and Deputy First Minister respectively, the stage was set for the North of Ireland to commence a political and commercial dialogue watched over by the English prime minister, Tony Blair, and the Irish Taoiseach, Bertie Ahern.

While the early release of many prisoners from both sides of the conflict occurred without any major difficulty, the issue of weapons decommissioning remained a point of contention. There are still die-hard pockets of extremists who resist violently any efforts at compromise, a fact evidenced by horrific events like the Omagh bombing of August 15, 1998. In many ways, the struggle for peace faces as many obstacles as the previous futile struggle for dominance by the gun.

In July of 1999, another stumbling block to eventual peace occurred when Unionists decided against taking part in the new Assembly's attempts to elect a power-sharing executive. Opting not to show up at Stormont on the appointed day to ratify the election of new ministers, the Unionists left rows of empty seats. The other parties were faced with the futile and ludicrous task of attempting to elect new ministers without the majority party present. Again, the problem boiled down to arms decommissioning and the reluctance of the IRA to hand over their weapons. Seamus Mallon, leader of the SDLP and First Deputy Minister, resigned his post on the day in despair of these political maneuvers. For the moment, Northern Ireland has arrived at another impasse, but one that most political pundits agree can be overcome in the months of lengthy and painstaking talks ahead. The return of American senator George Mitchell, the peace broker who did so much to bring a cessation of violence, may aid the reaching of a compromise. Ireland's Bertie Ahern, England's Tony Blair, and U.S. president Bill Clinton are also determined to support the talks that lie ahead. It does seem that the peace will prevail despite the extreme factions that still exist within this complex political landscape. One fact provides hope: Children from Protestant and Catholic communities in all parts of Northern Ireland are playing together for the first time in decades.

Northern Ireland's sporadic bursts of violence, armored troop carriers, and fortresslike police stations definitely cast a pall over the province but should not deter you from visiting. Northern Ireland has the lowest crime rate in the United Kingdom and Ireland, and you are far more likely to be mugged in Dublin or Cork than affected by terrorist activity in Belfast or Derry. Tourists are rarely ever harmed or affected by the Troubles. But be smart: If there seems to be a lot of civil unrest going on (such as in July and August, prime marching season for the Orangemen), it may be best to stay out of the province or, at the very least, to avoid the staunchly Catholic or Protestant areas after dark. Otherwise, when there's little civil unrest (i.e., 99% of the time), Northern Ireland can be a pleasant and intriguing place to visit: The country is beautiful and the people extremely hospitable. Particularly worthwhile is the Causeway Coast, with the celebrated Giant's Causeway, and the lush lake land around Enniskillen and Lough Erne. Derry and Belfast are also most worthwhile stops—Belfast for its architecture and art scene, Derry for its fortified city center and reasonably bacchanalian pub scene (Derry also makes a good base for exploring County Fermanagh and, in the Republic, County Donegal).

BASICS

PHONES

Country code: 011. British Telecom provides phone service in Northern Ireland. BT pay phones are easy to find throughout the province; the ones with a red stripe around them accept standard British coins, while phones with a green stripe require the use of a phone card, available at newsagents, train and bus stations, tourist information centers, and numerous other locations. Look for signs saying PHONE CARDS SOLD HERE. Phone cards come with a fixed number of units (10, 20, 50, 100), each valued at 10p. You cannot use Telecom Éireann phone cards in the North, just as you cannot use British Telecom cards in the Republic. Dial 192 for general inquiries, 153 for international inquiries, and 155 for an international operator. To call the Republic from the North, dial 00353, followed by the area code without the initial 0, followed by the remainder of the number. For emergencies dial 999.

VISITOR INFORMATION

Northern Irish tourist information centers are sprinkled throughout the country. Besides their requisite stock of maps and brochures, they also make lodging reservations for a £1–£3 fee. If you're planning an extended stay in Northern Ireland, consider purchasing their excellent pocket-size guides "Where to Stay in Northern Ireland" (£4) and "Where to Eat in Northern Ireland" (£3). In general, Northern Irish tourist centers are open weekdays 9–5 with extended weekday and weekend hours in the summer. Offices in large cities are usually open on Saturday afternoons and Sunday mornings.

For other basic information see Chapter 1.

COMING AND GOING

BY BUS

Northern Ireland's bus company, **Ulsterbus** (tel. 028/9033–3000), crosses the border to connect with Bus Éireann routes. The journey from Belfast to Dublin takes about 2¾ hours, with a change at Monaghan, and costs £10.

BY FERRY

The most convenient way to travel to Northern Ireland from the United Kingdom is via ferry. **SeaCat** (Donegall Quay, tel. 028/9031–3543 from the Republic of Ireland, or 0345/523523 from the North) ferries depart three to four times per day from Belfast's Donegall Quay to Stranraer, Scotland (90 mins, £22–£25). **Stena Line** (tel. 0990/707076 or 01233/647047) sends four to eight ferries per day between Belfast Harbour and Stranraer. Tickets cost £22–£26 (£30–£38 round-trip). P&O (Fleet St. Terminal, Larne Harbour, tel. 0990/9800888 or 028/2827–4321) offers daily service from Larne Harbour, 32 km (20 mi) north of Belfast, to Cairnryan, Scotland. **Isle of Man Steam Packet Co.** (Donegall Quay, Belfast, tel. 028/9035–1009) offers direct service from Belfast Harbour to the Isle of Man. Ferries sail from Belfast twice per week mid-April through September only, and tickets cost £25–£30. Students and Eurail and InterRail pass holders receive substantial discounts on most ferries, and bicycles are transported free on most routes. For more ferry information, see Coming and Going in Belfast, *below.*

Strange as it may seem, Northern Ireland is actually one of the safest places in Ireland for a tourist. With so many soldiers and police about, crime is not really a problem.

BY PLANE

Northern Ireland's principal airport is **Belfast International Airport** (Crumlin, tel. 028/9442–2888), 30 km (19 mi) northwest of the city, offering skeletal service to a handful of international destinations; call **Air UK** (tel. 01345/666777) or **British Airways** (tel. 01345/222111) for reservations. **Belfast City Airport** (Syndenham, tel. 028/9045–7745), 6½ km (4 mi) northeast of town, handles U.K. flights only. **Aer Lingus** (tel. 028/9031–4844) offers flights to Dublin, Shannon, and London; **British Airways** (tel. 0345/222111) flies to most major cities in the United Kingdom; Delta (tel. 028/9048–0526) goes to Dublin, London, and Manchester. Eight kilometers (5 mi) from Derry, Eglantin Airport (tel. 028/7181–0784) is served by British Airways, with flights to Scotland and England.

BY TRAIN

The only train arrivals at Belfast Central Station from the Republic are from Dublin (12–18 per day). The trip takes roughly 2½ hours and costs £15. There is no direct train service between Derry and the Republic of Ireland.

GETTING AROUND

Since Northern Ireland is rather small and trains and buses are relatively cheap, most discount passes aren't such a great deal. In 1999, Northern Irish Railways had the fantastic policy of offering a day of unlimited rail travel for £5 Monday through Saturday. On Sunday Northern Irish Railways' "Tracker" ticket offers unlimited travel for £3, and Ulsterbus offers the "Sunday Rambler," with unlimited travel for £5. Ask at any station for details. One last note: The Republic-issued Travelsave stamp is good for the Dublin–Belfast trip but not elsewhere in the North. The Youth Hostel Association of Northern Ireland (YHANI) and Translink offer a "Go As You Please" package for £69, which gives you seven days' unlimited travel by bus and rail and six nights' accommodation in any YHANI hostel. Contact **YHANI** (22 Donegall Rd., Belfast BT12 5JN, tel. 028/9032–4733).

BY BICYCLE

If the weather is good—and most of the year it isn't—touring Northern Ireland by bike is a great way to go. Stena Lines and the Isle of Man Steam Packet Co. ferries will transport your bike for free, while SeaCat charges £10. Taking your bike on the train or bus costs an extra 25% of your one-way fare (be sure to purchase a bike pass at the train station before getting on the train). Bus drivers are generally more lenient and will sometimes let you take your bike gratis if there is room. **ReCycle Bicycle Hire** (tel. 028/9031–3113) is a widely offered rental plan in which mountain bikes are £9 per day or £30 per week, with a £50 deposit.

BY BUS

Bus travel is both quick and fairly priced. The extensive bus network means it's easy to reach any town from a major hub like Belfast or Derry. The principal bus company is the state-owned **Ulsterbus** (tel. 028/9033–3000), which has offices scattered throughout the country. Comprehensive timetables are available free at any depot. An Ulsterbus trip from Belfast to Dublin costs £10 one-way; from Belfast to Derry the fare is £5.10 one-way. Ulsterbus gives substantial student discounts (10%–40% off) to those with an ISIC card. Ulsterbus also offers a range of day tours from Belfast for £7.50 to £18.50. A long-distance trip leaves around 9 AM and returns between 8:45 and 11:30 PM, depending on the journey you take. A number of the day tours explore the wild scenery of the Donegal Highlands (Mt. Errigal, Sheep-haven Bay, and Glenveagh National Park), while others head directly north to the Giant's Causeway and the Bushmills distillery. Specific day tours leave on specific days, so you'll need to pick up a booklet from a local Ulsterbus Depot or the **Travel Centre** (Europa Buscentre, Glengall St., tel. 028/9033–7006).

BY TRAIN

Northern Irish Railways (NIR), the Northern Irish train network, is sorely limited. In fact, there are only three main routes: Belfast–Derry via Coleraine, Belfast–Bangor along the shore of Belfast Lough, and Belfast–Dublin. If you're headed for the Causeway Coast and don't have your own vehicle, you'll definitely end up on a bus. On the plus side, Northern Ireland's trains are comfortable and efficient. Pick up free route maps and timetables at Northern Rail's main depot, **Belfast Central** (E. Bridge St., tel. 028/9089–9411).

WHERE TO SLEEP

By far, the cheapest beds in Northern Ireland can be found in youth hostels. But hostels fill up fast, especially during the summer, so be sure to book ahead. The best hostels are those run by Independent Holiday Hostels (IHH), a Republic-based operation with about 10 hostels scattered through Northern Ireland, and more popping up all the time. IHH hostels are cheap, with beds for £5–£7, and regulations are practically nil. A list of IHH hostels is available from tourist offices and member hostels.

More comfortable and private are Northern Ireland's numerous bed-and-breakfasts (B&Bs), which generally charge £12–£19 per person. A standard Northern Irish breakfast (called, appropriately enough, an Ulsterfry) consists of fried eggs, fried bacon, cornflakes, juice, fried bread or potato, and coffee. Purchase "Where to Stay in Northern Ireland" (£4) from any tourist office for a comprehensive list of B&Bs.

BELFAST

Northern Ireland's capital and largest city has been called everything from a well-armed wasteland to "Little Beirut." Yet take a stroll through the city center and you might wonder where the war-torn Belfast that you've seen on CNN is. With a well-respected university, a solid collection of performing-arts troupes, intriguing museums, and bustling industry, Belfast seems like any other vibrant, cosmopolitan capital—until an armored troop carrier rolls by. These tanklike vehicles are the main components of Northern Ireland's police force and are the most visible reminder that Belfast remains the traditional flash point for Northern Ireland's religious violence. Though 8,500 soldiers were sent to the city, in 1993 alone more than 125 residents were killed and at least 300 were wounded as a result of the Troubles. Some victims were targeted by the IRA, some by Protestant paramilitary groups, some even by the RUC and UDR, the province's ostensible peacekeepers.

Belfast greatly changed after the cease-fire of 1994. A spirit of optimism pervaded the city, as English troops were sent home, streets in "sensitive" areas and strategic points along the Peace Line—a 15-ft wall built by the military in the mid-1970s to separate the Shankill (Protestant) and Falls Road (Catholic) communities—were opened, and citizens opened new businesses to meet the growing tourist industry. This optimism and the progress of the all-party talks on Northern Ireland's future were dealt a harsh blow by the bombings in London and Manchester. In July of 1996, Belfast was rocked by some of the worst violence in the history of the Troubles in the wake of the Protestant Orange Order being allowed to march through a staunchly Catholic neighborhood in Portadown, south of Belfast in County Armagh. The present city climate is much more stable. If you visit the city in the hope of witnessing an incident or seeing any of the scars of its troubled history, you will be disappointed. For the time you are there, you might not even see a soldier or a roadblock. The Shankill and Falls Road will probably strike you as tiny in comparison to the giants that the world media has transformed them into, but the bright, political murals on many of the walls and the atmosphere on those streets will remind you that a huge divide separates the community. To understand the extent of this divide will take more than a casual visit and a few mural photographs.

Despite all its troubles, Belfast is a cultured and cosmopolitan capital. Helping to reinforce this image is the city center's vast, pedestrianized shopping district and its handful of galleries, theaters, and museums. Like Edinburgh and Glasgow, Belfast has bolstered its reputation as "The City of the Arts" with an impressive list of events: the Belfast Music Festival (March), the Guinness Jazz & Blues Festival (mid-June), the Royal Ulster Arts Exhibition (August), the Belfast Folk Festival (early September), and the Belfast Arts & Drama Festival at Queen's (mid-November).

Considering the province's small size, the capital also makes a good base for exploring the Antrim Coast or County Derry, both of which are frequently served from Belfast by Northern Irish Railways and Ulsterbus. Even if you're short on time, Belfast is close enough to Dublin—2½ hours by train—to merit at least a day trip. This holds doubly true if your impression of the city has been gleaned from the world press. Although remnants of the grim, Orwellian reality of Belfast strike people in different ways, the bottom line is best summed up by a Northern Irish tourist brochure: "Despite what you've probably heard, Belfast is not what you expect."

If you plan to camp, pick up the "Guide to Caravan and Camping in Northern Ireland" (30p) or the "Caravan and Camping Guide" (£1.50). Both are available at Northern Ireland tourist offices.

BASICS

AMERICAN EXPRESS

This office offers currency exchange, helps with lost or stolen cards and checks, and cashes personal checks for AmEx cardholders only. The office does not hold mail. *108–112 Royal Ave., off North St., BT1 1DP, tel. 028/9024–2341 or 020/8667–1111 for 24-hr emergency info. Open weekdays 9–5:30.*

BUREAU DE CHANGE

Tons of banks litter Donegall Square and Donegall Place. The post office (*see below*) also provides currency exchange and has an ATM outside that accepts Visa, MasterCard, Cirrus, and Plus.

EMBASSY

The **United States Consulate** (Queen St., Belfast, tel. 028/9032–8239) is open weekdays 1–5.

HOSPITALS

To reach **Belfast City Hospital** (9 Lisburn Rd., tel. 028/9032–9241), follow Bradbury Place out of Shaftsbury Square, taking a right at the fork. To get to **Royal Victoria** Hospital (12 Grosvenor Rd., tel. 028/9024–0503), go west from Donegall Square on Howard Street until you come to Grosvenor Road.

LAUNDRY

The cheapest place to wash clothes is the launderette in **Queen's University Student Union Building** (University Rd., no phone). A load of wash costs £1, a spin in the dryer 20p. It's open Monday–Friday 9–9, Saturday 9:30–4, and Sunday 2–9.

MAIL

Belfast's General Post Office provides the usual array of services and has a bureau de change. *25 Castle Pl., BT1 1BB, tel. 028/9032–3740. Open weekdays 9–5:30, Saturday 9–7.*

VISITOR INFORMATION

The **Northern Irish Tourist Information Centre** stocks walking guides, maps, bus and train info, and extensive accommodations listings for the province. Particularly useful are its pocket-size lodging and restaurant guides (£3–£4). It also has a bureau de change and will book a room anywhere in the United Kingdom for £2.50. From July to August, it offers a toll-free information and reservation line open 7 PM–10 PM; dial 0800/404050. *59 North St., tel. 028/9024–6609. From Donegall Sq., walk north on Donegall Pl., turn right on North St. Open July–Aug., Mon.–Sat. 9–7, Sun. 10–4; Sept.–June, weekdays 9–5:15.*

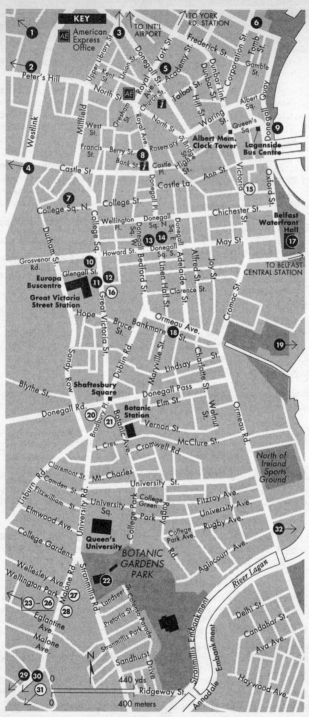

BELFAST

KEY

American Express Office

TO INT'L AIRPORT

TO YORK RD. STATION

Sights ●

Belfast Castle, 1
Belfast Waterfront Hall, 17
Belfast Zoo, 3
City Hall, 14
Cornmarket, 8
The Crown Liquor Saloon, 12
The Europa Hotel, 11
Falls District, 4
The Grand Opera House, 10
Linenhall Library, 13
Lagan Lookout & Visitors Centre, 9
Malone House, 29
Old Museum Arts Centre (OMAC), 7
Ormeau Baths Gallery, 18
Shankill District, 2
Sinclair Seamen's Presbyterian Church, 6
Sir Thomas & Lady Dixon Park, 30
St. Anne's Cathederal, 5
Stormont, 19
Ulster Folk and Transport Museum, 32
Ulster Museum, 22

Lodging ○

Belfast YHANI, 20
Botanic Lodge, 21
Eglantine Guest House, 24
Forte Postehouse, 31
The George Guest House, 26
Jurys Belfast Inn, 16
Lisdara Town House, 27
Liserin Guest House, 25
The Marine House, 23
McCauseland Hotel, 15
Pearl Court Guest House, 28

222

Bord Fáilte, the Irish Republic's national tourist office, has volumes of Republic-related information, from festival and transit schedules to maps, historical guides, and accommodations brochures. *53 Castle St., tel. 028/9032–7888. From Donegall Sq., walk north on Donegall Pl., turn left on College St. Open weekdays 9–5 (Mar.–Sept., also Sat. 9–12:30).*

COMING AND GOING

BY BUS

The very modern **Europa Bus Centre** (Glengall St., off Great Victoria St., tel. 028/9033–3000) provides service to Counties Tyrone, Fermanagh, Down, and all Irish Republic destinations. Buses depart from here to Omagh (10 per day; £6.00), Enniskillen (11 per day; £6.50), Derry (15 per day; £6.50), Newcastle (19 per day; £10.70), and Dublin (7 per day, 4 on Sun.; £10.50), among other destinations. The station has an info desk staffed weekdays 9–6 and Saturday 10–6. To reach Donegall Square and the city center, turn right out of the station, left on Great Victoria Street, and right on Howard Street—an easy 5- to 10-minute walk.

The new Laganside Bus Centre serves Antrim (i.e., the Causeway Coast and the Glens of Antrim), the area immediately surrounding Belfast, and parts of County Down. Six to eight buses per day travel to Portrush and Ballycastle (both £5.60) and Cushendall via Ballymena or Larne (£4.50). The station's info counter (tel. 028/9032–0011) is open Monday–Saturday 8:30–6. To get to Donegall Square, exit left on Albert Square, turn left on Victoria Street, and turn right on Chichester Street.

Belfast's location is striking: The city is nestled on the coast, buffered by green water on one side and by heath-covered hills on the other.

BY FERRY

Several companies sail directly from Belfast's Donegall Quay Terminal, on the north side of town near the York Street train station. **SeaCat** (tel. 0345/523523) runs daily ferries (5 per day in summer) to Stranraer, Scotland. Fares are £23–£26 (£16–£17 students). **Stena Line** (tel. 0990/707070 or 028/9061–5950) also offers daily ferry service (8 per day in summer) to Stranraer. Tickets cost £22–£26, and Stena Line offers a 50% discount to Eurail and BritRail pass holders. The **Isle of Man Steam Packet Co.** (tel. 028/9035–1009) offers service to the nearby Isle of Man; tickets are £25–£30. Ferries depart on Monday and Friday from mid-April to September. To reach Donegall Quay, take Bus 78 (£1.05) from Donegall Square or splurge on a cab (£2–£3.50). The terminal has no information line, so call the ferry companies directly or try the tourist office.

From Larne Harbour, 32 km (20 mi) north of Belfast, **P&O Ferries** (tel. 028/2827–4321) offers daily service to Cairnryan, Scotland. The 2½-hour crossing costs £21–£25 (students receive discounts of up to 50%). There is convenient rail service from Belfast Central to Larne Harbour's train depot (£2.90), adjacent to the Fleet Street Ferry Terminal.

BY PLANE

Belfast International Airport (Crumlin, tel. 028/9442–2888), 30 km (19 mi) northwest of town, offers service to a handful of international destinations—mainly Paris and Frankfurt. Airport shuttle buses (£3.70) leave Monday–Saturday every half hour (hourly on Sun.) from both the Europa Bus Centre and the airport, between 6 AM and 11:30 PM. Belfast City Airport (Syndenham, tel. 028/9045–7745), with U.K. flights only, is 6½ km (4 mi) outside town. To reach it, take Bus 21 (85p) from Donegall Square or a train (£1.50) from Central Station to Sydenham Halt, an easy 10-minute walk from the airport. For more information about airlines serving both airports, *see* Coming and Going, *above*.

BY TRAIN

Belfast has two main rail stations, Belfast Central and (ironically) the more central Great Victorian Street Station, as well as a handful of other depots convenient for intra-Belfast travel. Free red-and-white **Rail-Link** (tel. 028/9024–6485) shuttle buses travel between Belfast Central, the bus stations, Donegall Square, High Street, Oxford Street, Donegall Place, and the York Road depot. Outside each station—and along the streets—are shuttle stops marked RAIL-LINK; shuttles run every 10 minutes or so, Monday–Saturday only.

Northern Irish Railway's main depot, **Belfast Central** (E. Bridge St., tel. 028/9089–9400) is 1 km (½ mi) east of the city center; to get to Donegall Square take a Rail-Link shuttle, a city bus, or exit left on East

Bridge Street, turn right on Oxford Street, and turn left on May Street. Trains leave frequently for Dublin's Connolly (£15), Derry (£6.10), and Portrush (£5.15). If you're traveling to Scotland or England by ferry, a new rail link also provides direct service to Larne Harbour (17 per day; £3.10). Free train schedules are available at the ticket windows. The information counter is staffed Monday–Saturday 6:30 AM–11 PM, Sunday 9:15 AM–9:45 PM. With your purchase of train tickets, you also get free use of Centrelink buses, which connect all of the main areas of the city (see below).

Great Victoria Street Station (Great Victoria St., tel. 028/9043–4424) is adjacent to the Europa Bus Centre (see above) and conveniently located in the city center. All trains traveling to or from Belfast Central also stop here, except trains on the Belfast–Dublin line, which only stop at Belfast Centrál.

GETTING AROUND

Belfast's principal sights are grouped around Donegall Square, the city's official center. North of Donegall Square is Donegall Place, Belfast's minimall mecca, where the streets bristle with Victorian shop fronts and Georgian office blocks. Until 1997, Donegall Place and its tributaries—College Street, Castle Lane, Castle Place, and North Street—were off-limits to unauthorized vehicles and littered with RUC checkpoints and crowd barriers that helped ensure only peaceful pedestrians got through. With the recent improvement in political relations, many of these checkpoints have been removed, with a few appearing during the marching season or major football matches. From Donegall Square, walk south on Bedford Street (which becomes Dublin Road) to reach Shaftesbury Square and Queen's University (about a 10-minute walk), or take Bus 70 or 71. These areas are liberally sprinkled with pubs, cafés, and B&Bs.

BY BIKE

McConvey's (Pottinger's Entry, off High St., tel. 028/9033–0322) rents mountain bikes on the Raleigh Rent-A-Bike plan for £7 per day or £40 per week, with £30 deposit. **ReCycle Bike Hire** (1 Albert Sq., tel. 028/9031–3113) rents bikes for £11 a day on weekends, £9 a day on weekdays, or £30 for the week. A £50 or passport deposit is required. They will pick up bikes from hotels and B&Bs.

BY BUS

Belfast is well served by a variety of internal bus services. The **Citybus Network** (tel. 028/9024–6485) and **Ulsterbus** (tel. 028/9033–3000) deal mainly with the suburbs, where fares range from 70p to £1. Four-journey tickets cost £2.70 (senior citizens and kids £1.35), seven-day Gold Cards allow unlimited travel in the city (£10.50), and Silver Cards allow unlimited travel in either in either North, West, South, or East Belfast suburbs (£11). Tickets can be purchased at the kiosk in Donegall Square or at various points around the city. Centrelink buses (all green) connect all of the main areas of the city in a 12-stop loop that includes Donegall Square, Castlecourt Shopping Centre, and the Europa and Laganside bus stations. Tickets are 50p or free with rail tickets. **Nightline** (tel. 028/9033–3000) is handy if you have after-hours plans. Nightline buses cover five main routes fanning out from Shaftsbury Square to the main suburban sections of the city. Tickets must be purchased at the kiosk in Shaftsbury Square, which is open until 2 AM.

BY TAXI

Easily identifiable black cabs operate on set routes between the center and West and North Belfast for a standard 60p charge. In a nod to the differences within the population, cabs dealing with the mainly Catholic neighborhoods are marked with a Falls Road or Irish-language sign, while those going to Protestant neighborhoods will have a Shankill Road or red poppy sign. Both services are quick and equally efficient. The regular city-licensed cabs are identified by their yellow number plates and operate mostly around the city center. Unlike the cabs in many other large cities, whose drivers cruise relentlessly in search of fares, those in Belfast arrive more quickly when called to a specific destination. Try **City Cab** (tel. 028/9024–2000), **Diamond Taxi Service** (tel. 028/9064–6666), or **Jet Taxi** (tel. 028/9032–3728).

BY RENTAL CAR

Though the prices are prohibitive, you may want to splurge on a car rental. Rates run from around £40 to £45 per day, or around £200 per week. The main agencies are **McCauseland's** (Grovesnor Rd., tel. 028/9033–3777) and **Budget** (Great Victoria St., tel. 028/9032–0700).

BY TRAIN

The intercity train, used mainly by suburban commuters, leaves Belfast Central every 10–15 minutes on its way toward Botanic Station and the new Great Victoria Street Station, conveniently located near Donegall Square. Botanic Avenue is lined with some of Belfast's best pubs and restaurants, and if you turn right from the depot you'll quickly be funneled onto Shaftesbury Square.

WHERE TO SLEEP

BED-AND-BREAKFASTS

All of Belfast's best budget accommodations (including the hostels, YWCA, student residences, and B&Bs) are in the university neighborhood in South Belfast, generally considered the safest, most neutral section of the city. Most B&Bs are found on Eglantine Avenue and Wellington Park, off Lisburn and Malone roads. On Eglantine Avenue, you'll find five similarly priced B&Bs. The **Marine House** (30 Eglantine Ave., tel. 028/9066–2828) provides large, fluffy beds and enormous fried breakfasts; singles are £19, doubles £40 (£42 with bath). Across the street are **Eglantine Guest House** (21 Eglantine Ave., tel. 028/9066–7585), with singles for £20, doubles for £36, and triples for £51, and **Liserin Guest House** (17 Eglantine Ave., tel. 028/9066–0769), with lovely, clean rooms for £20 a single, £38 a double, and £57 a triple. The **George Guest House** (9 Eglantine Ave., tel. 028/9068–3212) has spacious single rooms for £20 and doubles for £38. **Pearl Court Guest House** (11 Malone Rd., tel. 028/9066–6145) is a cut above the rest, with a smart, plush lounge and breakfast room, and rooms for £23–£25. If being close to all the city-center action is important, try the **Botanic Lodge** (87 Botanic Ave., tel. 028/9032–7682), a tidy and compact B&B just a short walk from all the sights and distractions of the city. Singles are £22, doubles £40.

SMALL HOTELS

Forte Posthouse. This member of the large U.K. hotel chain is on 14 acres of woodland and gardens, 8 km (5 mi) south of Belfast. The rooms are en-suite. Also part of the hotel are Traders Restaurant and Thackeray's Bar. B&B rates range from £25 to £62 and include many different weekend and off-peak specials; call for details. *300 Kingsway, Dunmurry, Belfast BT17 9ES, tel. 028/9061–2101. 82 rooms.*

Jurys Belfast Inn. This large modern structure delivers the same high-quality facilities as its sister hotels in the Republic; every room has direct-dial phone, TV, radio, and tea/coffeemaker. Rooms can accommodate three adults or two adults and two kids and cost £65 a night. *Fisherwick Pl., Great Victoria St., Belfast BT2 7AP, tel. 028/9053–3500. 67 rooms.*

Lisdara Town House. In a converted town house situated on a tree-lined avenue in the university area of south Belfast, the Lisdara is a relic of past architectural grandeur. The bedrooms are large (one even has a four-poster bed), and the house is surrounded by mature gardens and private off-street parking. The B&B rates are £27.50–£32.50 per person. *23 Derryvolgie Ave., Malone Rd., Belfast BT9 6FN, tel. 028/9068–1549.*

McCauseland Hotel. Ads boast that this hotel is "an oasis of quiet elegance in the center of Belfast," and the place lives up to its claim. With a classical Italianate facade covering a tastefully converted contemporary interior, the McCauseland prides itself on state-of-the-art modernity with an old-fashioned warm welcome. Rates run £50 and upward per person. *34–38 Victoria St., Belfast BT1 3GH, tel. 028/9022–0200. 80 rooms.*

HOSTELS

Belfast YHANI. This large, institutional complex has dorm beds for £9 and singles for £15. Unfortunately there's no kitchen, but the hostel cafeteria, which doubles as a common room, serves reasonably priced meals. They also give out maps and sell discount train tickets to Dublin. *22–32 Donegall Rd., tel. 028/9031–5435. From Donegall Sq., walk south on Bedford St., turn right on Donegall Rd. 124 beds. Laundry.*

FOOD

Belfast's city center is littered with chippies, fast-food chains, and a number of pubs, as well as a few pricey hotel restaurants. A better option is to head for the Golden Mile, a triangular area famed for its variety of restaurants. The Golden Mile is bounded by Howard Street, Great Victoria Street, and Dublin

THE ABCS OF NORTHERN IRISH GROUPS

INLA: The Irish National Liberation Army, a splinter group of the IRA. IRA–INLA infighting was responsible for numerous murders in the 1980s.

IRA: The Irish Republican Army, an illegal paramilitary outfit whose ultimate goal is the reunification of Northern Ireland with the Republic. Staunchly anti-Brit. Responsible for hundreds of murders and bombings, including the 1996 bombs in Manchester and London's Canary Wharf.

IRISH REGIMENT: Formerly known as the Ulster Defense Regiment, this army unit—drawn from the local Protestant population—is responsible for keeping the peace in Northern Ireland. Set up by the British Crown when a group of paratroopers were accused of killing 13 unarmed Catholic civilians in the 1972 Bloody Sunday massacre in Derry.

LOYALIST: Anyone pro-British in outlook, generally also Protestant.

ORANGEMEN: A legal Loyalist group, named after the Protestant William of Orange, conqueror of the Catholic James II at the Battle of the Boyne in 1690.

REPUBLICAN: Anyone who supports Northern Ireland's union with the Dublin-based Republic, or, more specifically, a supporter of Sinn Féin.

RUC: Royal Ulster Constabulary, general name for the Northern Irish police force.

SINN FÉIN: Republican political party. Commonly assumed to be the IRA's political wing.

THE TROUBLES: Generic term for Northern Ireland's current Catholic-Protestant turmoil.

UFF: Ulster Freedom Fighters, an illegal Loyalist group often linked to the larger UDA (Ulster Defense Association). When the UDA was legal, the UFF was the group named responsible for the hundreds of sectarian murders commonly assumed to have been committed by the UDA.

ULSTER: Historic name of the northern province of Ireland. Used today to denote the six counties still governed by Britain.

UVF: Ulster Volunteer Force, another illegal pro-Brit paramilitary group.

Road (which becomes Bedford Street). If nothing here strikes your fancy, continue south from Shaftesbury Square down either Botanic Avenue or Bradbury Place (which turns into University Road), two student quarters peppered with good restaurants and cafés. Nearby Lisburn Road has a variety of ethnic eateries. For fresh produce, a small farmer's market is held daily on Castle Street near the Bord Fáilte office.

CITY CENTER

UNDER £5 • Bewley's. This link in the chain of Dublin-based coffeehouses is a sound stop for a fix of java and sticky buns or decent doorstop (big and overstuffed) sandwiches. There are also daily specials, usually along the lines of lasagna, salads, chicken potpie, and Irish stew, all priced in the £4–£6 range. Other draws are the replica of the famous Japanese tearoom and the good old-fashioned service. *Rosemary St., tel. 028/9023–2568.*

Café Deauville. You'll recognize this place by its arresting mosaic exterior. Open Monday–Saturday 8–4:30, this is a handy spot for inexpensive breakfasts and lunches. The menu includes good seafood (the prawn pancake is excellent), as well as the usual chicken and pasta dishes. *58 Wellington Pl., tel. 028/9032–6601.*

Roscoff Bakery & Café. Sophisticated fast food is served at this affordable offshoot of the decidedly upmarket and award-winning restaurant of the same name (*see below*). Superior sandwiches are made with the to-die-for breads baked on the premises and are well matched with tasty soups. It's a wonderful place to assemble a picnic for the park. *27 Fountain St., tel. 028/9031–5090.*

White's Tavern. Established in 1630, White's lays claim to being the oldest pub in Belfast. Dark oak wood, wrought-iron fixtures, and stained glass form the basic fabric of this venerable establishment. Along with the inevitable tourist crowd, there's always a strong representation of true Belfast types drinking at the bar. Try the chicken-and-corn crepes (£3) or roast pork with chips (£4.50*). High St., off Castle Pl., tel. 028/9024–3080.*

UNDER £10 • Deer's Head. Another good spot for pub fare, the Deer's Head has the unusual distinction of offering some vegetarian options, such as a veggie stir-fry and veggie burgers (both £4). The rest of the menu is heavy on pasta, chicken, and salmon dishes. Try the excellent chocolate cake or strawberry cheesecake for dessert. You can get dinner for two (not including drinks) for £20–£25. *76 North St., tel. 028/9023–9163.*

UNDER £20 • Kelly's Cellars. The home-style pub grub is the draw here, and it's been drawing guests since 1720. Hearty daily specials run the gamut from lamb and beef joints to salmon, cod, and prawn dishes. Entrées are £8–£10, starters around £4. You can also hear blues bands here on Saturday nights. *30 Bank St., off Donegall Pl., tel. 028/9032–4835.*

Nick's Warehouse. The city center's most famous restaurant is on a narrow cobbled street near the docks area. It's really two restaurants in one, a wine bar downstairs and a restaurant upstairs. The place looks frighteningly posh and has prices to match; a full meal upstairs runs upward of £12, and closer to £20 with drinks. Potato-herb soup and smoked haddock-and-salmon pasta are two of the many first-rate items on the menu. If you want to dine upstairs, make reservations. *35 Hill St., off Warring St., tel. 0232/439690. Closed Sun. No dinner Mon.*

Roscoff Restaurant. Run by chef Paul Rankin, who has spun off a TV show and many recipe books from his enterprise, this is one of only three restaurants in Ireland with the prized Michelin star (the other two are in Dublin). The set lunch is an extremely good value at £14.50. Dinner can easily cost £45 per person without wine, but if you're up for a splurge, you'll be treated to excellent service, unique food, and a romantic atmosphere. *7 Lesley House, Shaftsbury Sq., tel. 028/9033–1532.*

THE GOLDEN MILE

UNDER £5 • Cafe Booth. Don't be put off by this restaurant's location in the same building as the Salvation Army. Seriously generous portions of such home-cooked dishes as vegetable soup (£1.50), roast chicken (£3.50), and roast beef (£3.75) make it worth a stop. Painted in a bright yellow, the premises are clean and bright and make a particularly pleasing lunch stop. *40 Dublin Rd., tel. 028/9031–0854.*

Crown Liquor Saloon. A Golden Mile landmark, this Victorian-era pub is famous for its carved-oak ceiling and cozy, private snugs. A common call here is "Pint of Guinness, bowl of stew, please," but also try the beef-and-Cafferty's pie (£4) or the steak, pea, and chip plate (£3.50). *46 Great Victoria St., tel. 028/9024–9476.*

Ho Ho Chinese Restaurant and Takeaway. The huge selection of entrées here are tasty and affordable, and most are about £4. It's open until midnight most nights, so keep it in mind for late-night munchies. *71 Dublin Rd., tel. 028/9023–7811.*

Spuds. As the name implies, this establishment is devoted to making magical concoctions with that most enduring staple of the Irish diet, the potato. Huge spuds filled with your choice of toppings (£2.50) make for a warm glow from the lower depths. *23 Bradbury Pl., tel. 028/9033–1541.*

UNDER £10 • Harvey's. Pizzas (£5), chili (£2.55), and vegetarian dishes (£5.35) are the hits at this popular restaurant. They also serve some Tex-Mex dishes, including tacos and enchiladas, for £4–£7. The decor is of the cheap and cheerful kind, a mixture of wood, stone tiles, and pine tables. *95 Great Victoria St., tel. 028/9023–3433.*

Pizza Express. It might be just another eatery in a large chain, but that didn't stop Pizza Express from introducing a bit of Hollywood magic with a sweeping staircase and movie star memorabilia plastered around the place. Excellent pizzas from £5 make it a good stop on a tour of the pubs. *25 Bedford Rd., tel. 028/9032–9050.*

UNDER £15 • La Belle Epoque. If you don't mind spending £12–£15 on a meal, head to this relaxed, intimate, and charmingly French spot. Fresh seafood and meat dominate the menu in dishes such as smoked salmon stuffed with fish mousse in a horseradish sauce and fillet of beef with seed mustard cream sauce. The wine list is extensive. For a less expensive meal, go for lunch; three courses are just £7. If you're going for dinner, be sure to make reservations. *61 Dublin Rd., tel. 028/9032–3244. Closed Sun.*

UNIVERSITY AREA

UNDER £5 • Bishops. Exceptional fish-and-chips for £3 have made this the most famous chippy around. Residents of Belfast share Dubliners' near-religious veneration of the simple bag of chipped potatoes. This is a no-frills place where most opt for take-away meals to be eaten on one of the benches nearby. *34 Bradbury Pl., tel. 028/9031–1827.*

Bookfinders. The ultra-laid-back atmosphere, mellow music, and good food here are the reasons for a steady clientele that extends beyond the student crowd. A selection of soups and sandwiches ranges from £1.50 to £3.00; quiches, pastas, and chicken dishes are around £3.50. *47 University Rd., tel. 028/9032–869.*

Eatwell Health Food Delicatessen. This is a great place to build a picnic, with take-out foods like vegetarian spring rolls (60p) and pita sandwiches (£1.20–£1.60). *413 Lisburn Rd., tel. 028/9066–4362.*

Empire. This lively pub offers deals like a burger and chips or a 10-inch pizza for £2, and the ever-popular pizza-and-pint special for £4. The building, more than 100 years old, was once a church but has been revamped to resemble a Victorian-style music hall. Performers are invited to ply their trade, be it musical or comedy, on designated nights of the week. *42 Botanic Ave., tel. 028/9032–8110.*

UNDER £10 • The Attic Restaurant. Hearty portions of stews, quiches, and overfilled sandwiches make sure this small place is always crammed with a mix of office workers and students. Bright table cloths and large windows make for a cheerful atmosphere. *54 Stranmills Rd., tel. 028/9066–1074.*

Café Clementine. Cheap Continental dishes—pasta, pizza, quiches—and good weekend jazz sessions attract a crowd to this restaurant. The place is always buzzing with university students and a host of passing visitors. *245 Lisburn Rd., tel. 028/9061–1292.*

Jharna Tandoori. Spicy Indian cuisine, including tandoori chicken and beef dishes, fills the menu here, with entrées in the £7–£9.50 range. Indian wood carvings and wall hangings decorate the dining room. *133 Lisburn Rd., tel. 028/9038–1299.*

UNDER £20 • Saints and Scholars. At the upper end of the university-area scale, this is the sort of place students bring their visiting parents. The downstairs "library" has bookshelves on the walls, but the lively, noisy, and cheerful ambience could hardly be less studious. Upstairs are two calmer, more comfortable dining rooms. Choose from the large appetizer menu (£2.50–£5)—Alsace onion flan is particularly good—then move on to main courses (£8–£10), such as the hearty cassoulet and wok-roasted monkfish. Reservations are a must. *3 University Sq., just off University St., tel. 028/9032–5137.*

WORTH SEEING

The Northern Irish Tourist Information Centre (*see above*) stocks free "Belfast Civic Trail" brochures, which provide a series of five highly detailed, self-guided walking tours. Each covers roughly 2 km (1 mi) of the city center and takes about an hour to complete—strongly recommended for those with an eye for history. If you have a love of walking and drinking, check out the guided **Belfast Pub Walking Tours** (tel. 028/9065–8337), which depart from the Northern Irish Tourist Information Centre every Saturday at 2 PM. The cost is £5—not including drinks. **Citybus** (tel. 028/9045–8484) offers a 3½-hour "Belfast City Tour," which takes in Belfast Lough, the docks (where the *Titanic* was built), various parliament buildings, and the Belfast Zoo. The tour costs £8, £7 for students, including tea and scones, and runs from June to August; call Citybus for current schedules and details on other tours to North Down and East Antrim. For a no-frills excursion, consider a Black Cab Tour, in which one of the large, distinctive taxis ferries small numbers of people to the sights and sounds of the city that the big buses can't reach. Any hotel or B&B will be happy to put you in touch with their favorite driver, and the local commentary on these tours alone is worth the price of admission. At a cost of £5 per person in a six-person cab, it's a cheap treat well worth trying. Literary fans might consider doing the **C. S. Lewis Trail** (tel. 028/9067–2351), which traces the links to the famous Belfast-born writer. The guided tour is offered on the first Saturday of May, June, and September, and the first and third Saturday of July and August. The group departs at 10 AM from St. Mark's Church on Hollywood Road.

BELFAST ZOO

This place is fairly standard as far as zoos go. Its biggest draw isn't its collection of animals—though the underwater viewing room that looks out at sea lions, penguins, and seals is pretty cool—but rather its location: high above the city in a vast mountainside park, which is free and always open. Climb up nearby Cave Hill for an unbeatable view of Belfast Lough and the city center. **Belfast Castle** (tel. 028/9077–6925), on the wooded slopes adjacent to the zoo, is now an upscale restaurant open Monday–Saturday 9:30 AM–11:30 PM. *Antrim Rd., 6 mi north of city center, tel. 028/9077–6277. From Donegall Sq. W, take Bus 5, 10, or 45. Admission £4.50 in summer, £3.50 rest of yr. Open Apr.–Sept., daily 10–5; Oct.–Mar., Sun.–Thurs. 10–3:30, Fri. 10–2:30.*

BOTANIC GARDENS

Popular with students and families on the weekends, the Botanic Gardens is a well-kept city park with plenty of grass, trees, and wrought-iron benches. In the park is the Palm House, a cast-iron and glass house built in 1839 by the Marquis of Donegall, with tropical palms and flowers in the humid east wing and colorful blossoms in the west wing. The nearby Tropical Ravine houses jungle plants. Farther into the park, near Queen's University's Physical Education building, is the sweet-smelling rose garden, with rows of blooming bushes. *Stranmills Rd., just past Queen's University. Admission free. From Donegall Sq. E, take Bus 69 or 71. Gardens open daily until sunset. Palm House and Tropical Ravine open weekdays 10–noon and 1–4, weekends 1–4 (Apr.–Sept., daily until 5).*

CITY HALL

Belfast's city center is dominated by its Renaissance-style City Hall, built between 1898 and 1906. Its most impressive feature is the 173-ft Great Dome, which dominates Donegall Square and the city center. Inside, look for the oak-and-marble Grand Stairway and, off the second-floor landing, the Council Chamber, Banquet Hall, and Great Hall. The Great Hall was destroyed by German bombers during World War II and has since been meticulously restored. Of interest in the Council Chamber are the ornate chairs used by King George V and Queen Mary at the opening of Northern Ireland's first parliament on June 22, 1921. Portraits of previous Lord Mayors gaze imperiously down from the corniced walls, and brass, marble, and gilt gleam forth from all corners of the three elaborate reception rooms. Right in front of the main entrance, a massive statue of Queen Victoria gazes down upon visitors, while at her feet figurines representing the industries of shipbuilding and linen weaving curl in obedience. Another statue, commemorating the ill-fated *Titanic*, stands in the eastern side of the garden, and, possibly due to the popularity of the recent Oscar-winning film, has become something of a shrine. In another corner of the garden, a tall, gray, stone column commemorates the 1942 arrival of the U.S. Expeditionary Force to defend the North from the designs of Adolf Hitler. It was re-dedicated in 1996, during President Clinton's visit. Be sure to catch the 30-minute guided tour of City Hall, given weekdays at 10:30 AM and 2:30 PM mid-June–September, and Wednesday at 10:30 October–mid-April. *Donegall Sq., tel. 028/9032–0202, ext. 2346. Admission free.*

FALLS AND SHANKILL DISTRICTS

Belfast is littered with grim reminders of the Troubles. West Belfast is where the majority of violence occurred, specifically in Shankill, a Protestant enclave, and Falls Road, Shankill's Catholic counterpart. Though these neighborhoods used to be patrolled 24 hours a day by the RUC and UDR—impartial

TALKING ABOUT IT

In all of Ireland, Belfast included, the best information and folklore is always revealed through conversation with locals. While the city carries some deep-felt hatreds that will only soften as new generations learn to live together peacefully, under the right circumstances, most people are quite willing to talk to strangers about the recent history. Okay, sure, it's probably a bad idea to get into a deep political discussion after four hours in the pub and several pints of beer, but after decades of their home being a no-go zone, the population is keen to dispel the dangerous image. They do this the way they know best, by extending a warm hand to strangers. It also helps, it must be said, to play a little dumb about facts and events, as the residents seem to be even more willing to explain the history to visitors with no preconceived notions of how things should be. Take any questions of politics gently at first, smell the air of the company you're in, then play the gee-this-is-all-new-to-me card, and things should roll along fine. Whatever the other differences between North and South, they do both share one distinct quality—a love of words and their usage. Just flow with it and you'll be fine.

A highlight of any tour is Milltown Cemetery, the IRA's principal burial ground. Interspersed among the tombstones and makeshift memorials is a vast collection of pro-Republican murals. Along with the standard "We Will Never Surrender" and "Our Day Will Come" slogans, also note the IRA and Native American mural (a reference to the worldwide struggle against imperialism) and the faded handful of memorials depicting black-masked gunmen squashing the British Crown. Another hot spot for murals, this time pro-Brit, is along Donegall and Crumlin roads. Popular cries here range from "One People, One Country, One Crown" and "Ulster Welcomes the UDR" to the more inflammatory "God Bless the UVF." Other murals can be found on back streets and tenement walls just off Falls and Shankill roads, but many are being voluntarily whitewashed to help heal old wounds.

forces in theory, more supportive of the Protestant (and illegal) UVF in practice—unescorted forays are reasonably safe. Though it's unlikely you'll be affected by religious unrest in either neighborhood, they're not the nicest of 'hoods and petty crime is a possibility. Previously, the only way to explore these areas was on a taxi tour, unofficially restricted to the Catholic or Protestant district depending upon the religion of the driver. It's still not a bad way to learn about the areas; cabdrivers line up along Castle Street (west of Donegall Place), and most are well versed in the area's history (it's a simple fact of life that most will know someone who has died as a result of partisan violence). Fares for these informal tours vary from £6 to £15, depending on the driver's interest and your ability to barter. Citybus (tel. 028/9045–8484) also offers a comprehensive "Living History Tour" (£7), which offers an in-depth look at Belfast's history and includes most Troubles-related sites. Highlights include Fort Jericho (the most-bombed and shot-at building in Northern Ireland), the murals throughout the city, and, strangely enough, tea and scones at the Europa Bus Station halfway through. Tours depart from the General Post Office (*see* Basics, *above*) June–August, Tuesday, Thursday, and Sunday at 9:30 and 2.

THE MURALS

In the same way that Hanoi, Beirut, and possibly Sarajevo have engendered a unique type of post-conflict tourism, Belfast retains many reminders of its recent strife-torn past that prove a potent magnet for adventurous visitors. Even with the tide of commercial regeneration that began in earnest in 1997, there are still many bombed and derelict buildings, no-go peace lines, and acres of barbed wire. The large murals painted on the gable ends of many buildings in the Falls and Shankill districts have given rise to a whole sort of terrorist-tourism. These are generally safe places to go as long as you employ an appropriate guide, which will usually involve getting separate guides for the Catholic and Protestant areas. You should avoid unnecessary nighttime excursions and visits during the still-sensitive "Marching Season" of the 12th of July week.

Perhaps because of its younger population, the Falls Road area seems to have more outdoor graphic artists. You'll see murals everywhere, including those on the Divis Tower (nicknamed Little Beirut by the locals), on Divis Street, and on the Sinn Féin office, in a well-protected wire cage on the same street. Chief among the painted scenes are huge portraits of Bobby Sands, the Republican prisoner who died on hunger strike in the early 1980s. One particular mural on the corner of the Falls Road depicts the 10 hunger strikers who died with the words of Sands written boldly: "Our revenge will be the laughter of our children." Other pro-Republican murals seen in this area include stark black-and-white scenes of starving Irish people during the famine, ancient *Book of Kells*–type hieroglyphics, and colorful scenes of IRA freedom fighters in green battle dress, standing over the oft-used phrase "Tiocfaidh ar la," or "Our day will come." Other symbols with a Republican bias are green ribbons, usually accompanied by a "free the prisoners" statement; "Saoirshe," freedom, in Irish; green, white, and orange, the colors of the Republic's flag (usually painted on corners and lampposts to mark Republican territory); and the Phoenix, symbolizing a united Ireland breaking free of the shackles of English rule.

In the Shankill district, most of the pro-Protestant murals are found in the area encompassing Shankill Road, Crumlin Road, Sandy Row, and the Shankill Estate. Though this inner-city area shows many more signs of dereliction and migration than the flourishing Falls, there are still a good number of murals remaining. One, on Carnmore Street, depicts the Apprentice Boys shutting the gates of Derry in 1688, as the Catholic invaders under King James try to gain access. Other murals include the Red Hand of Ulster, a symbol found on the Ulster crest and used by extreme Protestants to emphasize their historical connection to English Rule; William of Orange, shown sitting on his white stallion, rallying his troops to the Battle of the Boyne, where he defeated King James in 1690; King Billy, another icon of Protestant defiance; and the red, white, and blue colors, used like the Republic's tricolor to mark the extent of Protestant areas.

LINENHALL LIBRARY

Belfast's oldest library was founded in 1788 by Wolfe Tone, legendary Irish revolutionary leader and staunch advocate for the freedom of speech. Since then, the staff has diligently collected virtually every scrap of Troubles-related propaganda and political commentary, no matter how inflammatory. This small but extremely intriguing library contains original underground newspapers, minuscule IRA messages smuggled into and out of prison (via various baked goods), threatening UFF calendars sent to Catholic "targets" as a vivid reminder that their days were numbered, and trinkets and posters crammed into every nook. As this is a place of research, access to the library is limited; call in the morning to try to arrange an afternoon viewing. *Donegall Sq. N, across from City Hall, tel. 028/9032–1707. Open by appointment only weekdays 9:30–5.*

SINCLAIR SEAMEN'S PRESBYTERIAN CHURCH

Somewhat off the beaten track beside a highway overpass lies this little gem of a church. The exterior is nothing special, but inside it's littered with objects from old ships, each with a story of its own to tell. The organ has port, starboard, and mast lights from an old Guinness boat that used to work the River Liffey in Dublin. There's a bell from HMS *Hood,* sunk to protect Portsmouth Harbour during the second World War. The bell is struck six times for the 7 PM service, just as it would be on a ship to call the watch. There is also an old brass wheel that faces the congregation and a brass binnacle (compass) that was used as a baptismal font, both of which were salvaged from a ship built in Detroit that sunk off the Northern Irish coast. The church was first set up in 1832 by an organization known as the Seamen's Friend Society, whose object was the religious improvement of seamen frequenting the port of Belfast. In those days Belfast was flourishing as a shipping port, and the church apparently proved very successful. It is normally open only Wednesday 2–5 PM, but if you give Ailsa Campbell a ring, she'll be happy to open it up for you, and if you're lucky, you'll be offered tea and scones and be given a personal tour of every fascinating object. *Corporation Sq., tel. 028/9071–5997. Head north up Victoria St.–Dunbar Link and then right up Corporation St. Admission free.*

CORNMARKET

This convenient and historic shopping district is just to the north of the city center, between Castle Street and Royal Avenue. Named for one of the commodities once traded there, the Cornmarket has been a retail market since the earliest days of the city, a fact best illustrated by the remains of the original 17th-century walls. Although the market is now taken up by modern shops, there are occasionally crafts or food stalls open on weekends. With many of the older buildings disappearing in the recent push for progress, the core of old Belfast can still be found by strolling down the small alleyways, or entries, that join the main thoroughfares in a crisscross pattern. The entries were once the thriving hub of commerce in the area, but they suffered badly in the bombing of World War II; now they contain a few pubs and provide linking walkways onto the Cornmarket. One of Belfast's oldest public buildings, the Old Stock Exchange, whose facade was designed by Charles Lanyon in 1845, sits on the corner of Waring Street, while close by the First Presbyterian Church of Belfast, the city's oldest church, is on Rosemary Street.

BELFAST CATHEDRAL

At the northern end of the Cornmarket is Belfast Cathedral, originally St. Anne's Church. In a gesture of civility that could only belong to a bygone age, the construction of the cathedral, which began in 1899, was carried out around the smaller church already on the site. This was to ensure that services would not be disrupted. Then, when the cathedral was completed, the smaller church was removed brick by brick from inside. There are 10 interior pillars in the cathedral meant to depict the 10 main professions that made Belfast great: Science, Industry, Healing, Agriculture, Music, Theology, Shipbuilding, Freemasonary, Art, and, believe it or not, Womanhood. A mosaic above the Chapel of the Holy Spirit depicts St. Patrick arriving in County Down to bring Christianity to Ireland. *Donegall St., tel. 028/9032–8332. Open daily 9–6.*

BELFAST WATERFRONT HALL

This pristine, new conference and concert center was completed in January 1997 and, with the peace dividend increasing, serves as a testament to a new era. In an architectural and aesthetic sense, it inspires hope in the future of Belfast. It's worth a visit just to look at its ornate exterior and walk around its vast interior. It has been compared to a very modern version of London's Albert Hall. Stars like Kiri Te Kanawa, James Galway, and Elton John have taken the stage underneath the awesome circular roof of the 2,235-seat auditorium. There's also the 400-seat BT Studio, where dance troupes and local theatrical companies often perform to a local audience before heading out on tour. Outside the front door, you can stroll along the River Lagan and enjoy a cup of coffee at the Terrace Café. *Oxford St., tel. 028/9033–4400.*

MALONE HOUSE

Malone House, 6½ km (4 mi) south of the city center, was built in the late 19th century to house Northern Ireland's growing national art collection and to serve as a high-class reception hall for visiting dignitaries. Although its prestigious art holdings have since been redistributed within the United Kingdom, it does contain a few historical portraits—mostly of long-forgotten dukes and earls—as well as a permanent exhibition on Belfast's city parks. More inspiring are the lush grounds, considered the best example of Victorian horticulture in the province. *Barnett Park, Upper Malone Rd., tel. 028/9068–1246. From Donegall Sq. W, take Bus 71 or 72. Admission free. Open Mon.–Sat. 9:30–6. Park open 24 hrs.*

OLD MUSEUM ARTS CENTRE

This excellent center has helped put Belfast on the world art map. Although it doesn't have a permanent collection, the OMAC, as it's known, is committed to the best in modern art and performance, both Irish and international. Events range from classical drama to controversial sculpture and photography installations. Shows generally change on a weekly basis, so call for current schedules. Admission varies with each event. *7 College Sq. N, tel. 028/9023–5053. From Donegall Sq. N, walk west to College Sq., turn right, then left on College Sq. N. Open Mon.–Sat. 10–5:30.*

ORMEAU BATHS GALLERY

Owned and operated by the city, this informal gallery hosts exhibitions of modern Irish and international art and strives to present innovative and contemporary installations. Recent exhibitions have included the more prominent of contemporary and traditional Irish artists, including Jack B. Yeats and William Orpen. *18A Ormeau Ave., tel. 028/9032–1402. Admission free. Open Tues.–Sat. 10–6.*

QUEEN'S UNIVERSITY

Dominating University Road is Queen's University itself. Most impressive is the Lanyon building, built in 1849, and the eye-catching, early Victorian University Square that surrounds it. The university was originally established as a college in 1845 by Queen Victoria, and it achieved full university status in 1908. Today, roughly 9,000 students, most from Northern Ireland, attend school here. The university's most recent claim to fame is alumnus Seamus Heaney, 1995 Nobel Prize winner for Literature. Inside the Lanyon Building is a visitor center (tel. 028/9033–5252) that can give you loads of info on the university. Free public lectures—more often than not dealing with some aspect of Northern Irish politics—are often given in summer by staff and visiting professors. *University Rd., south of Shaftesbury Sq., tel. 028/9024–5133.*

ULSTER MUSEUM

Belfast's biggest and most comprehensive museum, the Ulster Museum is definitely worth a few hours of your time. Located in the Botanic Gardens (*see above*) opposite Queen's University, it is a massive four-level complex with a host of permanent and temporary exhibits on subjects including Ulster history since the 1600s, a history of the post office in Ireland, Irish archaeology, local flora and fauna, and much, much more. Especially noteworthy are David West's "Venice Chair," the incredible Miervaldis Polis's "Self Portrait," the biggest ant farm you've ever seen, and a collection of artifacts pilfered from Egypt and the Middle East during England's imperial tenure. The top floor is dedicated to a rather small collection of Irish art and 20th-century painting and sculpture. If you're in Belfast for a while, you may want to tackle the museum in smaller doses and make several trips here, especially since the admission is free. *Botanic Gardens, tel. 028/9038–3000. Admission free. Open weekdays 10–5, Sat. 1–5, Sun. 2–5.*

THE GRAND OPERA HOUSE

Located on the Great Victoria Street strip known as "the Golden Mile," the Grand Opera House takes a place of pride among the monuments of the city's cultural heritage. Bombed on a number of occasions by the IRA and rebuilt at greater cost each time, it stands as an indomitable amalgam of stucco walls, corniced ceilings, and old-fashioned grandeur, as one of Belfast's crown jewels. This is a venue for musicals, dramas, and operas from major touring companies, as well as many high-profile Irish productions; and to spend an evening at the Grand Opera is indeed to experience theater in the grand fashion of generations past. Tours can be arranged by contacting the management. *Great Victoria St., tel. 028/9024–0411, 028/9024–1919 for tickets.*

THE EUROPA HOTEL

With the infamous tag of being "the city's most bombed hotel," the ultrasmart Europa Hotel survived its almost annual structural attacks by the IRA to enjoy a more commercial and peaceful future. It was also the site of many of the early peace talks between the warring factions in the province. Today, there's not much to see that's any different from any other modern hotel, but the accommodating doormen and bartenders are a great source of stories about the bad old days. *Great Victoria St. at Glengall St., tel. 028/9032–7000.*

THE CROWN LIQUOR SALOON

Directly opposite the Europa Hotel on Great Victoria Street is the Crown Liquor Saloon, a must-do stop at any time of the day. The place positively oozes history, with carved wood, stained glass, and gas lighting that date to the late 19th century. It's now owned by the National Trust, the United Kingdom's official conservation organization, and is kept immaculately. Try to get into one the snugs—quiet booths that provide privacy and convenience, with a direct hatch onto the bar. *46 Great Victoria St., tel. 028/9024–9476. Open daily 11:30 AM–midnight.*

THE LAGAN LOOKOUT & VISITORS CENTRE

The center tells the story of the important role of the River Lagan in the development of Belfast, via models, stories, and songs. Interactive displays and videos let you see the construction of the weir and the

VAN THE MAN

Another of the many areas in which North and South remain in complete agreement is that of appreciation for the music of Van Morrison. Belfast-born, "Van the Man," as he is universally known, has remained an enduring and groundbreaking purveyor of Celtic fusion, even in the present age of the 10-minute Rock Star. He began his career in Belfast in the 1960s with the short-lived group Them, and even in those early days he produced songs like "Gloria" and "Here Comes the Night," both of which still receive regular airtime. Having flirted with alternative lifestyles in the late 1960s—Woodstock, the Age of Aquarius, etc.—in one week in 1969 he laid down the tracks of his ultimate career marker, "Astral Weeks." The album launched Van Morrison onto the world stage that he still commands 30 years later. He's spent many years living in California, but his roots in the North are never far away. This is evident in the songs "Cypress Avenue" and "Madam George" on "Astral Weeks," in which he takes musical wanders through the city of his childhood. On his 1989, '90, and '91 albums, "Avalon Sunset," "Enlightenment," and "Hymns to the Silence," he trawls his adolescent days of the early 1950s, "the days before rock 'n' roll." His track "Coney Island" is a musical road map, with references to Downpatrick, Strangford Lough, Killyleagh, Ardglass, and Coney Island itself—"wouldn't it be great to be back there again." He also uses photographs of his native province on many of his album covers. Never the most media-friendly person, Van Morrison has been called irascible, stubborn, uncooperative, and a whole lot worse. In the end, he lets his music do the talking, in an eloquent way that sound bites could never match.

regeneration of the city and the surrounding areas. *Donegall Quay, tel. 028/9031–5444. Admission £1.50. Open weekdays 11–5, Sat. noon–5, Sun. 2–5.*

SIR THOMAS & LADY DIXON PARK

It's just a few miles south of the city (take Bus 70 from Donegall Square), but the serenity of Sir Thomas & Lady Dixon Park makes you feel much farther away. The gardens are crisscrossed by nature trails and streams, dotted with old monuments, and filled with plants from around the globe. Perhaps the most dazzling horticultural specimens are the collection of more than 20,000 rosebushes; one rare variety, China stud roses, were imported in the early 1800s and provided the foundation for today's British roses. The City of Belfast Rose Trials are held here during the first two weeks of July. Initially conceived in 1836, the gardens have grown over the decades in a carefully designed pattern in which wild gullies and manicured parterres reside happily side by side. A few miles north of the gardens, and a nice stroll along the riverside path, is the Giant's Ring, a raised circle of earth with a dolmen in its center. About 5,000 years old, the ring is thought to have been built around the same time as Stonehenge. *Upper Malone Rd., tel. 028/9032–0202. Admission free.*

BELFAST CASTLE

Located by one of the northern hills that surround the city, Belfast Castle was built by the Earl of Shaftsbury and presented to the city in 1934. While there has been a castle on the site since the 12th century, this particular construction in the Scottish Baronial style dates to 1870. A popular site for wedding receptions, the castle contains a restaurant, bistro, and shop. It also contains the Cave Hill Heritage Centre, which details the history of the area. Cave Hill Country Park, on which the castle is situated, covers 740 acres; and Cave Hill itself (1,182 ft) provides panoramic views over the city and Belfast Lough (on a clear day you can supposedly glimpse Scotland on the horizon). It was from the vantage point of Cave Hill that the Republican leader Wolfe Tone and his United Irishmen looked down over the city in 1795 and pledged to fight to the death for a free Ireland. An interesting legend surrounding the castle dictates that the residents will only experience good fortune as long as a white cat lives there—thus the many portrayals of cats in the gardens' mosaics, sculptures, and furniture. *Tel. 028/9077–6925. Admission free. Open Apr.–Sept., daily 9–9.*

STORMONT

Eight kilometers (5 mi) east of Belfast on the A20 is this magnificent 1932 building, once home to the Northern Ireland parliament, that now houses the recently formed Northern Ireland Assembly. The original parliament met here until 1972, when the increasing strife in the province forced its transfer to London. The building is at the end of a stately 2-km-long (1-mi-long) avenue, watched over by a statue of Lord Carson, the Dublin-born architect of the Ulster Unionists. The well-kept grounds are open to the public. Great stands of oak and beech shade the many walkways, and there are many quiet corners and conveniently located benches overlooking streams and bridges. *8 km (5mi) east of Belfast center, just off the A20, take Bus 22 or 23 from Donegall Square, tel. 028/9052–0600. Grounds open year-round, building tours by appointment.*

ULSTER FOLK & TRANSPORT MUSEUM

Located about 11 km (7 mi) east of Belfast on the Bangor Road, this open-air and indoor museum is situated on the grounds of Cultra Manor. At the Folk Museum (tel. 028/9042–8428), you can stroll through reproductions of typical Ulster buildings from the turn of the century, including shops, cottages, farmhouses, a flax mill, a forge, and a school. Inside, artists give demonstrations of spinning and weaving, and exhibitions on the domestic and agricultural practices of the time line the walls. The Transportation Museum (on the other side of the main road) houses many artifacts from Ulster's mechanical past, from horse-drawn carts to the museum's centerpiece Irish Railway Collection. There are also exhibits about great Belfast transportation firms like Shorts, the aircraft manufacturers, and Harland & Wolff, the shipbuilders who built the *Titanic*. A special section is also devoted to the ill-fated DeLorean sports car, briefly manufactured in the province and made famous by *Back to the Future* and the alleged criminal activities of its creator, John DeLorean. The car's production here was part of a project during the Margaret Thatcher era aimed at providing much-needed employment in the area. Unfortunately, the entire factory crashed spectacularly due to business malpractice and added further to the business woes of the North at a time when it needed it least. *11 km (7 mi) east of Belfast on the A2, tel. 028/9042–8428. Admission to both museums £4, £2.50 students. Open May–Sept., Mon.–Sat. 9:30–5, Sun. noon–6.*

AFTER DARK

Though the city center dies shortly after dark, Belfast still has a pretty lively nightlife. Head to the area between Shaftesbury Square and Queen's University, which is well endowed with pubs, movie theaters, and late-night coffeehouses. Old Museum Arts Centre (*see above*), **Grand Opera House** (Great Victoria St., tel. 028/9024–1919), **Crescent Arts Centre** (028/9024–2338), and **Lyric Players Theatre** (55 Ridgeway St., tel. 028/9038–1081) offer live entertainment ranging from opera and drama to dance and classical music. Tickets cost £6–£30, and student discounts of up to 50% are available. For more information on local goings-on, pick up the daily *Belfast Telegraph,* the free biweekly *That's Entertainment,* or the monthly *Arts Link,* available at the tourist office and local newsagents.

THE PUB SCENE

While the darkest days of the Troubles put a definite damper on pub crawling, the Belfast of today has a totally different atmosphere. The progressive peace has spurred the opening of new places almost every month; old warehouse conversions and smart bijou-style cocktail bars are the mark of the new city. You can drop in to witness for yourself the writing of this chapter in Irish history, all the while supping a favorite brew amidst a population that's keen to shake hands and hear about things where you come from. Depending on your constitution, you can engage in a lengthy crawl that'll occupy most of the twilight and darkness hours, or just have a few swift bevvies before or after a show. Here are a few places that are worth a look either way:

The **Morning Star** (Pottinger's Entry, tel. 028/9022–3976) is between Anne and High streets, hidden down the Cornmarket's historic Entries. An atmospheric stew of ancient wood paneling and wrought iron makes this Victorian masterpiece the perfect place to sup a pint. **Kelly's Cellars** (30 Bank St., tel. 028/9032–4835) is another old pub that has so far, thankfully, managed to avoid any attempt at gentrification. It's full of interesting old folk, as well as the passing parade of visitors, and hosts good traditional sessions on weekends. The **Hercules Bar** (63 Castle St., tel. 028/9032–4578) has a solid lock on the attentions of many of the best musicians around; there's always a good trad session in the offing on weekend nights, with some cool jazz on other days. The **Crown Liquor Saloon** (46 Great Victoria St., tel. 028/9024–9476) seems to grow better with age, despite the fact that it suffered regular bomb damage back in the bad old days. Gas lamps, hammered ceilings, and those old-style snugs that have disappeared everywhere else make this a tourist stop that still exudes character. **Lavery's Gin Palace** (12 Bradbury Pl., tel. 028/9023–3131) might not have too much ancient atmosphere, but it still has no problem attracting an exuberant student and music crowd. With a dance club upstairs and a packed bar downstairs, this is definitely an early 1920s kind of place. The **Fly** (5 Lower Crescent, tel. 028/9023–5666) is a new bar-nightclub-café mix, spread over three floors, that's aimed at a hip young crowd. Most nights it's filled with techno sounds from a live DJ—definitely the local dance scene. **Shine** (Queen's University Student Union, tel. 028/9032–4803) is, naturally, packed with students keen to forget their studies, but it's also very welcoming to visiting strangers. Again, resident DJs power up the volume to an ever-present crush of dancers keen to strut their attitude. The **Liverpool Bar** (Donegall Quay, tel. 028/9032–4796) is opposite the SeaCat terminal right on the docks. At various times a warehouse, a boardinghouse, and a brothel, it retains a certain rough-trade cachet as the home of some of the best trad and blues in the city. The Front Page (9 Ballymoney St., tel. 028/9032–4924) might be hard to find in its location down by the docks, but this tiny spit-and-sawdust establishment is another, like the aforementioned Liverpool Bar, where you'll find some great music and big crowds lapping up the slightly seedy nautical atmosphere.

MUSIC

Belfast Waterfront Hall (Oxford St., tel. 028/9033–4400) has a whole range of concerts and events throughout the year, from classical to Irish traditional and pop. Tickets range from £7.50 to £22.50. You can purchase them at the box office or over the phone (tel. 028/9033–4455). There's also a quiet café-restaurant called the **Terrace Café** (tel. 028/9024–4966), which looks out over the River Lagan. It's open from 10 AM to 8 PM and offers sandwiches (£3.50) and a two-course lunch (£7.95) with a good wine list, if you're feeling in the mood. To get there from the center, head down May Street toward the river and Belfast Central Station, and you can't miss it unless you're walking in thick fog. The nearest bus station is Laganside.

NEAR BELFAST

HILLSBOROUGH

COMING AND GOING • A regular Ulster Bus (tel. 028/9033–3000) service shuttles back and forth from Belfast, as well as Lisburn and Dromore.

WHERE TO SLEEP • Decent B&B accommodation can be found at **Growell House** (Dromore Rd., tel. 028/9753–2271), a friendly home where clean and comfortable rooms cost £20 per person. Farther down the same road, the **White Gables Hotel** (tel. 028/9068–2755) offers equally good accommodations and a well-appointed common room for a slightly higher price (£22).

FOOD • **The Plough Inn** (Main St., tel. 028/9768–2985) has been offering hospitality since 1758 in a wood-and-flagstone environment that fits in perfectly with the manicured and old-world atmosphere of the whole town. The pleasant wine bar upstairs allows you to take just a starter or indulge in a whole meal for a price around £10 a head. The menu includes meat and fish dishes and vegetarian options. Farther along Main Street, the Hillside Bar (tel. 028/9768–2765) offers excellent bar food, including superb hotpots and country soups. Its more formal restaurant at the back offers mostly seafood at around £15 a head.

WORTH SEEING • Sixteen kilometers (10 mi) south of Belfast stands Hillsborough, one of the province's most picturesque small towns. The town sprung up as the result of a visit from the Earl of Essex, who was sent to the area by Queen Elizabeth I to subdue the rebellious O'Neill clan. Construction originally took place around the fort that Colonel Arthur Hill built in 1650 to command commerce and traffic on the road from Dublin to Carrickfergus. From the ramparts of the fort, which was extensively remodeled in the 18th century, there are good views over the park's artificial lake and across to the elegant parish church. *Tel. 028/9268–3285. Admission to fort free. Open Apr.–Sept., Tues.–Sat. 10–7, Sun. 2–7.*

With stained glass by Joshua Reynolds and a memorial by Nollekens, St. Malachy's Parish Church does indeed live up to its local reputation as "the nicest little place of worship anyone could want." Originally dedicated in 1663 and improved in 1774, it sits at the bottom of Main Street, adorned by twin towers at the ends of its transept and an elegant spire at its west end. It contains two magnificent 18th-century Snetzler organs. The final resting place of Hamilton Harty—"the Irish Toscanini"—is found in the graveyard; he was born in Hillsborough, where his father was the church organist for 40 years. The church is open to visitors daily. Across the square, with its pretty market house and rows of Georgian town houses, is Hillsborough House, the official royal residence in the province. The wondrous wrought-iron gates that frame its entrance date from 1745 and were brought here from Richill Castle in Armagh. The mansion is now used for ceremonial occasions and was the site for many of the negotiations that began the present Peace Accord. It is not open to the public.

THE CAUSEWAY COAST

Stretching for 80 km (50 mi) along Northern Ireland's Atlantic shore, the Causeway Coast holds most of the province's "don't miss" attractions. Besides Belfast, the Causeway Coast is the most heavily visited region in the north and the focus of innumerable package and day-trip tours that depart from Belfast. These guided tours are an efficient way to take in the Causeway's sights—from Dunluce Castle and the world-famous Giant's Causeway to the endless string of whitewashed fishing villages along the coast—but consider staying longer if at all possible. Between Cushendall and Portrush, there's enough here to merit at least three or four days of exploration. Northern Ireland's train and bus network hits the important towns, but a mountain bike is ideal for the Causeway's flat terrain.

GLENS OF ANTRIM

The nine glens (or forests) of Antrim are steeped in Irish mythology. Hugging the coast in isolated pockets between Larne and Ballycastle, the glens were inhabited by small bands of Irish monks as early as AD 700. Since then, these peaceful old-growth forests have become synonymous with Irishness. Pro-Republicans proudly note that Ossian, one of the greatest Celtic poets, is supposedly buried near Glenaan, and that Moira O'Neill, Celtic poet and mystic, was born in the village of Cushendun. After a few pints, some locals reminisce incoherently about these two Irish cultural heroes while simultaneously lamenting the Glens' popularity with British tourists. For the most part, the people hereabouts are descendants of the ancient Irish and the Hebridean Scots who hail from across the narrow Sea of Moyle. The Glens were the last places in Northern Ireland where Gaelic was spoken. Working from south to north, the Glens are Glenarm, Glencloy, Glenariff, Glenballyeamon, Glenaan, Glencorp, Glendun, Glenshesk and Glentaisie. While their exact meanings have been lost in the winds of time, the popular translations are glen of the army, glen of the hedges, ploughman's glen, Edwardstown glen, glen of the rush lights, glen of the slaughter, brown glen, sedgy glen, and Taisie's glen. In legend, Taisie was a princess of Rathlin Island. Given the original remoteness of the area, a great tradition of storytelling still exists in the Glens area. Locals will often talk of "the wee folk" and the "gentle" (supernatural) places of Lurigethan Mountain and Tiveragh Hill. The fairies inhabiting these places are mostly mischievous creatures who mind their own business but are said to take devastating revenge on anyone rash enough to cut down a fairy thorn.

The Glens of Antrim are well worth several days of serious exploration. Marked trails stretch from Larne in the south to Ballycastle in the north, meandering at times through each of the nine unconnected glens. You'll need a full week and a rainproof tent to complete the nine-glen circuit, or you can stop for the day in Glenariff Park, the largest and most accessible of Antrim's glens.

GLENARM

Meandering out of the urban sprawl of Belfast and up the coast past Larne and Ballygally, both industrial locations with the former only used by visitors catching a ferry, the winding but flat A2 road gradually hits the real country as it hugs the coast. Big fields, grazing cattle, great clumps of forest, and a constant sea breeze eventually lead you into Glenarm (glen of the army). Once the headquarters of the McDonnells, this small village is little more than a collection of 100-plus-year-old houses and businesses, a jewel often passed over by the tourist throngs. This is the oldest village in the Glens and immediately stands out because of its pavements made from black and white pebbles (sounds awful on paper, but it works). Many of the buildings are coated white with the limestone dust from the local quarries.

BASICS • The **tourist office** (Coast Rd., tel. 028/2884–1087) is in the Town Council building and has an array of information on the surrounding area; it's open weekdays 9:30–5. The post office (tel. 028/2884–1218) is on Toberwine Street. It's open Monday, Tuesday, Thursday, and Friday 9–1 and 2–5:30; Wednesday and Saturday 9–12:30.

COMING AND GOING • Bus 162 from Laganside Station in Belfast (tel. 028/9033–3000) stops in Glenarm on its route through Larne, Ballygally, and Carnlough. It makes six runs a day on weekdays (5 Sat., 3 Sun.). In the summer, the Antrim Coaster (tel. 028/9033–3000), a bus operating along the coast from Belfast to Coleraine, makes daily trips, stopping at every town, including Glenarm.

WHERE TO SLEEP • **The Nine Glens B&B** (Toberwine St., tel. 028/2884–1590) is a period house, very much in keeping with the aged look of the town. The rooms, however, are modern and comfortable, each with their own bath and TV. Rates are £15 per person. **Margaret's B&B** (Altmore St., tel. 028/2884–1307) is a family-run place, with antiques in the public areas and modern, well-furnished bedrooms priced at around £14 per person.

FOOD • **Poacher's Pocket** (New Road, tel. 028/2884–1221) is festooned with pictures of the woodland creatures that adorn the dinner plates— pheasant, pig, rabbit—and offers hearty stews, burgers, and sandwiches from noon to 8 PM. The **Gallery Coffee Shop** (Toberwine St., no phone) is open 10:30 AM to 9 PM and specializes in baked goods, with quiches, pies, and pastries to tempt the palate.

WORTH SEEING • Glenarm Forest is the main attraction in the area, having a number of nature trails that follow the river through the trees. It's open 9 AM to 8 PM during the summer. The forest also contains Glenarm Castle, home of the present Earl of Antrim, which dates back to the 13th century. The castle itself is only open to the public on the 14th and 15th of July (meeting the minimum requirement by the National Trust to receive funding and tax breaks), but its well-tended gardens are a nice place for a stroll; reach them through the 17th-century gate at the top end of Castle Street. There is also a Heritage Trail through Glenarm (brochures at the tourist office), as well as a section of the Ulster Way, which offers a good 10-km (6-mi) hike.

CUSHENDALL

Farther up along the coast is Cushendall, another village of the picture-postcard variety. Called the capital of the Glens due to having a few more streets than the other villages hereabouts, it sits right in the center of moorland, graceful hills, and the jagged seashore. With a red sandstone tower built by Francis Turnly in the early 19th century dominating the main crossroads of the village, Chapel Road heads off toward Ballycastle; Shore Road back toward Glenarm; and the Coast Road down toward Waterfoot.

BASICS • **Glenariff Park Visitor Center** (tel. 028/2175–8232) is nothing more than a coffee–gift shop with a small unstaffed exhibit on the park. So take your questions to the Cushendall tourist office (24 Mill St., tel. 028/2177–1180) before you trek to the park. It has a small stock of hiking guides and maps (for Glenariff and all nine glens) and can help you find a B&B. It's open January–September, weekdays 10–1, and June–August, weekdays 2:30–5 and Saturday 10–1. The office doesn't exchange money, so try Northern Bank (5 Shore St., tel. 028/2177–1243), open weekdays 10–12:30 and 1:30–3:30. The post office is on Mill Street. It's open Monday, Wednesday, and Friday 9–1 and 2–5:30, and Tuesday and Saturday 9:30–12:30.

COMING AND GOING • Buses depart from the Mill Street post office to Belfast (£4.90), stopping at the gates of Glenariff Park (£1.30) four times a day weekdays and three times on Saturday, with additional buses in July and August. Two buses per day also run to Ballycastle (£2.80) July–August. Departure times are posted in the window of the post office. It's possible to walk the scenic 10-km (6-mi) road to the park, but be warned that this is an extremely steep trek.

WHERE TO SLEEP • The **Riverside Guest House** (14 Mill St., tel. 028/2177–1655) has three sumptuous, immaculate rooms for £15 per person, including Mrs. McKeegan's morning Ulsterfry. **Ryans** (9

Shore St., tel. 028/2177–1583) and Glendale House (46 Coast Rd., tel. 028/2177–1595) both have rooms from £13 to £17. The excellent campground at Glenariff Forest Park (*see below*) is adjacent to the park's upper gate and provides access to the park's signposted hiking trails, as well as showers. Its 40 tent sites (£8, including admission to the park) are hidden among trees and wildflowers. In Cushendall itself, **Cushendall Caravan Park** (62 Coast Rd., tel. 028/2177–1699), open April–October, has 20 tent sites (£4.50, £7.50 in summer), all within an easy walk of the village's pubs and chip shops.

FOOD • Cushendall's best pint is poured at the atmospheric **McCullum's** (Mill St., tel. 028/2567–1330), but for lunchtime grub (summer only) and spontaneous traditional music, head next door to **Lurig Inn** (tel. 028/2177–1293). The best restaurant in town is **Harry's** (Mill St., tel. 028/2177–1022), which serves dishes like tasty teriyaki chicken salad (£3.75) and vegetarian burritos (£7). Less expensive (and appetizing) is **Gillin's Coffee Shop** (Mill St., tel. 028/2177–1404). It serves good bread, decent sandwiches, simple salads, and a lot of fried stuff.

WORTH SEEING • **Glenariff Forest Park** (98 Glenariff Rd., tel. 028/2175–8232) is open daily from 8 AM to 8 PM, and admission is £1 for walkers, £1.50 for motorbikes, and £2.50 for cars. Often described as the most beautiful of the nine glens, the 1976-acre Glenariff was christened "little Switzerland" by Thackeray for its spectacular combination of rugged hills and lush valleys. Proud locals also call it "the Queen of the Glens." Inside are several easy hikes, including the Waterfalls Trail (follow the blue arrows), a 2½-km (1½-mi) path along wooden gangways past rain-forest-like waterfalls. Sadly, this, the most lush of Glenariff's trails, is often clogged with summer tourists. Brave them, and then flee to the longer and slightly more strenuous Scenic Hike (follow the red arrows), which gives views of the entire glen. Additional hikes from both Glenariff and Cushendall are described in the "Guide to the Glens" (£1), available at the Cushendall tourist office (*see above*).

The road from Cushendall to the small village of Waterfoot is barely 2 km (1 mi) long and worth the walk or cycle to see the coastal caves that line the route. The caves have been used for various purposes, housing everything from a schoolhouse to a farrier. One of the more colorful residents was a lady called Nun Marry who lived in one cave for 50 years, supplementing her income as one of the better poitín (an illegal local brew, similar to moonshine) makers in the region. The damp and windy conditions obviously agreed with her—she lived to the ripe age of 100.

As you travel from Cushendall and onward through Cushendun, the passing scenery gradually changes from romantic hidden glens to a more untamed and almost savage landscape. You're into serious hilly country here, where bicycling is definitely of the Tour de France variety, with stomach-churning ascents and descents and twisting narrow lanes. If you opt to stay with the main A2 route, as most visitors do, the road stays relatively flat and narrow and still provides great scenery around every turn. In fact, if you attempt to complete the journey to the Giant's Causeway in one day, you may find yourself ho-humming at your umpteenth view of the massive surf crashing upon pristine shores (no, probably not).

A better and much more remote option is the zigzagging scenic route, simply marked as Coast Road, that diverges from the A2 and leads to Murlough Bay, where the whole area comes under the environmental protection of the National Trust. Amid the contrast of land and water stands the medieval church of Drumnakill, a renowned pagan site. Moving along the coast you come to Torr Head, a long jutting peninsula that is Ireland's closest approach to neighboring Scotland. If you've got the time—and, really, in this most spectacular part of the Antrim coast you should make the time—you should do some hill-walking. Park your car at any of the three parks along the route and head towards Coolanlough, a 6-km (4-mi) round-trip. The views from Fair Head are about as good as it gets, with Rathlin Island on one side and the Isle of Arran, near the Mull of Kintyre, visible on the other side on clear days. It is from one of the small bays below that the legendary Deirdre of the Sorrows and the sons of Uisneach embarked for Scotland to escape the wrath of King Conor. This route also overlooks the eerie Lough na Crannagh, an island lake with an ancient crannog in the middle. Farther along the route, you'll find a memorial to Roger Casement, the Irish patriot hanged in 1916 for attempting to enlist the aid of Germany in the fight for independence. His last words, spoken to a relative who attended him before the hanging, were: "Take my body back with you and let it lie in the old churchyard in Murlough Bay." It was to be five decades before the British authorities would release his remains.

BALLYCASTLE

Ballycastle is where the Irish Sea meets the Atlantic Ocean and marks the final section of the Causeway Coast. A regular seaside town very popular with all kinds of holidaymakers and day-trippers from the

North, it has the feel of a friendly honky-tonk resort, with a decent beach and pubs jammed on weekends with music lovers. The castle after which it takes its name was destroyed in 1856. Its tourist popularity has always been guaranteed by being between the Glens to the south and the Giant's Causeway, Bushmills, and Rathlin Island to the north.

BASICS

Ballycastle's **tourist office** (Sheskburn House, 7 Mary St., tel. 028/2076–2024) is near the docks; from Quay Road, turn right on Mary Street and continue straight. The office has maps and brochures, can help you find a B&B, and will organize a Causeway Coast day trip. For currency exchange, head to one of the banks along Quay Road, Ann Street, or the Diamond. The **post office** (tel. 028/2076–2519) is also on Ann Street. You can rent bikes from **Stewarts** (30 Ann St., tel. 028/2076–2491) for £6 per day, £30 a week, or from **Northern Auto Factors** (Castle St., tel. 028/2076–3748) for £6 per day, £30 a week.

COMING AND GOING

Ballycastle's unstaffed bus depot is behind the Diamond on the west end of town. If you're staying at the hostel, a closer bus stop is near the intersection of Quay Road and Mary Street, opposite the Marine Hotel. Ballycastle is well connected by bus to most of Northern Ireland, including routes to Belfast (£5.50), Cushendall (£2.40), Larne (£4.50), Ballintoy (£1.30), the Giant's Causeway (£2), Bushmills (£2.20), and Portrush (£2.90). **McGinn's Coaches** (tel. 028/2076–3451) also runs a service to Carrick-a-Rede, the Giant's Causeway, Bushmills (£5), and Belfast (£3.50). A daily ferry service between Ballycastle and Campbeltown on Scotland's Mull of Kintyre peninsula is operated by the **Antrim Steam Packet Co.** (tel. 0990/523523); the fare is £25.

WHERE TO SLEEP

For the best breakfast on the island (with lots of fruit, yogurt, and cereal), stay at the superb **Glenluce Guest House** (42 Quay Rd., tel. 028/2076–2914) for £20 per person. **Cuchulainn House** (Quay Rd., tel. 028/2076–2252) is a little family-run jewel with wonderful rooms and terrific home-cooked breakfasts for £15 per person, £18.50 with bath. The cheapest beds (£6) in town are at the comfortable **IHH Castle Hostel** (62 Quay Rd., tel. 028/2076–2337), on the east side of town near the pier and a five-minute walk from the center of town. Private rooms are available for £7.50 per person.

FOOD

Try the popular **Wysner's Restaurant** (Ann St., tel. 028/2076–2372), a family-run bakery and coffee shop. The **Cellar Pizzeria** (The Diamond, tel. 028/7036–3037) squeezes wooden booths, pizza (£6–£7), and 1980s rock into a tiny whitewashed basement. **Strand Restaurant** (The Strand, tel. 028/2076–2349) is a casual place serving barbecued ribs (£4.80), pastas (£5), burgers (£3.50), and amazing ice cream and crepes (£2). **Herald's** (Ann St., tel. 028/2076–9064) does great food (pizzas, quiches, overstuffed sandwiches) at even better prices—about £6 a head for large portions—and the service is friendly.

Pub-wise, Ballycastle has a place to suit everybody, and all of them seem to do a roaring trade. **House of McDonnell** (Castle St., tel. 028/2076–2975) is a small place with ancient artifacts hanging from the walls, glowing fireplaces, and tourists squeezed into every corner to hear excellent traditional music; there are sessions most nights. The **Central Bar** (Ann St., tel. 028/2076–3877) also draws huge crowds to its equally good trad music, indeed some nights find an overflow of fans sitting on the backyard wall listening to the tunes drifting out. **McCarroll's Bar** (Ann St., tel. 028/2076–2123) is yet another trad haunt, but here impromptu ceidhlis and reels have patrons clutching their pints carefully to their chests as the dancers take the floor.

WORTH SEEING

Ballycastle, from the Irish Baile Caisleain (City of the Castle), lost its namesake ages ago, along with the staunch walls that once protected this seaside village from Norman and Viking raiders. Although the town's hostel draws crowds of backpackers and cyclists, tourists have largely ignored Ballycastle, despite the beautifully aged shops and pubs that line its Castle, Diamond, and Main streets.

Ballycastle is shaped like an hourglass, with its beach and dock at one end, its pubs and chippies at the other, and the 1-km-long (½-mi-long) Quay Road in between. There's not much to do here except gawk at old photographs and tarnished farm tools in the small, free **Ballycastle Museum** (59 Castle St., tel. 028/2076–2942), open Monday–Saturday noon–6. The local strand, accessed via a footbridge behind Mary Street, is popular when the weather's good, as is the footpath that meanders east along the coast. You can also stick around for a day trip to Rathlin Island or Ballintoy's Carrick-a-Rede (*see* Near Ballycastle, *below*), or for an after-dark crawl to one of Ballycastle's musty pubs. Just outside of town you'll find the ruins of the ancient Bonamargy Friary. Bushmills and Dunluce Castle (*see below*) are also day-trip possibilities, though they're slightly easier to get to from Portrush.

In mid-June, the town's two-day Fleadh Amhrán agus Rince, one of Northern Ireland's best dance and traditional-music festivals, draws performers from all over. The Ould Lammas Fair, held on the last Monday and Tuesday of August, is the biggest festival event in the local calendar. Originally a horse fair and a serious matchmaking event for the local farmers, now its focus is solely on equine trading, and it packs in crowds from all over the North and the Republic. One of the oldest fairs in the country, dating back to 1606, it is a blend of end-of-harvest merriment, great traditional music, and streets thronged with humanity. Booking a bed way in advance is vital. The fair is also famous for the sale of two unusual items, yellowman and dulse. The former is a soft toffee and the latter is a dried seaweed that's sold salted and ready to eat.

NEAR BALLYCASTLE

RATHLIN ISLAND

Rathlin Island lies in the middle of the treacherous North Channel, 9½ km (6 mi) north of Ballycastle and only 22 km (14 mi) from the Mull of Kintyre, Scotland. Lacking industry and agriculture, the islanders depend exclusively on the sea for their livelihood, evidenced by the number of scrawny fishing trawlers anchored in Rathlin's harbor. Rathlin's main attraction is its government-owned bird sanctuary—home to razorbills, fulmars, kittiwakes, puffins, buzzards, curlews, and peregrine falcons. The island provides a good sampling of Northern Ireland's terrain, with cliffs and boulders on the island's west end, circular sandy beaches near the harbor, and velvet green, rolling hills traversed by stone hedges in between. However, if you have already seen Inishbofin or the Aran Islands, and you are not a big fan of birds, the scenery may prove disappointing.

Bird-watching and hiking are Rathlin's main activities. At the west end of the island, Bull Point, with its Western Lighthouse, has the best cliff hiking and premier views of the bird-covered rocks below (bring binoculars). If you don't feel like forking out £3 for a round-trip bus ticket, you can walk from the harbor to the lighthouse in about an hour. A 3-km (2-mi) circuit to Bruce's Cave on the east coast takes you by the island's Catholic and Protestant churches and their shared graveyard. The cave—accessible only by boat and only when the weather cooperates—is where Scotland's Robert the Bruce lived in exile after being defeated by Edward I in 1306. During summer, competing islanders meet all incoming ferries and offer minibus tours of the island (£3). Also during summer, weather permitting, Mr. Tom Cecil (tel. 028/2076–3915) leads full-day scuba-diving trips to any of the dozen shipwrecks that litter Church Bay, the island's principal port. Trips cost £45 (including all gear); proof of certification is required. Accommodation is provided by **Rathlin Guesthouse** (The Quay, tel. 028/2076–3917), within two minutes of the docks. It is open April–September and has four rooms at £15 per person; guests can also arrange for light meals. With permission, you can camp for free in the adjacent campground. The lone pub **McCuaig's** (The Harbour, tel. 028/2076–3974) serves a small selection of meals, but your only other dining option is a glorified snack bar charging outrageous prices, so bring your own food.

Rathlin Ferry Service (tel. 028/2076–3915) runs boats to Rathlin Island (45 mins; £5.70 round-trip) year-round. From July to August, they depart Ballycastle Harbour daily at 10:30 AM and 12:15 PM and return from Rathlin at 9 AM, 11:15 AM, 4 PM, and 6 PM; January–March and November–December, they depart Ballycastle at 10:30 AM and 4 PM and return from Rathlin at 9 AM and 3 PM; April–June and September–October, they depart at 10:30 AM and 5 PM and return at 9 AM and 4 PM.

CARRICK-A-REDE

Between April and September every year, you can brave the Carrick-a-Rede rope bridge, which spans a 60-ft gap between the mainland and Carrick-a-Rede Island, off the coast 8 km (5 mi) west of Ballycastle. Carrick-a-Rede means "Rock in the Road" and refers to the island (the rock) that stands in the path of the salmon who follow the coast as they migrate to their home rivers to spawn. Salmon fishermen have set up this rope bridge in late April for the past 350 years, taking it down again after the salmon season ends. Crossing over to the rocky outcrop, they cast nets in the frothy water and catch throngs of salmon as they rush by. The creaky bridge is open to the public April–September 10–6 (June–August, until 8) and offers heart-stopping views of the crashing waves below. On Carrick-a-Rede itself, you can climb around the precarious terrain and revel in views of the stunning coastal cliffs and plenty of tourists. Be sure to look for the black-and-white razorbills on the cliff to your left as you cross

BLOODY SUNDAY

Bloody Sunday commemorates January 30, 1972, when British paratroopers opened fire on people participating in a nonviolent protest against the British policy of internment without trial. When the smoke cleared, 13 people, all Catholic and unarmed, had been killed. For the past 28 years, many have rallied in support of the victims, who were accused by the British Army of handling weapons. In an event known as the Bloody Sunday Justice Campaign, the supporters attained some success when the British government finally admitted that the victims were "innocent." Derry is filled with murals and memorials that serve as constant reminders of the struggle for justice, including the memorial at Free Derry Corner on Rossville Street carved with the inscription "Their epitaph is in the continuing struggle for democracy."

the bridge. There's a tea shop next to the parking lot, which has a small exhibit on the bridge and the cliffs and serves soups and sandwiches. Ulsterbus passes the bridge on its route between Portrush to Ballycastle; ask the driver to let you off at the entrance.

THE GIANT'S CAUSEWAY

The Giant's Causeway is Northern Ireland's premier tourist attraction. Spanning the coast for some 3 km (2 mi), the Giant's Causeway and its 40,000 basalt blocks are truly impressive. Geologists say these interlocking six- and seven-sided basalt columns, ranging from 4 inches to 6 ft long, were formed by cooling lava 2 million years ago. Others claim the Causeway was built by the mythic Irish figure Finn MacCool, who constructed the Causeway to do battle with Bennandonnar, Scotland's legendary Übermensch. Finn could pick thorns out of his feet while running and was capable of other amazing feats. In one particular fight with his Scottish adversary, he scooped up a huge clod of earth and flung it at his fleeing rival. The clod fell into the sea and formed the Isle of Man. The hole it left filled up with water and became Lough Neagh. And while this legendary figure chose a draughty Antrim headland as his home, "he lived happy and content, obeyed no law and paid no rent." The first historical accounts of the Causeway started appearing in the late 17th century when the Bishop of Derry made one of the first recorded visits. So impressed was the clergyman that he commissioned a number of paintings of the site that led to its eventual fame. To reach the Giant's Causeway, 3 km (2 mi) north of Bushmills on the B146, take Ulsterbus's Portrush–Bushmills–Ballycastle bus (Bus 172), which stops at the visitor center's front gate. Buses go from Portrush to the Causeway (£2.90 round-trip) four times per day Monday–Saturday (9 per day July–August). Buses also go from Ballycastle to the Causeway four times per day (except Sun.) and cost about the same. From the distillery, it's also an easy cycle or 30-minute walk.

One kilometer (½ mi) from the Causeway is a thoroughly modern visitor center (44 Causeway Rd., tel. 028/2073–1855), open daily 10–5 (slightly longer hrs in summer). The center runs a surprisingly good 25-minute audiovisual show (£1) dedicated to the site's geological and legendary history, has a tea shop (open mid-March–October) and a competitive bureau de change, and sells the best guide to walks in the area (50p). It also runs a bus to the Causeway itself every 15 minutes (90p).

The adjacent **Causeway School Museum** (tel. 028/2073–1777), open daily 11–5 July–August only, shows a video documenting the rigors of 1920s school life. Visitors are also encouraged to try their hand at copperplate handwriting or "whipping a pirie," a curiously enjoyable punishment. Admission to the school is £1. Afterward, walk or take the shuttle bus (80p round-trip) down to the Causeway itself. For excellent—and generally deserted—hiking, check the sign behind the visitor center. It outlines a half dozen easy hikes that skirt the pristine coastline and are unquestionably worth a few hours' exploration. The 5-km (3-mi) walk to Dunseverick Castle is one of the best as long as your interest lies with spectacular landscape—the one-tower "castle" isn't nearly as impressive as the land surrounding it.

PORTRUSH

BASICS

The **tourist office** (Dunluce Centre, Dunluce Ave., tel. 028/7082-3333), open daily 9–8 April–October, is adjacent to the bus station. Inside you'll find brochures, maps, and a helpful staff that can book you into a B&B or on a guided tour of the Causeway Coast and change your money. Twenty-four-hour computerized information is available outside. For currency exchange, head to any one of the banks that line Eglinton and Main streets or, on weekends, to the tourist office. **Bicycle Doctor** (104 Lower Main St., tel. 028/7082-4340) rents bikes for £7 per day, £30 per week, with a £40 deposit. The **post office** (tel. 028/7082-3700) is on Eglinton Street.

COMING AND GOING

BY TRAIN • Portrush's **train station** (Eglinton St., tel. 028/7082-2395) is within a five-minute walk of the town center; turn left from the station and keep straight. Except for its information counter (staffed June–August, Monday–Saturday 11–7:30 and Sunday 11–8), the station offers few comforts. Trains depart for Belfast (£5.90), Derry (£5 via Coleraine), and Lisburn (£5).

> "When the world was moulded and fashioned out of formless chaos, this must have been a bit over—a remnant of chaos."
> —Thackeray.

BY BUS • Portrush is well connected by bus to most destinations in Northern Ireland. The unstaffed Ulsterbus depot is near the traffic circle on Dunluce Avenue, across from the tourist office. An Ulsterbus representative can be found within the tourist office on weekdays for help with bus schedules. There's also an auxiliary stop adjacent to the rail station. If you're planning a Causeway Coast day trip, Bus 172 (Bushmills "Open Topper") is your best option. It leaves Portrush four times daily Monday–Saturday (9 times daily, July–August) and has scheduled stops at Bushmills and the Giant's Causeway visitor center. A ticket costs £2.60 round-trip. The first bus departs Portrush at 7:25 AM; the last returns from the Giant's Causeway at 6:35 PM. Other destinations from Portrush include Portstewart (85p), Belfast (£5.60), and Derry (£4.80).

WHERE TO SLEEP

Portrush has two reasonably priced, outstanding B&Bs with excellent views of the beach. The first is the **Clarence** (7 Bath Terr., tel. 028/7082-3575), an aged Georgian flat with 20 rooms (£14 per person) and a common lounge with truly knockout views of the ocean. To find it, turn left from the train depot and right on Bath Street. Next door is the **Rest-A-While** (6 Bath Terr., tel. 028/7082-2827), a similarly old and brightly colored Georgian relic with rooms for £14 per person. For an extra £5, they'll provide lunch and dinner in addition to breakfast. More formal is **Seamara** (26 Mark St., tel. 028/7082-2541), a prim family-run house that charges £17 per person. From the tourist office, continue straight down Mark Street to reach Seamara. **Beulah House** (16 Causeway St., tel. 028/7082-2413) is centrally located and comfortable. Bedrooms are brightly decorated and modern, with TV, hair dryer, and tea/coffeemaker. Singles range £15–£20, doubles £25–£35. **Alexander House** (23 Kerr St., tel. 028/7082-4566), a family-run establishment in the center of town, has singles for £15–£20 and doubles for £25–£35.

FOOD

Portrush teems with greasy chippies, kebab shops, and four-star tourist hotels with grossly overpriced dining rooms. There's hardly a decent meal to be found, and though the better of the rotten lot are reviewed below, they are mediocre at best. For a reasonable sit-down meal, try **Skerries Pantry** (Bath St., tel. 028/7082-2248) or **Singing Kettle Café** (3 Atlantic Ave., tel. 028/7082-3068). Both offer sandwiches, burgers, lasagna, shakes, and soups for less than £4. The **Singing Kettle's** veggie Ulsterfry is only £3. More elegant is **Rowland's** (92 Main St., tel. 028/7082-2063), which serves French onion soup (£2) and entrées such as peppered chicken breast (£6.35), best topped off with a bottle of reasonably priced wine. **Dionysus** (53 Eglinton St, tel. 028/7082-3855) is a Greek restaurant with a huge selection of vegetarian and vegan entrées in the £5–£6 range. **Don Giovanni** (13 Causeway St., tel. 028/7082-

5516) is owned by an Italian family and delivers the authentic goods in everything from pomodora to carbonara. The **Alamo** (Eglinton St., tel. 028/7082–2000) serves quick-fix pizzas and other speedy eats.

A discerning university crowd frequents the Portrush pubs, which range in atmosphere from old world to hip-hop. The **Harbour Bar** (Harbour Rd., tel. 028/7082–2430) is an old-fashioned seamen's hangout, where many of the story-telling oldsters while away the evenings spending their pension money. The **Alpha Bar** (Eglinton St., tel. 028/7082–3889) has a Victorian frontage inviting one into a cozy interior for good conversation and the odd single fiddle player. Things go decidedly into the early 20s age bracket at the **Atlantic Bar** (Main Street, tel. 028/7082–3693), a big conversion with wide open spaces, where DJ's spin records for a dance-orientated crowd. A huge selection of every kind of flavored vodka gives much rise to "cocktail-slamming." **Beetles Bar & Disco** (Bushmills Rd., tel. 028/7046–6930) is where everybody heads when the pubs close. It's got 11 bars and four discos and a real lively crowd that arrives with the sole intention of partying until dawn.

WORTH SEEING

Portrush may be the smarmiest, cheesiest, most touristy place in the British Isles. On summer week-ends the town's gorgeous beaches and quaint harbor are framed by a seemingly endless array of grimy video arcades, tacky amusement-park rides, and throngs of fortysomethings with their shrieking entourage of children. The prime reason to come here is the town's proximity to Dunluce Castle, Bush-mills, and the Giant's Causeway. All are within 11 km (7 mi) of Portrush and easily reached by bike or bus. If you're stuck here on a rainy day, you may want to visit the infamous Waterworld (The Harbour, tel. 028/7082–2001), a massive complex filled with indoor swimming pools, diving boards, water slides, "Swedish" saunas, and an army of overeager preteens. Open June–September, Waterworld is yours for a day for £3.75 (£2.50 in September).

Portrush is small and can comfortably be walked in less than 25 minutes. Most of the cafés, restaurants, and gift shops are between the Eglinton Street train station and the tip of Ramore Head. To the east are Strand Road's Georgian flats and crescent-shape public beach. Both Eglinton and Causeway streets, Portrush's principal commercial avenues, funnel into Main Street, forming a wishbone of sorts. At the northern end of Main Street, look for Waterworld and the town's harbor.

NEAR PORTRUSH

DUNLUCE CASTLE

Halfway between Portrush and the Giant's Causeway, Dunluce Castle is one of Northern Ireland's most evocative ruins. Built by the MacDonnell clan in 1550, it perches on the edge of a ragged cliff with a commanding view of the Atlantic coast. Most of its towers and battlements were destroyed cen-turies ago, and over the years cliff erosion has played havoc with what's left of this 3-acre complex. Still, Dunluce's surviving patchwork of walls and round towers remains intensely beautiful, especially at sunset or on a foggy, gray day. Guarding the castle entrance is a visitor center (tel. 028/2073–1938) where you can see a slide show or join a guided tour. Directly underneath the castle is a sea cave where the family hid their ship. The cave is definitely worth a look but is accessed (at your own risk) via a steep and slippery trail to the right of the castle entrance. The castle is open April–September, Monday–Saturday 10–7 and Sunday 2–7 (October–March until 4 PM) and costs £1.50. Call 028/7082–4444 for information.

Though Dunluce isn't officially served by public transportation, Ulsterbus's Causeway Coast Express drives right past it, and if you ask the driver, he or she will probably let you off at the castle entrance. Otherwise, you'll probably need to cycle the 5 km (3 mi) from Portrush to Dunluce along the A2 high-way or hike for one hour from Portrush along the beach.

BUSHMILLS

Bushmills, the oldest licensed distillery in the world, was first granted a charter by King James I in 1608, although historical records refer to a distillery here as early as 1276. Today, Bushmills is one of the busiest and most respected distillers in Ireland, even more so after its low-key merger with the Republic's own distillery, Jameson of County Cork. Bushmills's greatest appeal to the whiskey drinker, however, is its guided tour, topped off with a complimentary shot of uisce beatha, the "water of life." Tours begin in the mashing and fermentation room, then proceed to the maturing and bottling ware-house. After this brief but informative tour, all visitors are led to the visitor center–cum–gift shop for their free sample of either Black Bush, Old Bushmills, or Bushmills Malt, the three flagship spirits. To reach the distillery, take any Causeway Coast Ulsterbus between Ballycastle and Portrush; all stop in the center of Bushmills Town. From here, follow the signs to the distillery gate. Tel. 028/2073–1521. Admission: £3, students £2.50. Open June–Oct., daily 9–4; Nov.–May, Mon.–Thurs. 9–4 , Fri. 9–noon. Tours leave approximately every 15 mins.

DOWNHILL

Farther down along the A2 toward Derry is Downhill, a tiny village containing a few shops, one pub, and the remains of one eccentric man's architectural folly. Downhill Castle was built in 1774 by the very rich Fredrick Henry, Earl of Bristol and Bishop of Derry. Intent on building a structure that would match the grandeur of the Antrim cliffs, this man of the cloth fashioned a palace in the grand style of European aristocracy and filled it with paintings, ceramics, and rare tapestries from all around the globe. Burnt down in 1851 and rebuilt in 1870, the house was abandoned after World War II, when the roof was removed for the scrap value of its slates and lead. Nowadays the once-proud edifice sits forlornly in a field, fading once again into the landscape that it once commanded. Around the estate, which has become a magnet for visitors taking a slow and easy route into Derry, there are a few other gems of the eccentric Earl Bishop still standing. A short walk from the castle ruins is the Mussenden Temple, a circular library based on a similar building at Vesta in Italy, that sits on a promontory overlooking the sea. One body of historians has it that the bishop constructed it to house his rare book collection, while others maintain it was built for his mistress. This active cleric conducted a lifelong affair with the mistress of Frederick William II of Prussia. The views across Downhill Beach, Portstewart, and the hills of Donegal across the water are simply stunning; it's one of the best places you'll find to

The southeast tower of Dunluce Castle is haunted by Peter Carey, who was hung for three days over the cliffs in the 17th century.

have a picnic and take some photos. It was on the same Downhill beach, by the way, that the bishop commanded his priests to engage in horse races on the sand and then rewarded the winners by giving them the more lucrative parishes in his district. Though he may have been a delightful flavor of nutty fruitcake, the bishop did do some worthwhile deeds in the midst of his extravagances. The mountain road he built to Limavady gave much-needed work to the local people. It runs across the Binevenagh plateau and offers further splendid views across the Scottish coast and Donegal. The Temple is open in July–August, daily noon–6; April—June and September, Saturday and Sunday noon–6. The grounds are open year-round. Admission is free.

DERRY

What you call this city is more of a political issue than one of simple custom: While Republicans call it Derry, its official name, Londonderry is used by those in favor of British rule. The city's original Gaelic name was Daire Calgaigh (the Oak Grove of Calgach). Then, a few centuries later, it was changed to Doire Colmcille (the Oak Grove of Columb), the original founder. Thus it remained until 1609 when the English government decided to "plant" the city. It forged an agreement with the City of London to provide the necessary settlers and teams of master builders to rebuild the medieval town—hence the name Londonderry. Like many other places in Ireland such as Limerick, Galway, and Cork, Derry provides a curious amalgam of the bloody past and the progressive present. Ancient monuments sit comfortably beside modern office blocks, quiet and tranquil corners are often the sites of long-ago infamous deeds, and the inspiring skyline, dotted with cranes and industrial progress, bubbles underneath with a pervasive sense of history. The city's troubled past includes the 105-day siege of 1689, when the legendary Apprentice Boys closed the gates to the conquering columns of King James's army; the explosive street violence of the 1960s; and even the often-uneasy truce that prevails today between the sectarian divide. Yet in spite of it all, Derry continues to thrive. Since the mid-1990s, the city has made serious strides to cast aside the problems of the past in favor of a commerce and vitality that have seen entire sections of the previous urban decay flattened and replaced—progress that bodes well for the future. In the regenerated downtown area, explosions that were once of the petrol-bomb kind are now of the commercial kind, with new businesses proliferating.

Derry is one of Northern Ireland's most underrated towns. In contrast to the factories and low-income tenements along the banks of the River Foyle, the heart of the city is full of cultural artifacts and historic

THE BEST HOSTEL IN IRELAND

Situated in sheep country, 5 km (3 mi) outside Dungiven (southeast of Derry), the IHH Flax Mill Hostel (Mill La., Derrylane, Co. Derry, tel. 028/7174–2655) is a musty, 18th-century Irish cottage with no electricity. Conversations are held by candlelight and gas lamp within the gorgeously aged stone walls of the family room. There are 20 beds (£5 each), and tent sites go for £3. An amazing breakfast is only £1.70 extra and includes fresh eggs from the henhouse and homemade bread and rhubarb jam. The local pub—a five-minute walk—will pour your pint to go. Owned by a German-Irish couple who speak both languages fluently, the Flax Mill draws large crowds of backpackers during the summer, many on return trips specifically to this hostel. Reservations are advised. To get here, take one of Ulsterbus's six daily buses from Derry to Dungiven (£3). Once you arrive, give the hostel a call and they will pick you up. But be forewarned: You may end up staying for weeks rather than the day or two you planned.

beauty. This is particularly noticeable in the streets and alleys that fan outward from the Diamond—the historic center of Derry where St. Colomb founded his first monastery in 546 at the present-day site of Long Tower Church. Four main streets connect the four main gates of the city—Bishop's Gate, Ferryquay Gate, Shipquay Gate, and Butcher's Gate—to the Diamond. Another three gates—New Gate, Castle Gate, and Newmarket Street Gate—are the main arteries to the old city. Here, encircled by Derry's 20-ft-tall, 17th-century walls, fine examples of Georgian and Victorian architecture rub shoulders with a handful of old-style pubs, cathedrals, museums, and unpretentious shopping malls. Outside the city walls, a depressing collection of slums, barbed wire, and security-conscious suburbanites attests to the hard times of the past. But inside the walls, Derry is relaxed and confident and filled with quaint Georgian and Victorian town houses. Derry's cultured air can be sampled at **Orchard Street Gallery** (Orchard St., tel. 028/7126–9675), **Gordon Gallery** (7 London St., tel. 028/7137–4044), and **Foyle Arts Centre** (Lawrence Hill, tel. 028/7126–6657). All have secured solid reputations by showcasing the best in local and national art.

Derry has one of the largest college-age populations in Ireland, so the pub scene here is a pleasant change from the sterile sobriety of Northern Ireland's smaller towns. In mid-August, another good reason to come is the annual Busking Festival. With cash prizes topping £1,000, this bacchanalian event attracts some of the most bizarre and talented street musicians from the United Kingdom and Ireland.

BASICS

The tourist office houses both the Northern Irish and Irish Republic tourist boards and is a treasure trove of information. Besides free city maps, this office has heaps of brochures with details about B&Bs, trains, buses, and theater and art happenings. Pick up a copy of the free and helpful *Derry Tourist Guide*. It also organizes guided walks and bus tours of the city. *8 Bishop St., 1 block west of the Diamond, tel. 028/ 7126–7284. Open July–Aug., Mon.–Sat. 9–8, Sun. 10–6; Sept.–June, weekdays 9–5:15.*

Derry's student-run **USIT Travel Center** (33 Ferryquay St., tel. 028/7137–1888) is two blocks south of the Diamond. Come here for budget fares and tips on traveling cheaply. For a small fee, they can reschedule most airline tickets. The **main post office** (3 Custom House St, BT 48 6AA, tel. 028/7136–2563) is on the River Foyle's west bank, just outside the city walls, and offers Saturday currency exchange (9–12:30). During the week, head to any of the 20 banks that line Shipquay Street and the Diamond.

Laundry is less of a chore at **Duds 'n' Suds** (141 Strand St., tel. 028/7126–6006), where you can watch the big-screen TV or play a little pool while your clothes are spinning (wash £1.50, dry £1.80). It's open weekdays 8 AM–9 PM, weekends 8 AM–8 PM. **Webcrawler Internet Café** (52 Strand St., tel. 028/7126–8386) offers Internet access for £3 per hour, students £2.50.

COMING AND GOING

The symbolic heart of Derry is the Diamond, a small square inside the 17th-century city walls. Most of Derry's sights and nearly all of the pubs and eating establishments lie in or around the city walls, primarily on Strand Road and Shipquay Street.

BY BUS • Derry is well connected with Northern Ireland's major and minor towns. The **Foyle Street depot** (Foyle St., tel. 028/7126–2261) is on the River Foyle's western shore; here you can pick up a free route map and schedule booklet. A staffed info counter is open weekdays 6–5:30, Saturday 8–5:30, and for bus arrivals on Sunday. To reach the city center and the Diamond, turn right from the depot and immediately left on Shipquay Street. Ulsterbus destinations include Belfast (1 per hr; £6.50), Portrush (every 2 hrs; £5.20), Portstewart (every 2 hrs; £4.50), and Omagh (11 per day; £4). Republic destinations include Dublin (5 per day; £10.50), Letterkenny (6 per day; £4.30), and Donegal Town (6 per day; £7.70).

If you're Donegal-bound, the independent **Lough Swilly Bus Co.** (Foyle St., tel. 028/7126–2017) offers more frequent service than Ulsterbus to the Republic's northwest corner. Pick up a free booklet with fares and timetables from its office on the second floor of the bus station. All buses leave from the Foyle Street offices, down the road from Ulsterbus. Generally, destinations include Letterkenny, Fanad Head, and the Inishowen Peninsula; all fares are less than £10 one-way, and you get half off with an ISIC card.

On Halloween in Derry, the whole city turns out decked in their wildest homemade costumes. They have good reason: No pub will serve you a drink without one.

BY TRAIN • **Derry Station** (Duke St., tel. 028/7142–228) is on the River Foyle's eastern bank, across the water from Derry's walled city center. An information counter is open Monday–Saturday 9–5:30. A free shuttle whisks people across the river to the bus station after all major train arrivals. If you're heading to the train station, buses marked N.I.R. depart from the Foyle Street depot 20 minutes before most major train departures. Northern Irish Railway trains leave for Portrush (7 per day; £5), Lisburn (7 per day; £6.40), Belfast (7 per day; £6.40), and Dublin Connolly via Newry (4 per day; £17.30).

GETTING AROUND

Derry's old walls surround all of the main tourist areas except the Waterloo district, north of the walls, which is popular with shoppers. The Diamond is the main town square, and streets fan out from it to all sections of downtown. The famous Republican Bogside district is to the west of the walls, and the Loyalist Waterside is on the east side of the River Foyle.

BY BIKE • The YHANI hostel (see below) rents mountain bikes on the Raleigh Rent-A-Bike plan for £7 per day or £40 per week, with £30 deposit.

BY BUS • Bus fares within Derry range from 85p to £1.05, depending on the distance. Tickets can be purchased on board and at newsagents displaying a CITYBUS sign. Nearly all local buses start or end their journeys at the Diamond, the first at 6 AM and the last at 11 PM.

WHERE TO SLEEP

The **Trinity Hotel** (22–24 Strand Rd., tel. 028/7127–1271), right in the city center, is an ideal base for exploring the city and surroundings. It has 40 rooms, all with bath, and also has a café and bar on the premises. Rates are £40–£50 per person. The **White Horse Hotel** (Donnybrewer Rd., Campsie, Derry, tel. 1504/860606), 8 km (5 mi) outside of Derry City, on the road to the Giant's Causeway, is a pleasant place with plenty of gardens and parking attached. All rooms have bath, TV, trouser press, and tea/coffeemaking facilities. Rates are £25–£30 per person. The cheapest B&Bs in town are **Mrs. Cassidy's** (86 Duncreggan Rd., tel. 028/7137–4551) and **Groarty House** (62 Groarty Rd., tel. 028/7126–1403), which both have rooms from £15 per person, and **Mrs. Wiley's** (153 Culmore Rd., tel. 028/7135–2932), which has slightly spartan rooms from £13 per person. All of them are comfortable enough but are no-frills establishments (don't expect a hair dryer). **Florence House** (16 Northland Rd., tel. 028/7126–8093), near the university, is a cozy five-room B&B with rooms for £17 per person.

YHANI's Oakgrove Manor (4–6 Magazine St., tel. 028/7137–2273) is a big, modern complex located within the city walls. Its dorm rooms (beds £7.50–£9) and kitchen are institutional and bland but super-

THE SIEGE OF DERRY

The Catholic king James II seemed well prepared to conquer the Protestant enclave of Derry when he massed his troops around it in 1688. At the last moment, as the invading forces were about to enter the city, 13 Protestant apprentices stole the keys of the city and locked the gates against the advancing forces. Their motive was probably self-preservation, as they would have been among the first to be hanged if the siege were successful. Supporters of William III, who had deposed James from the English throne, rallied to the apprentices' cause and organized a defense of the city. The events that followed became the longest siege in English history, 105 days, during which time the city and its inhabitants withstood bombardment, disease, and starvation. Reduced to eating rotting horseflesh, dogs, and rats, the inhabitants declared that they would eat the Catholics first and then each other before they would capitulate. Offered peace terms from James, they raised a crimson standard signifying "No Surrender," a phrase that still adorns many of the banners and flags during the Orange Marching Season. Eventually, in July 1689, Captain Browning and his ship the "Mountjoy" broke the boom across the river and relieved the city; the captain perished in the act. At the end of the siege, almost 8,000 of the 30,000 inhabitants of Derry had died. In the long run, the siege worked in the Protestants' favor. During the months that King James was occupied with besieging the city, King William (or Billy as he's called hereabouts) regrouped and conscripted a much larger army, a factor that told fatally against the Catholic forces at the Battle of the Boyne on the 12th of July, 1690.

clean. It also has singles (£15) and doubles (£28) with shower. All rates include breakfast. The hostel has laundry facilities and a 2 AM curfew and is a short, well-signposted walk from the bus station. A much better choice is **Aberfoyle Independent Hostel** (29 Aberfoyle Terr., tel. 028/7137–0011), which occupies a brick Victorian town house. Beds in singles, doubles, and dorms all go for £7.50. Be sure to call ahead to snag the cheapest double on the island. To get here, exit right from the bus station, walk down Strand Road for 10 minutes, and keep a sharp eye out for the hostel on your left.

FOOD

Derry's most affordable eateries are clustered around Shipquay and Strand streets. At **Piemonte Pizzeria** (Clarendon Rd., off Strand St., tel. 028/7126–6828), open for dinner nightly and until 2:30 AM on weekends, an ultrafriendly waitstaff serves excellent pastas (£4) and pizzas (£3–£4) beneath a gaggle of plastic sea creatures clinging to a huge net. **Glue Pot** (36 Shipquay St., tel. 028/7136–7463) is a quiet, family-run pub with soup-and-sandwich combinations and lasagna for less than £4. Derry's best Chinese restaurant is **Mandarin Palace** (134 Strand Rd., tel. 028/7126–4613), where most dishes cost less than £6. At either branch of the **Sandwich Co.** (The Diamond, tel. 028/7137–2500; and 61 Strand Rd., tel. 028/7126–6771), you can choose from a creative list of sandwiches or design your own for £1.50 to £2.75. The best place for good, cheap eats is **Boston Tea Party** (in the Craft Village, tel. 028/7126–4568), which serves dishes like lasagna with a side salad (£2), quiche (£1.75), and chicken curry with a baked potato (£1.50). **Annie's Hot Bread Shop** (William St., tel. 028/7126–9236) is right by the city walls and is a local institution. Service is snappy but friendly, portions are enormous, and the place is almost always open (8 AM–4 AM). A nice place to write those cards home or update your diary is **Fitzroy's** (2 Bridge St., tel. 028/7126–6211)—good home cooking at around £7 a head, with great coffee and the perfect atmosphere in which to pass a wet afternoon.

WORTH SEEING

Most of Derry's attractions lie within its well-preserved city walls, which stretch for 1½ km (1 mi) from Foyle and Magazine streets in the north to Artillery and Market streets in the south. At 18 ft high and 20 ft thick, the walls were erected between 1614 and 1619 and have never been breached. The seven cannons along the northeast wall between Magazine and Shipquay gates were donated by Queen Elizabeth I to celebrate the "planting" and rebuilding by the London Guilds. On one section of the wall a plaque marks the water level of the River Foyle in the 1600s; nowadays the river is 500 ft away. The southwest wall is dominated by the Bishop's Gate, dedicated in 1789 to King William of Orange, victor at the Battle of the Boyne. On the northeast wall, a massive cannon called Roaring Meg (after an artillery man's wife, perhaps?) stands as a further reminder of the days of siege. Donated by, of all people, the London Guild of Fishmongers, it saw action in 1689. In another section of the wall, the Memorial Hall, the headquarters of the Apprentice Boys, stands between the Royal Bastion and Butcher's Gate. It is not open to the public. The walls were closed to the public until 1995, and though there is still a strong military presence in the northwest corner (video cameras and barbed wire), the walls now make a very pleasant walk, providing good views of the surrounding neighborhoods, along with descriptive plaques and informative markers. It's an area ideal for aimless, impromptu rambles.

In 1972, the Guildhall was partially destroyed by an IRA bomber who was later elected to an influential Derry city council.

One probably tall tale about the walls concerns the term "catwalk." Back in the old days, when the wealthy matrons and wives of the city's gentry ordered their dresses from London on a yearly basis, it was the practice for them to show off their new adornments by parading along the city walls. Down below, the chronically unemployed residents of the Bogside looked up at them and became incensed at the bold display of wealth. At one point, many of these residents took it upon themselves to write letters of protest to the *Times* in London, describing the ladies as "ostentatious cats on the prowl." Streetwise editors in England seized upon the term and, thus, the phrase "catwalk" entered the dictionary. So the story goes; it could be true.

The **Tower Museum** (Union Hall Pl., tel. 028/7137–2411, open Tues.–Sat. 10–5; also July–Aug., Mon. 10–5 and Sun. 2–5) is partially housed in the reconstructed O'Doherty Tower, which was built in 1615 by the O'Dohertys for their overlords (the O'Donnells) in lieu of tax payments. The intricate, well-planned "Story of Derry" exhibit takes you from the city's prehistoric origins to the present, hitting all the big events along the way, with loads of high-tech audiovisual displays. Admission is £3.50, students £1.50. To the south, **Derry Craft Village** (Shipquay St., tel. 028/7126–0329), open daily 9–5:30, offers a novel shopping experience. Instead of the standard minimall format, it combines retail establishments, workshops, and residential apartments in a medieval setting. St. Columb's Cathedral (off Bishop St., by courthouse, tel. 028/7126–7313) is one of the first Protestant cathedrals built in the United Kingdom after the Reformation. In addition to its intricate corbeled roof and austere spire, the church contains the oldest and largest bells in Ireland (dating from the 1620s). Notice the colorful procession of banners in the nave, a proud statement of pro-British sentiments. The £1 cathedral admission will also get you into the one-room, chock-full-of-history Chapter House Museum, which displays a few 16th-century bibles and the oldest surviving map of Derry (from 1600). The museum is open Monday–Saturday 9–5. Outside the walls, on Foyle Street, near Shipquay Gate, the redbrick **Guildhall** (Foyle St., tel. 028/7136–5151), originally built in 1890, is worth a visit for its impressive stained-glass windows; admission is free. Nearby, at the **Foyle Valley Railway Centre** (Foyle Rd. Station, tel. 028/7126–5234), you'll see mothballed locomotives, antique signal levers, and lots of railroad paraphernalia. The museum is open Tuesday–Saturday 10–4:30 (also May–September, Sunday 2–5:30). Admission is free, but the short train ride along the waterfront costs £2.

If you want a glimpse of Derry's ugly but fascinating underside, consider a trip to the Fountain and Bogside districts. The Fountain, a fiercely Protestant enclave, is best seen along Fountain Road; exit the city walls through the Bishop Street gate. Here you'll find smatterings of pro-British graffiti; red, white, and blue curbs and light posts; and lots of Union Jacks, all harsh reminders of the Troubles. To see the flip side of the coin, head north from the Diamond along Butcher Street, and veer left outside the city walls to reach the Bogside district, also known as Free Derry—a carryover from the days when this Rossville

THE SKELETON

As if it isn't enough to be reminded of the bloody history of the place by every rampart and bridge, the City of Derry coat of arms contains the sinister figure of a sad skeleton leaning to one side on a background of a castle and cross. While there are many stories concerning its origin, the most prevalent is that he represents Walter de Burgo, a Norman knight who was the nephew of the Red Earl, Richard de Burgo. Having fallen out with his relative over some land they were disputing, the Red Earl had him imprisoned in a dungeon in Greencastle in County Donegal where he eventually starved to death in 1332.

Street neighborhood was an IRA stronghold studiously avoided by the RUC. The Bogside (and some of the city center) saw horrendous rioting in July of 1996 in response to the so-called Siege of Drumcree: dozens of cars were hijacked and burned, and hundreds of plastic bullets and Molotov cocktails were exchanged between Nationalists and the RUC. Since then the area has been relatively quiet. The Bogside has more striking murals than the Fountain, some of which can be seen at a distance from the city walls.

Despite the present peace, you may feel more comfortable taking one of the many organized walking tours. As an introduction to the city, they are a great way to spend a half day early on in your stay. Most are around and about the walls and provide information of both a historical and anecdotal nature. Inter City Tours operate from the tourist office (*see above*) during the summer months, Monday–Friday 10:30 AM to 2:30 PM; they charge £3, students £1.75. McNamara Walking Tours (tel. 028/7134–5335), an award-winning company with enthusiastic guides, also operates out of the tourist office. Tours depart every two hours from 10 AM until 4 PM and cost £3, students £2.50. The Essential Walking Tour of Historic Derry (tel. 028/7130-=9051) has equally engaging guides who give tours focusing on the various stages of the city's history. They depart the Guild Hall every two hours from 10 AM to 4 PM and cost £3, students £2.50. If you're all tired out from rambling along the Glens and just want history from a comfortable seat, take the **Foyle Civic Bus Tour** (tel. 028/7126–2261), operated by Ulsterbus from the Foyle Street depot. The cost is £3.

AFTER DARK

PUBS • Derry is justifiably famous for its nightlife. Even during the darkest days of the Troubles (and possibly because of them), city dwellers have always been quick to forget their cares in the company of old friends. Back in the mid-1980s, the place almost had an air of the London Blitz about it, with normally respectable people greeting the dark with a devil-may-care attitude that still seeps through to this day. Most kinds of music from excellent trad to the best of Irish rock can be found seven nights a week. Check out the local listings on arrival. **Peadar O'Donnell's** (Waterloo St., tel. 028/7137–2318) is one of the hottest tourist hangouts and is named after a Union organizer who played a part in the 1921 Irish Civil War. With the interior always crammed with people, you'll have lots of time to admire the memorabilia tacked onto the ceiling. The **Strand Bar** (Strand St., tel. 028/7126–0494) is one of those total refurbishment/conversions covering three stories of eclectic space. It's constantly crammed with mellow locals, curious visitors, and yahoo-ing groups of university students having a ball. The music, which happens most nights, is reason enough to survive the crush—it's terrific. The **Carraig Bar** (Strand St., tel. 028/7126–7529) is a perfect Victorian bar in the university area. Bombed in 1973, it's been completely restored and is always thronged with students. There is also disco upstairs. The **Townsman Bar** (Shipquay St., tel. 028/7126–0820) is festooned with the paraphernalia of doctors and chemists of the 19th century; the awful-looking instruments are arranged here and there, offering a distraction if you can't find anyone to talk to (an unlikely prospect in this friendly spot). **Gweedore** (Waterloo St., tel. 028/7126–3513) is right next door to the aforementioned Peadar O'Donnell's (there's a back-door connection) and specializes in folk, trad, and some excellent toe-tappin' bluegrass pickin'. For entertainment listings, pick up the biweekly *Derry Journal* (50p) or the weekly *Londonderry Sentinel* (55p).

TYRONE AND FERMANAGH

South of County Londonderry, the counties of Tyrone and Fermanagh constitute the bulk of Northern Ireland's unheralded southern extreme. Despite the region's natural beauty, backpackers and budget travelers are rare here. Tyrone and Fermanagh have few well-known tourist sites and are completely ignored by Northern Irish Railway's train network. Cyclists may find this a boon rather than a drawback, since the region's uncrowded rural roads allow for some excellent sightseeing.

One of the least-explored counties in Northern Ireland, Tyrone is an ideal area to get off the beaten tourist track and kick back in the lazy, graceful countryside. With not a whole lot of attractions for the visitor, it's more a place for peaceful meandering. The people are friendly in that distinctly country way—a polite series of questions about your own heritage and where you're from will precede any conversation. Tyrone was the territory of the O'Neill clan until their defeat at Mellifont in 1603, when Red Hugh O'Neill, the Earl of Ulster, finally submitted to the dominion of British rule. This was the last breath of the old Gaelic Ireland. Shortly afterward, the Scottish planters moved in throughout the area, a group that was eventually responsible for the linen industry. Many of the Catholic Irish emigrated to the United States.

Fermanagh is big lake country with the Upper and Lower Lough Erne encircling Enniskillen and touching Donegal on one end and Cavan on the other. The River Erne wanders right across the county, attracting fishermen, sailors, hikers, and those interested in orienteering. If idling with a line in the water in the hope of catching the big one is your bag, this is your kind of country. "Once fished, never forgotten" is the local motto. A boon for two-wheelers is the new **Kingfisher Bike Trail** (tel. 028/6632–0121), which joins all the towns in the lake district, from Belleek in the south through Enniskillen, Belturbet, Leitrim, Belcoo, and Kiltycloguer. For walkers, the Ulster Way provides 37 km (23 mi) of well-marked paths on a route from Belcoo to Lough Navar. Due to its inaccessibility, Fermanagh always proved a difficult area for invaders to conquer; the Vikings, Normans, and Tudors all tried and failed. It was only in 1600, when the planters arrived in Enniskillen, that English rule began to flourish in the county, with numerous castles being built around the lake and the establishment of two royal regiments. With the coming of Partition, Fermanagh was forced to uneasily join the other counties that remained under English rule, but the Nationalist spirit continued to thrive. The hunger striker Bobby Sands was elected an MP for Fermanagh and South Tyrone in 1981. He died 66 days after beginning his fast and never took his seat in Westminster.

OMAGH

On August 15, 1998, the 29th anniversary of the arrival of British troops in Northern Ireland, a massive bomb blast in the center of Omagh left dozens dead and hundreds injured. In a province where urban atrocities have inured many of the population to such outrages, this was an event that overshadowed even the worst that had gone before. Planted by an extreme breakaway faction calling themselves the Real IRA, it was meant to underline the convictions of those who stood against the Peace Agreement. Instead, it galvanized those pursuing peace (the vast majority on both sides in the province) into hammering out their differences for the greater good. While the town of Omagh has now earned its own position in the roll call of infamy that has existed throughout the North for the last 30 years, it did, at least, emphasize the common bonds of survival and peaceful coexistence between the ordinary people of the province.

BASICS

Omagh's **tourist office** (1 Market St., tel. 028/8224–7831), open weekdays 9–5 (April–September, also Saturday 9–5), is in the easily navigated city center. Across the street, Conway's Cycles (Market St., tel. 028/8224–6195) rents bikes on the Raleigh scheme for £7 per day, £35 per week, plus a £40 deposit. The **Halifax Building Society** (High St., tel. 028/8224–6931) has an ATM and offers currency exchange services. It's open weekdays 9:30–5 and Saturday 9–12. The post office (7 High St., tel. 028/8224–2970) is open weekdays 9–5 and Saturday 10–12:30.

COMING AND GOING

The **bus station** (Mountjoy Rd., tel. 028/8224–2711), adjacent to the River Camowen, has an info desk open weekdays 9–5:45. Ulsterbus runs buses to Derry (hourly; £4.50), Enniskillen (8 per day; £4.20),

Belfast (9 per day; £5.90), and Dublin (6 per day; £9.50). If you're cycling between Derry and Omagh, take the scenic B48 rather than the congested A5.

WHERE TO SLEEP AND EAT

The only budget-friendly B&B in town is **Ardmore** (12 Tamlaght Rd., tel. 028/8224–3381), a neat family place that has a small library of books about the town and surrounding area. Rooms are £17 per person. The **Royal Arms Hotel** (51–53 High St., tel. 028/8224–3262) is in one of Omagh's oldest buildings, dating back to 1787. An old-fashioned establishment, it offers singles for £45 and doubles for £75. When it's time to eat try **Libbi's** (52 Market St., tel. 028/8224–2969), a cheap and wholesome sandwich shop, or **Pink Elephant** (19 High St., tel. 028/8224–9805), a reasonably priced greasy spoon. **Grant's** (Georges St., tel. 028/8225–0900) is a new addition to the restaurant scene, serving pastas and seafood in a Continental-style setting. Omagh has its share of lifeless run-of-the-mill pubs; three exceptions are **Gallagher's** (39 High St., tel. 028/8224–2698), the wonderfully musty **Bogan's** (20 High St., tel. 028/8224–2991), and **Sally O'Briens** (John St., tel. 028/8224–2521), which is worth a pint just to soak up the atmosphere of what was once a tea merchants. Wonderful aromas abound, with wooden tea chests and paraphernalia all around.

WORTH SEEING

Omagh, one of County Tyrone's largest commercial centers, sits in the Clogher Valley, 53 km (33 mi) south of Derry. Omagh is easily reached by bus from Derry, and it tends to attract a wealthy rental-car breed of tourists. You'll find few worthwhile attractions in Omagh proper, and even fewer inexpensive travel options—no cheap cafés, no hip hangouts or adventurous nighttime diversions.

Omagh's main attractions are the historically themed **Ulster-American Folk Park** (Mellon Rd., Castletown, 5 km/3 mi north of Omagh on A5, tel. 028/8224–3292) and **Ulster History Park** (Gortin Glen, 27 km/17 mi north of Omagh on B48, tel. 028/8264–8188). Ulster-American Folk Park is dedicated to Northern Irish emigrants who resettled in America during the 18th and 19th centuries. Exhibits include full-scale replicas of Irish peasant cottages, Pennsylvania farmhouses, a New York tenement, and immigrant transport ships. In the replica of a 19th-century Ulster village, staff dressed in 19th-century costumes talk about their trades (blacksmith, baker, weaver, etc.), answer questions, and pose for pictures. Admission is £3.50, and the park is open Monday–Saturday 11–6:30, Sunday 11:30–7 (October–Easter, weekdays 10:30–5). Ulster History Park, another open-air museum dominated by full-scale models, documents Irish history from the first known settlers to the 12th-century arrival of the Normans. It includes carefully replicated crannogs and dolmen, a monastery, and a plantation settlement. Admission is £3.50, and it's open April–September, Monday–Saturday 10:30–6:30, Sunday 11–7; and October–March, weekdays 10:30–5. Both parks are worthwhile if you happen to be in the neighborhood, but don't make a special trip to get here. For the Ulster-American Park, Ulsterbus's Omagh–Derry service stops outside the front gate 10 times daily; for the Ulster History Park, take one of Ulsterbus's twice-daily Omagh–Gortin coaches (£2.30 round-trip). The last admission to both parks is 1½ hours before closing.

Just a few miles north of Omagh is the small but very accessible Sperrin Mountain range. The mountains are full of twisting small roads, forested glens and hidden glades, and the many lookout spots, which offer views over the rolling countryside are ideal for a picnic. The Noble Prize–winning Irish poet, Seamus Heaney, grew up on the edge of the Sperrins and continues to write about their affect on his life. Back in the days when the "plantation" of Ulster was being sold to businessmen from the Empire, the guide who took the Four Citizens of London on a tour in 1609 was under strict orders from the First Deputy not to let them see the Sperrins. Officials feared that the mere sight of these inhospitable hills would put the could-be entrepreneurs off the project. For committed walkers, the Sperrins also contain a 40-km (25-mi) stretch of the Ulster Way, which meanders through the most beautiful heart of these mountains before joining A6 farther south at Dungiven. A copy of *The Ulster Way for Walkers* is available at any tourist office. The highest point is Mount Sawel (2,200 ft), at whose base stands the **Sperrin Heritage Centre** (tel. 028/8164–8142). The center has good computer graphics presentations about the historical and ecological aspects of the region. Small amounts of gold have been found in these mountains, and Barry McGuigan, a recent Irish world champion boxer, had his first medal made from it. The center also has a pleasant café. It's open April–September, weekdays 11–6, Saturday 11:30–6, and Sunday 2–7. Admission is £2.50.

COOKSTOWN

Founded in 1609 by planter Alan Cooke, this town was one of the smaller examples of the sectarian divide in Ulster, with Catholics living at one end and sharing an often-uneasy truce with the Protestants at the other. Having seen a number of explosive encounters during the dark days of the Troubles in the 1970s and '80s, the two groups have settled into a happier coexistence since the Peace Agreement. The two British Army checkpoints that stood at either end of Main Street have recently been removed, but the barbed wire around the courthouse and the army base next to the school remain as evidence of how things were.

BASICS

The **tourist office** (Molesworth St., tel. 0028/8676–6727) is open weekdays 9–5 and Saturday 9–1. It has all the usual info on the region, including walks, maps, historic sites, and accommodations.

WHERE TO SLEEP

The **Greenvale Hotel** (57 Drum Rd., tel. 028/8676–2243) has 12 rooms set in old-fashioned surroundings and carries a flavor of old-world welcome about it. Rates start at £35 per person. For B&B accommodations, try the **Central Inn** (William St., tel. 028/8676–2255), a family-run place where comfortable beds cost £14 per night. The **Edergole** (Moneymore Rd., tel. 028/8676–2924), which has rooms for £18 per person, also has a riding school. There is a campsite at **Drum Manor Forest Park** (tel. 01868/759664), with sites amid the lakes and woodland walks costing £7 a night. Facilities are basic, but the peace of the area is overpowering. The business includes a butterfly farm and an arboretum.

FOOD

For some strange reason, Cookstown has a fair selection of Chinese restaurants; the **Dragon Palace** (William St., tel. 028/8676–3311) and the **Gourmet Chinese** (Molesworth St., no phone) serve fresh and sizzling concoctions in the £6–£9 price range. **Joe Mac's Diner** (Molesworth St., no phone) is a cheerful café serving daily specials of the usual type—quiche, stews, soups, sandwiches—and a good range of coffees. For a white-tablecloth setting, go to the **Greenvale Hotel** (57 Drum Rd., tel. 028/8676–2243). Dinner, with entrées like cod fillets, roast chicken, and lamb with vegetables, runs about £15 a head.

WORTH SEEING

The **Wellbrook Beetling Mill** (tel. 028/8675–1735), maintained by the National Trust, is the last mill where hammers can be seen at work. Beetling refers to the final stage in linen making, when the cloth is beaten with hammers known as beetles to achieve a flattened sheen on the material. There were once six mills at Wellbrook, with all the machinery driven by water power. For the people who worked these mills, the noise often resulted in a permanent loss of hearing. The mill is on the A505 Omagh Road, about 5 km (3 mi) west of Kildress. It's usually open April–September, Wednesday–Saturday 2–6, but check with the tourist office (see above) before heading there.

About 13 km (8 mi) north of Cookstown, just off the A505, are the Beachmore Stone Circles, a series of Bronze Age circles and cairns dating back to 2000 BC. Buried deep in the bog land, the sites were only discovered in the 1950s and contain the so-called Dragon's Teeth, a circle of tightly set stones that jut out at regular intervals. While nobody knows for sure what the circles represent, most historians believe they had something to do with pagan astrological practices.

Three kilometers (2 mi) southeast of Cookstown off the B520 is Tullaghoge Fort, the site of an 11th-century burial ground of the O'Hagans, as well as the place the O'Neills were inaugurated as the Kings of Ulster. The stone inauguration chair, representing the throne, was destroyed by Mountjoy in 1602 during his pursuit of Hugh O'Neill, the last of the clan.

ENNISKILLEN

BASICS

Enniskillen's **tourist office** (Wellington Rd., tel. 028/6632–3110), adjacent to the Ulsterbus depot, has a bureau de change, books B&B accommodations (£1 fee), and will load you down with glossy brochures and information on transportation to Lough Erne and Devenish Island. It's open Monday–Friday 9–7, Saturday 10–6, and Sunday 11–5. First Trust Savings Bank (East Bridge St., tel. 028/6632–

BERNADETTE DEVLIN

Just as Gerry Adams, Mo Mowlam, and Tony Blair are the leaders that have shaped the present cease-fire and Peace Accord, Catholic political activist Bernadette Devlin was one of the strongest voices during the very troubled times in the 1960s and '70s. Born in Cookstown in 1947, she became an active member in the civil rights movement and was eventually elected to Westminster in 1969 as the youngest-ever member of parliament. Full of energy and zeal to right the wrongs of decades of bigotry and racism, she was imprisoned for taking part in the 1969 Battle of the Bogside in Derry and arrested for physically attacking the British Home Secretary in the House of Commons in 1972. She withdrew from active politics after an attempt was made on her life by a Protestant assassination squad in 1981. However, she is still deeply involved in the fights for prisoners' rights and social justice and against discrimination. Bernadette McAliskey, as she is now known, still lives in a council flat in her native Cookstown.

2464) has an ATM, as does the Halifax Building Society (High St., tel. 028/6632–7072). The post office (East Bridge St., tel. 028/6632–4525) is open weekdays 9–5:30 and Saturday 9–12:30. You can do laundry at Paragon Cleaners (East St., tel. 028/6632–5230) for £5 per load; it's open daily 9–5:30.

COMING AND GOING

Enniskillen's **bus station** (Wellington Rd., tel. 028/6632–2633) has an info desk open weekdays 9–5:30. To reach the city center from here, turn right out of the station and cross Wellington Road; High and Townhall streets are two blocks ahead. Buses leave Enniskillen for Omagh (8 per day; £4.20), Derry (7 per day; £6.30), Belfast (10 per day; £6.50), and Dublin (4 per day; £9.70).

WHERE TO SLEEP AND EAT

Rossole Guesthouse (85 Sligo Rd., tel. 028/6632–3462) is a modern town house on the banks of Rossole Lake, with rooms from £17 for a single to £34 for a double. This B&B is no-smoking, something that is becoming more common in lodgings throughout Ireland. The **Railway Hotel** (34 Forthill St., tel. 028/6632–2084) is another comfortable option, located on the east side of town, on the road to Omagh. The hotel is 150 years old and has a traditional feel to it, with interesting paintings and antiques decorating its lobby. Rooms are £33 per person.

The best restaurant for miles is **Oscar's** (29 Belmore St., tel. 028/6632–7037), open after 5 PM, a subdued place with lots of Oscar Wilde paraphernalia. Soups and sandwiches start at a reasonable £2, but splurge and try the seafood omelets (£6) or the chicken Kiev (£7). Slightly cheaper is **Golden Arrow** (23 Townhall St., tel. 028/6632–2259), which serves chicken pie and chips (£2.25) and sandwiches (£1.30). **Franco's Pizzeria and Seafood Bar** (Queen Elizabeth Rd., tel. 028/6632–4424) is a cozy place that serves pizza and pastas for around £6, in addition to a variety of reasonably priced fish dishes. The **Barbizon Café** (East Bridge St., tel. 028/6632–4556) is a coffee shop–cum–art gallery owned by a pair of Swiss artists. The **Crow's Nest** (High St., tel. 028/6632–5252) serves a gigantic breakfast all day for £4 as well as the standard grill fare, including steaks and burgers. **Blakes of the Hollow** (Church St., tel. 028/6632–2143) is a tourist landmark—an old-world institution with great trad music on weekends.

WORTH SEEING

Built on an island on the fringe of Lough Erne, Enniskillen is a pleasantly small and smart-looking town. The principal thoroughfares, Townhall and High streets, are crowded with old-style pubs and rows of redbrick Georgian flats, and the waterfront **Enniskillen Castle** (Wellington Rd., tel. 028/6632–5000) is one of the best-preserved monuments in Northern Ireland. This ancient stronghold, built by the Maguire clan in 1670, houses the Fermanagh County and Fusiliers Regimental Museum, as well as temporary exhibits. It's open May–September, Tuesday–Friday 10–5, Monday and Saturday 2–5; also July–August, Sunday 2–5, and admission is £2.

Nearby, look for the imposing St. Michael's and St. MacArtin's cathedrals, both on Church Street. Continue west down Church Street for High Street's pubs and restaurants. Farther west on Belmore Street, in another pocket of pubs and chippies, are **McCartney's** (17 Belmore St., tel. 028/6632–2012) and **McGee's Spirit Shop** (25 Belmore St., tel. 028/6632–4996), the city's best watering holes. **Bush Bar and Lounge** (26 Townhall St., tel. 028/6632–5210) often hosts live music.

Another good reason to visit Enniskillen is its location, nestled on the banks of Lough Erne in the heart of Fermanagh's stunning lake district. Cyclists in particular could spend a day or two exploring the lough's picture-perfect, 72-km (45-mi) shoreline. The rural A46/Bundoran road meanders along its pristine southern bank, and the equally scenic B82/Lisnarick road keeps to the east. Another good day trip is to Devenish Island, 3 km (2 mi) north of Enniskillen, which has a well-preserved medieval monastic settlement with a ruined abbey and an 82-ft-tall round tower. The M.V. *Kestrel* (Brook Park, tel. 028/6632–2882) runs 1¾-hour boat tours (£5) of Lough Erne that include a stop on Devenish Island.

On Lower Lough Erne, 40 km (25 mi) from Enniskillen on the A46, the small village of Belleek is worth a visit for its china, a delicate and paper-thin creation renowned for its intricate patterns. There are tours of the Belleek Pottery factory, which let you observe the tradesmen at work. The visitor center (tel. 028/6865–8501) contains both a museum and shop. For those looking for a bargain the pickings are slim, however, as there are no seconds—all rejects are destroyed. The factory is open weekdays 9–6 and Saturday 10–6.

Also consider a day trip to the **Marble Arch Caves** (Marlbank Scenic Loop, Florence Ct., tel. 028/6634–8855), the region's most popular tourist attraction. Inside the vast underground complex are subterranean rivers, waterfalls, and eerie passageways, all studded with the usual stalactite-stalagmite cave formations. You actually take a boat on an underground river for part of the tour. The caves are 30 km (19 mi) south of Enniskillen on the A32, a short but semi-steep cycle from town, and they're open late March–June and September, daily 10–4:30. Admission is £5. **Florence Court** (tel. 028/6634–8249) is an 18th-century Georgian mansion in the midst of the Florence Court Forest Park, 6 km (4 mi) beyond the Marble Arch Caves. Once the home of the Earls of Enniskillen, it contains an impressive fossil collection and the remains of a walled garden. There is little else of interest in the house. It's open April–September, Wednesday–Monday noon–6; hours sometimes vary, so call ahead. Admission is £2.80. You can get a ride from **County Cabs** (tel. 028/6632–8888) or **Cleenish Taxi Service** (tel. 0365/322255), both of which run daily service to the caves for £8 one-way.

Smack dab in the middle of Upper Lough Erne is Inis Rath Island, home to reclusive monks since the 6th century. Its current residents are members of the Hare Krishna sect. There's a nature preserve, where you can observe swans, peacocks, and herds of deer. A quick rowboat trip gets you there, but you have to call ahead to book your place (tel. 028/6672–1512). The food and lodging in the dormitory are free, as are the frequent prayer services, meditation, and recitation of the Hare Krishna mantra. It's an unusual experience.

ARMAGH

For its sheer unadorned and unspoiled beauty, the county of Armagh should be one of the favorite tourist destinations in Ireland. With a rich heritage of Gaelic culture, many prehistoric sites, and a wealth of monuments to both Protestant and Catholic religions, the place is a treasure trove of attractions surrounded by mountains, rivers, lakes, and nature in full bloom. The Troubles, however, made their mark on the county, with simmering resentments of a historical origin often boiling over into conflict. Apart from a few Protestant enclaves, the county is staunchly Catholic and has long proved a volatile member of the Northern six counties. Thankfully, like other flash points within the province, the Peace Accord has had a gentling effect on the passions of the past. The spiritual capital of Ireland for 5,000 years, and the seat of both Protestant and Catholic archbishops, Armagh is the most venerated of Irish cities. St. Patrick called Armagh "my sweet hill" and built his stone church on the hill where the Anglican cathedral now stands. On the opposite hill, the twin-spired Catholic cathedral, built in 1840, is flanked by two large marble statues of archbishops who look across the town.

BASICS

The **tourist office** (40 English St., tel. 028/3752–1800) is in the Old Bank Building and has all the information on the area you'll need. It's open Monday–Saturday 9–5 and Sunday 1–5. **Armagh Ancestry** (tel. 028/3751–0033), also on English Street, will help you trace your lineage; it's open Monday–Saturday 9–5. Banking needs are taken care of at **Northern Bank** (Scotch St., tel. 028/3752–2004); it has an ATM outside. Bike rental can be found at **Brown's Bikes** (Scotch St., tel. 028/3752–2782) for £5 per day, £25 per week. The **post office** (Upper English St., tel. 028/3751–0313) is open weekdays 9–5:30, Saturday 9–12:30.

COMING AND GOING

Buses stop on the east side of the Mall and offer regular services to Belfast (£5) and Enniskillen (£5.50). A chain of **Intercity buses** (tel. 028/3752–2266) services all points in the city.

WHERE TO SLEEP

The **Charlemont Arms Hotel** (63 Lower English St., tel. 028/3752–2028) is a standard country town hotel with all required basic facilities and a very friendly staff. Room rates are £28 per person. The spanking-new **IHH Hostel** (Abbey St., tel. 028/3751–1800) is a convenient and spotless place to stay. It has six-, four-, and two-bed rooms, each with TV and shower. Singles are £10, doubles £11.50; members get a £1 discount. There are also laundry facilities for £3. The **Padua Guest House** (Cathedral Rd., tel. 028/3752–2039) has clean, comfortable rooms for £12 a person. It's right by the Catholic cathedral and its ringing bells. The **Gosfard Forest Park** (tel. 028/3755–1277), 11 km (7 mi) southeast of Armagh off the A28, has camping space aplenty for £8.50 per two-person tent. Bus 40 from town will get you there.

FOOD

The town is definitely not big on restaurants. The **Basement Café** (English St., tel. 028/3752–4311), next to the library, serves cheap food of the wholesome variety. It specializes in hearty soups (£1.50), well-stuffed sandwiches (£2–£2.75), salads, and pasta. **Our Ma's Café**—say it quick—(Lower English St., tel. 028/3751–1289) is great for baked goods, including pastries, while **Rainbow Restaurant** (Upper English St., tel. 028/3752–3391) serves generous breakfasts and lunches at reasonable prices. The **Station Bar** (Lower English St., tel. 028/3752–3731) is a somewhat decrepit establishment, but that only adds to the popularity of the place, which is packed with locals. Likewise, the **Northern Bar** (Railway St., tel. 028/3752–7315) attracts many regulars to its good trad music and dancing weekend nights. McAleavey's, a roadhouse-style establishment 6 km (4 mi) south of town, in Keady, has a major reputation for excellent traditional music on Wednesday nights.

WORTH SEEING

English, Thomas, and Scotch streets form the core of the city center. Many of the public buildings and Georgian town houses along the Mall are the work of Francis Johnson, a native of Armagh, who also left his graceful mark upon the Georgian squares of Dublin. The builders of Armagh delighted in the warm-color local limestone called Armagh marble—it's everywhere to be seen. The archbishop's palace and the courthouse are prime examples.

This is a cathedral town, and a visit to the main structures is a must. The Church of Ireland Cathedral of St. Patrick (tel. 028/3752–3142) was originally built in the 13th century and then extensively remodeled in the 19th century. It is thought that the cathedral is on the site of a 5th-century edifice established by St. Patrick. Thackeray, who observed the church when he passed through the town in 1842, particularly admired the new building, which then, as now, included many monuments by Roubiliac, Chanterey, Rysbrack, and Nollekens. "It wants a hundred years at least," he declared "to cool the raw colours of the stones, and to dull the new brightness of the gilding, all which benefits, no doubt, time will bring to pass . . ." Brian Boru, who drove the Norsemen out of Ireland in 1014, is buried in the churchyard. The cathedral library, founded in 1771 by Archbishop Robinson, who also built the observatory, contains a copy of *Gulliver's Travels* corrected in Swift's hand. It also contains a copy of the *Claims of the Innocents,* the peasant pleas to Oliver Cromwell. The library is open April–September, daily 10:30–5. There are tours during the summer months. Admission is free.

Walking down Dawson Street from this cathedral, you'll come to the other St. Patrick's, St. Patrick's Roman Catholic Cathedral. It was built between 1838 and 1873, a period during which the trauma of the famine interrupted the work. Dark water stains on the lower sections of the outside walls bear testament to work having been stopped and marred by exposure to the elements. Built in the Gothic Revival style, the structure is dominated by huge twin towers piercing the skyline and rows upon rows of steps marking the approach. The interior walls are almost completely covered by brilliantly colored mosaics. The entire structure is more austere than the Church of Ireland and seems quite at odds with its own sanctuary, which was modernized in 1981 in a style that takes away from the history-rich atmosphere. The cathedral is open daily year-round; admission is free.

Heading up College Hill from the Mall brings you directly to the **Observatory & Planetarium** (tel. 028/ 3752–3689), two buildings set in extensive gardens ideal for strolling. The Armagh Observatory may be 200 years old, but it still contributes to astronomical research. A refractory telescope dating back to 1885 is on display, as is the modern weather station. In the Planetarium, you can observe the wonders of far-away galaxies and a global view of our home via the Eartharium Gallery. There's even a small chunk of Mars rock on display. Both buildings are open year-round, Monday–Saturday 10–5 and Sunday 1–5, with extended hours in peak season. Admission is £3.50, students £ 2.50.

In the center of town, right behind the tourist office, is **St. Patrick's Trian** (tel. 028/3752–1801). The ancient Presbyterian church has been turned into a heritage center that focuses on St. Patrick and his exploits in the place. "The Armagh Story" is a moving display and audiovisual presentation in which various "visitors" like the Vikings, pagan warriors, and priests relate the story of the town. There's also a "Land of Lilliput" exhibit with a well-detailed model of Gulliver pinned to the ground while little Lilliputians clamber on top of him. The story of his adventures works well with any little people that may be in your company. The center is open Monday–Saturday 10–5:30, Sunday 1–6. Admission is £3.35, students £2.50.

Just over 2 km (1 mi) west of Armagh town on the Killylea Road (A28) is the Navan Fort, home to the Kings of Ulster for more than 800 years and one of the principal archaeological sites in Ulster. It even appears in a map of the world made in the 2nd century by Ptolemy, the Egyptian geographer. Although its origins are open to all kinds of speculation, excavations have indicated that the hill was the site for houses and a temple during the Iron and Bronze ages, and later the site of a huge wooden structure that was filled with lime and burnt, possibly to prevent it from being sacked by invaders. It is thought that Queen Macha founded the fort, and there are many who claim that St. Patrick eventually chose it as another place to launch his assault on paganism. There is a **visitor center** (tel. 028/3752–5550) designed in the shape of a Bronze Age building where you'll find films, displays, and information about the site and the legends associated with it. The fort is open Monday–Saturday 10–7, Sunday 11–6. Admission is £3.95, students £3.

NEAR ARMAGH

SOUTH ARMAGH

Referred to during the Troubles as "Bandit Country," this staunchly Catholic area exemplified the disharmony between Catholics and Protestants. A collection of small towns and hamlets dotted about some of the most unspoiled (and obviously untraveled) country in Armagh, it was the scene of many ambushes, killings, and traumatic conflicts in recent years. Some villages became virtual garrisons, with British Army units on permanent patrol and the constant buzzing of military helicopters in the skies overhead. Again, with the Peace Accord, things have settled, and it's once again a peaceful pastoral environment. Towns like Bessbrook, Camlough, Crossmaglen, and Killnasaggart really have little to recommend them in terms of activities, just the open country and quiet roads as a soothing antidote to the other more bustling parts of the county.

NEWCASTLE AND THE MOUNTAINS OF MOURNE

Just 48 km (30 mi) from Belfast, Newcastle is a typical holiday-town resort with not a huge amount to recommend it other than being a prime position from which to explore the Mourne Mountains. Packed with holidaymakers from both the North and the Republic during vacation times, it does have 5 km (3 mi) of gentle sandy beaches but unfortunately also has the hurdy-gurdy atmosphere of amusement arcades, fast-food palaces, and seaside tackiness.

BASICS

The **tourist office** (tel. 028/4372–2222) is on Central Promenade just 500 yards from the bus station. It's open June–August, Monday–Saturday 9:30–7 and Sunday 2–6; and September–June, Monday–Saturday 10–5 and Sunday 2–6. The post office (tel. 028/4372–2418), also on Central Promenade, is open weekdays 9–5 and Saturday 9–noon. There are several banks on Main Street, including First Trust (tel. 028/4372–3476) and Northern Bank (tel. 028/9127–1211) both of which have ATM machines. You can do your laundry at Dirty Duds (Valentia Pl., tel. 028/4372–6190), open Monday–Saturday 9–6. A load costs £2.50. Bike rental can be had at Wiki Wiki Wheels (Donard St., tel. 028/4372–3973) by the bus station for £6.50 per day and £30 per week (passport or credit card deposit required).

COMING AND GOING

Ulsterbus (depot: Railway St., tel. 028/4372–2296) offers daily service to Belfast (£4.20), Downpatrick (£2.20), Newry (£3.30), and Dublin (£9.70). There is no train service to the town.

WHERE TO SLEEP

Given its main commerce as a holiday destination, Newcastle is jammed with B&Bs of all shapes and sizes with prices ranging from the sublime to the ridiculous in high season. The best bet, especially if you like glorious sea views, is **Drunrawn House** (Central Promenade, tel. 028/4372–6847), a tidy and looked-after Georgian town house where beds cost £16.50 per person. The **Glenside Farmhouse** (Tullybrannigan Rd., tel. 028/4372–2628) is a wonderful family-run affair about 3 km (2 mi) from the town proper. Rooms are £11 for a single and £22 for a double. The **YHANI Newcastle Youth Hostel** (tel. 028/4372–2133) is on Downs Road, a central location, close to transport, the seafront, and the town. While the rooms could be fairly described as cramped, they are comfortable and clean and come in at £7.50 for a dorm bed, and £30 for a six-person penthouse. **Tullymore Forest Park** (tel. 028/4372–2428) on Tullybrannigan Road, 3 km (2 mi) out along the A2, provides excellent camping facilities with showers, a café and 1,200 acres of walkway-filled gardens. Tent sites are £10 during the summer, £6.50 during the winter and early spring.

FOOD

It can seem like an impossible job to find a decent restaurant in the midst of the greasy burgers, candy floss, and ice cream cones that proliferate at most corners of Newcastle, but you'll succeed if you persist. **Mario's** (Central Promenade, tel. 028/4372–3912) does some decent Italian dishes, including spaghetti and pizza. Likewise, the **Cygnet Coffee Shop** (Savoy Lawn, right by the bus station, no phone) serves healthy home-cooked fare—stews, salads, and big sandwiches—for around £3.50–£5.50 an entrée. On Main Street is **Robinson's Restaurant** (tel. 028/4372–6259), where you can get good, light, bar food at reasonable prices. You won't find any quiet pubs in this vacation town, but you can find great trad music at the usually thronged **Quinn's** (Main St., tel. 028/4372–6400). Old retail products like boots and provisions decorate the walls and ceiling as the hard-pressed bar staff haul out rounds for the endless hands in the air. The **Anchor Bar** (Bryansford Rd., tel. 028/4372–3344) has some striking stained-glass fixtures evoking scenes of the nautical past. Down on the beach itself, many older patrons

Don't Forget To Pack A Nikon.

Nuvis S
The smart little camera in a cool metal jacket.

Slide the stainless steel cover open on the Nikon Nuvis S, and a new world of picture taking is in the palm of your hand. This pocket-sized gem offers a 3x zoom lens, three picture formats, and drop-in film loading. Slide the protective cover over the lens, slip it in your pocket, and you're ready for your next adventure. For more information, visit us at *www.nikonusa.com*

ADVANCED

Money From Home In Minutes.

If you're stuck for cash on your travels, don't panic. Millions of people trust Western Union to transfer money in minutes to 165 countries and over 50,000 locations worldwide. Our record of safety and reliability is second to none. For more information, call Western Union: USA 1-800-325-6000, Canada 1-800-235-0000. Wherever you are, you're never far from home.

www.westernunion.com

WESTERN UNION | MONEY TRANSFER®

The fastest way to send money worldwide.

prefer the more sedate surroundings of the **Percy French Bar** (Slieve Donard Hotel, Downs Rd., tel. 028/ 4423–175), where there's much memorabilia devoted to the man who penned those classic ditties about an Irish way of life that'll never come again.

WORTH SEEING

The most interesting site in Newcastle is not in the town itself but the Mountains of Mourne, which rise above it. Subjects of a song that is sung on every occasion from baptisms to funerals, the Mountains of Mourne must surely qualify as one of Ireland's best-known ranges. Distinctive and self-contained, they are tucked away in this southeast corner of Northern Ireland, their 12 shapely summits rising above 2,000 ft. Surrounded on all sides by towns and villages, the Mournes remain an isolated mass of unexplored corners and vistas, crossed only by the B27 road between Kilkeel and Hilltown. The steep and craggy peaks of the Mournes form a rough figure eight, with two great glens filling in the inner valleys. Slieve Donard, the tallest of the peaks, at 2,796 ft, has a peculiar blue hue when viewed from Newcastle at its base. A climb of the peak is a must-do. The reasonable three- to four-hour ascent is best approached from Donard Park on the southern edge of town. If the weather is right, the trip to the summit is rewarded with stunning views over the fields of County Down as well as parts of Scotland and the Isle of Man. The two ancient cairns you'll encounter right at the summit are believed to have been penance cells of St. Donard, who came here in early Christian times.

"Where the mountains o' Mourne sweep down to the sea"—Percy French

The Mournes are also a wonderful place for hiking. Any trek into the hills is better taken after a visit to the **Mourne Countryside Centre** (Central Promenade, tel. 028/ 4372–4059), where a helpful staff will provide info, maps, and advice on which route is best suited to your ability. They can also arrange for guides. The center is open Monday–Saturday 9–5 and Sunday 10–5. One good hike is along the Mourne Wall. Built early in the 20th century to provide employment, it stretches 40 km (25 mi), snaking around the midsections of the mountains' peaks, to enclose the Silent Valley reservoir, which acts as a water reserve for Belfast. Doing the whole wall in one day will require good footwear (decent boots a must) and a fairly determined pace—not too many breaks allowed. Many prefer to make a two-day jaunt of it and camp along the way; the best spots to pitch a tent are around Lough Shannagh, the Hare's gap, and the banks of Blue Lough. Another route full of historical atmosphere is the Brandy Pad, an old smugglers' path running right across the mountains through ever-changing terrain. If you'd like to trek in the company of experienced hillwalkers, contact the **Mourne Rambling Group** (tel. 028/4372–4315) for details on the trips they've got planned. There are also numerous guide books to the mountains; *St. Patrick's Vale: The Land of Legend* (£1 at most tourist offices in the area) is a good primer, listing more than 30 walks.

Tollymore Forest Park, 3 km (2 mi) northeast of Newcastle, is a wide-open-spaces kind of place with "a grand stroll" (as they'd call it hereabouts) available along the banks of the River Shimna. The park has a **visitor center** (tel. 028/4372–2428), housed in an old barn, that provides ample information of walks, vegetation, and the history of the region. The park is open daily 10 AM to sunset; admission is £2.50 per car. At the other end of Newcastle, just off the Dundrum Road, is **Murlough National Nature Reserve** (tel. 028/4375–1467). The sand dunes and woods here provide the habitats for seals, badgers, foxes, and all manner of birds. There's also excellent swimming (if you can handle the cold).

You can also take one of the frequent daily buses (15 a day) from Newcastle to the Castlewellan Forest Park (tel. 028/4377–8664), at the top of Main Street in Castlewellan. The park is spread out under and around the Mournes from the north and east sides. With the centerpiece being the impressively placed lake, the park has a number of low-lying attractions not requiring strong boots and a head for heights. There is a Sculpture Trail—a pathway along which are various sculptures made from local materials—and the National Arboretum, dating to 1760 and filled with rare shrubs, trees, and flora. The park is open weekdays 8:30–4:30 and weekends 10–5. Admission is £3 per car. Camping is £9.50 per tent.

THE YANKS IN THE NORTH

More than 300,000 Allied service personnel saw duty in Northern Ireland during World War II. The numbers that came across were so great, and the province so small, that there were soldiers, sailors, and airmen camped or billeted in every part of the province. The first wave of Operation Magnet arrived as a result of an agreement between President Roosevelt and Winston Churchill that the defense of Northern Ireland should be taken over by U.S. troops. Six weeks after the Japanese attacked Pearl Harbor on December 7, 1941, four American destroyers entered the Foyle at Derry. They were the first of hundreds, and Derry was expecting them: The city had been designated "Base One, Europe" by the U.S. Navy. American military personnel—called "technicians" and in civilian dress, since the United States was still ostensibly neutral at that time—had been hard at work since June on the construction of a huge anchorage at Lisahally. After Pearl Harbor, the "technicians" appeared in the streets in full uniform, their task almost completed. At the height of the Battle of the Atlantic in 1943, the city was host to some 50 warships of the American, Canadian, British, and other Allied navies. The fact that the province suddenly found itself populated with exotic gents from Mississippi and Missouri gave rise to many romantic entanglements, a fact exemplified by a song at the top of the hit parade in 1942, "Johnny Doughboy Found a Rose in Ireland." It was from Castle Archdale that "Catalina Z" of 204 Squadron took off to search for the "Bismark" on May 26, 1941. Co-pilot Leonard "Tuck" Smith of the U.S. Navy, on board to train RAF pilots, spotted the German battleship, eventually enabling the "Ark Royal" destroyer to sink it. The First Battalion of the U.S. Rangers was raised in Carrickfergus in June 1942; it was intended to be a U.S. equivalent of the British Commandos. Major William O'Darby, an aide to Major General Hartle, Commander of the U.S. Army in Northern Ireland, selected 500 men from about 2,000 volunteers. Barely two months later, 50 of the "Darby's rangers" took part in the raid at Dieppe in France. They also led the way in many other WWII operations, including the invasion of Italy at Salerno.

THE ARDS PENINSULA

Moving northeast from the Mourne Mountains, finishing the circle around Northern Ireland, you reach the Ards Peninsula. It begins at the town of Downpatrick in the south and arches north around the deep water of Strangford Lough to Belfast; along the way are the pleasant waterside towns of Portaferry, Killyleagh, and Bangor. The peninsula is crowded with historic sites and houses set against a varying backdrop of land, water, and gentle hills. Although the region long relied on fishing for its livelihood, quotas restricting the periods of the year when fishing is allowed have been introduced by the EU leaders in Brussels, much to the displeasure of the traditional fishermen. Now the Ards region is basically an agricultural domain, with little towns and villages creating their own commerce from tourism and the many small commercial enterprises that have flourished in the heady economics of the late 1990s.

DOWNPATRICK

One of the prime centers in the Ards, Downpatrick nestles between the low eastern hills of the Mournes and the big water of Strangford Lough to the north. Reputed to be the burial place of St. Patrick, the town and its outlying region have many relics and sites devoted to the famous saint. The town itself is a bustling center, with shops and offices being built at a rapid pace and old sectarian wounds being healed with the soothing balm of a unified commerce.

BASICS

The **tourist office** (Market St., tel. 028/4461–2233) is open weekdays 9–6 and Saturday 10–6. The **post office** (tel. 028/4461–2061) is also on Market Street; it's open Monday–Friday 9–5:30 and Saturday 9–12:30. **Northern Bank** (Market St., tel. 028/4461–4011) has an ATM.

COMING AND GOING

From the **bus station** (Market St., tel. 028/4461–2384) there are daily services to and from Belfast (£3.50), Newcastle (£2.15), and Strangford (£1.60).

WHERE TO SLEEP

Camping is available at the **Castle Ward Camping and Caravan Park** (tel. 028/4488–1680) near Strangford. The park, on a well-kept National Trust property, charges £7 per tent site; the showers are free, as are the fresh air and nature all around. A B&B of superior reputation is found at **Hillside** (Scotch St., tel. 028/4461–3134), where Mrs. Murray will treat you as one of her family in her friendly house with modern rooms. Cost is £13.50 per person, £15 with bathroom included.

FOOD AND DRINK

The **Daily Grind Coffee Shop** (St. Patrick's Ave., tel. 028/4461–5949) is a good stop for java, well-stuffed sandwiches, and regular specials. **Oakley Fayre's Bakery** (Market St., tel. 028/4461–5949) has all the pastry goodies one might expect (great croissants), as well as a full lunch and dinner selection in the restaurant right behind the shop. Pubs-wise, the town is well served. If you're after some more heritage to go with the sights you've seen during your day's travels, head for **Denvir's Hotel** (14 English St., tel. 028/4461–2012). Since its beginnings in 1642, it has attracted the likes of Jonathan Swift and Daniel O'Connell. It was also a favored meeting place of the outlawed United Irishmen before their rebellion in 1798. For music of all sorts from trad to blues and jive, get to **Hootenanny** (Irish St., tel. 028/4461–2222) where a mixed crowd of locals and visitors congregates amidst the swirling tunes. **The Russell** (Church St., tel. 028/4461–4170) is named after Thomas Russell, one of the leaders of the movement for Home Rule, who is said to haunt the place. Another attraction in the place is its reputation for serving the best Guinness in town.

WORTH SEEING

The **Down County Museum and Heritage Centre** (English St., tel. 028/4461–5218) is housed in the jail where many rebels were hanged. With an audiovisual history of County Down, some wax figures of prisoners, plus the obligatory history of St. Patrick, it endeavors to present a realistic version of the conditions that prevailed in those not-so-golden—particularly if you were Catholic—olden days. It's open weekdays 11–5 and Saturday 2–5. Admission is free. Down Cathedral (tel. 028/4461–4922) is right next door to the museum and has the Mound of Down close to its structure. The cathedral was erected on the site of a Bronze Age fort and is said to be the burial place of St. Patrick, although the claim still causes arguments among historians, who continue to disagree on the exact location. As declared by a plaque at its entrance, the site represents 1,500 years of Christianity, from its Celtic origins to its 1177 restoration by the Norman John De Courcy to the present. In addition to the alleged remains of Ireland's patron saint, the graveyard with its fine view over Downpatrick is also said to contain the remains of St. Brigid and St. Columbcille. The Mound, an elevated section of earth, rather like a large burial plot, stands in low-lying marshes just north of the Cathedral.

Three kilometers (2 mi) east of Downpatrick is the historical site of Saul, the spot where Saint Patrick is said to have landed in the 5th century. Having convinced the local chief to embrace the message of Christianity, Patrick was rewarded by being given a barn (a sabhal in Gaelic, which is pronounced saul) which he converted into the first parish church in Ireland. The church is open daily. Two kilometers (1 mi) from Saul, at the highest point of Slieve Patrick, is St. Patrick's Shrine, a massive granite statue of the saint and bronze panels depicting the major events of his life. The views from the summit, which take in all of the hinterland, the lough, and on a clear day, even the Isle of Man, are well worth the climb.

IRELAND AT A GLANCE: A CHRONOLOGY

CA. 6000 BC • Mesolithic (middle Stone Age) hunter-gatherers migrate from Scotland to the northeastern Irish coast.

CA. 3500 BC • Neolithic (new Stone Age) settlers (origins uncertain) bring agriculture, pottery, and weaving. They also build massive megaliths—stone monuments with counterparts in England (Stonehenge), Brittany (Carnac), and elsewhere in Europe.

CA. 700 BC • Celtic tribes begin to arrive via Britain and France; they divide Ireland into "fifths," or provinces, including Ulster, Leinster, Connaught, Meath, and Munster.

CA. AD 100 • Ireland becomes the center of Celtic culture and trade without being settled by the Romans.

432 • Traditional date for the arrival of St. Patrick and Christianity; in fact, Irish conversion to Christianity began at least a century earlier.

CA. 500–800 • Golden Age of Irish monasticism; as many as 3,000 study at Clonard (Meath). Irish missionaries carry the faith to barbarian Europe; art (exemplified by *The Book of Kells,* circa 700) and Gaelic poetry flourish.

795 • First Scandinavian Viking invasion; raids continue for the next 200 years. Viking towns founded include Dublin, Waterford, Wexford, Cork, and Limerick.

1014 • Vikings decisively defeated at Clontarf by Irish troops under King Brian Boru of Munster. His murder cuts short hopes of a unified Ireland.

1066 • Normans (French descendants of Viking invaders) conquer England and set their sights on Ireland as well.

1169 • Dermot MacMurrough, exiled King of Munster, invites the Anglo-Norman adventurer Richard FitzGilbert de Clare ("Strongbow") to help him regain his throne, beginning a pattern of English opportunism and bad decisions by the Irish.

1172 • Pope Alexander III confirms Henry II, King of England, as feudal lord of Ireland. Over the next two centuries, Anglo-Norman nobles establish estates, intermarry with the native population, and act in a manner similar to that of the neighboring Celtic chieftains. Actual control by the English crown is confined to a small area known as "the land of peace" or "the Pale" around Dublin.

1366 • Statutes of Kilkenny attempt belatedly to enforce ethnic divisions by prohibiting the expression of Irish language and culture and intermarriage between the Irish and English, but Gaelic culture prevails, and the Pale continues to contract. Constant warfare among the great landowners keeps Ireland poor, divided, and isolated from the rest of Europe.

1477–1513 • Garret Mor ("Gerald the Great") FitzGerald, eighth Earl of Kildare, dominates Irish affairs as lord deputy (the representative of the English crown).

1494 • Henry VII removes Kildare from office (he is soon reinstated) and initiates Statute of Drogheda (Poyning's Law), which is in force until 1782—Irish Parliament can only meet by consent of the King of England.

1534–40 • Henry VIII's break with the Catholic Church leads to insurrection in Ireland, led by Garret Mor's grandson Lord Offaly ("Silken Thomas"). He is executed with five of his brothers.

1541 • Parliament proclaims Henry VIII King of Ireland (his previous status was merely a feudal lord). Irish magnates reluctantly surrender their lands to him as their overlord. Hereafter, a constant English presence is required to keep the peace; no single Irish family replaces the FitzGeralds.

1558–1603 • Reign of Queen Elizabeth I; her fear of Irish intrigue with Catholic enemies of England leads to expansion of English power, including the Munster "plantation" (colony) scheme and the division of Ireland into English-style counties.

1580–88 • Edmund Spenser, an administrator for the Crown in Ireland, writes *The Faerie Queene*.

1591 • Trinity College, Dublin, is founded.

1595–1603 • Rebellion of Hugh O'Neill, Earl of Tyrone (Ulster). Defeats England at Yellow Ford (1598), but assistance from Spain is inadequate; Tyrone surrenders at Mellifont six days after Queen Elizabeth's death.

1607 • The Flight of the Earls, and the beginning of the end of Gaelic Ireland. The Earl of Tyrone and his ally Tyrconnell flee to Rome; their lands in Ulster are confiscated and opened to Protestant settlers, mostly Scots.

1641 • Charles I's policies provoke insurrection in Ulster and, soon after, civil war in England.

1649 • August: British leader Oliver Cromwell, having defeated Charles and witnessed his execution, invades Ireland, determined to crush Catholic opposition. Massacres at Drogheda and Wexford.

1652 • Act of Settlement—lands of Cromwell's opponents are confiscated, and owners are forced across the Shannon to Connaught. Never fully carried out, this policy nonetheless establishes Protestant ascendancy.

1690 • Battle of the Boyne—William of Orange lands in England and Catholic James II flees to Ireland to rally opposition. William pursues him with a large army and defeats him on the bands of the River Boyne in County Meath.

1678 • In the wake of the Popish Plot to assassinate King Charles II, Catholics are barred from British parliaments.

1683 • Dublin Philosophical Society founded, modeled on the Royal Society of London.

1689 • Having attempted, among other things, to repeal the Act of Settlement, King James II (a Catholic) is deposed and flees to Ireland. His daughter Mary and her husband William of Orange assume the throne.

1690 • James is defeated by William III at the Battle of the Boyne.

1704 • First laws of the Penal Code are enacted, restricting Catholic landowning; later laws prohibited voting, education, and military service among the Catholics.

1775 • American War of Independence begins, precipitating Irish unrest. Henry Grattan (1746–1820), a Protestant barrister, enters the Irish Parliament.

1778 • Land clauses of Penal Code are repealed.

1782 • Grattan's Parliament—Grattan asserts independence of Irish Parliament from Britain. Britain agrees, but independence is easier to declare than to sustain.

1798 • Inspired by the French Revolution and dissatisfied with the slow progress of Parliament, Wolfe Tone's United Irishmen rebel but are defeated.

1800 • The Irish Parliament votes itself out of existence and agrees to union with Britain, effective January 1, 1801.

1823 • Daniel O'Connell (1775–1847), "the Liberator," founds the Catholic Association to campaign for Catholic Emancipation.

1828 • O'Connell's election to Parliament (illegal, because he was a Catholic) leads to passage of Catholic Emancipation Act in 1829; later, he works unsuccessfully for repeal of the Union.

1845–48 • Failure of potato crop leads to famine; hundreds of thousands die, others emigrate.

1848 • "Young Ireland," a radical party, leads an abortive rebellion.

1856 • Birth of George Bernard Shaw, playwright (d. 1950).

1858 • Fenian Brotherhood founded in New York by Irish immigrants with the aim of overthrowing British rule. A revolt in 1867 fails, but it compels Gladstone, the British prime minister, to disestablish the Anglican Church (1869) and reform landholding (1870) in Ireland. The government also increases its powers of repression.

1865 • Birth of William Butler Yeats, the great Irish poet (d. 1939).

1871 • Isaac Butts founds parliamentary Home Rule Party, soon dominated by Charles Stewart Parnell (1846–91, descendant of English Protestants), who tries to force the issue by obstructing parliamentary business.

1881 • Gladstone's second Land Act opposed by Parnell, who leads a boycott (named for Captain Boycott, its first victim) of landlords.

1882 • Phoenix Park murders—British officials murdered by Fenians. Prevention of Crime bill that follows suspends trial by jury and increases police powers. Acts of terrorism increase. Parnell disavows all connection with Fenians. Birth of James Joyce, novelist (d. 1941).

1886 • Gladstone introduces his first Home Rule Bill, which is defeated. Ulster Protestants fear Catholic domination and revive Orange Order (named for William of Orange) to oppose Home Rule.

1890 • Parnell is named corespondent in the divorce case of Kitty O'Shea; his career is ruined.

1893 • Second Home Rule Bill passes Commons but is defeated by Lords. Subsequent policy is to "kill Home Rule with kindness" with land reform, but cultural nationalism revives with founding of Gaelic League to promote Irish language. Yeats, John Synge (1871–1909), and other writers find inspiration in Gaelic past.

1898 • On the anniversary of Wolfe Tone's rebellion, Arthur Griffith (1872–1922) founds the Dublin newspaper *the United Irishman,* preaching sinn féin ("we ourselves")—secession from Britain; Sinn Féin party founded 1905. Socialist James Connolly (executed 1916) founds the Workers' Republic.

1904 • Abbey Theatre opens in Dublin.

1912 • Third Home Rule Bill passes Commons but is rejected by Lords. Under new rules, however, Lords' veto is null after two years. Meanwhile, Ulster Protestants plan defiance; the Ulster Volunteers recruit 100,000. Radical Republicans such as Connolly, Patrick Pearse, and others of the Irish Republican Brotherhood (IRB) preach insurrection and recruit their own volunteers.

1914 • Outbreak of war postpones implementation of Home Rule until peace returns. Parliamentarians agree, but radicals plan revolt.

1916 • Easter Uprising—IRB stages insurrection in Dublin and declares independence; the uprising fails, but the execution of 15 leaders by the British turns public opinion in favor of the insurgents. Yeats writes "a terrible beauty is born."

1919 • January: Irish Parliamentarians meet as the Dail Éireann (Irish Assembly) and declare independence. September: Dail suppressed; Sinn Féin made illegal.

1920–21 • War breaks out between Britain and Ireland: the "Black and Tans" versus the Irish Republican Army (IRA). Government of Ireland Act declares separate parliaments for north and south and continued ties to Britain. Elections follow, but the Sinn Féin majority in the south again declare themselves the Dail Éireann under Eamonn de Valera (1882–1975), rejecting British authority. December 1921: Anglo-Irish Treaty grants the south dominion status as the Irish Free State, allowing the north to remain under Britain.

1922 • De Valera and his Republican followers reject the treaty; civil war results. The Irish Free State adopts a constitution; William T. Cosgrave becomes president. Michael Collins, chairman of the Irish Free State and Commander-in-Chief of the Army, is shot dead in his County Cork, not far from where he was born. In Paris, James Joyce's Ulysses is published.

1923 • De Valera is arrested and the civil war ends, but Republican agitation and terrorism continue. William Butler Yeats is the first Irish writer to be awarded the Nobel Prize in Literature.

1925 • George Bernard Shaw wins the Nobel Prize in Literature.

1932 • De Valera, who had founded the Fianna Fáil party in 1926, begins a 16-year term as Taioseach (Prime Minister).

1932–36 • Tariff war with Britain.

1938 • New constitution creates Republic of Ireland with no ties to Britain.

1939–45 • Despite strong pressure from Britain and the U.S., Ireland remains neutral throughout World War II.

1947 • The statue of Queen Victoria is removed from the courtyard in front of the Irish Parliament in Dublin.

1963 • John F. Kennedy, the first Irish-American President of the U.S., visits Ireland.

1969 • The annual Apprentice Boys' march in Derry, Northern Ireland, leads to rioting between Catholics and Protestants. British troops, called in to keep the peace, remain in Northern Ireland to this day. Samuel Beckett is awarded the Nobel Prize in Literature but declines to travel to Oslo to receive it.

1972 • Republic of Ireland admitted to European Economic Community. Troubles continue in the north: In Derry on January 30, British troops shoot 13 unarmed demonstrators on "Bloody Sunday." Stormont (the Northern Parliament) is suspended and direct rule from London is imposed. Acts of terrorism on both sides leads to draconian law enforcement by the British. "The Troubles," as the conflict becomes known, will last 26 years and claim more than 3,000 lives.

1979 • Pope John Paul II visits Ireland and celebrates mass in Phoenix Park; more than a million people attend.

1986 • Anglo-Irish Agreement signed, giving the Republic of Ireland a stronger voice in northern affairs.

1988 • Dublin celebrates its millennium.

1991 • Mary Robinson becomes the first female President of the Republic of Ireland. Peace talks begin between the British and Irish governments and the main political parties of the North, excepting Sinn Féin.

1992 • Ireland approves European Union. Sixty-two percent of the Irish vote in a referendum in favor of allowing pregnant women to seek an abortion abroad.

1994 • The IRA, in response to advances made by the Irish, British, and U.S. governments, announces a complete cessation of activities. Protestant paramilitary groups follow suit one month later.

1995 • After 25 years, daylight troop patrols are discontinued in Belfast. Seamus Heaney receives the Nobel Prize in Literature, the fourth Irish writer in less than 75 years so honored.

1996 • The IRA, in frustration with the slow progress in the peace talks, explode bombs on the British mainland, throwing the whole peace process into doubt.

1997 • The Republic of Ireland legalizes divorce. Ireland is rated the fastest growing economy in the industrialized world. IRA declare new ceasefire and are admitted into all party talks.

1998 • On Good Friday all sides in the conflict agree on an arrangement for power-sharing that guarantees the rights of the Catholic minority. Referenda in the North and the Republic show overwhelming support for the agreement. A splinter IRA group opposed to the deal explodes a bomb in Omagh, killing more than 20 people. Catholic leader John Hume and Protestant leader David Trimble share the Nobel Peace Prize.

1999 • Preparations for a new power-sharing executive are delayed over disagreements about the decommissioning of weapons. Sporadic violence by splinter loyalist groups keeps tensions high.

IT'S ALL IN THE NAME

BY FIONN DAVENPORT

In a small coffee shop outside of Galway town, Seamus D., a young man from Dublin, sat eating a warm scone and drinking a hot cup of tea. He had driven that morning from home, crossing from coast to coast—from east to west—in a matter of hours, on a trip that brought him from the familiarity of Dublin to the excitement of what was to him, despite his irishness, a foreign place. He had never been to this part of the country—was it possible that he was a foreigner here? the feeling in his stomach seemed to say so.

Along the journey he fought the notion that he was being irrational; he had listened to tapes of Irish traditional music and had recognized many of the tunes (though the names of the different jigs, reels, and laments meant nothing to him); he knew the history of the area as well as his own family past; he could imitate the gruff lilt of the Galway accent to the point where he might actually pass as a local, if only for a couple of minutes, in a crowded bar where conversation and the effects of the stout would surely dull a quick ear. But as he finished the rest of his snack, he felt slightly lost—and thrilled at the thought of what lay ahead.

His acquaintance with the west of Ireland, and Galway in particular, was that of a pen pal. His knowledge was secondhand and was locked in a cage of big-city ideas about "minor" towns. It was no accident that, as a rule, the Irish talked about trips to and from the capital as going up to Dublin and going down to the country. Dubliners have a tendency of looking at non-Dubliners as though they were a kind of ancient grandparents, to be loved—and sometimes hated—with a tinge of superiority that one usually feels toward the old and slightly out of touch. Dublin was the new Ireland, the rest of the country a land of verdant beauty and peculiar customs; it was where you could "get away from it all"; it was the greatest backyard in the world.

If it was a backyard, he had spent too long indoors. He settled into the driver's seat for the last leg of the journey, now less than an hour away. He was going to Kinvara, a small fishing port on the Atlantic coast that was home and final resting place of his paternal grandfather, a hamlet described in his guidebook as a "delightful village tucked away on the southeast corner of Galway Bay."

He had come in search of traces of his grandfather Seamus, a man in a grave not quite forgotten, but ignored. Perhaps the sight of their shared name—once proudly engraved in the elegant stone, now hidden by weeds and moss—would make everything seem less foreign to him and more a reminder of home and a past he knew little about.

His grandfather had died in the late 1950s, and nobody had visited his grave since the day of the funeral, when a resigned widow and a puzzled boy—his father—buried a man they never really knew. His death brought little grief to wife and son, despite the fears of the woman and the tears of the child, now alone after so many years of being left alone by a man whose beds and favorite pubs were in faraway London, Chicago, New York, or wherever the creditors could be kept at bay. The widow and the son mourned respectfully but not excessively: the family had declared Seamus a "bad" man and his passing was met with stoic indifference.

In Kinvara, Seamus the younger was struck by the picturesque quality of the village: The houses were wrapped around a small bay used as a port by the local fishermen. Wooden longboats were run aground on the pebbled beach, idle through the long winter months when challenging the merciless sea would have been suicidal. On a small hill to one side of the bay was Kinvara's most famous landmark, Dungaire Castle, a stronghold of the O'Brien family before it was captured by the Tourist Board and turned into a curiosity, complete with a souvenir shop and nighttime medieval banquets. But sightseeing was not Seamus's priority, so he turned his attention to the matter at hand. He had to find the graveyard but needed directions. He decided to go to the pub.

The pub was a small terraced house, undistinguishable from the houses on either side except for the "Lynch's" sign over the door. Its pebble-dash front was painted in a pastel yellow that, along with the colored shades of the other houses, gave the whole town an almost fairy-tale look, as though it were an Irish version of a Lego village. He stepped inside and over to the bar. He waited a moment before the barman looked up from his newspaper to acknowledge his presence.

"A pint of plain, please."

The barman pulled a glass from beneath the bar and rested it under the tap. A flick of his wrist and the glass began to fill up with black, creamy liquid. When it was about three-quarters full he pushed the tap back and sat the glass on the bar. Within a couple of minutes the pint had settled and a thin white head had formed. He held it a second time under the tap and filled it to the rim, and once again the barman sat the pint on the bar. He did all of this without once stirring from his stool, only looking up from his newspaper to make sure that the glass didn't overflow.

"And a packet of peanuts, please. Oh, and could you be so kind as to tell me where the cemetery is?"

The barman raised his eyes. "What kind?" Seamus stared back, a little perplexed. The barman spoke again. "Salted or plain? Do you want salted peanuts or plain ones?"

"Plain, please." But what about the cemetery?

"Two, please," the barman said. Seamus took out a five-pound note from his wallet and left it on the bar.

"Which graveyard are you lookin' for? The new one or the old one?"

Ah, some information. "I don't know which one. I'm trying to find my grandfather's grave. . ."

"What was his name?"

"Seamus." The barman looked at him. "Seamus D."

"He can't be buried around here," the barman said firmly. "That's a Clare name, not a Galway name. Are you sure you have the right town?" The barman's tone bordered on the bored, which brought the risk of an end to the conversation and would leave him with no clue as to where to go.

"I knew Michael D. well." The voice came from behind Seamus and startled him. He turned around, and in the corner there was a small man dressed in a dark suit at a small table full of empty pint glasses. Seamus had not seen him against the dark walls when he came in. Perhaps this fellow had been a local for so long that his molecules had fused with those of the bar, and had become a rural version of Flann O'Brien's The Third Policeman.

"My grandfather's name was Seamus, not Michael," Seamus responded politely. Despite his visions of men who were half-human and half-pub, he feared that he was wasting his time. Ah, but big-city time and country time were two different things altogether.

"That's right," the man said, "but your great-grandfather was Michael. I knew him well and his son, too, that is, your grandfather," the man continued. "Julia's husband he was, at least before he died and she took her brood up to her people in Dublin." Seamus smiled at the man, but he ignored the gesture and continued talking. "He commanded a brigade in the war against the British, I remember. A tallish fellow, and he liked his pint. By God, he liked his pint. He once told me a story about how the Black and Tans were chasing him and he hid in a stream for three days and four nights so that their dogs wouldn't catch his scent." Seamus had heard this story from his own father, but in his version he had stayed in the stream only a couple of hours.

The barman listened intently, and then declared "Oh, I remember him now. He drank in here when Da was running things!" Seamus turned to the barman and was surprised to see a smile come across his face as he spoke. "He was a fine man, if I remember correctly." He was an awful man, Seamus thought to himself, but he who is fond of the drink will be one thing to the person serving him and another to his family. "Great with the stories, generous with friends, gracious with his enemies, and a bit of a charmer with the ladies." The barman looked at Seamus. "So, he was your grandfather, then?"

"He was."

"Well then, my young Dub, you've come home, haven't you?" He offered his hand. "You'll be needing a few and a bit of a rest before you tackle the cemetery. A grave and sullen place it is. The first pint is on me. Taidgh O Shaughnessy at your service."

IRISH FAMILY NAMES

Antrim
Lynch
McDonnell
McNeill
O'Hara
O'Neill
Quinn

Armagh
Hanlon
McCann

Carlow
Kinsella
Nolan
O'Neill

Cavan
Boylan
Lynch
McCabe
McGovern
McGowan
McNally
O'Reilly
Sheridan

Clare
Aherne
Boland
Clancy
Daly
Lynch
McGrath
McInerney
McMahon
McNamara
Molon(e)y
O'Brien
O'Dea
O'Grady
O'Halloran
O'Loughlin

Cork
Barry
Callaghan
Cullinane
Donovan
Driscoll
Flynn
Hennessey
Hogan
Lynch
McCarthy
McSweeney
Murphy
Nugent
O'Casey
O'Cullane
(Collins)

O'Keefe
O'Leary
O'Mahony
O'Riordan
Roche
Scanlon
Sheridan

Derry
Cahan
Hegarty
Kelly
McLaughlin

Donegal
Boyle
Clery
Doherty
Friel
Gallagher
Gormley
McGrath
McLoughlin
McSweeney
Mooney
O'Donnell

Down
Lynch
McGuinness
O'Neil
White

Dublin
Hennessey
O'Casey
Plunkett

Fermanagh
Cassidy
Connolly
Corrigan
Flanagan
Maguire
McManus

Galway
Blake
Burke
Clery
Fah(e)y
French
Jennings
Joyce
Kelly
Kenny
Kirwan
Lynch
Madden
Moran
O'Flaherty
O'Halloran

Kerry
Connor
Fitzgerald
Galvin
McCarthy
Moriarty
O'Connell
O'Donoghue
O'Shea
O'Sullivan

Kildare
Cullen
Fitzgerald
O'Byrne
White

Kilkenny
Butler
Fitzpatrick
O'Carroll
Tobin

Laois
Dempsey
Doran
Dunn(e)
Kelly
Moore

Leitrim
Clancy
O'Rourke

Limerick
Fitzgerald
Fitzgibbon
McKeough
O'Brien
O'Cullane
(Collins)
O'Grady
Woulfe

Longford
O'Farrell
Quinn

Louth
O'Carroll
Plunkett

Mayo
Burke
Costello
Dugan
Gormley
Horan
Jennings
Jordan
Kelly
Madden
O'Malley

Meath
Coffey
Connolly
Cusack
Dillon
Hayes
Hennessey
Plunkett
Quinlan

Monaghan
Boylan
Connolly
Hanratty
McKenna
McMahon
McNally

Offaly
Coghlan
Dempsey
Fallon
(Maher)
Malone
Meagher
Molloy
O'Carroll
Sheridan

Roscommon
Fallon
Flanagan
Flynn
Hanley
McDermot
McKeogh
McManus
Molloy
Murphy

Sligo
Boland
Higgins
McDonagh
O'Dowd
O'Hara
Rafferty

Tipperary
Butler
Fogarty
Kennedy
Lynch
Meagher
(Maher)
O'Carroll
O'Dwyer
O'Meara
Purcell
Ryan

Tyrone
Cahan
Donnelly
Gormley
Hagan
Murphy
O'Neill
Quinn

Waterford
Keane
McGrath
O'Brien
Phelan
Power

Westmeath
Coffey
Dalton
Daly
Dillon
Sheridan

Wexford
Doran
Doyle
Hartley
Kavanagh
Keating
Kinsella
McKeogh
Redmond
Walsh

Wicklow
Cullen
Kelly
McKeogh
O'Byrne
O'Toole

BOOKS AND VIDEOS

AUTOBIOGRAPHY

Since it was published in September 1996, *Angela's Ashes,* Frank McCourt's enormously affecting memoir of growing up desperately poor in Limerick, has garnered every major American literary accolade, from the Pulitzer Prize to the National Book Critics Circle Award, and has become a fixture at the top of American bestseller lists. In *An Only Child* and *My Father's Son* (1969), Frank O'Connor, known primarily for his fiction and short stories, recounts his years as an Irish revolutionary and later as an intellectual in Dublin during the 1920s. Christy Brown's *My Left Foot* is the autobiographical account of a Dublin artist stricken with cerebral palsy (*see* Movies and Videos, *below*).

GUIDEBOOKS AND TRAVEL LITERATURE

Exploring Ireland (2nd ed.), also published by Fodor's, a full-color guide packed with photographs, is an excellent companion guide to this edition.

Peter Somerville-Large's *Dublin* is packed with anecdotes relating to the famed Irish city. *Georgian Dublin,* by Desmond Guinness, the founder of the Irish Georgian Society, explores the city's architecture, with photographs and plans of Dublin's most admirable buildings. The most up-to-date work on the Aran Islands is Tim Robinson's award-winning *The Stones of Aran*: *Pilgrimage.* Robinson has also written a long introduction to the Penguin edition of J. M. Synge's 1907 classic, *The Aran Islands.* Tomas Ó Crohán's *The Islandman* provides a good background on Dingle and the Blasket Islands.

In *Round Ireland in Low Gear* (1988), famed British travel writer Eric Newby writes breezily of his bicycle journey with his wife around the wet Emerald Isle. Fifty years older but no less fresh is H.V. Morton's *In Search of Ireland* (1938). Rebecca Solnit uses Ireland as a sounding board for her meditations on travel in *A Book of Migrations: Some Passages in Ireland* (1997).

HISTORY AND CURRENT AFFAIRS

For two intriguing studies of Irish culture and history, consult Constantine FitzGibbon's *The Irish in Ireland* and Sean O'Faolain's *The Irish: A Character Study,* which traces the history of Ireland from Celtic times. J. C. Beckett's *The Making of Modern Ireland,* a concise introduction to Irish history, covers the years between 1603 and 1923. *Modern Ireland,* by R. F. Foster, spans the years between 1600 and 1972. An up-to-date analysis of the making of modern Ireland can be found in *Ireland 1912–1985 Politics and Society,* by J. J. Lee. For an acclaimed history of Irish nationalism, try Robert Kee's *The Green Flag.* Peter De Rosa's *Rebels: The Irish Rising of 1916* is a popularly written, novelistic history of the defining event of modern Irish history. Irish country-house devotees should read *Aristocrats: Caroline, Emily, Louisa and Sarah Lennox, 1740–1832,* by Stella Tillyard; Louisa was the force behind Castletown House.

John Ardagh's *Ireland and the Irish: Portrait of a Changing Society* (1997) is the best current sociological and economic analysis of modern Ireland. *"We Wrecked the Place": Contemplating an End to the Northern Irish Troubles* (1996) by Belfast-based journalist Jonathan Stevenson is the best recent book on the subject. John Conroy's *Belfast Diary: War as a Way of Life* (1995) was reissued with a new afterword on the ceasefire. Neither Colm Toibin's *Bad Blood: A Walk Along the Irish Border* nor Carlo Gebler's *The Glass Curtain: Inside an Ulster Community* is published in the U.S., but both are worth tracking down.

Rosemary Mahoney, a young Irish-American writer, moved to Ireland, where she wrote *Whoredom in Kimmage: Irish Women Coming of Age* (1993), a collective portrait of Irish women and men in the early 1990s.

LITERARY BIOGRAPHY AND CRITICISM

Richard Ellman's *James Joyce* (1959) is recognized as the finest literary biography ever written and is easily the best introduction to the man and his work. Ellman completed his second biographical masterpiece, *Oscar Wilde* (1988), shortly before his death, after more than 20 years of research. Ellman also wrote *Yeats: The Man and the Masks* (1978), although the first volume of Roy F. Foster's new biography, *W. B. Yeats: A Life—The Apprentice Mage 1865–1914, Vol. 1* (1997), has been welcomed as definitive, on the caliber of Ellman's Joyce and Wilde bios. Michael Holroyd's exhaustive, four-volume biography of George Bernard Shaw (1988, 1988, 1991, and 1993) will tell you everything you want to know about the larger-than-life, Nobel Prize–winning dramatist, critic, and social reformer. Samuel Beckett himself asked James Knowlson to write his biography; the result, *Damned to Fame: The Life of Samuel Beckett,* was published in 1996 and is widely regarded as the definitive life of the writer. William Trevor's *A Writer's Ireland: Landscape in Literature* (1984) explores the influence of Ireland's changing landscape on its writers. *Inventing Ireland: The Literature of Modern Nation* (1995) by Declan Kiberd is a major literary history of modern Ireland.

LITERATURE

Ulysses (1922) is the linguistically innovative masterpiece by James Joyce, one of the titans of 20th-century literature. Emulating the structure of *The Odyssey,* and using an unprecedented stream of consciousness technique, Joyce follows Leopold and Molly Bloom and Stephen Daedalus through the course of a single day—June 16, 1904—around Dublin. (Joyce set *Ulysses* on the day he and his future wife, Nora Barnacle, had their first date.) More accessible introductions to Joyce's writing include *A Portrait of the Artist as a Young Man* (1916) and *Dubliners* (1914), a collection of short stories (its most accomplished story, "The Dead," was made into a movie starring Angelica Huston in 1988). Joyce aficionados may want to tackle his final, gigantic work, *Finnegan's Wake* (1939), which takes the linguistic experimentation of *Ulysses* to an almost incomprehensible level. Arguably the greatest literary challenge of the 20th century, its pages include word plays and phonetic metaphors in more than 100 languages. To prepare you for reading Joyce, you might seek out audio recordings in which he reads in his inimitable lilting tenor voice.

Samuel Beckett fills his story collection *More Pricks than Kicks* with Dublin characters; if you enjoy literary gamesmanship, you may also want to try Beckett's trilogy—*Molloy* (1951), *Malone Dies* (1951), and *The Unnamable* (1953).

If you're drawn to tales of unrequited love, turn to Elizabeth Bowen's stories and her novel, *The Last September* (1929), set in Ireland during the Irish Civil War. Coming-of-age novels include *Under the Eye of the Clock,* a somewhat autobiographical work by Christopher Nolan, which takes as its subject a handicapped youth discovering the pleasures of language, and *Fools of Fortune* (1983), by William Trevor, which treats the loss of an ideal childhood, brought about by a changing political climate. Trevor's *The Silence in the Garden* (1988) is also worth looking for.

If you prefer reading more magical novels, take a look at James Stephens's *A Crock of Gold* (1912), a charming and wise fairy tale written for adults, and Flann O'Brien's *At Swim-Two-Birds* (1939), a surrealistic tale full of Irish folklore.

One of Ireland's foremost fiction writers working today, Edna O'Brien began her career with the comic novel, *The Country Girls* (1960), and has published 17 books since, most recently *House of Splendid Isolation* (1994) and *Down By the River* (1997). Like many of her compatriots, she is a superb short-story writer. Her collection, *A Fanatic Heart* (1985), is one of her best. Other superbly crafted story collections, full of acute observations of Ireland's social and political landscape, include Benedict Kiely's *The State of Ireland, Mary Lavin's Collected Stories,* Frank O'Connor's *Collected Stories* (1952), William Trevor's *Collected Stories* (1993), and John McGahern's *Collected Stories* (1993).

Thomas Flanagan's *The Year of the French* is a historical novel about the people of County Mayo, who revolted in 1798 with the help of French revolutionaries. *A Nest of Simple Folk,* by Sean O'Faolain, follows three generations of an Irish family between 1854 and 1916. Leon Uris's *Trinity* covers the years 1840–1916, as seen through the eyes of British, Irish Catholic, and Ulster Protestant families. In *No Country for Young Men,* Julia O'Faolain writes of two Irish families struggling to overcome the effects of the Irish Civil War. In John McGahern's prizewinning novel *Amongst Women,* modern-day Ireland attempts to reconcile itself to the upheavals of the early years of this century. For a more contemporary look at life in urban Ireland, try the phenomenally successful Roddy Doyle: All three works from his "Barrytown Trilogy"—*The Snapper, The Commitments,* and *The Van*—have all been made into films;

Paddy Clarke Ha Ha Ha, another success, is sure to follow. Shortlisted for the Booker Prize, *Reading in the Dark* (1997) marks the novelistic debut of Seamus Deane, a poet, critic, and editor. It covers famil- iar territory—a family in 1920 Ireland riven by political strife—but does so with extraordinarily evocative language.

MOVIES AND VIDEOS

There has been a plethora of movies made in or about Ireland, and the number of Irish characters on screen is legion (the most numerous being priests, drunks, New York cops, and Old Mother Riley). *Juno and the Paycock* (known in the United States as *The Shame of Mary Boyle*) and *The Plough and the Stars* (1936), about the months leading up to the Easter Uprising, are early screen adaptations of Sean O'Casey's theatrical masterpieces. John Ford's superb *The Informer* (1935) is a full-blooded and highly stylized tale of an IRA leader's betrayal during the struggle for independence by a simpleminded hanger- on who wants to emigrate to the United States. Ford's boisterous comedy *The Quiet Man* (1952) is an Irish-village version of *The Taming of the Shrew,* with John Wayne playing a boxer who returns to his ancestor's village in the West of Ireland to claim local beauty Maureen O'Hara, and Barry Fitzgerald. David Lean's epic, *Ryan's Daughter* (1970), is a four-hour pastoral melodrama of a village schoolmas- ter's wife falling for a British officer in the troubled Ireland of 1916; the film was a critical and commer- cial disaster for Lean, who didn't make another film for 14 years.

Daniel Day-Lewis and Brenda Fricker give Oscar-winning performances in Jim Sheridan's *My Left Foot* (1989), a biography of Christy Brown, the Irish writer and painter crippled from birth by cerebral palsy. Alan Parker's *The Commitments* (1991), from Roddy Doyle's best-seller, humorously recounts the efforts of a group of young, working-class northside Dubliners trying to make it as a soul band. A made- for-TV version of another of Doyle's best-sellers, *The Snapper* (1993), is a touching, funny tale of a Dublin girl's struggles to be a single mother in the face of an orthodox and often unforgiving society. *The Van* (1997) completes the "Trilogy," as the books that were the basis of these three films are known. In *A Man of No Importance* (1994), Albert Finney plays a sexually repressed bus conductor whose passion for poetry leads him to stage Wilde's *Salomé.* John Sayles hooked up with acclaimed cinematographer Haskell Wexler to make *The Secret of Roan Inish* (1996), a magical realist fable about a Selkie—a crea- ture from Celtic folkore who is a seal in the water and a woman on land—and the fisherman's family whose lives she changes.

Some of the best movies made in Ireland deal with the Troubles that have afflicted Northern Ireland. *Four Days in July* (1984), directed by Mike Leigh in classic cinema verité style, is a poignant and com- pelling portrayal of the sectarian divide in working-class Belfast. Based on actual events, Ken Loach's *Hidden Agenda* (1990) is a hard-hitting thriller about the murder of an American lawyer working for Amnesty International in the troubled North. As the plot unfolds, it becomes clear that the highest ech- elons of the British government and secret services are involved. Helen Mirren stars as the widow of an executed Protestant policeman in *Cal* (1984), based on Bernard MacLaverty's masterful novel about the Troubles. Daniel Day-Lewis was nominated for an Academy Award for his portrayal of Gerry Conlon, the wrongfully imprisoned Irish youth, in Jim Sheridan's *In the Name of the Father* (1993). Neil Jordan's *Michael Collins* (1996) depicts the turbulent life of the heroic commander-in-chief of the Irish Republi- can Army from the Easter Uprising in 1916, when Collins was 25, until his assassination in West Cork six years later; it went on to become the highest-grossing film ever in Ireland. Helen Mirren again plays a widow in *Some Mother's Son* (1997), set during the 1981 Maze Prison Hunger Strike that claimed Bobby Sands.

PERIODICAL

Billing itself as "a magazine for the Irish diaspora: An ongoing celebration of Ireland and the Irish around the world," *The World of Hibernia* (issued quarterly; US $50, Canada US$60, and rest of the world US$80: 340 Madison Ave., Suite 411, New York, NY 10164-2920; Ireland and Britain £32: 22 Crofton Rd., Dun Laoghaire, Co. Dublin) has savvy, solid editorial coverage. Its quality is also high (on par with that of the finest art magazines), making it a magazine you're likely to keep on your coffee table months after the issue date.

POETRY

The poems of William Butler Yeats, Ireland's most celebrated poet, often describe the Irish landscape, including the Sligo and Coole countryside. A favorite poet among the Irish is Patrick Kavanagh, whose distinguished career was devoted to writing exceptionally about ordinary lives. Winner of the Irish Times– Aer Lingus Literary prize in 1993, Derek Mahon is the author of *Selected Poems* (1992) and many other books. Northern Ireland serves as the setting for many of Seamus Heaney's poems. *Selected Poems 1996–1987* (1990) and *The Spirit Level* (1996), his first collection published since he won the Nobel Prize in Literature in 1995, are both highly recommended introductions to his work. Though not as well known outside Ireland as Heaney, Paul Muldoon is another major Irish poet. His *Selected Poems: 1968–1986* (1987) and his most recent volume, *The Annals of Chile* (1994), are both good places to start. Eavan Boland is widely regarded as among the top tier of Irish poets, and the finest woman writing poetry in Ireland today. *An Origin Like Water: Collected Poems 1957–1987* (1996) and *Object Lessons: The Life of the Woman and the Poet in Our Time* (1995) are two of her recent books.

THEATER

Ireland's playwrights are as distinguished as its novelists and short story writers. Samuel Beckett, who moved from Ireland to Paris and began writing in French, is the author of the comic modernist masterpiece *Waiting for Godot* (1952), among many other plays. Oscar Wilde's finest plays, *The Importance of Being Earnest* and *An Ideal Husband* (both 1895), were playing to packed audiences in London when he was charged by his lover's father as a somdomite [sic, setting in motion the trials that lead to his downfall. Among the many plays of George Bernard Shaw, who grew up in Dublin, are *Arms and the Man* (1894), *Major Barbara* (1905), *Pygmalion* (1913), and *Saint Joan* (1923).

The history of Irish theater includes a good number of controversial plays, such as J. M. Synge's *The Playboy of the Western World*, which was considered morally outrageous at the time of its opening in 1907 ("Playboy riots" took place in Dublin when the play was produced at the Abbey Theatre) but is appreciated today for its poetic language. Sean O'Casey wrote passionately about social injustice and working-class characters around the time of the Irish Civil War in such plays as *The Plough and the Stars* (1926) and *Juno and the Paycock* (1924). *The Quare Fellow* (1956), by Brendan Behan, challenged accepted mores in the 1950s and at the time could only be produced in London. Behan is also well known for his play *The Hostage* and for *Borstal Boy* (1958), his memoirs. Two more recently recognized playwrights are Hugh Leonard (*Da* and *A Life*) and Brian Friel (*Philadelphia, Here I Come!*, *The Faith Healer*, and *Dancing at Lughnasa*), whose work often illuminates Irish small-town life.

INDEX

NOTES

NOTES

IT'S YOUR TURN TO TALK BACK!

FILL OUT THIS QUICK SURVEY AND RECEIVE A FREE COPY OF FODOR'S *HOW TO PACK*.*

Which Fodor's upCLOSE guide did you buy?

_____

What was the duration of your trip?

_____

How much did you spend per day, not including airfare?

❑ $100 ❑ $300
❑ $150 ❑ Other_____
❑ $200

Why did you choose Fodor's upCLOSE?

❑ Budget focus
❑ Fodor's reputation
❑ Opinionated writing & comprehensive content
❑ Other_____

Would you use Fodor's upCLOSE again?

❑ Yes ❑ No

Which guides have you used in the past two years?

❑ Frommer's $-A-Day ❑ Let's Go
❑ Rough Guides ❑ Rick Steves'
❑ Lonely Planet ❑ None
❑ Other_____

Did you like Fodor's upCLOSE better?

❑ Yes ❑ No

Please rank the following features (1 = needs improvement / 2 = adequate / 3 = excellent).

Accommodations listings	1	2	3
Dining listings	1	2	3
Major sights	1	2	3
Off-the-beaten-path sights	1	2	3
Shopping listings	1	2	3
Nightlife listings	1	2	3
Public transportation	1	2	3

Please feel free to elaborate. _____

_____

_____

_____

Which of the following destinations would you like to see Fodor's upCLOSE cover?

❑ Alaska ❑ Pacific Northwest
❑ Australia ❑ South America
❑ Austria ❑ Southeast Asia
❑ Eastern Europe ❑ Switzerland
❑ Greece ❑ Turkey
❑ Israel ❑ More European cities
❑ New Zealand ❑ More U.S. cities
❑ Other_____

You are ❑ Male ❑ Female

Your age is
❑ 18-24   ❑ 45-54
❑ 25-34   ❑ 55-64
❑ 35-44   ❑ 65+

You are ❑ Single ❑ Married

Your occupation is
❑ Student (undergraduate)
❑ Student (graduate)
❑ Professional
❑ Executive/managerial/administrative
❑ Military
❑ Retired
❑ Other_____

Which choice best describes your household income?
❑ Under $10,000
❑ $10,000-$19,999
❑ $20,000-$29,999
❑ $30,000-$49,999
❑ $50,000-$74,999
❑ $75,000+

Your name and address are

_____
_____
_____

Your E-mail address is

_____

Would you like to receive informational E-mails from Fodor's?
❑ Yes   ❑ No

Please return this survey to Fodor's Travel Publications, Attn: Fodor's upCLOSE Survey, 1540 Broadway, New York, NY 10036, for a free copy of Fodor's *How to Pack* (while supplies last). You can also fill out this survey on the Web at www.fodors.com/upclose/upclosesurvey.html.

The information herein will be treated in confidence. Names and addresses will not be released to mailing-list houses or other organizations.

* While supplies last